THE SECOND WORLD WAR
1939—1945
ARMY

AIRBORNE FORCES

COMPILED BY
LIEUTENANT-COLONEL T. B. H. OTWAY, D.S.O.,
The Royal Ulster Rifles.

The Naval & Military Press Ltd

Published by

The Naval & Military Press Ltd

Unit 5 Riverside, Brambleside
Bellbrook Industrial Estate
Uckfield, East Sussex
TN22 1QQ England

Tel: +44 (0)1825 749494

www.naval–military-press.com
www.nmarchive.com

Acknowledgment is made for permission to quote from the following sources :—

" Prelude to Glory "

by Group Captain Maurice Newnham, O.B.E., D.F.C., published by Messrs. Sampson Low Marston and Co.

" Born of the Desert "

by Malcolm James, published by Messrs. Collins, Sons and Co.

FOREWORD

This book is one of a series of volumes, compiled by authority of the Army Council, the object of which is to preserve the experience gained during the Second World War, 1939–1945, in selected fields of military staff work and administration. The author has been given access to official sources of information, and every endeavour has been made to ensure the accuracy of the work as an historical record. Any views expressed and conclusions drawn are those of the author, and do not necessarily reflect those of the Army Council, which, so far as they relate to current training, are to be found in the official manuals, training memoranda, etc., issued from time to time by the War Office.

For the operational background, the reader is referred to the Official History of the War.

THE WAR OFFICE

December, 1951.

CONTENTS

CONTENTS—*continued*

v

CONTENTS—*continued*

vi

CONTENTS—*continued*

CONTENTS—*continued*

APPENDICES—*continued*

MAPS
(at end of Volume)

1. TUNISIA
   1 Parachute Brigade, November, 1942–April, 1943.

2. SOUTH EAST SICILY
   1 Airborne Division, July, 1943.

3. SOUTHERN ITALY
   11 S.A.S. Battalion, February, 1941—1 Airborne Division, September–November, 1943—2 Parachute Brigade, November, 1943–May, 1944.

4. NORTHERN MEDITERRANEAN
   2 Parachute Brigade, August, 1944—3 Squadron, 2nd S.A.S. Regiment, December, 1944, to May, 1945.

5. CENTRAL GREECE AND CRETE
   2 Parachute Brigade in Greece, October, 1944, to January, 1945—German Invasion of Crete, May, 1941.

6. DIAGRAM OF COMMUNICATIONS FROM H.Q., 1 AIRBORNE CORPS

7. NORTHERN FRANCE, NORMANDY
   6 Airborne Division, June–August, 1944.

8. NORTHERN FRANCE, NORMANDY
   6 Airborne Division, 17th–26th August, 1944.

9. FRANCE
   2nd Parachute Battalion, February, 1942—S.A.S. Brigade Operations, 1944—Projected Airborne Operations, June to September, 1944.

10. HOLLAND AND BELGIUM
    S.A.S. Operations, 1944—Projected Airborne Operations, June to September, 1944.

11. HOLLAND
    Second Army Advance, and 1 British Airborne Corps Landings, 17th September, 1944.

12. HOLLAND, ARNHEM
    1 Airborne Division, September, 1944.

13. THE RHINE
    Allied Armies, March, 1945.

14. THE RIVER RHINE, REES–WESEL
    XVIII U.S. Airborne Corps, March, 1945.

15. WESTERN GERMANY, RIVER RHINE TO THE BALTIC
    6 Airborne Division, March–May, 1945.

ix

LIST OF ILLUSTRATIONS

Title

xi

" . . . a tribute to the man who is looking for no better drop zone for tomorrow than the heartland of the enemy, the Allied airborne soldier. As future commanders, you will find that he is a useful fellow to have around."

MAJOR-GENERAL MAXWELL D. TAYLOR,
United States Army.

CHAPTER I

INTRODUCTION

The Object of the History

1. This history is intended to tell the story of British airborne forces during the war of 1939–45 and includes a chapter on the activities of the Dominions in this sphere. British airborne forces were in action frequently with our Allies, under one command, carried into battle by British and American air forces. The closest co-operation was maintained in training and development, particularly with the Americans, to achieve common methods. Therefore, the history cannot be complete without considerable reference to our Allies. However, it will be appreciated that precedence must be given to the British airborne forces and space does not allow adequate emphasis to be placed on the great achievements of the Allies. Similarly, it is written mainly on behalf of the Army, and the exploits of the Royal Air Force, the Dominion Air Forces and the American Army Air Force are therefore described only so far as they directly affected the airborne troops.

2. No history of any particular period, nor of the growth of a new branch of the Services, can be properly understood unless a preliminary explanation is given of the ideas and developments which led up to that period. The story starts with a very brief account of the beginnings of the theory and practice of airborne warfare before the outbreak of war in 1939. It includes mention of the first large scale exercises held by the Russians and leads up to enemy airborne technique and methods of operations learnt as a result of them, to which a chapter is devoted. The information contained in this chapter on the enemy was obtained after the war, but had we had that information available as we developed our own airborne forces it would probably have helped the airborne staffs considerably in persuading the mass of doubters with whom they had to contend in the early days. From there, this volume proceeds to the history of the British airborne forces first formed in 1940 and to their development, training and operations until the end of the war. Where it has been possible to obtain the information, the German reaction to our airborne operations has been included in the appropriate chapters. In the appendices are included descriptions of the parachutes, the gliders and the aircraft used by British airborne troops, and the story of their development. There is also an appendix (F) which is a reprint of an official pamphlet entitled " Standard Operating Procedure," as it was issued by Supreme Headquarters, Allied Expeditionary Forces, before the Normandy landings, in 1944. This pamphlet outlined the staff procedure during the planning, mounting and operating of airborne operations agreed by Headquarters, Airborne Troops, 38 Group R.A.F. and IX United States Troop Carrier Command and was the essential link which ensured good Allied and army–air co-operation at all stages and levels.

Early Airborne Ideas and Development

3. There are probably many examples in past centuries of individuals and nations who dreamed of the possibility of airborne operations of one kind and another ; one or two will serve to illustrate the lines on which their thoughts ran. First there is the story in Greek mythology of Pegasus and Bellerophon, in which the Warrior Bellerophon mounted his winged horse Pegasus in order to make his successful attack on the fire-breathing monster, the Chimaera. From this story, as depicted in art, was taken the sign of the airborne division in 1941 and that same sign was later extended to represent all British airborne forces. Then there was the idea of a great fortress suspended from balloons which Napoleon is reputed to have considered for his planned invasion of Great Britain, a fortress which would drift with the wind across the Channel and provide a modern means of transport for a part of his armies. Later, during the 1914–18 war when, for the first time, the idea of flying was translated into a military fact, Allied agents were dropped by parachute or landed by aircraft behind the enemy lines. In addition, a plan was made in 1918 to drop part of the American 1st Division commanded by Brigadier-General W. Mitchell, behind the German lines in the Metz sector. The officer-in-charge of the planning was Lieutenant-Colonel Lewis H. Brereton, later destined to command First Allied Airborne Army in the Second World War. However, the armistice arrived before the plan could be put into action. All these examples had one object in mind, to use a new method—aircraft of some kind—to transport troops over the enemy's defences so that they could attack a vital objective which could be reached in no other way. That object remains the " raison d'etre " for airborne forces to-day, forces which can take advantage of the open flank to place themselves in such a position that they can strike a mortal blow in the most economical manner. As with any tool destined for a vital role, it must be made of the finest material or the great effort put into its production will be wasted ; such tools, or even their parts, are difficult to replace and only the best can do the job properly.

The Russians

4. Although the American army carried out small scale experiments in dropping parachutists and weapons at Kelly and Brooks Fields, Texas, during 1928 and 1929, the first nation to realize the possibilities of airborne forces on a large scale, in addition to their value as guerilla fighters, and to apply theory to actual tests, was Russia. After the 1914–18 war, she began to develop parachuting and gliding as a national sport for young and old and by 1935 she had gone a long way towards creating an effective airborne force, including parachute troops carried in gliders (the air-landing troops of to-day). Although little was known about this outside Russia, she had developed the technique of towing several small gliders behind a single aircraft and proposed to use them for special tasks such as carrying troops and supplies to otherwise inaccessible areas. She had also developed a parachute force which demonstrated its power during the Red Army manœuvres in September, 1936, and which was described by Major-General A. P. Wavell (later Field-Marshal The Earl Wavell) as follows, in his official report as head of the British Military Delegation to these manœuvres :—

> " We were then taken to see a force of about 1,500 men dropped by parachute ; they were supposed to represent a ' Blue ' force dropped to occupy the passages over a river and so delay the advance of the ' Red '

2

Infantry Corps which was being brought up for the counter-offensive. This parachute descent, though its tactical value may be doubtful, was a most spectacular performance. We were told that there were no casualties and we certainly saw none ; in fact the parachutists we saw in action after the landings were in remarkably good trim and mostly moving at the double. They are, of course, a specially picked force and had had some months training. It apparently took some time to collect the force after the landing ; about one and a half hours after the first descent began, a part of the force was still being collected, though the greater part had already by then been in action for some time. The personal equipment seemed to consist of a rifle or light automatic with a small supply of ammunition. The less experienced parachutists, we were told, landed without rifles, their rifles being parachuted separately. No mechanical vehicles were landed by aeroplane, as was done at Kiev in 1935."

5. In a later paragraph of the same report, Major-General Wavell stated :—

" . . . the Central Flying Club, Tushino. This club is the headquarters of the flying activities of the Society of Air and Chemical Defence, Oscaviakhim. The club provides instruction in flying, gliding and parachute jumping. The members are mostly recruited from factories and devote their spare time to training in one or all of these branches."

Reaction to Russian Developments

6. The reaction of other nations to these Russian manœuvres and experiments is particularly interesting in the cases of Great Britain and Germany. The official view of the War Office appears to have been that there was little scope for the employment of airborne forces on a scale sufficient to exert any major influence on a campaign or battle. Although there may have been a feeling that parachutists might be usefully employed as saboteurs and that they would be a nuisance if so employed by an enemy, no action was taken to investigate the possibilities of airborne troops in practice and no airborne unit or experimental establishment was formed. In any case no interest was shown, which may have been owing to financial stringency in times of peace which discouraged expenditure on apparently rather fantastic new ideas. Alternatively, it may have been owing to a feeling that the number of suitable aircraft and gliders required to carry an effective force would never be forthcoming, particularly in competition with demands for bombers and fighters, and because relations between the Army and the R.A.F. were not then so close as they became later. There were few Army officers who did more than read occasional glamorous newspaper articles on gliding and parachuting, though it is interesting to note that General Sir Cyril Deverell, General Officer Commanding-in-Chief, Eastern Command did hold a series of anti-parachutist training exercises in 1935 and 1936 and instructed all his commanding officers to do the same. Among these was Lieutenant-Colonel F. A. M. Browning (later Lieutenant-General Sir Frederick Browning), then commanding 2nd Battalion the Grenadier Guards and later destined to command all British airborne troops.

7. The Germans, on the other hand, apparently realized fully the possibilities of this new form of warfare and secretly encouraged its development. As the aggressor nation, they had every incentive to devise some new means of surprising their future victims and of quickening the pace of modern warfare.

Furthermore, a new technique of this kind was particularly suited to methods of warfare aimed at destroying the morale of an opponent in the early, decisive stages of a campaign. Good base areas were available within reach of prospective vital objectives, and prepared linear ground defences of the fashionable static type of those days encouraged airborne operations in rear areas. The Germans, therefore, developed airborne forces secretly, both parachutists and glider-borne, and allotted them a major role in any operations which it might be necessary to initiate against the great Western European powers. The story of the operations they carried out is told briefly in Chapter II.

8. Nor were the Germans the only people to realize the possibility of airborne troops. In 1936 the Poles opened a parachute training school at Legionowo near Warsaw, run on similar lines to the Russians. They also included the study of the use of airborne troops in the syllabus at some of their senior officers' schools. Colonel Sosabowski (later Commander of 1 Polish Independent-Parachute Brigade Group) said :—

" It would be wrong to consider the parachutist only as a soldier who has learned an extremely important kind of modern warfare. Parachute training is a school of character and a test of leaders' capacities."

9. By 1939 it was known that Germany was carrying out trials with gliders and parachutists, so the Deputy Chiefs of Staff requested the Inter-Services Training and Development Centre to investigate the subject and report. One sentence of the report sums it up " and it is for consideration as to whether the present is the time to direct effort to the production of a weapon which may never be used." This opinion was expressed only some six months before war broke out. In the meantime the French had formed two companies of " Infanterie de l'Air " with a total of some 300 men. In April, 1939, it was suggested that two British officers should visit these units and study their techniques. Whether it was lack of interest on the part of the Service Ministry concerned we do not know, but whatever the reason, arrangements for the visit had not been completed by the outbreak of war. In October, 1939, the visit was cancelled.

Difficulties regarding the development and use of British Airborne Forces during the 1939–45 War

10. The difficulties inherent in forming an entirely new branch of the Services during the greatest war in history are apparent in the chapters which follow. No attempt is made to hide or belittle faults of initiative, organization, production or operational use. Similarly, there is no intention to lay the blame for all or even the majority of these faults on any one Service or Ministry, because to do so would be invidious and would be unfair to the great efforts made by all concerned.

11. There is one fact that is paramount. That is that at a time when national resources were strained as never before (in the short period between autumn, 1941, and autumn, 1944) there were created a British airborne corps of two complete divisions, one independent parachute brigade group and a special air service brigade, with one Polish Independent Parachute Brigade Group and units of parachutists from Belgium, France, Holland and Norway. In support, there was a complete organization of depots, training establishments and

4

experimental establishments. In lifts totalling on each of two separate occasions no less than 2,000 Allied aircraft and gliders, they were transported to battle in the Mediterranean, Normandy, Holland and Germany with a success which had a major effect on operations. In addition in the Far East, Major-General Orde Wingate had transported two brigade groups in gliders and had landed them in the Burmese jungle behind the Japanese lines during the winter of 1943–44 and an Indian airborne division was being raised for operations against the Japanese.

12. These achievements silence factional criticism and clearly evidence the co-operation, energy and imagination of all those, both in the Army and the R.A.F., who strove to create this new weapon of warfare.

CHAPTER II

ENEMY AIRBORNE FORCES

General

1. This chapter describes in some detail the growth of German airborne forces, and includes brief descriptions of the main operations in which they took part. There are also short accounts of Italian and Japanese airborne forces. The accuracy of the statements made in connection with these enemy forces is not guaranteed in all cases, but at least they serve to provide some comparison with our own and Allied airborne forces.

German Airborne Forces

2. Unlike the British, the Germans realized that there was a future in the development of parachute troops after they had seen the Russian demonstrations. Initial experiments were carried out in great secrecy, and in the spring of 1936 an experimental staff was set up at Stendal under Major Immanns consisting of 15 officers and about 80 other ranks, most of them drawn from the Regiment " General Goering ". The tasks of this staff were to decide whether a manual or automatic parachute was to be used, and what form a basic parachute course should take. A year later these problems had been solved, the automatic parachute having been taken into use. In the spring of 1937, a parachute school was opened at Stendal under command of Generalmajor Bassenge. Later that year a parachute battalion within the German air force was formed from volunteers from the Regiment " General Goering ". The battalion commander was Major Brauer. At the same time an S.S. platoon was being trained as parachutists, and the Army was also planning to have its own parachute force. However, political jealousy was widespread and there was no real policy in either the German Air Force or the army concerning parachute troops or transport aircraft.

3. In the autumn of 1937, at manœuvres in West Prussia and Pomerania, parachute troops took part in an exercise for the first time. Fourteen demolition squads were dropped by night to cut railways and generally disrupt communications, and were to be picked up by aircraft at secret landing grounds. They succeeded in their tasks, and delayed the advance of the " enemy ", but they were not picked up as the pilots could not find the landing grounds. The following day a parachute infantry company was dropped to co-operate with ground troops, but the tactical value of the exercise was lost as it was turned into a demonstration for Hitler. At the end of 1937 the first tactical experiments were carried out with cargo gliders. However, there was still much hesitation and indecision in high places, and many proposals by the commander of the parachute school for the use of parachutists and airborne troops remained unanswered.

4. Early in 1938 the parachute school at Stendal was expanded to 12 training companies, with 180 parachute instructors. The basic course lasted for two months, during which pupils had to complete six jumps to qualify as parachutists. In general the training was carried out on similar lines to the training of the British parachutist as we know it today. There were two main

differences. The first was that the German soldier was given practice in landing in a wind before he actually jumped, *i.e.* by carrying out ground training in the slipstream of an aircraft engine. The second difference was that he was taught to pack a parachute and jump with it. The output of the school was 4,000 parachutists a year in peace, but during the war three branch schools were formed, and by the end of the war their total annual output was about 57,000 men. On the tactical side, the German airborne experts realized at once that the use of the individual parachute had two essential weaknesses. The first was that the man was very vulnerable immediately after landing, before he had released his parachute harness. The second was the length of time it took for units and sub-units to assemble on the ground in sufficient strength to carry out an operation. It was always realized that troops carried in aeroplanes or gliders had a great advantage over parachute troops as soon as they touched the ground, providing suitable landing places could be found, because they did not suffer from the drawbacks mentioned above. However, it was accepted that normally parachute troops must land first in order to secure landing places.

5. On 30th May, 1938, Generalmajor Bassenge was ordered to organize, equip and train the S.A. Standarte " Feldherrnhalle " as a normal infantry regiment in preparation for an airborne operation against Czechoslovakia. On 4th July Generalmajor Student was ordered to form by 1st September an airborne division to take part in airborne operations to " liberate " the Sudetenland. The intention was to land a strong airborne force in the area of Freudenthal (Moravia) which is east of the Altvater mountain range. The division was to be known as 7 Flieger Division and was to consist of :—

Parachute Units
> Parachute Jäger Battalion—Five companies, signal platoon, engineer platoon.
> Parachute Infantry Battalion—Four companies, signal platoon, engineer platoon.

Airborne Units
> Airborne Battalion " Hermann Goering "—Three companies and a signal platoon.
> 16 Infantry Regiment—from 22 Infantry Division.
> S.A. Standarte " Feldherrnhalle "—Three Battalions.
> One Airborne Artillery troop with four Skoda guns.
> One Airborne Medical Company.

German Air Force Flying Units
> One Reconnaissance Echelon.
> One Combat Squadron—Heinkels 123.
> One Fighter Squadron—Heinkels 51. and Aeronautica Regias 68.
> Eight Transport Groups, 250 Junkers 52.
> One Glider Echelon—12 DFS 230.
> The total strength of the division was 9,000 men (not including air crews) and it was to be carried in three lifts.

The division was not required in an operational role, as the Sudetenland was annexed peacefully on 30th September. However, as an exercise, the first lift of 16 Infantry Regiment were landed on 1st October in fields, on the hills and in valleys near Freudenthal, as there were no airfields. Of the 250 transport aircraft used, only 12 were so badly damaged that they had to be removed by motor-transport and no personnel were lost. The exercise proved the possibility of landing troops in transport planes in open country without airfields.

6. Towards the end of 1938 it was decided that 7 Flieger Division was to be a parachute division and that 22 Infantry Division was to be an airborne division. Generalmajor Student was appointed Inspector of Parachute and Airborne Forces in addition to his duties as Divisional Commander of 7 Flieger Division, and worked directly under the German Air Force High Command. Reichsmarschall Goering took a personal interest in parachute forces. The occupation of Czechoslovakia took place in March, 1939 and had there been fighting 7 Flieger Division was to have occupied the airfields round Prague in an airborne landing. The build-up of 7 Flieger Division was slow. Many important personalities doubted the value of a parachute force and there was a shortage of personnel, especially of officers. 16 Infantry Regiment returned to 22 Division and S.A. Standarte " Feldherrnhalle " went back to the S.A. However, 1 Parachute Regiment was formed under Oberstleutnant Brauer from the Parachute Infantry Battalion and the Airborne Battalion " Hermann Goering ". By 1st September, 1939, I and II Battalions of 2 Parachute Regiment had been formed as independent battalions and two parachute anti-tank companies and a light parachute anti-aircraft troop had also been formed. In addition, what existed of the division was completely " motorized ". During the period up to September, 1939, a large number of airborne exercises took place. The largest was in July on the training grounds at Bergen near Celle, in which the bulk of 7 Flieger Division and 22 Infantry Division participated. On this occasion a complete parachute battalion, 1,000 strong, jumped for the first time, and for the first time dummy parachutists were used for deception. In the first week of September, 7 Flieger Division, reinforced by 16 Infantry Regiment, was assembled in the area east of Liegnitz (Lower Silesia), and held there as High Command Reserve for the Polish campaign. The division was earmarked for three tasks, but did not go into action. The tasks were the blocking of the Vistula River crossings near Pulawy and Deblin, the seizing of the bridges over the River San near Jaroslaw, and the capture of the Polish Government and High Command at Krzemieniewice (S.E. Poland).

7. In October, 1939, Hitler personally ordered Generalmajor Student to prepare for airborne operations in the offensive in the west, which was to begin in the spring of the following year. Between October and the end of 1939 various tasks were considered, among them the capture of the " Reduit Nationale ", the line of concrete fortifications near Ghent, by 7 Flieger Division and 22 Infantry Division. Five parachute battalions were available and 400 Junkers 52 for the airborne troops, who would have to make forced landings in open country. At the same time smaller units of 7 Flieger Division in the only 50 gliders then available were to capture the Fort of Eben Emael near Liege, and three bridges over the Albert Canal to the north of Liege, which were to be kept open for the advance of 6 Army. An alternative task considered was to capture the crossings of the River Meuse between Namur and Dinant. It is typical of German methods that in training for these operations one company was flown for two and a half hours in 15 degrees of frost and then made to jump.

8. On 9th April, 1940, one company of a parachute battalion of 7 Flieger Division jumped on to the airfield at Stavanger, Norway, and captured it in 35 minutes. Another company jumped in Denmark and without any fighting occupied the crossings near Aalberg. The remainder of the battalion flew into Oslo. On 14th April, one company took off from Oslo to drop near Dombas to block a road and destroy a railway, both of which ran through a narrow pass. The drop took place at 1830 hours in twilight into deep snow which caused the loss of a number of men and containers. By the following morning only two officers and 61 other ranks were available, the attack was unsuccessful and all survivors were finally captured by the British.

9. On 10th May, 1940, the airborne invasion of Holland began. 7 Flieger Division, commanded by Student, now Generalleutnant, with under command 16 Infantry Regiment and 72 Infantry Regiment, was to capture the bridges at Moerdijk, Dordrecht and Rotterdam. The only landing field available was at Waalhaven, near Rotterdam. One company of 16 Infantry Regiment was to land in seaplanes (Heinkel 59) near the Rotterdam bridges in the middle of the city. 22 Infantry Division under command of Generalleutnant Graf Sponeck with one parachute battalion and one parachute company attached was to occupy the Hague and capture the Royal Family, the Army High Command and the Government. Landing fields existed at Ypenburg, Katwijk and Loosduinen on the three open sides of the city. If necessary motor roads were to be used as landing strips. The operations of 22 Infantry Division failed, but those of 7 Flieger Division were more successful. The bridges at Moerdijk and Rotterdam, and the Waalhaven airfield were captured easily, but Dordrecht was only taken after a severe battle. All the German positions were then counter-attacked by the Allies, but were held successfully. Approximately 7,000 men of the division were landed with heavy weapons and artillery over a period of four days with comparatively light losses in personnel. Losses in transport aircraft were severe, 170 Junkers 52 being destroyed or badly damaged. On the same day the attacks were made on Fort Eben Emael and the bridges over the Albert Canal. A total of 600 troops took part, of whom 150 jumped while the remainder travelled in 50 gliders, which were released in darkness 35 kilometres from their objectives. In the attack on the fort 78 parachute engineers landed on the roof and blasted their way in with pole charges. Other troops landed in the fort by glider, and in 24 hours it had been captured for the loss of six men killed. Two out of the three bridges over the canal were captured intact.

10. As a result of the operations in Holland, the German High Command realized that there was a future in parachute and airborne forces, and the expansion of 7 Flieger Division and the production of equipment were accelerated. Headquarters, XI Flieger Corps was established with corps troops to command all parachute and airborne troops. General Student was appointed corps commander with Generalleutnant Putzier as his deputy. By 1st September, 1940, 7 Flieger Division consisted of :—

Divisional Headquarters.
7 Parachute Signals Battalion (one telephone company and one wireless company).
7 Parachute Medical Battalion (four companies).
7 Parachute Artillery Battalion (three troops).
7 Parachute Anti-Aircraft Battalion (four troops).

7 Parachute Anti-Tank Battalion (four companies).
7 Parachute Machine-Gun Battalion (four companies).
7 Parachute Engineer Battalion (four companies).
1 Parachute Regiment ⎫
2 Parachute Regiment ⎬Each of three battalions.
3 Parachute Regiment ⎭
Supply Troops.

In addition, there was an assault regiment which was independent of 7 Flieger Division. All ranks in the division and the assault regiment were parachutists and all except heavy weapons could be dropped in containers. A new glider unit was formed, the Luftlandegeschwader, consisting of three squadrons, each with 53 tug aircraft and gliders (DFS 230) which were for the primary use of the assault regiment.

11. For the invasion of England, which was to have taken place in September, 1940, all parachute and airborne troops were to take part under command of Generalleutnant Putzier. They were to establish a comparatively deep bridge-head on the south-east coast of England. In order to transport as large a force as possible in the first lift, those aircraft towing gliders were also to carry parachutists. However, Generalleutnant Putzier reported that the area was so well covered with anti-airborne obstacles that even if the invasion had taken place the airborne operations would have been impracticable. It is true that anti-airborne obstacles were constructed in the area, but it is doubtful whether they would have stopped any determined airborne assault.

12. By the end of 1940 XI Flieger Corps consisted of the following :—

(a) *Corps Troops*
XI Reconnaissance Unit (all flying units).
XI Parachute Signals Battalion.
Assault Regiment.
XI Parachute Anti-Aircraft/Machine Gun Battalion.
XI Airborne Field Hospital.
XI Airborne Supply Battalion.

(b) *7 Flieger Division.*

(c) *22 Infantry Division.*

(d) *XI Air Command* (comprising all air transport units)
Air Transport Squadron (with Supply Groups attached).
Combat Squadron Zb V I (Junkers 52).
Combat Squadron Zb V II (Junkers 52).
Glider School at Langendiebach.

(e) *Reserve Units and Schools*
Parachute Training Regiment (four battalions).
Convalescent Battalion.
Motor Transport Training Battalion.
Parachute School at Stendal (later Wittstock) which had attached to it an experimental unit.
Parachute School at Brunswick.
Main Experimental Staff.

10

During this period the solutions were found to the problems of dropping the 3·7 cm. Pak gun, the light anti-aircraft gun, the L.G.2, a lightweight gun, and motor-cycles.

13. During the Balkan campaign it was originally intended that one parachute regiment should be used to capture Lemnos, and it was assembled at Plovdiv, Bulgaria. The operation was cancelled by Hitler. Shortly after this, on 21st April, 1941, the decision was taken to attack Crete by parachute and airborne forces, on the suggestion of General Student. The original date of the attack was to be 16th May, 1941. XI Flieger Corps was moved from central Germany to the Athens area, where it came under command of 4 Air Fleet. The whole movement was slowed up owing to the impassability of the roads and railways in Greece, and the original date could not be achieved. 22 Infantry Division could not be released from its commitments in the Balkans and its place was taken by 5 Mountain Division, and a regiment of 6 Mountain Division which were attached to XI Flieger Corps. Both these formations were completely inexperienced in airborne operations. Although the Germans had reports of about 100,000 British and Allied troops on the island, they were unaware of the presence of the whole of 2 New Zealand Division and part of 6 Australian Division. For the operation about 530 Junkers 52. were available, and about 100 gliders were to be used. The airfields at Maleme, Heraklion and Retimo were to be captured by parachute troops, and Allied reserves were to be pinned down by a parachute regiment jumping south of Canea. The assault was to be carried out in two waves.

14. In the meantime, at 0930 hours on 26th April, 1941, parties of German parachute troops and airborne troops in gliders landed at either end of the bridge connecting the Isthmus of Corinth with the mainland. Although some of the gliders went into the water, the troops seized the bridge after a short fight and occupied the neighbouring town without much difficulty. This operation speeded up considerably the German occupation of the Peloponnese.

15. The attack on Crete began at 0715 hours on 20th May, 1941. Two companies of I Battalion of the Assault Regiment in gliders overran two anti-aircraft positions near Maleme and Canea. At the same time other companies of the battalion landed on the high ground south of Maleme and on the Akrotiri Peninsula to occupy the high ground there. These attacks were a failure and the companies destroyed. At 0730 hours the remainder of the Assault Regiment under Generalmajor Meindl jumped near Maleme and 3 Parachute Regiment jumped south-west of Canea. At the same time 7 Parachute Engineer Battalion dropped near Alikianou to cover the rear of 3 Parachute Regiment while it attacked Canea. These forces formed the " Gruppe West " under General-leutnant Süssmann, commander of 7 Flieger Division. However, he and his staff were shot down by Allied aircraft shortly after taking off. The drops were scattered, some being right among the British troops. III Battalion, Assault Regiment was almost annihilated. The survivors regrouped and the Assault Regiment attacked Maleme airfield but failed to capture it. Luckily for them the British did not counter-attack or they would have been wiped out. 3 Parachute Regiment attacked Canea, but I Battalion was only able to capture the heights above the town, where it dug in, reinforced by 7 Parachute Engineer Battalion.

16. The second lift was scheduled to follow as soon as possible in the afternoon of 20th May, and was to consist of 1 Parachute Regiment with under command II Battalion of 2 Parachute Regiment, to drop at Heraklion, and I and III Battalions of 2 Parachute Regiment to drop at Retimo. However, the take-off was considerably delayed owing to slow refuelling of the aircraft. In an effort to make up for lost time, the starting order as planned was not maintained. Some units arrived over the battlefield in the wrong tactical order, and some companies did not take off at all. To add to the confusion, corps headquarters did not know what was happening, as Greek saboteurs had cut the telephone lines. VIII Flieger Corps could not be informed, so they carried out their preliminary bombing attacks on the original time-table, more than an hour before the troops actually dropped, which was useless. I Parachute Regiment's attack on Heraklion airfield failed, and the regiment remained " dug in " on the defensive outside the town. The attack on Retimo airfield also failed, the commander and staff of 2 Parachute Regiment being dropped within the Allied lines, and captured. The regiment remained in position around the town for ten days until relieved by ground forces. Wireless communications between regimental and corps headquarters did not work. However, the regiment managed to cut a road which was important to the Allies.

17. On the morning of 21st May two parachute infantry companies and 7 Parachute Anti-Tank Battalion dropped west of Maleme airfield, which was eventually captured. The Germans could not clear the Allies from the fortified village of Maleme, so at first the airfield remained under Allied small-arms fire. In the afternoon two more companies were dropped in the area and, after bitter fighting, the village was captured and the airfield could now be used by the Germans. Mountain troops were flown in at once, and during the night 21st/22nd May heavy counter-attacks were repulsed. The battle-groups at Canea, Heraklion and Retimo were supplied from the air, but many containers dropped in the Allied lines. Attempts were made to bring in more supplies by sea, but were prevented by the British Navy. After 22nd May operations proceeded more or less according to plan until the Allies evacuated their forces on 30th May. Canea and Suda Bay were captured on 27th May. After some difficulty Retimo was captured on 29th May. The casualties in the fighting for Crete were heavy, about 4,000 men being killed or missing alone. Of the 530 Junkers 52 employed, some 170 were lost or so heavily damaged that their repair took a long time. It is interesting to note that General Student considered that these losses " were not very heavy."

18. In July, 1941, 7 Flieger Division was brought back to Germany from Crete, was re-formed and, less 2 Parachute Regiment, was sent into action as infantry near Leningrad. It was taken out of the line in November, by which time it had suffered heavy losses. 2 Parachute Regiment went into action in a ground role at the end of 1941 in the Stalino area, and later in the Volkhov Sector, east of Leningrad. The Assault Regiment was split up into battalions and distributed over the Eastern Front. As a result of the Russian successes in the winter of 1941–42 on the Eastern Front, even the parachute training units and the parachute schools had to send many of their best personnel into the line. Headquarters, XI Flieger Corps remained in Germany, in the Berlin–Tempelhof area, and had to administer the widely dispersed parachute units. In addition it had to train six special German air force infantry regiments which had been newly formed and were required at the Eastern Front as soon as possible.

19. During the period experiment and development continued. Despatchers were introduced in parachute aircraft and they were also made responsible for the correct approach to the dropping zone. These men were called " Fallschirm Kampfbeobachter " and were trained at a special Parachute Observers School which was established at Freiburg, under Corps Headquarters. The Heinkel 111 superseded the Junkers 52 as a parachute aircraft. It also held 12 parachutists, but was a better all-round aircraft. Formation night jumps were practised on a large scale. Troops were trained to jump with rifles and machine-guns, and later, in 1943, with mortars. The quick-release box on the parachute harness was introduced. Efforts to obtain a new glider failed, but the old D.F.S. 230 was improved, being equipped with machine-guns and parachute brakes. Later, a rocket brake was developed at Peenemünde, which would stop a glider on the ground within a few yards. The German official attitude at this time to the development of parachute forces appears to have been negative, but General Student was left very much on his own. To carry out his experiments and tests he formed a Lehr Battalion, out of which developed later the Parachute Lehr Regiment, but he was handicapped by a lack of aircraft. Towards the end of 1941, 4 and 5 Parachute Regiments were formed and another parachute engineer battalion.

20. During 1942 a number of airborne operations were planned. In the spring of 1942 Hitler and Mussolini decided to attack Malta. The attack was to take place in August, 1942, under the overall command of Marshal Cavallero, Italian Commander-in-Chief, and was to be carried out by 7 Flieger Division, two other German parachute regiments, the Italian parachute division " Folgore " and the Italian marine regiment " San Marco," all under the immediate command of General Student. Five-hundred Junkers 52 and Heinkels 111, and 80 Savoia 82 were to be used. Then an airborne attack on Gibraltar was considered, and soon after this 7 Flieger Division was moved from Normandy to the eastern front to take part in an airborne operation against the Russians. They were to be dropped and landed behind the Russians to open up an important coastal road along the Black Sea near Adler, south-east of Tuapse. However, the situation deteriorated and the division was committed in a ground role near Smolensk. In July, 1942, a parachute brigade was formed under Oberst Ramcke, and was sent to Africa where it fought under General Rommel. In November, 1942, all available German parachute units, including training establishments, were assembled and transported by air to Bizerta and Tunis. They went into action in a ground role and suffered very heavy losses.

21. At the beginning of 1943, XI Flieger Corps undertook the formation and unit training of Bulgarian parachute units. The Bulgarians were trained at the Parachute School at Brunswick and a small German detachment went to Sofia to assist them on the spot. All jumping equipment was supplied by Germany. By the beginning of 1943 Hitler had at last been convinced that the Allies were forming strong airborne forces, and he reconsidered his opinion about German parachute forces. He gave General Student the task of training the German Army in the west in defence against possible Allied airborne operations. For this purpose Headquarters, XI Flieger Corps, was moved to Quintin, Brittany. A new formation, 2 Parachute Division, was formed in Brittany and 1 Parachute Division was transferred from the eastern front to Normandy. A parachute school was set up at Dreux and an infantry battle school for parachutists was opened at La Courtine near Limoges. A number of

exercises were carried out in France by the Parachute Lehr Battalion and a glider unit, to give practice to the German forces in anti-airborne defence. Meanwhile, possible action in the event of an Allied invasion of Italy and the latter's defection was being considered. If this occurred Marshal Rommel was to march in over the Alps with a strong force while XI Flieger Corps was to hold the Brenner Pass and was concentrated for this purpose on the southern coast of France as High Command. When the Allies did land in Sicily only 1 Parachute Division was used as reinforcements because of the expected superiority of Allied fighters. Mussolini was arrested at the end of July, 1943, and preparations were made for the desertion of Italy from the Axis. All available formations of XI Flieger Corps and 3 Panzer Grenadier Division were concentrated near Rome. 2 Parachute Division and a few newly formed parachute battalions were brought by air from Nimes and camped in the area of the Pontine marshes. 3 Panzer Grenadier Division went to Orte, north of Rome. On the evening of 10th September an Allied radio station reported the capitulation of Italy and that night the Germans disarmed two Italian divisions on the coast and near Frascati. Early next morning a parachute battalion dropped near Monte Rotondo and attacked the Italian headquarters, which were stubbornly defended. 3 Panzer Grenadier Division attacked north of Rome and during the day 2 Parachute Division advanced into the suburbs from the south. Shortly after this all Italian forces in the area capitulated to the Germans. The rescue of Mussolini was then carried out by the Parachute Lehr Battalion under Oberstleutnant Skorzeny. One company in gliders landed on the Campo Imperatore, where Mussolini was imprisoned, while the main body of the battalion advanced to the foot of the plateau by motor transport. The operation was successful and Mussolini was evacuated to Vienna in a Storch aircraft. XI Flieger Corps was then employed to defend the western coast of Italy between Orbetello and Terracina, and in disarming the Italian forces in Central Italy. One parachute battalion of 2 Parachute Division dropped and captured the island of Elba. In November, 1943, the division was transferred to the eastern front, except for one battalion, which was dropped in an attack on Leros. 1 Parachute Division was employed in Italy until the end of the war.

22. At the end of 1943 it was found that large numbers of redundant German Air Force ground personnel were available. Reichsmarschal Goering therefore decided upon a considerable increase in parachute forces. General Student was promoted to Generaloberst and was made Commander-in-Chief of a new Parachute High Command which was formed out of the bulk of XI Flieger Corps Headquarters. I and II Parachute Corps and 3, 4, 5 and 6 Parachute Divisions were to be formed at once. The authorities realized that these formations would have to be employed in ground operations, and that it was unlikely that they would be used in a parachute role owing to Allied superiority in the air. In spite of the sudden increase in numbers the volunteer system was kept in being until the middle of 1944. Training in jumping was continued as far as possible and about 30 per cent. of the new formations qualified as parachutists. At that time there were parachute schools at Wittstock, Frieburg (formerly at Brunswick, later at Salzwedel) and Dreux (later at Lyons). Difficulty was experienced in setting up the new formations, as the work was carried out in occupied territory where there were operational commitments. The two existing parachute divisions were in action and it was only possible to withdraw from them a very few men as cadres. Also, equipment was scarce.

23. At the beginning of 1944 the remainder of Headquarters, XI Flieger Corps, was withdrawn from Italy, and finally lost its identity, being replaced by 1 Parachute Corps. 4 Parachute Division, consisting of 10, 11 and 12 Parachute Regiments was formed in Italy, and went into action almost immediately against the Allied landings at Nettuno. With 1 Parachute Division it formed 1 Parachute Corps and also remained in Italy until the war ended. In March, 1944, the Parachute High Command was moved to Nancy, France. 3 Parachute Division (5, 8 and 9 Parachute Regiments) was raised in Brittany, and was part of II Parachute Corps. 5 Parachute Division, consisting of 13, 14 and 15 Parachute Regiments was formed in the Bourges area, later moved to eastern Brittany, and at the time of the invasion it was not complete. In April, 2 Parachute Division was brought from the eastern front to Köln-Wahn for re-forming, and sent to Brittany, where it formed the garrison at Brest. 16 Parachute Regiment was formed at Köln-Wahn in May and was sent to Normandy. This regiment was the first and only formation of 6 Parachute Division. The parachute training organization was also expanded. The Parachute Weapon School was reorganized and transferred from La Courtine to Valdahon (Franche Comte). Another school was opened at Pontà Mousson. Two more Parachute Training Regiments, Nos. 2 and 3, were formed, each having four battalions, and a large training camp for parachute artillery units was set up in Luneville. When the Allies invaded Normandy the Parachute Army consisted of about 160,000 men.

24. A few days after the start of the invasion, Generaloberst Student was ordered to prepare an airborne counter-attack against the Normandy bridgehead, using 15,000 parachute troops. However, the Allied build-up and advance was so fast that the operation was abandoned. The remains of 3, 5 and 6 Parachute Divisions retreated *via* Rouen–Mons–Liege, being used chiefly as rear-guards and suffering severe losses. By September they consisted of a few thousand men only and were withdrawn to reform under Headquarters II Parachute Corps at Köln-Wahn. In the meantime, because of the losses and defeats on both fronts, the Parachute High Command was ordered to raise new parachute divisions for ground roles, and the Headquarters moved from Nancy to Berlin—Wannsee. Five independent parachute regiments were formed, four of which later formed 7 Parachute Division, but had no artillery. They occupied a sector on the Albert Canal between Antwerp and Maastricht. On 1st November, Generaloberst Student was made Commander-in-Chief, Army Group H, but also remained as Commander-in-Chief of parachute forces. The Parachute High Command was taken over by General Schlemm, and the training and replacement organizations were commanded by General Conrath who later commanded all home parachute formations. At this time a parachute training division was formed and other divisions were commanded as follows :—

2 Parachute Division ..	.. ..	Generalleutnant Lackner.
3 Parachute Division ..	.. ..	Generalleutnant Schimpf.
5 Parachute Division ..	.. ..	Generalmajor Heilmann.
6 Parachute Division ..	.. ..	Generalleutnant Plocher.

They were all put into Army Group H.

At the end of 1944, 8 Parachute Division, under Generalmajor Wadehn (22, 24 and 32 Parachute Regiments) was formed in Holland. The last German parachute operation took place on 17th December, 1944, during the Ardennes offensive. A battalion, 1,000 strong, under the command of Oberstleutnant von der Heydte was to drop by night at Mont Rigi, between Eupen and Malmedy to occupy an important road network. However, the aircrews were inadequately trained for night work and the drop was dispersed, with high casualties. Only about 300 men arrived at the rendezvous, and eventually most of them were killed or captured. Another parachute battalion, under Oberstleutnant Herrmann, stood by to establish a bridgehead over the River Meuse, but the operation was cancelled.

25. On 1st February, 1945, Generaloberst Student was ordered to form more parachute units. 9 Parachute Division (16, 25 and 27 Parachute Regiments) was already forming, and was then committed on the eastern front near Stettin. Later it was transferred to the Kustrin area and was believed to have been annihilated in the Battle of Berlin. The first new formation to be raised was a " Jagd-Brigade," followed by 10 and 11 Parachute Divisions and a parachute " Stamm-Brigade." In the meantime a Parachute Army (Fallschirm Armee) had been set up to control a sector of the front in southern Holland. It was quite distinct from the Parachute High Command and, under General Schlemm, consisted of 2, 6, 7 and 8 Parachute Divisions and some army formations. General Schlemm was wounded in March and was succeeded by General Blumentritt. On 31st March, Generaloberst Student was ordered by Hitler to carry out a counter-offensive on the western front with II Parachute Corps. The attack was to start from the area south of Enschede in the direction of Haltern, but the situation had deteriorated so badly that the project was abandoned.

26. When the war ended the following German parachute forces existed :—

I Parachute Corps	General Heidrich.
1 Parachute Division	Generalmajor Schulz.
4 Parachute Division	Generalleutnant Trettner.
2 Parachute Division	Generalleutnant Lackner.
3 Parachute Division	Oberst Becker.
5 Parachute Division	Oberst Gröschke.
6 Parachute Division	Generalleutnant Plocher.
II Parachute Corps	General Meindl.
7 Parachute Division	Generalleutnant Erdmann.
8 Parachute Division	Generalmajor Wadehn.
9 Parachute Division	Oberst Herrmann.
10 Parachute Division	Oberst von Hofmann.
11 Parachute Division	Oberst Fuchs.

Italian Airborne Forces

27. The Italians appear to have considered the possibilities of parachute troops rather earlier than most nations, though they did not follow up their experiments to any great extent. In 1927, nine men, carrying equipment, dropped on Cinisello airfield, and in the same year a course was started for training about 250 parachutists. Air Marshal Balbo then gave his backing to airborne forces, and we next hear of them in 1937, when parachute units took part in manœuvres at Gefara, Libya. The main parachute training centre was at Castel Benito airfield, near Tripoli, but the Italians found that it was not worth while to continue training native troops as parachutists, and so they opened a training centre in Italy at Tarquinia.

28. By 1939 there were two trained parachute battalions in Libya, but their total strength was only about 500 all ranks, and the following year they had an additional battalion of native parachute troops, between 200 and 300 strong, stationed at Castel Benito. On 30th April, 1941, less than a week after the German airborne attack on the Corinth Canal, the Italians carried out a small parachute operation to occupy the Island of Cephalonia, off the west coast of Greece, about 150 miles south-east of the " heel " of the Italian " boot."

29. In the spring of 1942 Italian parachutist headquarters were at Florence, with Tarquinia still a large training centre. There was one parachute division, the Folgore, in Italy, consisting of two parachute regiments each about 2,500 strong. One was at Civitavecchia, on the coast 40 miles west of Rome and the other at Viterbo, 40 miles north of Rome. Within the regiments each battalion was made up of 29 officers and about 300 other ranks, formed into three companies ; a mining platoon or company for demolition work, a communication section and a medical section.

30. In March, 1942, the Parachute Division, Folgore carried out rehearsals at Viterbo for the projected attack on Malta, mentioned in paragraph 20 above, which never took place. For the remainder of Italy's participation in the war her parachute troops did not function as such and were only used operationally in a ground role.

Japanese Airborne Forces

31. As with everything they undertook, when the Japanese started to organize parachute troops they did it thoroughly. They began in the early part of 1940 by setting up four parachute training centres at Shimonoseki, Shizuoka, Hiroshima and Himeji at which they ran courses lasting for six months. During the summer some German parachute instructors arrived and at their suggestion the courses were reduced to about two months but were highly intensified.

32. By the autumn of 1941 about 100 German instructors had arrived and there were nine training centres and some fourteen or fifteen thousand men under training. Both the Army and the Navy had their own separate forces of parachute troops, but the naval training period was very short in comparison with the army programme. By 1st November, 1941, the naval parachute force consisted of 2,000 men divided into the Yokosuka 1st and Yokosuka 3rd Special Naval Landing Forces, which were later called the Hariuchi (Karashima) and Fukumi Forces. When war broke out on 7th December, 1941, both these forces were ready for operations.

33. The army parachute units were part of the Japanese Army Air Force and were known as raiding units. Eventually these units were organized into various formations, the largest of which was the raiding group, the equivalent of a division. It was commanded by a major-general and consisted of a group headquarters, a raiding flying brigade, a raiding brigade, two glider infantry regiments, a raiding machine cannon unit, a raiding signal unit and a raiding engineer unit. The total strength was just under 6,000 all ranks. The raiding brigade consisted entirely of parachute troops, was commanded by a colonel or lieutenant-colonel and was composed of headquarters, and two raiding regiments, the total strength being about 1,500 all ranks, and that of a regiment being some 700. Other units could be attached as required. Each glider regiment was just under 900 strong, and corresponded to our air-landing battalion.

34. The transport aircraft attached to a group were controlled by a raiding flying-brigade, which consisted of two raiding flying regiments, one glider flying regiment and a brigade signal unit. The duties of the glider and raiding flying regiments were to transport the glider and parachute units. The raiding flying regiment had a headquarters unit and three squadrons, and a strength of about 500 all ranks and 35 aircraft. The size of the sticks varied from 10 to 13 according to the type of aircraft.

35. Japanese parachute troops took part in several operations, a few of which are described briefly in the following paragraphs. The first on record, and the only one by naval parachute units, was an operation by Yokosuka 1st Special Naval Landing Unit against Menado airfield on the north-east tip of Celebes Island. The unit was based on Davao and on 11th January, 1942, three companies were dropped from about 900 feet. The transport aircraft were preceded by bombers and escorted by Zero fighters. After five hours fighting the Japanese had captured the airfield. The native troops fled and the small force of Dutch regulars was annihilated with the exception of about 30 who were taken prisoners.

36. When the Japanese entered the war the army had planned to use their parachute troops for about three months in practice operations in China before they used this particular type of warfare against the Allies. However, when the campaign against Java and Sumatra began they soon realized that the only way of seizing the oil refineries at Palembang before the British and Dutch destroyed them was to employ parachute troops. Therefore they decided to use a raiding regiment for the purpose, though the training of the unit was by no means complete. The Allied anti-aircraft defence consisted of 16 3·7 inch and 15 40 mm. Bofors guns, of which eight 3·7 inch and seven Bofors were on the airfield and four 3·7 inch and four Bofors each at the refineries at Pladjoe, four miles east of Palembang and Soengei Gerong. In addition to seizing the refineries the Japanese unit was ordered to capture the airfield.

37. On 14th February, 1942, the area was bombed from a high altitude by medium bombers, but there was no strafing. At about 1830 hours on the same day some 70 Hudsons, with R.A.F. markings, flew over Palembang in two waves at 600 feet, each wave dropping 350 troops. Two planes were detailed to drop equipment but one was shot down. The troops were armed with rifles, pistols, sub-machine guns and light machine guns and were dropped about five miles from the aerodrome in an area astride the River Moesi. The Allied anti-aircraft fire was so effective that the enemy pilots flew too high so that the troops were scattered very wide. After great difficulty in finding their equipment they assembled in three groups, one of 300 and two each of 200. The larger group moved off to attack the airfield, and split into three parties, one attempting to cut the road leading to the town and the others attacking the gun positions. After severe fighting and two further drops of Japanese reinforcements on 15th February, the airfield was eventually captured from the Allies. The attacks on the refineries were a complete failure, all the parachute troops being killed, and 16 aircraft being shot down. The demolition work which the Allies had already started was not stopped, so that when an enemy sea-borne force finally took Palembang on 15th February both refineries had been badly damaged.

38. A week after the Palembang operations the Japanese again used parachute troops, this time on Timor, on 21st February, 1942, in conjunction with the main attack on Koepang. The operation was divided into two parts, the first being a drop by five aircraft over the southernmost top of Timor as a feint to distract attention from the main attack. The object of the main attack was to secure a position astride the Allied line of communication. On 21st and 22nd February some 20 or 25 Douglas type transport aircraft dropped about 350 troops one and a half miles from the Allied forward positions. The drops were preceded by heavy bombing and strafing of the ground defences from a low level, which continued until the troops were on the ground. There was no air opposition and no wind, so that the operations were successful and the sea-borne landing of 18,000 men on 22nd February overran the defenders.

39. After an interval of 18 months a successful small operation was staged against the Chinese at Taoyuan, Hunan, when 60 troops were dropped. This was followed the following year, on 6th August, by the dropping of several plain clothes agents, and on 26th November by another small operation against the Americans at Leyte. Three planes flew over at midnight to drop parachutists whose task was to carry out acts of sabotage against American aircraft based at Leyte so that they would not be able to interfere with a Japanese convoy due to enter Ormoc Bay on 28th November. One plane was shot down with all occupants killed, and the other two crash-landed, the parachute troops scattering and being eventually hunted down and killed.

40. Another attack was carried out against Leyte in December, 1944, in a further effort to prevent American aircraft from interfering with convoys in the Ormoc area and with Japanese air operations based on Luzon. The Japanese therefore decided to capture the Buri, San Pablo and Bayug airstrips on 6th December in conjunction with the landing of troops in Ormoc Bay on 7th December, the anniversary of Pearl Harbour. The Japanese plan was for the main effort to be made against the three airstrips mentioned above so that they would be captured in conjunction with ground troops attacking from the west. Smaller, suicidal attacks were to be made against the airstrips at Dulag and Tacloban where as many American planes as possible were to be destroyed and the airstrips held at least until midnight, 7th December.

41. Just before 1800 hours on 6th December the first wave of transport aircraft appeared over the targets and 18 aircraft were shot down out of a total of about 51, including bombers. However, after bombing and the laying of a smoke screen about 300 parachutists were dropped. Unfortunately for the Japanese the strips at San Pablo and Buri were non operational at the time. As the parachute troops dropped they called out various threats in English such as :—" Kill a Yankee ! " ; " Go to Hell Beast " ; " Have done, all the resistance " ; " Lay down arms, surrender quickly, if don't shall die ! ; It is resistless, so that get away from here in this night ; do what I say, must help your life. If don't shall die all these captives ! " As aids to assembling, harmonicas, jewsharps, wooden clappers, flutes, gongs and a pigeon whistle were used. Two or three L-5 aircraft and a jeep were burned and a truck was upset, but no important demolitions were carried out. The Japanese rushed around firing into wash-bowls and other non-military objectives but did not touch petrol supplies and ammunition dumps.

42. Part of a Japanese division had begun to attack from the west on 5th December, but the attack was broken up before the parachute troops dropped and only scattered remnants succeeded in joining the airborne force. On 7th December the parachutists, having been driven off the other airstrips, concentrated near Buri where they held out for several days with survivors of the infantry division. An attempt to relieve them by a battalion of another division came to nothing. In the meantime the attacks on Dulag and Tacloban were a complete failure. Two transport aircraft appeared over Dulag, one dropping five troops and then crashing, and the other crashing without dropping any troops. Two aircraft also arrived at Tacloban and lowered their wheels and flaps as if to land, but one was shot down and the other crashed. By 12th December, all parachute troops had been liquidated.

43. At first the Americans thought that the Japanese airborne force was a loosely organized group of picked fanatics who had little or no special training for an airborne operation. But it was learned later they they belonged to a well organized and trained raiding regiment and had rehearsed the operation in considerable detail, the aircraft having come from a raiding flying regiment. The attacks were a complete failure, for a Japanese convoy attempting to put into Ormoc Bay was smashed by planes from Tacloban on 7th December, while American amphibious forces landed on the very beach which the Japanese had selected for this disembarkation.

CHAPTER III

THE ORIGIN OF BRITISH AIRBORNE FORCES

JUNE, 1940, to OCTOBER, 1941

The Initial Requirement

1. The evacuation of Dunkirk and the collapse of France took place in the middle of 1940. Less than three weeks later, on 22nd June, 1940, when the Empire was more on the defensive than it had ever been in its history, and while Hitler awaited the French reply to his terms of surrender the Prime Minister of Great Britain, Mr. Winston Churchill, directed the War Office to investigate the possibility of forming a Corps of at least 5,000 parachute troops, including a proportion of Canadians, Australians and New Zealanders, together with some trustworthy men from France and Norway. He was anxious that advantage should be taken of the summer to train these troops which would, if required, still be available for home defence.

2. The Director of Combined Operations, who was responsible for the development of airborne forces, had already formed the Central Landing School, details of which are given later, which was to investigate the technical problems concerned with parachuting and the carriage of troops by glider. Shortly after this the Air Ministry and War Office agreed on four types of gliders and placed initial orders for their production. The decision as to which type or types were to be finally adopted was left until prototypes had been made and flown. Only a few civilian gliders, too light for military purposes, existed in 1940. On 6th August the Chiefs of Staff informed the Prime Minister that out of 3,500 volunteers, 500 specially selected men were being trained as parachute troops, but that their training was held up through lack of suitable aircraft. Efforts were being made to obtain the use of four K.L.M. (Royal Dutch Air Lines) Dakotas. The Prime Minister noted " I said 5,000 ". On 10th August he was informed that limitations in training equipment and aircraft made it impossible for the time being to go beyond the first 500 parachute troops. He was also told that it had not been possible to obtain the K.L.M. machines, but that the possibilities were being examined of using other types or of obtaining Dakotas from America.

3. Mr. Churchill immediately asked " When will this figure be achieved according to plan ? " On 31st August he was informed that with existing facilities the target of 5,000 parachute troops would not be reached for 12 months. He was told that the crux of the matter was aircraft. The Air Ministry stated that two principles had been adopted by the Air Force in developing the training of parachute troops :—

" (a) That owing to the need for as rapid as possible a development of the Bomber Force, and our shortage of personnel, there can be no question within the predictable future of our being able to afford to have squadrons of aircraft solely for the purpose of dropping parachute troops. Parachute dropping must therefore be an alternative role for heavy bomber squadrons.

21

(*b*) In training it is obviously necessary to use the same sort of aircraft as are to be used for operations—*i.e.*, it is no good training on an aircraft which the personnel leave by means of a door if in operations they are going to have to leave by means of a hole in the floor."

The only aeroplane which met these requirements was the Whitley bomber, which was far from ideal technically or tactically. Several other types had been examined and found to be of no use. The Bombay and Dakota were aircraft with doors and were suitable, but the former was out of production, there being only 21 in the country, only three of which had engines. Every effort was being made to obtain Dakotas from the United States of America. The Air Ministry also stated that they did not consider a totally unarmed aircraft acceptable for dropping parachute troops in active operations. They were beginning to believe that dropping troops from the air by parachute was a clumsy and obsolescent method, and that there were far more important possibilities in gliders. Although the Germans had been successful with their parachute troops in the Low Countries the Air Ministry considered " that it was at least possible that this was the last time that parachute troops are used on a serious scale in major operations ". In addition, they thought that the glider might be used for such purposes as refuelling heavy aircraft in the air, or for carrying an additional load of bombs.

4. The Prime Minister agreed that if it were considered that gliders were preferable to parachutes, the scheme should be taken up seriously, but he feared that by pursuing a doubtful and experimental policy we might be losing one which had already been proved. He asked for a full report of what had been done about the gliders.

On 9th September, a report was submitted to the Prime Minister containing the following main points :—

(*a*) There appeared to be three types of raid for which airborne troops might be used :—

    (i) A raid on a selected position, to be followed by the evacuation of the raiding force by air.

    (ii) A raid to be followed by evacuation by sea.

    (iii) The dropping of parachutists as saboteurs, pure and simple.

(*b*) For the first two roles the best method would be to use a small force of parachutists, who would be followed by a larger body landing from gliders.

(*c*) For any particular operation about 1,000 men would be required, of whom 100 would be parachutists, and 900 glider-borne. To enable more than one raid to be carried out, plans were being made to train three such forces by the spring of 1941, plus 200 parachute saboteurs.

(*d*) The total airborne force envisaged, therefore, was :—

    500 parachute troops.
    2,700 glider-borne troops.
    360 glider pilots to fly the glider-borne troops.

This was a force very much reduced from Mr. Churchill's original conception but our resources at that time would not permit of anything larger, so he accepted it.

5. Even with this greatly reduced commitment the problems of training such an airborne force by the spring of 1941 were numerous.   The position was summed up neatly by a senior officer of the Royal Air Force who said :—

"There are very real difficulties in this parachute business.   We are trying to do what we have never been able to do hitherto, namely to introduce a completely new arm into the Service at about five minutes' notice, and with totally inadequate resources and personnel.   Little, if any, practical experience is possessed in England of any of these problems and it will be necessary to cover in six months what the Germans have covered in six years."

The General Situation at the end of 1940

6. By the end of 1940 the situation was as follows :—

(a) The 500 parachute troops would probably be trained by the spring of 1941.   This figure of 500 was, however, purely arbitrary and bore no relation to any existing unit establishment, the internal organization being left to the discretion of the unit commander.   No arrangements had been made for any increase.   The equipment was confined to purely personal weapons, as dropping trials for any heavier types were not yet completed.

(b) No definite units or personnel had been allotted as air-landing troops.   It was considered better to provide them when their means of transport was ready.   The general view was that any ordinary troops could be called on for this role with little or no specialist training.   It was realized, however, that they would need to be very lightly equipped, with little transport, though as far as possible they were to use only standard army issues.   They would probably have to do with less equipment, rather than take normal scales of specialized airborne equipment.   The specifications put forward for the gliders bore little relation to the carriage of vehicles and supporting weapons, with the exception of one type of glider to carry a light tank.

(c) The Air Ministry and War Office had agreed to produce four types of gliders (for details *see* Appendix A) :—

(i) An eight-seater, subsequently named the " Hotspur ".   This glider was originally intended as an operational type, 250 of them being kept for this purpose, but later became a trainer.   It had the great advantage that it could be towed by a small aircraft.

(ii) A 25-seater operational type, subsequently named the " Horsa ".

(iii) A 15-seater operational type, to be produced in small numbers purely as an insurance against the 25-seater proving unsuitable, subsequently named the " Hengist ".

(iv) A tank-carrying type.   Only two of these were to be produced as an experimental measure, from which a general purpose weight-carrying glider could be developed for an alternate use as a 40-seater troop-carrier, subsequently named the " Hamilcar ".

23

The " Horsas " were originally intended to act purely as troop-carriers.   It is interesting to note, however, that when it was first suggested that they should carry equipment, the maximum load considered was one motor-cycle and side car.   Later the suggestion was made that they might be able to carry a load of four motor-cycle combinations fully equipped, or one scout car, or one 3·7 howitzer. The " Hengist " was definitely a troop-carrier only.   Any heavier arms required by an airborne force, *e.g.* 15-cwt. trucks or Bren carriers, would be transported in the general purpose glider to be developed much later from the " Hamilcar ".   The design of this general-purpose glider would be hastened directly the composition of the future airborne force was known and the loads to be carried could be defined.

Estimated production figures at December, 1940, were as follows :

| Type. | Prospective Cumulative Production Dates. | | | | | | |
| | 1941. | | | | | 1942. | |
	May.	Aug.	Sept.	Oct.	Nov.	Mar.	Apr.
Hotspur..	50	—	330	390	—	—	—
Horsa ..	—	2	—	—	50	330	390
Hengist ..	18	—	—	—	—	—	—
Hamilcar	Two prototypes to fly in May 1941.						

Most of the production of these gliders, which were of all-wooden construction, was to be done by furniture-making firms and so save skilled munitions labour.   Because they were made of wood, they would not compete unduly with the materials required for aircraft and most other weapons and munitions of war.   Some doubt was now arising, however, as to the competition to be expected from the new " Mosquito " and other " wooden aircraft ".

(*d*) The only glider pilots under training were some 37 army and 18 R.A.F. personnel under Squadron-Leader W. E. Hervey (*see* para. 34), and there were no definite provisions for more.   The 37 army pilots were reduced to 24 shortly for various reasons.   Whether even these few were being trained to a sufficiently high standard was doubtful.

(*e*) The only British aircraft so far found to be suitable for dropping parachute troops were Whitley twin-engine bombers, which at first carried eight, and then ten troops.   It was expected, too, that they would be able to tow the lighter gliders.   The Whitley was the slowest and structurally the most easily modified of the operational bombers, but only about six could be spared from operational bombing duties.   Except for some old Bombays there were no British transport aircraft and none could be produced as the Air Ministry was forced to concentrate on purely operational types.

By December, 1940, the few Whitleys that had been provided for the Central Landing Establishment were busily engaged in training and in technical trials. In addition one or two Stirling and Wellington bombers had been loaned for technical investigation. (*See* Appendix B for details of airborne forces aircraft.)

7. There were three overriding factors which delayed the development of airborne forces :—

(*a*) *Priority to manpower.* In 1940, with the threat of Nazi invasion, priority was given to the defence of the United Kingdom. Despite the Prime Minister's original instructions, many people doubted whether there was yet time to spare for the creation of a force which could exert no major influence on the war for some time to come. Indeed there were those who considered that airborne troops would never be more than a nuisance value to the enemy and their own side.

(*b*) *Priority to material.* The Army was reorganizing and re-arming, at home and abroad, after Dunkirk. The R.A.F. was looking for fighters to defend Great Britain, bombers to bomb the Germans and other aircraft to defeat the submarine. The factories were not yet generally organized on a war footing and not enough raw materials were available for production purposes. In fact there was a desperate shortage of every kind and airborne forces had to take the turn of the youngest arm of the Service.

(*c*) *Lack of policy.* There was no clear idea as to how airborne forces would fit into the developing picture and therefore how they should be organized. Throughout 1940, and most of 1941, ideas on their employment were by no means definite and were not agreed either in principle or in detail by the two main organizations—the War Office and the Air Ministry. This was probably the main factor in the delay that ensued.

The Views of the War Office and the Air Ministry up to June, 1941

8. Between June and November, 1940, the planning staffs at the War Office and Air Ministry were engaged in working out the requirements for two invasion corps, one at home and one overseas, to take part in offensive operations when more favourable circumstances arose. On 11th November, 1940, the War Office presented to the Chiefs of Staff the Army requirements for these corps. They included in each corps an Aerodrome Capture Group, of which the following units were to be airborne assault troops :—

H.Q.
Two battalions (with 10 carriers and five trucks each).
One light tank squadron (18 tanks).
Two 3·7-in. howitzer sections (four guns each).
Two light Anti-Aircraft Troops (four guns each, Bofors or Hispanos).
Signal Section.
Medical Detachment.
Supply Detachment.

This was a total of about 1,730 troops and 600 tons air-lift, requiring, if most of it was to be carried in gliders, up to 350 aircraft for the force to travel in one lift. Although they realized that this number of bombers, the only suitable type of aircraft, would not be available for some time, the War Office adhered to these requirements, in general, throughout the discussions that followed. They agreed that the Air Ministry should be responsible for producing a joint paper on all airborne requirements, to be presented to the Chiefs of Staff as soon as possible.

9. The first concern of the Air Ministry was to define clearly the Army and Air Force responsibilities in regard to the provision and control of airborne forces. On 30th December, 1940, they sent to the War Office, a memorandum which was intended as a basis of discussion between the Vice-Chiefs of Staff. It was founded on the following ideas :—

(a) The development of technique and equipment for airborne forces should proceed as rapidly as possible in the United Kingdom. However, it was unlikely that large forces of troop carrier aircraft would be available in the United Kingdom for a long time. Therefore the provision of trained airborne or air-transported units in the United Kingdom should be kept to a minimum. This was even more important because of the shortage of resources for current air operations and the expansion of operational squadrons. This minimum was to be sufficient for demonstration and training purposes until an operation requiring airborne forces, based on the United Kingdom, was planned to take place.

(b) The Mediterranean theatre was likely to require the employment of airborne forces in the future. Resources for such operations should be built up on the further side of the Mediterranean, rather than in the United Kingdom, in order to conserve shipping which would barely be adequate to meet other commitments for that area.

(c) The staging and conduct of airborne operations would involve the co-ordination of the majority of the remainder of the air forces in the theatre of war concerned. This would require high standards of skill and technical air organization. For these reasons, and for economy of resources, the staging and conduct of airborne operations should be a Royal Air Force responsibility planned to meet Army requirements.

The Air Ministry stated that they would not agree to any proposal to form an independent service for airborne forces, with its own separate organization and uniform.

10. On 10th January, 1941, the War Office stated that they considered that the development of airborne forces should be based on the principle that the Army would present their requirements for airborne forces to the Air Force, who would do what they could to meet them. The War Office did not agree that the Air Ministry memorandum should be used as a basis for discussion between the Vice-Chiefs of Staff. They re-affirmed the requirements set forth in paragraph 8 above. They suggested that the Air Ministry should consider these requirements with a view to the production of a joint Air Ministry–War Office paper on which the Chiefs of Staff could base their policy. The date by which airborne forces would be required would be as early as production would allow.

11. The Air Ministry agreed in general with the War Office proposals and asked the latter to draw up the first draft of the joint paper, bearing in mind the principles mentioned in paragraph 9 above. They suggested that the paper should recommend the action required for raising airborne forces, and that any questions not agreed by the Ministries should be left to the decision of the Chiefs of Staff. They asked the War Office to suggest the requirements for an airborne establishment in the United Kingdom which would cover development and training in Home Forces, as distinct from any requirements for offensive operations overseas. They still believed that parachute troops should form only a small proportion of an airborne force, in order to economize in aircraft, and because air-landing troops would have an advantage on the ground, landing in tactical groups and carrying heavier equipment.

12. From the middle of January until May the drafts continued to travel backwards and forwards between the Air Ministry and the War Office in what has aptly been described as a " shuttle-cock " service. On 26th April Mr. Churchill visited the Central Landing Establishment (*see* para. 14) and was very depressed by the lack of progress made. On his return to London on 28th April he asked urgently for the latest proposals for increasing the parachute and glider forces together with a time-table showing the expected results.

On 20th May the Germans began their airborne assault on Crete, and on 26th May the Prime Minister drew the attention of the Chiefs of Staff to this, saying that the same thing might soon be happening in Cyprus and Syria. He regretted the slow progress we had made in the formation of airborne forces and that we still had nothing more than 500 parachutists. He felt that a whole year had been lost and urged the Chiefs of Staff to press on with the provision of 5,000 parachutists and an airborne division on the German model with any improvements that experience suggested.

13. Fortunately the Joint Memoranda was almost complete and on 31st May the Chiefs of Staff submitted it to the Prime Minister. However, in fairness, it must be remembered that despite the delay the Central Landing Establishment had been functioning to some extent, the initial manufacture of gliders had begun and a small parachute operation had been carried out in Italy in February, 1941 (*see* Chapter VII). The main points in the joint paper, which was accepted by the Prime Minister, are summarized below :—

(*a*) Airborne forces could only be used successfully in localities where air superiority has been firmly established and where the flow of rein-forcements could be assured. It was impossible to foresee these conditions in the immediate future, but by the middle of 1942 airborne forces might be required.

(*b*) The existing 500 parachutists were picked volunteers. The policy to date had been to keep this body up to strength and to train, in addition, a limited number of parachutists among whom were special agents chosen from Polish and French soldiers in the country. There would be no difficulty in raising further British volunteers, and expanding the present parachutists' training organization to an output of 400 a month. This would produce some 5,000 British parachutists by May, 1942. If these were required earlier a considerable expansion in both personnel and material would be necessary, but the programme would be assisted by the institution of a parachute school in the Middle East or India.

(*c*) In future all Wellingtons were to be modified for parachuting. It was hoped that by spring, 1943, there would be an additional ten squadrons of transport aircraft, with a total air-transported lift of about 3,000 men, which would also be suitable for parachuting.

(*d*) The 25-seater operational glider, which could also carry some supporting weapons and light cars, was in the prototype stage. Production was expected to begin not earlier than January, 1942, and the total would carry approximately a brigade and ancillary troops without armoured fighting vehicles, or Bren carriers, on one operation, with no reserves. The intention was to place an order for a further 400 gliders in India as soon as possible. It might be possible to increase output later.

(*e*) The tank carrying glider was in the " mock-up " stage. At the most optimistic estimate, the delivery of a sufficient number to carry a squadron of light tanks would probably not be before November, 1942.

(*f*) For the future, Army requirements were :—

    (i) One brigade of parachute troops to be located at Home, and one in the Middle East with the necessary transport aircraft. The strength of each brigade would be approximately 2,400 men.

    (ii) Sufficient gliders to carry two air-landing brigades each approximately 5,000 strong, including ancillaries and armoured fighting vehicles. One air-landing brigade would be at Home and one in the Middle East, with their glider pilots and tug aircraft.

    (iii) Sufficient transport aircraft to lift an air-landing brigade in an air-transported role, both at Home and in the Middle East.

(*g*) The provision of the Army requirements would make considerable inroads on Bomber Command and might involve crews and aircraft being absent from bomber operations for as long as two months. It would also mean reserving up to five airfields exclusively for airborne operations, and the setting aside of a considerable amount of motor transport for moving gliders.

(*h*) The Chiefs of Staff agreed to the existing programme for airborne forces and this was being pressed on as fast as possible. With regard to the additional Army requirements, and in particular to the provision of a large number of transport aircraft, this raised the question as to how far the building up of Army support as a whole, of which airborne forces were only a part, was to be allowed to interfere with the expansion of the main Royal Air Force effort. They proposed to submit their views on this subject separately.

The Central Landing Establishment

14. The Central Landing School opened at Ringway airfield, near Manchester, on 21st June, 1940. Under the command of Squadron Leader L. A. Strange, it was designed mainly as a parachute training school and was equipped

initially with six Mark II Whitley aircraft and 1,000 R.A.F. training type parachutes. In addition, on the same airfield, there was a small detached flight of glider pilots, with light civilian-type gliders, commanded by Wing Commander G. M. Buxton, which assisted in Radar Direction Finding experiments during the summer of 1940, and No. 110 Wing commanded by Wing Commander Sir Nigel Norman, Bart, who was posted to the school within a few weeks. Major John Rock, R.E., was appointed by the War Office on 24th June, 1940, to organize the Army side of airborne forces and he joined the school immediately. Among others, he and Squadron Leader Strange were assisted in their early experiments by Captain M. A. Lindsay, of Arctic exploration fame, Captain W. P. B. Bradish, Captain J. Lander, some R.A.F. enthusiasts and a few ex-professional " stunt jumpers." At this time enthusiasm rather than experience was the keynote. Technical trials and the practical testing of many theories started, with any resources that were at hand or which could be acquired in spite of the national shortage. The greater part of the credit, on the Army side, for the success of the initial experiments and trials must go to Major Rock, whose unfailing courage and determination in the face of all difficulties was an inspiration to others. It should be remembered that when this officer was sent for by the War Office to begin parachute training he was a brigade-major in Scotland with no previous air experience.

15. The only British aircraft then available for parachute dropping was the Whitley bomber. Accordingly most of the early trials were developed to suit this aircraft, and the British parachute and methods of using it were designed for jumping through the hole in the floor of the aircraft fuselage. It was unlikely that any aircraft with a door would be available for some considerable time. Various difficulties regarding " hole jumping " were discovered and overcome, holes were improvised and aircraft modifications agreed, parachute packs were made to suit, and methods of ground training for parachuting became ever more numerous and complicated. The majority of the original " live " experiments were carried out by personnel of No. 2 Commando, and most of the Parachute Jumping Instructors were non-commissioned officers from the Army. There were not sufficient instructors available from the R.A.F. until much later. It is interesting to record how the first parachute jumps were made. The original pioneers, using the R.A.F. type parachute, began by standing in the open tail of a Whitley from which the rear gun turret had been removed, holding on to a bar ; the parachute was then opened by a normal ripcord and the man was pulled off the aircraft by the slip-stream. The R.A.F. parachute was superseded by an American statichute and jumping through a hole began, at first with the static line attached to a bar running down the top of the fuselage, and later with the static line attached to the side of the hole. At this time the static line was a tape and not strong webbing as we know it to-day. Training of troops began on 8th July, the first " live " jump being made by instructors on 13th July. Pupils began to jump on 21st July but on 25th July Driver Evans, Royal Army Service Corps, attached No. 2 Commando was killed when jumping with an American-type statichute, owing to his rigging lines becoming twisted and preventing the canopy from developing. Training was suspended temporarily, but was recommenced on 8th August using a British statichute known as the "G.Q." This statichute, with modifications, is used to-day, and was designed by Mr. Raymond Quilter, an ex-officer of the Grenadier Guards, who was Managing Director of the G.Q. Parachute

29

Company. Airborne forces owe a great deal to both Mr. Quilter and Mr. L. L. Irvin of the Irving Parachute Company, Ltd. Details of the development of the parachute for airborne forces are given in Appendix C.

16. On 19th September, 1940, the Air Ministry took over most of the responsibility for the development of what may be called " the flying side " of airborne forces. The Central Landing School was expanded to the Central Landing Establishment, R.A.F. ; Group Captain L. G. Harvey was the Station Commander immediately assisted by Wing Commander Sir Nigel Norman as Commandant, and an Army staff was attached under Lieutenant-Colonel John Rock, reporting direct to the War Office. The Establishment was now divided into a Parachute Training School (Squadron-Leader Strange), a Technical Unit (Wing Commander Buxton), and a Glider Training Squadron (Squadron-Leader H. E. Hervey). The functions of the Establishment were to train parachute troops, glider pilots and aircrews for airborne work, to develop the tactical handling of airborne troops, to carry out technical research, and to recommend operational requirements.

17. To discharge its responsibilities the Central Landing Establishment had the few Mark II Whitley twin-engined bomber aircraft modified for dropping, an assorted collection of other aircraft including Tiger Moths, Avro 504 N. and British Airways Swallows, and various requisitioned single-seater gliders. The difficulties of maintenance of these varied type of aircraft with a small staff, the general shortage of spares and the notoriously bad weather of Manchester delayed development and training to a serious extent. However, during 1940 and the early part of 1941 parachuting progressed reasonably well. By February 500 individuals had been trained as parachutists. In April, 1941, the first Service glider, a Hotspur, appeared, and 15 had been delivered to the Central Landing Establishment by 22nd August. On 6th May Squadron-Leader Strange was transferred to another appointment and was succeeded in command of the Parachute Training School by Squadron-Leader G. Benham. However, at the end of the month Ringway was informed that a similar school was to be formed in India and that they were to provide the nucleus staff (*see* Chapter XXIII). Squadron Leader Benham, at his own request, was placed in charge of the Indian counterpart though he did not actually go to India as he was found to be medically unfit. He was succeeded at Ringway by Squadron Leader Maurice Newnham, hitherto Administrative Officer at the Central Landing Establishment, who took over command of the Parachute Training School on 9th July.

18. On 26th April, 1941, a parachute and glider demonstration was given at Ringway for the Prime Minister, Mr. Churchill. He was left in no doubt as to the hopelessness of accomplishing the ambitious programme laid down six months earlier, if the existing priorities for allotment of resources were to remain. A formation parachute drop by six Whitleys, a formation landing by five sailplanes, and a fly-past of one Hotspur, was the total so far possible. In fact, upwards of 800 parachute troops had been trained by now, but the size of the drop for this demonstration was limited entirely by the number of aircraft available. Nevertheless, the Central Landing Establishment received little more in the way of resources for many months to come, except that a few more Hotspurs appeared and Stirling and Wellington type aircraft were tested for the dropping of parachute troops.

19. Among the subjects under investigation at the Central Landing Establishment during 1941 were glider towing problems, including multiple, blind and night towing ; the possibilities of ground recognition and navigational aids for airborne operations, including smoke and light signals and radio beacons ; army loading and organization problems ; parachute container design and development ; individual descent by rotorchute (a man sitting in a cradle suspended from a propeller, which resembled and acted in a similar manner to a falling leaf).

20. On 1st September, 1941, the Central Landing Establishment was renamed the Airborne Forces Establishment, the task of which was to—

" investigate problems of technical development, to establish the principles of glider and parachute training and to form the first units carrying out this training."

In preparation for the inevitable expansion of airborne forces, the R.A.F. were getting ready to form self-contained units to carry out separately the training of parachute and glider troops. However, by October, 1941, the situation at Ringway was not encouraging, particularly on the flying side. The task which should have been accomplished by the spring of that year, was still not within sight, except for the training of the parachute troops themselves. The Establishment, now under the command of 70 Group R.A.F., of Army Co-operation Command, was hard put to it to keep it going, owing to the shortage of equipment. Nevertheless, much invaluable and vital work had been done, without which the later expansion of airborne forces would have been delayed beyond the end of the war. Above all, sufficient had been done to convince the War Office that expansion was justified.

21. Before leaving the story of the Establishment it is worth noting, not for reasons of sentiment but from a purely practical point of view, that excellent co-operation had been achieved between the two Services. The R.A.F., in general terms, were responsible for producing the aircraft, gliders and parachute equipment, developing and teaching the methods of dropping, training the glider pilots, teaching the troops their air technique, flying or towing them to the target area and putting them down correctly at the right time. The Army had to submit to the teaching of this new art, organize and arm itself to suit its means of conveyance, and still, by training and the careful selection of personnel, produce a good worth-while fighting force for the battle. Theirs was an expensive " approach march " to the battle field and only the best was worth carrying. Each Service learned to rely implicitly upon the other, and from this trust was developed an intimate co-operation at all levels which formed the basis of careful planning for the future. It was this co-operation which was largely responsible for the success of the major airborne operations later in the war.

No. 11 Special Air Service Battalion

22. In June, 1940, No. 2 Commando, which was under command of the Director of Combined Operations, was turned over to parachute duties, and was moved to the area of Knutsford, near Ringway. On 3rd July Lieutenant-Colonel I. A. Jackson arrived at Ringway and assumed command of the unit, and on 21st July the first parachute descents were made by commandos. The

31

unit was organized into headquarters and a varying number of troops, each about 50 strong, the total strength averaging about 500, all ranks. They remained on commando terms of service, with extra parachute pay of 4s. 0d. a day for officers and 2s. 0d. a day for other ranks, which was granted after the completion of three parachute jumps when they would qualify to wear the parachute badge, a pair of wings with a parachute in the centre, on their right arm. They were not quartered in camps or barracks but were granted a daily subsistence allowance and left to find their own accommodation and food. By 21st September 21 officers and 321 other ranks had been accepted as being physically fit to undergo a course of instruction in parachute duties. These men were tough, but even so all of them could not manage parachuting. Though they were of the highest quality, and though they did only an average of two or three jumps a man, there was a wastage of some 15 per cent. over a period of two months. Of the total number who were accepted from the original No. 2 Commando, 30 men refused to jump, two were killed through parachute failures and 20 others were found unsuitable or sustained medical injuries. As Group Captain Maurice Newnham, says in his book " Prelude to Glory " :—

> " most of the men were of a good type and were a loss to the Commando. The majority got to the edge of the hole in the aircraft before refusing. Four men fainted in aircraft, while a number jumped in a state of collapse having forced themselves to do so by sheer will-power ". He quotes Wing Commander Strange as saying that " the wastage was due to the fear of the unknown, launching oneself into space and fear that the parachute would not open . . . . the Whitley fuselage is dark and gloomy with its hole in the middle, and is bad for the nerves. The sight of other men disappearing through the hole is an unpleasant one and the prospect of scraping one's face on the side is not encouraging ".

The School was then using an old Bombay for jumping as well as Whitleys and although over 200 jumps were made from this aircraft, it is significant that there were no refusals—the Bombay had a door, not a hole. These original parachutists, who did a great deal of the pioneer work by which later members of airborne forces benefited, deserve great credit and praise for the way in which they carried out their tasks in the face of unpleasant and discouraging conditions.

23. On 21st November, 1940, the name of the unit was changed to 11 Special Air Service Battalion, and the establishment was altered to battalion headquarters, one parachute wing and one glider wing. Initially most of the time of 11 Special Air Service Battalion was spent in completing the parachuting training of the unit, and in carrying out demonstration drops for the Central Landing Establishment. However, by 17th December, 1940, 22 teams of eight men each had been trained to sub-section standard, which corresponded to section training in an infantry battalion. It was then suggested that the sub-section would consist of ten men, based on the Whitley " stick " of ten. From then onwards sub-units of the battalion took part in demonstrations and exercises all over the United Kingdom. On 6th April, 1941, 92 men were dropped on pin-point targets in Northern Command without previous reconnaissance by the pilots and without the use of air photographs. On 15th August, 1941, the battalion, still stationed at Knutsford, was reorganized into battalion headquarters and four companies, and a month later it became 1st Parachute Battalion and part of 1 Parachute Brigade.

1 Parachute Brigade

24. One of the Army requirements mentioned in the Joint Memorandum by the Chiefs of Staff at the end of May, 1941 (*see* para. 13*f*) was for the existing 11 Special Air Service Battalion to be expanded into a parachute brigade as soon as possible. The War Office immediately started investigating the Army problems connected with raising this force. As a first step, in July the Chief of the Imperial General Staff authorized the raising of brigade headquarters, four parachute battalions and one air troop of Royal Engineers. The raising of the other special units required to complete the brigade (artillery, signals, medical, supply and possibly light tanks), although approved, would be left until later.

25. The immediate problems were considered under the following headings :—

(*a*) The method by which the new units would be formed.

(*b*) The terms of service, with special reference to the continuance of subsistence allowance, the right of return to parent units after six months, and the rate of parachute pay.

(*c*) Training and the means of co-operation with the Central Landing Establishment.

(*d*) A timed programme for raising the new units.

(*e*) Questions of accommodation.

26. Parachuting had not been accepted as a normal duty of soldiers and was confined to volunteers on a six monthly basis. It is an individual act requiring considerable determination and great physical fitness. It was expected in 1941, and has been amply proved since then, that if an ordinary unit is turned over *en masse* to parachuting there would be a very high proportion of men who would be physically or psychologically unfit for the task, many of them being too old. Yet there are very many obvious advantages, particularly as regards administration and *esprit-de-corps*, in turning over a complete unit. It is also a quicker way of producing a trained team. However, the War Office, influenced by the fact that no airborne operations on a brigade scale were contemplated before the spring of 1942, decided to form the battalions now required as new units.

27. As regards the terms of service, the experiences of 11 Special Air Service Battalion showed that the system of granting subsistence allowance to all ranks was bad because the battalion could not function operationally owing to the lack of cooks and messing staff, accommodation was difficult to find and the civilian rationing system suffered. Personnel of the new brigade, therefore, were not to be granted a special subsistence allowance but were to be accommodated and fed in the normal manner.

28. The option of returning to their previous units after six months parachuting service was also withdrawn and the new terms included no fixed period of service with a parachute unit. Battalion commanders were empowered to deal with men who refused to jump, either because they had lost their nerve or because they wished to return to their units, in the same way as any other unit commander could deal with compassionate release, and no special regulations were introduced for this purpose.

33

29. After consideration of the rates of pay for comparable duties in the Royal Navy (*e.g.* submarine service) and the R.A.F., the rate of parachute pay remained at 4*s*. 0*d*. a day for officers and 2*s*. 0*d*. for other ranks, as was in force with 11 Special Air Service Battalion, subject to the discretion of unit commanders and on completion of three jumps. The low figure of three jumps, after which a man is not fully trained as a parachutist, was agreed owing to the limited number that could be done in the near future with the few aircraft available.

30. It was further agreed that it was more economical to carry out all parachute training at the Central Landing Establishment so as to make the best use of available aircraft, parachutes and instructors and the somewhat specialized ground training equipment required. The course would last three weeks and the capacity at Ringway would be 100 a week, which should be sufficient to meet an operational date of readiness for a three-battalion brigade (including its reserves) by 1st March, 1942. Brigade headquarters initially would be a small administrative and training headquarters only. Accommodation was required as close as possible to Ringway and in good training country and was allotted at Hardwick Hall Camp, near Chesterfield, Derbyshire.

31. The decision to form the new brigade was promulgated on 31st August, 1941, and volunteers, up to a maximum of ten other ranks a unit so as not to deplete any one unit unduly, were requested from all British infantry resources in the United Kingdom. The individual standards of fitness required were much the same as for 11 Special Air Service Battalion. They were high standards, including a normal age limit between 22–32 years, a top weight limit of 196 lb., good eyesight without glasses and good hearing.

32. Headquarters 1 Parachute Brigade was formed early in September, 1941, and command of the new brigade was given to Brigadier R. N. Gale, who was instructed to form a parachute brigade of four parachute battalions. It was left to Brigadier Gale to decide whether 11 Special Air Service Battalion should be disbanded or not, with such of its personnel as volunteered being absorbed into the four new battalions that were to be raised. However, after inspecting the unit, and discussing the matter with then Commander-in-Chief, Home Forces, General Sir Bernard Paget, Brigadier Gale decided that the battalion should remain in being, and should become 1st Parachute Battalion. The change-over took place on 15th September, 1941. There were many problems arising out of controlling so many new volunteers and so General Paget and Brigadier Gale decided that only two new battalions would be raised at first, making a total of three, and leaving the fourth battalion to be raised later. Lieutenant-Colonel E. E. Down was appointed to command 1st Parachute Battalion, Lieutenant-Colonel E. W. C. Flavell to 2nd Parachute Battalion, and Lieutenant-Colonel G. W. Lathbury to 3rd Parachute Battalion. Major P. E. Bromley-Martin was brigade major and Captain J. G. Squirrel was staff captain. The new units formed on a war establishment based on a three-company battalion, and sections of ten men, each section being commanded by a serjeant. No. 1 Air Troop, Royal Engineers, was also formed in September, 1941, and a skeleton brigade signal section at the same time, as new units. They did not become part of the Special Air Service Regiment but remained in their own corps, detached for parachute duties.

33. Thus for the first time airborne forces were given an army formation commander who was not immediately concerned with the raising and training of a unit of his own. He had more time to spare for the hundred and one questions affecting general, though detailed, policy and could begin to co-ordinate the parachuting requirements of units other than infantry. He was able to see on the spot, what was required and held equivalent rank with the air commodore commanding 70 Group R.A.F. He was able to take a great deal of the weight of outside affairs off the shoulders of his unit commanders, particularly 1st Parachute Battalion, although for the time being they had to spend a lot of time doing their own recruiting. Brigadier Gale was authorized to deal direct with the War Office on all matters of policy, to maintain liaison with the Airborne Forces Establishment and 70 Group R.A.F. for technical and domestic training purposes, and to utilize the normal army command channels for routine matters.

Glider Pilots

34. We have seen how the Glider Training Squadron was set up at Ringway in September, 1940 (*see* para. 16), and how in the early days there were no gliders other than light civilian types. During the summer of 1940 the policy regarding the supply of glider pilots had been discussed several times by the Air Ministry and War Office without either party arriving at any satisfactory solution. On 5th September it was decided to call for volunteer glider pilots from men of No. 2 Commando who had flying experience, and 37 men were selected and attached to Army Co-operation Squadrons during the autumn of 1940. However, most of the volunteers did not have much experience in the air, and no syllabus for their training existed. It was difficult to include glider-flying training at the Army Co-operational Schools without interfering with the normal training of R.A.F. squadrons. The system was not satisfactory but the resources of Army Co-operation Command were not adequate to provide special schools. On 11th December, 1940, the Deputy Chief of the Air Staff, looking ahead to the time when troop-carrying gliders would be coming off production, said :—

" The idea that semi-skilled, unpicked personnel (infantry corporals have, I believe, even been suggested) could with a maximum of training be entrusted with the piloting of these troop carriers is fantastic. Their operation is equivalent to forced landing the largest sized aircraft without engine aid—than which there is no higher test of piloting skill."

He suggested that they should be R.A.F. or Army seconded personnel who would complete the course for powered aircraft at the R.A.F. Elementary Flying Training Schools and the Service Flying Training Schools ; only then would they be trained to fly gliders. However, in view of the urgent need for operational pilots in R.A.F. Bomber, Fighter and Coastal Commands, it was not possible to implement this policy yet.

35. In January, 1941, because Ringway was unsuitable for dual glider training, a flight of the Glider Training Squadron, known as the Glider Exercise Flight, moved to Haddenham, near Oxford. In March, 12 of the more advanced ex-commando pupils arrived for training and they were followed the next month by the remainder. There was only one Hotspur available and the civilian gliders were used. The glider situation improved slightly during the summer, but the number of pilots dwindled steadily until 1st September, 1941, when

there were only 19 on flying duties. However, it had been possible to carry out a number of small glider exercises at Ringway with six Hotspurs which were available, carrying troops of 11 Special Air Service Regiment as passengers. Small as these exercises were they enabled Lieutenant-Colonel Rock and Flying Officer P. B. N. Davis (Hervey's second-in-command) to learn many valuable lessons from which a basic procedure for glider flying was evolved. They were able to solve such problems as the connecting of tow-ropes, signals for take-off, circuit procedure before casting off and landing, and the dropping of tow ropes by tug aircraft.

36. During 1941 the delivery of gliders, especially Horsas, had fallen far behind schedule. Hotspurs were coming off production the more quickly, as in July, 1941, there was no expectation of the first delivery of Horsas until the early part of 1942. As a result of this the Air Ministry arranged for increased production of Hotspurs to cover the gap made by the lack of Horsas. Being a smaller glider this meant that many more were necessary—a total of 990 were ordered—with a consequent increase in the number of glider pilots required. Until 22nd August, 1941, the Air Ministry had always maintained that gliders should be flown by fully trained R.A.F. or Army seconded pilots who would be withdrawn from normal duties for any airborne operation. They had not been able to put this policy into effect owing to the lack of personnel and gliders. It was now decided that glider pilots would be Army volunteers, trained by the R.A.F., who would remain in the Army and would not be employed on any flying duties other than glider flying. The first 600 were to be selected from the initial batch of volunteers from the Army for R.A.F. aircrew duties, but would not be transferred to the Air Force.

37. On 26th September, 1941, the War Office and Air Ministry decided that glider pilots would conform to the mental and physical standards of R.A.F. aircrews and would be interviewed by combined Air Force/Army selection boards. From the Army point of view the glider pilot was to be the " total soldier," a man who would fly and could also fight on the ground with any weapon with which airborne troops were armed ; who could take his part if necessary with any body of troops travelling in his glider in any action they might fight ; who was a trained signaller and liaison officer. It was a high standard of intelligence, initiative and discipline but experience proved that it could be achieved and it has been well maintained by the Glider Pilot Regiment ever since. The Air Ministry were determined that the glider pilot should reach a first class standard in the air, and at last were able to put into practice the theory advanced by the Deputy Chief of the Air Staff in December, 1940 (see paragraph 34). Glider pilots were to begin their training with a 12-week course at an R.A.F. Elementary Flying Training School, where they would learn to fly light aircraft. Then they would move on to a Glider Training School where, during a further 12-week course, they would learn to fly Hotspur gliders. After this they would spend six weeks at a glider Operational Training Unit when they would be taught to fly a Horsa glider, when they would qualify to wear the Army Flying Badge, which was also worn by the Air Observation Post Pilots of the Royal Artillery.

CHAPTER IV

THE FORMATION OF 1 AIRBORNE DIVISION, OCTOBER–NOVEMBER, 1941

General

1. As described in the preceding chapter, the decision to form 1 Parachute Brigade in the United Kingdom had been taken in July, 1941, and by September action was well under way. The parachute side of airborne forces was now reasonably well organized and advantage could be taken of the early experiments and trials carried out by the Central Landing Establishment and 11 Special Air Service Battalion. The Airborne Forces Establishment remained to carry out technical development, the training of R.A.F. crews and glider pilots and the initial parachute training of army recruits. 1 Parachute Brigade was available for "user" trials of equipment and methods, and was to be ready for operations, as a brigade, by the spring of 1942.

2. However, although the commander 1 Parachute Brigade was also given, at first, some general responsibility for the glider side of airborne forces, he was in fact completely occupied with parachuting. No glider-borne troops existed and the real responsibility for glider development still rested entirely with the R.A.F., the Airborne Forces Establishment and the War Office. Largely owing to the inevitable delay in the production of gliders, this side of airborne forces was lagging far behind.

1 Air-landing Brigade Group

3. The War Office believed that troops carried by glider or aircraft were required to support parachutists for any except the most limited operations. On 10th October, 1941, they selected 31 Independent Brigade Group, a formation of regular units recently returned from India, for the role of an air-landing brigade group. The brigade had just completed mountain warfare training in Wales, and was already trained to operate in a light role. They were to carry out the initial investigations into the problems of organization, equipment and training of an air-landing formation. They were to be prepared to travel in gliders, or in aircraft landing on an airfield, hence the name " air-landing " as opposed to " glider-borne " troops.

4. The general background upon which the experiments, training and planning was to be based was as follows :—

    (a) The roles of the air-landing brigade group might include :—

        (i) The capture of vital enemy communication centres.

        (ii) The attack of enemy field formations in the rear, in conjunction with the advance of the main force.

        (iii) The capture of an airfield or airfields.

        (iv) Subsidiary operations in conjunction with seaborne expeditions.

    (b) The brigade group might be required to operate in an area up to 500 miles from its base airfields, in the first instance against moderate resistance consisting of small arms fire, though subsequently it might have to meet an attack by armoured fighting vehicles. It had to be prepared to be self-contained up to a period of at least three days, but in certain circumstances might be isolated for longer periods and might have to depend on supply by air for its maintenance.

(c) A parachute detachment would probably work in conjunction with the air-landing force, to secure the landing zones and for pathfinding duties. The size of this parachute component would vary according to the circumstances and might consist of as much as three battalions.

5. It was realized that it might not be possible, owing to the shortage of aircraft and gliders, to lift the whole of the brigade group simultaneously. However, the intention was to provide sufficient aircraft to carry essential fighting troops in one flight.

6. The formation, subsequently re-named 1 Air-landing Brigade Group, was composed initially of the following units :—

> Brigade H.Q. and Signal Section.
> 1st Bn. The Border Regiment.
> 2nd Bn. The South Staffordshire Regiment.
> 2nd Bn. The Oxfordshire and Buckinghamshire Light Infantry.
> 1st Bn. The Royal Ulster Rifles.
> 31 Independent Reconnaissance Company.
> 223rd Anti-Tank Battery, R.A.
> 9th Field Company, R.E.
> 181st Field Ambulance, R.A.M.C.
> 31 Independent Infantry Brigade, Ordnance Workshop and Field Park, R.A.O.C.
> 31 Independent Infantry Brigade Company, R.A.S.C.
> 31 Independent Infantry Brigade, Provost Section.
> One Company troop carrying vehicles, R.A.S.C.

The details of the organization for the future were to be settled when trials had been carried out. It was also realized that under varying operational circumstances the brigade group might need some modifications. In particular, it was considered that a reduction in the scale of air-landing infantry might be necessary when a large parachute component was working in co-operation with air-landing troops.

7. Command of the brigade group was given to Brigadier G. F. Hopkinson, who took over from Brigadier H. E. F. Smyth, on 31st October, 1941. He was authorized to use the same channels of command and liaison as commander, 1 Parachute Brigade (*see* Chapter III). Major W. T. Campbell was brigade major and Major P. J. Luard was deputy assistant adjutant and quartermaster general.

Headquarters 1 Airborne Division

8. The War Office now decided that a separate airborne headquarters was required to co-ordinate the whole development and training of airborne forces under a senior officer, who would have no other responsibilities and who would be able to see for himself what was actually happening. The Commander-in-Chief, Home Forces, General Sir Alan Brooke (later Field Marshal, The Viscount Alanbrooke) advocated a more definite operational responsibility for the " divisional commander " than was suggested by War Office. It had not yet been decided whether airborne forces would operate eventually in formations larger than brigades. For reasons of morale, to impress the enemy, and for convenience, General Brooke recommended that a divisional rather than a " force " commander should be appointed and that his headquarters should

be called divisional headquarters from the start. The original establishment recommended was designed to cover the supervision of training and the investigation of the many problems of organization and equipment which would have to be faced in the near future. Personnel of the headquarters would be attached initially to General Headquarters, Home Forces, in London. The Commander-in-Chief also considered that, when the division concentrated and the headquarters took over operational control, it would be necessary to expand the staff considerably.

9. On 29th October, 1941, the War Office selected Brigadier F. A. M. Browning, then commanding 24 Guards Brigade, for appointment as " Commander Para-Troops and Airborne Troops " with the acting rank of major-general and ordered him to report to General Headquarters, Home Forces for duty on 3rd November. Lieutenant-Colonel A. G. Walch was ordered to report as General Staff Officer, 1st Grade, on the same date. The following day Wing Commander Sir Nigel Norman, from Ringway, joined divisional headquarters as air adviser. Major-General Browning would have under his command 1 Parachute Brigade, 1 Air-landing Brigade and the glider pilots. The headquarters war establishment recommended, as a temporary measure, by Home Forces on 1st November, allowed three General Staff Officers, one first, one second and one third grade, one deputy assistant quartermaster general and one assistant director of medical services with one staff officer, Royal Engineers and one staff officer Royal Signals attached. As the result of further recommendations, it was expanded by the War Office on 2nd December to include one assistant adjutant and quartermaster general, one deputy assistant adjutant-general, one chaplain, one assistant director of ordnance services, with a deputy, and one camp commandant with administrative staff. Several of the officers filling these appointments had a great share in the development of airborne forces for a long time and their names are therefore given here.

A.A. and Q.M.G.		Lt. Col. J. A. Goschen.
S.O., R.E.		Lt. Col. M. C. A. Henniker.
S.O., R. Sigs.		Major D. Smallman-Tew.
A.D.M.S.		Colonel A. Austin Eagger.
A.D.O.S.		Lt. Col. G. M. Loring.
D.A.D.O.S. (O.M.E.) ..		Major R. T. L. Shorrock.

The airborne headquarters was first established in one of the lower basements of King Charles Street in London, its original members being known as the " Dungeon Party ".

10. On the strong recommendation of Major-General Browning, who visualized airborne operations of the future on at least a divisional scale, the Chief of the Imperial General Staff, General Sir Alan Brooke, decided during November that the airborne divisional headquarters should be operational, though it would only be made up to operational strength gradually as the situation required. It was recognized that, apart from any other reason, it was bad for the morale of the formation, and of the personnel of divisional headquarters that the latter should not be able to go into action with the troops they commanded. In addition the Director of Military Operations at the War Office, Major-General J. N. Kennedy, expressed the opinion that there would be occasions upon which airborne forces would be employed during the war as a complete division.

11. From the first, the Airborne Division Headquarters (which will in future be referred to as Headquarters, 1 Airborne Division) was under command of Home Forces and for routine army matters used the normal army chain of command. For technical airborne problems, however, direct liaison was permitted with the War Office, the Air Ministry, Army Co-operation Command R.A.F., 70 Group R.A.F. and the Airborne Forces Establishment provided that all demands affecting policy were eventually submitted officially through Home Forces. Direct liaison and planning for small operations was also permitted with Headquarters, Combined Operations. This system worked well until it threw too heavy a load on 1 Airborne Divisional staff. By reason of his position as the senior British airborne officer, Major-General Browning also became responsible, in fact if not in theory at first, for assistance to Allied parachute contingents forming in the United Kingdom (Poles, French, Dutch, Belgians, Norwegians) and for advising everyone else as to the possibilities of our own and the enemy's airborne troops. The latter commitment particularly was, as might be imagined, no easy one at that time.

12. One other high authority who should be mentioned at this stage is the American Embassy. Although the United States of America was not yet at war, no-one could have given more enthusiastic assistance to British airborne forces than their Embassy in London. It was, for example, to Lieutenant-Colonel Tom Wells, United States Military Attaché, that we owe the early trials of the " jeep " as airborne transport and the chance to place an immediate order for their provision. He produced and lent to Divisional Headquarters the first " jeep " within a few days of its arrival in England in November, 1941, and a day or two later several very senior officers forced it into the Horsa Glider " mock-up " at Ringway.

CHAPTER V

AIRBORNE FORCES IN THE UNITED KINGDOM, NOVEMBER, 1941–APRIL, 1942

General

1. In Chapters III and IV it will have been seen how airborne forces originated in the United Kingdom from a very small nucleus, and how they grew to a parachute brigade. This was followed rapidly by an air-landing brigade, a firm policy on the supply and training of glider pilots and the formation of an airborne divisional headquarters. The next two chapters deal with the expansion of 1 Airborne Division, the steps taken by the R.A.F. to keep pace with the Army side of airborne forces, and the severe check in development which occurred in the autumn of 1942 because of a difference of opinion between the War Office and Air Ministry. During the period covered by these chapters, two small but important airborne operations took place in France and Norway. To avoid mixing policy with battles, and for the sake of clarity, these operations, and one in Italy in February, 1941, have been placed together in Chapter VII.

1 Parachute and 1 Air-landing Brigades, and The Glider Pilot Regiment

2. By November, 1941, 1 Parachute Brigade consisted of brigade head-quarters, three battalions and an air troop R.E., all concentrated in the area of Ringway and Hardwick Camp. 4th Parachute Battalion also existed in skeleton and was part of the brigade, having formed under Lieutenant-Colonel M. R. J. Hope Thomson. The greater proportion of 1st Parachute Battalion had completed their basic parachute training, and they were busy carrying out ground training as companies before they could start battalion training. The 2nd, 3rd and 4th Parachute Battalions were still in the process of forming and the problems of obtaining and hardening recruits before sending them to Ringway for individual parachute training occupied most of their time. Commanding officers had to compete with the fact that units supplying volunteers used the new airborne units as an excuse for getting rid of their " bad types ", and many new recruits to parachuting thought they were coming to an " Eldorado " where discipline did not exist. The process of disillusion-ment took up much of a parachute commanding officer's time. The air troop R.E. were in the same state and brigade headquarters was by no means complete so that, with their operational date of readiness set at the following spring, the brigade had little time to spare. They thought out and used enthusiastically all sorts of methods and equipment to harden their muscles, to improve their battle-craft, and to make up for the shortage of training aircraft—such as parachute jumping from towers and stationary balloons by day and night, jumping from moving lorries to get used to landing at speed (a practice later prohibited because of injuries) training under simulated battle conditions and long, fast marches. In fact for the next few months the parachute brigade and battalion headquarters more than had their hands full.

3. Thirty-one Independent Brigade Group (later 1 Air-landing Brigade) were spread over a large area of South Wales, where they had been training for mountain warfare partly on a pack basis. Experienced units, strong in personnel,

they were well-suited to their new role, but they were no better trained or equipped than the majority of the British Army at home at that time and were far from fit for modern war. Their immediate problem was to sort out the personnel because, although service in the air-landing brigade was not to be on a voluntary basis, it was obviously necessary to retain only the right type of men who were suitable and willing for the proposed training. Consequently commanding officers were allowed to get rid of whom they wished and a considerable turn-over took place. The brigade had to be moved to a good air and ground training area and unit staffs given the job of working out an organization to suit their role and their means of travel, which was primarily by glider. Salisbury Plain was occupied by other troops and for the moment little accommodation was available, so the brigade moved to the area Newbury–Basingstoke–Barton Stacey, the nearest available places, during November and December 1941. With the aid of " mock-up " gliders, by means of close liaison with the Air-borne Forces Establishment and in the course of many tactical exercises on paper, the brigade and unit staffs worked out their organization and decided on the weapons and equipment they wanted. Training in units concentrated on the individual, his initiative and his fitness for war. Every use was made of opportunities to get air experience of any kind, including the provision of " live loads " for glider pilots under training at the Glider Training Schools and Glider Operational Training Units.

4. Agreement having been reached during the summer and autumn of 1941, as to how glider pilots were to be provided and trained, it was up to the War Office to implement the army side of the bargain as soon as possible. The high standard laid down meant that a unit *esprit de corps* would be necessary for these troops as much as for any others, and in any case they had to be administered by someone. The War Office realized that these arguments might apply to other units of airborne forces—for example the parachute battalions, though self-contained units, had as yet no parent regiment—and so on 21st December, 1941, they decided to form the Army Air Corps, and within it, the Glider Pilot Regiment. The new regiments were announced in Army Orders on 24th February, 1942, but in the meantime work had gone ahead on getting them started. Lieutenant-Colonel Rock was given command of 1st Battalion, the Glider Pilot Regiment, with Major G. J. S. Chatterton as his second-in-command, who was given the task of raising the regiment, while his commanding officer took the first 40 members of the regiment to a course at No. 16 Elementary Flying Training School on 2nd January, 1942. It will be seen later how the regiment grew to a strength of some 2,500.

5. With this background in mind the formations of 1 Airborne Division will be left for the time being and the problems that faced Major-General Browning on his appointment as Commander of the Division will be examined.

The Problems confronting the Commander, 1 Airborne Division

6. On taking over his new command, one of the first things that Major-General Browning did was to discuss with Air Marshal Sir Arthur Barrett, Commander-in-Chief, Army Co-operation Command, various factors affecting both the Army and Air Force aspects of airborne forces. They decided that there were two immediate necessities, the first of which was the provision of a complete Air Force organization which would provide, in addition to the

schools for individual training, special exercise squadrons for collective training, a problem which is dealt with later in this chapter. The second was the concentration of the whole force of the two Services in one area, and for this they chose Salisbury Plain which was suitable for the tactical training of troops, open enough to provide good dropping and landing zones, and enabled gliders to be retrieved easily after exercises. The salvaging of gliders and the collection of parachutes was an important factor when considering areas for airborne training, as the gliders were valuable and liable to be damaged in close country, or bogged in soft ground, while parachutes had to be loaded into lorries which had to get on to or near the dropping zones.

7. There were many other problems, connected with the formation, organization, equipping and building up of airborne forces, and they can be summarized as follows :—

- (*a*) General policy which included the role and composition of airborne forces and of the air forces which carried them.
- (*b*) The creation of an airborne morale based on the assumption that airborne forces formed a *corps d'élite* and would be the spearhead of the British armies.
- (*c*) Detailed organizations and war establishments.
- (*d*) Detailed unit equipment tables.
- (*e*) Experiment and technical development in connection with operational requirements and " user " trials.
- (*f*) Co-ordination of Army and R.A.F. ideas and technique.
- (*g*) Planning, launching, and carrying out of operations.
- (*h*) Air and ground training.
- (*i*) Recruiting.
- (*j*) All the tasks of a normal formation, including a part in the defence of the United Kingdom.

This list does not include the " unofficial " duties that also had to be done, such as helping Allied parachute contingents and advising on defence against possible enemy airborne attacks. Yet 1 Airborne Division Headquarters staff were many fewer in numbers than an ordinary divisional staff and were not all experienced staff officers. Hours of work were long, and that there were some mistakes and some delay in working out the many problems was inevitable. At that time there were no branches at the War Office or the Air Ministry primarily designed to look after the interests of airborne forces, whose rapid and recent expansion meant that there were not enough officers with even a slight knowledge of airborne matters to go round, while the few with knowledge were busy with the new units and the technical establishments and not many of them were trained staff officers. In the War Office air subjects generally were dealt with by the Staff Duties Directorate, and in the Air Ministry a Lieutenant-Colonel looked after subjects connected with airborne forces.

8. Having spent some six weeks at General Headquarters, Home Forces, Headquarters 1 Airborne Division moved to Syrencote House, near Netheravon, Wiltshire, on 22nd December, 1941. A lot of detail had been investigated and the first essential and immediate requirements had been stated. It was now time for the staff, who had little or no experience of the practical side of airborne forces, to join the troops and work out the problems with them on the spot. One member of the staff had already completed his parachute course and one

had flown in a glider, but in these early days of parachuting it was found that the excitement and glamour of a parachute course quite definitely spoilt for some weeks most men's ability to concentrate on the detail or on the more boring routine tasks required of a staff officer. For that reason, and because they were really busy on other duties, few staff officers were allowed to jump until the pressure of work eased over a year later.

9. The first concern of Major-General Browning and Wing Commander Norman was to establish in their own commands the *esprit de corps* of a *corps d'élite*. Airborne forces have an expensive means of transport to battle and the skill and courage of the R.A.F. personnel and glider pilots handling that transport must be very great. Usually leading the assault for tasks that no other means could accomplish, only the very best troops were worth the effort involved. Since the parachute troops would probably lead the air-landing troops, they had to be the *élite* of the *corps d'élite*, but since the air-landing troops would have a responsibility hardly less important, they, too, must be special troops. All airborne forces, though emphatically not " suicide " troops, should at all times be prepared to fight under unusual circumstances, to gain a vital objective, for the initial battle was theirs, and theirs alone. They should expect as a matter of course to be surrounded by the enemy, cut off for some time from all except supply by air and to have to defeat a more heavily-armed opponent before being relieved by ground troops. This was as much a matter of morale as of skill and training ; and complete self-confidence in their cause, their country, their unit and themselves, was the essential requirement. In addition to that, physical fitness, endurance and personal initiative were as necessary in training as in operations. Experience from 1941 to 1945 proved that only about one man in three of all volunteers possessed the necessary physique and morale to become and remain a parachute soldier. It did not take long to evolve standards of physical fitness and before the invasion of North-West Europe airborne troops were regularly carrying out marching tests which stood them in good stead later—five miles in one hour, ten miles in two hours, 15 miles in three hours, 20 miles in four hours, some in battle order and some in games kit but wearing marching boots, and finally 50 miles in 24 hours in full fighting order, carrying all personal and light automatic weapons and ammunition.

10. The next point to be emphasized was that parachuting and gliding were only a means to an end, even though it is a vital means as the object is to defeat the enemy after approaching him. There was a certain glamour attached to these variations of a normal military approach march and at first the glamour outweighed the necessity for extreme battle efficiency on the ground producing an attitude of mind that had to be changed radically if airborne forces were to achieve their full stature. The change was a long and sometimes painful process and it had to be achieved without spoiling the enthusiasm of those concerned.

11. There was also an apparent impression amongst the Services generally that airborne forces, once landed, were supermen who could do things that lay far beyond the capabilities of ordinary troops and that they were desperadoes who did not mind being killed fighting against hopeless odds. This had to be denied forcibly on occasions and the strength of the airborne force had to be related to the task to be carried out. It was a rule in all planning of airborne

operations up to 1945 that, for one reason or another, one-third of the airborne force that started from the base would not be expected to arrive at the objective in time to influence the operation. This was owing to the normal risks of flying, weather, technical failures of aircraft or gliders, loss of direction, difficulties of recognizing landing areas, enemy action *en route*, and landing losses. It was a safe general guide and will probably remain so until flying technique and navigational aids are further improved and supremacy is gained against enemy ground and air action from base to target area. The only alternative to supremacy is surprise but unless the operation takes place in one concentrated lift, surprise is lost with the arrival of the first aircraft, and the enemy is alert and waiting for the following flights.

12. The problems concerned with evolving war establishments and equipment tables were involved and at times appeared endless and exasperating. Once the requirement had been agreed by the War Office, the proposals were put up by the unit concerned and were sifted and examined at all levels until they finally arrived at the War Office through Divisional Headquarters and General Headquarters, Home Forces. Once in the War Office they were examined by all branches concerned, and were then placed before a meeting of the War Office War Establishments Committee at which representatives of Home Forces and Headquarters 1 Airborne Division, as the " experts ", would be present. This procedure was slow admittedly, but with national resources of manpower and material so limited, and so much at stake, it is difficult to see how it could have been shortened by very much. It did ensure that there was no unnecessary waste and it gave a fair hearing to both sides when there were conflicting claims. A normal divisional headquarters does not become involved to any great extent in such procedure, because the establishments concerned are common throughout the Army and have been evolved over a long time, but, in the case of a new arm the " founders " are bound to be involved, and at the beginning Headquarters 1 Airborne Division had to deal with over 20 new types of war establishments.

13. Unit equipment tables were not only dependent upon fixed war establishments, but upon the development of new equipment, most of which, at first, had to be done by the Division in conjunction with the R.A.F. The latter was concerned chiefly with aircraft, parachutes, gliders, and containers for dropping arms and equipment, while the Army had to produce weapons, vehicles and equipment which were sufficiently light, small and yet efficient to be carried either by parachute or glider. A great deal of the credit for the development of Army equipment is due to Colonel Eagger, Lieutenant-Colonel Shorrock and their staffs, and to the scientific research section of the Ministry of Supply which was assisting the Division, and a large part of their time was taken up with field trials and conferences with manufacturers. Some examples of weapons, vehicles and equipment are given below :—

(a) *Weapons* had to be dropped by parachute and/or carried in Horsa Gliders until the Hamilcar became available some two years later. Weapons, ammunition and spare parts would not be easy to replace in action, so that they had to be strong, and their ammunition scales had to be economical in weight in relation to their effect. At the same time, in order to economize in resources, wherever possible they had to be similar to those used by the remainder of the Armed

Forces. The rifle, the Bren light machine gun and the 3-inch mortar, with little modification, remained the best and basic infantry weapons. Carbine sub-machine-guns were also required in large numbers, particularly for parachute troops in the initial drop to provide concentrated fire-power, and Stens were found to be the most suitable, being light, and using 9-mm. ammunition which the enemy also used, so that supplies could usually be found. The Royal Artillery were armed with the American 75-mm. pack howitzer, this gun being more easily available than the British 3·7-inch howitzer and slightly better suited to the very general tasks required. For anti-tank purposes the 2-pounder was discarded in favour of the 6-pounder as soon as the axle had been modified so that it would fit into the Horsa, and a small proportion of high explosive was included in its ammunition scales. 20-mm. Hispanos and 40-mm. Bofors guns were provided for anti-aircraft purposes, the latter requiring some dismantling for carriage in the Horsa and consequently taking longer to get into action. It was originally proposed that air-landing battalions would have isolated roles and, so that they might have their own supporting weapons, a few anti-tank and 20-mm. dual purpose guns were included in their establishments, the idea being that the action of these guns would be co-ordinated by the commander, Royal Artillery as the battle developed. The air-landing battalions were, in fact, the most heavily armed infantry in the British Army, in accordance with the principle that as far as possible gliders should carry heavy material rather than more light infantry of the parachutist type.

(b) *Vehicles.*—Some form of cross-country vehicle capable of being carried in a Horsa, and if possible of being dropped by parachute as well, had to be found to provide mobility for key personnel, signals and weapons. The existing heavier vehicles of the Army were too big for the Horsa, and light cars of the Austin Seven type were not sufficiently powerful. The problem was solved by the lucky arrival of the American jeep, which by good fortune and with very little modification could just be squeezed into the Horsa. Every kind of experiment was undertaken to make full use of this vehicle and a shorter working life with a greater strain than normal was accepted. Eventually, and after much argument with the more orthodox experts, the jeep was used successfully and continuously to tow such heavy weapons as the 6-pounder anti-tank gun and Bofors anti-aircraft gun, and it was not long before the gun and detachments were able to drive and manhandle these guns over really rough country. Apart from the jeep, and until the Hamilcar Glider became available, there were no other four-wheeled airborne vehicles but large numbers of light and a proportion of heavy motor-cycles were included in the Division. An ultra-light folding motor-cycle was also developed to drop by parachute in a container. In addition both the parachute and the air-landing troops were equipped with folding bicycles. To overcome difficulties of removal of supplies and medical stores, various types of trailer were developed to be towed by jeeps, and there were also hand-drawn two-wheeled trolleys to carry such things as mortars, ammunition, supplies, and other stores. In addition, every unit had a certain amount of normal army transport which was used to save wear and tear to jeeps on training and was intended to join the unit in action as soon as ground conditions permitted, if immediate evacuation of the airborne troops were not possible or was not intended.

(c) *Equipment.*—The type of personal equipment was dictated by the roles. The troops would often be exposed to extreme cold in the aircraft *en route* to the battle area. On arrival they might have to depend for several days almost entirely on what they carried themselves. All available transport was required for weapons, ammunition and certain essential stores such as medical supplies. For all except the sick and wounded, such "luxuries" as greatcoats, blankets and tents were out of the question until the land communications were opened. Furthermore, the clothing and equipment worn by parachutists had to be so designed that they would not catch in any projections from the aircraft or foul the parachute rigging lines. Personal clothing was therefore based on what might be called the "aertex" system as used in the Arctic. A string vest, loosely-woven and loosely-fitting, was worn next to the skin, with a closely-woven, semi-waterproof smock over the battle-dress giving a combination which was suitable for cold or warm non-tropical weather and was light, without a "tail" or other loose piece of cloth. The beret was chosen as the headgear most likely to stay on the head and the steel helmet was designed as a crash-helmet, the edge of which did not protrude so as to cut a neighbour during a forced landing, or interfere with the exit from a parachute aircraft. Otherwise the clothing was practically the same as for the remainder of the Army, except that more pockets were provided in the battle dress, two shell dressings being carried in pockets in the seat of the trousers, to act both as spinal shock-absorbers for parachutists after landing and as medical equipment. Rubber-soled boots, considered necessary in the early days to take the shock of a parachute landing and to assist stealthy movement, were replaced later by ordinary army boots, as there was a shortage of rubber and rubber soles were not suitable for long marches. Such extras as knee-pads and ankle bandages were available if required.

To foster the principles of high morale and a *corps d'élite*, the formation sign of the Division, later extended to all airborne forces, was chosen by Major-General Browning to show Bellerophon astride a winged Pegasus, in sky-blue on a maroon background, the beret also to be maroon so that members of airborne forces would be recognized as such wherever they might be.

Light medical and surgical equipment of all kinds was produced from stock or manufactured to new design. Before the advent of airborne forces the Army had always worked upon the principle that a casualty should be picked up in battle by stretcher bearers, evacuated from the regimental aid post to a dressing station and then to progressively improving hospitals. Airborne forces accepted this principle as far as the dressing station but no further in the initial stages of a battle because it was impracticable. Normal evacuation was only possible after the ground forces had linked up with the airborne troops. But major surgical operations might have to be performed and therefore the only solution was to take the doctors and the surgical teams to the troops instead of *vice versa*. This is in fact what happened and the surgeons jumped with their instruments, performing their operations often in the front line. Airborne field ambulances held the casualties and kept them in good condition for eventual evacuation when conditions permitted. By this means many lives were saved and it was expected, and later proved, that such excellent medical arrangements would be a very great factor in establishing and maintaining morale and battle efficiency.

Equipment for the Royal Engineers varied comparatively little from that of the rest of the Army, but only certain types could be taken by air. Generally, until land communications opened or more supplies were air-landed, each engineer unit or sub-unit could do one main task and one only. They could lay a small minefield, or carry out demolitions, but they could not normally carry the equipment for more than one of these tasks. Therefore, even more than in a normal division, the personnel were trained to be able to do anything, and the Field Park Company held a great variety of stores which could be used as required in any particular operation. Equipment was designed so that engineers could operate either as sub-units with infantry battalions in the early stages of a battle, or be concentrated under higher control.

There was also considerable development of equipment connected with the R.A.F. side of airborne forces. Blind-flying instruments for gliders, for use at night or in cloud, were developed jointly by 38 Wing, by the R.A.F. Technical Establishments and by the Glider Pilot Regiment themselves. Pathfinding radar equipment and ground location devices, *e.g.* " Rebecca " and " Eureka " (*see* Appendix D), were used by the pilots of 38 Wing and 21st Independent Parachute Company together, personnel of the latter being dropped ahead by special aircrews to set up wireless or other location devices on the ground to guide the remaining aircrews to the correct dropping or glider landing zones. Although many of these devices did not materialize in 1942, they were under continuous development and trial the whole time, and all equipment, whether dropped by parachute or landed by glider, had to be designed, packed and loaded to the satisfaction of the R.A.F. For example, parachute containers had to be packed to specified weights, and glider loads had to be individually lashed to certain strong points in the glider. One of the greatest problems was to distribute the loads evenly over the floor of the glider, at the same time conforming to R.A.F. centre of gravity requirements. When the hundreds of trials in this connection had been completed, all troops had to be instructed in packing and lashing the loads and for this purpose many tons of lashing equipment were held by army units and in the Ordnance Field Park. The development of equipment used for dropping stores by parachute is given in Appendix E.

The Expansion of the Air Training Organization and the Formation of 38 Wing, R.A.F.

14. While Major-General Browning was dealing with the problems of training and organizing his rather " ad hoc " division of two brigades and a few divisional troops, the R.A.F. were endeavouring to keep pace with the Army side of airborne forces. In Chapter III we saw how, in September, 1941, they anticipated the inevitable expansion by ordering the reorganization of the Airborne Forces Establishment. By 1st November, the reorganization had been completed, the new self-contained units were ready to be formed, and the R.A.F. assumed full responsibility for the training of parachute troops, all Army instructors being replaced by R.A.F. personnel. The first course under the new system began on 3rd November and consisted of 18 officers and 237 other ranks who had been carefully selected and hardened at Hardwick Camp, there being only seven injuries and two refusals. On the following day No. 1 Glider Training School formed at Haddenham round the old Glider Exercise Flight, and was thereby divorced from the Airborne Forces Establishment which now consisted of the Headquarters, the Parachute Training School, the Technical Development Unit and an experimental flight.

15. On 28th November the Air Ministry stated that the R.A.F. training organization for airborne forces would be as follows :—

    (a) *For individual training of glider pilots*
        One Elementary Flying Training School.
        Two Glider Training Schools. (No. 1 Glider Training School already existed.)
        Two Glider Operational Training Units.
    (b) *For individual training of parachute troops*
        One Parachute Training School. (In existence at Ringway.)
    (c) *For collective training*
        One Parachute Exercise Squadron.
        One Glider Exercise Squadron.
    (d) A Technical Development Section. (In existence at Ringway.)

For administrative purposes the five schools for training glider pilots were placed under Flying Training Command, the remainder being under Army Co-operation Command.

16. Immediate steps were taken to implement the new organization and No. 1 Glider Training School opened at Weston-on-the-Green on 1st December, No. 16 Elementary Flying Training School turned over to glider flying training on 31st December, and Nos. 1 and 2 Glider Operational Training Units opened at Netheravon and Kidlington on 1st January and 1st February, 1942, respectively. Of the two exercise squadrons formed at Netheravon during January, No. 296 (Glider Exercise) Squadron (Squadron Leader P. B. N. Davis) was to have 8 plus 3 Hectors, 20 plus 6 Whitleys, 30 plus 10 Horsas and 16 plus 14 Hotspurs, and No. 297 (Parachute Exercise) Squadron (Wing Commander B. Oakley) was to have 12 plus 4 Whitleys. Aircrews were immediately available, but aircraft and gliders were very slow in arriving and the squadrons were not nearly up to establishment by April. Even if the aircraft had been available the numbers in the two exercise squadrons would have been quite inadequate.

17. On 15th February, 1942, the Airborne Forces Establishment ceased to exist and No. 1 Parachute Training School became a self-contained unit, remaining at Ringway. The Headquarters, the Technical Development Unit and the Experimental Flight were merged into a new unit known as the Airborne Forces Experimental Establishment under Group Captain Harvey, whose charter was " to carry on the Technical Development programme in connection with the R.A.F. side of Airborne Warfare," and which remained at Ringway until 1st July, 1942, when it moved to Sherburne-in-Elmet, near Harrogate.

18. It was now obvious that some form of headquarters was necessary to co-ordinate the activities of 296 and 297 Squadrons, and to work with Headquarters 1 Airborne Division, as there would be common problems which would have to be solved jointly and the two squadrons could not be under command of the Army formation. On 15th January, 1942, therefore, Headquarters 38 Wing was established. Wing Commander Sir Nigel Norman was promoted to Group Captain and appointed to command and opened his headquarters alongside Headquarters 1 Airborne Division at Syrencote House, Netheravon. The Air Ministry later ordered the wing headquarters to move to Netheravon airfield so that the conception of a combined Army/R.A.F. airborne headquarters never fully materialized. The wing headquarters was to work with Headquarters 1 Airborne Division and was to be responsible to Army Co-operation Command for the air training of the division and for any operations that might take place. Group Captain Sir Nigel Norman was authorized to establish liaison direct with the Airborne Forces Establishment (and later with No. 1 Parachute Training School and the Airborne Forces Experimental Establishment) and with Flying Training Command regarding the training of glider pilots. He was given a very small operational and training staff whose duties were to include the evolving of a technique of training that could be applied to Bomber Command aircrews and squadrons as they became available, because the Air Ministry would not permit the squadrons of the wing to be operational, but laid down that airborne operations would be carried out by aircraft lent from Bomber Command. As a result the Bruneval raid (*see* Chapter VII) was carried out by No. 51 Squadron of Bomber Command.

19. One of the first problems that Group Captain Norman had to face was that of air training for the troops and particularly for glider pilots. 38 Wing was desperately short of aircraft and gliders. Bomber Command could not spare any aircraft or crews for training with troops and the only other resources available were the few aircraft at the Airborne Forces Experimental Establishment and No. 1 Parachute Training School which, in any case, were fully occupied with training individuals and with technical development. To add to this Allied airborne contingents in the United Kingdom—Poles, French, Dutch, Belgians and Norwegians—were clamouring in vain for their share of resources. The allotment and best use of the available aircraft, therefore, were problems that taxed the ingenuity of 38 Wing, division, and brigade headquarters to the utmost, particularly as the glider pilots leaving the R.A.F. schools also had to continue their training and keep in practice. Eight hours flying a month each pilot had been considered a reasonable minimum to keep a glider pilot at a good operational standard, but, during 1942, 1943 and 1944 they were lucky if they averaged five hours. It was obvious that when the units were ready for air training and a steady flow of glider pilots started from the schools, the resources would be totally inadequate unless the strength of 38 Wing could be greatly increased or Bomber Command squadrons could be loaned.

The Position by mid–April, 1942

20. Since the inception of airborne forces there had always been two widely differing points of view regarding their use. One school of thought considered that their value lay in small operations, either independent of the main force or in close co-operation with them in the tactical battle, to cut communications and harass the enemy's rear areas. The other school did not deny their value for this purpose, but were convinced that their greatest importance lay in their power to attack the enemy in force on his open flank—over the top and they considered that the first and most important requirement was a well-balanced force of all arms concentrated on vital objectives which land or sea-borne forces could not reach. In fact this school insisted that the first, though not the only requirement, was a fully trained, fully equipped and well balanced division. Major-General Browning supported this view and never varied his policy, treating his command as an operational division, which he considered could provide any raiding or sabotage parties for the time being, special guerrilla units being formed after the division was complete. As a first step in this policy the following units which had been part of 1 Air-landing and 1 Parachute Brigade Groups had been removed from these brigades and designated as Divisional Troops on 15th December, 1941 :—

> 458 Independent Light Battery, R.A. (redesignated 1 Air-landing Light Battery, R.A., on 27th July, 1942).
>
> 1 Air-landing Brigade Group Reconnaissance Squadron (redesignated 1 Airborne Reconnaissance Squadron, 28th April, 1942).
>
> 1 Air-landing Brigade Group Company, R.A.S.C. (redesignated 1 Airborne Composite Company, R.A.S.C., 7th August, 1942).
>
> 261 Field Park Company, R.E.

21. Eventually the second school prevailed and steps were taken to build 1 Airborne Division up to its full strength, though this took some considerable time, and the process lasted until December, 1942. On 3rd February, 1942, Headquarters Royal Engineers was formed around those sappers who had been originally attached to Division Headquarters, in March, 1 Parachute Brigade moved to Bulford Camp, Salisbury Plain, and in April, 1 Airborne Divisional Signals and 16 Parachute Field Ambulance were formed.

22. On 16th April, Mr. Winston Churchill visited 1 Airborne Division and was shown a demonstration of parachute troop dropping and gliders, in which were used the maximum number of aircraft then available from 38 Wing. There were 12 Whitleys for the parachute troops and nine Hectors each towing one Hotspur Glider. The Prime Minister was most disturbed at this lack of aircraft for airborne forces and on his return to London took immediate action which resulted in the expansion of 38 Wing and the setting up of the Airborne Forces Committee, both of which events will be discussed in the next chapter.

CHAPTER VI

AIRBORNE FORCES IN THE UNITED KINGDOM, APRIL TO OCTOBER, 1942

The Build-up of the Air Training Organization

1. Mr. Churchill returned to London from the demonstration at Netheravon on 16th April determined that the R.A.F. side of airborne forces should keep pace with that of the Army. He directed the Chief of the Air Staff to make proposals for increasing the number of discarded bombers which could rapidly be placed at the disposal of the Airborne Corps. He hoped that at least 100 could be found within the next three months.

However, the problem was not quite so simple, because as bombers became obsolete they were urgently required by Bomber Command Operational Training Units. At a meeting of the Chiefs of Staff on 6th May, at which both Mr. Churchill and Major-General Browning were present the latter put forward a suggestion originally made by Group Captain Sir Nigel Norman that a self-contained force should be formed, to consist of four squadrons with a total of 96 aircraft, whose primary task would be to train and operate with 1 Airborne Division. This proposal was agreed and the Air Ministry were instructed to go ahead with the detailed plans.

2. In the meantime, other steps were being taken to assist the expansion of the air side of airborne forces. On 1st May, at the instigation of the Prime Minister through Colonel J. J. Llewellin, Minister of Aircraft Production, the Airborne Forces Committee was established under the chairmanship of Sir Robert Renwick, Bart, with the following terms of reference :—

> " to co-ordinate arrangements for the development, production, supply, transport and storage of all equipment for airborne forces, and to secure rapid decisions ".

The chairman had direct access to the Prime Minister and the members were the Assistant Chief of the Air Staff (Technical), the Director of Military Co-operation, Air Ministry, the Director of Staff Duties, War Office (later succeeded by the Director of Air), Major-General Browning, and from the Ministry of Aircraft Production Mr. M. Rosenburg (Technical) and Mr. S. V. Connolly (Production). Originally composed of senior members, meetings were later held on a branch level and were used as a means of taking decisions on this level and of sorting our inter-ministry difficulties without resorting to unnecessary correspondence. The committee existed until the middle of 1943, and during that period covered a lot of very useful ground and considerably speeded up the supply of equipment to airborne forces.

3. During May, Mr. Churchill cabled to the President of the United States explaining the position and asking for an immediate stepping-up of the allocation of transport aircraft, even at the expense of deliveries due later in the year. President Roosevelt replied that it was impossible to supply aircraft owing to the heavy demands of the American forces, but he promised that four transport groups of the United States Army Air Forces would sail for England as soon as

possible, two arriving in June, and the other two a month or two later, having a total of 208 aircraft. It was hoped that four more groups would arrive by November, increasing the total to 416 aircraft, all of which would be available to assist the British forces both in training and in operations.

4. On 4th June, members of the Parliamentary Committee on National Expenditure under the chairmanship of Sir Ralph Glynn, visited Headquarters 1 Airborne Division and Headquarters 38 Wing at Netheravon to :—

" ascertain whether the resources provided by the Army and R.A.F. were economically related to each other so as to produce a balanced force, and, if not, to make recommendations ".

They found that there were insufficient R.A.F. resources for the force required, and recommended the immediate allotment of some Albemarle aircraft, of which there were about 60 available, and it was agreed that technical trials for airborne purposes should be carried out with this type. Such was the deficiency of aircraft in 38 Wing at the end of June when 1st Parachute Battalion were to take part in the Dieppe raid, that the wing could not even lift one battalion and had to borrow Nos. 12 and 142 squadrons from Bomber Command. The men were actually in their aircraft when the airborne part of the operation was cancelled.

5. On 19th June, the Prime Minister approved the Air Ministry's proposals for implementing the self-contained R.A.F. element of airborne forces. Whitley aircraft were to be withdrawn from Bomber Command and supplied to 38 Wing on the following programme :—

May	June	July	August	September	Total
10	10	20	23	23	86

As Whitleys could not tow the Hamilcar Glider, the first of which was due to be delivered in July, five Halifaxes would be supplied to 38 Wing in August, and a further five in September, by which time eight Hamilcars were due. 38 Wing was to have its own operational training unit and squadrons were not to specialize in parachute dropping or glider towing but were to be prepared to do either. To enable the policy to be implemented a glider flight of 30 Horsas was to be established at each 38 Wing station. A Glider Exercise Unit was formed at Netheravon on 2nd August, and on the next day No. 295 Squadron (Wing Commander G. P. Marvin) began to form there around a nucleus taken from 296 Squadron, with an establishment of 24 plus 6 Whitley aircraft at full strength, which was the same as Nos. 296 and 297 Squadrons, who were now at Hurn near Bournemouth. On 10th August, No. 298 (Wing Commander D. H. Duder) formed at Thruxton from personnel of 297 Squadron with an establishment of 16 plus 4 Whitleys and 8 plus 2 Halifaxes, and all squadrons were due to be complete to establishment by 21st October.

6. The enlarged 38 Wing would relieve Bomber Command of the commitment of supplying aircraft for training airborne forces and for smaller operations. As it was likely that bomber aircraft would be turned over to 38 Wing as they became obsolete for bombing purposes and as the Air Ministry considered that, as a long-term project only, additional aircraft for larger operations would have to be supplied by Bomber Command, they ordered all bomber aircraft which came off production after mid 1942 to be modified for glider-towing by

53

the addition of certain fixed fittings which strengthened the rear of the fuselage and provided strong points to which glider-towing attachments could be fixed. In addition certain types, such as Stirlings, Halifaxes, and Albemarles, were modified for parachute dropping. The wisdom of this decision was apparent in December, 1943, when 38 Group (as it was then) took over two squadrons of Stirlings from Bomber Command. Normally the modifications to these aircraft would have taken months and there would have been no possibility of them being ready for the invasion of North-West Europe in 1944, but as it was, the necessary fittings were completed in a week or so. The Air Ministry intention was that bomber crews should practise glider-towing when not on operations and to this end, in the summer of 1942 orders were issued for the erection of two T.2 ("Blister") hangars at each of the 22 heavy-bomber airfields for the storage of gliders, thus making sure, also, that gliders would be on tug-aircraft airfields in the event of large-scale airborne operations.

7. In the meantime Flying Training Command had been watching the growth of the Glider Pilot Regiment and during June, July and August increased the arrangements for glider pilot training accordingly. On 29th June, 1942, the Heavy Glider Conversion Unit was formed at Shrewton, later moving to Brize Norton, to cover the conversion of glider pilots to Horsa and Hamilcar Gliders, previously carried out by the glider operational training units.

8. During July and August additional elementary flying training flights were allotted from Nos. 3, 21 and 27 Elementary Flying Training Schools ; No. 1 Glider Training School moved from Haddenham to Croughton ; No. 3 Glider Training School opened at Stoke Orchard on 21st July ; and Nos. 1 and 2 Glider Operational Training Units were closed down and became Nos. 4 and 5 Glider Training Schools which opened at Kidlington and Shobden respectively. By the end of the summer it appeared that the air component of airborne forces was well on the way to be able to play a full part in the training of the airborne troops who were still expanding and were settling down rapidly.

1 Airborne Division

9. The process of expansion of the airborne troops continued steadily throughout the summer side by side with the R.A.F. Gradually problems of organization and establishments were settled and the division got down to something like normal training.

10. In the spring the War Office had agreed that as for any ordinary division, a third brigade was necessary. There was at this time a shortage of aircraft and gliders, and all gliders likely to be available for some time to come would be required to carry 1 Air-landing Brigade and the heavier supporting arms, so that the new formation was to be a parachute brigade. On 17th July, 1942, Headquarters, 2 Parachute Brigade was formed, with Lieutenant-Colonel Down, from 1st Parachute Battalion, promoted to Brigadier and appointed to command. The 4th Parachute Battalion was transferred from 1 Parachute Brigade as the first unit to join, and on 1st August, 7th Battalion The Cameron Highlanders became 5th (Scottish) Parachute Battalion, and on 14th August, 10th Battalion The Royal Welch Fusiliers was redesignated 6th (Royal Welch) Parachute Battalion.

11. The following list shows how the divisional troops, services and supporting arms were built up by the end of 1942 :—

May, 1942

1 Airborne Division Postal Unit.

June, 1942

1 Air-landing Anti-Tank Battery, R.A. (redesignated from 223 Anti-Tank Battery, R.A.).

1 Airborne Division Provost Company (formed around 1 Air-landing Brigade Group Provost Section).

1 Air-landing Brigade Group Defence Platoon (redesignated from 1 Independent Brigade Group Defence Platoon).

July, 1942

21 Independent Parachute Company.

1 Airborne Light Tank Squadron (converted from " C " Special Service Light Tank Squadron).

August, 1942

H.Q., Glider Pilot Regiment.

1 Glider Pilot Regiment (redesignated from the Glider Regiment).

2 Glider Pilot Regiment.

September, 1942

2 Air-landing Anti-Tank Battery, R.A. (redesignated from 204 Anti-Tank Battery, R.A.).

October, 1942

H.Q., R.A. Airborne Division.

2 Parachute Squadron, R.E. (redesignated from Holding Company, Kent Corps Troops, R.E.).

December, 1942

127 Parachute Field Ambulance.

12. By the end of the summer most of the detailed work of preparing the Division's war establishments had been completed. The credit for this must go mainly to the second-grade staff officers of Divisional Headquarters— Majors Sir Richard des Voeux, F. H. Lowman, N. S. L. Field and J. M. B. Cowan, whose hard work and sympathy with the wishes of the brigades deserve the greatest praise. However, the establishments had yet to receive the approval of Home Forces and the War Office ; the Division's demands were not backed by operational experience, and there was no guiding precedent, so that discussions took somewhat longer than they might otherwise have done. During the resultant delay units had to do the best they could to organize and train themselves on anticipated establishments without, in many cases, the necessary equipment and it is a tribute to all concerned during this difficult period that their keenness never faltered in the slightest degree.

13. Recruiting for the Glider Pilot Regiment went ahead steadily until, in August, 1942, a second battalion was formed. Lieutenant-Colonel Rock was killed while piloting a glider in October, 1942, and Major Chatterton took

55

command of the Regiment. He remained in command until he retired after the war had ended, and he was in action in every airborne operation from Sicily onwards. He saw the regiment grow from nothing to a final strength of 2,500 all ranks, and he planned every glider operation. He insisted on the necessity for the glider-pilot being " the total soldier " and played a large part in the development of the tactical handling of gliders. With the shortages of aircraft and gliders, for a long time to come it was impossible to give the glider-pilots adequate flying practice, and it is a tribute to the men themselves that they managed to fly gliders from England to North Africa, and to take part successfully in operations with so few flying hours to their credit. They were an exceptionally fine type of man, and so high was their standard that on an average only a third of those who volunteered were accepted.

14. We have already mentioned that the parachute battalions had no parent regiment or corps, and in this respect the Glider Pilot Regiment was better off, being part of the Army Air Corps. On 1st August, 1942, the War Office formed the Parachute Regiment, which was also to be part of the Army Air Corps, and which was to consist of all parachute infantry units, thus simplifying their administration, and increasing their already good *esprit de corps*.

15. Further relief to the Division in general and to commanding officers in particular had been welcomed in April when the Airborne Forces Depot and School was formed at Hardwick after 1 Parachute Brigade had moved to Bulford. This establishment was quite unofficial but it was created as a properly organized unit, and by mid-summer its effect was beginning to be felt. Although it was still under command of the Division it relieved it from much of its work in training and holding recruits before they went to the Parachute Training School, and in rehabilitating the temporarily unfit.

16. During the summer the Division was honoured by visits from Royalty and from senior officers of our own and Allied Services. It was assisted and encouraged in many ways by other headquarters, and a close liaison with American and other Allied parachute units was started. Loading trials began with gliders, and the Airborne Forces Security Fund was founded.

17. The first visitors were the Secretary of State for War, the Chiefs of the Imperial General and Air Staffs and General Marshall, Chief of Staff, United States Army. They were followed on 21st May by Their Majesties The King and Queen, who watched parachute and Hotspur Glider exercises and encouraged everyone while inspecting the troops and their equipment. All possible help was given to the Division by Headquarters Southern Command, particularly as regards training and accommodation matters, and Headquarters, Combined Operations showed continued interest and were always ready to assist with special training and equipment. The Military Attachés of the American Embassy kept in constant and friendly touch. 1 Polish Parachute Brigade and the parachute contingents of the Free French, Norwegian, Belgian and Dutch Armies were most enthusiastic and grateful for any assistance that the Division and the Wing could give them.

18. In May, soon after General Marshall's visit, Headquarters 1 Airborne Division had been told that an American parachute battalion would shortly be leaving for England as a result of a personal invitation from Mr. Churchill to Mr. Roosevelt, and that it would come under the operational command of

56

the Division on arrival. On 11th June, 2nd Battalion 503 Parachute Infantry Regiment, United States Army, under the command of Lieutenant-Colonel Edson D. Raffe, arrived at Chilton Foliat, near Newbury, where a camp and billets had been arranged for them. They were very welcome and the closest relations were immediately established, many officers and men being attached to British parachute units and *vice versa*, so that they could learn each other's ways. Organized and equipped on parallel lines to the British parachute battalions and trained with the same objects in view, co-operation with them was easy in spite of certain differences in types of parachutes, wireless sets and weapons. It was a great compliment, sincerely appreciated, that they should have been placed so readily under British command. The arrival of this battalion was followed in July by the attachment to 1 Airborne Division, of the Commander, Major-General William C. Lee, eleven officers and three enlisted men of the United States 101 Airborne Division, then training in America, who stayed for three weeks, to study British airborne methods. During the same month, Major-General Browning visited America to establish liaison with their airborne troops and to tell them how the British Airborne Division was organized and trained.

19. Although no Horsas had been delivered to 38 Wing, loading trials with these gliders had begun during the period, and in March at Ringway, Major-General Browning, among others, watched the staff of the Airborne Forces Experimental Establishment attempt to load a jeep into the first Horsa prototype. Their attempt was frustrated by the managing director and chief designer of Messrs. Airspeeds Ltd., of Portsmouth, the makers, who said that it would break the glider as the floor and loading ramp had been constructed for the motor-cycle combination which had been called for in the specifications. This caused consternation all round and shortly afterwards 1 Air-landing Brigade was ordered to provide samples of all equipment for loading trials to Airspeeds Ltd. So began a close liaison between the makers and the users, initially working out methods of fitting the equipment into a Horsa mock-up at Portsmouth, and ascertaining the necessary loading and lashing gear required, and subsequently, beginning on 6th July, proving the loads and lashing in one of the six prototypes at Netheravon. Brigadier Hopkinson and his Brigade Major, Major Campbell, who became the acknowledged airborne expert on the subject, spent many weeks personally on these trials. This, incidentally, is an example of how much guess-work had to be done by the Division in the early days in that they had no opportunity of testing loads in an actual Horsa Glider until eight months after the Division was formed.

20. In about August or September, the confidence of 1 Air-landing Brigade, and indeed of the Division was somewhat shaken by the discovery that the Whitley could not tow a loaded Horsa. As these two types of aircraft were the basis of 38 Wing and of our air-landing troops this caused no small concern for it meant that in operations, of whatever size, Horsas would have to be towed by heavy bombers until a more powerful transport type became available.

21. It would be invidious to leave this account of the happenings of the Division during the summer without telling the story of the Airborne Forces Security Fund, which, though not an official Army institution, probably did more than any other organization to assist the welfare of the airborne soldier and to maintain his morale at such a high standard. Major-General Browning had always realized the importance of doing anything that would improve the

morale of the troops, so when Captain J. M. Pearson suggested to him that some form of benevolent fund should be started, he agreed at once. Captain Pearson had been attached to the Glider Pilot Regiment at Tilshead and while there he studied the problem of the individual's private affairs, especially those needing monetary assistance. There were many of all ranks, but in the initial stages more especially officers, who were born leaders in war but who, in civilian life, had not so far achieved great heights. They found themselves in the Army as officers, or senior non-commissioned officers, leading a life with a standard of living far above that to which they had been accustomed. Many of them being young, got into financial difficulties. These men, like those of the Parachute Regiment, came from all units in the Army and so Captain Pearson investigated the possibility of help from the regimental funds of most regiments of the Army. He found that many of them were small and had so many other commitments that it was doubtful if they would be able to give very much assistance to anyone who needed it urgently in 1 Airborne Division, and so, as an experiment, he established the Glider Pilot Benevolent Association, which was extremely successful. On 1st May, 1942, a meeting was called at Headquarters, 1 Airborne Division by Major-General Browning to discuss the formation of a benevolent or welfare fund, and was attended by Lieutenant-Colonel Walch, Major Chatterton and Captain Pearson. Captain Pearson was entrusted with the creation of an airborne division benevolent fund, and those present agreed to serve as trustees, Colonel Eagger and Lieutenant-Colonel Goschen also being appointed as temporary trustees. In starting the fund, Captain Pearson had to bear in mind that no matter how good the individual officer or soldier was, he could be completely put off his work if he were worried financially, matrimonially or in any other way by his private affairs. The fund would have to be strong enough to enable Major-General Browning to assure troops going into battle that no matter what happened to them, behind them was an organization which would look after their dependants, and indeed on one occasion in the early days he did this when addressing several hundred troops, using the words " I give you my word of honour . . . ".

22. Through the aid of Mr. Gordon Boggon, a philanthropist, who had great experience of various charitable organizations, especially the Children's Hospital in Great Ormond Street, the services were secured of Mr. D. K. I. King, who at the time of writing is still the deputy controller. Two rooms in Fleet Street were obtained as offices and a trust deed was drawn up by Mr. Claude Rivers, K.C. The trust stated :—

" That the Fund be formed for the benefit of all ranks of Airborne Forces, their dependants, and/or next-of-kin who find themselves in need of assistance, financial or otherwise. Grants may also be made for any welfare project which would assist in maintaining the high morale of the Airborne Soldier."

Three honorary appointments were made, Mr. E. P. Rugg, as Honorary Solicitor, Major the Hon. Patrick Kinnard, Barclays Bank, as Honorary Treasurer and Messrs, Graham, Smart and Annan as Auditors. The first meeting of the trustees was held at Headquarters, 1 Airborne Division on 2nd November, 1942, and after this one of the objects was to make the board so representative of industry, banking and the like that not only would they be able to operate the funds successfully, but after the war would assist in finding employment for those who required it.

23. The Fund soon met with very generous support from a wide circle of the general public as well as from many friends engaged in the production of airborne equipment, and before long many thousands of pounds had been subscribed. The Fleet Street rooms became too small and the Fund moved several times, first to offices lent free by William Beardmore & Co. Ltd., at 3, St. James's Square, then to No. 70, Eaton Place, which was lent, again free, by Lady North, until finally permanent offices were obtained at Greenwich House, 10, Newgate Street, London, E.C. The Fund, now known as the Airborne Forces Security Fund, became and remained an important part of the life of the personnel of airborne forces and their families and did an untold amount of good. It lessened considerably the problems of morale and welfare that confronted airborne commanding officers in all parts of the world. Major-General Browning supported the Fund from its beginning, and remained as its Chairman until December, 1944, when he had to resign on being posted to the Far East and was succeeded by Mr. Harvey Bowring, one of the earliest trustees. Sincere gratitude is due to those civilian men and women who throughout the war years, gave so much of their time, mostly unpaid, to organize the Fund's offices and many local committees. In particular, Captain Pearson's energy and initiative will always be remembered by many grateful members, of whatever rank, of airborne forces.

The Air Directorate at the War Office

24. In June, 1942, the War Office took a step which had a far-reaching and lasting effect upon the development of airborne forces. A new Air Directorate was formed to look after and sponsor the affairs of airborne forces and to act as a special link between the War Office and Air Ministry on all air matters. The head of the Directorate was a brigadier, responsible to the Director of Staff Duties, and it was divided into two branches, the second of which, Air 2, dealt with all airborne matters. This was a great advance, as it meant that for the first time airborne forces would have one man at the War Office whom they could consult and soon resulted in a great saving of time and work for the Divisional Headquarters staff. It had a great effect on maintaining some degree of continuity of policy and co-ordination of requirements. It was essential that the Director of Air should have a real knowledge of airborne needs and a practical experience of airborne matters in order to carry conviction both inside and outside the War Office, and for this reason Brigadier Gale was appointed from commanding 1 Parachute Brigade. His first team in Air 2, who did such a lot for airborne forces in the early days was :—

G.S.O. I	Lieutenant-Colonel G. W. Lathbury.
G.S.O. II	Major W. P. B. Bradish.
G.S.O. III	Captain V. S. Bazalgette.
	Captain R. G. Collins.

The Need for more Airborne Forces

25. While the Division and the Wing were settling down to their problems of expansion and training, Major-General Browning and Group-Captain Norman were looking ahead and insisting on the strategic, long-range possibilities of employing large formations of airborne forces. Every opportunity was taken to accustom the troops to long distance flying and many plans were

made with the Headquarters Combined Operations for raids on the Continent. For various reasons they were cancelled and the troops disappointed, but they provided many valuable lessons and much useful experience.

26. The War Office also believed that in the near future large scale airborne operations would be necessary, probably on a divisional level, and possibly on an even greater scale. They maintained this opinion consistently and it was encouraged by the rapidly increasing resources of American troop-carrying aircraft and, later, by the success of 1 Parachute Brigade operations in North Africa, but it led to the development of two diametrically opposed points of view between the War Office and the Air Ministry.

27. It has been pointed out already that 38 Wing, even at its increased strength, would have to obtain assistance from Bomber Command for large-scale operations. The War Office wanted to be sure that they would in fact, receive this additional assistance, and so they submitted a paper to the Chiefs of Staff in which they recommended :—

> " that the Commander-in-Chief, Bomber Command, be asked to report to the Chiefs of Staff upon the implications of the assistance which will be required from Bomber Command, and in particular, upon the effects he considers the necessary preliminary training and subsequent operation of the division, or of a brigade group will have on the bomber effort ".

In a paper submitted to the Chiefs of Staff on 11th September, the Air Officer Commanding-in-Chief, Bomber Command, Air Chief Marshal Sir Arthur Harris, said that he considered that parachute or glider operations were not a practical operation of war other than against practically unarmed or unprotected troops, that the weather in Europe was generally unsuited—except on casual and almost unpredictable occasions—to airborne operations, that the casualties incurred in transporting airborne troops were bound to be enormous, that only one parachute brigade could be carried at a time and that airborne troops could not be employed with any prospect of material contribution to victory. In addition, Air Chief Marshal Harris stated that to set aside aircraft to transport a substantial airborne force would cripple Bomber Command's offensive, and that he considered that the employment of airborne troops at this stage of the war would be a side-show. The only alternative to the employment of Bomber Command aircraft would be to set up a separate transport organization, which he dismissed as " fantastic ".

28. The Chief of the Air Staff, Marshal of the Royal Air Force Sir Charles Portal, agreed with some of the views expressed by Air Chief Marshal Harris. He did not deny the value of airborne forces in war, but he did not agree that a complete airborne division would ever be used from the United Kingdom for any re-entry into the Continent. He considered that small airborne forces, and in particular parachutists, would be valuable for raiding operations. He said :—

> " I regard the bombing of German industry as an incomparably greater contribution to the war than the training and constant availability of the airborne division, and as the two things at present seriously conflict I would certainly accord priority to bombing . . .".

The War Office maintained, however, that 1 Airborne Division must be made ready for operations as soon as possible, that another airborne division might soon be required and that the operational airborne formations must be free from all responsibilities not directly aimed at their own readiness for war.

29. At the beginning of October, Sir Charles Portal circulated a paper to the Chiefs of Staff in which he recommended that the maximum airborne force which we could afford to maintain was that of two parachute brigades plus a small glider-borne force to carry supporting weapons, and that our existing airborne division should be reduced to this size. The Chief of the Imperial General Staff did not agree with this and, as it was obvious that, for the time being at any rate, the two points of view were irreconcilable, on 14th October, the Chiefs of Staff decided to submit the matter to the Prime Minister for arbitration.

30. The Prime Minister's decisions, and the events that followed, will be described in Chapter IX, but in the meantime, pending the result of the arbitration, on 19th October the Air Ministry issued orders that no more aircraft or personnel would be posted to R.A.F. airborne forces units until further notice. The situation then was that 295 Squadron had two flights complete in personnel and 21 aircraft, 296 and 297 Squadrons were at full personnel strength, the latter also being complete in aircraft, but 296 Squadron only had 21 Whitleys. The formation of 298 Squadron had been held up owing to lack of aircraft, while three Albemarles had been provided for trials.

31. The standstill order was a bitter blow and most disheartening for the Wing and the Division, especially when so many things had occurred during the summer to encourage them. Inevitably it meant that for an indefinite but necessarily long period the Division, including its glider pilots, would not receive adequate air training and the prospect of airborne operations, except for those in North Africa, receded into the dim future. It was all the more disappointing as the division was really beginning to shake down and had just completed its first field training exercise as a formation. However, the setback was not allowed to interfere with the arrangements for getting 1 Parachute Brigade ready for North Africa, and it will now be seen what these were.

Preparations for the North African Campaign

32. Major-General Browning had been appointed the official British adviser on airborne forces to Commander-in-Chief in all theatres of war, and towards the end of September, 1942, he was informed that the North African campaign was to take place in November and that 2nd Battalion, 503 U.S. Parachute Infantry Regiment, would be required to take part. He suggested that more than one parachute battalion was required for such a campaign which was to be conducted over great distances with the probability that, at any rate in the early stages, only comparatively light opposition would be encountered in country where there were obviously tremendous possibilities for airborne troops. The Commander-in-Chief, Home Forces, and the War Office, then approved the addition of 1 Parachute Brigade to the force already allotted for the campaign, and as strategic troops the brigade was placed under command of General Dwight Eisenhower, the Supreme Allied Commander, and sub-allotted by him to First British Army for specific operations. The Air Ministry were unable to provide any aircraft or crews to work with the brigade, although 38 Wing R.A.F. were the only airmen, British or American, fully trained to drop British parachutists, whose parachute equipment and technique varied in important details from the Americans. The United States Army Air Force immediately and enthusiastically took over responsibility for the Air side of the

operations and combined training with 60 Group of 51 Wing (Dakotas) which had arrived in England, resulted in the first drop of a British unit from that type of aircraft on 9th October, 1942. Unfortunately, although all concerned, including 38 Wing, had worked overtime in the short period available, the technique was not then completely understood and three men were killed out of the 250 who dropped that day. This had a most unfortunate effect as further practice drops had to be delayed for a few days while the technique was corrected and resulted in a large number of the personnel of 1 Parachute Brigade going overseas to the campaign without having had the opportunity to do any practice jumps from a Dakota aircraft. Most of their jumps beforehand had been through apertures in the floors of bombers, whereas they now had to use the entirely different method of exit through a door in the side, but these difficulties did not deter them and co-operation with the Americans was excellent, though necessarily limited by the time factor.

33. In order to complete 1 Parachute Brigade as nearly as possible to war establishment it was necessary to take many personnel and much equipment from the remainder of the Airborne Division. This was complicated by the fact that the brigade had not yet been able to sort out all its unfit personnel, most of them training casualties who needed a few weeks to recover but who could not be ready in time, and because no up-to-date official equipment or staff tables had been approved. Hurried improvisations, the cross-posting of personnel from 2 Parachute Brigade and from other units in the Division, priority in allotment of recruits, and the surrender of much of the Division's resources did, however, enable 1 Parachute Brigade to leave England at the beginning of November, in fairly good shape, though without reinforcements, which would have to follow them later as they became available. In Chapter VIII it will be seen how they fared after their arrival in North Africa.

CHAPTER VII

THE EARLY AIRBORNE OPERATIONS—ITALY, BRUNEVAL AND NORWAY

General

1. While airborne forces were expanding during 1941 and 1942, three small operations took place, with varying success, the lessons of which assisted in many ways the development of the new arm of the Service. These operations, which are described in this chapter, were an attempt to blow up an aqueduct in Italy in February, 1941, the Bruneval raid in February, 1942, and an attack on a heavy water plant in Norway, in November, 1942.

"Colossus"—The Parachute Operation against the Tragino Aqueduct in Southern Italy, 10th February, 1941

2. At the beginning of 1941 there were few airborne resources available, either Army or R.A.F., and these were concentrated at the Central Landing Establishment. Whitley bombers were the only approved parachuting aircraft, but even their modification for this purpose was in its infancy, and there were very few of them. There were no service gliders. There were few R.A.F. crews with any experience of parachute dropping and none with operational experience. The only troops were 11 Special Air Service Battalion, formed from No. 2 Commando during the previous November. There were no facilities at overseas bases for airborne operations, other than the normal, and strained, servicing facilities for aircraft.

3. At this period of the war, however, it was most desirable to do anything which would hamper the Italians in their campaigns in North Africa and Albania. One of the plans to this end envisaged the temporary dislocation of the water supplies for their departure ports of Taranto, Brindisi and Bari. A study of the map and of various Italian reports revealed the possibility that this might be done by cutting the Acquedetto Pugliese, the great system that carried the waters of the River Sele through the Apennines to the arid province of Apulia. The only vulnerable and vital points of this system were, however, many miles from the coast and it was unlikely that they could be reached by sea-borne raiding parties. Bombing of the pin-point and strongly constructed targets was also likely to be ineffectual. It was therefore decided to use parachute troops against the Tragino Aqueduct, apparently a suitable target on the pipeline near Calitri.

4. Preparations and training, under the direction of Lieutenant-Colonel Rock, for the Army, and Wing Commander Sir Nigel Norman for the R.A.F., started in January, 1941. A party of seven officers and 31 other ranks, including one Italian, of 11 Special Air Service Battalion were selected. They were commanded by Major T. A. G. Pritchard, Royal Welch Fusiliers, with Captain G. F. K. Daly, R.E., in charge of the demolition party. Eight Whitleys from 91 Squadron, commanded by Wing Commander J. B. Tate, were allotted for the parachute troops and two for a diversionary bombing raid against Foggia. Training in the United Kingdom, with excellent models of the target area and approaches, "mock-ups" and sketches of the viaduct, was intensive

63

and enthusiastic. On 24th January, Lieutenant A. J. Deane-Drummond, Royal Corps of Signals, was ordered to fly to Malta in a Sunderland to prepare for the expedition. The party would take off for the operation from there on 10th February and would be evacuated by His Majesty's Submarine " Triumph " from the mouth of the River Sele during the night of 15th/16th February. These evacuation plans, until take-off, were known only to Major Pritchard, Lieutenant Deane-Drummond, the submarine commander and a few of the naval staff. They were not divulged at all to the crews of the aircraft carrying out the diversionary bombing.

5. The aircraft and all personnel, with their parachutes, flew to Malta, where they assembled. Each of the six Whitleys for the parachute troops was allotted a sub-section of one officer and five other ranks, with arms, ammunition and explosives.

6. The operation began when these aircraft left Malta at 1830 hours on the night 10th/11th February, as planned. They were due over the target at 2130 hours. The moon was full, visibility excellent, and the journey was calm and uneventful except for slight enemy flak over Sicily. The intention was to run up to the target from Calitri across the River Ofanto and to drop the parties on Hill 427 about half a mile north of the aqueduct.

7. At 2142 hours the first aircraft, flying at 400 feet above the ground, dropped its complete load within 250 yards of the target. Four other aircraft dropped their troops up to three-quarters of a mile short of the target within a few minutes but two failed to drop their arms and explosives. The sixth aircraft, carrying Captain Daly and five sappers, did not drop its sub-section until two hours later and then some two miles to the north-east in the next valley. The party could not take part in the operation and were captured 13 miles from the mouth of the River Sele five days later. Dropping casualties were small, only one man being seriously injured, but Major Pritchard was short of his senior R.E. officer and five sappers and a considerable proportion of his arms and explosives. But it was a great effort by the R.A.F. to drop so many men so accurately at a little over 400 miles from base with such limited technical flying resources.

8. There were difficulties in finding the containers, as the lighting devices did not work satisfactorily and only one arms container was picked up. However, enough explosives to do considerable damage were found and were carried to the aqueduct with the impressed aid of some local Italians, including the Railway Transport Officer at Calitri Railway Station. Second Lieutenant A. Paterson, R.E., took charge of the demolition of the main viaduct. There were no Italian troops in the immediate neighbourhood and the peasants gave no trouble. The viaduct was found to be much as expected, except that the centre pier and abutment was found to be of reinforced concrete instead of masonry. It was too strong to tackle with the resources in the time available. Nevertheless, at 0030 hours on 11th February the further pier of the main viaduct and a smaller bridge over the River Ginestra nearby were blown up. These demolitions were effective, the pier collapsed, the waterway was broken in two where it had been supported by the pier and water flooded down the ravine. The operation was successful. Major Pritchard now organized his party into three sections and gave them orders to move independently to the

64

rendezvous with the submarine. In spite of their efforts, however, all were captured on 12th February without getting very far. After this Lieutenant Deane-Drummond began an amazing series of escapes, whereby he rejoined 1 Airborne Division in 1942 and was captured and escaped again after the battle of Arnhem in 1944.

9. In the meantime one of the Whitleys carrying out the diversionary raid on 11th February developed engine trouble between Sicily and Italy. The pilot sent a wireless message in an insecure code saying that he would make for the mouth of the River Sele in the hope that he could be picked up. This message was considered to endanger the submarine due to rendezvous there and its move was cancelled. The point is mentioned because there was a widespread rumour that the parachute troops were captured owing to a breach of security in this message. In fact the pilot did not know of the rendezvous, selected the same place by pure chance, and the parachute troops were captured before they could get there. The other Whitley, with Wing Commander Sir Nigel Norman on board, bombed Foggia and returned safely to base *via* the aqueduct, seeing the troops in action there.

10. Operation " Colossus " had, in the end, a negligible effect on the war in North Africa and Albania. It did not achieve a serious interruption to the water supplies of the ports, as the water in the local reservoirs lasted for nearly the whole of the period of repair to the aqueduct. It did, however, spread great alarm in southern Italy and caused considerable effort to be wasted on more stringent air raid precautions and on unnecessary guards. This was a lasting effect. It provided useful experience for parachute raids in the future and showed the wide flexibility and range inherent in airborne troops—and their ever-present threat to the enemy. It also provided valuable technical experience on which were based many of the later developments for parachute aircraft and their equipment. For example, it was found that the soft-skinned containers previously used sagged so much that the bomb doors could not be closed. The metal containers manufactured especially for this operation provided the pattern for containers used in the later stages of the war. Similarly, the large numbers of containers which were not dropped in this operation, but were taken back to Malta were the result of unsatisfactory electrical connections, later put right.

The Bruneval Raid, 27th February, 1942

11. On 8th January, 1942, Headquarters, 1 Airborne Division and 38 Wing R.A.F. were asked by the Chief of Combined Operations (Admiral Lord Louis Mountbatten) whether they could carry out a raid on a German radio-location station on the French coast at Bruneval, near Le Havre. A series of these stations had been discovered along the coast but their exact purpose and the type of equipment they used were not known. Consequently no proper action could be taken against them although it was suspected that they produced information leading to many losses among our bomber aircraft. Furthermore, they were well guarded against assault from the sea and a commando raid against them would probably be expensive in casualties and too slow to capture any of the equipment before it could be destroyed. Surprise and speed were the essential requirements of any raid. An airborne assault, followed by sea-borne evacuation, seemed to be the only method by which specimens of the equipment and possibly a radio-location technician, could be captured.

12. As such an operation would require only a small force, and as only an airborne operation offered the best chance of success, Major-General Browning agreed that his Division should attempt the task, Group Captain Sir Nigel Norman agreeing that the air aspects were satisfactory. A successful operation at this stage in the development of airborne forces would be excellent as an incentive to the troops and as a demonstration of their value. Major-General Browning and Group Captain Norman, with the approval of the Commander-in-Chief, Home Forces, the Air Officer Commanding-in-Chief, Army Co-operation Command, and the Chief of Combined Operations decided that training could be completed by the end of February, when the right moon conditions would be suitable, provided one experienced squadron from Bomber Command could be made available to carry the troops. It was unfortunate and very disappointing for all concerned that 38 Wing were not yet ready to produce their own aircraft and crews, but any attempt to do so would have meant an over-hasty preparation and a complete stoppage of airborne training for the remainder of the Division for some six weeks. However, 51 Squadron (Whitleys), under the command of Wing Commander P. C. Pickard was allotted by the Air Ministry and detailed planning for the operation started within a few days.

13. It will be appreciated that the utmost secrecy was essential to the success of such an operation, particularly as there had been a long interval since British airborne troops had been engaged and the enemy had no reason to expect their imminent use. There were two aspects to be considered. The troops taking part in the operation must know every detail that would help them, in time for them to absorb that knowledge and use it in their rehearsals and training. No one else, whatever his rank or appointment, should have the slightest inkling that an airbourne operation was even contemplated unless he had a definite part to play in its preparation, and then he should know only as much as was necessary. As an example in this case, the essential members of the crews of 51 Squadron and the company of parachute troops taking part were fully briefed some days before the operation was due to take place, while the parachute battalion and brigade commander were told nothing until it was about to start. Only the army commander and a few field security personnel at Headquarters, Southern Command knew of the project, while the majority of Headquarters, 1 Airborne Division, where the detailed planning was done, were entirely ignorant of the matter. This led to many amusing incidents and some criticism of Headquarters, 1 Airborne Division for their insistence on certain requirements, but was well worth while. For example, a complaint by a farmer whose land was temporarily disfigured, and an indignant protest on his behalf by the training and compensation staffs at district and command headquarters were withdrawn wholeheartedly when some troops who had taken part in the raid helped the farmer to repair the damage a month later.

14. To return to the actual preparations for the raid, the Commander, 1 Parachute Brigade, was asked to provide a company for special training in combined operations. Wishing to keep 1st Parachute Battalion intact for an operation when called for, he ordered 2nd Parachute Battalion to provide the company and Major J. D. Frost and " C " Company were selected. It is of interest to note that they were so recently formed that the company commander and many of his men had not then completed their parachute jumping course

and they had done no training as a company. They moved to Tilshead Camp on Salisbury Plain on 24th January to start their training and to be near 51 Squadron, the latter moving to Thruxton airfield, their departure station for the operation. The next few days were spent by the unit commanders in planning while their respective commands did their own training and 38 Group instructed 51 Squadron in parachute dropping and carried out the necessary modification to the aircraft. Major Frost was also introduced to Commander F. N. Cook, Royal Australian Navy, who was to command the naval force destined to evacuate the parachute company back to England, and to the commander of a party of 32 officers and men of the Royal Fusiliers and the South Wales Borderers whose duty was to cover from landing-craft the withdrawal of the company to the boats. Flight Serjeant C. W. H. Cox, R.A.F., an expert radio mechanic, and a volunteer for hazardous operations, also joined the company for the operation, having done a quick parachute training course since he was warned for impending action.

15. Planning, training and equipping now proceeded fast. Excellent intelligence, including air photos and large scale models of the target area and its approaches, were provided by or through Headquarters, Combined Operations. Radio-location experts assisted with elementary training in the recognition of important parts of the machinery likely to be required from the German station. Major Frost's force did their first parachute training drop as a company on 15th February, from the aircraft of 51 Squadron. It was successful and complete confidence was established between the two units. Rehearsals with the naval force, although relations were good, were not so successful and many difficulties were experienced in arranging times to suit the tides and in getting the communications to work. Constant journeyings to secret places on the sea coast, as well as to the airfield at Thruxton, took up a disproportionate time of the company. It would have been far easier to get ready quickly if it had been possible to accommodate the company alongside the airfield and if all personnel had been trained previously in the elementary routine of combined sea-borne operations. These are facts to be remembered when the general situation may require a small airborne operation to be carried out, as always, at short notice.

16. After some postponement, owing to weather conditions unsuitable for either air or sea operations, the night 27/28th February provided an excellent opportunity. The moon was bright, with very light haze and little cloud ; there was no wind or sea swell, and visibility for 51 Squadron in the target area was two to four miles, with good definition. The naval force sailed in the afternoon and later in the evening " C " Company, 2nd Parachute Battalion, six officers and 113 other ranks strong, including nine sappers, four signallers and Flight Serjeant Cox, emplaned at Thruxton. Airborne sleeping bags were used for the first time to keep the men warm in the aircraft. Complete secrecy had been maintained despite the postponements. Even the Royal Artillery quartermaster, who looked after the company at Tilshead Camp, had no idea that an operation was starting.

17. The flight to the dropping zone was uneventful except for some slight enemy flak along the French coast. They arrived soon after midnight, having been airborne for over two hours. A diversion by aircraft of Fighter Command drew away any enemy fighters that might have been in the area. The flak did,

however, cause the Whitleys to take evasive action and was probably the main reason why two aircraft mistook the correct area by about two miles. All other aircraft dropped their troops accurately and well. First reports coming in from returning aircraft indicated that all was going well. No special path-finding aircraft were used, but all aircraft flew individually, and relied on accurate navigation to locate the dropping zone. Dropping was from 500 feet above ground level.

18. The radio-location apparatus had been assembled and erected by the enemy between the cliffs and a lone villa, which stood about 100 yards from the edge of the cliffs. To the north, and approximately 400 yards away from the villa, was an enclosure containing buildings and trees which was called " La Presbytère ". To the east and inland, the country was gently undulating grassland, intersected in places by thin belts of trees and sparse hedgerows. To the south lay the village of Bruneval, the houses of which were built on the sides of a steep ravine that led down to a pebble sea-shore.

19. Extremely accurate information concerning the enemy defences had been obtained from the local French. The radar station was permanently manned by signallers and surrounded by various posts. " La Presbytère " housed approximately 100 enemy troops, including signallers and infantry for local defence. One platoon was billeted in Bruneval and was responsible for manning the beach defences, which comprised a strongpoint near the beach and pillboxes and machine-gun posts on the shoulders of the cliffs leading down to it. The area was patrolled at intervals during the night. The beach was not mined and wire defences were incomplete. A mobile reserve was thought to be available at one hour's notice and this was stationed some distance inland.

20. The company group was divided into three main parties each consisting of approximately 40 men and each named after a famous sailor as a compliment to the senior service. The " Nelson " party, under the command of Lieutenant E. B. C. Charteris were to drop in the first wave and were to take the beach defences and mop up the enemy in Bruneval. " Drake " party, under command of Lieutenant P. A. Young for the initial assault were to drop next and were to capture the radar station. Major Frost, the force commander, Lieutenant C. D. H. Vernon in charge of the R.E. detachment and Flight Serjeant Cox, R.A.F. were also in this party. " Rodney " party under the command of Lieutenant V. Timothy were to arrive last, their task being to contain the enemy in " La Presbytère " and to act as a reserve. When the apparatus had been dismantled the whole force would withdraw to the beach and would be evacuated in the order " Drake ", " Rodney ", " Nelson ".

21. As the aircraft arrived over France it was seen that the ground was covered with snow. The drop went according to plan with the important exception that one half of " Nelson " party, which included Lieutenant Charteris, was dropped some two miles short of the correct place. This was not known to the force commander at the time. The other parties assembled at the edge of the dropping zone and moved off to their allotted tasks. " Drake " party experienced no difficulty in capturing the villa and the radar station. The enemy was taken completely by surprise and the majority were killed at their posts. The R.E. party took a little time to reach the area with their equipment, as there were a number of wire fences to negotiate and the going was heavy through the snow.

22. The enemy in " La Presbytère " were slow to react to the noise of explosives and automatic fire coming from the radar station, but gradually fire was opened and some casualties were inflicted on our force, a man being killed coming out of the villa and two others wounded, while Lieutenant Vernon and the engineers completed their tasks of dismantling parts of the apparatus under increasingly heavy fire. Just before the order to withdraw was given vehicles were seen to be moving up behind " La Presbytère ". Presumably this was the enemy mobile force.

23. " Drake " party moved down towards the beach at about 0145 hours, but on reaching the shoulder of the cliff came under fire from a machine gun on the far side of the valley which caused some casualties. At the same time the company commander realized that the beach defences had not yet been captured. Shortly after this, the enemy were reported to be advancing from the radar station, but were dealt with effectively. At about the same time Lieutenant Charteris arrived at the beach with the remainder of " Nelson " party. Under his vigorous leadership the beach defences were quickly subdued. Throughout the action, wireless communications failed to function and all information had to be passed by shouting. All attempts to communicate with the naval force had also failed. These factors added greatly to the difficulty of control and command as the enemy reaction was increasing and the ground leading down to the beach sloped far more steeply than was expected. Deep snowdrifts made movement extremely difficult in places.

24. The whole force was concentrated on the beach by 0215, but there was still no sign of the arrival of the Naval force. Accordingly, " Nelson " party were ordered to take up positions to cover the approaches to the beach from inland and the final emergency signal was fired from the beach. Soon after this, the flotilla was seen approaching. The plan was that the landing craft would beach two at a time so that the evacuation could take place gradually, party by party, but unfortunately during the period of training this had never been satisfactorily achieved. In the event all six landing craft arrived at the beach at the same time under cover of intense supporting fire from the sea-borne parties of the Royal Fusiliers and South Wales Borderers. There was considerable confusion on the beach as a result and this part of the operation did not go according to plan. Some of the craft were overcrowded and some left the beach half empty. However, the radar apparatus, prisoners of war and wounded were safely evacuated in the first boats away and the beach was clear before the last boat left. Meanwhile the enemy fire onto the beaches continued. Approximately two miles from the shore, the apparatus, prisoners of war, and the company were transhipped to motor gunboats. Major Frost discovered that the naval force had received no signals, except for the emergency red verey lights, during the whole period of the raid. They had been nearly discovered by an enemy naval patrol consisting of one destroyer and two " E " boats which passed close to them. The voyage back to Portsmouth was uneventful and from dawn onwards the flotilla was escorted by four destroyers and a squadron of Spitfires.

25. The casualties amounted to three killed, two missing and seven wounded. Three prisoners of war were brought back to Portsmouth, one of whom was a radar expert who was able to supply information about any parts of the apparatus which had been left behind. However, the R.E. party had been able to secure

95 per cent. of what was required. Such was the interest taken in the raid that the Prime Minister assembled the War Cabinet on 3rd March to hear the full story from those who took part, and he reasserted before them his belief in the future of airborne forces.

Operation " Freshman "—Norway, 19th November, 1942

26. Quite early in the war it was known that the Germans were experimenting in the production of an atomic bomb, of which a compound described as " heavy water " was an essential part, and it was believed that they had made considerable progress. It was most important that these experiments should be dislocated and the production of the bomb delayed as long as possible. In 1942 attacks by special troops were to be made on German research installations with the object of destroying existing stocks of " heavy water," which was extremely difficult to produce in any large quantity. The main enemy installation was the Norsk Hydro plant at Vermork, a village some two and a half miles to the west of Rjukan, about 60 miles due west of Oslo and some 80 miles from the west coast. A considerable quantity of explosive and a high degree of technical training would be required to destroy the installations. Rjukan was a very isolated town situated in a very deep valley, the thickly forested sides of which rose almost vertically from a narrow river bed for over 3,000 feet. The valley was overlooked by Gaustal Fjell, a mountain 5,400 feet high. The heavy water plant was built on a broad shelf of rock which rises sheer from the river bed to a height of 1,000 feet, the climb above being dangerously steep, through a thick pine forest. It was a most difficult area for glider or parachute landings and the surrounding country was little better, but it was possible to land by either means within about five hours marching distance.

27. Headquarters, Combined Operations, had been given the responsibility for all attacks on objectives of this type and they considered three methods—by bomber aircraft, by saboteurs and by airborne troops. The first, although used with partial success late in 1943, was ruled out because of the difficulty in finding the target, as night bombing was then the R.A.F.'s chief method of attack, and also because bombing might cause heavy casualties among the Norwegian population. Attack by Norwegian saboteurs was also ruled out, although it was by this method that success was eventually obtained. Landing troops by flying boat on Tinnsjön, a lake some 15 miles from the objective, was also considered but the steepness of the surrounding mountain slopes made this impracticable. An attack by airborne troops was considered to have the best chance. Because of the heavy loads to be carried and the risk of too great dispersion in that country if parachutes were used, Major-General Browning and Group Captain Norman decided, when given the task in the middle of October, 1942, that gliders were probably the most suitable form of transport. They had found a difficult but probably possible landing zone which was not too far from the objective and which could be marked by Norwegian agents. However, in case gliders were found to be unsuitable when detailed planning had been done, the party had to be prepared to go by parachute.

28. Technical considerations demanded a minimum force of 12 to 16 men for the operation, and they had to be skilled engineers. Because of the difficulties inherent in such a long flight to such a pin-pointed area, and because

of the importance of the task, it was decided to duplicate the party. The troops were provided by 9th Field Company (Airborne), R.E. and 261st Field Park Company (Airborne) R.E., being selected from volunteer parachutists in these units as the only engineer parachute unit at that time, 1st Parachute Squadron, R.E., was already committed to the North African campaign. One party was commanded by Lieutenant A. C. Allen, R.E., and the other by Lieutenant D. A. Methven, R.E., who replaced Second-Lieutenant M. D. Green, R.E., when the latter was injured in an accident three days before the operation was due. Lieutenant-Colonel M. C. A. Henniker, R.E., then Commander, Royal Engineers, of the Division, was in charge of the army side of the planning.

29. For 38 Wing, Group Captain T. B. Cooper was put in charge of the operation and a special allotment of three Halifax aircraft was made by the Air Ministry. These were the only existing British aircraft capable of towing Horsa Gliders for the required distance, about 400 miles, and returning to base. Practice long-distance tows with gliders were started immediately and, in spite of the weather being very variable, they were sufficiently successful to confirm the decision to use gliders for the operation. Two of their original pilots, Staff Serjeant M. F. C. Strathdee and Serjeant P. Doig, were provided by The Glider Pilot Regiment, and the other glider pilot team consisted of Pilot Officer Davies, R.A.A.F., and Serjeant Fraser, R.A.A.F., also two of the old glider pilots. Squadron Leader Wilkinson, R.A.F., captained the first aircraft and was accompanied by Group Captain Cooper, and Flight Lieutenant Parkinson, R.C.A.F., captained the second aircraft. The force thus included an important element of Dominion representatives.

30. Training was comprehensive and concentrated, and included technical specialist training, the use of snowboots and hard physical exercise. Not only had the " heavy water " and the plant to be destroyed as effectively as possible but the men had to reach the objective through difficult and probably snow-covered country and then make their way over the mountains to Sweden to avoid capture. Norwegian agents would act as guides throughout. Both the aircraft crews and the Norwegian agents on the landing zone had to be trained in the use of the radar-location device, " Rebecca—Eureka ", while the " Eureka " instrument itself had to be got to the agents in the area before the operation started. The latter task was arranged by Headquarters, Combined Operations, with complete success.

31. Security was a most important aspect of the operation. Bad security would not only prejudice the lives of 34 men, but also make a further attack more difficult should this one fail. A " cover story " was put out telling of the challenge of a company of American engineers for a mythical " Washington Cup " which involved a long approach march by either glider or parachute, followed by a complicated demolition task and concluded with a strenuous endurance test. Talked about openly, it was completely successful until a training establishment visited by the force insisted that they should come without airborne division signs and wearing the ordinary army field service caps instead of berets. It is common knowledge among airborne troops that when an airborne soldier puts on a field service cap " something is up ". Apart from this cover story, there were the normal security precautions such

71

as sealing the departure airfield, censoring mail and telephone calls, etc. The field security personnel detachment which accompanied the force until take-off never once heard a whisper of the real intention of the raid.

32. The whole force moved to the departure airfield at Skitten, a satellite of Wick in Scotland, on 17th November, the operation being scheduled for the night of 19/20th November or the first suitable night following within that moon period. The final decision to take off lay, as always in any flight, with the R.A.F., in this case Group Captain Cooper. He had to assist him a meteorological expert on Norway, and to advise him he had the latest reports from the agents on the spot. The forecast for the night 19/20th November was reasonable enough, though not ideal, and with the possibility of a deterioration in the weather for the remainder of the moon period it was decided to mount the operation that night. All was ready and morale was very high. The first aircraft and glider took off at 1750 hours and the second at 1810 hours, while it was still light, and after circling the airfield each party flew individually out across the North Sea, towards their objective. The first news to reach the base airfield was a faint signal at 2341 hours that night, which was believed to have come from the second aircraft (Flight Lieutenant Parkinson), asking for a course to bring it back to base. By intersection of bearings with another R.A.F. station it was found that this signal originated over the North Sea. At 2355 hours a second signal was heard, this time from the first aircraft (Squadron Leader Wilkinson and Group Captain Cooper) saying " glider released in sea ". By intersection, however, it was found that the aircraft was then over the mountains of southern Norway and this was confirmed by a careful check when the aircraft returned. The glider had been released just over the coast but nowhere near the target.

33. The actual course of events, as discovered in part when the war was over, was as follows. The first aircraft and glider, flying with great skill in the moonlight through patchy clouds, made landfall over Norway and flew on towards the target. But as the aircraft approached the coast " Rebecca " had become unserviceable and they were without any means, except map-reading, of locating the landing zone. On a second attempt to find the right place, the aircraft flew into thick cloud about 40 miles northwest of Rjukan and was unable to climb out of it. By this time there was barely sufficient petrol to get the tug and glider home. Ice was forming on the craft, and worse still, on the towing rope. Both tug and glider lost height rapidly and eventually in the area of the Norwegian coast just north of Stavanger the rope completely iced up and broke. It was at this point that the wireless operator had sent out his signal. The aircraft, unable to do any more, just succeeded in returning to base before its petrol ran out. The glider crash-landed at Fylesdalen, on top of the snow-covered mountains overlooking Lysefjord. The weather was extremely bad and it was snowing at the time. Of the 17 men in the glider, eight including Lieutenant Methven and the two glider pilots, Staff Serjeant Strathdee and Serjeant Doig, were killed immediately, four were severely injured and five were uninjured. The four injured were poisoned later by a German doctor on the orders of the Gestapo and the five uninjured were shot by the Gestapo on 18th January, 1943, all having been captured before they could get away from the area of the crash. The Norwegian agents on the landing zone had heard this aircraft flying almost directly over the landing

zone on its first attempt but, as previously explained, the " Rebecca " radio-location device in the aircraft had failed and the crew were thus unable to pick up the " Eureka " signals. The failure of a small piece of equipment completely spoilt a very gallant and otherwise successful flight.

34. The second aircraft and glider crashed immediately after crossing the Norwegian coast after they, too, had successfully achieved the difficult task of crossing some 350 miles of the North Sea by night. Landfall was made near Egersund and the tug and glider headed towards Rjukan. For some reason still unknown the glider crash-landed in the mountains north-east of Helleland and the tug, after just clearing the mountain there, crashed into the next range of mountains to the south, near the farm of Helleven. In the glider, three men were killed immediately and the remainder were captured and shot within a few hours under the terms of a general order issued by Hitler. In the aircraft all the crew were killed immediately.

35. The local Norwegians, friendly and anxious to assist to their utmost, were not able to prevent the German action but they showed every consideration in burying the dead and tending their graves. 1 Airborne Division were able to check the full story of these operations when they moved into Norway in 1945, and, with the co-operation of the Norwegians, they re-buried the bodies at Egenes (Stavanger) and Oslo with full military honours. A memorial stone has been erected at Egenes. Effective action was also taken to bring to trial the Germans responsible for the murders.

36. Operation " Freshman " failed, but in spite of its failure it demonstrated again the range, flexibility and possibilities that lay within the scope of airborne forces in this, the first glider operation. It is not easy to imagine a set of circumstances more hazardous and difficult than a glider flight over 340 miles of the North Sea during a winter night, with a further 60 miles over mountains to a small landing zone in a deep valley, but the attempt failed by only a very narrow margin. It is believed that the secret of the objective was well kept and that the Germans never knew what the target was, so that security for the next operation against it was not compromised.

CHAPTER VIII

1 PARACHUTE BRIGADE OPERATIONS IN NORTH AFRICA, NOVEMBER, 1942, TO APRIL, 1943

General

1. The events leading up to the inclusion of 1 Parachute Brigade in the Allied forces destined to invade North Africa have been described in Chapter VI. It is only necessary to repeat that they had not been included until the last moment, that they had been hurriedly completed to establishment by drawing on the resources of the remainder of 1 Airborne Division, that their war establishment and equipment tables were out of date and new ones had not yet been approved, that no R.A.F. aircraft or crews were available to carry them, and that they relied for their air transport on American Dakota (C47) squadrons with whom they had had little or no time to train or overcome technical difficulties.

2. General Eisenhower allotted 1 Parachute Brigade to the First British Army (General Sir Kenneth Anderson) for specific operations, retaining the right to withdraw them for use as strategic troops on any part of the front of the Allied Expeditionary Force as required. From this moment, the Commander, 1st Parachute Brigade, Brigadier E. W. C. Flavell, dealt direct with Headquarters, First Army in connection with all operational planning, administration and movement. Major-General Browning and Headquarters, 1 Airborne Division, advised and assisted where necessary but concentrated mainly on getting the brigade itself ready for war. In spite of repeated requests by Major-General Browning for the appointment of a senior airborne adviser to represent 1 Parachute Brigade at Headquarters, First Army, or at any other senior headquarters which might command the brigade at another period, this was not granted by the War Office. The result, both during planning in England and during operations in North Africa, was that the brigade commander was available neither to plan on a high level nor command his brigade to the proper extent. He could not be in two places at once.

3. After the landings were successful First Army intended to keep 1 Parachute Brigade in reserve for opportunity tasks as they occurred. General Anderson was anxious to get the brigade to Africa as soon as possible, but there were not enough aircraft to lift even one complete battalion. It was therefore decided to fly out 3rd Parachute Battalion (Lieutenant-Colonel Pine-Coffin), at the maximum strength that the available aircraft would permit, which was a small headquarters and two rifle companies. The remainder of the Brigade moved to Algiers by sea, taking with them an R.A.F. parachute packing detachment. 3rd Parachute Battalion took off for Africa on 10th November, 1942, in aircraft of 60 Group, 51 Wing, United States Transport Command. They landed at Gibraltar on the way, where the commanding officer was told that they must arrive in Africa combat loaded. This presented a problem that was far from easy to solve. The battalion was flying in more aircraft than would be needed for an operational drop, and were carrying a good deal of heavy kit. Two aircraft failed to arrive at Gibraltar, and as every available pound of payload had been taken up it took a great deal of sorting

out to try and load up the aircraft required for a drop with their correct containers. However, by working late into the night the task was completed by the light of searchlights—there was no blackout at Gibraltar. They took off that night for Maison Blanche, an airfield some 12 miles from Algiers, where they arrived at 0800 hours on 11th November.

4. When the battalion left England they had been briefed, and carried models and photographs for two alternative plans :—

    (*a*) In the event of French resistance to capture the airfield at Djidjelli in conjunction with a sea-borne landing by 36 Infantry Brigade.

    (*b*) In the event of French co-operation to land on the airfield at Bizerta and hold it.

At Maison Blanche Lieutenant-Colonel Pine-Coffin was given fresh orders personally by General Anderson on board the headquarters ship. These orders were to take off on the following morning, 12th November, and drop at 0830 to capture Bone airfield. This they did after a very sketchy briefing, capturing the airfield without opposition. One man was killed during the drop and two aircraft came down in the sea, causing a further three fatal casualties to the battalion. Dropping was scattered over about three miles and was not entirely accurate, but about 90 per cent. of the parachutes and containers were recovered. The operation was successful and there is no doubt that the presence of the battalion helped considerably to raise the morale of the local French population and to confirm them in their support of the Allies. In some ways it was an example of the perfectly planned airborne operation, in that mobility was exploited to forestall the enemy.

The Capture of Tebessa and Souk el Arba by 2nd Battalion 503 U.S. Parachute Regiment and 1st Parachute Battalion

5. The main body of 1 Parachute Brigade arrived at Algiers by sea on 12th November, some of the stores arriving a little later. By that night reconnaissance parties were at Maison Blanche airfield, and on 13th November the brigade (less 3rd Parachute Battalion) had moved to billets at Maison Blanche, Maison Carrée and Rouiba. On the same day 2nd Battalion 503 United States Parachute Regiment (Lieutenant-Colonel Edson D. Raffe) was placed under the brigade's command. This battalion had flown direct from Cornwall to drop in the area of Oran on 8th November, in support of United States Fifth Army, and had then concentrated for further operations to the east under First Army.

6. The original intention of the Commander-in-Chief, First Army, had been to drop one parachute battalion on Tunis airfield, and 1st Parachute Battalion was actually issued with the necessary briefing material for the operation. The arrival of the battalion at Algiers was delayed for three days, and by this time intelligence reported that the Germans had air-landed between 7,000 and 10,000 troops on Tunis airfield, so the operation was cancelled. However, at 0930 hours on 14th November, First Army ordered that on 15th November one parachute battalion should drop at Souk el Arba, contact the French forces stationed at Beja, hold the cross-roads at Souk el Arba, and patrol east to harass the enemy, resorting to guerilla warfare if necessary. First Army also directed that 2/503 United States Parachute Battalion should drop on 15th November in the area of Tebessa and Youks les Bains to seize and

hold the airfields at those places. Both operations were hampered by the lack of time and transport and by the comparative inexperience of both the troops and the air forces. Equipment and parachutes had to be unloaded from the ships and moved to the airfield by the operational troops during the 24 hours preceding take-off. Only a limited amount of transport was available as First Army had been unable to allot shipping space for any of the brigade's own transport. Air photographs were non-existent as these particular operations had not been foreseen and only one small-scale map of Souk el Arba was available for the whole battalion. Information was extremely vague. But both these operations offered good chances of again forestalling the enemy if they were carried out quickly.

7. 1st Parachute Battalion, with detachments of 1st Parachute Squadron, R.E., and 16th Parachute Field Ambulance, R.A.M.C., were selected for the Souk el Arba operation and by 0500 hours on 15th November all packing and loading into aircraft had been completed at Maison Blanche. This in spite of the fact that all stores had not arrived from the docks until 1630 hours on 14th November and that they then had to be repacked operationally into parachute containers. The parachutes for the operation had travelled packed 12 together wrapped in greased paper in plywood cases lined with balloon fabric, and 38 Wing's parachute packing section (Flight Lieutenant Hare) had improvised packing tables from the parachute cases. They laid out the containers on the floor of a hangar, and inspected all parachutes and containers before loading them on to aircraft. Thirty-two Dakota aircraft were provided by 64 Group, 51 U.S. Wing (Colonel Dorset) and as no more aircraft were available one company of the battalion could not take off at 0730 hours on 15th November. However, by 1100 hours the battalion had returned to Maison Blanche as thick cloud *en route* to the objective forced the aircraft to turn back. The operation was postponed to 16th November, and it was intended to drop the remainder of the battalion on 17th November. Owing to shortage of aircraft this did not take place.

8. In the meantime 2/503 United States Parachute Battalion took off for Tebessa at 0730 hours on 15th November and later in the day all aircraft returned and reported that the drop was successful. The battalion now passed from command of 1 Parachute Brigade and remained dominating the Tebessa area and further east for some time. Two teams of 1 Parachute Brigade Signal Section, carrying No. 65 wireless sets, dropped with the battalion and provided the only effective communications with First Army, through 1 Parachute Brigade Headquarters

9. At 1100 hours on 16th November, 1st Parachute Battalion took off again under much the same arrangements. Their task was now altered to the extent that they were ordered to establish battalion headquarters at Beja and push out patrols to contact the enemy, thus securing the Souk el Khemis–Souk el Arba plain for use by the R.A.F. It was expected that the French would be able to supply transport. The actual orders issued to the battalion commander were to seize and hold the town of Beja, to bring the French forces in on our side, and to patrol to the east and harry the enemy wherever they might be found. In addition the army commander told the brigade commander that even if clouds and fog on the mountains prevented the battalion from reaching the Souk El Arba plain, they were not to return the second time. This meant that they had

to jump at some unknown spot in the middle of North Africa and advance in what they thought was an easterly direction to make contact with the enemy. By 1630 hours all aircraft had returned and reported a successful drop, having completed a round trip of some 800 miles. In fact no air or ground opposition was encountered. The map used for navigation purposes and for general selection of the dropping zones was a $\frac{1}{4}$-inch to the mile French motoring map. Owing to this and the lack of photographs, the actual dropping zone near Souk El Arba was selected by the battalion commander, Lieutenant-Colonel S. J. L. Hill, who travelled in the leading aircraft and, followed by his battalion, jumped when the ground looked suitable. This is not a good method when early enemy opposition is expected. There was one parachute dropping fatal casualty and five injuries, and 90 per cent. of the containers were collected in spite of the attempts of local Arabs to steal them first. A reconnaissance party from 1st Parachute Squadron, R.E., reconnoitred the area for landing grounds and reported favourably to the R.A.F. at Maison Blanche. 1st Parachute Battalion advanced through Beja to Medjez el Bab, in contact with enemy patrols. the first Allied troops to meet the enemy in the Tunisian campaign, successfully raising the French and assisting them. As enemy opposition stiffened, they withdrew to good defensive positions about Oued Zarqa, halfway between Medjez and Beja. The battalion then came under orders of " Bladeforce," the first ground troops to arrive, and operated about that area and to the east until 11th December. Wireless communication on No. 65 sets was maintained with 1 Parachute Brigade Headquarters throughout. Lieutenant-Colonel Hill was wounded on 24th November and Major A. S. Pearson took over command.

10. A detailed account of the activities of 1st Parachute Battalion during this period has appeared in " The Army Quarterly " of January, 1946. Space does not allow many details here. Certain points must, however, be included. In order to carry out the orders of First Army it was essential that the local French troops, poorly armed and equipped and dominated by the Germans for the past two years, should be rallied and encouraged to the utmost extent possible. In addition, it was essential to the further advance of First Army that the country should be dominated as far to the east as possible and that the enemy should be given the impression of formidable Allied forces operating in the area. 1st Parachute Battalion achieved both these tasks by hard fighting, great boldness and mobility in spite of a shortage of local transport, and by various ruses designed to magnify in the minds of both the French and Germans the real strength of the battalion. Such success was only made possible by the initiative of all ranks at all times and continuous though small-scale, offensive action. A successful ambush by " S " Company (Major P. Cleasby-Thompson) on 17th November, during which the enemy suffered 19 casualties and lost six armoured vehicles, was of particular value to impress the French in the early stages. The enemy was dissuaded from advancing westwards through Medjez until the night of 19th/20th November, and by that time the battalion together with certain French forces and the leading ground troops of First Army had taken up strong positions about Oued Zarqa, covering Beja from the north-east as well. Continuous offensive patrols from these areas kept the enemy uncertain of the situation and prevented any major enemy advance. The whole of the important plain, with its possibilities as an advanced air base west of Beja, was held intact until taken over by " Bladeforce " and 78 Division of First Army.

11. During these operations, too, the value and efficiency was proved of the medical and surgical teams, who were dropped by parachute with all their equipment. They rendered excellent service under their commander Captain C. G. Robb, R.A.M.C., both to the battalion they were with and to many units of " Bladeforce."

The Drop at Depienne and Move on Oudna by 2nd Parachute Battalion

12. At 1000 hours on 17th November, Brigadier Flavell was ordered by the Commander-in-Chief, First Army, to despatch the remaining company of 1st Parachute Battalion to drop in the area of Enfidaville and harass the main route from Tripoli to Tunis. Although reports showed no enemy troops stationed in that area, there was unimpeded movement of staff cars and transport. Guerilla tactics were to be adopted, the company was to be lightly armed and self-sufficient for ten days. This operation was cancelled at 1300 hours the same day on the urgent representations of Brigadier Flavell, who considered that a force of one company was entirely inadequate for the task. On this day, too, orders were received to move 3rd Parachute Battalion from Bone to concentrate at Maison Blanche.

13. On 18th November, orders were received from First Army to prepare 2nd Parachute Battalion to drop at Sousse and in the area of Kairouan, to deny the port and airfield to the enemy. Aircraft availability being limited, take-off for two companies was ordered for 1100 hours 19th November and the remainder of the battalion were to follow on 20th November. Ten days supplies were to be taken. At 2330 hours 18th November, this operation was postponed for 24 hours and Brigadier Flavell recommended that the size of the force should be increased if possible. Sousse was several miles ahead of the nearest British forces and these forces themselves were small and isolated. More aircraft became available on 19th November and Brigadier Flavell decided to send the remaining company of 1st Parachute Battalion with 2nd Parachute Battalion. At 1430 hours that day, the operation was postponed for at least three days. At 1000 hours on 19th November 3rd Parachute Battalion arrived from Bone and moved into billets vacated by 1st Parachute Battalion at Maison Blanche. Repacking of their parachutes salvaged from Bone started on the next day.

14. During the nights, 20th/21st and 21st/22nd November, enemy aircraft bombed Maison Blanche airfield with some success. A few casualties were caused, parachute containers of one company were destroyed and several aircraft damaged on the ground. Casualties might have been far higher had not the bulk of the personnel and stores been held some distance away from the airfield, and the lesson was confirmed that, as a general rule, airborne troops should not be concentrated on airfields in the operational area for longer than necessary. They should be held reasonably close to the airfield and transport provided on the scale of one truck each aircraft, so that men and stores can be emplaned quickly and efficiently.

15. On 22nd November, First Army ordered that both 2nd and 3rd Parachute Battalions should be prepared for operations on 25th November. 62 and 64 groups of 51 U.S. Wing (Dakotas) would be available but Brigadier Flavell warned the army commander that both groups would be required by each battalion if they were to drop at full strength in one lift.

16. On 27th November 1 Parachute Brigade received a warning order for one battalion group to stand-by with effect from dawn on 28th November, for an unknown task. 2nd Parachute Battalion (Lieutenant-Colonel J. D. Frost) was selected. At 1500 hours on 27th November, Brigadier Flavell at First Army Headquarters received orders that the battalion would drop in the area of Pont du Fahs to destroy enemy aircraft and stores on the airfields at that place, at Depienne and at Oudna. Only light enemy opposition was expected and the operations would be timed by First Army to coincide with a general advance of our ground forces from Medjez, now in our hands, and Mateur towards Tunis and Bizerta. They should join up with 2nd Parachute Battalion within five days in the area of Tebourba. The number of aircraft to carry the battalion was a doubtful factor, but it was hoped that 40 Dakotas would be available. At 2230 hours on 27th November, the operation was postponed until 29th November. There was great difficulty in getting air photographs. At 2300 hours on 28th November First Army informed 1 Parachute Brigade that Pont du Fahs had been occupied by reconnaissance elements of 78 Division after its evacuation and destruction by the enemy. Depienne airfield had been ploughed up and 56 Reconnaissance Regiment of 78 Division were operating west of a line Pont du Fahs–Oudna. On an enquiry by 1 Parachute Brigade whether 2nd Parachute Battalion were still required to drop at Pont du Fahs, First Army ordered them to drop at Depienne instead. Oudna airfield remained the objective and the link up with First Army would be at St. Cyprien.

17. Forty-four aircraft of 62 and 64 Groups carrying 2nd Parachute Battalion started to take off at 1130 hours on 29th November. There was much confusion over the emplaning and loading of containers as many aircraft arrived late, markings of aircraft were different from those expected, there was a last-minute change in the number of aircraft available, and heavy rain turned the airfield into thick mud. However, all except one, which was bogged in the mud, were off by 1245 hours. The flight was uneventful and unopposed, though both the Dakotas and their fighter escort had to fly high to avoid the mountains and the temperature dropped to zero. The first aircraft dropped its troops at 1450 hours on Depienne airfield, the actual dropping zone being selected by the pilot of the leading aircraft. The total area over which the battalion was dropped extended to about one and a half miles by half a mile and a large watercourse running through the middle delayed concentration on the ground. One man was killed during the drop, there were a few other dropping casualties and some containers failed to come off the aircraft or their parachutes failed to open. There was no enemy opposition, which was fortunate in the circumstances. In accordance with brigade standing orders at the time, caused by the shortage of equipment available in the theatre, parachutes and containers were salvaged and collected on the dropping zone in case they could be removed later and used again, while the battalion took up defensive positions and sent out patrols. A search for local transport produced a few mule carts. The local French were very friendly and assisted with the dropping casualties, also informing Lieutenant-Colonel Frost that the Germans had withdrawn northwards three days earlier.

18. At about 1600 hours three armoured cars of 56 Reconnaissance Regiment appeared on the road running north from Depienne and patrolled northwards towards Cheylus. At 1700 hours they returned and reported a German road block midway between these places and four miles north of the battalion, which

had prevented them going further. Arrangements were made for the presence of the battalion to be reported to 78 Division and for the dropping casualties to be collected later. The troops had had a strenuous time assembling from the scattered drop and carrying their containers and parachutes over the rough country. The commanding officer decided to remain as long as possible at Depienne to rest the men and to reach the neighbourhood of Oudna soon after first light.

19. At about midnight on 29th November the battalion, less a small party left to collect stragglers dropped wide and to complete arrangements regarding the casualties and salvage, moved north towards Oudna, some miles distant, marching by rough tracks over steep hills. Loads of equipment and weapons, including 3-inch mortars, were heavy in spite of the use of the mule carts. By 0430 hours the battalion had covered 12 miles unopposed and were halted ; it was bitterly cold and little real rest was possible. At 0715 hours the advance continued and more mules, donkeys and horses were commandeered from local Arabs to carry some of the loads now proving far too heavy on the men for movement of this nature.

20. At 1430 hours the leading company met opposition from Germans just south of the landing ground near Oudna railway station, and a short while later the battalion, having suffered a few casualties, had captured the landing ground and consolidated around it. It was found that the Germans were not using the landing ground as such and there were no aircraft or stores in the area. At 1530 hours five heavy German tanks attacked and Messerschmitt fighters made low-flying machine-gun attacks, but the tanks were held off and the camouflage smocks and nets worn by the parachute troops were successful in hiding them from the aircraft and in avoiding casualties. At 1730 hours a flight of six Stuka dive bombers were equally unsuccessful in locating the battalion.

21. As the whole object of the battalion's mission had been to destroy aircraft and stores on the landing ground and as there were in fact none to destroy, Lieutenant-Colonel Frost decided to move west to join up with the other troops of First Army, before the enemy could launch a major attack. There was no sign of First Army's projected armoured thrust on Tunis. Accordingly the battalion withdrew to the neighbouring hills during darkness that night. A wireless message received next morning stated that First Army's advance to Tunis had been postponed.

22. Threatened by greatly superior forces, including German tanks and lorried infantry, only about nine miles from the German base at Tunis, and being several miles over the hills from the nearest British formation, there was no alternative except to withdraw, avoiding action as far as possible. From now, the morning of 1st December, until 3rd December, the battalion moved generally westwards over very difficult hilly country. They were continually attacked by tanks, infantry and aircraft but maintained cohesion and made every use of cover by day and night. At 1600 hours on 3rd December the leading elements of the battalion reached the Allied lines at Medjez. Small parties, who had been isolated in the withdrawal, continued to arrive until 5th December. The strength of the unit was now about 200 all ranks, having suffered some 260 casualties, including killed, wounded and missing. They remained in action in the Medjez area with 78 Division until withdrawn to Souk el Khemis on 11th December, about 50 of the missing having rejoined by that date.

23. The operation suffered from a lack of information, and from a lack of adequate arrangements for a link-up between the ground forces and too lightly armed and comparatively immobile airborne troops. A speedy link-up in all such cases is vital. The battalion carried out its orders and its presence at Oudna must have had a considerable effect on German operations elsewhere, but the cost was high.

Lessons of the Airborne Operations of 1 Parachute Brigade

24. The operation by 2nd Parachute Battalion was the last airborne operation during the campaign in North Africa. From this date until the end of April, 1943, 1 Parachute Brigade fought as infantry in a purely ground role. It is therefore a suitable moment to consider the main lessons of the airborne operations so far. They were included in reports made by Major-General Browning and Group Captain Norman, commanding 1 Airborne Division and 38 Wing R.A.F. respectively, after their visit to 1 Parachute Brigade, 5 Corps, First Army and Allied Force Headquarters in December, 1942.

25. The operations by 1st and 2nd Parachute Battalions were handicapped very severely by a complete lack of air photographs, a severe shortage of maps, and by the fact that 62 and 64 Groups United States Army Air Force had little or no experience of dropping parachutists using British equipment. The lack of British aircraft and crews, trained with the men they would carry into action, was felt in a concrete operational form for the first time, though training and projected operations had suffered earlier. In spite of the gallant efforts of the American air crews, the drops were inaccurate and men were widely dispersed. Had the troops met enemy opposition immediately on landing, the effects might well have been disastrous. 60 United States Group, the only group training in England with British troops, had no container racks available in the theatre and therefore containers could not be used. Furthermore, none of the American groups had been trained in dropping by night, so that fighter escort had to be provided, at the expense of other operations for day flights.

26. 51 Wing, to which all three groups belonged, were very fully occupied carrying stores and personnel all over North Africa. They had not sufficient experience with British troops, and the combined airborne–air ground base organization was not good enough, to enable them to switch efficiently from one task to the other at short notice. Great credit is due to Squadron Leader Potter, 38 Wing R.A.F., who was attached to brigade headquarters and without whose help it would have been impossible to co-ordinate army–air requirements.

27. There was no doubt that the lack of an expert in airborne matters at either Allied Force Headquarters or First Army had the inevitable result that 1 Parachute Brigade were not used to their full airborne capacity and arrangements before each drop were not as good as they should and could have been. An independent commander or adviser of airborne forces at the senior headquarters concerned, aided by a very small Army and R.A.F. staff, was required urgently if full value was to be obtained from airborne forces. No one else had the time or knowledge to tie up all the Army and Air Force capabilities and requirements.

28. The distances, the nature of the country, and the type of warfare involved, all offered great opportunities for airborne forces in North Africa. There were no other troops who could compare in strategic mobility and their mere presence somewhere within range of an objective had paralysing effects on the

enemy. Even if large numbers of gliders could not be provided in this theatre, owing to the difficulty of moving them from England, the air-landing part of the Airborne Division which was still in England, when equipped and brought up to strength, was ideally suited by training, armament and equipment for ground operations in these areas. Major-General Browning was convinced that if 1 Airborne Division, completed and properly equipped, had been given the responsibility from the first, for the campaign from Bone to Tunis, they could have forestalled the Germans by themselves and ended the campaign at one blow. It was generally agreed in the theatre at the time that had it been possible to drop 1 Parachute Brigade on Tunis before about 23rd November, the city would have been captured, the French would have been roused to vigorous co-operation and the campaign would have been virtually at an end. In fact the whole brigade was available then but it was used in small parties for comparatively minor objectives. The brigade commander had made almost daily requests that it should be used as a brigade and conditions in the theatre were such that the delay caused by the necessity to use the same aircraft for several lifts could have been accepted.

29. The armament and equipment of the brigade was found to be generally suitable, except that there was a need for better light anti-tank weapons. The lack of a fourth company in the parachute battalion organization was a serious handicap, particularly when operating surrounded by the enemy. This had been represented to the War Office already and was represented many times later, but it was not granted until 1946, owing to manpower shortages throughout the Army. 16th Parachute Field Ambulance R.A.M.C. had proved the soundness of its organization and the great value of parachute surgical teams operating at the front.

1 Parachute Brigade in a ground role, December, 1942 to April, 1943

30. On 2nd December, 1 Parachute Brigade, less 1st and 2nd Parachute Battalions received a warning order to move forward to Souk el Arba by air, taking equipment for one brigade parachute drop with them. Eastern Air Command, when consulted by Brigadier Flavell, objected however, for the reason that ground conditions in the winter made it impossible for aircraft to take off from Souk el Arba. First Army then warned Brigadier Flavell that his brigade might have to be used as infantry in the first instance and issued instructions for a move by rail on 6th December. Parachute equipment was not to be moved forward from Maison Blanche and a rear party would stay behind to look after it. At 1730 hours on 7th December Brigadier Flavell reported to Commander 5 Corps, now in effective command of the forward battle, at Souk el Khemis and by the night of 11th December the brigade was complete there, 1st and 2nd Parachute Battalions having returned from the forward areas. 173 men of 1st Parachute Battalion, the third company and reserves, arrived from the base on 10th December. No. 1 Commando and 2nd Battalion, 9th Regiment, Tiralleurs Algeriennes were placed under command of the brigade.

31. A defensive position covering Beja was taken up and active patrolling, particularly towards Mateur, started on 12th December, the Germans having advanced from the east and north-east, while 5 Corps still held Medjez. On 21st December the brigade was placed under command of 78 Division in order to take part in a general attack from the area of Medjez on to Tunis. This operation was cancelled owing to rain before the brigade was committed.

32. By 26th December it was realized that any further major attack by 5 Corps towards Tunis must be postponed until after the rainy season and on that date Brigadier Flavell suggested that the brigade should be withdrawn from the forward area to reform and train as parachute troops. Many of the reserve personnel were comparatively untrained and their absorption into the battalions required time. In addition, the whole brigade would benefit from combined training with the American transport squadrons. This proposal was supported by Commander 78 Division but 5 Corps were unable to agree owing to the shortage of troops to replace them. During the period up to 7th January, the brigade remained in the same general area, taking over command of further units and being responsible for the defence of the whole Beja area. 3rd Parachute Battalion were particularly heavily engaged during this period. In an attack on a feature known as " Green Hill," " A " Company, under Major S. Terrell, made a very gallant effort. They had been placed under command of a battalion of 36 Brigade for a night attack. The attack failed but " A " Company reached the top of the hill, being the only attackers to do so. 3rd Parachute Battalion was then placed under command of 36 Brigade and was ordered to attack the hill the following night, in co-operation with the battalion of 36 Brigade. " C " Company was already committed to a task in another area. The orders for the attack were issued late and the approach was so difficult that the mortars and other supporting weapons could not keep up. In the end the only attacking force left was " B " Company under Major D. T. Dobie. They got a footing on the hill and beat off one counter-attack, but were driven off the hill by a second and stronger enemy effort. On 3rd January, however, the first warning was received that the whole brigade might be required to move back to base in the neighbourhood of Algiers so as to be ready for further parachute operations.

33. This warning was confirmed, except that, in spite of Brigadier Flavell's protests, 2nd Parachute Battalion was retained under 78 Division owing to the lack of other troops to replace them. The remainder of the brigade moved back to Algiers by rail between 7–8th January. Allied Force Headquarters had decided to place 1 Parachute Brigade, less 2nd Parachute Battalion, unless it too could be released in time, under the command of II U.S. Corps for operations in the area of Sfax and Gabes to cut the German lines of communication from Tunis to Tripolitania. Headquarters, II U.S., Corps were at Constantine and Brigadier Flavell reported there while his brigade moved back to Algiers. Between 9th–18th January various plans were made with II U.S. Corps but on the latter date Allied Force Headquarters decided that 1 Parachute Brigade would not be required for this operation, which in fact never took place. It was then expected that the brigade would remain at Algiers for a considerable period, but on 24th January it was once more on the move to 5 Corps, this time by the sea *via* Bone, for further duty as infantry.

34. On 28th January, 1 Parachute Brigade, still less 2nd Parachute Battalion, came under command of 6 Armoured Division. 3rd Parachute Battalion relieved 10th Battalion The Rifle Brigade at Argoub, while brigade headquarters were at Bou Arada and the remainder of the brigade in the general area of El Aroussa. This sector was quiet except for some shelling and patrolling.

35. Two days later at 1330 hours, Brigadier Flavell received warning from 6 Armoured Division that 1 Parachute Brigade, less 2nd Parachute Battalion would be transferred to the command of General Mathinet, Commander XIX

French Corps, with 17 Field Regiment, R.A., in support. This transfer was completed at 1800 hours on the same day, the intention being that the brigade would relieve certain French battalions who needed re-equipping.

36. On 1st February, General Mathinet placed the Groupement Tremeau (4 Regiment Tirailleur Tunisien, 43 Regiment Infanterie Coloniale, six batteries of artillery, 4 Chasseurs d'Afrique, 4 Spahis) under command 1 Parachute Brigade, who side-stepped slightly to the right from their original positions but remained between 36 Infantry Brigade on their right and 1 Guards Brigade on their left, from Bou Arada to Roubia. The next day it was decided that 1st Parachute Battalion would attack the important massif of Djebel Mansour and its neighbouring feature Djebel Alliliga, with one company of the French Foreign Legion under command and one battery 17th Field Regiment R.A. in support. In addition one other company of the Foreign Legion would create a diversion on the southern end of Djebel Alliliga. 3rd Battalion Grenadier Guards, less one company, would be ready to assist 1st Parachute Battalion to hold the objective when captured. To cope with the extremely difficult nature of the country 11th Pack Transport Company was placed under command 1 Parachute Brigade for supplies. The supply route would be very precarious, often suitable only for pack mule transport or carriers and likely to be under observed fire for long stretches until both objectives were held. 1st Parachute Battalion having been relieved in their old position by 3rd Battalion Grenadier Guards, moved to their assembly area during 2nd February, advanced during that night to the foot of Djebel Mansour and by 0700 hours the following morning had captured it and most of Djebel Alliliga. The objective was only taken after very heavy fighting against strong opposition and over most difficult country in an action which was one of the finest ever fought by 1st Parachute Battalion during the war.

However, by about 0900 hours casualties and a shortage of troops forced them to give up Djebel Alliliga and concentrate on Djebel Mansour. The mule supply column was unable to reach them until the afternoon owing to enemy machine gun fire. An enemy threat elsewhere had the effect that only one company of 3rd Battalion Grenadier Guards were able to reinforce 1st Parachute Battalion. An attack later that afternoon by troops of 1 Guards Brigade, under command of 6 Armoured Division on El Alliliga, at the urgent request of 1st Parachute Battalion, failed and General Mathinet gave permission for 3rd Parachute Battalion to be moved up into immediate reserve. On 4th February at 1500 hours 3rd Battalion Grenadier Guards attacked Djebel Alliliga and captured most of it by dark. By 0700 hours on 5th February 1st Parachute Battalion were again being attacked heavily. They were badly enfiladed from that part of Djebel Alliliga not captured by 3rd Battalion Grenadier Guards, they were very short of men and ammunition, and the enemy threatened to infiltrate between them and the Guards. At 1100 hours it was decided to withdraw both battalions under cover of a smoke screen laid by tanks of 26 Armoured Brigade and by 1600 hours the withdrawal was complete. 3rd Parachute Battalion took up a covering position and 1st Parachute Battalion withdrew into reserve.

37. During the evening of 7th February, 2nd Parachute Battalion, which had been under the command of several different formations and been moved from one end of the front to the other since 7th January, reverted to command

of 1 Parachute Brigade, actually rejoining them at 1500 hours on 8th February. By 0900 hours on 9th February, 1 Parachute Brigade had passed under command of 6 Armoured Division and the Brigade handed over to 36 Infantry Brigade part of the right of their front. From then until 2nd March, the situation remained comparatively quiet and static, though several minor enemy attacks were defeated and our night patrols took many prisoners. On 14th February the Brigade received very welcome though inadequate reinforcements to the extent of 12 officers and 164 other ranks. On 16th February, 1 Parachute Brigade were placed under " Y " British Division (an *ad hoc* division), who relieved 6 Armoured Division ; very active patrolling was necessary to hide from the Germans the weakness of " Y " Division and all available troops, including Royal Engineers, were used to hold the front. It is of interest to note that on 26th February, the whole Allied front was attacked in force. 1 Parachute Brigade held all their positions, inflicted over 400 casualties on the enemy and took in addition over 200 prisoners, at a cost to themselves of 18 killed and 54 wounded. 3rd Parachute Battalion alone counted several score enemy dead on their front. The brigade on their left, however, had had its position penetrated by enemy armour, which reached 1 Parachute Brigade's administrative transport 12 miles in rear before a part of 6 Armoured Division restored the situation.

38. At 1200 hours on 3rd March, 1 Parachute Brigade received orders to move, after relief by 26 U.S. Regimental Combat Team, to the Beja sector and came under command of 46 Division. During the night of 4/5th March the relief was completed and by daylight on 5th March the brigade had withdrawn into harbour at Teboursouk. That night the Brigade took up defensive positions astride the road Tamera—Sedjenane, with the exception of 2nd Parachute Battalion who did not arrive until 2000 hours on 7th March as they had been ordered to carry out certain minor operations *en route*. At 0730 hours on 8th March the enemy attacked all three parachute battalions in force but by 1600 hours that day they had been counter-attacked, driven off and everything was quiet. 198 German prisoners were taken. On 9th March the Brigade patrolled actively, took more prisoners and caused the enemy considerable casualties. By now, however, the Brigade was weak in numbers and had been in action continuously for a long period. Furthermore, Commandant Durand reported that 1st and 2nd Battalions of the Corps Francs d'Afrique, now under command, were not in a fit state to offer much resistance to the enemy, and there were no reserves in the area. Early on 10th March the enemy again attacked in force along the whole brigade front, but in spite of his efforts all day the Brigade held their ground. At 1345 hours Brigadier Flavell was placed in command of the whole sector, some 30 miles long, with 139 Infantry Brigade also under command, and his force consisted of :—

1 Parachute Brigade Group.	One Company R.A.S.C.
French Brigade (three battalions).	139 Infantry Brigade.
6th Battalion The Royal Lincoln-shire Regiment.	No. 1 Commando.
	70th Field Regiment, R.A.
457th Light Battery, R.A.	15/17th Medium Battery, R.A.
B/72nd Anti-Tank Battery, R.A.	Two Troops " C " Squadron,
One Squadron, 46 Reconnaissance Regiment.	North Irish Horse (Churchills).
	One Field Ambulance, R.A.M.C.

His only means of command was his own brigade headquarters, the staff of which at that time consisted of the brigade major, staff captain, defence platoon commander, parachute training instructor, two signals officers and two R.A.S.C. officers. The acting commander, Royal Artillery, was the commanding officer of 70 Field Regiment and one officer was loaned for intelligence duties. 1 Parachute Brigade maintained their positions again on 11th March against sustained attack and during 12th March a dangerous high feature called Djebel Harch was attacked by 5th Battalion The Sherwood Foresters, supported by one company of 1st Parachute Battalion. This attack failed after a successful beginning. From 13–16th March matters were fairly quiet but it became necessary for No. 1 Commando to assist the weakened French battalions. On 17th March the enemy attacked again in strength all along the front, forcing their way through the positions of 139 Brigade and the French, and at 2100 hours it was decided to make a slight general withdrawal.

39. 1st and 3rd Parachute Battalions, who had been withdrawn into sector reserve a short time previously, were ordered to hold a new line including the position still held by 2nd Parachute Battalion, and to cover the withdrawal of 139 Brigade, No. 1 Commando and the French battalions. By 1000 hours on 18th March the new line was established but very heavy attacks were developed against it immediately. By 1300 hours that day the divisional commander authorized a further withdrawal to take place that night to the general line running east and west through Djebel Abiad. This withdrawal and the occupation of the new position was successfully achieved during the night of 19th March.

40. The next morning the corps and divisional commanders visited 1 Parachute Brigade and indicated that the offensive would be resumed in about five days time. Brigadier Flavell repeated that the Brigade was very weak in numbers and tired from long and continuous fighting and asked that they should be given some rest in the meantime. 138 Brigade took over the sector on the east of 1 Parachute Brigade and 2nd Parachute Battalion was withdrawn into reserve. The area was fairly quiet now and 3rd Parachute Battalion also withdrew into reserve during the night 20th/21st March, being relieved by 1 Thabor Goums, French Colonial Army. At 1400 hours on 21st March, it was decided, however, that 3rd Parachute Battalion must relieve 2/5 Leicesters of 159 Brigade who had sustained severe casualties, and retake an important feature known as the " Pimple ". At the same time the divisional commander outlined his plan for a general offensive, in which 1 Parachute Brigade would take part, timed to start about 25th March if the weather were suitable. At 2245 hours on 21st March 3rd Parachute Battalion attacked the " Pimple ", but by 0600 hours on 22nd March, they had been forced to withdraw after heavy fighting and when their ammunition was practically exhausted. At 1200 hours that day the army commander confirmed a decision to attack the " Pimple " again, as it provided an essential stepping-off place for any future attack, and to use 1st Parachute Battalion for this purpose after they had been relieved in their present positions. This attack started at 2230 hours on 23rd March, and was successfully concluded by 0230 hours on 24th March. The next night 24/25th March, 3rd Parachute Battalion took over the " Pimple " from 1st Parachute Battalion, who withdrew into reserve.

41. At 1800 hours on 24th March, the Commander, 46 Division issued orders for a new general offensive by 1 Parachute, 36 and 138 Brigades to begin on 27th March. The object was to capture the Tamera position within a period of about 48 hours, with two intermediate objectives. 36 and 138 Brigades would be on the right of the road and 1 Parachute Brigade, with 1 Thabor Goums, under command and 70th Field Regiment, R.A., in support, on the left of the road. 1st and 2nd Parachute Battalions attacked their first objectives, starting at 2300 hours on 27th March, and captured them, taking many German and Italian prisoners during the night and early morning. Soon after first light the German's immediate reserve, who were also parachute troops, put in a heavy counter-attack against 2nd Parachute Battalion. The attack was held but caused many casualties to our troops. By 1015 hours on 28th March, both battalions were pushing on to their second objectives and 1 Thabor Goums had taken their first objective. Fighting was heavy and confused but the enemy were losing many casualties and about 400 prisoners had been taken. At 1125 hours "A" and " B " Companies of 3rd Parachute Battalion were placed under command 2nd Parachute Battalion, to reinforce them as they were now very weak in numbers. By 1830 hours 1st Parachute Battalion had captured their second objective, taking more prisoners and six enemy guns. At 1845 hours 2nd Parachute Battalion reported that their strength was now equivalent to only about one company, but that enemy opposition was weakening and they intended to capture their second objective during the night. At 2300 hours that day, 28th March, the divisional commander authorized a further advance to the third and final objectives of the brigade on 29th March, although 36 and 138 Brigades had not yet reached their second objectives. 1 Parachute Brigade were convinced that organized enemy resistance on the brigade front had ceased. They attacked again at first light on 29th March and by the end of the day had captured all objectives and a further, 770 prisoners. These prisoners included German parachute troops as well as 550 Italians. Patrols on 30th March reported no enemy seen on their front and the next day the whole brigade took up new positions to cover the left flank of 46 division while 36 Brigade attacked east of Sedjenane.

42. From 1st to 14th April, 1 Parachute Brigade remained in the same general area, carrying out very active patrolling but encountering little opposition. The few enemy patrols encountered were practically annihilated and the area completely dominated. During the night 14/15th April, the brigade was relieved by 39 Regimental Combat Team of 9 U.S. Division and withdrew into 5 Corps reserve west of Beja. On 18th April, orders were received for the brigade to move back by road and rail to Boufarik, near Algiers, and this was completed by 24th April. On 27th April, Brigadier Flavell, left by air for a new appointment in England, and Brigadier G. W. Lathbury arrived on 28th April to take over command.

The " Red Devils "

43. 1 Parachute Brigade had completed their three parachute operations and five months operations as infantry with the First Army in North Africa. In the course of the campaign, the brigade captured over 3,500 prisoners of war and must have caused over 5,000 additional enemy casualties. They had fought in every sector of the British front in Tunisia during the course of which they had suffered · 1,700 casualties. They had more battles than any other

87

formation and in the Tamera valley, in the period 6th March to 14th April, did most of the fighting for 46 Division. In fact, it may be safely said that the brigade bore the brunt of the original operations of First Army. The brigade was now to rejoin 1 Airborne Division for training, reorganization, reinforcement and re-equipping before taking part in further airborne operations during the invasion of Sicily. It is a suitable moment to consider some of the more important lessons of those past few months, as regards the use of parachute troops as normal infantry.

44. However, before doing so it is well to mention some points of general interest.

(*a*) It is not generally realized that during 1 Parachute Brigade's operations in North Africa they had to contend with frightful weather conditions in some of the grimmest and most forbidding country in the world. Add these factors to a tenacious, brave and well-trained enemy, and the distances involved, and some measure of the great tasks which the brigade accomplished can be realized.

(*b*) In addition, they had another problem to face. This was the unfriendliness and general unpleasantness of the Tunisian Arabs, who not only looted wounded and dead, but also gave away information to the enemy on many occasions.

(*c*) It is a measure of the very great respect in which the brigade was held by the enemy that the Germans gave them the name " Red Devils ", which was confirmed by General Alexander (later Field Marshal The Viscount Alexander). Later, this name was applied to all airborne troops in honour of the exploits of 1 Parachute Brigade.

Lessons Resulting from the Use of 1 Parachute Brigade as Normal Infantry

45. The training of the brigade in England had been successful in producing a very live and fit brigade with great morale and *esprit-de-corps*. They were, as might be expected in a formation of very carefully selected volunteers, particularly rich in personal initiative and resource. Such tasks as patrolling, night operations and guerilla warfare in difficult country showed these qualifications to great advantage. Furthermore, their tenacity was exploited in many awkward situations where the presence of first-class troops was required to encourage less well-trained or poorly equipped units. They were not, however, accustomed to the close co-operation of medium and field artillery and tanks as there had been little time to train with these other arms in England, and they had to learn by war experience.

46. There was a natural desire on the part of the War Office to husband airborne troops for airborne operations and not to replace casualties in the brigade by trained parachutist reserves during ground operations It should be understood that at this time only about one volunteer in three was finally accepted into the parachute units, owing to physical or mental unsuitability. The cost of this was high and the intake of recruits was limited Furthermore, the remainder of 1 Airborne Division in England were far below strength and could ill spare large numbers of replacements for 1 Parachute Brigade. No recruits could be obtained from First Army as they could not be spared. There

were no parachute training facilities in North Africa. First Army supported as far as possible the desire of the War Office to retain all parachute reinforcements for airborne operations and this resulted in many of them being kept at the base near Algiers for considerable periods, together with the minimum brigade staff required to maintain the airborne equipment there. Therefore 1 Parachute Brigade was never at full strength and it is doubtful if its battalions averaged more than 300 strong during the ground operations from January, to April, 1943. This placed a great strain on all units and also had the inevitable effect that when they were eventually withdrawn from the fighting they needed a long period to absorb their many new reinforcements. In addition, the personnel who had been fighting for so long needed a thorough course in parachuting before they were again fit for airborne operations.

47. The equipment of the whole brigade, including its R.E. and R.A.M.C. units, was on the whole excellent and well suited to both airborne and ground operations. It was, however, a disadvantage that the brigade did not have its own services under command. The R.E. equipment was necessarily very light.

48. Practically speaking, the brigade had no first-line transport of its own and had to rely on captured vehicles, impressed mules and R.A.S.C. transport borrowed on occasion for particular purposes. There was very seldom sufficient available. This reduced its mobility, caused it much physical exertion and sometimes made it impossible to employ its full complement of 3-inch mortars and machine guns.

49. For all these reasons, it was evident that it was most uneconomical and inefficient to employ a parachute brigade in ground operations unless it were decided to increase it to a brigade group with its own services under command and a suitable amount of transport. In addition, the brigade headquarters itself needed a bigger staff to cope with ground operations and simultaneous preparations for airborne operations. A senior commander or adviser at Army or Supreme Headquarters was required to look after its interest there, and to advise on its use in an airborne role.

CHAPTER IX

AIRBORNE FORCES IN THE UNITED KINGDOM FROM OCTOBER, 1942, UNTIL APRIL, 1943

1 Airborne Division

1. Towards the end of 1942, after 1 Parachute Brigade had left for North Africa, the remainder of 1 Airborne Division, particularly 2 Parachute Brigade, fell to very much below establishment, having been drained to make 1 Parachute Brigade up to strength. With the possible exception of 1 Air-landing Brigade, the Division was very far from being ready for war, but a divisional exercise, brigade and unit training, and a concentrated series of technical trials of all descriptions had provided suitable experience on which to base the organization and armament needed for the future. However, there was little operational experience to confirm these requirements, and being expensive in men and material they had to be discussed in detail with General Headquarters, Home Forces, and the War Office. In addition, Headquarters 1 Airborne Division were continually altering their establishments so that discussions went on for several months. As a result divisional headquarters and units wasted a lot of valuable time, for it was by no means certain that they would go into action with the establishments on which they were training. But in view of the experimental nature of things it is difficult to see how this could have been avoided. In addition, many improvisations had to be made owing to inadequate numbers of vehicles, as full scales were not issued until war establishments were firm. In fact, when the Division moved overseas in May, 1943, some units were still without an approved war establishment.

2. Nevertheless, a certain amount of progress was made and the formation of 3 Parachute Brigade was authorized on 5th November, 1942, its composition being as follows :—

> 10th Battalion, Somerset Light Infantry became 7th (Light Infantry) Battalion, The Parachute Regiment.
>
> 13th Battalion, The Royal Warwickshire Regiment became 8th (Midland) Battalion, The Parachute Regiment.
>
> 10th Battalion, The Essex Regiment became 9th (Eastern and Home Counties) Battalion, The Parachute Regiment.

A new R.E. unit was raised and named 3rd Parachute Squadron, R.E 224th Field Ambulance became 224th Parachute Field Ambulance, R.A.M.C The brigade was commanded by Brigadier Lathbury, the former commander of 3rd Parachute Battalion, now released from his appointment in the Air Directorate at the War Office, and became part of 1 Airborne Division which once again, on paper at least, included three Brigades—1 Air-landing Brigade, 2 Parachute Brigade and 3 Parachute Brigade. But there was no possibility of 3 Parachute Brigade being ready for operations before the end of June, 1943, as recruiting was slow, equipment was scarce and very little unit air training could be provided. The conversion of a battalion of infantry to a parachute role was not a simple process of a change of role. The existing personnel of the battalion had to be given the opportunity of volunteering for parachute duties and many did not satisfy the exacting physical standard. Wide changes of command and establishment and the complete re-equipping of units were involved.

3. On 11th January, 1943, Major-General Browning submitted a report to General Headquarters, Home Forces, and the War Office, giving his views regarding the state of 1 Airborne Division and 38 Wing, R.A.F. at that time. In brief, he stated that :—

(*a*) 2 Parachute Brigade, having lost 600 trained personnel to 1 Parachute Brigade in North Africa, was considerably under strength and had few experienced leaders.

(*b*) 3 Parachute Brigade was only then forming.

(*c*) 1 Air-landing Brigade, except for serious deficiencies in equipment, was trained and ready for war, though not completely up to strength.

(*d*) The divisional artillery consisted of one light battery armed with only two guns, and two anti-tank and one light anti-aircraft battery nearly at full strength.

No decision had been taken regarding the formation of further light artillery units and it was not known whether they would be armed with the British 3·7-inch howitzer or the American 75-mm. pack howitzer.

(*e*) The Royal Engineers were seriously under strength, except for 9th Field Company, and short of much equipment, and a decision was still awaited regarding the formation of the field park company.

(*f*) Divisional signals were far below strength, their organization was uncertain and the situation regarding wireless sets was deplorable.

(*g*) The parachute field ambulances were recruiting personnel very slowly and were nearly 200 under strength, with no reserves.

(*h*) Divisional headquarters was overworked, under-staffed and responsible for too many duties apart from the Division itself.

(*i*) The divisional troops were, in general, very short of personnel and equipment, and there were not enough R.A.S.C., R.A.O.C. and R.E.M.E. resources to administer the division properly.

(*j*) All units were organized on out-of-date establishments and equipment tables, and the delay in considering and approving the new ones submitted was having very serious repercussions both as regards training and readiness for war.

(*k*) 38 Wing, R.A.F., had not sufficient serviceable aircraft to provide simultaneous training for even one battalion and serious formation air training was out of the question. The aircraft were obsolescent Whitleys, and no decision had been made regarding their replacement. When that decision had been made, the aircraft would have to be provided and crews converted to their use. During that period there would probably be even less air training for the division. No single aircraft on the strength of 38 Wing was capable of towing a fully-loaded Horsa Glider on operations.

(*l*) The production of Horsa Gliders, the basic operational type, was far behind schedule and the necessary modifications to carry equipment and weapons were progressing very slowly.

(*m*) The air resources for the operational training of the glider pilots and for keeping them in flying practice after they left the flying training schools were totally inadequate.

91

As a result of Major-General Browning's letter, the Commander-in-Chief, Home Forces, pressed the War Office to obtain an agreed policy whereby the R.A.F. should provide sufficient aircraft to carry out air training for units of the Division and operational training for the glider pilots. It will be seen later how improvements were made in this respect.

4. Meanwhile, examination of the organization of the Division had been carried out by Headquarters 1 Airborne Division, and on 25th February, 1943, Major-General Browning submitted proposals for reorganization. These proposals were largely based on experience gained in the North African operations, the main lessons of which were given in Chapter VIII, and they were designed to allow the Division to be employed as such. All his proposals were agreed, except the increase in establishment of parachute battalions to four companies, and the formation of a parachute light regiment, Royal Artillery. It was also considered that an anti-tank regimental headquarters was unnecessary and that the training of the batteries could be supervised by the commander, Royal Artillery. However, on 13th February, 1943, 458th Independent Light Battery R.A. was expanded to form 1st Air-landing Light Regiment, though it was not for some considerable time that the anti-tank regimental headquarters was formed. It is interesting to note that the lack of the fourth company in parachute battalions was found to be a severe handicap by unit commanders and was introduced after the war had ended.

5. At this time the target date for the operational readiness of the Division was taken as 1st July, 1943. Major-General Browning impressed upon the War Office and Home Forces, that if this date were to be achieved it was essential that firm war establishments should be agreed by the end of March, and that the full numbers of personnel, both officers and other ranks, should be posted to the Division at the earliest date.

6. On 9th March, 1943, 1 Airborne Division less 3 Parachute Brigade, 2nd Battalion, The Oxfordshire and Buckinghamshire Light Infantry, 1st Battalion, The Royal Ulster Rifles, and the Airborne Light Tank Squadron were ordered to mobilize, and to complete mobilization by May, 1943. On this date there were still nine major war establishments of the Division outstanding, which had not yet been considered by the War Establishments Committee at the War Office. Shortly after this the Division came under direct War Office control insofar as war establishments and provision or equipment were concerned. In addition, the Director of Air at the War Office assumed responsibility for scrutinizing all war establishments proposed by the Division, so that by the time they were placed in front of the War Establishments Committee all queries had been settled. Both these measures assured a considerable saving of time in completing the mobilization of the Division. There was one other factor which Major-General Browning continually impressed upon the War Office and that was the necessity for the formation of some headquarters to take over all non-divisional work at present being carried out by the Division.

7. While the Division was completing its readiness for war it received a further visit from Major-General Lee, the Commander, 101 U.S. Airborne Division, on 29th March, 1943, and on 2nd April His Majesty the King carried out an inspection. By the end of April, Major-General Hopkinson had succeeded Major-General Browning as divisional commander on the latter's

appointment as Major-General, Airborne Forces, and Brigadier Lathbury had been appointed to command 1 Parachute Brigade, having carried out a direct change of appointments with Brigadier Flavell. The new divisional commander and Brigadier Lathbury left England for North Africa on 25th April. The Division completed mobilization by 1st May, 1943, and shortly afterwards the first unit sailed for North Africa in Convoy WS. 30.

8. It is necessary to emphasize again the amount of time that divisional headquarters, from the commander to clerks, had to spend on matters connected with equipment, strengths, recruiting, experiments and other such subjects, all outside the scope of a divisional headquarters. As a consequence very little time was available for training the headquarters, and when it left the United Kingdom only one very skeleton exercise had been held to test its mobility.

6 Airborne Division

9. The reader will remember that in Chapter VI the events were studied which led to the conflict of views between the Chief of the Imperial General Staff and the Chief of the Air Staff being placed before Mr. Winston Churchill for arbitration. This was on 23rd October, 1942, and two days before, the War Office, adhering to its policy had decided that the Army order of battle for 1944 should include one airborne division in the United Kingdom, one more for Western Europe, and one for India and Ceylon. Mr. Churchill gave his decision on 18th November, 1942.

He felt that it was a question of balance and emphasis. He had himself always been anxious for an airborne division, but saw that there was no prospect in the near future of our being able to provide the necessary aircraft for a force of the size contemplated by the War Office. He was also worried by the large construction of gliders and the difficulty of storing those wooden machines which might be spoilt by rain and damp before we had any opportunity of using them. He thought we should find out how many C.47s we could expect to get from the U.S.A., as it was not possible to accept a heavy drain upon our bomber offensive. In any event he was sure that the Horsa programme would have to be drastically curtailed.

The Prime Minister said that our immediate target should be of the dimensions recommended by C.A.S., *i.e.* two parachute brigades plus a small glider-borne force to lift the heavier supporting weapons and vehicles which could not be dropped by parachute. He directed that the details be worked out forthwith, and a standstill order for gliders issued at once. He considered that the whole position should be re-examined in about six months' time, say 1st June, 1943.

In effect this meant that 1 Air-landing Brigade would have to be disbanded, but on the following day General Sir Alan Brooke stated that whatever might be the shortage of transport aircraft he had no intention of breaking up 1 Airborne Division, which was a most valuable formation. In addition, to stop glider production completely would mean that skilled personnel would be dispersed throughout the country, so the War Office and Air Ministry recommended that it should be slowed down, which would enable certain modifications to be made to the Horsa during production. The Prime Minister agreed.

10. In January, 1943, Mr. Roosevelt and Mr. Churchill held their historic conference at Casablanca. It was decided that Anglo-American strategy against Germany in 1943 should be based on an offensive against the Axis forces in the

Mediterranean after North Africa had been cleared. Should an opportunity occur, a re-entry into North-West Europe should also be made in 1943. In either or both of these contingencies the employment of adequate airborne forces would be an essential factor for success. As a result of this decision, on 24th February, the Chief of the Imperial General Staff decided that the minimum British airborne requirements for operations in 1943 and 1944 would be :—

(a) *North Africa.*—One airborne division and one parachute brigade. The division was to consist of two parachute brigades, one air-landing brigade (two battalions) and divisional troops, including artillery and gliders.

(b) *United Kingdom.*—One airborne division on the same establishment as the division for North Africa.

However, the Chief of the Air Staff did not agree with Sir Alan Brooke and maintained his previous view that, although he was far from denying the value of airborne forces, he was strongly of the opinion that the large drain on our resources, which would result from Sir Alan Brooke's proposals, could not be justified from the results likely to be obtained. He further stated, on 4th March, 1943, that he considered that developments in strategical and in operational experience over the past three months did not warrant the Chiefs of Staff asking the Prime Minister to reconsider his decision of November, 1942. However, the General and Air Staffs were ordered to examine in detail the implications of the Chief of the Imperial General Staff's proposals.

11. On 21st April the examination was complete and considered by the Chiefs of Staff. It then became apparent that although there had been a difference of opinion, there had also been a misunderstanding. The air staff had been working on the assumption that an air-landing brigade would consist of four battalions, whereas the War Office intended it to contain only two. Therefore the number of gliders to lift an airborne division, and consequently the number of tugs required, had been reduced from 760 to 630. A second pilot was considered necessary for each glider and the total number of glider pilots for the British division was estimated at 1,800. Under existing arrangements 1,000 of these would be trained by October, 1943, although 300 would not be up to full operational standards. The overall reduction in aircraft and gliders on the previous calculations was 260 for the two British divisions, or 390 if the division in the Far East was added. The Chief of the Air Staff, therefore, agreed with the War Office proposals to form an additional division. He suggested that as the first real test of Allied airborne forces was about to be made in the attack on Sicily, preparations should be made to train the extra 800 glider pilots required, but that a final decision should not be made until the results of the forthcoming operations were known. The delay would not be more than one month, and training would begin in July and August, 1943, and be completed by August, 1944. To this the Chief of the Imperial General Staff agreed.

12. On 23rd April, 1943, the War Office issued orders for the formation of 6 Airborne Division on a phased programme, the number " 6 " being chosen for security reasons. The phased programme allowed for 30 per cent. of the divisional headquarters to be formed immediately, 30 per cent. to be formed on 1st June, 1943, and the remainder to be reviewed in September, 1943. Of the formations and units in 1 Airborne Division, 3 Parachute Brigade, including

3rd Parachute Squadron, R.E., and 224th Parachute Field Ambulance R.A.M.C., was to be transferred into 6 Airborne Division. Headquarters, 6 Air-landing Brigade, was to be formed immediately and the brigade was to consist of 2nd Battalion, The Oxfordshire and Buckinghamshire Light Infantry and 1st Battalion, The Royal Ulster Rifles, who had originally been in 1 Air-landing Brigade. A new 5 Parachute Brigade and the majority of the divisional troops were to be formed on 1st June, 1943, any outstanding units being reviewed in September, 1943. There, we may leave 6 Airborne Division about to form, and turn to the happenings in 38 Wing, R.A.F.

38 Wing, Royal Air Force, and the Glider Pilot Regiment

13. When, on 19th October, 1942, all further issues of aircraft to 38 Wing were stopped, the Wing's total strength was 60 obsolescent Whitleys and a few Albemarles. As a result of the shut-down order No. 298 Squadron was disbanded, No. 295 Squadron remained at Netheravon, No. 296 moved to Andover, No. 297 went to Thruxton and No. 42 Operational Training Unit was moved to Ashbourne, Derbyshire. At about this time discussions were taking place within the War Office regarding the possible replacement of Whitleys as tugs for Horsas by other types of aircraft. It was considered that the best replacement was the American Dakota C.47 (transport version of the Douglas D.C.3) as it was unlikely that any heavy bombers would be available for a considerable time. The War Office estimated that the requirements by 1st April, 1943, would be :—

(a) *United Kingdom*
    400 tugs for Horsas.
    30 tugs for Hamilcars.

(b) *Middle East*
    200 tugs for Hadrians (U.S. CG–4A) in tropical conditions. (These gliders were known as the " Waco " by the Americans. *See* Appendix A.)

It was expected that 690 Hadrian gliders would be available from the United States by that date.

14. By 23rd December, 1942, the position had improved sufficiently to allow of a modification to the standstill order regarding the posting of personnel and the issue of aircraft to units of 38 Wing. The Air Ministry stated that personnel within the Wing would be increased as much as possible, and that the policy for provision of aircraft would be as follows :—

(a) *No. 1 Parachute Training School.*—To be built up to the full establishment of 12 + 4 Whitleys.

(b) 38 *Wing.*—Not to be allowed to fall below a total of 48 + 12 aircraft between the three squadrons.

(c) *Glider Pilot Exercise Unit.*—To be built up to 18 Masters, 15 Moths and 30 Hotspurs.

(d) *No. 42 O.T.U.*—To be maintained on a scale sufficient to provide wastage of the existing 38 Wing.

(e) *Glider Training Schools.*—To be maintained at their present strength.

(f) *Heavy Glider Conversion Unit.*—To be built up to the full establishment of 10 Albemarles and 24 Whitleys by January, 1943.

Although these figures fell far below the numbers considered necessary to provide continuous air training for 1 Airborne Division, they were a great improvement on the situation as it had existed two months previously.

15. In the meantime, great difficulties had been experienced in maintaining the morale and training of the Glider Pilot Regiment, which was receiving its full quota of volunteers. Many pilots who had completed their initial training were becoming out of practice because of the lack of aircraft to provide them with further training. Despite this, a number of glider exercises were held and on 26th January, 1943, a demonstration was given to a party of Members of Parliament, who flew in the gliders. Unfortunately, an accident occurred when one of the gliders landed and two Members of Parliament, one being Dame Ellen Wilkinson, and Major-General Browning, were injured.

16. On 1st March, the situation as regards the further training of glider pilots had become so serious that the War Office requested the Air Ministry, as a matter of urgency, to provide facilities for the further exercising of the 550 glider pilots of 1 Airborne Division who, in the opinion of the divisional commander, required 100 hours further flying before being fit for operations. About this time, Major I. A. Murray, was appointed to command the 2nd Battalion, the Glider Pilot Regiment, and promoted to Lieutenant-Colonel.

17. By the end of March, the figures of glider pilots who had completed training, and those who were undergoing training, were as follows :—

(a) Passed Heavy Glider Conversion Unit 510
(b) Passed Glider Training School, but awaiting H.G.C.U. 209
(c) At the Glider Training Schools 116
(d) At the Elementary Flying Training Schools 200

Approx. Total 1,035

There was thus a bottle-neck between the Glider Training Schools and the Heavy Glider Conversion Unit, and of those who had learned to fly the heavy gliders over 78 per cent. were still below operational standard. In order to cut down training and save time the War Office and Air Ministry now agreed that there should be two distinctive gradings of glider-pilots, first pilot and second pilot. The more experienced and capable of the pilots already trained were graded as first pilots and were " crewed up " with a less experienced man as second pilot. Glider crews were then formed into flights and each flight was attached to a flight of one of the tug-squadrons for a period of one month at a time, at the end of which they were replaced by new flights, and left the tug-squadrons. They returned to the tug-squadrons after two months for more training. By this means each aircrew had attached to them three glider crews in turn, whom they got to know well. During the period of attachment, they were encouraged to regard themselves as one crew of six men, four aircrew and two glider crew. During the two months rest period, the glider pilots either went to the Glider Pilot Exercise Unit for refresher Hotspur training or to the Glider Pilot Regiment Depot for military training. As second pilots became more experienced they were sent to the Heavy Glider Conversion Unit to complete their first pilot's course.

18. The mobilization of 1 Airborne Division and the likelihood of the formation of another airborne division had made it essential that 38 Wing be increased in aircraft as soon as possible. The War Office therefore requested the Air Ministry to make up 38 Wing to a total of 90 aircraft. The Air Ministry agreed to this informing the War Office that the Albemarle had been cleared for the tropics and that 38 Wing would be completely re-equipped with a total of 80 Albemarles and ten Halifaxes, all in lieu of Whitleys, by September, 1943. In addition, a further 66 Albemarles would be available for the Operational Training Unit, the Heavy Glider Conversion Unit and No. 1 Parachute Training School by October, 1943.

19. During this period the effect of the shut-down order on provision of aircraft and personnel for 38 Wing was being felt by the squadrons themselves. They realized fully that it was essential to provide as many flying hours as possible for the dropping of parachute troops and towing of gliders, but through no fault of their own, they were compelled to devote a high proportion of flying hours to the training of air crews. As an example, during February, 1943, squadrons of 38 Wing flew 1,404 flying hours, of which they were only able to devote 340 to dropping parachute troops or towing gliders.

20. There were other factors besides the training of aircrews which affected the number of flying hours allotted to airborne forces. The three squadrons of the Wing were engaged on the dropping of leaflets in France on behalf of the Foreign Office, and this task took up a great deal of their time. In February, 1943, No. 296 Squadron began re-equipping with Albemarles in order to take part in the Sicily campaign. From then on it was gradually withdrawn from the air training programme. Its establishment was increased from two flights to three so that additional aircrews—and the most experienced— had to be posted in from the remainder of the Wing. This left Nos. 295 and 297 Squadrons to carry out the increased glider flying commitment. Both were depleted, while within No. 295 Squadron a flight of Halifaxes was formed to tow Horsas to North Africa for the Sicily operations, and had priority over all other squadron demands.

21. Despite these drawbacks the Wing made an effort to help the airborne troops, especially the glider pilots, and in many cases a dual purpose was served when various R.A.F. squadrons changed station by moving their personnel and equipment in gliders. One station commander, being accustomed to frequent moves, had the officers' mess bar so constructed that it could be dismantled and fitted into a Horsa ! In April, 1943, a Bomber Command Stirling forced-landed at night on the Isle of Man through engine trouble. The following morning a new engine was flown over in a Horsa Glider, with a saving of time amounting to days.

22. Although the airborne commanders were naturally very anxious to obtain a high proportion of flying hours for the air training of their formations, a lack of which always causes dissatisfaction, it must be remembered that it was an Air Force responsibility for ensuring that the troops, whether parachutists, or glider-borne, arrived on the ground at the correct place and the correct time. Highly trained air crews are essential for this and time was to prove that the R.A.F. decision was right.

The first Colonels Commandant of the Glider Pilot Regiment and the Parachute Regiment

23. While 1 Airborne Division had been mobilizing, the brigades in the Division had been going through, once again, the experience of 1 Parachute Brigade before it went to North Africa. Volunteers for parachute duties were not coming forward in sufficient numbers, and of those that did come forward a large number were unsuitable and had to be rejected. In particular, this applied to 3 Parachute Brigade, which had to contend with these difficulties in addition to forming and training new units. Particular attention was paid by Major-General Browning to the maintenance of a high standard of morale and the fostering of a regimental *esprit-de-corps* in both the Glider Pilot Regiment and the Parachute Regiment. To this end the first meeting of the Trustees of the Airborne Forces Security Fund was held in November, 1942 (*see* Chapter VI), and on 24th December, 1942, General Sir Alan Brooke was appointed Colonel Commandant of the Glider Pilot Regiment, Army Air Corps, and Field Marshal Sir John Dill, British representative on the Combined Chiefs of Staff, Washington, was appointed Colonel Commandant of the Parachute Regiment, Army Air Corps. He was succeeded on his death by Field Marshal Viscount Montgomery.

Technical Development and Problems

24. Several important technical developments took place in the period and among these was the first jump carried out by a parachutist with a loaded kit-bag strapped to his leg. The parachutist was Major John Lander, later killed in Sicily, Commander, 21 Independent Parachute Company, and it was as a result of his jump that the kit-bag later came into common use, largely super-seding containers for carrying weapons and equipment. At the same time, officers of Headquarters, 1 Airborne Division and the R.A.F. were working out details of " Rebecca "/" Eureka " radar devices (*see* Appendix D) for pin-pointing and landing on to dropping-zones. A standard operating procedure for parachuting from American aircraft was worked out by Lieutenant-Colonel W. T. Campbell and circulated to all concerned. In addition to developments, there were several problems which had to be faced. When 1 Airborne Division was mobilized, all parachute troops had been trained to jump out of American Dakota aircraft—the majority had one jump from these aircraft before leaving England, but some were not so lucky. Standard glider loads had to be worked out, tested and approved officially by the Airborne Forces Experimental Establishment, but in some cases time did not permit of official approval being obtained and the Division carried out its own tests. Disturbing reports came back from Africa that the Horsa glider would not stand up to hot weather—" the glue melted," but luckily this was a false alarm.

The Director of Air, Major-General Airborne Forces, and Training Establishments

25. Major-General Browning was always of the opinion that a separate airborne headquarters was necessary to relieve Commander, 1 Airborne Division of the many responsibilities outside that of a normal divisional commander. He had consistently maintained this point of view from June, 1942, and in a letter on 19th November he put his views once again to General Headquarters, Home Forces, and to the War Office. He stated that the whole

development of British airborne forces was being delayed to such an extent that we were in great danger of falling behind our Allies, when a short time previously we had been ahead of them. This was entirely owing to the fact that the Army lacked officers with any experience of airborne formations, so that those few officers who had got experience, namely, the staff officers of Headquarters, 1 Airborne Division, were grossly overworked. In addition to their normal duties as divisional staff officers, they had to cope with problems of experiment and development. As a result of this letter, on 21st November, Home Forces asked the War Office for approval to set up a brigadier and staff at General Headquarters in an advisory capacity for the purpose of dealing with all air matters, including airborne. This staff would work in conjunction with the Army co-operation staff of General Headquarters and the object of the airborne members would be to relieve the Commander of 1 Airborne Division of his many responsibilities outside the duties of a divisional commander. Major-General Browning did not agree with this proposal and stated that, as this air staff was to be divorced from the Division and was not to consist of specialist airborne officers, it would, in fact, become a mere post office and would not relieve Headquarters, 1 Airborne Division of work to any great extent. Eventually, it was proved that he was right in this view. However, the manpower shortages were acute at the time and the War Office decided that Home Forces' proposals would be met, and they were approved on 23rd December.

26. In addition to a separate headquarters, or staff, Major-General Browning had always considered that a separate airborne forces depot was necessary, whose duty would be the training and holding of all reinforcements for the airborne formations. This depot had been formed unofficially at Hardwick in April, 1942, from the details of 1 Parachute Brigade when the brigade moved from Hardwick to Bulford. On 25th December the War Office approved a war establishment for the depot. Lieutenant-Colonel W. Giles, Oxfordshire and Buckinghamshire Light Infantry, became the first commanding officer, being succeeded later by Lieutenant-Colonel R. W. Campbell, The Royal Ulster Rifles. The depot consisted of a depot company, a parachute training company, an air-landing training company, a battle school, a holding company, and an airfield detachment which was stationed at No. 1 Parachute Training School, Ringway.

27. In the meantime, the growing importance to the Army of air matters generally was shown by the upgrading of the Air Directorate at the War Office from a Brigadier to a Major-General's level, and the appointment of Major-General K. N. Crawford. During his term of office he did a great deal for airborne forces and was instrumental in bringing about a very close liaison between all the ministries concerned. He received every encouragement from his " opposite numbers " in the Air Ministry and the Ministry of Aircraft Production. In the Air Ministry, Air Commodore J. D. I. Hardman was Director of Military Co-operation. He did invaluable work for the Army, and had a military staff officer to assist him, at first Lieutenant-Colonel A. J. H. Cassels, who was later succeeded by Lieutenant-Colonel R. H. N. Bray. There was an army staff officer at the Ministry of Aircraft Production and the direct interest taken in Army matters by Air Marshal Sir F. G. Linsell, who was later killed in an air crash, did an enormous amount to help.

28. One of the main lessons of the North African campaign had been that a separate airborne adviser, not the divisional commander, was necessary at any headquarters controlling the use of airborne troops ; Major-General Browning emphasized this point again in January, 1943, on his return from a visit to 1 Parachute Brigade, and he continued to press for the formation of a separate airborne forces headquarters. Once a decision had been taken to form 6 Airborne Division, the necessity for such a headquarters became even more urgent, and War Office approval was finally given in April, 1943, the orders for the formation of Headquarters, Major-General Airborne Forces (*see* Chapter XII for duties) , being issued early- in May.

Situation on the Departure of 1 Airborne Division for North Africa, May, 1943

29. 1 Airborne Division had completed mobilization by 1st May, 1943, and on that date the situation was as follows :—

(*a*) The Air Directorate at the War Office was now under a first-grade director with the rank of Major-General.

(*b*) Approval had been given for the formation of 6 Airborne Division, which absorbed the following formations and units left behind by 1 Airborne Division :—

  3 Parachute Brigade.

  2nd Battalion, The Oxfordshire and Buckinghamshire Light Infantry.

  1st Battalion, The Royal Ulster Rifles.

  The Airborne Light Tank Squadron.

  2nd Battalion, The Glider Pilot Regiment.

  224th Parachute Field Ambulance.

(*c*) Approval had been given for the formation of Headquarters, Major-General Airborne Forces, which had started to form.

(*d*) An Airborne Forces Depot and School had been established.

(*e*) 38 Wing were re-equipping with Albemarle and Halifax aircraft, both of which were suitable for dropping parachute troops and towing gliders. The rank of the Commander had been raised to that of Air Commodore and Group Captain Sir Nigel Norman had been promoted on 23rd March.

(*f*) The training of glider pilots was proceeding apace in order to provide the necessary additional pilots for 6 Airborne Division.

Illustration 1.   The Radar Station, Bruneval.

Illustration 2.   The Coast-line, Bruneval.

Illustration 3.   Loading supplies into a Hadrian (USCG4–A) Glider before the invasion of Sicily.

Illustration 4.   Loading a Car, 5-cwt., 4 × 4, into a Hadrian (USCG4–A) Glider before the invasion of Sicily.

Illustration 5. The Caen Canal Bridge.

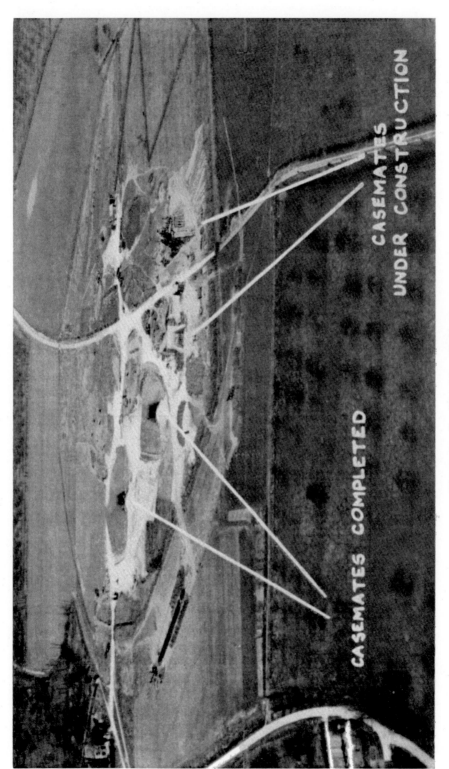

Illustration 6. The Merville Battery.

Illustration 7.   The Main Bridge, Arnhem.   Enemy tanks destroyed, 18th September, 1944.

Illustration 8.   Arnhem Bridge.   Enemy tanks destroyed, 18th September, 1944.

Illustration 9.   The Hotspur Glider.

Illustration 10.   The Hotspur Glider (in flight).

Illustration 11.   Albemarle Aircraft towing Horsa Glider at moment of take-off.

CHAPTER X

THE FORMATION OF THE SPECIAL AIR SERVICE (S.A.S.), AND AIRBORNE FORCES IN THE MIDDLE EAST

General

1. While airborne forces were being expanded and developed in the United Kingdom and while 1 Parachute Brigade was fighting in North Africa much was being done in the Middle East. This chapter covers the formation of the Special Air Service, 4 Parachute Brigade, No. 4 Middle East Training School, R.A.F., the Parachute Company of the Royal Air Force Iraq Levies, and a brief description of some small operations that took place in 1943.

" L " Detachment, Special Air Service

2. In January, 1941, a Commando formation known as Layforce, under Brigadier R. E. Laycock (later Major-General and Chief of Combined Operations), arrived in the Middle East to carry out a combined operation on the Island of Rhodes. However, German successes in the Western Desert and in Greece caused the operation to be cancelled. Layforce was split up and its units were used independently in a variety of roles, including holding a small section of the Tobruk perimeter, covering the evacuation of Crete, an opposed landing on the Syrian coast and raids on the coast of Cyrenaica. No. 8 Commando, a unit of Layforce based on Mersa Matruh, provided three forces of about 200 all ranks for three different sea-borne raids, by destroyer or gunboat. One raid failed through rough weather and two because of loss of surprise.

3. In the meantime the decision had been taken to disband Layforce, but just before this happened Lieutenant A. D. Stirling, of No. 8 Commando, obtained permission from Brigadier Laycock to experiment with some parachutes that had arrived in the Middle East. (That they had reached the Middle East at all was an error on someone's part, for they were destined for India, which may explain why India only had some 200 parachutes by March, 1942) (see Chapter XXIII). Assisted by Lieutenant J. Lewis, also a Commando, he borrowed an old Valencia aircraft for an afternoon, and the two officers and six volunteer other ranks each did a jump, their static lines being secured to the legs of the aircraft seats. Lieutenant Stirling was unlucky and injured his back, spending the next two months in hospital. While there he devoted his time to considering how the Commando role of raiding behind the enemy's lines could be carried out by a special unit. He sent his ideas to the Commander-in-Chief, based on the following arguments :—

(a) Because of his long lines of communication the enemy airfields, transport parks, etc., all on or near the coast, were extremely vulnerable.

(b) The scale on which previous raids had been planned prejudiced surprise at the outset, and the method of transport—i.e., destroyer—risked valuable naval units unnecessarily.

(c) The raids could best be carried out by a unit organized and trained on the principle of the fullest exploitation of surprise, with the minimum demands on manpower and equipment. This meant that five properly selected, trained and equipped men could more easily carry out a raid on an enemy airfield to destroy 50 aircraft, than could 200 men—because they would obtain surprise. Carried a stage further, 200 of these special troops should be able to attack at least 30 different objectives in one night, compared to only one objective using the Commando technique.

(*d*) The unit must be prepared to arrive at its objective by land, sea or air. By land, it should be ready to infiltrate on foot or be carried by the Long Range Desert Group, by sea in submarines, caiques or folboats, and from the air by parachute.

(*e*) The unit should be responsible for its own training and equipment, and the commander should be directly under the Commander-in-Chief. Lieutenant Stirling strongly resisted any suggestion that the unit should be placed under G(R), the Middle East equivalent of the Special Operations Executive, the Director of Combined Operations or any existing branch of the General Staff. At the same time Lieutenant Stirling submitted proposals for the employment of such a unit in the forthcoming offensive, the preparation of which appeared to have been no secret.

4. Lieutenant Stirling's suggestions were accepted, he was promoted to Captain and was authorized to form the unit from Layforce, and if necessary from certain formations in the desert. This was about the end of July, 1941, when Brigadier Dudley Clarke was responsible for a branch in the Middle East which dealt with deception, and was endeavouring to persuade the enemy that there was a fully equipped parachute and glider brigade in the Middle East. He had dummy parachutists dropped in the enemy lines, parked " bogus " gliders about the desert and invented a non-existent 1 Special Air Service Brigade. Naturally he welcomed the appearance of real parachutists, and to help his deception Captain Stirling's unit was named " L " Detachment, Special Air Service Brigade.

5. After some difficulty Captain Stirling obtained Lieutenant Lewis as his second-in-command, and chose as his base Kabrit, a headland situated on the western shore of the Bitter Lake near its junction with the Suez Canal. He recruited the majority of the unit from Layforce, which had by this time been largely disbanded, and obtained a few men from his own regiment, the Scots Guards, who had a battalion in the desert. Most of the men had considerable operational experience and had done a good deal of night training. By August, 1941 the formation of the unit was complete on an establishment of seven officers and about 60 other ranks with a high proportion of non-commissioned officers. It was divided into a headquarters and five troops, each consisting of two sections of four men and an officer or non-commissioned officer in charge.

6. Then they came up against the problem of training the troops in parachute jumping. Lieutenant Lewis was put in charge of this training, and was quite tireless. He carried out all experiments himself and it was due to him that success was eventually achieved. The authorities at home could not provide any assistance initially, for they were fully committed with their own problems of training 1 Parachute Brigade. However, by some means or other Captain Stirling managed to obtain an old Bombay aircraft and someone was persuaded to modify it for dropping parachute troops. By perseverance and by trial

and error they improved their technique and found out what equipment was required for ground training but there was an accident in which two men were killed. The S.A.S. then sent a further appeal to Ringway for assistance and received in return some training notes and general information which unfortunately arrived at the end of October, after the end of the S.A.S. parachute course. The notes disclosed that Ringway had had a fatal accident caused by exactly the same reason as in the case of the S.A.S. However, Captain P. Waugh arrived out from Ringway two days before the Gazala operation and was a great help in the final preparations. During training " L " Detachment worked on the principle of setting a minimum standard to be reached by all personnel, and any who did not reach the standard were returned to their unit. A Brigade of Guards standard of discipline and turn-out was insisted upon.

7. General Auchinleck's offensive against the Germans began in November, 1941, and immediately before it, on the night of 17/18th November, 1941, the first parachute operation of the S.A.S. took place, as proposed by Captain Stirling earlier. The plan was that five parachute parties were to be dropped on the night of " D "—2 day to attack the five main forward fighter and bomber enemy landing grounds at Timini and Gazala. The dropping zones were to be about 12 miles south of the objectives, and the drop was to be at night, with no moon. The R.A.F. were to carry out a heavy attack on the Gazala and Timini areas, dropping a number of flares so that the parachute aircraft could get direction to the dropping zones. From the dropping zones parties were to move to a laying up place and were to spend all " D "—1 day in observing their objectives. On the night of " D "—1/" D " day the parties were to attack, arriving at their objectives simultaneously. Each party was to carry a total of about 60 incendiary *cum* explosive bombs equipped with two-hour, half-hour and ten-minute time-pencils and also a 12-second time fuse. After the attack the sections were to retire into the desert to a pre-arranged meeting place south of the Trig el Abd where a patrol of the Long Range Desert Group would pick them up.

8. Unfortunately the night was quite unsuitable for a parachute operation. The wind was so strong that when the parachute aircraft arrived over the Gazala area the flares dropped by the bombers were not strong enough for the navigators to identify any fixed point because the sand and dust was obscuring the whole coastline. As a result no party was dropped within ten miles of the correct spot.

The story is best told in the words of Captain Malcolm Pleydell, who was the " L " Detachment medical officer, writing under the name of Malcolm James, in his book " Born of the Desert "—54 men took part in five Bombays and . . . .

" They got into their planes and left Kabrit in the early evening flying to Bagoush airfield in order to refuel, and taking off again at about ten o'clock. Their course took them out to sea, and then they turned inland when they reached the gulf of Bomba. Apart from a certain amount of flak sent up at them as they crossed the coast, they received no attention from the enemy ; but the weather, which had been good when they started, deteriorated steadily throughout the flight and by now had become really foul. It was on account of this that the Air Force pilots lost their way and the men were given the orders to jump while the planes were over the wrong area. In the stormy blackness of that night, broken only by an occasional flash of lightning, the men jumped out of the planes into a wind that was blowing at half-gale strength. They drifted down fast, striking the ground heavily when they landed, and being dragged hard along the stony surface before they had an opportunity to find their feet. Little wonder, then that they were widely scattered and separated, and had great difficulty in finding one another.

" Serjeant Bennett was fortunate in only grazing himself when he landed. As he tried to struggle to his feet a fresh buffet of wind caught his 'chute, billowing it out and dragging him along once more. At last he managed to release the safety-box round his waist and rolled out of his harness. Then he got to his feet wondering what to do next. There was not a soul to be seen, nor the slightest sign of a land feature ; in the pitch blackness and the blustering wind, he told me, he might have been the only person in the desert that night. It was a full half-hour before he found any one else, for under these circumstances whistle-blowing and shouting were of little value in personal location. But at length nine of the men had joined one another, although of this number, two had been crippled by injuries in falling and were unable to walk. The remaining seven went out in different directions searching for the ammunition and supplies which had been dropped with them in parachute containers. They found only three of the sixteen containers which had been dropped, and from these they sorted out the explosives and ammunition they would need. When they had done this they made the two injured men comfortable, leaving them most of the food and water ; and then, after saying good-bye, they marched off on a north-easterly bearing which by rights should have taken them to the airfield. In the remaining hours of darkness they covered 15 miles, and with a grey dawn lighting up the desolate scene of the open desert they began to search round for a hiding-place.

" The weather continued to be stormy throughout the day, and at five-thirty that afternoon, just as it was getting dark, there was a sudden cloudburst. They had three blankets between the seven men and they lay there shivering, doubtless feeling very miserable in their isolation. The rain kept on during the night, beating down with the wind, driving into their faces as they trudged northwards once more, until daylight the next morning showed the water fairly cascading down the rough stony slopes of the small wadis. They were wet through ; but what was far worse was the depressing fact that their sticky bombs had been rendered quite useless. For this meant that they were no longer effectual as far as the raid was concerned. Accordingly they decided to march back to the prearranged rendezvous area where a patrol of the Long Range Desert Group had been detailed to stand by and pick them up.

" For the next two days and nights they walked south, with occasional halts for resting and sleeping. At the end of that time they stopped, since they had covered more than the distance which had been given to them in their instructions. It should be borne in mind that these men did not know they had been dropped in the wrong place. Further, one should realize that it required a considerable amount of courage and determination to decide to stay in one place like this. For their food supplies were dwindling, and if the weather turned dry their water would soon become another problem. Perhaps it might be compared to a person swimming out to sea and waiting, say half a mile out, not knowing whether he had sufficient strength to swim back to shore again ; only for these men the shore would be represented by the enemy held coastline.

" They kept a good look-out the next day and saw nothing ; but soon after darkness had fallen they caught sight of a light low down on the horizon. After about half an hour it went out, and thinking it to be a star, they did not investigate. By now they were feeling ' very tired,' as Serjeant Bennett expressed it.

" On the following morning they noticed smoke where previously they had seen the light. Their spirits rose, and they trudged wearily across the intervening miles. It was the patrol of the Long Range Desert Group which had arranged to come and pick up the Special Air Service operatives after the raid. For the next three days they all searched the area for the rest of the men ; but of the fifty-four who started out, only twenty-one were picked up. Realizing that there was no object in remaining longer, they turned south and drove down to the oasis of Siwa which, at this time, was in British possession, and was being used by the L.R.D.G. as their head-quarters.

" So this, their first raid, was a most complete and utter failure. They had been dropped in the wrong area ; they had been scattered all over the place by the storm ; their explosives had been ruined by the rain. It was uncertain whether any of them had ever reached the aerodrome. Several of the officers and men had to be left where they had fallen. A few of them were in a critical condition, and were almost certain to have died before they were found by the enemy ; . . . "

Later unconfirmed reports claimed that 19 aircraft had been destroyed on the airfields, presumably by other members of the party. One of the Bombay aircraft actually landed on the airfield that its passengers were briefed to attack, complete with the troops who were going to do the job. The captain of this aircraft had decided that conditions were too bad to drop his party and was returning to base when engine trouble occurred, so he had to make a forced landing in the desert. After the engine was repaired he radioed a request for an indication of direction. This was promptly provided—but, unknown to the aircrew, by the German Staff on one of the Gazala landing fields. The un-suspecting R.A.F. officer accepted the course, but a little later discovered that his Bombay was being escorted by German fighters who forced him to land on the main fighter airfield at Gazala.

9. Although they continued with parachute training the S.A.S. did not carry out any more parachute attacks in the Middle East. Between December, 1941, and March, 1942, they undertook about 20 raids, all in conjunction with the Long Range Desert Group, who provided the means of transport and all on the lines of the Gazala–Timini attack, except for the method of approach. About 115 enemy aircraft and a number of vehicles were destroyed for only a few casualties, which unfortunately included Lieutenant J. Lewis.

10. By April, 1942, " L" Detachment had been built up again to its original size and Captain Stirling, now promoted to Major, also had under his command a unit of 60 Free French parachutists under Captain Berget, all Ringway trained, and a unit, under Captain Buck, of 12 ex-members of the German regular army, who had escaped from Germany before the war. By June,

" L" Detachment, with its Allies under command, had raided all the important enemy aerodromes within 300 miles of the forward area. One of the raids was undertaken by a party of the French squadron being marched to their objective as " prisoners of war " " escorted " by Captain Buck's German Detachment. They had also assisted in the safe passage of a vital sea-borne convoy from Alexandria to Malta by attacking seven airfields in Cyrenaica and two in Crete, destroying 75 aircraft and grounding many more. As the enemy defences were now getting stronger the S.A.S. now developed the jeep as an unarmoured machine-gun carrier, armed with two sets of twin Vickers " K " machine-guns, or one set of Vickers and one Browning ·5 machine-gun. By the end of July ·' L" Detachment was entirely " motorized ".

11. From July to October, 1942, landing grounds continued to be the main objectives, but for the last quarter of the year all efforts were directed at Rommel's lines of communications. A large scale raid against harbour installations and shipping in Benghazi during the first period was a failure, about 50 three-ton lorries and 50 jeeps being lost, but luckily only a few personnel. In the period immediately before the Battle of El Alamein an S.A.S. base had been established between Siwa and Mersa Matruh, and had been supplied by infiltration through the El Alamein position. When the Germans established an organized line, a route was made through the Quattara Depression, but this was mined and patrolled by the enemy at the Cara end. The S.A.S. then took their supplies and reinforcements up the River Nile, across the desert *via* El Kharga to the Kufra Oasis and then north through the Great Sand Sea at Howards Cairn to the base at Siwa—which was only 40 miles from Eighth Army's forward positions, though its supply route was 1,800 miles long. After Rommel had been defeated at El Alamein the objectives were communications between Tripoli and El Agheila, and at least three or four raids were carried out each night.

12. In January, 1943, Lieutenant-Colonel Stirling, as he was then, was captured by a German reconnaissance unit near Sfax in Tunisia. By this time he had under his command the following units :—

   (a) 1st S.A.S. Regiment, formed from " L" Detachment with an establishment of five squadrons, and a total of some 50 officers and 450 other ranks.
   (b) The French S.A.S. Squadron of about 14 officers and 80 other ranks.
   (c) The Greek Sacred Squadron of about 14 officers and 100 other ranks.
   (d) The Folboat Section of 15 officers and 40 other ranks.
   (e) The Middle East Commando, consisting of 30 officers and 300 other ranks.

13. Between January and April, 1943, the S.A.S. carried out various deep penetration, harassing and reconnaissance tasks in conjunction with the advance of Eighth Army. 1st S.A.S. Regiment was split into the Special Raiding Squadron (Major R. B. Mayne) and the Special Boat Squadron (Major The Lord Jellicoe), each of about 250 all ranks, and these units were placed under command of Raiding Forces, Middle East Forces (Brigadier Turnbull), which organization also took command of the Middle East Commando.

14. In May, 1943, 2nd S.A.S. Regiment (Lieutenant-Colonel W. S. Stirling) was formed in North Africa from a detachment of No. 62 Commando (Small Scale Raiding Forces) which had been sent out from England a few months previously. For the remainder of the year the Special Raiding Squadron, the Special Boat Squadron and 2nd S.A.S. Regiment took part in raids on Crete, Sardinia, the Dodecanese and the Greek islands, and in the invasions of Sicily and Italy, where they operated with 1 Airborne Division. During the summer Major-General Browning, in his capacity as Major General Airborne Forces and adviser to Generals Eisenhower and Alexander, arranged that some of the Special Raiding Squadron and 2nd S.A.S. Regiment should come under command of 1 Airborne Division for a short period so as to make the best use of the troop carrying aircraft available. During this period a close liaison was started between Headquarters, Major-General Airborne Forces and the commanders of these special units with a view to eventual co-operation in the assault on the western front. We shall see the results of this co-operation when we follow the activities of 1 Special Air Service Brigade in Chapters XVIII and XIX.

The Formation of 4 Parachute Brigade and No. 4 Middle East Training School, R.A.F.

15. The reader will remember that throughout 1941, discussions had been proceeding at home between the War Office and Air Ministry regarding the eventual size of airborne forces (*see* Chapters III and V). After much delay an agreed Joint Memorandum was submitted to the Prime Minister on 31st May, 1941. Two points in this paper affected the Middle East :—

    (*a*) " . . . . the programme (of training parachute troops) would be assisted by the institution of a parachute school in the Middle East/India."*

    (*b*) " For the future, Army requirements were :—

        (i) One brigade of parachute troops to be located at home, and one in the Middle East with the necessary transport aircraft . . . . "

16. Although the Joint Memorandum was accepted by the Prime Minister, various other factors arose which led to further differences of opinion between the two Services and more discussions and delays, as we have already seen in earlier chapters. However, the S.A.S. operation in November, 1941, drew the attention of the Home authorities to parachuting in the Middle East. They had already sent out Captain Waugh to assist the S.A.S., but he joined the S.A.S. himself eventually. There was still an acute shortage of instructors in the United Kingdom, but Ringway managed to spare three—Captain Weir, Staff Serjeant Kennedy and Flight Serjeant Spencer R.A.F. who were given the tasks of placing parachute training in the Middle East on a sound basis.

17. On 3rd May, 1942, No. 4 Middle East Training School was opened at Kabrit and, despite the difficulties of the shortage of instructors and equipment, training continued throughout most of the summer, the majority of the pupils coming from the S.A.S. and agents who had to be dropped behind the enemy lines. In August, the school was merged temporarily with No. 2 Middle East Training School to carry out ferry work, but recommenced parachute training in September with a small staff and three Wellington aircraft.

---

* In fact, parachute schools were established both in the Middle East and India—*see* Chapter XXIII.

18. In the meantime, in September, 1941, orders had been issued for the formation of a parachute brigade in India, the first battalion of which was to be British—151 Parachute Battalion (*see* Chapter XXIII). In November, 1942, this battalion was moved to the Middle East, under Lieutenant-Colonel H. C. R. Hose, where it went to Kabrit and where its name was changed to 156 Parachute Battalion. It was in November, 1942, also, that the decision was taken to form 4 Parachute Brigade in the Middle East. Lieutenant-Colonel J. W. Hackett, was promoted to Brigadier and appointed to command, and did his parachute course in December with his Brigade Major, Major P. H. M. May. The brigade headquarters and signal section began to form during December at Kabrit, and 2nd Battalion The Royal Sussex Regiment was earmarked for conversion to a parachute battalion as the second battalion of the brigade.

19. In the following month 4th Parachute Squadron R.E. and 133rd Parachute Field Ambulance began to form, and it was decided that as 2nd Battalion, The Royal Sussex Regiment was a regular unit it could not be transferred to the Army Air Corps. Those men who did not volunteer for parachute duties, therefore, remained as the regular battalion, the volunteers being formed into 10th Parachute Battalion under Lieutenant-Colonel K. B. I. Smyth. In the same month Lieutenant-Colonel Hose left 156 Parachute Battalion and was succeeded by Lieutenant-Colonel Sir Richard des Voeux from the Staff of Headquarters 1 Airborne Division.

20. The Kabrit area had never been satisfactory as an airborne training centre because the airfield facilities were inadequate, the country was unsuitable for tactical training, the dropping zone was too hard for basic training and caused many casualties, the weather conditions were bad, with wind, sandstorms and periodical great heat, and accommodation was unsatisfactory. Accordingly, at the end of February, the brigade and No. 4 Middle East Training School moved to the Ramat David area in Northern Palestine.

21. By this time No. 4 Middle East Training School had obtained six Hudsons and two civilian Dakotas (C53) which were similar to the Service version but had a small door. Basic training was going well, the average time taken to train an individual being ten days, but there were many personnel problems. Only about 100 men of 2nd Battalion, The Royal Sussex Regiment had volunteered to parachute, and there were few coming in from elsewhere. The average length of overseas service in 156 Parachute Battalion was five or six years, and so the main problem was how to build up 10th Parachute Battalion and replace the repatriations in 156 Parachute Battalion. To help in this a recruiting drive was started all over the Middle East.

22. Soon after the brigade arrived at Ramat David, 7 United States Troop Carrier Squadron with 12 Dakotas was attached to the brigade, and company training became possible and continued throughout the next few months. Exercises took place chiefly in the Lake Tiberias area by night, and in Cyprus by day. One of these exercises took the form of a demonstration to the Emir Abdullah of Transjordan at Shune, where a company of 156 Parachute Battalion was dropped and " captured " a fort belonging to the Arab Legion. After the exercise the Emir had the flag pulled down and presented it to the company commander, and it was carried by the company in Italy and at Arnhem and was

kept by the company commander while he was a prisoner of war in German hands. The Emir also watched another exercise in which the dropping zone was 1,000 feet below sea-level, so that the troops actually jumped from the aircraft at about 500 feet below sea-level.

23. At the end of March, 11th Parachute Battalion began to form at Shallufa, on the Suez Canal, under Lieutenant-Colonel R. M. C. Thomas, who had been second-in-command of 156 Parachute Battalion and took with him a cadre from that battalion. From then on recruiting for the whole brigade improved, and volunteers arrived from places as far apart as Malta and Khartoum.

24. By the middle of May the brigade was more or less up to strength, except for 11th Parachute Battalion, who remained behind in Palestine, and during the next month it moved by rail to Port Said, then by sea to Tripoli, in Tripolitania, and then by road to Msaken, between Sousse and Kairouan, where it joined 1 Airborne Division. The story of the remainder of the life of 4 Parachute Brigade is bound up with 1 Airborne Division, and so there we shall leave it for the time being.

The Parachute Company of the Royal Air Force Iraq Levies

25. While the Special Air Service had been training in the desert and 4 Parachute Brigade had been growing, small but interesting developments had been taking place further East. In 1942 Air Marshal H. V. Champion de Crespigny, the Air Officer Commanding in Chief, Iraq, impressed by the potential value of airborne troops in a country like Iraq, asked for volunteers to form a parachute company, from the R.A.F. Iraq Levies.

26. Unlike the British system, where additional pay was given, in order to attract the right types no inducement was offered in the way of extra pay or special promotion. Despite this nearly 1,000 men volunteered for the 150 vacancies, and of those selected, 80 per cent. were Assyrians and 20 per cent. were Kurds. There were only four Valencia aircraft available and the men were trained and commanded by their own officers, of whom the company commander, two officers and several non-commissioned officers came from 156 Parachute Battalion. Among the latter were one or two who had been instructors at Ringway in the early days.

27. During the existence of the company only one man was killed in parachute training and there were no refusals to jump. In 1943, when the German threat to Iraq had lessened, the company was offered to the Middle East and gladly accepted, and was attached to 11th Parachute Battalion.

11th Parachute Battalion Operation at Cos, and Miscellaneous Small Operations

28. When 4 Parachute Brigade left Palestine for North Africa, 11th Parachute Battalion moved from Shallufa to Ramat David to complete its formation and basic parachute training, where it was joined by the Parachute Company of the Royal Air Force Iraq Levies.

29. Between August and December, 1943, several small parachute operations were carried out. During August, the Iraqi Parachute Company was dropped in a raid on the Adriatic coast near Corfu, which was successful, but for the loss of one British officer and 14 Levies killed.

30. On 15th September, a company group of 11th Parachute Battalion took part in an operation against the Island of Cos. Six Dakotas were used, the operation was completely successful and in three days 14 Dakotas and three Hudsons carried out supply by air. One of our aircraft came down in the sea, but the crew were picked up by a Turkish ship, interned for a short period and allowed to return to their base. Four more supply drops took place, two by night, and the troops were finally withdrawn on 25th September. Another operation was planned to take place in the same month against Rhodes but was cancelled when it was known that the Germans were in complete control of that Island.

31. A night operation took place on 31st October and 1st November and was successful. Two hundred troops of the Greek Sacred Squadron, who had negligible experience of parachuting, were dropped on Samos, 100 on each night from five Dakotas. There were no other operations worth mentioning in the Middle East, and 11th Parachute Battalion moved to Port Said in December, 1943, and sailed to rejoin 4 Parachute Brigade in England, leaving behind the Iraqi Parachute Company to be disbanded. However, the Middle East Training School continued to run courses for special agents and other individuals. Special attention was paid by the school to supply dropping, and many exercises were carried out in conjunction with the Army, until in May, 1944, the unit was finally disbanded.

CHAPTER XI

1 AIRBORNE DIVISION IN THE MEDITERRANEAN FROM APRIL TO DECEMBER, 1943

Preparations for the Move to North Africa

1. The state of 1 Airborne Division during the winter of 1942–43 has been described in Chapter IX. It was only by great efforts by all concerned that the Division was brought to a reasonable strength in personnel and equipment at the last possible moment. Its preparation for a move overseas and subsequent operations was extremely hurried. Even its order of battle and the organization of its units were not firm at the time of sailing. It had been brought almost up to personnel strength by the last-minute inclusions of all available recruits. Many of them were only half-trained and some 650 of the parachutist recruits had not been able to complete the full parachute jumping courses. It would therefore be necessary to do as much training as possible in North Africa before operations were undertaken.

2. As regards glider pilots, the training situation was really desperate. The very limited resources of 38 Wing R.A.F. could produce a maximum of 50 trained Army glider pilot crews with concentrated training resources in England. The only solution was to send as many glider pilots as possible to North Africa to complete their training there, using such resources as the United States Troop Carrier Command could provide. This number, in consultation with the Americans, was fixed at 60 additional crews and they arrived at Oran, in the area administered by Fifth U.S. Army, on 26th April, 1942. None of the glider pilots of either party had been trained in flying Hadrian (U.S. CG–4A) gliders and few had been trained on Horsas, which were only then being provided for 38 Wing in reasonable numbers. It was certain that Hadrians would be the gliders normally available in the theatre, with a few Horsas if they could be got out there in time. Furthermore, there had not been time to train any glider pilots in night landings under operational conditions.

3. The 50 crews trained by 38 Wing in England arrived in North Africa about the middle of June without any training in night landings. This was not the fault of 38 Wing but was owing to a combination of the lack of resources available to the wing and to continuous bad weather conditions. When they reached North Africa the 60 crews who were due to be trained there found that the Hadrians were still *en route* from America. However, a sufficient number arrived to enable training to start three weeks later, most of them being assembled and erected from crates by the glider pilots themselves, but the delay resulted in a loss of valuable moon periods for practice in night landings and a consequent last-minute rush in the operational training of the crews, especially as the first stage naturally had to be conversion to the Hadrian. This very unsatisfactory situation was a direct result of the earlier delays in expanding and equipping 38 Wing R.A.F.

4. In addition to the hurried training of glider pilot crews, 38 Wing was faced with two other major tasks. It had to provide a maximum effort to take

part in operations in North Africa with 1 Airborne Division, at the same time retaining in England sufficient resources to train 6 Airborne Division, now forming. It was decided that wing headquarters and two squadrons would remain in England for the latter task, and that a tactical headquarters, " A " flight of 295 Squadron (Halifaxes) and the whole of 296 Squadron (Albemarles) would go to North Africa and come under the orders of XII U.S. Troop Carrier Command for airborne training and operations. It should be realized that the Wing itself was in the throes of expansion, it was very short of experienced crews, it had to convert from Whitleys to Albemarle and Halifax aircraft, and its maintenance resources were deplorable. To those airborne soldiers who knew the facts it was a wonder that the Wing achieved as much as it did and it was a tribute to them that 1 Airborne Division did not lose all confidence in its ability to drop and tow them efficiently. Mutual confidence between airborne troops and the R.A.F. formations with whom they work is an essential factor for success in all airborne operations.

5. These Hadrian Gliders could not carry all the loads required in operations by 1 Airborne Division and it was important that some Horsa Gliders should be available for the heavier and larger weapons (*e.g.* 6-pr. anti-tank guns with jeeps). It was not possible to allot shipping space for this purpose and the only alternative was to fly them out. The Air Ministry at first refused to permit this as impracticable, but were eventually persuaded by 38 Wing and Major-General Browning to allow an attempt to be made. The only suitable aircraft that could be made available for this purpose were 12 Halifaxes allotted to 295 Squadron. Intensive training of selected R.A.F. and glider pilot crews started about 1st May and ferrying started on 3rd June. For this the enthusiasm and skill of Air Commodore Sir Nigel Norman, Group Captain T. B. Cooper, Squadron Leader Wilkinson, who commanded " A " Flight of 295 Squadron responsible for the ferrying, and Major A. J. Cooper, commanding the glider pilot detachment, were mainly responsible. Even so, three Halifax crews were lost during the hurried conversion training. But the problem did not end with the arrival of the Horsas at Froha, ten miles south of Mascara, *via* Sale in Morocco, after a direct ten-hour flight of 1,400 miles mainly over the sea from Portreath in Cornwall. The distance from Froha to the operational airborne base near Sousse in Tunisia was another 600 miles and the route lay over high mountains and desert where bumpy conditions were very bad. However, by 8th July there were 19 serviceable Horsas ready at the airborne operational base, out of 29 which left England. Of the balance three came down into the sea *en route* from England, one of which was the result of enemy action, three force landed in Africa and could not be recovered in time, two were under repair and two had been destroyed in crash landings at Sale.

It is of interest to note that one of the Horsa Gliders that came down in the sea required considerable efforts by the Royal Navy to sink it, and eventually sank only after a combination of gun-fire and ramming. Eight Halifax aircraft were also ready at Sousse on 8th July. It was a remarkable successful performance under existing conditions especially when it is remembered that the towing route was well within the range of German aircraft, and the Horsas proved invaluable in the subsequent operations, but it had its disadvantages in wear and tear to the aircraft and over-work for Squadron Leader Wilkinson's flight before they took part in the Sicilian operations on 9th/10th July.

112

6. 296 Squadron, under the command of Wing Commander May, flew out from England in time to concentrate with 30 aircraft in 1 Airborne Division area near Mascara by about 10th June and were able to do a little training there with the Division and with 51 Wing of XII U.S. Troop Carrier Command. Although their Albemarles were capable of dropping parachute troops and towing light gliders, their range towing a loaded Horsa Glider was very limited.

7. 51 Wing, now under Brigadier-General Dunn, as Brigadier-General Paul L. Williams had taken over the Command of XII U.S. Troop Carrier Command, had been in North Africa since the beginning of that campaign and some of the crews had dropped 1 Parachute Brigade in November, 1942. However, many crews had not had that experience and none had been properly trained with British troops. 52 Wing (Brigadier-General H. L. Clark), the other component of XII U.S. Troop Carrier Command, were fresh from the United States, where they had been training with 82 U.S. Airborne Division, which was also due to take part in the Mediterranean operations and had arrived in North Africa in April. On about 6th May it was decided that for the initial airborne landings in Sicily, 51 U.S. Wing (consisting of 60 and 62 Groups, each of about 52 Dakota aircraft), with the detachment of 38 Wing R.A.F. under command, would be allotted to 1 Airborne Division. Extra aircraft from 52 U.S. Wing, allotted initially to 82 Airborne Division, would be provided for subsequent operations by 1 Airborne Division. It was therefore necessary that both 51 and 52 Wings should be trained with British troops and equipped to drop them. The towing of gliders by these wings presented only comparatively minor difficulties, concerned mainly with co-operation with the British glider pilots, as only Hadrian Gliders would be towed by the Dakota aircraft.

8. Every effort was made to release 51 Wing from the heavy and continuous freight and general transport duties on which they were employed all over North Africa, so that they could train with 1 Airborne Division in the Mascara area. However, they were not really available to start combined training until early May. In the one moon period then and in the final rehearsals for the operations in Sicily they had to do air crew night training, night training of parachutists and night landings of gliders, and the time was not long enough for efficiency. The situation was further complicated by the fact that the aircraft of 51 Wing needed much overhaul after their heavy work of the past eight months. Engine hours were mounting up, and if the aircraft were used too much on training they would not be available for operations. This necessity to conserve engine hours · complicated and reduced all training programmes.

The Move to the Training Area of Mascara

9. 1 Airborne Division moved to North Africa in two main convoys from England. 2 Parachute Brigade arrived at Oran on 26th April and 1 Air-landing Brigade on 26th May, a proportion of divisional troops accompanying each brigade, and moved to their training area near Mascara. No. R.A.S.C. units could move with the first convoy as 250 Company was converting from a divisional composite company to a light company on a jeep basis, 253 Troop Carrying Company was converting to a divisional composite company and 93 Company only was allotted to 1 Airborne Division on about 10th April. 1 Parachute Brigade, having fought in the Tunisian campaign, rejoined

1 Airborne Division near Mascara on 10th May. Their need for airborne training and time to reorganize has been explained at the end of Chapter VIII. The whole Division was located in an area administered by Fifth U.S. Army, the nearest British bases being many hundreds of miles away with very poor intermediate communications. Although the Americans were most helpful, this separation from their normal supply and equipment resources greatly complicated the problem for the Division and caused many delays, particularly as regards R.A.O.C. and R.E.M.E. requirements.

10. There were several reasons for the choice of Mascara as the training area, instead of one much further east near the eventual operational bases. Security had to be preserved, and, from the enemy point of view, airborne troops located at Mascara might be intended for use anywhere from the western Mediterranean to Italy, but situated in eastern Tunisia they might indicate Sicily or Italy as the objective. In addition, Allied Force Headquarters had ordered the establishment of an airborne training centre at Oudja under Fifth Army in anticipation of co-ordinating both British and United States airborne training. In fact this co-ordination never materialized. The only other area offered was in a " hot belt " about 50 miles to the north where there were only three airfields spread over 30 miles. The Mascara area was suitable for camps and had four airfields fairly well concentrated. Other reasons were the crowding of Army and Air Force units in the whole area from Algiers to Sousse and the congestion of the ports. Therefore, it was decided to move to the operational bases near Sousse at the latest possible date.

11. The various senior headquarters with which planning had to be done were :—

(a) Allied Forces Headquarters at Algiers.

(b) Force 141, later 15 Army Group, under General Alexander at Algiers and then just outside Tunis.

(c) Eighth Army Planning Staff at Cairo for most of the time.

(d) Fifth U.S. Army at Oran.

(e) 13 Corps, who would be in direct command of 1 Airborne Division for the initial operations in Sicily, in Egypt.

(f) The equivalent Allied Naval and Air Headquarters in the same areas.

A glance at the map will show how impossible it would have been for one man to command his division and at the same time plan with all these headquarters.

12. Major-General Browning visited 4 Parachute Brigade, commanded by Brigadier J. W. Hackett, near Haifa, in Palestine, on 13th April. They had been training there for some time but had suffered from an even greater shortage of equipment and aircraft than 1 Airborne Division in England (see Chapter IX). It was decided to place them under command of 1 Airborne Division and they actually arrived at the airborne operational base near Sousse on 10th June. Thus the Division consisted temporarily of one air-landing and three parachute brigades.

13. As far as the airborne operations were concerned, high level planning in North Africa and Egypt for the invasion of Sicily started in March. There was, however, a radical change in the whole invasion plan at the beginning of May

and the proposed airborne operations had to be completely re-cast. Instead of a divisional airborne assault on the coast defences in close co-operation with the sea-borne troops, 1 Airborne Division was now required to carry out three successive brigade assaults against selected objectives ahead of the leading British troops, 13 Corps. There were not enough aircraft available for a divisional operation. The first of these assaults would be during the night preceding the sea-borne landings and the others on the two following nights subject to postponement according to circumstances. The fourth brigade would be held in reserve. 82 U.S. Airborne Division would also attack on the first two nights, practically the whole Division being landed then. Such aircraft as became spare after 82 U.S. Airborne Division's assault would be used to replace casualties amongst those originally available for 1 Airborne Division and to keep the number available at sufficient strength to lift approximately a brigade.

14. The objectives allotted in south-eastern Sicily to 1 Airborne Division were, in outline, the Ponte Grande (*see* Map 2) just south of Syracuse, the port of Augusta and a bridge nearby, and the Ponte di Primosole over the River Simeto, in that order. They are described in more detail later. 82 U.S. Airborne Division was given objectives to cover the landings of Fifth U.S. Army in south-western Sicily. Once these decisions had been made, detailed planning was passed as far as possible to the brigade commanders concerned and they or their representatives were put in touch with 13 Corps and 5 Division. However, as both these formations were in Egypt it was impossible for the brigades to maintain close liaison with them and much co-ordination had to be done by the Commander, 1 Airborne Division. 1 Airborne Division also controlled the sub-allotment of all aircraft and shared the control of the airborne base with XII U.S. Troop Carrier Command and 51 U.S. Wing. Major-General Browning arranged all plans with the Allied navies, including the routeing of the airborne aircraft so as to avoid the sea convoys, and also the overall plan with the Allied air forces. In addition, Group Captain Cooper was available to represent 38 Wing R.A.F. but it should be remembered that their squadrons were under the operational command of 51 U.S. Wing. Once the three planned operations were concluded, 1 Airborne Division would revert from command of 13 Corps to command of 15 Army Group.

15. Photographs and information regarding the enemy had to be collected from various sources many thousands of miles apart. Photographs and some information were provided by Force 141 (15 Army Group) at Algiers and Tunis, but most of the information was obtained from Eighth Army Staff in Cairo. Members of the intelligence staff of 1 Airborne Division were attached to each headquarters and the divisional mobile photographic enlargement unit was located near Tunis. In spite of the distances and the consequent delays, the information and photographs were provided efficiently and proved to be accurate and reliable in most cases.

16. While all this planning and preparation was going on, 1 Airborne Division was doing its training, collecting from many North African ports and dumps the equipment sent out by the War Office, setting up the operational base near Sousse and moving there itself. This was all done between the beginning of June and 9th July, when operations started.

Training, the Move to the Sousse Area and Administrative Problems

17. Much useful training was accomplished at Mascara and liaison with 51 U.S. Wing improved rapidly. 1 and 2 Parachute Brigades completed individual parachute training and managed some battalion and brigade exercises. Between 8th May and 30th June, 8,913 parachute jumps were done, and considering the conditions the accident rate was surprisingly low. Only two men were killed, 100 seriously injured and 200 sustained minor damage, such as a twisted ankle or knee. 1 Air-landing Brigade was given a surprising amount of glider experience in the time available and all brigades were soon fit for operations. However, XII U.S. Troop Carrier Command, the detachment of 38 Group R.A.F. and the British glider pilots, had less chance of becoming a cohesive and co-ordinated force in time and they suffered from the serious disadvantage that, owing to the lack of suitable landing zones in the coastal area of North Africa, they were unable to rehearse glider releases from a short distance off the coast. The aircraft pilots had little or no practice in the difficult art of judging distances under such circumstances. Sufficient British glider pilots were available and were considered good enough to provide the number of first pilots required for planned operations, but several second pilots had to be provided by XII U.S. Troop Carrier Command to make up numbers. Between 21st May and 13th June, the British glider pilots in North Africa completed 1,873 training flights, 510 of them by night, with and without live loads, making a total of 522 hours flying for 116 crews. An agreed combined Army–Air Force airborne base procedure was worked out and established by Headquarters 1 Airborne Division and 51 Wing. Though far less elaborate and complete than the Standard Operating Procedure (*see* Appendix F) drawn up early in 1944, it laid the foundation for future practice and worked well. On the Army side, the organization was under the control of Lieutenant-Colonel W. T. Campbell, then General Staff Officer 1st Grade (Air), 1 Airborne Division, with a make-shift staff drawn from the Division itself.

18. The move of 1 Airborne Division from Mascara to the vicinity of Kairouan, west of Sousse, was done by rail, road and air over a distance in a straight line of 600 miles. The move started on 19th June and ended on 5th July, training continuing except when units were actually *en route*. On 27th June about 1,200 men of 1 Air-landing Brigade were moved in five hours some 600 miles across desert and mountains, in 84 Hadrian gliders. Two of the gliders made forced landings and one suffered a fatal crash through structural failure but 81 arrived safely. Each tug aircraft had sufficient petrol to return to Mascara without refuelling. It is significant to note that none of the glider pilots had previously experienced more than one hour's continuous flight. More gliders were ferried subsequently and the number available at Kairouan for 1 Airborne Division rose to 140 Hadrians and 19 Horsas by 8th July. The remainder of 1 Airborne Division moved by rail, although the local railways were not in good condition, except for the vehicle parties which went by road and the average time taken was six days.

19. Amongst the administrative complications at the time, mention must be made of parachutes and parachute containers. No 1 Mobile Parachute Servicing Unit, R.A.F., had been attached to 1 Parachute Brigade during the Tunisian operations and moved to the Mascara area before 1 Airborne Division arrived there. It had with it some 2,000 serviceable parachutes and, although

capable, if necessary, of maintaining these parachutes without the use of buildings, it set up an establishment in a local cinema. No. 2 Mobile Parachute Servicing Unit joined it from England on about 1st May with further parachutes. During the period 8th May to 18th June, some 12,688 parachutes were used for dropping troops and containers, and, unsuccessfully, one donkey, and had been repacked. No. 3 Mobile Parachute Servicing Unit arrived later and moved straight to the operational base near Sousse. It had been estimated that these units were required on the scale of one for each parachute brigade and this proved to be correct, but the rate of packing could not exceed a maximum of about 250 parachutes a day each servicing unit.

20. Parachute containers, although R.A.F. stores, were held by units of 1 Airborne Division on a scale sufficient for one drop and a large divisional reserve was held under R.E.M.E. arrangements. They were held by the Army because they were so bulky that the R.A.F. organization could not manage them and because in any case some were required by the airborne units for use during normal ground training. As far as possible units were responsible for the maintenance of their own containers, but in fact there were a very large number of repairs and much maintenance that they could not do. No. 3 Light Aid Detachment R.E.M.E., 1 Airborne Division, were made responsible for such repairs and maintenance and were assisted by the divisional R.E.M.E. workshops. Work included painting the containers white (for recognition by night), modifying and maintaining newly devised lighting sets, repairing catches and buffers and many smaller jobs not possible in units. This was a very large commitment and strained the R.E.M.E. resources to an undesirable extent. The establishment of a separate small container maintenance unit for the Division was recommended as a result of this experience.

21. At the actual airborne base near Sousse and Kairouan, 51 U.S. Wing and the detachment of 38 Wing shared six airfields set up over a wide area in the open desert. Each airfield consisted of one broad dusty runway strip and very little else. There were, of course, no hangars and accommodation was in tents. 1 Airborne Division was located as centrally as possible to these airfields and their camps were hidden in the local olive groves. 82 U.S. Airborne Division and 52 U.S. Wing were around Kairouan, and Headquarters XII U.S. Troop Carrier Command was in Sousse itself. The work in preparing airfields and camps had been done for the most part by an Army organization known as Kairouan Area, set up after the German retreat from the neighbourhood about the beginning of April, and was remarkably successful. The whole airborne force was complete there by 8th July although the majority had arrived some days earlier.

22. Another complication was the fact that the Division was made responsible for the supply by air of Eighth Army should it be necessary. This involved a large dumping programme, the collection of quantities of containers and their move from Algiers to Kairouan, for which tank transporters were used. Later, just before "D" day there was a disastrous fire and fresh stores had to be rushed from Algiers. They arrived in time, to the great credit of the "Q" staff.

Final Planning for Operations in Sicily

23. For the first of the three brigade operations, the attack in the neighbourhood of Syracuse, both 4 Parachute Brigade and 1 Air-landing Brigade were warned as it was not at first certain that gliders could be used. The decision

to use 1 Air-landing Brigade was made about the middle of June, when it was confirmed that sufficient gliders and pilots would be available and adequate landing places had been found in the target area. It was considered that air-landing troops were more suitable than parachute troops for the tasks involved. The retention in reserve of 4 Parachute Brigade provided more flexibility at greater flying ranges for subsequent operations. It was hoped that by releasing their gliders out at sea the tug aircraft would avoid casualties. 2 Parachute Brigade was allotted to the Augusta operation and 1 Parachute Brigade to the Ponte di Primasole operation. All three would be withdrawn to the airborne base immediately they had completed their tasks, in readiness for further airborne operations. Main divisional headquarters and all troops not taking part in these operations would remain at the airborne base, while a small tactical divisional headquarters sailed with the sea convoys from Egypt. The airborne base itself would be prepared to move to Sicily at a later date, when the prior requirements of the Allied fighter and bomber units on the few airfields in that Island had been met.

24. The necessity for central planning and control of airborne operations by one staff is shown very clearly by the following facts. This centralization covers all stages except the detailed ground planning between the airborne formations and the ground forces with whom they will be working after they have landed.

(a) 1 Airborne Division was placed under command of Eighth Army and 82 U.S. Airborne Division under command of Seventh U.S. Army.

(b) The allotment of aircraft and gliders was decided by Allied Force Headquarters, Mediterranean Air Command and 15 Army Group. The allocation of wings and divisions and the detail of control and training was carried out by XII U.S. Troop Carrier Command under the direction of North-West Africa Air Forces (Lieutenant-General Carl Spaatz).

(c) Major-General Browning advised the higher commanders and co-ordinated inter-services requirements. The divisional commanders were given tasks and objectives after they had given their expert airborne advice to their Army commanders as to what could and could not be done for technical reasons.

(d) From then on, detailed planning as regards direct co-operation between airborne and ground forces with, or under whom, the former would be operating on landing, was carried out by divisions.

(e) Apart from this planning of the battle on the ground, all information, photographic cover, aircraft routeing, which intimately concerned the Navy as well as the Air Force, offensive air support, dropping of dummy parachutists, provision of stores and equipment, reconnaissance and setting up of training and airborne bases, was dealt with direct between Major-General Browning, in his capacity as Airborne Forces Adviser to 15 Army Group, and 1 Airborne Division. 82 U.S. Airborne Division, however, tended to do everything through the Headquarters, Seventh U.S. Army. The experience gained of working direct with a large headquarters which could not be expected to have expert airborne knowledge and which had little time to deal with many particular details, caused them to revise their opinion in time for the operations in Europe in 1944.

(*f*) The responsibility for sanctioning the launching of all airborne operations rested with the Air Commander-in-Chief or the senior air officer at the air headquarters controlling the air operations concerned. This was the only possible course, as airborne operations are air operations until the landings are made.

Operations by 1 Air-landing Brigade, near Syracuse

25. 13 Corps were due to assault the south-eastern coast of Sicily and advance northwards as fast as possible. They needed the ports of Syracuse and Augusta quickly, so that all their supplies and reinforcements would not have to be landed over open beaches and then moved over long land lines of communication. In addition they foresaw strong enemy opposition on the line of the River Simeto, guarding vital airfields not far to the north, near Catania, unless a crossing could be seized by a surprise attack before the enemy were ready. To achieve such a swift advance it was essential that they should not be delayed in defiles formed by bridges and they needed the resources of the two ports undamaged. In the case of the initial landings they also required some assistance to overcome the beach defences.

26. 1 Air-landing Brigade, Commanded by Brigadier P. H. W. Hicks, were given the following tasks :—

(*a*) The capture intact of the Ponte Grande over the double canal one mile south of Syracuse.

(*b*) Subsequently, the capture of the harbour of Syracuse and a portion of the town adjoining it.

(*c*) The destruction or capture of one coastal defence battery which could cover the sea-borne landings.

27. They had at their disposal a total of 109 Dakota aircraft from 60 and 62 Groups of XII U.S. Troop Carrier Command, with 28 Albemarle and seven Halifax aircraft from 296 and 295 squadrons of 38 Wing detachment, R.A.F. This provided a tug force for 136 Hadrian and eight Horsa Gliders, the latter being towed by seven Halifaxes and one Albemarle. The Hadrian payload was 3,700 pounds and the majority of loads were 14 men with one handcart. The Horsa payload was 6,900 pounds, 32 men being carried. The force was dispersed on six airfields and times of take-off were arranged to compensate for varying distances to the objectives and to allow for the varying speeds of the different types of aircraft. All flights were to be made individually and not in formation, but they were to form a continuous stream of aircraft on the same route and were designed to land all gliders within a period of 20 minutes between 2210 and 2230 hours. The route was *via* the south-east corner of Malta to Cape Passero, thence north along the East coast to the landing zones, keeping 3,000 yards out to sea to avoid anti-aircraft fire. The gliders would be released out at sea and would glide in while the tug aircraft returned on the same route. This release would require very accurate judgment by the aircraft pilots. Diversionary bombing attacks and dummy parachute dropping were arranged to confuse the enemy and disguise the true purpose of the airborne attack. British night fighter aircraft were to operate in the area to discourage enemy air action. Enemy anti-aircraft batteries were known to exist but on a very light scale compared with Western Europe. It was hoped that the tug

119

aircraft would avoid them altogether by remaining out over the sea, while the gliders made silent surprise approaches. Air/sea rescue arrangements were made by the Air Officer Commanding, Malta.

28. 1 Air-landing Brigade could not be at full strength for this operation as the air lift was not sufficient and units were reduced accordingly. Brigade Headquarters, 1st Battalion The Border Regiment (Lieutenant-Colonel R. G. Britten), 2nd Battalion The South Staffordshire Regiment (Lieutenant-Colonel W. D. H. McCardie), 9th Field Company, R.E. (Major Beazley), less one and a half sections and 181st Field Ambulance (Lieutenant-Colonel G. M. Warrack) took part. The total strength was 148 officers and 1,927 other ranks, including 1,550 infantry. In addition, there were two naval bombardment detachments to direct the naval supporting fire available, and a detachment of 4th Army Film and Photo Section. Practically no transport was taken except some handcarts and light motor cycles, as distances during operations on the ground would not be great. No Royal Artillery units, light or anti-tank, were taken, particularly as no enemy tanks of any size were expected to be in the area before 13 Corps arrived and the infantry battalions had their own 6-pounder anti-tank guns available, a total of six, with jeeps, being taken.

29. 13 Corps were due to make their sea-borne assault landings two hours before nautical twilight on 10th July and they expected to reach the Ponte Grande about 1000 hours or earlier that day. 1 Air-landing Brigade were to attack the previous night, 9/10th July, their operations being planned in three phases :—

> *Phase one*, the capture of the Ponte Grande at 2315 hours 9th July by two companies of 2nd Battalion South Staffordshires to be landed in eight Horsas in the immediate vicinity.

> *Phase two*, the landing of the main force and its advance to the bridge by 0115 hours, 10th July, except for one company to deal with the coastal defence battery *en route*.

> *Phase three*, 2nd Battalion South Staffordshires to hold the bridge while 1st Battalion The Border Regiment passed through at 0145 hours to capture Syracuse by 0530 hours 10th July.

80 Wellington Aircraft were to bomb Syracuse at 0200 hours, 10th July, to coincide with the advance of 1st Battalion The Border Regiment. In the event, this bombing was highly effective and was an excellent direction indicator for the crews of scattered and lost gliders.

In addition to the normal communications within the brigade, direct wireless links were arranged to the airborne base, tactical divisional headquarters (temporarily with 13 Corps), 13 Corps Headquarters and 17 Infantry Brigade who were the leading ground troops.

30. Approximately two hours before take-off, the latest weather forecast from Malta gave an estimated 30 or 35 miles an hour off shore wind blowing in the target area. This was some 15 or 20 miles an hour stronger than had been anticipated. After a hasty conference between the commanding officer of the glider pilots, Lieutenant-Colonel Chatterton, and Brigadier-General Dunn, it was decided that the selected point for releasing the gliders 3,000 yards off the coast should remain the same. However, the heights of release were to be increased to between 1,400 and 1,800 feet for Hadrians and 4,000 feet for Horsas.

This information was passed on immediately to all airstrips. The start from the base airfields was good, although of the 444 gliders seven failed to leave the mainland of Africa. The actual take-off in daylight between 1848 hours and 2012 hours on 9th July was most impressive in its speed and efficiency, in spite of the thick clouds of dust which often completely blinded the pilots. Several glider pilots could not see their tug aircraft until they were well off the ground but, as expected, the moon was bright and clear and lights on Malta provided a valuable check-point. Unfortunately, however, the strong opposing wind that had sprung up shortly before take-off lasted all the way to the landing zone. Conditions were very bumpy and unpleasant. Many of the telephone communications between tugs and gliders broke and some of the wing-tip lights of the tugs failed and made it difficult for the gliders to keep position. The Hadrians had no blind flying instruments. An unusual mist or haze over some of the landing zones made it difficult for the glider pilots to recognize them after release in spite of the bright moonlight.

31. These weather conditions, combined with the inexperience of the tug pilots in judging distance off a coastline and the lack of operational experience of some of the American pilots against anti-aircraft fire, had the most unfortunate results. The difficulty of following the route selected was also emphasized by some pilots but opinions on this point varied. There is little doubt that the use of navigational aids to find the actual landing zones and to mark the point where the gliders should have been released, even at the loss of some degree of secrecy, would have been of great value. This might have been done by stationary submarines on the route. 75 Hadrians and three Horsas landed in the sea, the remaining 61 Hadrians being scattered over a distance of some 25 miles along the coast from Cape Passero to Cape Murro di Porco, though the majority were within five miles of the landing-zone. One Horsa only reached the correct landing zone, making a perfect landing about 300 yards from the bridge, although two more Horsas exploded nearby in the air as the result of anti-aircraft fire. The majority of the glider landings on Sicily were made in very rough country but few of the passengers were hurt. The glider pilots were not so lucky, several being killed or having their legs broken owing to the noses of the Hadrians hitting obstacles such as walls. The total number of 6-pounder anti-tank guns available for action were three out of six and there were four jeeps effective out of nine. Unfortunately, guns and jeeps were separated.

32. The ground operations of 1 Air-landing Brigade obviously could not go according to plan, but much was done. The Ponte Grande was captured intact by 2300 hours by Lieutenant L. Withers and 15 Platoon, 2nd Battalion South Staffordshires, landing in the one Horsa already mentioned and killing or capturing the Italian garrison. Reinforcements of Lieutenant Welch and seven other ranks of the brigade headquarters defence platoon arrived at 0430 hours and about the same time a counter-attack by three Italian armoured cars was beaten off easily. At 0500 hours Lieutenant-Colonel A. G. Walch, and Major Beazley, R.E., also arrived with a very mixed party of about 30 other ranks. Lieutenant-Colonel Walch, took command of the whole force and Major Beazley completed the removal of all demolition charges on the bridge. At 0630 hours the party at the bridge was further increased to about seven officers and 80 other ranks by the arrival of Lieutenants Deucher and Reynolds with another small mixed force. Most of these parties had moved

some four or five miles through the enemy defences at night, generally avoiding battle *en route* as much as possible so as to reach the main objectives. This was made easier by the reluctance of the Italian troops to leave their pill boxes and trenches. The miscellaneous British force had no serviceable wireless sets with them and apart from rifles and Stens they had only one 3-inch mortar, with six rounds of ammunition, four Bren light machine-guns, two 2-inch mortars, with a few rounds of smoke only, and one anti-tank bomb. There was little enemy activity until 0800 hours, when heavy and accurate mortar and machine-gun fire began. The Italians held the dominating ground all round the bridge and had several posts within 400 yards of it. From 1000 hours to 1200 hours the enemy fire increased, field guns being brought into action as well. From 1200 hours onwards the enemy attacked with infantry estimated at about one battalion. At 1530 hours they overran the few survivors, who by that time had practically exhausted their ammunition, though Lieutenant Welch and seven other ranks managed to escape by hiding under a small culvert nearby. There were no signs of the arrival of 13 Corps and nothing was known of their movements or of those of the remainder of 1 Air-landing Brigade. Nor, as communications were non-existent, did anyone in these formations know that the bridge had been captured and held. As it happened, 2nd Battalion Royal Scots Fusiliers of 17 Infantry Brigade reached the vicinity of the bridge at about 1615 hours and recaptured it half an hour later still in good enough condition to carry all transport. Lieutenant-Colonel Walch and others of his party who were taken prisoner, escaped at 1700 hours with the assistance of a patrol of 17 Infantry Brigade and returned that evening to resume the defence of the bridge.

33. In the meantime the other parties of 1 Air-landing Brigade who reached Sicily took violent offensive action wherever they happened to be and caused the utmost confusion amongst the Italian defenders. The coastal battery which had been one of the brigade's objectives was captured after daylight by a force of seven officers and about ten other ranks from two Hadrians. Six Italians were killed, six wounded and 40 taken prisoner, while the five field guns were destroyed and the ammunition blown up. This British force included Colonel O. L. Jones, Deputy Brigade Commander, Lieutenant-Colonel M. C. A. Henniker, Commander, Royal Engineers, Major R. Tomkins, Deputy Assistant Adjutant and Quartermaster General, Captain D. G. Clarke, Brigade R.A.S.C. Officer, Captain R. S. Roberson, Brigade Signal Officer, The Reverend D. F. Hourigan, Lieutenant Budgeon, 1st Battalion, The Border Regiment and other ranks from brigade headquarters, The Glider Pilot Regiment and 1st Battalion The Border Regiment.

34. Another example of initiative and determination was the action of one Hadrian Glider load of 2nd Battalion, South Staffordshire Regiment. Their glider landed in the sea 250 yards from the shore. One man was drowned and one killed by machine-gun fire from the land. The remaining ten reached the shore safely though still being fired on while swimming. Four were exhausted and remained where they landed till daybreak, but four officers and two other ranks moved off to rejoin their battalion. This involved a crawl through 20 feet of barbed wire, covered by a pill box only 100 yards away. Eventually, during the evening of 10th July, after marching 10 miles and picking up three more other ranks *en route*, the party did rejoin their battalion. By then they had captured two pill boxes, 21 Italians, three machine-guns and an anti-tank gun.

35. Other small parties attacked the Italians over a very wide area to such an extent that the enemy reported a landing by at least a corps of airborne troops on a front of 25 miles. Their action materially assisted the sea-borne landings, which were practically unopposed.

36. The medical arrangements for the airborne troops were based on local medical and surgical treatment by advanced dressing stations of 181st Air-landing Field Ambulance R.A.M.C. and the normal regimental arrangements. All evacuation and hospital arrangements were the responsibility of the relieving ground formations, assisted by Colonel A. A. Eagger, Assistant Director of Medical Services, 1 Airborne Division. This system was the only practical one under the circumstances and worked well. It became the normal system for airborne operations, though the resources of the airborne R.A.M.C. units are not great.

37. The total casualties in 1 Air-landing Brigade were, however, high. Approximately, they were :—

Killed in action on land	61
Wounded	133
Missing	44
Drowned	252
Total	490

Original reports of over 500 probably drowned were reduced, as many survivors clinging to floating gliders were rescued by passing ships and subsequently landed all over the Mediterranean seaboard. Less than half the original forces had been able to take part in the land battle.

38. The brigade had, however, achieved its main objects as the Ponte Grande was not destroyed, 13 Corps were not delayed there, and the coastal defence battery was put out of action. General Montgomery and Lieutenant-General Dempsey, commanding 13 Corps, were very satisfied with the assistance given to their main forces.

39. The casualties of the Glider Pilot Regiment were :—

	Officers	Other Ranks
Killed ..	3	11
Wounded	4	25
Missing ..	6	52
Total	13	88

40. Three important structural defects of the Hadrian were, however, demonstrated. They were first, a weakness in the floor resulting in such loads as 6-pounder anti-tank guns and jeeps being inextricably mixed with broken floors when landing on poor surfaces ; second, a weakness in the attachment loads to strong points in the glider, resulting in heavy loads breaking loose or shifting in flight and on landings ; and third, insufficient strength in the nose to protect the glider pilots during heavy landings. In addition, it was evident that a more reliable intercommunication system between tug aircraft and glider was required. All these faults were taken in hand immediately by XII U.S. Troop Carrier Command, and Hadrians used in subsequent operations were much more satisfactory. The Horsa Glider had done all that was required of it and carried a better tactical load.

41. As regards the aircraft, which suffered no casualties and which were all available for any further operations required the next night, the Dakotas and Albemarles had proved their ability to tow fully loaded single Hadrians a distance of 400 miles against a strong wind and return to base without refuelling *en route*. The Halifaxes had given every satisfaction. One Albemarle, with a very expert crew, had towed a fully-loaded Horsa rather more than 400 miles and returned to base, but the margin was too narrow to be acceptable in normal operational conditions.

42. There is no reliable information to show how effective was the dropping of parachute dummies, though they must have added to the general confusion amongst the enemy. A total of 620 dummies were dropped as a diversion near Catania at 2140 hours on 9th July, 16 Boston aircraft of 326 Wing R.A.F. and 3 Wing South African Air Force being used. Bombing in support of the ground actions of 1 Air-landing Brigade was not sufficiently heavy to influence the battle appreciably, but 70 aircraft of 205 Bomber Group R.A.F. attacked the targets given them. Although 205 Bomber Group was in fact most co-operative with the planning staff of 1 Airborne Division, it did not receive any official instructions through Air Force channels regarding its tasks until the morning of 9th July and 1 Air-landing Brigade were in doubt until then regarding the assistance they might expect. The gliders carrying two Naval bombardment units, designed to direct fire from warships on to targets required by 1 Air-landing Brigade, went astray and thus no naval gun support was available.

43. 1 Air-landing Brigade, having reorganized its scattered forces, took over the defence of Syracuse during the morning of 11th July from 17 Infantry Brigade, which had captured the town and harbour intact the previous night. 1 Air-landing Brigade was then about 800 strong. At 2000 hours on 13th July they embarked at Syracuse in four landing craft and arrived at Sousse at 2100 hours on 14th July, *en route* for the airborne base. During the next few weeks, survivors from gliders which had landed in the sea continued to rejoin the brigade from ports all along the Mediterranean coast, but it was some time before it was once more made up to strength.

Cancelled Operations of 2 Parachute Brigade

44. As mentioned previously, 2 Parachute Brigade had been allotted the task of capturing an important road bridge south-west of Augusta and subsequently operating to capture the harbour and town. They were to land from 102 parachute aircraft, 12 Hadrian and six Horsa Gliders. The Horsa Gliders would carry six 6-pounder anti-tank guns and jeeps of 2nd Air-landing Anti-Tank Battery. These rather unexpectedly large numbers of aircraft and gliders had been made possible by the fact that there had been no casualties to aircraft during 1 Air-landing Brigade's operations.

45. 2 Parachute Brigade loaded their containers on to the parachute aircraft at 1100 hours on 10th July. The gliders, except those allotted with the extra aircraft, had been loaded the day before. Troops then rested near the air strips, ready for emplaning. Take-off for the operation was timed for 1845 hours on 10th July, provided a confirmatory executive order was received at Airborne base from 13 Corps by 1800 hours. In fact no message was received until 1945 hours, when a postponement of the operation for 24 hours was ordered.

2 Parachute Brigade left their aircraft and gliders loaded and stood by again on 11th July. The operation was, however, finally cancelled at 1707 hours that day, as 13 Corps were able to secure the objectives themselves and Eighth Army wished to hold the airborne troops in reserve for vital opportunity tasks that might occur later.

46. It was a disappointment for 2 Parachute Brigade, who had not so far been in action, but it provided valuable experience for the staff at the airborne base and enabled a check to be made of the signal arrangements to Sicily and Malta. However, the disappointment turned to thankfulness later when an examination of the ground was possible. The areas that had been chosen from maps and photographs were quite unsuitable as they were covered with rocks and stones and seamed with steep-sided gullies.

Operations of 1 Parachute Brigade near Catania

47. With the cancellation of the Augusta operation, 2 Parachute Brigade unloaded their equipment and 1 Parachute Brigade stood by instead. By the afternoon of 12th July, they had loaded all equipment and gliders and were ready to carry out their previously planned operation to capture the bridge over the River Simeto on the main road from Augusta to Catania. At 1745 hours that day, however, a message was received from 13 Corps postponing the operation for 24 hours. It had always been realized, of course, that the actual date of the operation would be governed, subject to the weather, solely by the speed of 13 Corps' advance. However, this particular bridge was a vital defile and only exceptional circumstances would render an airborne operation unnecessary. By this time 82 U.S. Airborne Division did not require so many aircraft for their operations, so some of the aircraft of 64 Group, XII U.S. Carrier Command, were available to strengthen 51 U.S. Wing. On 13th July, 1 Parachute Brigade had at their disposal 116 parachute aircraft, eight Hadrians and eleven Horsa Gliders. Four of the Horsas, at full payload of 6,900 pounds, but having jettisoned their undercarriage after take-off, were towed by Albemarles of 296 Squadron R.A.F. The troops taking part were 1 Parachute Brigade under Brigadier G. W. Lathbury consisting of 1st Parachute Battalion, 2nd Parachute Battalion, 3rd Parachute Battalion, 1st Air-landing Anti-Tank Battery, R.A. less one Troop, 1st Parachute Squadron R.E., less one Troop, and 16th Parachute Field Ambulance. There were also detachments from 21st Independent Parachute Company and 4th Army Film and Photo Section, two parachute naval bombardment units, for control of naval gun support, a forward observation officer from 1st Air-landing light Regiment, R.A., for liaison with the artillery of 13 Corps as they advanced, and the glider pilots. The total force was some 1,900 all ranks.

48. The route of about 400 miles from the airborne base was to a rendezvous point over the Kuriate Islands east of Sousse, thence to the south-east corner of Malta and up round the south-east corner of Sicily past Syracuse and Augusta keeping at least five miles off shore, to the mouth of the River Simeto and inland about three miles to the bridge. The return route for the aircraft was similar but slightly south and east. The approach flight was to be at 500 feet and the return at from a 1,000 to 3,000 feet. Both routes had been cleared with the Naval Force as avoiding their danger zones, and warning had been given to all ships that friendly aircraft would be using these routes at stated times. This was

125

stressed particularly as parachute aircraft carrying troops of 82 U.S. Airborne Division had been fired on by the Allied Naval Forces in operations south of Sicily and casualties had resulted. Four parachute dropping zones and two glider landing zones had been selected west of the main road in the area of the bridge, within a radius of about two and a half miles. The two nearest dropping zones were each about one mile from the bridge, north and south of the river. Dropping was to begin at 2220 hours, after a flight of about three and a half hours and the first gliders would land at 0100 hours, being guided in by lights of the detachment of 21st Independent Parachute Company.

49. In the few days before the operation took place, information was received that the enemy anti-aircraft defences in the target area had been increased considerably but the risk was considered acceptable in view of the importance of the objective. However, no aircraft could be spared for diversionary bombing and preliminary bombing near the bridge might have forfeited surprise for the airborne assault. The result was that no appreciable action was taken to neutralize the enemy anti-aircraft defences and in fact no definite bomber or fighter support was organized to assist the ground operations. Liaison between the Army and Air Force formations concerned at all levels was not well organized at this period and the importance of air support for airborne forces, whereby to some extent the Air Force can replace the artillery support normally lacking to airborne troops, was not fully realized.

50. The plan of 1 Parachute Brigade was that 1st Parachute Battalion was to capture the Ponte di Primosole itself, while 2nd and 3rd Parachute Battalions held the approaches from the south and north respectively. Of the anti-tank guns, to be landed in the gliders after the bridge had been seized, six would be allotted to 3rd Parachute Battalion, four to 2nd Parachute Battalion and two to brigade headquarters in reserve. It was expected that the leading troops of 13 Corps, advancing up the main road, would make contact with 1 Parachute Brigade that morning. This was important, as considerable enemy opposition was expected and German as well as Italian units were known to be in the area, with some armour.

51. The confirming order for the operation to take place that night was received at the airborne base at 1540 hours on 13th July, *via* tactical divisional headquarters then with 13 Corps. The first parachute aircraft took off at 1901 hours and the first glider at 2143 hours. One hundred and thirteen parachute aircraft and 16 gliders with their tugs left the African mainland for Sicily, three parachute aircraft and three gliders having returned for various technical reasons soon after take-off. The weather was clear and favourable, with a light wind of some 14 miles an hour.

52. The first trouble to be met was anti-aircraft fire from the Allied Naval Forces, 55 of the aircraft pilots reporting that they had been fired on when approaching the coast of Sicily and when following its contours up to ten miles out at sea. There is no doubt, however, that some at least of these aircraft were actually within the five mile danger zone and they all experienced great difficulty in judging their distance from the coast. A considerable amount of damage was done to the aircraft, some being forced to return to base before reaching the dropping zones, and the taking of evasive action caused others to lose their way and arrive late. It seems that a bombing attack by the enemy

at about the same time, combined with the serious difficulty of quick aircraft recognition in moonlight, caused the Allied Naval Forces to take no chances and fire at all aircraft which were not immediately obvious as friendly. This experience emphasized the necessity for accurate navigation by the aircraft, the setting of a route which must be very easy to follow, an even wider allowance for mistakes, and a really efficient recognition system in emergency.

53. On turning inland to the dropping and landing zones, pilots again reported considerable anti-aircraft fire and many searchlights, this time from the enemy. It should be remembered that the Dakota aircraft was not then designed to meet these dangers as they were unarmed, unarmoured and their petrol tanks were not self-sealing. Many Dakota pilots in particular, therefore, were forced to take evasive action near and over the dropping zones and the consequent violent movements of the aircraft made it very difficult for the parachute troops to jump out. In many cases the latter were being thrown about inside the aircraft, some were wounded, and some were prevented from jumping owing to the chaos between them and the door through which they had to pass. For the same reasons, a considerable number of parachute containers were not released. The final result was that only 39 parachute aircraft dropped their troops on or within half a mile of their dropping zones, 48 more dropped them over half-a-mile away and 17 returned to base with some troops still on board. A further 12 were unable to reach or find their dropping zones at all. A total of 11 parachute aircraft were shot down, eight of them after dropping their troops and many more were badly damaged. Of the gliders, four Horsas landed successfully on their landing zones, three Horsas and four Hadrians landed successfully but away from their landing zones, two Horsas and four Hadrians crashed on landing, two Horsas and one Hadrian were lost at sea. Of the tug aircraft, all provided by 295 and 296 Squadrons, R.A.F., two, both towing Horsas, were lost.

54. Very few of the parachute aircraft dropped according to planned timings and the arrival of the troops in the battle area was spread between 2205 hours and 2340 hours, except for those in two aircraft which dropped at 0150 hours after failing to locate the dropping zones at their first attempts. Less than 20 per cent of 1 Parachute Brigade were dropped according to plan and nearly 30 per cent, through no fault of their own, returned to base without dropping. Twelve officers and 283 other ranks, out of a total of 1,856 all ranks who left North Africa, were available for the battle for which they were intended. They collected 147 out of the 428 parachute containers which started. The detachment of 21st Independent Company which dropped with the brigade put out landing aids for the glider element, but they were of little value, as the glider pilots could not distinguish the lights from the fires.

55. As in the case of 1 Air-landing Brigade outside Syracuse, the ground operations of 1 Parachute Brigade could not proceed according to plan. In this case, however, they were able to keep to the main programme so far as the capture of the bridge was concerned, though there was no central control of the battle until much later than intended. The account of the operations may be divided conveniently into two parts, the first dealing with the action up to the establishment of brigade headquarters on the south bank of the river at 0615 hours on 14th July and the second with subsequent developments.

56. In the first phase about 170 all ranks of 2nd Parachute Battalion collected at the battalion rendezvous near their dropping zone by 2240 hours on 13th July. At 0215 hours, having failed to find any more of their men as they were expected to be in their positions holding the southern approaches to the bridge by 0400 hours, the battalion moved off to its forming up position to attack the enemy. Soon after 0330 hours their leading platoon captured their first objective, and by 0500 hours the battalion held all the positions allotted to them and the high ground about 1,300 yards south of the bridge was firmly in their hands. Enemy opposition had been overcome without much difficulty and 100 prisoners had been taken, but the battalion had no heavy weapons and no wireless sets for communication with other units.

57. In the meantime the leading party of 1st Parachute Battalion had been dropped at 2230 hours, ten minutes late. By 0215 hours Captain Rann and 50 men of the battalion, the total strength then available, had attacked and captured the bridge without much difficulty from the north, taking some 50 Italian prisoners. By 0400 hours the bridge positions had been consolidated and the strength of 1st Parachute Battalion had risen to about 120 all ranks. The bridge demolition fuzes were cut and the charges thrown into the river by one officer and nine other ranks of 1st Parachute Squadron, R.E. By 0630 hours three 6-pounder guns of 1st Air-landing Anti-Tank Battery were in position, as well as one captured Italian anti-tank gun. Other weapons available besides personal weapons, were two 3-inch mortars, one Vickers machine gun and three P.I.A.Ts., but no wireless sets had arrived. The defensive perimeter included some buildings about 500 yards north of the bridge.

58. 3rd Parachute Battalion, whose task was to capture and hold the northern approaches to the bridge, had been dropped most unsuccessfully of all. One officer and three other ranks, having been dropped on the wrong dropping zone, joined 1st Parachute Battalion near the bridge about 0130 hours. By 0400 hours the battalion strength had grown to about two platoons, who were with 1st Parachute Battalion at the bridge. It was quite impossible for them to attempt their task to the north.

59. Brigadier Lathbury dropped amongst enemy positions at 2332 hours, but by 0315 hours he, the brigade major and part of brigade headquarters arrived at the southern end of the bridge. To discover whether the bridge was held, Brigadier Lathbury went forward to reconnoitre and was wounded by a grenade thrown by a stray Italian. By 0630 hours brigade headquarters was established on the south bank of the river but, although one No. 22 wireless set was available and in working order, they could not get communication with any of the relieving ground troops who still did not know whether the bridge had been captured. Lieutenant-Colonel Wheatley and some of 16th Parachute Field Ambulance established a main dressing station south of the river in 2nd Parachute Battalion's area.

60. Thus the general situation on the early morning of 14th July was that the bridge was held and the demolition charges had been removed, the southern approaches were held, the northern approaches were wide open to attack. A much reduced 1 Parachute Brigade, with very few heavy weapons and remarkably poor communications, had achieved its object but was not in a good position to resist strong enemy counter-attack. The expected early relief by the advancing ground formations was essential.

61. At 0630 hours on 14th July, German parachute troops, supported by machine guns and mortars, counter-attacked 2nd Parachute Battalion from the west. At 0700 hours the forward observation officer from 1st Air-landing Light Regiment R.A. (Captain V. Hodge) arrived and started to open communications with a British 6-inch gun cruiser lying off shore in support. By 0900 hours 2nd Parachute Battalion were in difficulties as their light weapons could not reply to the longer range weapons of the enemy and it was very hard to dig cover in the rocky ground. By 1000 hours, however, the cruiser had opened accurate fire and the enemy, closing in, were forced to withdraw. Light enemy howitzers found in 2nd Parachute Battalion's position, were also now used against the Germans north of the bridge, although the situation there was still fairly quiet and only enemy patrols had advanced. At 0930 hours the brigade major, by searching all wavelengths had accidentally contacted 4 Armoured Brigade of 13 Corps. He received the information that relief was not yet possible, but by 1000 hours, 4 Armoured Brigade told him that his information regarding the bridge being held intact had been passed to 13 Corps. Wireless contact was then lost and never regained.

62. Preceded by shelling and an attack by two fighter aircraft, the enemy counter-attack against the bridge from the north developed at 1310 hours. Infantry advanced astride the road under cover of smoke and with close support from their fighter aircraft. The attack was met by 3rd Parachute Battalion, now five officers and 35 other ranks strong, and by 1500 hours they had held two attacks by Germans and Italians amounting to about company strength. By 1530 hours, however, the enemy strength had grown to about one battalion, with considerably more supporting weapons, and the bridge itself was also under direct gunfire. At 1705 hours, under heavy enemy pressure, all troops of 3rd and 1st Parachute Battalions were withdrawn to the southern bank of the river, but, although decreasing ammunition supplies prevented heavy fire being maintained against the enemy, the latter were still prevented from reaching the bridge itself.

63. Realizing that he could make no more progress frontally, the enemy kept up a heavy fire while crossing the river further to the east. By 1845 hours the situation at the bridge became untenable as the British position was exposed owing to the burning of cover provided by reeds and cornfields and the enemy was firing heavily from north, east and south. There was still no sign of relief and communications with 2nd Parachute Battalion were cut. At 1935 hours orders were given for the whole force to withdraw south in small parties under cover of darkness and join up with 2nd Parachute Battalion if possible. This was done and Brigadier Lathbury contacted Lieutenant-Colonel Frost, in his position at 0600 hours on 15th July.

64. While the battle was being fought at the bridge, the enemy had kept up continuous pressure against 2nd Parachute Battalion but without dislodging them. Fighting was hard but the battalion held its own, although it could not spare any reinforcements for the bridge even if they could have got there. They took over 100 Italian prisoners. The shelling of the cruiser in support was a very valuable aid and the forward observation officer was able to direct fire against the enemy attacking the bridge. At 1945 hours on 14th July, the first tanks of 4 Armoured Brigade arrived in 2nd Parachute Battalion's area and at 2359 hours more tanks and the infantry arrived. One company of 9th Battalion, Durham Light Infantry joined 2nd Parachute Battalion in their position.

65. At 0600 hours on 15th July, Brigadier Lathbury met the Commander, 4 Armoured Brigade and explained the position. At 0915 hours he was admitted to the Main Dressing Station for an operation and command of 1 Parachute Brigade was taken over by Lieutenant-Colonel Frost. Meanwhile, at 0800 hours, 9th Battalion, Durham Light Infantry, supported by tanks and field guns, made an unsuccessful and costly attack on the bridge, being held between there and 2nd Parachute Battalion's position 1,200 yards to the south. Artillery duels continued throughout the day and at 2359 hours the Durham Light Infantry withdrew and relieved 1 Parachute Brigade on the positions of 2nd Parachute Battalion. After further artillery preparation during the night, the Durham Light Infantry, supported by tanks and guided by Lieutenant-Colonel Pearson crossed the river at 0600 hours and recaptured the bridge in good condition. At 0700 hours the same day 1 Parachute Brigade left by motor transport for Syracuse where they embarked at 1600 hours. By 0700 hours on 19th July the had arrived back at Sousse, *en route* for the airborne base.

66. Casualties amongst the 12 officers and 280 other ranks of 1 Parachute Brigade who took part in the ground battle for the bridge were :—

Killed	27
Wounded	78
Missing	10

The medical arrangements were based on the same principles as at Syracuse though the advanced dressing station intended to be set up north of the bridge never arrived and the main dressing station dealt with all casualties direct from units. One hundred and nine wounded personnel were treated during the operations, including 38 enemy who were admitted, 92 were evacuated through 13 Corps ; ten returned to unit ; seven died. Thirty-five surgical operations were performed in 21 operating hours by two officers.

67. Once again the airborne troops had captured their objective in spite of all handicaps and had held it for longer than the time stipulated in the plans. There is no doubt, too, that in this case the bridge was finally captured in working order only because 1 Parachute Brigade had removed the charges and held the vital high ground dominating it from the south.

Lessons of 1 Parachute Brigade's Operations

68. In addition to these points which have appeared in the narrative, 1 Airborne Division reported several other lessons which had been brought out. It would have been better to have accepted fewer dropping zones, with the consequent crowding as a greater concentration of troops on the ground would have been ensured and the aircraft navigational problems would have been easier. They considered that if at all possible, a previously rehearsed plan for ground operations should be adhered to, so that even if major accidents were to occur everyone would know what to do and stragglers could rejoin units. They found that night operations were not welcomed by the enemy and little effective counter-action was taken until after daylight. A good knowledge amongst all ranks of the enemy weapons likely to be used against them was of value as there were many examples of Italian guns, mortars and machine-guns so used. The care, use and evacuation of the many prisoners taken was a problem.

69. As regards supply by air for 1 Parachute Brigade, arrangements were made for this to be done on receipt of a request by wireless to the airborne base. No wireless link was, however, established as the sets were missing or damaged. It would have been more prudent to have arranged for at least one automatic supply drop unless cancelled by wireless, as then 1 Parachute Brigade would have been temporarily independent of maintenance through delayed ground formations. This was subsequently established as a rule for all airborne operations.

70. Again, as in the case of 1 Air-landing Brigade at Syracuse, no definite arrangements were made for tactical reconnaissance aircraft to establish liaison closely with the airborne troops and report their activities and requirements. Normal fighter aircraft were not an efficient substitute for such tactical ground reconnaissance and they did not see the yellow recognition flares used by 1 Parachute Brigade.

71. The value of good medical attention in the forward areas was again proved and the airborne medical equipment was again found to be most satisfactory. Evacuation by 13 Corps, assisted by Colonel Eagger, when the relief was complete, worked well.

72. There were, however, two lessons which were outstanding and which had already been emphasized by the experience of 1 Air-landing Brigade. They were, first, the requirement that the Air Forces must be able to land a substantial proportion of the airborne forces at the right place and the right time and that this was an Air Force responsibility having priority over all else. This would have been assisted materially if a pathfinder force had been dropped ahead of the main body to put out navigational aids even at the expense of secrecy. Second, the requirement that the Air Force transporting airborne troops must be trained to a fully operational standard and must work intimately and as a team with the troops they are carrying. The satisfaction of both requirements could be achieved only by combined training and the simultaneous preparation of Army and Air Force plans at all levels.

Subsequent Operations in Italy

73. The Catania operations were the last airborne operations carried out by 1 Airborne Division in the Mediterranean. The whole Division was reconcentrated at the airborne base in North Africa by 30th July, though it took some time to obtain from England the numerous reinforcements required to bring 1 Air-landing Brigade and 1 Parachute Brigade up to strength, as reserve personnel in the theatre were insufficient. That, however, was not the reason why they ceased temporarily to be airborne.

74. It will be appreciated that the airfields available to the Allies in Sicily and, later on, in southern Italy were few and that most of them were poorly developed for medium and heavy aircraft. As it was essential that the armies should have fighter and bomber support in all their battles, and as the range of fighters and many bombers was very limited, the transport aircraft had to take second priority in the allotment of these airfields. Thus, in the main, the airborne base could not move forward until the fighters and bombers no longer required all the advanced airfields. Furthermore, the shipping resources were limited and there was considerable congestion of space in Sicily for all the

army formations involved in the campaign. In these circumstances the American and the British adopted two different methods. 82 U.S. Airborne Division had employed from the beginning the greater part of the parachute assault troops of the Division in their airborne operations against Sicily and all those troops remained in Sicily. The remainder of the Division, including most of its administrative and air-landing troops, were shipped to Sicily to join them at an early date. The Division was then assigned the ground duties of a normal Division until such time as the airborne base could move forward from North Africa. This was made easier because the Americans suffered from no shortage of reinforcements or reserve equipment and they could afford to risk their specialist troops for normal duties. 1 Airborne Division, on the other hand, were held back until more airborne operations became possible and would only be used for normal ground operations in emergency. The result in this case was that when the airborne base and the " airborne aircraft " could move forward, 82 U.S. Airborne Division was ready and available, while 1 Airborne Division was left behind. This was one good reason why troops of 82 U.S. Airborne Division alone were used in parachute operations in the Salerno beachhead in Southern Italy. It was also a discouraging factor in the contemplation of various airborne assaults, all abortive, planned in the area of north-east Sicily, and south-west Italy. Another effect of holding 1 Airborne Division back in North Africa was that divisional headquarters and headquarters, Eighth Army, were completely out of touch with each other. In order to mitigate this as far as possible the Division sent a staff officer and a wireless set to Sicily to act as a link with Eighth Army.

75. Realizing these circumstances, and being in urgent need of light troops who could be carried mainly in naval warships, General Alexander issued orders that 1 Airborne Division would capture the port of Taranto, in south-east Italy, and exploit to the north, on the eastern flank of his main advance. The advance of the main armies were proceeding swiftly in the south-west " toe " of Italy, but they had far to go. In the meantime it was known that German reinforcements were moving down from the far north and it was necessary to forestall them as far north as possible. All ports, particularly a good one such as Taranto, were important and the enemy must be harried wherever he could be reached.

76. On 4th September, Major-General Hopkinson was in Sicily where he had to see General Alexander about future airborne operations. While he was at Headquarters, 15 Army Group, he met the Italian plenipotentiaries and was told that 1 Airborne Division was to embark in 1st Cruiser Squadron at Bizerta on or about 11th September for Taranto. However, Admiral Cunningham (later Admiral of the Fleet, The Viscount Cunningham), Commander-in-Chief Mediterranean, stated that the Taranto units of the Italian Fleet must be safely in British ports before he would order 1st Cruiser Squadron to sail, which would delay sailing and so Major-General Hopkinson returned to the airborne base that night. On 7th September, he went to Bizerta where he was told that plans had been changed and that 1st Cruiser Squadron would sail as soon as loaded. 1 Airborne Division had been ordered to move by road to transit camps at Bizerta on 9th and 10th September, but a hurried telephone message set them moving at once. The whole of the first half of the Division was concentrated at Bizerta that night. Loading took place the following day and the convoy sailed in the afternoon. The second half of the Division arrived in Bizerta on

9th September, and sailed the next day, arriving in Taranto on 11th September. The composition of the convoys had been left to the discretion of the divisional commander, depending on the carrying capacity of the ships and their readiness for loading, but very few guns and practically no transport, even light airborne transport, could be taken in the early stages. On landing at Taranto the Division would have to rely on local resources and any captured enemy equipment. The necessary personnel and stores required to maintain the airborne base in its present position, or to move it forward at a later date, would be left behind.

77. As this history is intended to deal mainly with airborne operations, and as the operations against Taranto and subsequently in Italy brought out few lessons except the need for initiative and improvisation, no attempt will be made to describe the actions of 1 Airborne Division in detail during the next few months. They secured Taranto on 9th September, with no opposition, although a mine blew up one ship in the harbour and 129 officers and men were drowned. As the Royal Navy entered the port, units of the Italian fleet steamed out under the British guns to their surrender at Malta. The Division advanced quickly north and north-west, inflicting casualties on a retreating enemy. During this period, soon after the capture of Taranto, Major-General Hopkinson was killed while observing one of his forward units in action and Brigadier Down, from 2 Parachute Brigade, took over command of the Division.

78. The Division's improvised transport included an Italian railway train and, for the field park company, R.E., a steam-roller and trailers. When their lines of communication were stretched beyond the limit, they halted at Foggia, while other formations passed through them and continued the advance.

79. During these moves and the advance to Foggia, the administration of the Division was, as may be imagined, complicated in the extreme. Frequently they advanced with only one day's rations within reach and with only the ammunition that they could carry on their persons, with no guarantee of further supplies at any definite time. Yet somehow the machine worked and the determination to succeed carried them through. Not only did they advance and maintain themselves, but they also played the major part in organizing the working and repairs of the ports of Taranto and Brindisi for the first few weeks after its capture.

80. While waiting in the general area of Gioia, north of Taranto, after they had been relieved at Foggia, 1 Airborne Division assisted in the escape of Allied prisoners who were trying to reach our lines from prison camps in Italy. The surrender of the Italians had resulted in the release of many of these prisoners and they were trying in large numbers to avoid the German attempts to recapture them.

81. In October, 1 Airborne Division were informed that they would return to England shortly, leaving behind one of their three parachute brigades to remain under the command of 15 Army Group. In addition, 1st Air-landing Light Regiment, R.A., as yet untried in battle, would remain in Italy for the time being in order to gain operational experience. Remembering the experiences of 1 Parachute Brigade in Tunisia, the War Office and Allied Force Headquarters agreed that the parachute brigade remaining in Italy should be enlarged to independent brigade group status, including the essential

133

administrative units and a nucleus staff for a small airborne base, but excluding any artillery. 2 Parachute Brigade, now commanded by Brigadier C. H. V. Pritchard, in succession to Major-General Down, were selected and administrative units for them were also provided by the Division. The detailed order of battle is given in Chapter XVII. Further instructions included the return of the R.A.F. squadrons to rejoin 38 Group in England and the information that 2 Independent Parachute Brigade Group would be carried by units of XII U.S. Troop Carrier Command in any airborne operations that might materialize.

82. 1 Airborne Division, consisting of 1 and 4 Parachute Brigades and 1 Air-landing Brigade, but less 1st Air-landing Light Regiment, R.A., left for England from Taranto during November. The personnel with the airborne base in North Africa sailed about the same time, bringing with them all stores and equipment not required for 2 Independent Parachute Brigade Group. 1st Air-landing Light Regiment, R.A., rejoined 1 Airborne Division in England in February, 1944, the story of that Regiment's deeds in Italy in the meantime being told in Chapter XVII, with those of 2 Independent Parachute Brigade Group.

CHAPTER XII

AIRBORNE FORCES IN THE UNITED KINGDOM AND AMERICA, MAY TO DECEMBER, 1943

General

1. Chapter XI described the operations of 1 Airborne Division in Sicily and Italy during 1943. While these operations were taking place, great strides were being made in the development of airborne forces in the United Kingdom and they will be described in this chapter. It covers that most important period from May to December, 1943, deals briefly with American airborne forces, and leads up to the initial planning for the Normandy operations preceding the invasion of North-West Europe.

Major-General Airborne Forces and Commander Airborne Forces Depot and Development Centre

2. In Chapter IX the point had been reached where the War Office had agreed to the necessity for a Headquarters, Major-General Airborne Forces, and on 5th May, 1943, authority for its formation was issued, although it had actually begun to form at Brigmerston House, Durrington, Wiltshire on 1st May. Major-General Browning was appointed as the first Major-General Airborne Forces and was succeeded in command of 1 Airborne Division by Major-General Hopkinson.

3. On 11th May, the War Office finally approved the war establishment for an Airborne Forces Depot and Development Centre under the command of a brigadier, to be known as Commander Airborne Establishments, though the organization had begun to form on 3rd May around the old unofficial airborne forces depot. On 5th July, Brigadier Flavell was appointed Commander Airborne Establishments and was succeeded in command of 5 Parachute Brigade by Brigadier J. H. N. Poett. He set up his headquarters at Amesbury, near Salisbury, moving to Alderbury in 1944. The Airborne Forces Depot remained at Hardwick, being the nearest available place to No. 1 Parachute Training School, Ringway. The Development Centre was established at Amesbury Abbey under a General Staff Officer, 1st Grade, who had under him staff officers of all arms and services and an experimental section R.E.M.E. workshops, etc. Later the appointment was changed to that of commandant, and later still upgraded to full colonel. The original appointments at the centre which was to work in very close conjunction with the Technical Development Unit, R.A.F. were filled by :—

G.S.O.1 Lt.-Colonel J. G. Squirrell.	D.A.A. and Q.M.G. Major F. R.
G.S.O.2 Major J. D. Irvine.	Dubery.
S.O.R.A. Major G. A. Stogdon.	D.A.D.S.T. Major. J. C. Morris.
S.O.R.E. Major Ae. J. M. Perkins.	D.A.D.M.E. Major A. F. L. Pollit.
S.O.R. Sigs. Major R. J. F. Whistler.	D.A.D.O.S. Major J. S. Allison.
Staff Secretary W.O., J. V. Jolly.	S.C. " Q " Captain H C. Byng.
Camp Commandant Captain E. Ritchie.	D.A.D.M.S. Major R. West.

4. Major-General Browning had been pressing continually for a charter to be issued setting out the duties of Major-General Airborne Forces and Commander Airborne Forces Depot and Development Centre as soon as possible as,

without such a charter, it was not possible for the staffs of these two head-quarters to be organized on an economic basis. However, it was not until 12th June that it was issued. The duties of Major-General Airborne Forces and of Commander Airborne Forces Depot and Development Centre as given on that date are set out below :—

" *Duties of Major-General Airborne Forces*
1. The Major-General Airborne Forces is responsible to the War Office (Director of Air).
2. His duties are :—
    (*a*) To advise the War Office and Commanders-in-Chief at home and abroad on all airborne matters.
    (*b*) To be responsible for the Airborne Forces Depot and Development Centre. (*See* Appendix G.)
    (*c*) To maintain liaison with all airborne formations at home and abroad. (He will communicate with them direct on questions of technical development.)
    (*d*) To maintain liaison with Allied airborne force commanders and staffs and to assist them in co-ordination of their training and equipment. When discharge of this responsibility necessitates calls on the services of an airborne division or 38 Wing, Major-General Airborne Forces will apply in the first instance to the Force Commander concerned.
3. In carrying out his duties, Major-General Airborne Forces will have personal access to all War Office branches and to Service and other Ministries but official communications will be addressed through the Director of Air. He will communicate direct with Allied contingents through the appropriate British Military Mission on technical matters.

Duties of Commander Airborne Forces Depot and Development Centre
1. The Commander Airborne Forces Depot and Development Centre will be responsible to Major-General Airborne Forces.
2. His duties are :—
    (*a*) To command the Airborne Forces Depot and Development Centre.
    (*b*) To issue progress reports to the War Office through the Major-General Airborne Forces when the latter is in England.
    (*c*) To prepare drafts of training pamphlets and instructions as required and submit them to the War Office.
    (*d*) To assist the War Office branches concerned in all matters affecting the recruitment and administration of personnel for airborne forces.
    (*e*) To keep in touch with commandants of experimental establishments and schools on matters affecting airborne forces.
    (*f*) In the absence of Major-General Airborne Forces to deputize as adviser to the War Office on airborne matters.
3. In carrying out his duties he will have personal access to all War Office branches but official communications will be addressed through Major-General, Airborne Forces to the Director of Air ".

5. By August, Headquarters, Major-General Airborne Forces, had been established long enough for Major-General Browning to determine whether or not it was organized on the right lines, and on 20th August he forwarded a letter to the War Office in which he stated that he did not consider that the present organization was correct and giving his views on improvements that could be made. This letter is so important and has such a bearing upon the future organization of airborne forces, their development and their training for the re-entry into North-West Europe that extracts from it are given in some detail. Major-General Browning pointed out that :—

(a) Major-General Airborne Forces had been established to deal with all matters outside the concern of the airborne divisional commander but the present organization crippled his value as he was not a commander. His powers were only advisory and limited at that.

(b) To cope with immediate requirements for airborne forces in the Mediterranean, staff officers had been appointed to various headquarters in that area and these appointments had not been co-ordinated.

(c) For the Sicilian operations, airborne forces had been used in strength for the first time under Army and R.A.F. commanders who had no experience of them, and with headquarters staffs who had had no chance of learning their problems and requirements. This, combined with the necessity to set up a large and completely new airborne base and training organization in a strange country and over great distances, had made necessary the presence overseas of Major-General Airborne Forces, and the whole of his small staff.

(d) Therefore, except for the brigadier commanding the Airborne Forces Depot and Development Centre, there was a period during which there was no adequate representation at home of the views of Major-General Airborne Forces. Under the present organization this situation was likely to be repeated.

(e) Major-General Airborne Forces, although the adviser to the Director of Air at the War Office, was in fact in a subordinate position to the divisional commanders, since he was of the same rank, did not exercise a function of command and was not given any authority over them whatever.

(f) The Commander Airborne Forces Depot and Development Centre was fully occupied in command of these establishments and had not time to spare to deputize to any appreciable extent for Major-General Airborne Forces, when absent. His own commitments grew every day, e.g., glider pilot depot and training of R.A.S.C. personnel in airborne supply.

(g) It was desirable to use airborne forces in as large concentrations as possible, preferably as a corps, and the division should be the minimum force used for each operation, even though it might not be possible to take it to war in one lift of aircraft.

(h) A headquarters was required which had the ability and authority to command more than one division in operations and to prepare them during training.

137

(*i*) There was no one with authority to whom 38 Wing R.A.F. could turn to decide the allotment of aircraft between divisional training, the training of Allies, the training of glider pilots for home and abroad, Army requirements regarding standards of training and many other points. In fairness to them, and to produce efficient results, the R.A.F. must be able to work with one senior authority who would tell them what the Army required.

(*j*) Higher authority had already accepted that there was need for an organization outside the divisions to supervise and co-ordinate the work which did not properly fall within the scope of divisional commanders, thus leaving them free to concentrate on their normal duties. Part of this work was done by the Commander Airborne Forces Depot and Development Centre, but there was a further part which had hardly been attempted and which was extremely urgent, *i.e.*, that connected with the preparation and execution of operations. These duties would be divided as follows :—

Airborne Forces Depot and Development Centre

The training and holding of personnel until posted to units, technical research and development and staff duties.

Airborne Forces Headquarters duties connected with Operations

The command of airborne formations, airborne operations and planning, and the provision of a nucleus for a Headquarters, Airborne Corps, as required.

(*k*) To remedy the faults Major-General Browning recommended the revision of the existing organization under a Lieutenant-General Airborne Forces, as an urgent requirement to prevent further waste of time and experience.

6. The War Office took several months to consider these recommendations as many people, including Headquarters, 21 Army Group, had to be consulted, and it was not until some time later that the recommendations were put into force. In the meantime, Major-General Browning, accompanied by Lieutenant-Colonel Walch, Major Bradish and Lieutenant-Colonel A. B. Harris, who was a liaison officer from the United States Army Air Force (*see* Chapter XXIV), visited India, Italy, North Africa, Sicily and Palestine to acquaint themselves at first hand with the airborne problems in those theatres, particularly India. While they were away a new and much stronger charter was issued on 8th October, 1943, as follows :—

" *Charter for Major-General Airborne Forces*

1. The Major-General Airborne Forces is responsible to the War Office (Director of Air).

2. His duties are :—

(*a*) To advise the War Office on all airborne matters, including policy, doctrine, planning, organization, training, equipment, research and development, both tactical and technical.

(b) To be available for consultation on all airborne matters, including planning by supreme commanders, commanders-in-chief and other interested authorities at home and abroad.

138

(c) To keep the War Office informed on all points connected with the training and efficiency for war of all airborne forces and he is empowered to carry out inspections for this purpose.

(d) To assist Allied airborne force commanders at home and abroad in co-ordination of their training and equipment.

(e) To co-ordinate, in consultation with the R.A.F., training capacity for army airborne training.

(f) To command all training, holding, depot and army experimental establishments in connection with airborne forces, except those training establishments which are the domestic concern of airborne formations as such."

On 26th December, 1943, Major-General Airborne Forces was disbanded on the formation of Headquarters, Airborne Troops, incorporating the same charter as given above and in addition the command of all airborne forces, but with the rank of the Commander raised to that of Lieutenant-General. On the same date Headquarters, Airborne Troops (*see* Chapter XIV), came under command of, and was set up in close proximity to, 21 Army Group at Hammersmith, later moving to Ashley Gardens to be near Headquarters 1 Corps during planning for the Normandy Operations. Two weeks later, on 10th January, 1944, the designation of " Commander Airborne Forces Depot and Development Centre " was changed to " Commander Airborne Establishments ", and the organization was brought under direct control of the War Office. Thus in two years airborne forces had grown from a small beginning to a force of two airborne divisions and an independent parachute brigade group under the command of its own headquarters which had full authority and world-wide responsibility in airborne matters and which also commanded all Allied (less United States) airborne forces in the United Kingdom. It also had under its command the Special Air Service Brigade, formed in January, 1944, details of which are given in Chapter XVIII.

Technical Developments

7. During the period under review, continual experiments and developments connected with airborne forces were being carried out. First among these were thoughts on a non-oscillating parachute, which was only partially successful, parachuting from Horsa Gliders, which was unsuccessful, and experiments to improve the technique for blind and night flying and towing of gliders. Successful experiments were carried out in dropping a jeep and a 6-pounder anti-tank gun from a Halifax, and it was considered that these would be ready for operations by the autumn of 1943. Specifications were given to the Air Ministry for experiments in constructing a new medium troop-carrying glider and instructions were given to the Airborne Forces Development Centre for work to go ahead on a 2,000-lb. container for dropping from heavy aircraft. Further improvements were made to " Rebecca/Eureka " radar equipment for homing aircraft on to dropping zones, and United States aircraft began to come into more frequent use for British troops. During this period the question was raised whether a reserve parachute, similar to that used by American airborne forces, should be introduced into British airborne forces and it was decided that it should not be used.

6 Airborne Division

8. We left 6 Airborne Division about to be formed on a phased programme. The first arrivals were 3 Parachute Brigade, under command of Brigadier S. J. L. Hill, the Airborne Armoured Reconnaissance Regiment, 2nd Battalion the Oxfordshire and Buckinghamshire Light Infantry and 1st Battalion the Royal Ulster Rifles, who had all been left behind when 1 Airborne Division went to the Mediterranean. The last two units were to form 6 Air-landing Brigade. On 2nd May Brigadier Gale who, it will be remembered, had been Director of Air at the War Office, was promoted to Major-General and appointed to command 6 Airborne Division. Divisional headquarters began to form at Syrencote House, near Netheravon, on 3rd May and the first officers to arrive on 7th May were Major-General Gale, Lieutenant-Colonel W. S. F. Hickie, Assistant-Adjutant and Quarter-Master General and Lieutenant-Colonel J. Fielding, Assistant Director of Ordnance Services. They were followed shortly afterwards by the General Staff Officer, 1st Grade, Lieutenant-Colonel R. H. N. C. Bray, while Headquarters, 6 Air-landing Brigade formed at Amesbury under command of Brigadier the Honourable H. K. M. Kindersley. This was followed on 1st July by the formation of the second 30 per cent. of the Division, which included 53rd (Worcestershire Yeomanry) Air-landing Light Regiment R.A. and the new 5 Parachute Brigade under command of Brigadier J. H. N. Poett. The headquarters of this brigade was formed from 72 Independent Infantry Brigade and two new parachute battalions, the 12th and 13th Battalions of the Parachute Regiment, were formed from the 10th Battalion The Green Howards and the 2nd/4th Battalion South Lancashire Regiment respectively. On 28th July, 1st Canadian Parachute Battalion arrived in England earmarked to be the third battalion of 5 Parachute Brigade. In fact when this battalion did join 6 Airborne Division on 11th August, it went to 3 Parachute Brigade, and 7th (Light Infantry) Parachute Battalion was transferred to 5 Parachute Brigade so that there would be an experienced nucleus for the new formation. One of the lessons of the invasion of Sicily was that the air-landing brigade of an airborne division should be increased to three battalions and, on 18th September, the War Office issued orders for 12th Battalion The Devonshire Regiment to join 6 Air-landing Brigade as the third battalion. On 22nd September, War Office orders were issued for the formation of the remainder of 6 Airborne Division less the second composite company R.A.S.C. which was to begin forming in cadre in November, 1943, for expansion later, and less the Air-landing Reconnaissance Squadron, the requirement for which was to be reviewed at the end of October, 1943, though it was never formed.

9. During this period 6 Airborne Division was carrying out unit training while it was forming so that a considerable strain was placed upon all ranks, especially unit commanders and staff officers. Despite this, by the end of the year considerable progress had been made, formations and units were beginning to take shape as efficient teams and a considerable number of large scale exercises had been held. The hard work put in by all ranks only just achieved results in time and on 23rd December, 1943, less than eight months after its formation, 6 Airborne Division was ordered to mobilize and to complete training in readiness for operations by 1st February, 1944, by which date it would be less than

one year old. This was no mean achievement, but mobilization was completed on time and in the ensuing Normandy operations, as will be seen in a later chapter, complete success was achieved.

38 Group R.A.F. and the Glider Pilot Regiment

10. In April, 1943, 38 Wing had begun to re-equip with Albemarle and Halifax aircraft, both of which were fairly suitable for dropping parachute troops and towing gliders, and the training of the additional glider pilots for 6 Airborne Division was proceeding. Nevertheless, the Wing was still unable to devote a sufficient number of flying hours to airborne forces, and so the Air Ministry suggested that the squadrons should be relieved of their leaflet dropping commitment. This was an unpopular suggestion as the Foreign Office were insistent upon the value of the work and said that they must have other squadrons to do it. Army Co-operation Command and 38 Wing were in favour of the raids because they served as " flak inoculation " for the aircrews and maintained their morale, and the squadrons themselves were highly indignant at the thought that their one operational activity should cease. However, their primary role was to function with airborne forces and, on 15th May, the Air Ministry ordered that their entire effort was to be directed to this end, and leaflet dropping ceased. On 19th May, the Wing and airborne forces generally suffered one of their greatest losses, when Air Commodore Sir Nigel Norman was killed in a flying accident in Cornwall, on his way to North Africa. He was succeeded by Air Commodore W. H. Primrose.

11. While more modern aircraft were being provided, the position as regards the provision of gliders was being examined by the War Office and the Air Ministry, and on 7th July, the number of gliders available in the United Kingdom was as follows :—

(a) *Horsa Gliders—*

Operationally equipped, 312.
Not operationally equipped, 209.
Unserviceable, 25.

(b) *Hamilcar Gliders—*

16 Gliders assembled, of which 3 were operationally equipped and 1 unserviceable.

(c) *Hadrian Gliders (U.S. CG–4A)—*

There were 6 Hadrian gliders in the United Kingdom.

The above figures give an approximate total of only 550 Horsa Gliders available in July, 1943. The number of glider pilots which had reached heavy glider standard was rising rapidly and from about 650 in May had increased by September to nearly 900. In addition, the Americans had stated that they would need approximately 300 additional Horsa Gliders and a special production programme to meet this demand was put into force immediately. It was assumed that the Americans and British would each need about 470 gliders each division for any operations in North-West Europe in 1944 and on this assumption it was calculated that, at the existing rate of production, by the spring of 1944 there would only be sufficient Horsa Gliders for two operations by British airborne divisions and for one operation by an American airborne division. The War Office pointed out that unless the number of Horsa Gliders was increased for subsequent operations and supply by air, American gliders would have to be used and steps were therefore taken to increase production. It is worth noting here that one of the main causes of the delay in getting gliders off the production line was undoubtedly the incessant number of modifications which had to be put in, amounting at one time to no less than 2,000. The fault was nobody's but was owing to the newness of the whole enterprise and consequent lack of real experience. Of the gliders that had arrived, a certain number had been distributed round Bomber Command airfields in accordance with the Air Ministry policy of 1942. However, building of the hangars was slow, the gliders were standing out in the open, and maintenance was difficult, so in July the R.A.F. formed No. 2 Heavy Glider Maintenance Unit for this purpose, sections being placed at each Bomber Command Station.

12. In August, 1943, as the result of a request from the War Office the Air Ministry gave the latest position regarding the re-equipping of 38 Wing. They stated that it had been hoped that the production of the Albemarle, Mark IV, would have coincided with the withdrawal from service of Albemarle, Marks I and II, thereby ensuring continuity of re-equipping aircraft. However, there had been delays in the production of the Albemarle, Mark IV, at the assembly centre and so full production of this model would not start until October, 1943, thereby considerably delaying the re-equipping of 38 Wing. The Air Ministry gave a new forecast of re-equipment, by which they hoped that all units of 38 Wing, including the Parachute Training School and Heavy Glider Conversion Unit would be fully re-equipped by May, 1944. However, they were being pressed on all sides to increase the *tempo*, the War Office continuing to demand urgently more Albemarles, while Air Commodore Primrose asked for the return of his detachments in North Africa, and for the wing to be completely re-equipped at once. It so happened that there were 100 Albemarles, which had been allocated to Russia, but had not been definitely accepted for delivery, and these were re-allocated by the Allied Supplies Executive to the R.A.F. for 38 Wing. On 30th September, the Chiefs of Staff Committee considered a Joint Memorandum on Airborne Forces which had been prepared by the War Office and Air Ministry and agreed with the main recommendations of the paper which were the result of lessons learned in the Sicily operations. The memorandum formed the basis of future joint Army/R.A.F. policy for airborne operations and a summary is given below :—

    (a) The airborne operations in Sicily were the first large-scale airborne operations to be undertaken by Allied forces, and the first to be undertaken at night. The difficulties were not fully appreciated nor was the necessity for placing such operations under an Air Force commander fully recognized.

    (b) In consequence inadequate training was given to the air forces participating, and the air tactical plan was weak. As a result only a small percentage of the assault forces were brought into action as planned.

    (c) The airborne assaults were successful or partially successful in attaining their object. They contributed greatly to the quick success of the sea-borne attacks and the subsequent advance inland was speeded up and many lives saved.

(*d*) Airborne operations were air operations and should be entirely controlled by the Air Commander-in-Chief, assisted by a joint staff representing all three Services.

(*e*) Airborne operations should be planned well ahead to allow adequate training for both air and ground forces participating and for the issue of warning to all friendly forces.

(*f*) Aircraft with specially trained crews were required to act as " Pathfinders ". All aircraft crews taking part should be trained to normal standards required in bomber squadrons and have had some operational experience.

(*g*) Airborne operations should be concentrated in time and space and also in respect of numbers and lifts of aircraft. Glider-borne troops should be preceded by a parachute party.

(*h*) Operations in the European theatre would probably have to be carried out at night.

(*i*) Airborne forces should be used in conjunction with a main attack by land, sea or air, and supply a means of turning the enemy's ever-open flank by using the door over the top.

(*j*) Gliders entailed considerable demands on R.A.F. resources and were difficult to launch. They should be limited to 430 for one divisional operation.

(*k*) No major changes were required in the existing organization of an airborne division, but the air-landing brigade should be increased from two to three battalions.

(*l*) In planning an operation, it should be stated whether the role of airborne forces were a vital part of the plan because of their dependence on weather.

(*m*) Air crews should be specially trained and aircraft modified during production for operations with airborne forces.

(*n*) No. 38 Wing should be increased to 180 aircraft.

(*o*) Airborne forces were likely to be required in continental operations, in any further Mediterranean operations, and in Burma, and the Far East.

(*p*) It was not practicable to use surplus pilots in Fighter Command in an airborne forces role.

(*q*) The existing training programme would provide sufficient glider pilots.

(*r*) The existing production programme substantially met requirements, subject to American demands.

(*s*) A few gliders should be sent to India for trials.

13. As a result of this report, on 19th October, the Air Ministry issued instructions for a new phased programme for the re-equipment of 38 Wing, in which they stated that the strength of the wing was to be nine squadrons—four of Albemarles, one of Halifaxes and four of Stirlings, each with an aircraft establishment of 16 plus 4, a total of 180 aircraft. A wing headquarters was not large enough to control so many squadrons and so, at the same time, Headquarters 38 Wing became Headquarters 38 Group within the Tactical Air

Force, Fighter Command. The first phase in the reorganization of 38 Group, to be completed by 4th November, was the re-equipping of 295, 296 and 297 Squadrons with Albemarles. 298 was to be a Halifax Squadron formed from the Halifax flight of 295 Squadron, and 299 Squadron was to have Venturas initially, but was to be turned over to Stirlings later. The Ventura was totally unsuitable for airborne work and was not fitted for glider towing or for parachute dropping. All that it would be used for would be to keep the pilots in flying practice.

14. On 6th November, Air Vice-Marshal L. N. Hollinghurst, took over command of 38 Group, and shortly afterwards the Group was placed under command of Headquarters Allied Expeditionary Air Forces, which had just been formed. On 16th November, a new squadron No. 570 began to form with Albemarles, drawing their personnel from 295 and 296 Squadrons, and on 22nd November, 196 and 620 Squadrons, both with Stirlings, were transferred from 93 Group, Bomber Command, to 38 Group.

15. One of the first things that Air Vice-Marshal Hollinghurst observed on taking over 38 Group was that the aircrews had insufficient sympathy with the tribulations of the glider pilots. This was mainly because the glider pilots, except when they were doing their attachments, were not then accommodated on the R.A.F. station, or even near it, so there was no opportunity for the personnel to " hob-nob " off duty, which is so important. Thanks to the co-operation of Brigadier Chatterton this was quickly remedied. The Glider Pilot Regiment was reorganized into Headquarters, Commander Glider Pilots, and two separate wings which took the place of the old battalions. The wing headquarters was so designed as to be completely independent, so that if necessary it could work on its own overseas. The squadron and flight headquarters were also independent, the squadron commander being at the disposal of the R.A.F. Squadron commander. The ideal aimed at was for a flight to consist of 20 glider crews, each of two pilots, where an R.A.F. squadron consisted of 16 plus 4 aircraft—one glider crew for each aircraft. A glider pilot wing consisted of a flexible number of squadrons and a squadron of a flexible number of flights. No. 1 Wing was attached to 38 Group with all glider pilots living on the R.A.F. stations, while No. 2 Wing was given refresher training on return from North Africa, and in January, 1944, was attached to 46 Group on its formation. Brigadier Chatterton himself, and his staff, lived at Headquarters 38 Group. During the period two innovations were introduced which increased the already high standard set by the Glider Pilot Regiment and the promotion incentive. The first was that all first pilots who were not officers should be staff-serjeants with the full flying badge, and that second pilots should be serjeants with special second pilots wings. The second was that the Air Ministry approved glider pilots passing a test, after which they would be allowed to inspect their gliders for airworthiness, a task hitherto carried out by the R.A.F.

16. Despite the expansion and re-equipping of 38 Group, several exercises were carried out with troops during the summer of 1943, in which the training of the aircrews improved considerably. One of these exercises was such a remarkable demonstration of accuracy that it must be mentioned. On 9th August, 1943, 15 aircraft of No. 295 and 297 Squadrons took part in a daylight exercise with 9th Battalion, The Parachute Regiment. The dropping

zone was alongside the River Spey between Nethybridge and Grantown in Scotland, a distance of between 400 and 500 miles and a flight of some five hours from the take-off airfield at Thruxton, Salisbury Plain. The object of the drop was to accustom the troops to long distance flying and to combine a demonstration before several thousand personnel of 52 (Lowland) Division with a series of exercises. Brigadier Hill accompanied the troops. The battalion's second-in-command was on the ground to give a running commentary to the audience over loud-speakers. The drop was timed for 1500 hours. The aircraft took off at 1000 hours and encountered some bumpy weather on the way which made a number of troops airsick. A smoke-candle had been placed on the dropping zone to mark the place where the first men should land. At exactly ten seconds past 1500 hours the first parachutist, Brigadier Hill, left the leading aircraft, the navigator of which was Flight Serjeant L. Meller of 297 Squadron. To the amazement of the crowd, the delight of the commentator and the surprise of the brigadier himself, he landed right on the smoke candle. The remaining aircraft were at their correct interval behind the leader and there was only one minor injury.

Personnel

17. Despite all efforts sufficient numbers of parachute volunteers were not being obtained. Certain anomalies in the award of additional pay for parachute and glider duties had become apparent during the last six months and to rectify these, and to encourage recruiting, the War Office brought out two important rulings on 1st June, 1943 :—

(a) Additional pay for parachute duties and glider pilots was to continue for any period of captivity in which a man might be held as a prisoner of war.

(b) Additional pay for parachute duties and glider pilots was to continue up to 91 days spent in hospital as a result of wounds or injuries which might be attributable to parachute or glider duties.

(c) Airborne pay received by troops employed as glider or airborne troops in a non-parachute role was to be admissible up to 91 days spent in hospital as in sub-para. (b) above.

(d) The acting rank of glider pilots was to continue both for prisoners of war as in sub-para. (a) above, and for those in sub-para. (b) above.

In addition, on 19th July, the minimum age for parachute volunteers was lowered to 18½ years. The following month parachute pay for Royal Artillery personnel and men of other units not specifically designated as parachute units was authorized and between then and the end of the year various new methods of selection of parachute volunteers were brought into force as the result of experiments carried out at the Airborne Forces Depot with a twofold object— first to improve recruiting and second to ensure a higher standard of recruit. During this period a proposal was put forward, again as a means to attract volunteers, that the parachute badge should be worn on the right breast as opposed to the right arm. However, this was opposed by the Air Ministry, who maintained that only members of the Royal Air Force, Army pilots (air observer post) and glider pilots, were permitted to wear wings, or half-wings on their chest. After some discussion it was decided that the badge should remain on the right arm.

Allied Airborne Forces

18. During the latter part of 1943, 6 Airborne Division spent a great deal of their time training with 101 U.S. Airborne Division (Major-General Maxwell D. Taylor) and other Allied airborne contingents. Towards the end of the year there were also in the United Kingdom 1 Airborne Division and 82 U.S. Airborne Division (less one regimental combat team), both of which returned from the Mediterranean in December, 1943. It is of interest to digress at this point to trace briefly the history of the American airborne divisions :—

(a) 82 *U.S. Airborne Division.*—After World War I, 82 All American Infantry Division returned to the United States where it remained during the intervening period during the two wars. The Division was " activated* " at Camp Claiborne, Louisiana on 25th March, 1942, and at that time Major-General Omar N. Bradley was the commanding general with Brigadier-General Matthew B. Ridgway as the assistant divisional commander. On 26th June, 1942, Brigadier-General Ridgway assumed command of the Division with the rank of Major-General. On 15th August, the Division was converted into 82 Airborne Division. It proceeded overseas to North Africa on 29th April, 1943. When Major-General Ridgway assumed command of XVIII U.S. Airborne Corps he was succeeded in command of the Division on 15th August, 1944, by Major-General James M. Gavin. The division took part in the Sicily operations, the invasions of North-West Europe, the Arnhem–Nijmegen operations and the Battle of the Ardennes.

(b) 101 *U.S. Airborne Division* was " activated " on 16th August, 1942, and formed from a nucleus of 82 U.S. Airborne Division. The Commanding General was Major-General William C. Lee, who was one of the originators of airborne forces in the United States. The Division sailed for England in September, 1943. In the spring of 1944 Major-General Lee had a heart attack from overwork and was invalided back to the United States. He was succeeded by Major-General Maxwell D. Taylor who had been 82 Airborne Division artillery commander. This Division also took part in the invasion of North-West Europe, it was in the Arnhem–Nijmegen operations and became famous at Bastogne in the Battle of the Ardennes.

(c) 11 *U.S. Airborne Division* was " activated " on 25th February, 1943, under command of Major-General J. M. Swing. It sailed for the Pacific on 8th May, 1944, and took part in the Philippine Islands operations. It was joined by 503 U.S. Parachute Infantry Regiment which had already taken part in several operations in the Pacific, and finally jumped onto Corregidor Island, Manila. The Division later took part in the occupation of Japan.

(d) 17 *U.S. Airborne Division*, under the command of Major-General W. M. Miley was " activated " on 15th April, 1943, and arrived in England during the autumn of 1944. Like 6 Airborne Division they were rushed over to Europe from England to help in the battle of the Ardennes and took part with 6 Airborne Division, in the crossing of the River Rhine.

" Mobilized."

(e) 13 *U.S. Airborne Division*, Major-General E. G. Chapman, was
" activated " on 13th August, 1943, and though it arrived in France
on 26th January, 1945, it never saw active service as a division.

19. Co-operation between the American and British airborne troops was
very close. When 101 U.S. Airborne Division arrived in England it went into
camp in the Newbury area close to the training ground of 6 Airborne Division.
The camps for the reception of the Division were prepared by parties from
6 Airborne Division and from then until the invasion of Normandy in June,
1944, a very close liaison was maintained between the two formations and an
almost identical similarity of training and operational technique was achieved.
Officers were made honorary members of each other's messes and clubs, and
inter-unit exchanges of officers and non-commissioned officers took place,
usually on the scale of one officer a company and one non-commissioned officer
a platoon. Common exercises, rifle meetings, social functions, etc., were held
to further the spirit of friendship. This was also typical of the liaison between
82 U.S. Airborne Division and 1 Airborne Division. Naturally, rivalries were
keen but were quickly subordinated to a common airborne spirit when mutual
benefit would result as the following story shows. On one occasion, rather late
in the evening, British and American airborne troops were having a considerable
argument which became rather noisy. Some military police (nationality
unknown) advanced upon them and tried to stop the noise. With cries of
" up the airborne ! " the American and British troops combined together
and—it is alleged—violently assaulted the military police !

20. By December, 1943, also, the Parachute Section of the Infantry Training
Centre, Fort Benning, Georgia, in the United States, had got well into its
stride. Approximately 48,000 volunteers began the basic airborne course at
the school during the year, of which some 30,000 qualified as parachutists.
Of the remainder, not all were rejected entirely, a number being retained as
air-landing troops.

21. As well as United States airborne forces, there were in the United
Kingdom towards the end of 1943, several Allied airborne contingents. The
strongest of these was the Polish Parachute Brigade which consisted of a brigade
headquarters, a light battery, a parachute squadron of engineers, a parachute
field ambulance, a signals section and four parachute battalions, of which only
three were formed initially, the fourth being formed when further recruits were
received from the Middle East. There were two French parachute battalions
of the Special Air Service Brigade, a Norwegian, a Dutch and a Belgian parachute
company. All these units showed extreme keenness but until Headquarters,
Major-General Airborne Forces, was properly established it was virtually
impossible for Major-General Browning and his staff to give them the assistance
for which they continually asked, as 1 Airborne Division's hands were full with
training our own troops. However, as the headquarters got into its stride, all
available assistance was given to these Allied contingents and on the formation
of Headquarters Airborne Troops at the end of 1943 they came under its
command. Before this they had assisted airborne forces in many ways, *e.g.* the
Belgian parachute company volunteered for and carried out experiments for the
Airborne Forces Experimental Establishment. Considerable difficulty was
experienced initially with the Polish Parachute Brigade as they were stationed
in Scotland a long way from the main British airborne centres and no transport

aircraft were available for them other than their own Polish bomber squadrons, which were fully occupied in bombing Germany under Bomber Command. On the formation of Headquarters, Airborne Troops, these problems were solved and the brigade was given adequate training.

United States Troop Carrier Command

22. The Chiefs of Staff had agreed to an American proposal to send to England four groups of United States troop carrier aircraft in the early part of 1944 in order to work with 38 Group in the training of British and Allied airborne forces. This programme was soon accelerated and by December, 1943, there were already two groups of American transport aircraft in the Doncaster area, four and a half groups were due to arrive in England in January, 1944, from North Africa and seven groups were due to arrive from the United States at the rate of one group every 14 days starting on 1st January, 1944. Thus, within a few months the aircraft situation had undergone a fundamental change from a picture of shortage to one of an abundance of aircraft. However, it must be remembered that by the beginning of 1944 there would be in the United Kingdom a total of four airborne divisions (two British, two American) and other Allied airborne contingents which would require training.

Standard Operating Procedure

23. As a result of experience in England, in training in North Africa and in the operations in Sicily, 1 Airborne Division had produced certain Standard Operating Procedures for use in airborne operations and these had been issued in the form of a pamphlet by Headquarters, Major-General Airborne Forces. When the American divisions arrived in this country they were not in possession of any Standard Operating Procedure, with the result that they borrowed the British version and adapted it to their own use. Later, British and American Army and Air Force staff officers produced a combined procedure which was suitable for the airborne forces of both countries in any circumstances. When General Eisenhower's Headquarters was established in the United Kingdom this Anglo-American Standard Operating Procedure was reproduced by Supreme Headquarters Allied Expeditionary Force as an operation instruction (*see* Appendix F).

The Overall Picture at the Beginning of 1944

24. By the beginning of 1944, the situation generally as regards airborne forces was as follows :—

(*a*) Headquarters, Airborne Troops, under Lieutenant-General Browning, had been formed in order to command, train and advise on all British airborne forces throughout the world, and Allied airborne forces in the United Kingdom, except those of the United States of America. The headquarters worked directly under 21 Army Group.

(*b*) The designation of "Commander Airborne Forces Depot and Development Centre" had been changed to "Commander Airborne Establishments". This organization, dealing with the personnel, research and development side of airborne forces, had been placed directly under War Office control.

(*c*) Considerable progress had been made in technical developments, especially in the dropping of heavy equipment from aircraft, and in the technique of jumping from American aircraft (C.47 Dakota).

(*d*) 6 Airborne Division had been formed, had completed a great part of its training and had been ordered to mobilize in readiness for operations by 1st February, 1944. 1 Airborne Division had returned from the Mediterranean and was re-organizing and training in preparation for operations in North-West Europe.

(*e*) 2 Independent Parachute Brigade Group had remained in Italy.

(*f*) 38 Wing R.A.F. had been increased to a group and was re-equipping with Albemarles, Halifaxes and Stirlings to a total of 180 aircraft, organized in nine squadrons—four of Albemarles, one of Halifaxes and four of Stirlings.

(*g*) Production of Horsa and Hamilcar Gliders continued on a scale sufficient to provide for a substantial number of airborne divisional operations, though it was still uncertain whether this scale would be sufficient to meet all requirements.

(*h*) The training of glider pilots, continued in order to provide sufficient pilots for 1 and 6 Airborne Divisions with a substantial reserve.

(*i*) Conditions of service had been improved to increase recruiting and maintain morale.

(*j*) 82 U.S. Airborne Division, less one regimental combat team, had arrived in the United Kingdom from the Mediterranean, and was re-organizing. 101 U.S. Airborne Division had arrived in the United Kingdom from the United States, and was training hard in co-operation with 6 Airborne Division for European operations. 11, 13, and 17 U.S. Airborne Divisions, and large numbers of parachute reinforcements were training in America and would be ready for operations during 1944. There were in the United Kingdom one Polish parachute brigade, two French parachute battalions of the Special Air Service Brigade and parachute companies of Norwegian, Dutch and Belgians, all training to take their part in European operations.

(*k*) One regimental combat team of 82 U.S. Airborne Division remained in Italy.

(*l*) Two groups of American transport aircraft were already in the United Kingdom for training with airborne forces and a further $11\frac{1}{2}$ groups were due to arrive in the early part of 1944.

(*m*) An Anglo-American Standard Operating Procedure had been produced for British and American airborne forces, in order to achieve a common method of training and a common airborne battle technique.

(*n*) The Special Air Service Brigade was forming under Brigadier R. W. McLeod.

(*o*) As a result of the operations in Sicily, considerable thought was being given to the setting up of an airborne base for the mounting of airborne operations. Details of its organization will be given in Chapter XIV.

149

CHAPTER XIII

DOMINION AIRBORNE FORCES

Introduction

1. So far we have traced in detail the development and expansion of British airborne forces, and in outline of American airborne forces, up to the end of 1943, but only passing references have been made to Dominion and Indian airborne forces. Before beginning to describe the activities of airborne troops in North-West Europe, Italy, Southern France and Greece the reader should know the Dominion background, which is given in this chapter. The growth of Indian airborne forces and operations in the Far East are dealt with separately in Chapters XXIII, XXIV and XXV.

Australia

2. In September, 1942, Australian Army Headquarters, in conjunction with the Royal Australian Air Force, decided to raise an independent parachute company for use in jungle operations. The original intention was that this company would be raised and trained in New Guinea but at that time New Guinea was very much in the battle area and this, combined with the difficulties of carrying out parachute training under jungle conditions, led to all training being confined to the mainland of Australia. In October, the United Kingdom was asked to send out suitable instructors for the new unit. In the meantime a composite Parachute Training Centre was formed at Laverton, Victoria, on 3rd November, 1942, and moved to Tocamwal, New South Wales, on 16th November. This unit was commanded by Wing Commander C. P. Glasscock, R.A.F., and consisted of six officers and 80 airmen of the R.A.A.F., and seven officers and 90 other ranks of the Australian Army. The original object was to train the necessary instructors for the Parachute Training Centre and then to produce 100 qualified parachutists a week.

3. On 6th April, 1943, Wing Commander W. H. Wetton, R.A.F., took over command of the centre, having arrived out from the United Kingdom. He brought with him Major H. Roberts of the British Army who was to be chief Army instructor, and Major T. R. B. Courtney, R.A.M.C., who was to be the centre medical officer. The weather conditions and training facilities at Tocamwal were not good and on the recommendation of Wing Commander Wetton and Major Roberts, the centre was moved to the R.A.A.F. Station at Richmond, New South Wales, on 13th April, 1943. Richmond had good climatic conditions by day for 70 per cent. of the year, good accommodation and good dropping zones and training areas. From then onwards the training centre was organized on the lines of No. 1 Parachute Training School in the United Kingdom. D.C.2 (Dakota) aircraft were used for training.

4. In April, 1943, the Australian Army Staff decided to raise a parachute battalion less one company and a parachute troop, Royal Australian Engineers, and on 15th August, 1st Australian Parachute Battalion was formed under the command of Major J. W. Overall, with Major J. M. Atkinson, as second in command ; 1st Parachute Troop, R.A.E., was raised at the same time. On 24th September, the two units moved from the R.A.A.F. Station, Richmond, to Scheyville Camp which was about eight miles away from the school. At that time the battalion consisted of 360 officers and men.

5. In October, approval was given to raise the complete parachute battalion and first reinforcements for it, and it was also decided to raise a further five men for the engineer parachute troop to form the nucleus of a parachute squadron headquarters, and to act as first reinforcements for the troop. In that same month, on 14th October, Major A. C. Smith, who had taken over the duties of second in command from Major Atkinson, and Lieutenant D. L. Govett were killed in an aircraft and as a result of this Major D. I. H. McClean was appointed second in command. By December, 1943, 770 officers and men had been trained for 1st Australian Parachute Battalion, and the output of the school was 50 parachute troops a month as reinforcements for the battalion and additional parachutists for other arms and special agents. By May, 1944, the battalion and the engineer parachute troop had been completely formed with their first reinforcements and had moved to a forward training area at Mareeba, Queensland. Here the battalion group carried out operational training whenever possible and took part in exercises with formations which were training close by. This type of training continued until September, 1945.

6. In May, 1944, one troop of parachute pack artillery was raised and was found from within the establishment of 1st Australian Mountain Battery. It was not detached as a separate parachute unit but remained within its own battery available on call for use in a parachute role, and was trained to jump with its guns, which were 75-mm. pack howitzers or alternatively short axled 25-pounders.

7. In August, 1945, a detachment of 120 parachute troops went to Singapore to represent Australia on the return of British troops to that base. In September, the strength of the detachment was increased to 200 and it remained in Singapore until February, 1946. Meanwhile, 1st Australian Parachute Battalion and the Parachute Troop, R.A.E., less the Singapore detachment, were disbanded.

8. 1st Australian Parachute Battalion consisted of a battalion headquarters, a headquarters company and three rifle companies. Within headquarter company there were an intelligence section, signal platoon, mortar platoon, pioneer platoon and an administrative platoon. Each rifle company consisted of a company headquarters, an anti-tank section, a mortar detachment and three rifle platoons each of three sections, the total strength all ranks being 637. 1st Parachute Troop, R.A.E., consisted of troop headquarters and three sections, a total strength of 40 all ranks. Throughout their history these units were essentially part of airborne forces as a whole and wore the maroon beret and the airborne forces signs. A detachment of 2nd/4th Australian Field Regiment was dropped into action in the Markham Valley, New Guinea, in September, 1943 (*see* Chapter XXV), where they were under the direct command of First Australian Army, who were responsible for their training and organization. Although the other units did not go into action, they did provide a large number of trained parachutists for operations with the special reconnaissance detachments of " Z " Force (Special Agents) which was employed extensively throughout the South-West Pacific area. Working in co-operation with the Army units was 38 Transport Squadron, R.A.A.F., which was part of 244 Group, R.A.A.F., and at Richmond, New South Wales, one flight of 38 Squadron was permanently attached to the Parachute Training Centre, and at Mareeba, Queensland, one flight of the squadron was available on call when required for training purposes. In addition, at Mareeba, there was 1 Mobile

Parachute Maintenance Unit, which was responsible for the care, maintenance and packing of all parachutes used by the airborne troops. The order of battle of Australian airborne forces is given at Appendix O.

Canada

9. The Canadian Army first considered the possibilities of raising airborne troops in November, 1940. At that time Colonel E. L. M. Burns, in a paper prepared for the Chief of the General Staff at National Defence Headquarters, Ottawa, expressed the opinion, which is interesting in view of the tendency for airborne troops then to be considered as highly specialized forces, that

> " Airborne troops are merely the most mobile form of land forces, and the fact that some of them land by parachute is due to the characteristics of the aeroplane ".

The suggestion that Canada might make a contribution towards the training of parachute troops in the United Kingdom was forwarded to Canadian Military Headquarters, London, in December, 1940. A meeting was held on 20th December, and among those present were Lieutenant-General A. G. L. McNaughton, Commander Canadian Corps, and Major-General H. D. G. Crerer, Chief of the General Staff, who was at that time on a visit to the United Kingdom. The opinion was expressed that no action should be taken to organize or train airborne troops except at the request of the War Office.

10. In August, 1941, the question of organizing Canadian parachute troops was raised again at National Defence Headquarters, but the time was not considered ripe for the establishment of any separate parachute troops within Canadian forces. With changing conditions, however, the matter was kept under discussion, and subsequently a decision was taken to provide a Canadian parachute battalion with effect from 1st July, 1942. The war establishment for this unit was published in November, 1942. The unit was to consist of a battalion headquarters, headquarter company, and three rifle companies, with a total strength of 26 officers and 590 other ranks. Later, minor alterations were made to this establishment to bring it into line with that of a British parachute battalion.

11. In July, 1942, volunteers for parachute duties were requested from the Canadian forces then in the United Kingdom and between the 23rd August and 12th September, 1942, 23 officers and 60 other ranks attended a parachute course at No. 1 Parachute Training School, Ringway (*see* Appendix O). Soon afterwards a large group of volunteers recruited from other ranks in training centres and infantry units in Canada was despatched from Canada to the U.S. Parachute Training School at Fort Benning, Georgia. When 1st Canadian Parachute Battalion was raised, Lieutenant-Colonel G. F. P. Bradbrooke was appointed to command, and the officers came mainly from those who had completed the course in England. By 22nd March, 1943, the battalion had completed four months training at the U.S. Parachute Training School, Fort Benning, and then moved to a Parachute Training Wing at Shilo, Manitoba. At the conclusion of the training at Fort Benning, all officers and 97 per cent. of the other ranks, including first reinforcements, had qualified for their parachute wings, but no collective training had been carried out. They had been trained by American methods on American aircraft using American equipment, which included carrying a reserve parachute in addition to the main statichute.

12. In March, 1943, discussions took place between the Canadian Military Headquarters and the War Office as to whether 1st Canadian Parachute Battalion could be included within British airborne forces. The War Office welcomed the offer. The unit was to remain part of the Canadian Army in the United Kingdom, but would be placed under command of 6 Airborne Division, to the staff of which Canadian administrative officers would be attached. Standard British equipment would be used in the same way as for British units but personal clothing and battle dress would continue to be a Canadian issue. On 7th April, 1943, authority was given for the inclusion of 1st Canadian Parachute Battalion in 6 Airborne Division and the battalion arrived in the United Kingdom on 28th July, 1943, and went to No. 1 Canadian Base Staging Camp, Chobham, Surrey. On 11th August they moved to Carter Barracks, Bulford, and became part of 3 Parachute Brigade under Brigadier S. J. L. Hill and from then on their training conformed to the remainder of the units in 6 Airborne Division and has been covered elsewhere in this history. They were sent by detachments to No. 1 Parachute Training School, Ringway, to undergo a conversion parachute course so that they would become familiar with British methods. The battalion did well in training, as is evident in a message from Brigadier Hill to the commanding officer after a large-scale brigade exercise in February, 1944 :—

" I feel I must write and congratulate you on the excellent show your battalion put up from the Albemarles on Exercise ' Co-operation '. If they continue to make progress in this connection at this rate they will soon be the best jumping exponents in our airborne corps and I should very much like to see them achieve this end for themselves. Well done."

13. During October, 1943, it was pointed out that the existing organization for providing reinforcements for Canadian units in the United Kingdom did not provide the facilities for the training of reinforcements for 1st Canadian Parachute Battalion. It was decided to form a Canadian parachute training company which would be a separate unit but would be linked with and under command of 1st Canadian Parachute Battalion while that unit was in the United Kingdom. The permanent staff of the training company consisted of five officers and 32 other ranks who were to hold and train 14 officers and 348 other ranks as reinforcements.

14. 1st Canadian Parachute Battalion wore the maroon beret and signs of airborne forces but they had the badge of the Canadian Parachute Regiment. As with other units of 6 Airborne Division they wore a distinctive flash on their battle dress and this consisted of a gold strip worn on the shoulder straps. They fought with 6 Airborne Division from Normandy to the Baltic and won the following decorations :—

VICTORIA CROSS
    Corporal F. G. Topham . .   The Crossing of the River Rhine.
OFFICER OF THE ORDER OF THE BRITISH EMPIRE
    Lieutenant-Colonel J. A. Nicklin.
MILITARY CROSS
    Captain J. P. Hanson.
    Captain P. R. Griffin.
    Captain J. A. Clancy.
MEMBER OF THE ORDER OF THE BRITISH EMPIRE
    Lieutenant L. J. G. Brunelle.

DISTINGUISHED CONDUCT MEDAL
Company Serjeant-Major G. W. Green.

MILITARY MEDAL

Serjeant A. Bray.

Serjeant G. H. Morgan.

Serjeant J. A. Lacasse.

Serjeant W. P. Minard.

Serjeant G. W. Green.

Private W. Noval.

Private R. A. Geddes.

Private W. D. Ducker.

Private J. C. Quigley.

MENTIONS IN DESPATCHES

Lieutenant-Colonel J. A. Nicklin.

Lieutenant J. L. Davies.

Company Serjeant-Major H. K.
Duckett.

Company Serjeant-Major J. Kemp.

Serjeant G. Caprara.

Corporal G. H. Jickels.

Corporal J. L. Chambers.

Lance/Corporal L. L. Weatherson.

Private M. M. Petrow.

During the Rhine crossing the commanding officer, Lieutenant-Colonel J. A. Nicklin, who had taken over from Lieutenant-Colonel Bradbrooke in Normandy, was killed while hanging from a tree suspended in his parachute harness. Of the battalion's part in this operation, in a letter to the Chief of Staff at Canadian Military Headquarters, London, Brigadier Hill said :—

"The battalion really put up a most tremendous performance on 'D' day and as a result of their dash and enthusiasm they overcame their objectives, which were very sticky ones, with considerable ease killing a very large number of Germans and capturing many others. During the advance the battalion have shown the same enthusiasm and yesterday's effort was typical of them. Having marched 20 miles over very bad roads the day before, they marched a further 14 yesterday morning and were then called to put in an assault on a small village. This they successfully did. Meanwhile an S.O.S. had been sent out for them to try and rescue a small reconnaissance detachment which was holding an important bridge just to the south of Hanover, and in order to do this the leading company of the battalion doubled pretty well non-stop for two miles with full equipment and stormed the bridge over an extremely open piece of ground under fire from three or four German S.P. guns without turning a hair. They got the bridge intact, but the reconnaissance regiment unfortunately had been unable to hold out."

15. After they returned from Germany, the battalion was granted nine days leave in the United Kingdom but were recalled only three days later on 27th May, 1945, and then embarked on the "Ile de France" for Canada. They were the first complete Canadian unit to return to Canada from overseas, and received a tumultuous homecoming reception. After a short period at Niagara-on-the-Lake, Ontario, the battalion was disbanded. Field Marshal Lord Alanbrooke, Chief of the Imperial General Staff, sent the following message to the Chief of the General Staff, Ottawa :—

"I hear that the 1st Canadian Parachute Battalion received a great welcome as the first unit to arrive back in Canada. I realize that circumstances have made it inevitable that the battalion should now cease to form part of the 6 Airborne Division, but I would like to tell you how sorry we all are to lose this magnificent battalion, which has taken such a distinguished part in the great battles of the past year. I know how high is the regard and affection of all ranks of the 6th Airborne Division for their Canadian parachute battalion. The battalion played a vital part in the heavy fighting which followed their parachute descent on to French soil on 6th June, 1944, during the subsequent critical days, and in the pursuit to the Seine. It was well to the fore in the fighting which checked the Runstedt offensive in December, 1944. In the battle which followed the crossing of the Rhine on 24th March, 1945, its performance was again of the highest quality, in spite of the much regretted death in action of their fine commanding officer, Lieutenant-Colonel J. A. Nicklin. Finally, it played a great part in the lightning pursuit of the German army right up to the shores of the Baltic. It can indeed be proud of its record. I understand that it may not be possible for you to keep the 1st Canadian Parachute Battalion in being as a full battalion. Nevertheless, I hope that the close ties formed in battle between the Canadian parachute troops and the airborne troops of the British Army may be retained in future."

New Zealand and the Union of South Africa

16. The available manpower resources of New Zealand from the beginning of the war were dispersed for four main purposes :—

    (a) A land force of one infantry division and a large number of corps troops units. These were deployed in the Middle East theatre.

    (b) A manpower contribution to the effort in the air.

    (c) A manpower contribution to the effort at sea.

    (d) A manpower contribution to the production of supplies and munitions, particularly food.

With the entry of Japan into the war, New Zealand found herself faced with the possibility of invasion. This called for an increased effort as regards the land forces. It was decided to leave the division in the Middle East, to despatch another infantry division to the Pacific theatre and to mobilize three divisions for home defence. The other three demands, of course, continued. Under these conditions, which existed about the time of the expansion of airborne formations, it was found impossible to accept any other commitments without seriously affecting the fighting efficiency of units in the field. Therefore, New Zealand did not raise any airborne forces during the war, although individual officers and other ranks from the Dominion were to be found serving with British and Indian airborne units wherever there were airborne forces.

17. South Africa also suffered from a shortage of manpower and was unable to raise any airborne forces as such. However in 1944, 2 British Independent Parachute Brigade Group, which was serving in Italy, was very short of officers and volunteers were asked for from South African Forces in Italy. As a result of this appeal, between 30 and 40 South African officers were posted to 2 Independent Parachute Brigade Group. They served with the British units in Italy, France and Greece, and some accompanied the brigade to England, and were with it still when it joined 6 Airborne Division in Palestine. In addition, there were individual South African officers and other ranks serving with airborne forces in other parts of the world.

CHAPTER XIV

PREPARATIONS FOR THE INVASION OF NORTH-WEST EUROPE, JANUARY TO JUNE, 1944

The Second Front

1. When President Roosevelt and Mr. Churchill held their conference at Casablanca in January, 1943, it was apparent that the campaign in North Africa would be successful, and so they discussed what operations should follow the withdrawal of the Germans from Tunisia. From all points of view the most desirable course of action would have been an immediate invasion of North-West Europe, but at that time the Allied resources did not permit this. In particular, there was insufficient time to allow the build-up of the American forces in the United Kingdom. Therefore, it was decided that the next step should be the capture of Sicily followed by the invasion of Italy. At the same time the Prime Minister and the President decided that the concentration of all available forces in the United Kingdom should continue and that the planning of the invasion of North-West Europe should begin at once. To this end a joint Anglo-American staff was established under the direction of Lieutenant-General Sir F. E. Morgan, who was known as the Chief of Staff to the Supreme Allied Commander (designate) (C.O.S.S.A.C.). At a further conference between Mr. Roosevelt and Mr. Churchill held at Washington in May, 1943, the decision was confirmed to undertake a full-scale invasion of North-West Europe at an early date. The operation was given the code name of " Overlord," with a target date of 1st May, 1944.

2. In August, 1943, Lieutenant-General Morgan produced a tentative plan which was approved by the Combined Chiefs of Staff but which was later altered by General Eisenhower, in his capacity of Supreme Allied Commander (designate), in consultation with General Sir Bernard Montgomery (later Field-Marshal The Viscount Montgomery), who was to be Commander-in-Chief, 21 Army Group, and was also to command all Allied ground forces in the initial stages of the invasion.

Higher Planning

3. As a result of a conference which took place in November, 1943, at Teheran between Mr. Churchill, Mr. Roosevelt and Generalissimo Stalin, General Eisenhower was appointed Supreme Allied Commander for operation " Overlord ". He arrived in the United Kingdom with General Montgomery, in January, 1944, to assume his command. Both Supreme Headquarters, Allied Expeditionary Force (S.H.A.E.F.) and 21 Army Group, had been established towards the end of 1943, the former based on Lieutenant-General Morgan's headquarters and the latter being a new headquarters. Official recognition was not given to S.H.A.E.F. until 15th February, 1944, the day after General Eisenhower received his directive from the Combined Chiefs of Staff. As soon as they arrived in England, Generals Eisenhower and Montgomery, in conjunction with Admiral Sir Bertram Ramsay, Commander of the Allied Naval Expeditionary Force, and Air Chief Marshal Sir Trafford Leigh-Mallory, Commander of the Allied Expeditionary Air Force, examined in detail the plan produced by C.O.S.S.A.C., and as a result several major changes were made in it. These involved an increase in the assault forces and an increase in the

width of the front. In the original plan the target date for " D " day had been 1st May, 1944, but a shortage of assault craft brought about by an increase in the numbers of assault formations caused the postponement of " D " day by one month, and its was agreed eventually that 5th June would be the official date. Additional factors influenced the postponement of the date and, to quote the " Report by the Supreme Commander to the Combined Chiefs of Staff on the Operations in Europe of the Allied Expeditionary Force, 6th June, 1944, to 8th May, 1945 ", these were that :—

> " from the air point of view the extension of the target date would afford a longer opportunity for the strategic bombing of Germany and the wearing down of the German air strength. In addition, the tactical bombing of railheads and transportation centres, the preliminary softening of fortifications on the Channel coast and the diversionary heavy air attacks in the Pas-de-Calais could be undertaken with greater thoroughness. The training of the invasion forces, and particularly the troop-carrier crews for the airborne operations, could also be carried out more thoroughly. The Navy, moreover, desired additional time for the training of the assault craft crews and for the delivery and assembly of the extra vessels needed in the enlarged attack. From the naval viewpoint a postponement of the target date to 1st June, was preferable to any briefer postponement, say of two weeks, since an early June date guaranteed the favourable tides necessary for the beach operations as well as a full moon. From the strategic point of view the postponement seemed desirable, since weather conditions at the end of May would be likely to be more favourable for the mounting of a large scale Russian offensive to assist the ' Overlord ' operation. Additionally, the situation in the Mediterranean might be sufficiently resolved by that time to preclude the necessity of an operation against the south of France closely co-ordinated with our western assault. The German forces in that theatre might be so heavily engaged by our armies that a diversionary and containing assault would not be required in direct and immediate assistance to ' Overlord '."

4. The original invasion plan included a sea-borne assault by one corps of three divisions, on a front between Grandcamp in the west and the River Orne in the east, but the air lift allotted for the airborne assault was only sufficient for two-thirds of an airborne division and was to be used for an attack on Caen on " D " day. General Montgomery, when studying the original plan, considered that the eventual capture of the Cherbourg Peninsula was essential for the success of the invasion and that the original forces allotted were too weak to cover this front. He therefore recommended, and General Eisenhower agreed, that the front be increased to the west to cover an area from the base of the Cotentin Peninsula, between Varreville and the Carentan Estuary, to inclusive of the River Orne. This frontage amounted to some 50 miles. General Montgomery considered that airborne forces would play an extremely important role in the assault and that a greater air lift should be allotted as there would be three or four airborne divisions available for operations on " D " day. To quote the General's own words* :—

> " Extension of the invasion frontage to the base of the Cotentin Peninsula resulted in increased commitments for airborne forces as they were

---

* " Normandy to the Baltic " by Field-Marshal The Viscount Montgomery of Alamein.

157

required on the western flank to ensure the capture of the causeways leading across the inundations behind the assault beaches. The Supreme Commander strongly supported the need for additional air lift and, as a result of his recommendations, the availability of transport aircraft and gliders was materially increased. The extension of the target date helped in this matter, for the extra time made it possible to concentrate more aircraft and to train additional crews ".

As will be seen in Chapter XV the airlift finally made available was sufficient for three airborne divisions, although 6 Airborne Division only had sufficient aircraft to carry it in two lifts.

5. The airlift would be provided by 38 Group R.A.F. with under command 46 Group R.A.F., and IX U.S. Troop Carrier Command. These Air Forces would provide a common pool of aircraft available for lifting British, American and Allied airborne forces, and therefore it was essential that a common headquarters, with common communications, should be established where the staff officers of both nations could work together. To this end, in April, 1944, a Combined Troop Carrier Command Post (C.T.C.C.P.) was set up at Eastcote, Middlesex, where the Air Officer Commanding 38 Group and the Commanding General IX U.S. Troop Carrier Command both had their headquarters and operated through combined staffs. How the Combined Troop Carrier Command Post fitted in with the general system of command, and in particular with 6 Airborne Division and the Royal Air Force transport groups is shown at Appendix J.

The Airborne Base

6. At the beginning of 1944, there were four airborne divisions assembled in the United Kingdom, 1 and 6 British Airborne Divisions and 82 and 101 U.S. Airborne Divisions, all of which were to be available, if necessary, for use in the invasion of North-West Europe. This was the largest concentration of airborne forces and troop-carrier aircraft ever achieved. Up to that date airborne divisions had been more or less responsible for launching themselves into battle and this meant providing the necessary Army personnel from within divisional resources to establish control sections at the various airfields. An airborne division was not, and is not, designed to provide these in addition to the fighting and administrative personnel and, therefore, they had been found from troops who would be going into battle in later lifts. However, circumstances for the invasion of North-West Europe were quite different, in that airborne divisions would be despatched into battle either in one lift or in lifts spread over a maximum of 48 hours from at least 18 widely spaced airfields. Their administrative units would be required to assemble in sea-transit camps sometime before the take-off of the airborne element. It was evident, therefore, that some organization outside the airborne divisions was needed to mount, control and despatch these formations into battle so that if necessary consecutive divisions could be dealt with by the same base organization.

7. On 1st February, 1944, Lieutenant-General Browning submitted to Headquarters 21 Army Group and the War Office a paper on the airborne base organization with a request that the organization should be able to start functioning adequately on 1st March, 1944, when large scale training with the

British and American Air Forces was due to begin. This paper had been agreed with the Allied Expeditionary Air Force, IX U.S. Troop Carrier Command and 38 Group. Lieutenant-General Browning pointed out that :—

(a) For the Sicily operations the limited number of aircraft available restricted the size of the force to be carried in one lift to a brigade group. The brigade groups were despatched in succession, but even this strained the resources of the division particularly in signals.

(b) For the invasion of North-West Europe it was the intention, agreed with the Commander, Allied Expeditionary Air Force, that both British airborne divisions should, in their turn as required, use all British and American troop carrying aircraft as a common pool for a simultaneous lift of one division. A second division could be lifted 24 hours later.

(c) The British and American troop carrying aircraft in the initial stages of such an invasion would start from 18 or more airfields scattered from Lincolnshire to Dorset. They should be prepared to operate from a similar number of airfields overseas at a later date.

(d) Airborne divisions should be prepared to operate in support of the sea assault landing or at short notice either for a previously unconsidered task or for a task previously considered but liable to much alteration at the last moment.

(e) In either of these cases the commanders and staffs on all levels within the divisions should be sufficiently free from other matters to be able to concentrate on the tactical tasks involved. They had not the extra personnel within their establishments to organize and control the whole of the base and airfield despatching organization.

(f) Now that circumstances had changed and each division would be required to operate as a division in one lift, it was essential to set up a base organization to make this possible.

(g) As each division would be using the same aircraft, it was obviously more economical and more efficient to have one base organization used by the airborne divisions in turn. In addition, as Headquarters Airborne Troops would be controlling the despatch of the divisions on operations and would be directing large scale exercises, it was essential that the airborne base should be established directly under that headquarters.

8. Lieutenant-General Browning stated that the main responsibilities of the airborne base would be as follows :—

(a) To marshal troops and equipment on airfields.

(b) To organize the Army side of the reception of the troops at airfields.

(c) To organize the Army side of air supply for airborne forces.

(d) To arrange for distribution of last minute information to troops and, where necessary to Air Force personnel.

(e) To control the despatch of any reinforcements or special task troops standing by to go into action at short notice.

(f) To organize the second and subsequent aircraft and glider lifts, and to allot troops, equipment or supplies as required.

159

(g) To maintain a record of all troops, equipment and supplies despatched and any reserve remaining.

(h) To move the Army part of the airborne base to any new location ordered.

(j) To provide communications as necessary.

9. The duties outlined above fell naturally into three requirements ; airborne control sections at airfields, transit camps for troops near the airfields and a separate network of communications, all under Headquarters Airborne Troops. Lieutenant-General Browning summarized the need for airborne control sections thus :—

> " Whenever airborne troops are operating from an airfield it is necessary for a control staff of airborne personnel to be provided in order to ensure the simplicity and smooth running of all arrangements for the despatch of these troops. This section must work in the closest possible touch with the Air Force formation on the airfield and, if possible, work alongside the operations staff. In all exercises or operations there will be an Air Force controller and this section should work under his orders. In order to differentiate between this section and the various other controls normally operating on an airfield, it is recommended that this section be known as an Airborne Control Section."

10. These proposals were agreed by the War Office on 19th February, and in order to co-ordinate the airborne control sections established at the various airfields, the two General Staff Officers, 1st Grade (Air) of 1 and 6 Airborne Divisions came under command of Headquarters Airborne Troops on 10th March. They were established, each with a small staff, respectively at Headquarters IX U.S. Troop Carrier Command and Headquarters 38 Group, but they were instructed to give every possible assistance to their respective divisional commanders when required. They had under their command all personnel of the airborne control sections on those airfields controlled by the Air Headquarters to which they were attached. From 10th March onwards airborne control sections were formed at 38 and 46 Groups and IX U.S. Troop Carrier Command airfields (*see* Map 6). Each section consisted of an air liaison officer, a captain, with a clerk and batman provided by one of the British airborne divisions and a non-commissioned officer and driver provided by Commander Airborne Establishments. A provost staff of four for each airfield was to have been provided by 21 Army Group, but the airborne divisions had to meet this commitment as well, owing to the heavy demands on police throughout the Army and Air Force. The Commander, Glider Pilot Regiment, allotted one officer and four other rank advisers to each section. These were all flying personnel and three of the five were normally available at any time. The difficulty of staffing these sections was shown by the fact that it was decided to close the Airborne Development Centre, if necessary, to find sufficient men to cover the launching of operation " Overlord."

11. During March, IX U.S. Troop Carrier Command was reorganized into three Wings, 50, 52 and 53 Troop Carrier Wings, of a varying number of groups, each containing four squadrons. At this time 38 Group had 46 Group under command, and the latter consisted of five squadrons. Thus Headquarters 46 Group within 38 Group corresponded to a wing headquarters in IX U.S.

Troop Carrier Command. Training exercises carried out during March showed that the existing organization was not practical and that airborne representatives were also required at headquarters of American wings and 46 Group, British Transport Command. Therefore, Lieutenant-General Browning asked Headquarters, 21 Army Group if four additional sections could be established for this purpose. He also requested that these four officers should be General Staff Officers, Grade 2, as they would command up to five airborne control sections each and would be responsible for co-ordinating the despatch of up to 232 aircraft and 4,000 airborne troops in one lift. These proposals were agreed by Headquarters, 21 Army Group, though it is not clear whether they were ever put into effect.

12. The accommodation commitment was met by setting up a series of transit camps which were established near an airfield or a group of airfields. By 20th April, 1944, eight transit camps had been established to cater for the airfields used by British troop-carrier aircraft. These camps were near the 38 Group stations of Harwell, Brize Norton, Tarrant Rushton, Keevil and Fairford, and for 46 Group at Blakehill Farm, Down Ampney and Broadwell, and were built by personnel of 1 and 6 Airborne Divisions. Each transit camp was in charge of a camp commandant and administrative staff and was designed to accommodate up to 1,000 troops at winter scales, with the appropriate accommodation stores, for a period of up to ten days either for training or for operations. During the time that units spent in camps they were relieved of all administrative duties. The staffs were found to a large extent from unfit or first reinforcement personnel of 1 and 6 Airborne Divisions, but the camps were run on lines similar to those at the main ports of the United Kingdom, details of which are given in other official histories of the war.

13. Existing R.A.F. and United States Air Force communication facilities were insufficient to carry the additional traffic, so three new signal offices were opened. This meant providing well over 100 trained signals staff at a month's notice and as the invasion of Normandy was only ten weeks off, the scanty resources available were severely taxed. Headquarters, 1 Airborne Corps, at Moor Park, Rickmansworth, was given a full signal office and also a detachment for a tactical headquarters. At Headquarters 38 Group, Netheravon, a combined message centre was opened and was manned jointly by Army and R.A.F. signalmen. This arrangement was considered impracticable at Headquarters IX U.S. Troop Carrier Command at Eastcote because of the difficulties that might arise in the use of unfamiliar terms between British and American signalmen. A signal office was accordingly provided by General Headquarters, Home Forces. Telephone and teleprinter connections and an emergency wireless system were set up between Headquarters, 1 Airborne Corps, the two Air Force headquarters and their local airfields and transit camps. On each airfield there were airborne control section report centres at the various Air Force squadron dispersal areas, and a central airborne control office, which was normally alongside the station operations room. Both the control offices and report centres were connected to the communications system so that any last minute alterations could be received up to the time of take-off for an operation (see Map 6). The report centres also provided a meeting place where representatives of air crews and airborne troops could make arrangements for aircraft or glider loading.

The Maintenance Project

14. Once the airborne base had been established it was possible for Headquarters, Airborne Troops to issue instructions concerning administrative arrangements for the maintenance of the British airborne troops taking part in operation " Overlord." These instructions were issued on 23rd and 24th March, 1944, and covered the establishment of the supply base for maintenance by air of airborne operations and general administrative instructions for airborne formations following a successful landing on the Continent, until normal maintenance conditions had been established. The general principles remained in force until the end of the war although they were altered in detail for each operation according to circumstances.

15. The supply base for the mounting of airborne operations was founded upon seven airborne supply dumps, six of which were for Royal Army Service Corps stores in the area between Oxford and Salisbury and one for ordnance stores at Great Missenden, Bucks. The policy for holding stocks was that ten days maintenance of all requirements, except medical stores, for two airborne divisions was moved to depots in the vicinity of the airborne dumps. Five days maintenance was drawn from the depots by divisional R.A.S.C. and was moved by motor transport to the dumps. The remaining five days continued to be held in the depots until quantities were required to replace the amounts despatched by air. These quantities were then drawn by the R.A.S.C. and moved to the dumps concerned on instructions of the Deputy Director, Supplies and Transport, Headquarters Airborne Troops.

16. The responsibility of the R.A.S.C. for loading aircraft began when they examined the rollers, and other equipment in the aircraft to ensure that they were correctly fitted and in working order. Divisional R.A.S.C. provided staffs for each corps dump on the scale of one officer, one non-commissioned officer and five issuers or technical personnel of a composite platoon, and one non-commissioned officer and six drivers as a guard. In addition, labour for packing stores and stocking the dumps and for subsequent issues in operations was provided by divisional R.A.S.C. Panniers and containers were pre-packed in certain standard loads identified by code serial numbers and labels. Detailed lists of these standard packs were issued to all concerned so that any formation requiring certain stores only had to quote the code serial number and the amount required.

17. Stirling, Halifax and C.47 Dakota aircraft were to be used for supply by air of airborne formations. R.A.F. Dakota aircraft were to be loaded with six containers and ten panniers but aircraft of IX U.S. Troop Carrier Command were only to carry four containers and ten panniers. R.A.F. Stirlings were to carry 24 containers and four panniers. Headquarters Airborne Troops were responsible for issuing the actual orders to R.A.S.C. to carry out the maintenance by air according to the progress of operations. All dumps and transport for maintenance of airborne forces by air and divisional R.A.S.C. units were placed directly under Headquarters Airborne Troops as the R.A.S.C. commander would be overseas on operations. Sufficient R.A.S.C. personnel, trained as air crews, to man 200 C.47 Dakota aircraft, i.e., 800 R.A.S.C. personnel for this purpose alone, were to be provided by 1 and 6 Airborne Divisions, and kept in the vicinity of the supply by air base. In actual fact, however, only about 400 R.A.S.C. personnel were so trained.

18. The general maintenance policy was that airborne formations would land with sufficient rations for 48 hours, ammunition and petrol, oil and lubricants to last for 36 hours, and that on the night following the airborne landing one day's re-supply and one second line refill of ammunition would be dropped to formations. After this, maintenance was to be the responsibility of the formation of 21 Army Group under whose command the airborne division would have been placed, *i.e.*, the corps headquarters commanding the sea and land operations. Further maintenance by air was pre-planned but would take place only if a special requirement were put in by the division concerned before or during the operation.

19. Whenever possible the balance of divisional transport which could not be taken by air would be sent by sea under arrangements of 21 Army Group Build Up Control Organization and would join the division concerned as soon as possible after the link-up with the main forces. If this were not possible, and airborne divisions were operating at such short notice that administrative assistance could not be given by 21 Army Group, sufficient transport would be taken by air to ensure that the formation could operate efficiently. Divisional second line transport sent by sea would be limited to the balance of the light composite company R.A.S.C. not sent by air and to one 3-ton company R.A.S.C. One 3-ton company R.A.S.C. would remain in the United Kingdom for assisting at the airborne base. A reasonable allotment of ambulances and water trucks would be included with the transport by sea. To enable second line transport to be embarked loaded, if this were necessary, arrangements were made for second line requirements of ammunition, supplies and petrol, oil and lubricants to be available on demand in depots within reasonable reach of the normal divisional locations in the United Kingdom before they moved to transit camps. Otherwise second line commodities were held by divisional R.A.S.C. in the normal way. At least two and, if possible, three days " compo " rations were included in first and second line vehicle loads.

20. In the case of medical supplies, field ambulances drew panniers from divisional R.A.S.C. and were responsible for packing the contents and for handing the panniers back to the divisional R.A.S.C., who moved them to corps dumps. Panniers so packed were unit packs designated specifically for the field ambulances which packed them and were marked in blue with the day for which they were required. Deputy Assistant Directors of Medical Services were responsible for arranging provision of blankets, stretchers and sleeping bags in conjunction with the " Q " Staffs and Assistant Directors of Ordnance Services concerned. These were to be sent to R.A.S.C. by Ordnance and would then be packed by R.A.S.C. Stretchers, blankets and medical stores were to be dropped as part of the daily supply by air pack on the following scale—50 sleeping bags, 50 stretchers, 100 blankets, and five panniers of medical stores for a brigade each day.

21. The following are the main points given in Headquarters Airborne Troops administrative instructions for airborne operations, with particular reference to operation " Overlord " :—

    (*a*) *Water.*—Water would not be dropped.

    (*b*) *Ammunition.*—Whenever possible units were to land either from the air or the sea carrying 100 per cent. of first line ammunition. A proportion of second line ammunition might be landed in pre-loaded second line vehicles. Where necessary, second line ammunition could be dropped by air, subject to aircraft being available.

(c) *Petrol.*—Petrol tanks of vehicles travelling by air would not be less than 80 per cent full, but those travelling by sea would be 90 per cent full.

(d) *Ordnance.*—Divisional headquarters would have the following sources of ordnance supply from which they would demand as applicable :—

" D " day to " D " + 7 day.
   (i) Non-controlled stores from Ordnance Beach Detachments.
   (ii) Controlled stores from 1 Corps Ordnance Field Park.
   (iii) Items not obtained through (i) or (ii) would be demanded from airborne base supply dump and would be dropped by air.

From " D " + 8 day onwards.
   (i) A stores transit sub-depot would be established by " D " + 8 day. Indents for items not available in the beach maintenance area would be received by the stores transit sub-depot and flown back to the United Kingdom. Stores would be despatched to the stores transit sub-depot and issued to units through the Ordnance dump.
   (ii) However, " Q " Branch was still able to demand urgently required items from the Airborne Corps base supply dump.

(e) *R.E.M.E.*—R.E.M.E. Light Aid Detachment personnel would accompany formations and units and would carry a hand kit of tools.

(f) Units would carry first line scales of spares for jeeps and motor-cycles, and R.E.M.E. detachments would carry light scales based on unit first line scales but would depend on Ordnance Field Park for supply of mechanical transport spares.

(g) First line scales of armament spares would be carried by units, but where this was not possible owing to the weight involved, divisions would apply to Headquarters, Airborne Troops for these spares to be held pre-packed at the supply airfields. R.E.M.E. detachments would draw on Ordnance Field Park for second line spares and unit armourers would carry in their tool chests sufficient spares to carry out first line repairs to small arms in the field. Divisional R.E.M.E. would carry spares for second line small arms repairs in the field.

(h) *Medical.*—Airborne medical transport* would be taken on as high a scale as available gliders would allow. Medical services attached to units as well as parachute field ambulances would be responsible for the evacuation of casualties from the forward area to main dressing stations established by airborne medical units. Evacuation of casualties from these main dressing stations would be the responsibility of the medical services of the link-up formations. Wet plasma blood and penicillin would be included in stores taken in the initial drop or landing and in second line supplies by sea or air. In addition, wet plasma would be contained in each medical maintenance block. Blood would be available at the advanced blood bank located in one beach sub-area of each corps from " D " + 2 day onwards.

---

* Jeeps modified to take stretchers and trailers.

164

(*i*) *Sea-borne Element.*—With regard to the movement of airborne divisional units, personnel and vehicles by sea, infantry divisions were responsible for the assembly on " D " day of the airborne troops landing under their command. Airborne troops landing by sea on " D " + 1 day and later would be passed through transit areas to assembly and concentration areas and thence to the airborne divisions as soon as possible.

(*j*) *Mail.*—Once airborne formations had taken off, mail would not be forwarded to the battle area until it was clear that the formation would be out of the United Kingdom for more than 14 days. This was to avoid delay in mail " chasing " units backwards and forwards should they be withdrawn from the line unexpectedly.

(*k*) *Salvage.*—It was the intention that, as soon as the situation permitted, divisions would arrange for the collection and dumping in suitable areas near traffic routes of all airborne equipment—parachutes, containers, panniers, harnesses, etc., and if possible, to leave a guard to look after the equipment. It was stressed that it was important to recover from damaged gliders such flying instruments as cable angle indicators, etc., and that it must be considered an operational necessity that every possible piece of airborne equipment was salvaged for future use. (In action, however, it was found not practicable to carry out this instruction and little equipment was salvaged, as will be seen in Chapter XV.) Further, it was stated that when airborne formations were withdrawn from the line for reorganization for a subsequent airborne operation, it was essential that all airborne equipment and all transport, less 3-ton lorries, should be brought back. Equipment normally carried in 3-ton vehicles would be brought back in jeeps and trailers which would be emptied of all supplies, ammunition, petrol, oil and lubricants, to enable this to be done. If such a withdrawal took place before the collection of airborne salvage, divisions would be responsible for removing as much salvage equipment as possible and handing over the balance to the relieving formation.

(*l*) *Reinforcements.*—First reinforcements of all arms of airborne troops would remain in unit locations in the United Kingdom and would not be transferred overseas unless the airborne base moved. Airborne trained reinforcements would not be used to reinforce units who had just carried out an airborne operation. Once units were fighting on the ground reinforcements would come from reinforcement pools of their own arms under instructions from Second Echelon. When units were withdrawn from the line to reorganize for another airborne operation their own airborne trained first reinforcements would join them and any ordinary reinforcements acquired in the line would have to be returned to the reinforcement holding unit from whence they came, unless they had volunteered for parachute duties in the meantime. Airborne trained first reinforcements thus absorbed would be replaced from airborne establishments under arrangements made by the War Office.

165

22. An important administration factor was the decision by the Commander, 6 Airborne Division, to employ the " Jettison Drop " (*see* Chapter XV) by which all spare bomb-rack space on parachute aircraft was made up with containers of ammunition, medical and ordnance stores.   These containers were to be dropped either just before or immediately after troops jumped and were to be collected as additional dumps by divisional R.A.S.C. or, where this was not possible, by units on the spot.

The Transport Air Forces

23. The expansion of 38 Group (*see* Chapter XII), continued throughout the early months of 1944.   Early in the new year 190 Squadron was formed at Stoney Cross with 16 plus 4 Stirlings, and 299 Squadron began to replace their Venturas with Stirlings.   By 16th March, all operational units of 38 Group had moved to their new stations and the order of battle was as follows :—

Station.	Squadron.	Aircraft.
Brize Norton	296	22 + 4 Albemarles
	297	22 + 4 Albemarles
Harwell ..	295	22 + 4 Albemarles
	570	22 + 4 Albemarles
Keevil	196	22 + 4 Stirlings
	299	22 + 4 Stirlings
Fairford ..	190	22 + 4 Stirlings
	620	22 + 4 Stirlings
Tarrant Rushton	298	18 + 2 Halifaxes
	644	18 + 2 Halifaxes

24. In the meantime it had become obvious that 38 Group would not be large enough to carry out airborne operations on its own or even with the assistance of IX U.S. Troop Carrier Command.   On 17th January, 1944, therefore, 46 Group was formed within Transport Command.   The Group was to be under the operational control of 38 Group for airborne operations, and Air Commodore A. L. Fiddament, was appointed to command.   It differed from 38 Group in that it was not constituted for the sole purpose of working with airborne forces.   When not employed on airborne operations, or in training for them, it was to carry on with normal transport duties.   The group was formed with a unit equipment of 150 Dakotas, and the original squadrons were 271 and 512.   By 1st March, three more squadrons had been added, 48 and 233, which were transferred from Coastal Command, and 575 which was formed around a nucleus from 512 Squadron.   By this date also, the group had moved to Wiltshire and the order of battle was :—

Station	Squadron	Aircraft.
Broadwell ..	512	30 + 0 Dakota
Broadwell ..	575	30 + 0 Dakota
Down Ampney ..	48	30 + 0 Dakota
Down Ampney ..	271	30 + 0 Dakota
Blakehill Farm ..	233	30 + 0 Dakota
Reserves		25 Dakotas

25. The period immediately before operation " Overlord " was taken up with intensive training, in all units within 38 and 46 Groups. The large-scale exercises are described separately later. Great stress was laid on navigational training and in order to give aircrew practice under operational conditions, 46 Group took part in leaflet dropping operations. 38 Group in their turn were gaining operational experience by dropping Special Agents on the Continent at frequent intervals and during May alone about 200 sorties were flown for this purpose. A high proportion of the sorties of both groups were routed into France over the Caen sector with the dual object of familiarizing aircrews with the landfall and of accustoming the Germans to the passage of small numbers of aircraft. The pathfinders of 21st Independent Parachute Company would have to be dropped half an hour ahead of the main body of 6 Airborne Division and if they were to have a chance of doing their work undisturbed it was important that the enemy should not associate their planes with anything but the normal passage of " resistance " aircraft. These sorties were invaluable in another way as by the reports of drops received from the agents in the field, Headquarters 38 Group were able to check up on the reports made by each pilot and navigator. From this they were able to compile a comprehensive record which was very useful when it came to selecting crews for the more important tasks, such as pathfinders.

26. The system of glider-marshalling and take-off and landing aircraft in rapid succession and marshalling them so that they could take off again as soon as possible, were all improved. At one demonstration of take-off, 18 aircraft were marshalled at the end of the runway in threes in V-formation and were all in the air in 56 seconds. During the period 1st January–31st May, 1944, the following had been achieved in training units :—

    (a) *No. 1 Parachute Training School, Ringway.*—58,990 jumps were made, and the 200,000th jump since the school opened took place.

    (b) *Glider Pilot Regiment.*—774 first pilots and 718 second pilots were available. Of these, 320 first pilots and 215 second pilots completed refresher training at the Heavy Glider Conversion Unit despite the move of the unit from Brize Norton to North Luffenham.

    (c) *Gliders.*—1,946 Horsas and 114 Hamilcars had been erected but were not all available owing to wastage.

    (d) *Fatal Accidents.*—During the period there were three fatal accidents in parachute jumping and 14 in gliders.

For the two weeks immediately before " D " day all aircraft and gliders, except those used for special agent activities, were grounded to obtain maximum serviceability.

27. IX U.S. Troop Carrier Command was also getting ready to carry British troops and had made every effort to have all their aircraft fitted with British type bomb-racks and the British parachute anchor-cable. They had estimated their requirements some months before " D " day but they had to take second place to the fitting of 46 Group aircraft. However, by 5th June, about two-thirds of the command's aircraft had the anchor-cable, and the bomb-racks were put in very quickly at short notice.

Final Preparation

28. The period between January and June, 1944, was one of intense activity for all airborne forces stationed in the United Kingdom. Plans were being made for the invasion, detailed training and rehearsals were carried out and preparations were made for the very careful briefing that would be necessary for an operation of this type. Headquarters, Airborne Troops was established at Ashley Gardens, London, in January, and in April moved to Moor Park, near Rickmansworth, when it became Headquarters, 1 Airborne Corps. It coordinated the training and planning of all British airborne forces, and received a great deal of help from the United States Forces. The organization of the Headquarters as it was in June, 1944, is given in Appendix H.

29. On 17th February, Major-General Gale received orders from Lieutenant-General Browning, who later flew on a reconnaissance over the operational area, to place a parachute brigade and one anti-tank battery under command of 3 British Infantry Division to plan for operations on the Continent. The Air Officer Commanding 38 Group was briefed at the same time. The task was given to seize intact, if possible, the bridges over the River Orne and the Caen Canal near Ranville. 3 Parachute Brigade was selected for the task and the size of the force was limited by the number of aircraft that could be allotted to the British airborne effort. However, the airlift was increased considerably and the whole resources of 38 Group and 46 Group were placed at the disposal of Commander, 6 Airborne Division, so a divisional operation became possible in two lifts. On 24th February 6 Airborne Division was placed under command of 1 Corps (Lieutenant-General (later General Sir John) Crocker) for the operation. The following members of the staff joined 1 Corps planning headquarters which was established alongside Headquarters, Airborne Troops at Ashley Gardens :—

G.S.O.1 (Ops.)	..	Lt.-Col. R. H. N. C. Bray.
G.S.O.2 (Int.)	..	Major G. A. C. Lacoste.
G.S.O.3 ..	..	Captain N. H. P. Pratt.
C.R.E. ..	..	Lt.-Col. F. H. Lowman.
A.A. & Q.M.G. ..		Lt.-Col. W. S. F. Hickie.
A.D.M.S. ..	..	Col. M. McEwan.
C.R.A. ..	..	Lt.-Col. J. S. L. Norris.
Two Clerks.		

By mid-April planning had advanced considerably, 6 Airborne Division had established a planning headquarters at The Old Farm, Brigmerston House, Netheravon, whose official code name was " Broadmoor ", six officers of 38 Group had been briefed and a war room opened at Netheravon. Later the planning staff moved to Scotland to plan with 3 British Infantry Division.

30. The four British and American airborne divisions in the United Kingdom with the transport Air Forces of both nations spent their time concentrating on formation training and the specialized training of aircrews. It was vitally important that the Air Forces should have as much time to themselves as possible to train their own crews and the glider pilot crews. On the other hand, somewhat naturally, the airborne commanders were constant in their demands for more and more flying exercises. The exercises required by the Army might not suit the Air Forces at the time, and more than once the divisional commander had to arbitrate in favour of the Air Forces to allow them more time to themselves.

31. 6 Airborne Division carried out several large scale exercises. They experimented with the various methods of putting a brigade group down on one or several dropping or landing zones. Everything possible was dropped, from men to patrol dogs. On 6th February, 3 Parachute Brigade carried out a mass drop at Winterbourne Stoke from 98 aircraft of 38 Group and 435 Group, IX U.S. Troop Carrier Command. Special brigade and unit exercises were held to test the ability of commanders. At the end of March 284 aircraft of 38 and 46 Groups and IX U.S. Troop Carrier Command took part in Exercise " Bizz II " in which the whole of 6 Airborne Division was dropped or landed by glider. Between 21st and 25th April, Headquarters 1 Airborne Corps set and supervised exercise " Mush " which was in fact a rehearsal over similar ground for 6 Airborne Division's task in the invasion of North-West Europe, although this was not known to the majority of those taking part. Approximately 700 British and American aircraft took part, dropping and landing 1 Airborne Division and 1 Polish Parachute Brigade Group, who represented the enemy, while 6 Airborne Division went by road. The aircraft were controlled by the Combined Troop Carrier Command Post at Eastcote. In May an operational rehearsal for the divisional supply-by-air was held in which all stores were dropped, or landed and collected.

32. On 19th May, 6 Airborne Division was visited by Their Majesties the King and Queen, and Her Royal Highness the Princess Elizabeth, accompanied by Air Chief Marshal Sir Trafford Leigh-Mallory, and on another occasion by General Montgomery. During the Royal visit a massed glider landing took place, and the King showed great interest. The glider pilots were all briefed as to their point of landing, as in operations. His Majesty happened to see the Senior Air Staff Officer of 38 Group, Air Commodore Bladin, referring to a " crib " which showed exactly where each glider was to land. The King pointed out that whereas gliders, 53, 55, 56, etc., had landed in their correct places, No. 54 was not to be seen. After a wait which seemed like years to the anxious R.A.F. officers, their faith was rewarded and No. 54 appeared and landed in the right place. Whereupon the Air Staff breathed again.

33. Shortly after exercise " Mush ", brigade and unit commanders of 6 Airborne Division and senior R.A.F. commanders were briefed for their operational tasks in Normandy and specialist training for these tasks began. A special " X " list was maintained of those personnel who were permitted to be briefed and therefore allowed to hold the special pass to enter Brigmerston House, and each application had to be approved by Headquarters, 21 Army Group, who also laid down the scale of briefing. In the first instance only the divisional commander and the special planning staff were let into the secret, then the intelligence staffs of divisional headquarters, brigade commanders and brigade majors, who were followed by the commanding officers of 2nd Battalion The Oxfordshire and Buckinghamshire Light Infantry and 9th Parachute Battalion, responsible for the Orne bridges and the Merville battery, the capture of which were among the tasks given to the Division. Day after day gliders could be seen circling over airfields, practising " spot " landings for the *coups de main* on to the bridges and the battery. Once they had perfected their day landings, the glider pilots practised continually at night. Dozens of poles were erected on the divisional dropping zone to represent anti-glider obstacles put up by the Germans in Normandy, and windows in Bulford rattled while the engineers of 5 Parachute Brigade Group blew them up as fast as

they were erected, in practise for their role of clearing the landing zones for 6 Air-landing Brigade. 9th Parachute Battalion with detachments from 4th Anti-Tank Battery, R.A., 591st Parachute Squadron, R.E., 224th Parachute Field Ambulance, divisional signals, the Glider Pilot Regiment and the Royal Navy went into a special camp for a fortnight where they erected a replica, complete in every detail, of the Merville battery and carried out several rehearsals for their operations with the utmost secrecy. 7th Parachute Battalion and the six platoons of 2nd Battalion The Oxfordshire and Buckinghamshire Light Infantry who were to be under their command for the capture of the Orne bridges went to Exeter. There they carried out intensive training on the bridges over the River Exe and the canal immediately south of the city.

During the training period the troops were told all details of the operations which were about to take place except actual locations, and very strict security measures were taken throughout the division in checking mail and the reaction of local inhabitants and by the introduction of security personnel, but there were no breaches. One unit even went so far as to employ some 30 attractive, well-dressed W.A.A.Fs. in civilian clothes in order to test whether the troops could keep a secret. All concerned had an excellent time and the integrity of the troops was proved to be complete—at any rate as regards security. The results justified the methods as all ranks went into action with complete confidence in the job in hand and with a morale that was outstandingly high.

34. The innumerable inter-service meetings and conferences included two held by Lieutenant-General Crocker, in the form of model exercises, one at the Royal United Service Institution, London, and one at Bagshot and ended with a final " check-up " conference at Headquarters, 1 Airborne Corps where the Army and Air Commanders concerned went through their respective plans, and at which any minor discrepancies and alterations were brought to light and dealt with. This was followed by a meeting held by Major-General Gale at Brigmerston House where all formation and unit commanders of the Division gave their plans so that everyone was " in the picture ".

35. The problem of collecting, sorting, issuing and re-issuing the thousands of maps and photographs was enormous, especially if there were to be no breach of security. Maps at the scale of 1/50,000 were issued at least to every section commander, with larger scales to all officers. Defence overprints were on the scale of not less than 50 per cent of unit war establishments, with one for each glider pilot and each member of R.A.F. aircrews. New issues were dependent on new information as it came in and the divisional intelligence staffs were kept hard at it, motoring hundreds of miles. The peak was reached on " D "— 3 day when complete new sets of photographs of the dropping zones were taken and had to reach units at once.

36. Preparations for briefing both troops and air crews had begun early in the year with constant photographic reconnaissance over the operational area. Thousands of prints, both vertical and oblique, were produced, and wherever necessary, enlargements up to six feet square were made. The Central Interpretation Unit, Medmenham, with whom the Division was permitted to deal direct, made models of the dropping and landing zones and objectives of such accuracy and detail that they were works of art in themselves. As soon as a bombing raid took place on an objective during the preliminary period such was the care taken by the Central Interpretation Unit that every bomb-crater,

accurate to the last foot, was plotted on the models.   A plasticene model of the whole area was made with great skill by Corporal Jones of 6 Airborne Division Intelligence Section.   For briefing aircrews a model of the area was made to the scale of 1/5,000 and kept at Netheravon.   It was not possible to duplicate this model to stations, but all aircrews were able to study it at least once.   With its aid and of others at Brigmerston House, a coloured film was produced by 38 Group.   By moving the camera at the correct height and speed over the models, runs-in over the dropping and landing zones were accurately simulated and this film was shown to all aircrews.

37. Units of 6 Airborne Division moved to their transit camps towards the end of May, 1944.   Security precautions in transit camps were strict, and each camp was wired in, and heavily guarded.   Once inside no one was allowed out whether they were taking part in the operations or not, unless in formed bodies under command of officers for such purposes as proceeding to airfields, or unless they were in possession of special passes signed by the camp security officers.   The issue of these passes was strictly limited to commanding officers and other key personnel.   Mail could be written in the camps but would not be posted until after the invasion had begun, and no communication by telephone or other means was allowed with " the outside world ".   While at the transit camps troops carried out refresher training in aircraft drills and met their aircrews and glider pilots.   Each unit in camp had a special briefing hut in which were displayed models and photographs, large and small.   Briefing of troops began about 31st May and of aircrews three days before the operation. Complete sets of photographs were issued on the scale of one set each section and one set an aircrew and glider crew.   R.A.F. officers attended army briefing, and where necessary, senior army officers attended, and sometimes assisted in, the briefing of aircrews.

38. By 5th June, 1944, all members of airborne forces, both Army and Air Force, had been thoroughly drilled in what they had to do and had studied maps, models and photographs so often that they could almost draw the operational areas blindfold.   Their morale was as high as it could be and they were ready to " GO TO IT ", to use the divisional motto introduced by Major-General Gale with the words :—

"This motto will be adopted by 6 Airborne Division and as such should be remembered by all ranks in action against the enemy, in training and during day-to-day routine duties ".

Their confidence was typified in the following extract from a letter written later in Normandy by a private soldier to his parents :—

" . . . . nearly three weeks of really hard work by day and night, doing the same thing over and over again meant that we could do the whole thing without thinking . . . .   Can one wonder that we knew and were confident that if everything went according to plan we could not fail . . . . "

CHAPTER XV

THE NORMANDY OPERATIONS, JUNE–SEPTEMBER, 1944

The Allied Plan and the Airborne Tasks

1. The Allied plan for the invasion of North-West Europe, from the Army point of view, was based on a " D " day assault on a five-divisional front over the beaches between Varreville in the west and Ouistreham at the mouth of the River Orne in the east. The initial objectives included Carentan, Isigny, Bayeux and Caen, the airfields in the vicinity of these towns, and the port of Cherbourg. Thereafter the plan envisaged an advance into Britanny with the object of capturing the ports southward to Nantes, then a drive eastward along the line of the River Loire in the direction of Paris, and north-east across the River Seine. The assault was to be carried out on the right by the United States First Army* consisting of VII U.S. Corps and V U.S. Corps, on the left by the British Second Army† consisting of 1 Corps and 30 Corps. Airborne forces were to be dropped on the flanks of the area. Owing to the vital importance of capturing the beaches and exits on the American sector leading to the base of the Cotentin Peninsula, priority of air-lift was given to the American airborne formations, the remainder, sufficient for two-thirds of a division, being allotted to the British.

2. The airborne tasks for the assault on the right were that in the early hours of " D " day, 82 and 101 U.S. Airborne Divisions were to drop in the area south-east and west of Sainte Mère-Église. The task of the former was to capture the crossings of the Merderet river and secure the line of the River Douve as a barrier against the movement of enemy reserves, while the latter was to assist the landing of troops‡ of VII U.S. Corps on the beaches. On the left 6 Airborne Division, less one brigade, was to land on the night of " D " —1 day/" D " day east of Caen with the task of seizing the crossings over the River Orne at Benouville and Ranville, and, in conjunction with commando troops, was to dominate the area to the east of Caen in order to delay the movement of enemy forces towards the town.

6 Airborne Division Plan

3. 1 Corps was the left assault corps of Second Army, and the corps commander's plan was to land two assault divisions, between Graye-sur-Mer and Ouistreham, with 3 Canadian Infantry Division on the right and 3 British Division on the left. The left flank of the sea-borne assault was bounded by a double water obstacle, consisting of the River Orne and the Caen Canal and was overlooked by high ground to the east. Any sea-borne attack on this high ground would have to be made over beaches whose sea approaches would come under the fire of the defences of Le Havre and was to be avoided if possible. An attack across the river and canal themselves might have been a costly operation. The quickest way to seize the dominating ground, therefore, was by an airborne assault. The Commander, 6 Airborne Division, was given the following tasks (*see* Map 7) :—

    (*a*) *Primary Tasks*

            (i) The capture of the bridges (intact if possible) at Benouville and Ranville and the establishment of a bridgehead sufficiently deep to enable them to be held.

---

* General O. M. Bradley.   † General Sir Miles Dempsey.   ‡ 4 U.S. Infantry Division.

(ii) The destruction or neutralization of the coastal battery at Franceville Plage (later known as the Merville battery) by dawn minus 30 minutes, before the sea-borne assault craft came within its range.

(iii) The destruction of the bridges over the River Dives at Varaville, Robehomme, Bures and Troarn in order to impose the maximum delay on any enemy movements from the east.

(*b*) *Secondary Tasks.*—As soon as the resources permitted, but without prejudice to the success of the primary tasks, to develop the operation east of the River Orne in order to :—

(i) Mop up and secure the area between the Rivers Orne and Dives, north of the road Colombelles–Sannerville–Troarn. This was to include the capture of the towns of Sallenelles and Franceville Plage, and the clearing of as much as possible of the coastal strip between these places and Cabourg, at the mouth of the River Dives.

(ii) Having secured a firm base east of the River Orne, to operate offensively against any reserve attempting to move towards the covering position from the east and south-east.

In order to assist 6 Airborne Division to carry out these tasks 1 Special Service Brigade (Commandos) was to be placed under command after it had been landed by sea.

4. Although the resources of 38 Group, with under command 46 Group, were at the disposal of 6 Airborne Division, the total airlift available did not permit of the carrying of the whole Division in one lift, and the divisional commander had to decide, therefore, which troops were to be carried by air in each of two lifts and which were to be brought in by sea. The task of seizing the bridges required a rapid concentration of effort, if they were to be seized intact, and therefore in the original plan this task was allotted to 6 Air-landing Brigade, as the more heavily armed units of this brigade were better fitted for a prolonged defence of the bridges after their capture. The more dispersed tasks towards the east including the destruction of the Merville battery were allotted to 3 Parachute Brigade, while 5 Parachute Brigade, with some divisional troops, including the tanks of 6 Airborne Armoured Reconnaissance Regiment, was to be brought in on a second lift. Divisional headquarters, with some anti-tank and light artillery units, was to land after 6 Air-landing Brigade.

5. The terrain was such that no time was wasted between the Army and R.A.F. in deciding on the dropping zones and landing zones, which would meet both the Army and Air requirements. However, on 17th April photographic reconnaissance revealed that the Germans were erecting poles as anti-air-landing obstacles on all the available landing zones. As a result the plan had to be altered and parachute troops had to be landed before the main glider force in order to remove sufficient of the obstacles to make the landing of gliders a reasonably safe proposition. The assault on the bridges, therefore, was allotted to 5 Parachute Brigade, instead of 6 Air-landing Brigade which was to come in with the second lift. A small glider *coup de main* party of 2nd Battalion, The Oxfordshire and Buckinghamshire Light Infantry was placed under command of 5 Parachute Brigade. The idea of a direct assault

by gliders on to the bridges had come to Major-General Gale as a result of reading the reports of the German attacks on Fort Eben Emael, in Holland and on the Corinth Canal in Greece, although Brigadier Hill had also thought of it at about the same time. One air-landing battalion, the Light Regiment, less one battery, and various divisional troops together with a " sea-tail " were to come by sea.

6. The fact that the primary tasks of the Division had to be accomplished before dawn on 6th June, meant that the first lift would have to be dropped after dark on 5th June, if surprise were to be obtained. To make this surprise complete the troops would have to be on the ground for the shortest possible time before they attacked their objectives. 3 Parachute Brigade's job of destroying the Merville battery was one of the most difficult and would need careful synchronization, so that the timing of the operations of the Division virtually depended on the plan for the destruction of the battery. It is not always easy for the Air Forces to drop troops accurately in daylight, and with a night drop of this description there was a risk that only a proportion of the forces might be available in the right place at the right time. Major-General Gale had to accept this risk.

7. On 18th March, the divisional commander held a conference at the planning headquarters, Brigmerston House, Netheravon, and gave commanders their tasks in the form of operation instructions (*see* Appendix K).

8. Intelligence of the enemy's dispositions was detailed and accurate. It was known that the German strength in the area consisted of 711 and 716 infantry divisions, possibly two armoured squadrons, and an unknown number of infantry and artillery units which could be produced from training schools in the area. Both these divisions had a miscellaneous collection of anti-tank guns, static field and medium guns, with a sprinkling of German and French obsolescent tanks and self-propelled guns. Compared with a first class line infantry division their efficiency was assessed at 40 per cent. in a static and 15 per cent. in a counter-attack role. In addition to these troops, 352 Infantry Division and 12 S.S. Panzer Division (Hitler Jugend) were situated fairly close to the area in counter-attack roles. They were believed to be up to strength and fully equipped with modern weapons, the armoured division having Panther tanks. It was estimated that the infantry division would be able to concentrate and be ready to operate in the area Caen-Bayeux by " H " + 8 hours and that the armoured division could arrive east of Caen by " H " + 12 hours. In fact 352 Infantry Division never intervened on 6 Airborne Division front as it was drawn off to the west. Of other counter-attack formations, the most noteworthy were 21 Panzer Division in the area of Rennes and 3 Parachute Division in western Brittany. 21 Panzer Division later moved towards Caen during May, and at the time of the invasion was on manœuvres in that area with an anti-invasion role.

9. It appeared that, having ascertained the limits of the landing and failed in the initial counter-attack, the obvious line on which the enemy would hold the invading forces would be the high ground to the east of the flooded valley of the River Dives. Although it would weaken the estuary defences of the River Seine, which were a definite part of the German system, it was likely that once the threat had clearly declared itself west of the River Seine estuary, part of the

infantry division earmarked for the defence of these areas would move west to take up position along the high ground east of the River Dives. It was thought that no serious large scale enemy attack would be launched against the airborne troops for 24 hours.

10. 5 Parachute Brigade was commanded by Brigadier J. H. N. Poett, and consisted of Brigade Headquarters, 7th, 12th and 13th Parachute Battalions, 4th Anti-Tank Battery, R.A., less one section, D Company, 2nd Battalion Oxfordshire and Buckinghamshire Light Infantry, 591st Parachute Squadron, R.E., less one troop, detachment 286th Field Park Company, R.E., and 225th Parachute Field Ambulance. The tasks given to the brigade commander were :-
- (a) By a *coup de main* with glider-borne troops to seize the crossings over the River Orne and the canal at Benouville and Ranville.
- (b) To secure and hold the area Benouville-Ranville-Le Bas de Ranville.
- (c) To clear the landing zones north of Ranville of obstructions sufficiently to allow 68 gliders to land by two hours before daylight on " D " day and 146 Gliders to land by the evening of " D " day.
  The brigade was also responsible for the protection of the larger of the two landing zones.

11. 3 Parachute Brigade commanded by Brigadier S. J. L. Hill, and consisting of 1st Canadian, 8th and 9th Parachute Battalions, one section 4th Anti-Tank Battery, R.A., 3rd Parachute Squadron, R.E., one troop 591st Parachute Squadron, R.E., and 224th Parachute Field Ambulance, was to drop south-east of the River Orne. The brigade tasks were :—
- (a) To silence the Merville battery and destroy its equipment one and a half hours before the first landing craft were to touch down on the beaches.
- (b) To demolish the bridges over the River Dives at Varaville, Robehomme, Bures and Troarn.
- (c) On completion of the above tasks to deny the enemy the use of the roads leading into the Ranville bridgehead area from the east, by establishing the brigade on the high ground from north of Troarn to Le Plein.

12. On the evening of " D " day, 6 Air-landing Brigade commanded by Brigadier The Hon. H. K. M. Kindersley, and an Armoured Reconnaissance Group under Colonel R. G. Parker, Deputy Commander of 6 Air-landing Brigade was to land by glider in the vicinity of Ranville. 6 Air-landing Brigade consisted of :—

    2nd Battalion Oxfordshire and Buckinghamshire Light Infantry, less one company and two platoons

    1st Battalion Royal Ulster Rifles

was to take over command of 4th Anti-Tank Battery and one parachute battalion from 5 Parachute Brigade on arrival, and was to occupy and hold the bridghead to the south-west of Ranville on the line Longueval–St. Honorine la Chardonnerette Escoville–Les Bas de Ranville. 5 Parachute Brigade was then to come into divisional reserve in the Ranville–Le Mariquet area. 6 Air-landing Brigade was to be joined by 12th Battalion, The Devonshire Regiment, less one company, and 3rd Anti-Tank Battery which were to arrive by sea. The Armoured Reconnaissance Group was a mobile column and was to be prepared to operate south of the bridgehead area in a reconnaissance role if the tactical situation permitted. It consisted of 6 Airborne Armoured Reconnaissance Regiment, 211th Air-landing Light Battery, one company 12th Battalion, Devonshire Regiment, and would be joined by one troop of 3rd Air-landing Anti-Tank Battery on arrival by sea.

13. Commander 6 Airborne Division gave 1 Special Service Brigade the task of holding the area of Le Plein as a base with the object of mopping up as far as possible along the coast towards the area Franceville Plage and Cabourg. The Brigade was under command of Brigadier The Lord Lovat, and consisted of No. 3 Commando, No. 6 Commando, No. 45 (Royal Marine) Commando, No. 1 and 8 Allied Troops and one troop Engineer Commando. It was joined later by No. 4 Commando.

The Air Plan

14. The total available air-lift of 38 and 46 Groups was 15 squadrons, providing 423 aircraft. The available glider force consisted of 1,040 Horsas (50 each squadron) and 80 Hamilcars which were allotted to Halifax squadrons, of which 6 Airborne Division would probably use 350 gliders, the majority being taken up by 6 Air-landing Brigade (220 Horsas and 30 Hamilcars).

In addition, 6,000 man dropping " X " type parachutes and 10,000 containers were needed for the main operation with a further 10,000 containers or panniers for supply by air. All 38 and 46 Group aircraft were fitted with " Gee " as an aid to navigation to the approximate target area and with Rebecca II as a short-range homing device on to pinpoint targets marked by Eureka radar beacons, set up by personnel of 22nd Independent Parachute Company. The flight plan was as follows :—

(a) 0020 *hours 6th June*

Pathfinders on all D.Zs.—two Albemarles to each D.Z.

Coup de Main party—three Horsa gliders on each bridge towed by three Halifaxes of 644 Squadron and three Halifaxes of 298 Squadron.

Advance parties of 3 and 5 Parachute Brigades—16 Albemarles of 295 and 570 Squadrons for 3 Parachute Brigade, and five Albemarles of 296 and 297 Squadrons for 5 Parachute Brigade.

(b) 0050 *hours 6th June*

Main body of 3 and 5 Parachute Brigades.

3 Parachute Brigade to be dropped by 108 Dakotas of 46 Group and to use 17 Horsas towed by Dakotas and Albemarles of both groups for heavy equipment. 5 Parachute Brigade to be dropped by 131 aircraft, Dakotas and Stirlings, of both groups.

(c) 0320 *hours 6th June*

Divisional Headquarters including H.Q. R.A., H.Q. R.E., H.Q. R.A.S.C., F.O.O. and F.O.B. parties and 4th Anti-Tank Battery, R.A., to be landed in 65 Horsas and four Hamilcars.

(d) 0430 *hours 6th June*

Three Horsa Gliders towed by Albemarles of 297 Squadron to land for a direct assault on the Merville coastal battery.

(e) 2100 *hours 6th June*

      Headquarters, 6 Air-landing Brigade, 2nd Battalion Oxfordshire and Buckinghamshire Light Infantry, less one company and two platoons.

      1st Battalion Royal Ulster Rifles, 211th Light Battery, R.A., and the Armoured Reconnaissance Regiment. The total lift for this party was to consist of 220 Horsas and 30 Hamilcars towed by ten squadrons of 38 Group and four squadrons of 46 Group.

15. The Air plan was the responsibility of the R.A.F., but in every case alterations were made only after consultation with 6 Airborne Division. Requests for offensive support and diversions were put forward by the Division through Army channels after consultation with 38 Group. The most important of these was to be a bomber attack by 100 Lancasters with 4,000 and 8,000 lb. bombs on the Merville battery from 0030 hours to 0040 hours in support of the eventual assault by 9th Parachute Battalion. There were also to be intruders on inland night-fighter airfields in the shape of standing patrols from 2345 hours on " D " — 1 day to 0430 hours on " D " day. Ground straffing by fighters was to be carried out, the fighters patrolling to draw light flak and searchlights and to attack these, but they were to be instructed to be clear of the area before the first landings. To confuse the enemy radar system until the last possible moment ten " window " dropping aircraft were to simulate an airborne attack in the direction of the River Seine estuary. The six aircraft towing the gliders for the *coup de main* party on the bridges were each to carry two general purpose bombs which they were to drop on a powder factory a short distance to the south-east of Caen in order to deceive the enemy as to the real reason for the presence of six aircraft in more or less close formation. It will be remembered that in the preparation period (*see* Chapter XIV) aircraft had been " dribbled " in over this area by ones and twos. On the evening of " D " day, close fighter escort was to be provided for 6 Air-landing Brigade by 15 squadrons of No. 11 Group, R.A.F., and routine high and low level fighter cover was to be provided for the beach-head ; escorted bomber operations and fighter sweeps were to take place to the south and south-east of the beach-head area. Aircraft of No. 3 (Bomber) Group were to drop parachute dummies and noise simulators near the Dieppe–Boulogne area to confuse the enemy defence as to the real area of the attack.

16. There were many spare bomb-racks on both parachute and tug-aircraft, and these were filled with stores containers, known as " jettison " containers, on the principle that no effort should be spared to take in everything possible that might be useful. The jettison drop is dealt with in more detail later.

The Airborne Assault of 6 Airborne Division

PATHFINDERS

17. Two sticks of pathfinders from 22nd Independent Parachute Company should have been dropped on each dropping zone but in each case only one stick was accurately dropped. In three cases two or more runs over the target were needed to get all the troops out, one aircraft completing its drop on the third run, 14 minutes later. All the radar and visual beacons for dropping zone " V " (1st Canadian and 9th Parachute Battalions) were lost or damaged, and one aircraft carrying a pathfinder team intended for dropping zone " K "

(H.Q. 3 Parachute Brigade and 8th Parachute Battalion) put its passengers down on dropping zone " N " (5 Parachute Brigade). Not realizing that they were on the wrong dropping zone, the " K " pathfinders set up their beacons and lights on dropping zone " N ". The result was that 14 sticks, with their jettison containers, of Headquarters 3 Parachute Brigade and 8th Parachute Battalion dropped on to dropping zone " N ", before the " N " pathfinders, who had been dropped some distance away, arrived and erected the correct beacons about 30 minutes later. In addition some of the pathfinder personnel set up their lights in standing crops, and they were not seen from the air.

5 Parachute Brigade

18. The seizure of the bridges over the Caen Canal and the River Orne was carried out by a glider-borne *coup de main* party of six platoons of 2nd Battalion Oxfordshire and Buckinghamshire Light Infantry under command of Major R. J. Howard, with a detachment of Royal Engineers, supported by 7th Parachute Battalion dropping half an hour later. Of the six gliders, five landed exactly on time at 0020 hours 6th June, 1944, four with great accuracy and one half a mile away. The sixth was put down on a bridge over the River Dives seven miles way. The surprise obtained in this initial landing, coupled with the degree of speed with which the assault was delivered, resulted in the enemy's defences being overrun immediately. Both bridges were captured intact and a close bridgehead was established on the western bank. Of the 131 aircraft allotted to 5 Parachute Brigade two became unserviceable at the airfield, and were unable to take off, and six failed to reach Normandy, among them five Stirlings later reported missing. Flight conditions were similar to those of the pathfinder aircraft, the sky being covered most of the way with layers of cloud between 4,000 and 6,000 feet, with no moon. Average visibility was under three miles, and the wind was ten to twenty miles an hour from the west. However, the crews carrying 5 Parachute Brigade had the advantage of being able to use the battle for the bridges as a land-mark, and although some sticks were dropped short of the target, on the whole the dropping was fairly accurate. Of the 750 jettison containers carried, 702 were dropped.

The drop of 7th Parachute Battalion was scattered, but by 0300 hours, 40 per cent. of the battalion had reached the bridges and more men continued to come in throughout the day. The battalion assumed responsibility for the position on arrival and enlarged the bridgehead on the western bank to a depth of 800 yards. Enemy counter-measures, consisting of isolated and uncoordinated counter-attacks by tanks, armoured cars and infantry, began to develop at 0500 hours and continued with increasing intensity during 6th June. 7th Parachute Battalion, with the glider force, successfully beat off these attacks and at 1900 hours 6th June, Major-General T. G. Rennie, Commander 3 British Infantry Division, arrived at the bridges. He issued orders for troops of his Division to take over from 7th Parachute Battalion, and the relief was completed by about 0100 hours 7th June. Among other things, while holding the bridges, 7th Parachute Battalion had a " naval battle " with two German coastal craft, which had retired from Ouistreham, and were on their way up the canal to Caen. The first information they had that we owned the bridges was when our troops opened fire. The vessels went aground and the crews were captured. During 6th June the Germans made an unsuccessful air attack on the bridge, a 1,000 lb. bomb actually hitting it, but bouncing off without exploding.

178

19. Meanwhile 12th and 13th Parachute Battalions had dropped at 0050 hours and were also scattered. When they moved from their rendezvous each battalion was not more than 60 per cent. strong, though odd parties joined up during the day, but 12th Parachute Battalion seized the Le Bas de Ranville area and 13th Parachute Battalion the Ranville–Le Mariquet area. The Germans reacted swiftly against these units and attacked Ranville almost at once, but they were repulsed with the loss of a number of enemy prisoners of war and one German tank destroyed. At 1045 hours a further attack developed supported by self-propelled guns, which penetrated the village but was beaten off by 12th Parachute Battalion while 4th Air-landing Anti-Tank Battery accounted for three self-propelled guns and one tank. By 1300 hours the enemy attacks had increased and the position of 12th and 13th Parachute Battalions was critical, with the result that the leading commando of 1 Special Service Brigade was diverted to the area to assist the airborne troops and was not released until the evening. This diversion, necessary and successful though it was, curtailed the offensive action of 1 Special Service Brigade and subsequently delayed their penetration into Franceville Plage. In the fighting at Ranville there were many gallant actions but one was outstanding. Lieutenant J. A. N. Sims, 12th Parachute Battalion, was in charge of a position held by a few men. German infantry attacked, supported by two self-propelled guns, one of which Lieutenant Sims knocked out. The other gun killed his men one by one at point-blank range. However, the officer held his ground until the gun withdrew, leaving him with only three men.

3 Parachute Brigade

20. When addressing some of his officers on the day before the operation Brigadier Hill proved himself to be somewhat of a prophet. He said " Gentlemen, in spite of your excellent training and orders, do not be daunted if chaos reigns. It undoubtedly will."

21. The advance party of 3 Parachute Brigade included elements of Brigade headquarters and of each battalion, and one company of 1st Canadian Parachute Battalion, whose duty it was to clear dropping zone " V " of enemy posts. Two of the 14 Albemarles carrying the advance party dropped only three and nine troops respectively ; from a third aircraft six men went out as it crossed the coast, and only four jumped over the dropping zone ; and a fourth aircraft, under enemy fire, had to make a second run over the area, so that it dropped late. Two more aircraft reported " Gee " failure, one losing time flying along the coast to find the point of entry, and the other having to return to base after being hit by flak on its seventh run-over in search of the dropping zone. In the latter aircraft was Major W. A. C. Collingwood, brigade major of 3 Parachute Brigade, who was waiting to jump when the aircraft was hit. He was knocked through the hole and remained hanging underneath the fuselage for half-an-hour suspended by his static line which had become wound round his leg. He had a 60 lb. kit-bag attached to his leg, but was eventually pulled into the aircraft. Despite his hair-raising experience he arrived in Normandy by glider later in the day.

22. Most of the pathfinder equipment for dropping zone " V " was damaged in the drop, so only two green lights were exhibited when the main body arrived there and few crews saw them, in addition to which they were hampered by dust and smoke blowing across the run-in from the bombing of the Merville

battery by the Lancasters. The main body had a very scattered drop, Brigadier Hill and several sticks of 1st Canadian and 9th Parachute Battalion being dropped near the River Dives. Their position of course was not known and unfortunately on their way to join their units later in the day, this party suffered heavy casualties in killed and wounded from our own bombing, Brigadier Hill being slightly wounded. Of the gliders carrying the heavy equipment of the brigade, three parted from their tugs in cloud off the French coast, the remainder being released to the north of the landing zone. Three gliders landed on dropping zone " N ", the others ending up in a semi-circle about a mile and a half to the south-east of their correct landing zone.

23. 9th Parachute Battalion, with under command detachments of anti-tank artillery, forward observation bombardment units to control naval gunfire, Royal Engineers and field ambulances, was given the task of destroying the Merville coastal battery. The battalion was given the secondary tasks of seizing and holding the high ground on which stood the village of Le Plein until relieved by commandos, of blocking the roads leading from Franceville Plage to the Le Plein feature, and, finally, of capturing a German naval headquarters at Sallenelles near the mouth of the River Orne. The battalion dropped at 0050 hours over an enormous area. They moved off from their rendezvous under the commanding officer at 0245 hours with only 150 all ranks out of an approximate total of 700, and having only one Vickers machine-gun, no 3-inch mortars, no vehicles, no artillery, Royal Engineers or field ambulance personnel, no mine detectors, a few anti-tank weapons, no special stores and barely sufficient wireless sets. The glider-borne element of the battalion which carried the anti-tank guns, jeeps and special stores for the assault on the battery, had failed to arrive and the battalion reconnaissance party reported that the preliminary heavy bomber attack by Lancasters had completely missed the target.

The battalion plan included a direct assault on the battery by three Horsa Gliders carrying 58 officers and men of the battalion, and one officer and seven other ranks of the Royal Engineers. The commander of this party was Major R. Gordon-Brown, and the arrival of the gliders was timed to coincide with the attack of the remainder of the battalion from outside the battery defences so that they could be guided in by 3-inch mortar flares. Of the three gliders detailed for this task, one had instrument trouble and turned back to land in England. There were no flares to guide the other two glider-crews as the battalion had no 3-inch mortars, the majority of the mortar-platoon having been dropped in or near the River Dives, and one glider landed close to the battery, the other landing about three miles away. In spite of these handicaps, the battalion penetrated the minefields and outer wire defences of the battery in the face of heavy enemy fire, and finally assaulted and overran the position, destroying two out of four guns completely and rendering two useless for 48 hours. At the close of this action they had lost 65 killed, wounded or missing from the assaulting 150, and had captured 22 enemy prisoners. The remaining personnel of the German garrison of 200 were either killed or wounded. Subsequently, on approaching Le Plein, it was found that the village was strongly held by the enemy. The battalion's strength had now increased to approximately 100 all ranks, but it suffered further casualties and in any case was too weak to evict the enemy from the village completely, so that after it had captured half the village both sides settled down to a period of watching and waiting. On the arrival of No. 3 Commando on the afternoon of 7th June, a combined airborne-commando attack finally forced the enemy to withdraw.

24. 1st Canadian Parachute Battalion was allotted the primary task of destroying the bridges at Varaville and Robehomme after which they were to assist in forming the bridgehead in the area of the Bois de Bavent. Most of this battalion was also dropped some distance from the dropping zone but the enemy offered only slight opposition, except in the area of the chateau near Varaville where a sharp action took place, with the result that the primary tasks were successfully carried out without difficulty. The battalion then reverted to brigade control and occupied a position in the Le Mesnil area.

25. 8th Parachute Battalion was given the task of destroying two bridges at Bures and one east of Troarn. Then they were to assist in forming the bridgehead, by occupying an area south of Le Mesnil. The drop of this battalion was also scattered, a number of sticks being dropped in 5 Parachute Brigade's area, as has already been mentioned, with the result that the Royal Engineer detachments became separated and could not reach the battalion rendezvous in time. They therefore proceeded direct to the objective independently. One serjeant, a Serjeant Jones, was captured, but snatched a machine-carbine from a German, killed eight of the enemy and escaped. At Bures the sappers linked up with the advance elements of 8th Parachute Battalion, did not meet any enemy, and blew both bridges successfully. At Troarn the leading elements of the battalion encountered opposition on the northern outskirts of the town. The engineer detachment of seven, with Major J. C. A. Roseveare in charge, mounted in a jeep and trailer, heard this action in progress as they approached Troarn from the west. They decided to rush through the town, and this they did, firing blindly from their vehicles as they went, and being in turn heavily fired upon by the Germans. At a level crossing in Troarn they ran into a barbed wire knife rest, and took 20 minutes to cut themselves free. They went on and reached the bridge and successfully blew the gap. After this feat they ditched the jeep and made their way back to Le Mesnil on foot. The gap in the bridge was subsequently widened by 8th Parachute Battalion later in the day. The battalion then moved north and occupied its position in the bridgehead.

H.Q. 6 Airborne Division, 6 Air-landing Brigade and the Armoured Reconnaissance Group

26. Headquarters 6 Airborne Division landed by glider on the main landing zone in the Ranville area at 0335 hours, though a few gliders were scattered, and moved to the Le Bas de Ranville area. Contact with Headquarters, 5 Parachute Brigade was established at 0500 hours, and with 3 Parachute Brigade at 1235 hours. As stated above, enemy pressure gradually increased during the morning culminating in the attack on Ranville at 1300 hours. However, by 1353 hours 1 Special Service Brigade had crossed the bridges, where it came under command of 6 Airborne Division, and the situation was in hand. By 1700 hours it was known that the Merville battery had been destroyed, that the bridges at Varaville, Robehomme, Troarn and Bures had been blown and that 1st Canadian Parachute Battalion was established in the area of Le Mesnil. 6 Air-landing Brigade less one battalion, the Airborne

181

Armoured Reconnaissance Regiment and 211th Light Battery, R.A., landed by glider on the Ranville and " W " landing zones at 2100 hours without incident. Few casualties were sustained, either by enemy action or from crash landings, and all obstructions had been removed as planned by the sappers of 5 Parachute Brigade. A few days after landing, a Frenchman was observed laboriously digging holes in the fields on the landing zone, and erecting large poles. When asked why, he replied that the Germans had paid him to do it and no one had told him to stop.

27. A summary of the 85 gliders of the Division, not including the bridge and battery assault gliders which landed by night is as follows :—

Correctly landed on L.Z.	52
Within two miles of L.Z.	6
Over two miles from L.Z.	10
Missing ..	17

Of the 17 missing gliders, three landed in England, and one in the sea, personnel of all four joining the Division later. It is impossible to give the accurate strength of units in the first few hours of darkness, but the battalions of 3 Parachute Brigade had to carry out their tasks at well below 30 per cent strength. In the case of 5 Parachute Brigade, some 16 men were killed and 80 wounded during the drop, and the number of all ranks finally missing after rallying was complete was 432, of whom a substantial number re-joined during the next few days. One serjeant-major came in on a bicycle, wearing civilian clothes and carrying a Frenchman's identity card. A French girl was with him, as she had accompanied him through the German lines in case he was stopped, in which case she was going to do the talking. The clothes and papers belonged to her brother. The final figures of missing for the two parachute brigades, as a result of the initial airborne operations, was 30 officers and 628 other ranks. Parachute drops were not as concentrated as might have been expected.

One unforeseen repercussion of this unintentional scattering of troops was that great confusion was caused to the Germans who were misled as to the area and extent of the airborne landings. Some of our own troops got a bit mixed up too, especially in regard to the passwords. One staff officer of divisional headquarters whose glider landed a long way from the correct place, was challenged by an officer of the parachute troops, accompanied by several of his men. The staff officer had to confess that he didn't know the counter-sign. After several bursts of sten-fire had missed him identities were established. The staff officer then came into his own for he knew where he was and the parachutists did not. On another occasion an officer was challenged with the password " Punch " by a raucous voice. The officer froze into frightened immobility, too shaken to reply. The voice then said " if you don't . . . well answer Judy I'll . . . shoot " and a large British warrant officer appeared.

28. In fact the air plan worked, although weather conditions were by no means ideal. All tasks allotted to 6 Airborne Division were carried out up to time, and such scattering of personnel as there was did not cause failure in any part of the operation of the plan.

The American Airborne Assaults

29. While the attack by 6 Airborne Division had been proceeding east of the River Orne, at the other end of the long front, near the base of the Cotentin Peninsula, the American airborne assaults had been taking place with much the same difficulties from the weather as those of their British comrades. 101 U.S. Airborne Division began dropping south-east of Sainte Mère Église at about 0130 hours, 6th June, 1944. Owing to the weather the pathfinders had failed to locate the exact areas of the dropping zones, and this, combined with the inexperience of some of the pilots and their method of formation flying (*see* para. 76 (*c*)) led to a very wide dispersal of troops and supplies. The Division went into action at an approximate strength of only 6,600 and was scattered over an area some 25 by 15 miles as a result of which 60 per cent of their equipment was lost. However, despite these difficulties the troops fought with great gallantry and quickly seized the two villages of Pouppeville and Saint Martin de Varreville behind the beaches. 82 U.S. Airborne Division landed west of the Carentan-Cherbourg main road from 0230 hours onwards, and was also very widely scattered for the same reasons but had the added difficulty that the troops were dispersed astride the River Merderet. In addition they came under very heavy shell fire but despite these hardships the town of Sainte Mère Église was captured before daylight and by the early hours of 6th June contact had been established with the sea-borne troops pushing inland from the beaches. Gliders were flown in during the day and suffered considerable casualties, but reinforcements reached the hard-pressed airborne units during the night of 6/7th June. The element of surprise achieved by the American airborne troops was as effective as that achieved by 6 Airborne Division and great confusion was caused by the cutting of enemy communications and the disorganizing of the German defences. More important than this, the American airborne troops succeeded in capturing the causeways across the inundated areas behind the beaches, thereby giving the Allies control of the routes into the Cotentin Peninsula, upon which depended the capture of Cherbourg.

Holding the Flank East of the River Orne

30. The period from 7th June until 16th August, 1944, was spent by 6 Airborne Division in consolidating the bridgehead in the first stage and in holding it against enemy attacks in the second stage. During the first week the Germans kept up a continuous and increasing pressure on the Division's position in determined attempts to force the crossings over the River Orne so that they could attack the left flank of the British Second Army. The Germans realized that once they obtained possession of the high ground running south from Le Plein through the Bois de Bavent to Troarn they could dominate all crossings over the River Orne, the low ground on either side of the river and the canal, the beaches used for the build-up, and to a certain extent the high ground to the west of the river, which was the area over which 3 British Division was operating.

31. Major-General Gale's original plan had envisaged the use of the Armoured Reconnaissance Group in a long range reconnaissance role to the south of the bridgehead on the east of the Orne, but owing to the strength of the enemy this plan was abandoned. The Airborne Armoured Reconnaissance Regiment was employed in reconnaissance forward to Troarn and Sannerville and obtained a considerable amount of information that was of value both to 6 Airborne Division and to 1 Corps.

183

32. During the night 6th/7th June, 1st Battalion Royal Ulster Rifles and 2nd Battalion Oxfordshire and Buckinghamshire Light Infantry moved to the southern portion of the bridgehead and by 0900 hours, 7th June, had occupied Longueval and Herouvillette respectively. During the morning of 7th June, 1 Special Service Brigade occupied Sallenelles and attacked and captured Franceville Plage, but the village of Breville which lay between the commando brigade and 3 Parachute Brigade and overlooked the Ranville area, remained in enemy hands. While the commandos were attacking Franceville Plage troops of 6 Air-landing Brigade were putting in attacks on St. Honorine and Escoville. These attacks penetrated the enemy defences but they encountered such stiff opposition from enemy self-propelled guns and tanks that it was decided to fall back and consolidate in the original positions. Shortly after the troops had done this the Germans developed a determined infantry and armoured attack on 1st Battalion The Royal Ulster Rifles in Longueval which was repulsed after heavy fighting. At 1815 hours, 12th Battalion The Devonshire Regiment, which had crossed the Channel by sea, entered the divisional area and took over positions from 12th Parachute Battalion in the area of Le Bas de Ranville. By the night of 7th June, 6 Airborne Division had secured all its objectives with the exception of the small coastal strip between Franceville Plage and Cabourg which was beyond its resources to occupy. The enemy remained in possession of Breville.

33. During the morning of 8th June, the Germans attacked in strength against No. 4 Commando in the Hauger-Sallenelles area. This attack continued throughout the day at intervals and was renewed in strength at 2130 hours in the evening but the Germans made no progress. On 9th June enemy pressure was maintained on the front of 1 Special Service Brigade and 3 Parachute Brigade. Some infiltration was achieved on 1 Special Service Brigade front and the attacks on 3 Parachute Brigade front increased in strength throughout the day with the enemy endeavouring to locate the exact positions of our troops. At 2000 hours, 9th June, a strong enemy attack was delivered against 12th Battalion the Devonshire Regiment and 2nd Battalion Oxfordshire and Buckinghamshire Light Infantry in the south of the bridgehead. The Devon front was penetrated but the enemy was driven out by an immediate counter-attack, and he lost four tanks which were destroyed by the Light Infantrymen. Enemy self-propelled guns also penetrated Longueval but withdrew when engaged.

34. During the early morning of 10th June, 1 Special Service Brigade front was subjected to heavy mortar fire, and concentrations of mortar and shell fire came down in the Longueval area, accompanied by bombing. Shortly after this infantry probing attacks developed along the commando front and infil-trated through the Breville gap between the brigade and 3 Parachute Brigade. This was followed by the main attack from the Breville area in two directions, north-west against the commandos in Le Plein and south-west across the landing zone towards Le Mariquet which was held by 13th Parachute Battalion. The attack against Le Plein failed, the enemy being driven back into Breville with great loss. While crossing the landing zone the Germans took advantage of the cover afforded by our gliders but this did not worry 13th Parachute Battalion who held their fire until the enemy emerged into the open at close range. Great losses were inflicted on the Germans who immediately halted and took cover. At 1600 hours a counter-attack was launched by two

companies of 7th Parachute Battalion supported by one squadron 13th/18th Hussars (Sherman Tanks) from the Le Hom area north-west of Ranville. The enemy was taken completely by surprise and offered no organized resistance. Two hundred dead were left on the ground and over 150 were taken prisoner, the remainder streaming back in the direction of Breville where they were caught between cross-fire from the commandos on one side and 9th Parachute Battalion on the other.

35. During the whole of this period of heavy fighting between 8th and 10th June, 6 Airborne Division was given invaluable assistance by the divisional artillery of 3 British Infantry Division. Whenever this fire was called for it came down in the required place accurately and rapidly and the volume was far in excess of any fire that could be produced from the airborne artillery, and was annihilating in its effect. Although the enemy did penetrate slightly into the divisional positions on occasions, the weight had been taken out of his attack by artillery fire before he could do much damage and in every case local counter-attacks restored the situation very soon.

36. It was the intention of Commander, 1 Corps to extend the bridgehead south and to this end the southern sector was to be taken over by 51 (Highland) Division. However, no serious attack south was safe with the Breville gap still in German hands. 6 Airborne Division had not the resources to fill this gap and the 1st Battalion 5th Black Watch (Royal Highland Regiment) was therefore to be placed under command for this purpose. During the night 10th/11th June, 153 Infantry Brigade of 51 (Highland) Division crossed the River Orne and entered the divisional area. 1st and 5th/7th Battalions, The Gordon Highlanders took over the southern half of the Bois de Bavent sector while 1st Battalion 5th Black Watch was placed under command 3 Parachute Brigade in order to attack and capture Breville. However, this attack was carried out without daylight reconnaissance despite warnings issued by the airborne troops on the ground and as a result the Black Watch encountered heavy opposition and suffered considerable casualties. The attack was a failure and the battalion withdrew into 9th Parachute Battalion area to reorganize. The remainder of 153 Infantry Brigade was in position by the night of 11th June and at the same time 4 Special Service Brigade (Commandos) under Brigadier B. W. Leicester, consisting of Nos. 41, 46, 47, and 48 (Royal Marine) Commandos, entered the divisional area and came under command 6 Airborne Division. On 12th June, enemy attacks from Breville and further east began at 0500 hours supported by tanks and heavy mortar and artillery fire on to the positions held by 9th Parachute Battalion and 1st Battalion 5th Black Watch. These attacks continued throughout the day and several defensive tasks were fired by the artillery of 3 British Division and 51 (Highland) Division, and by cruisers of the Royal Navy, to repel them. At 1700 hours the Germans put in yet another very determined attack against 1st Battalion 5th Black Watch which forced part of this unit to fall back on to 9th Parachute Battalion positions. By this time 9th Parachute Battalion was less than 200 strong and had no reserve with which to counter-attack, so Brigadier Hill, despite the fact that he was still suffering from the effects of his wound, personally led one company of 1st Canadian Parachute Battalion in a counter-attack which partially restored the situation. The only divisional reserve at this time was 12th Parachute Battalion which was very weak and which was resting, and one squadron 13th/18th Hussars.

37. The divisional commander decided that Breville must be liquidated once and for all and that an attack that evening was a vital necessity despite the short time available. Major-General Gale calculated that an attack in the last light and after a very heavy day's fighting would catch the Germans unprepared and would give the assaulting troops time to reorganize in the dark. Orders were issued at 1900 hours for an attack on Breville to be launched at 2230 hours by 12th Parachute Battalion with under command one company 12 Devons, one squadron 13th/18th Hussars and 22nd Independent Parachute Company, supported by four field regiments and one medium regiment. An immediate counter-attack was anticipated. Our attack was to go in from the west, the start line being the outer edge of Amfreville. While the troops were forming up our artillery fire fell short, and caused a number of casualties, among them being Lieutenant-Colonel Johnston and Major J. Bampfylde, the Devon Company Commander, killed, and Brigadiers Kindersley and Lord Lovat, seriously wounded. In addition the Germans put down heavy defensive fire causing still more casualties to the leading troops, " C " Company, under Major C. W. Stephens. The second company also suffered heavy losses. Nevertheless, led by Colonel Parker, himself wounded, who had taken over command when Lieutenant-Colonel Johnston was killed, the attacking troops pressed on, and were successful, owing to the determination of the troops and close co-operation between the infantry and tanks. When we had captured half the village heavy enemy defensive artillery fire came down, causing casualties to both sides. After this enemy resistance ceased suddenly and Breville was ours, at a cost of eight officers and 133 other ranks.

The battle was the deciding factor on this front, as from then on the enemy did not attack again. There is some doubt as to the real reason why our artillery fire came down on our own troops, but one explanation offered is that the various lifts were signified by the same codeword with the addition of " I " or " II ", *i.e.,* " Blank ", " Blank I " or " Blank II ". The report says that a signaller was told to send " Blank I " to the naval ships but that owing to the noise of battle he did not hear the " I " and only sent " Blank " with the result that the barrage came down in the same place again. In these circumstances the gunners would be quite justified in assuming that the infantry had been held up and therefore wanted a repeat.

38. During the night 12th/13th June, 152 Infantry Brigade of 51 (Highland) Division crossed the River Orne and 5th Battalion Cameron Highlanders attacked the village of St. Honorine. The village was captured but lost a few hours later to a determined enemy counter-attack. Later that day 7th Battalion The Argyll and Sutherland Highlanders of 154 Infantry Brigade also came under command of 6 Airborne Division and moved to the Ranville area, and during the night 13th/14th June, 51 (Highland) Division finally assumed responsibility for the southern portion of the bridgehead.

39. The remainder of the period during which 6 Airborne Division held the flank, from 14th June to 16th August, was spent in further consolidating the bridgehead and operations settled down to a period of static warfare and intense patrolling, with every advantage being taken to push the front forward even though advances of only a few yards were involved. During this phase 6 Airborne Division, with 1 and 4 Special Service Brigades still under command, held the left flank of the bridgehead from the Sallenelles-Breville area to approximately three miles north west of Troarn.

40. This was a period of static defence in which great attention had to be paid to maintaining an aggressive spirit. In spite of the fact that the Division realized the valuable part it was playing in holding the left flank, the role was an unexpected one for the troops who had been under the impression that they would be withdrawn from action fairly early in order to prepare for another early airborne operation. The result was a sense of disappointment and frustration which was countered by encouraging sniping, patrolling, a few minor raids and by training whenever troops could be taken out of the line. Unfortunately it was not possible to undertake extensive raiding. Owing to the length of the line few troops could be rested at a time but as the advance increased so the line could be thinned. Generally speaking it was possible to keep one parachute brigade and one air-landing battalion out of the line in a comparatively quiet sector. One of the interesting problems studied was that of counter-mortar and an organization similar to that later used in infantry and armoured divisions was evolved. Air photographs were of great value in detecting hostile battery and mortar positions and were extensively used. At the end of July, a divisional rest centre and battle school was opened at Ouistreham, under Colonel Parker. Unfortunately two of the houses of the centre were demolished when a German bomber crashed on to one of them, and 22 men were killed. During this period Brigadier E. W. C. Flavell had arrived from England to take command of 6 Air-landing Brigade, and Lieutenant-Colonel D. Mills-Roberts had been promoted to Brigadier and had assumed command of 1 Special Service Brigade.

During the period, too, the Germans did their best, which was not very good, to intimidate our troops by various means, including leaflets. One such leaflet read :—

" BRITISH AND CANADIAN SOLDIERS !

Did you know what's going on in England ?

Since June 15 Germany's new terrific weapons are in action against London and Southern England. London is in flames for days now. If you don't believe go over the hills nearby and look for yourselves. At night you can observe the great fire."

The troops had a very appropriate answer to this, which is perhaps best not put in print.

40A. In the last week, when 1 Corps began to break out to the south-east the front was extended considerably further south and in fact just before the advance began, the Division, augmented by the Royal Netherlands Brigade " Princess Irene " and the Belgian Brigade under command, held as far south as the railway line Troarn–Caen, with the Armoured Reconnaissance Regiment holding some 4,000 yards still further south.

41. On 7th August, 1 Corps Commander directed that plans be prepared for an operation to be carried out in the event of a general withdrawal of the enemy. It was not anticipated that 6 Airborne Division could do more than follow up a withdrawing enemy since the vehicles available were insufficient to make the Division mobile. However, by borrowing from here and by improvising there, plans were made and on 16th August all formations of 6 Airborne Division were put at short notice. In the early hours of 17th August, operation " Paddle " began, being the advance across the marshes of the River Dives.

The Advance to the River Seine

42. The First Canadian Army, under whose command 1 Corps had been placed, was ordered to break out of the Normandy bridgehead south-east from Caen towards Falaise, and as the main German armies withdrew the Canadian Army was to swing eastwards towards the River Seine. During the subsequent advance the main axis of 1 Corps ran through Lisieux some 15 miles inland from the coast, the German forces swinging back to the River Seine keeping their right flank on the sea. If a constant pressure was kept up on the enemy's right flank the whole advance of First Canadian Army would be accelerated and it was even hoped that by taking the crossings near the mouth of the River Seine quickly, large numbers of Germans would be captured. The task of keeping up this pressure on the enemy's right flank was given to 6 Airborne Division with under command 1 and 4 Special Service Brigades and the Belgian and Royal Netherland Brigades. During the advance there were periods when there was a gap of up to ten miles between the right flank of 6 Airborne Division and the left flank of the remainder of 1 Corps. Therefore, the Division was left to fight an operation which, although it was an important part of the whole plan, was in effect an isolated series of actions.

43. The final objective given to the Division was the mouth of the River Seine, and to reach it a series of river crossings had to be made. Since these crossings were carried out near the sea the rivers were wide and deep and frequently tidal. Two main roads led to the River Seine, the first through Troarn–Dozule–Pont L'Évêque–Beuzeville to Pont Audemer, the second along the coast through Cabourg–Trouville–Honfleur. Both routes ran through similar types of country which consisted of small undulating hills covered with scrub woods and thickly hedged pasture land, the coastal road running through most of the old beach defences of pillboxes and minefields. There were two main rivers across the routes, the River Dives and the River Touques. The River Dives lay in a broad marshy valley and had an additional obstacle running parallel to it, the derelict Dives Canal, both the river and the canal being overlooked by a formidable range of hills to the east. The River Touques and the River Risle, though not formidable obstacles in themselves, ran through deep gorges that afforded excellent delaying positions. The total distance from Troarn to Pont Audemer was 35 miles as the crow flies but nearer 45 miles by road.

44. During the night 16th/17th August, the enemy began to withdraw on the 6 Airborne Division front. At 0300 hours on 17th August, 3 Parachute Brigade moved forward and by 0600 hours a general advance along the whole divisional front was taking place. 4 Special Service Brigade advanced towards Troarn and St. Pair, 3 Parachute Brigade towards Bures, 1 Special Service Brigade towards Bavent and Robehomme and 6 Air-landing Brigade towards Cabourg. 6 Air-landing Brigade met large numbers of craters and mines on their way to Cabourg with the result that their advance was considerably delayed and they were ultimately held up just east of the town by well placed enemy pillboxes. There were only two routes across the swampy Dives valley, one through Cabourg and the other north-east through Troarn up a long narrow feature in the direction of Dozule. As 6 Air-landing Brigade had been held up at Cabourg, the divisional commander decided to make his main effort of advance up the narrow island from Troarn. By the evening of 17th August, 3 Parachute Brigade had reached the area of Goustranville after some quite

heavy fighting, and during that night 5 Parachute Brigade began to advance. The movement was held up at the Troarn bridges, but eventually a way was cleared through for the transport. By the evening of 18th August 3 Parachute Brigade, 5 Parachute Brigade and 4 Special Service Brigade were concentrated on the island.

45. At 2200 hours on 18th August 3 Parachute Brigade attacked the four main bridges over the Dives Canal and had captured these by 0220 hours on 19th August. One bridge was intact, another was passable to infantry, but the remaining two had been blown up by the enemy. The brigade made full use of the good bridges and the line of the railway east of the Dives Canal was reached by 0235 hours. 5 Parachute Brigade then passed through 3 Parachute Brigade at 0400 hours and at 0845 hours had captured the village of Putot-en-Auge, taking 120 prisoners. Although these night attacks had been carried out so quickly, they were undertaken in the face of strong enemy opposition and with little opportunity for reconnaissance, and the fact that they achieved such success reflects great credit on the two brigades.

46. The divisional commander's main object at this stage was to get his troops clear of the River Dives valley as soon as possible so that advantage could be taken of the more open ground to the east. With this in view, on the night of 19th/20th August, 4 Special Service Brigade attacked the hills to the south-east of Putot-en-Auge and 1 Special Service Brigade attacked the high ground to the north of the main road, both attacks being successful. 4 Special Service Brigade continued to fight their way over difficult scrub covered hills while 1 Special Service Brigade became involved in heavy fighting and were cut off by enemy penetration down the valley. Nevertheless the brigade continued to fight hard and managed to maintain artillery communication throughout the greater part of the day so that its positions were successfully held. By the night of 20th August their ammunition was running low and the Division prepared an escorted convoy to take up reserves. In addition, 6 Air-landing Brigade was brought forward in order to capture the high ground north of Dozule and east of the commandos. However, in the early hours of 21st August, the Germans began to withdraw and 4 Special Service Brigade captured Dozule ; at the same time the Belgian Brigade began attacking Cabourg and had begun to get patrols across the River Dives.

47. Early on 21st August, 3 Parachute Brigade started their advance towards Pont L'Évêque. Stiff opposition was encountered on the route and the enemy, supported by tanks, held the village of Annebault. The resistance was overcome after fierce fighting by 8th Parachute Battalion. That night 5 Parachute Brigade moved through 3 Parachute Brigade and on the morning of 22nd August, continued the advance, reaching the line of the River Touques by mid-day. During the afternoon of 22nd August 5 Parachute Brigade attacked Pont L'Évêque with the object of getting across the River Touques. Fighting in the town was bitter and in spite of the most gallant efforts of 12th and 13th Parachute Battalions and of the Royal Engineers, no progress could be made across the easterly branch of the River Touques and the attack across the valley to the north was held on the river line.

48. At this point the main river flows from Pont L'Évêque in two channels approximately 200 yards apart. The houses of the town are built largely of wood and are therefore inflammable. On both sides of the valley predominating

189

hills, well covered with trees, rise to approximately 450 feet, and on either side of the town the river runs through flat water meadows. On the easterly bank the railway line runs along the embankment, from which the whole valley could be covered.

49. On the night 22nd/23rd August, a wind was blowing from the east and the enemy took advantage of this by setting fire to large parts of Pont L'Évêque and burning out most of the forward positions. The combined efforts of the fires and the enemy resistance made it impossible for any further advance to take place through the town next day, despite the fact that close support had been given to the infantry by the Cromwell tanks of the Armoured Reconnaissance Regiment. Nearer the coast, 6 Air-landing Brigade, who had captured Vauville and Deauville on 22nd August, taking many German prisoners and releasing many Allied prisoners, had managed to get small patrols across the river in one or two places but in each case they were met by heavy opposition. On the night of 23rd/24th August, the brigade forced the crossing of the River Touques at its mouth. However, early on 24th August, the Germans withdrew from the whole line of the River Touques leaving behind a very thorough belt of demolitions. Our troops followed up quickly but it was not until the late afternoon of that day that the vehicles could get across the river.

50. The main axis of the advance continued eastwards through Pont L'Évêque and all the bridging resources of the Division were concentrated on this route. All transport had to cross the River Touques at Pont L'Évêque except for a small number of vehicles ferried over at Touques and Trouville. By the evening of 24th August, the Division was in possession of the high ground to the east of the valley with 5 Parachute Brigade on the right, 3 Parachute Brigade in the centre and 6 Air-landing Brigade on the left. That night 1 Special Service Brigade passed through the right of our front towards Beuzeville, and early next morning 6 Air-landing Brigade advanced east along the coast. 12th Battalion The Devonshire Regiment made a spectacular dash and captured Honfleur. The Germans had carried out all their demolitions thoroughly and considerable delay was imposed on the Division in getting forward, involving the sappers in a great deal of hard work before further advance became possible. At this point mention must be made of the valuable work done by the Airborne Armoured Reconnaissance Regiment with under command the Belgian and Dutch Reconnaissance Units. The information these units provided was accurate, up to date and of great value, and in addition, they kept in touch with 49 Division to the south and so provided a connecting link with the remainder of 1 Corps.

On 25th August, 1 Special Service Brigade were held up west of Beuzeville and both 3 Parachute Brigade and 4 Special Service Brigade attacked in an effort to break through the enemy defences, and he was finally forced to withdraw by the capture of Honfleur. That evening the Commander, 6 Airborne Division, decided to push forward during the night to capture Pont Audemer in the hope of cutting off those German forces which were withdrawing north-east in front of 49 Division. 1 Special Service Brigade advanced during the night and at dawn 26th August, 5 Parachute Brigade with under command the Royal Netherlands Brigade attacked through to Pont Audemer. After heavy fighting, the town was captured but the bridges had been demolished and few Germans were captured. However, in spite of this disappointment there is little doubt that the rapid advance of the Division hustled the Germans and made the task of those Allied formations to the south considerably easier. Meanwhile 6 Air-landing Brigade, with under command the Belgian Brigade, had cleared the area up to the coast, and the River Risle. The remainder of this period was spent in re-organizing and mopping up small parties of the enemy who still wandered about the area.

51. This was the end of the advance by 6 Airborne Division, and attached troops, of approximately 45 miles in nine days, carried out largely on foot against heavy enemy opposition and through difficult country, aggravated by well-planned enemy demolitions. The original plan had envisaged the Division following up a withdrawing enemy. Far from this, the Division had literally pushed the enemy back into the River Seine, liberating more than 400 square miles of France and capturing over 1,000 prisoners. Lieutenant-General Crerar, Commander-in-Chief, First Canadian Army stated quite clearly how great had been the value of the assistance rendered by 6 Airborne Division when he sent the following signal to Lieutenant-General Crocker, Commander 1 Corps :—

> " Desire you inform Gale of my appreciation of immense contribution 6 Airborne Division and all Allied contingents under his command have made during recent fighting advance. The determination and speed with which his troops have pressed on in spite of all enemy efforts to the contrary have been impressive and of greatest assistance to the Army as a whole."

And what of the original landing on " D " day ? The following extract from a newspaper published on 22nd June, 1944, probably sums up public opinion :—

> " British armoured divisions are fighting south-east of Caen. That is the outstanding feature of the news. For it is the very development that Rommel has fought his hardest to postpone. . . . . all springing from that grand operation on the day of the landing when the 6th Airborne Division descended on the canal and river bridges between Caen and the sea . . . . the bridges were seized unbroken and held for weeks against the utmost the Germans could do to turn them out.
>
> It is doubtful whether there has ever been a body of troops in which the individuals had been brought to a higher pitch of physical fitness, self-reliance and fighting skill. The gallant deeds of that magnificent division made history, for they made possible the stroke that cut through the German right flank on Tuesday morning . . . . It should have been a proud moment for the 6th Airborne Division to see the outcome of their sacrifices. As General Montgomery said yesterday : ' the men of that division who died did not die in vain '."

The Division embarked for England at the beginning of September, disembarked at Southampton and proceeded to their barracks in the Bulford area to re-organize. The total casualties they had suffered were (as known at the time) :—

	Officers.	Other Ranks.
Killed	76	745
Wounded ..	199	2,510
Missing ..	41	886

Administration

52. The administrative planning for the operation was based on the instructions summarized in Chapter XIV issued by Headquarters, 1 Airborne Corps which laid down the general policy for all airborne operations. It was overshadowed by three factors :—

(a) The shortage of aircraft which did not permit of the Division being flown in at full strength either in one or two lifts.

(b) The allocation of shipping space for vehicles which could be allotted to the Division during the first eight days of the invasion.

(c) The verbal understanding that the Division would be withdrawn from Normandy within three weeks of " D " day, which gave rise to the Divisional policy not to ask for shipping space after " D "+ 7 day.

The effect of this lack of shipping space was that units had to be kept to a minimum and in fact it meant that divisional R.A.S.C., R.A.O.C. and R.E.M.E. were available in Normandy at a minimum scale only. Medical units were brought in at full scale by " D "+ 1 day. The result of these administrative shortages was that help had to be sought from second and third line administrative units of 1 Corps, 3 British Division and 27 Armoured Brigade. This help was given willingly but third line assistance could not be provided at the correct army scale since no provision had been made by higher authority for 1 Corps to be allotted an additional increment to its basic corps troops from which to provide for the Division.

53. Administrative planning for the operation was carried out under two headings, the first being the sea/land side under Headquarters, 1 Corps and the second being the air side under Headquarters, 1 Airborne Corps. 1 Corps' operational plan envisaged the link up between 6 Airborne Division and 3 British Division taking place during the afternoon of " D " day, and the divisional administrative plan was based on this assumption. 3 British Division was made responsible for administrative assistance reaching 6 Airborne Division as soon as possible and to this end they undertook to deliver stores required by the Division east of the River Orne.

54. As the days went by more and more of 6 Airborne Division's administrative transport, which was to be phased in by sea up to " D "+ 7 day became available, but in the meantime 3 British Division made an allocation to the airborne division of 20 pre-loaded 3-ton lorries, the loads being laid down by 6 Airborne Division. One of the difficulties that 3 British Division had to face was that if the bridges over the river and canal were not captured intact all stores would have to be ferried across the two water obstacles until military bridges could be built, but this risk was accepted. It was agreed between the two divisions that 70 tons of stores would be delivered at " H "+ 20 hours, 196 tons on " D "+ 1 day and thereafter full daily tonnages demanded by 6 Airborne Division up to a daily maximum figure of 245 tons. 1 Corps undertook to meet the requirements of the Division if 3 British Division moved forward beyond Caen more quickly than anticipated, and if necessary Second Army troops would in turn be prepared to accept the responsibility from 1 Corps. Workshop facilities were to be provided from " D "+ 1 day by 27 Armoured Brigade workshops and also by 1 Corps Troops Workshops, to which the sea-borne element of 6 Airborne Division Workshops would be

attached. 3 British Division were made responsible for the evacuation of casualties from the area immediately east of the River Orne, and to do this they were to establish a casualty clearing post close to the bridges, 6 Airborne Division being responsible for evacuation up to this point. A divisional maintenance area was to be established as early as possible east of the River Orne to hold two days' requirements of all commodities as a " buffer " in case 6 Airborne Division was cut off from the beach-head as the result of enemy action.

55. Planning on the air side followed on in general from the arrangements made on the sea/land side, one of the objects being to cover any breakdowns in the sea/land plan. Units flew in with the following scales of stores :—

Rations	for 48 hours.
Water ..	Water bottles and sterilizing equipments.
Ammunition..	Hard scales. In practice this meant enough 3-inch mortar and ·303, Mk. VIIIZ, for short actions only but approximately enough of other types to last for 24 hours.
Petrol, oil and Lubricants.	Approximately 200 miles a vehicle.

All available space was taken up on parachute and tug aircraft flying in on the morning of " D " day with bomb-cell containers loaded with stores, the more important types being loaded in parachute aircraft because these flew in at a lower altitude and therefore there would be a greater chance of recovering their containers. This supply was known as the " jettison drop " and consisted largely of 3-inch mortar ammunition, anti-tank mines, wire and medical stores. All available lift on tug aircraft flying in on the evening of " D " day was also taken up with bomb-cell containers loaded with stores, and a maintenance mission of 50 aircraft was provided for the night " D " day/" D "+ 1 day, no more aircraft being available. In addition, maintenance missions to cover the requirements of the complete division or a parachute brigade group were pre-planned and could be demanded by code word. Final arrangements were made whereby demands for special items would be met and flown in within approximately 18 hours of demands being received at the airborne base.

56. The " jettison drop " was reasonably successful and by 0600 hours on 6th June, 6 Airborne Division R.A.S.C. had a dump operating, from which units were able to draw direct and this dump continued to operate all day. Demands made at the dump were mostly for anti-tank mines, wire, 3-inch mortar ammunition and medical supplies, all available quantities of these stores being issued, while more would have been drawn had they been available. Small arms ammunition was not in big demand but medical stores, particularly blood and plasma, were very much needed and only just enough was found. It was estimated that 60 per cent. of the containers dropped from 5 Parachute Brigade aircraft were collected but very few of those dropped from tug aircraft were seen as they apparently fell wide in enemy occupied territory. Those carried on 3 Parachute Brigade aircraft were very dispersed and only a small number were found by R.A.S.C. units, though the contents of a number of others were collected and used by units or sub-units which had been cut off.

57. The flow of stores to the east bank of the River Orne from 3 British Division area began at about " H "+ 23 hours, the link-up between the two divisions having taken place on the evening of " D " day according to plan, and the bridges over the River Orne and canal having been captured intact. Initially, full stocks as planned could not be provided because of losses in the sea-borne landings, but this did not cause any shortages to 6 Airborne Division and by " D "+ 2 day full requirements were being delivered with the exception of ordnance stores, chiefly weapons and wireless sets. Supplies continued throughout the operations with a 100 per cent efficiency, drawing from the Beach Maintenance Area being taken over by 6 Airborne Division R.A.S.C. on " D "+ 6 day. There was one exception to this easy flow of stores and that was the provision of 75-mm. pack howitzer ammunition which caused much worry in the early stages, the guns drawing every round that could be produced. Expenditure by eight guns was 1,500 rounds on " D "+ 1 day, 1,300 rounds on " D "+ 2 day and 2,500 rounds on " D " + 3 day. This type of ammunition was peculiar to 6 Airborne Division in the British sector and difficulty arose over finding it on the beaches.

58. The container drop from the tug aircraft of 6 Air-landing Brigade group on the evening of " D " day fell in 3 British Division's area west of the River Orne. Owing to lack of transport these containers could not be collected until " D "+ 1 day, by which time the contents of approximately 50 per cent had been used by the troops on the ground. The maintenance mission carried out by 50 Dakotas on the night of " D " day/" D "+ 1 day was a failure due to the dispersion of the aircraft which were fired on by ships of the Royal Navy before they were able to drop. The Dakotas unfortunately arrived shortly after enemy aircraft had been in the vicinity. Of 116 tons despatched, only some 20 tons were collected. It was not found necessary to demand the pre-planned maintenance missions although great assistance was given by air maintenance in the re-equipping of units with weapons lost in the initial drop, and in addition, large quantities of sand bags were dropped on four separate occasions between " D "+ 6 day and " D "+ 30 day. In most of the latter missions, Stirling aircraft were used, carrying 24 containers and four panniers, and the drops were very successful. Halifax aircraft were used for dropping jeeps and 6-pounder guns and six each of these were dropped, in some cases being in action within a few minutes of reaching the ground. There were two supply dropping points, one being east of the River Orne and one being west. The area to the east of the River Orne was under aimed enemy rifle fire until " D "+ 5 day and was therefore used only once, on " D "+ 1 day. The area west of the River Orne was used for all other drops but remained within range of enemy artillery fire for some weeks. However, it was never seriously interfered with although R.A.S.C. clearing parties were shelled on several occasions.

59. From " D "+ 2 day until the beginning of 6 Airborne Division's advance to the River Seine, there was a period of approximately 70 days during which maintenance followed the normal army procedure and during which 6 Airborne Division R.A.S.C. drew stores initially from the Beach Maintenance Area, and later from roadhead, holding a " buffer " of two days estimated requirements of all commodities in the divisional maintenance area immediately east of the River Orne. The divisional maintenance area also operated as a bulk breaking point from where either divisional R.A.S.C. supplied forward to units in

R.A.S.C. transport, or units drew stores in their own transport. This system also operated for 1 and 4 Special Service Brigades and the Belgian and Dutch Brigades, but it did not operate for artillery regiments of other formations which were under command of 6 Airborne Division, as these regiments were administered by their parent headquarters. There was a constant threat of brigades or units being isolated by enemy action during the period of static warfare and therefore dumps, holding 48 hour requirements, were established in forward brigade areas as reserves, not to be drawn from except in cases of emergency.

60. Ordnance services were provided by a detachment of 6 Airborne Division Ordnance Field Park which operated close to the Division's maintenance area. The only difficulty experienced in this connection was in obtaining spare parts for issue to R.E.M.E. workshops once the small stocks which had been brought in by the Division's ordnance detachment had been exhausted. In fact these stores had to be obtained from England. The detachment of the divisional Ordnance Field Park was separated from 6 Airborne Division Workshops by some ten miles. This caused certain provision difficulties because the workshop had not got an ordnance stores section forming an integral part of it and the detachment of the Division Ordnance Field Park was not strong enough to provide the necessary personnel. 6 Airborne Division Workshops had been phased in at light scales and as time went on it was found more and more difficult to carry out repair work efficiently, this difficulty being aggravated when 1 Corps Troops Workshops advanced, leaving 6 Airborne Division Workshops with no heavy machinery with which to do their work. An advanced workshops detachment was established in the divisional maintenance area to carry out light second echelon work and this it did satisfactorily. Light aid detachments operated with brigades and units as far as possible, but the lack of a brigade Electrical and Mechanical Engineer was acutely felt and affected adversely the repair of equipment. However, recovery work was carried out efficiently with a captured enemy break-down vehicle and with the aid of beach recovery vehicles loaned by 1 Corps. Later on it was found advisable to centralize light aid detachments.

61. The divisional provost suffered a number of casualties and as a result of this and the subsequent difficulty of obtaining reinforcements they were greatly overworked, their difficulties being further increased by lack of vehicles. The divisional postal unit, on 75 per cent. war establishment operated effectively in the divisional maintenance area, the first mails being despatched on " D "+ 2 day and the first delivery being made on " D "+ 7 day. At times, when an air supply took place, mail only 48 hours old was delivered to the front line.

62. There was an acute shortage of tentage for headquarters and for medical units, owing once again to the fact that the Division had planned on a short stay in the line and therefore was not ready to provide its own, and the stocks at base were very small.

63. Once the Division began to advance and undertook a mobile role, the problems of maintenance assumed an entirely different aspect from hitherto. While it had been static, the small amount of first and second line transport which was available within the Division had proved adequate for the maintenance task, but now a very great strain was placed upon available resources.

Assistance in transport had to be given to 6 Air-landing Brigade, to parachute battalions, field squadrons, R.E. and to field ambulances, and additional transport was necessary to carry the divisional pool of bridging material. Only 77 3-ton lorries were available with a few 15-cwt. trucks and some jeeps to do this and to provide second line services for the Division plus 1 and 4 Special Service Brigades. Luckily the Belgian and Royal Netherland Brigades were self-supporting in second line transport. The tasks which this small number of 3-ton lorries had to carry out included drawing from Corps Field Maintenance Areas up to a distance of 40 miles along a line of communication which had four bottle-necks in the form of one-way bridges and bombed areas, providing load carrying vehicles to move non-mobile elements such as divisional headquarters, workshops and Ordnance Field Park, and providing troop carrying transport from time to time. The problem was partially solved by withdrawing transport from the Belgian and Royal Netherland Brigades and by borrowing one transport platoon from 1 Corps, which was all they could provide. The system of maintenance adopted during the advance was to establish as far forward as possible jeep mobile observation posts and to follow these up with composite points which were always well forward within brigade areas. Units drew from these points either in their own or in a brigade pool of jeep transport. The lack of workshop equipment was felt more acutely than previously by Ordnance and R.E.M.E. services and was partly made up by the attachment of an armoured light aid detachment from 1 Corps.

64. When the advance began the provost company's strength was only four officers and 45 other ranks and the shortage of transport was acute, but this was relieved by the provision of four Lloyd towing vehicles. There were a number of diversions at each river crossing during the advance and the problem of policing these placed such a strain on the unit that eventually sections were withdrawn from brigades and placed under divisional control.

65. Owing to the original policy that the Division would be withdrawn early, Headquarters 21 Army Group laid down that it would not be reinforced in the field as trained airborne reinforcements were precious and had to be conserved. As time went on and casualties increased, more and more strenuous efforts were made to obtain reinforcements but without much success, although some were provided to fill vital gaps, particularly in infantry units, but they were non-airborne. The situation in artillery, engineer and provost units remained serious.

66. The medical plan was based upon the general instructions issued by Headquarters, 1 Airborne Corps before the operation, the principle being that field ambulances dropped or landed in support of brigades, each field ambulance to establish a main dressing station in their area as soon as possible. Sections landed with units but reverted to field ambulance control as soon as possible. Field ambulances came under divisional control on landing, except 224th Parachute Field Ambulance, which was to remain under 3 Parachute Brigade until communication was established. Casualties were to be collected, held and treated at main dressing stations until evacuation to 3 British Division was possible, and a medical officer from 6 Airborne Division was to accompany the leading medical unit of 3 British Division. Additional medical stores were included in the " jettison drop " and the automatic supply by air mentioned above, and thereafter stores were to be provided through 3 British Division and

Illustration 12.   6-pr., Mk. 2, on Carriage, Mk. 3, being loaded into Horsa, Mk. 1.

Illustration 13.   Car, 5 cwt., 4 × 4, lashed in Horsa.

Illustration 14.   Horsa, Mk. 2.

Illustration 15.   Hamilcar " X."

Illustration 16. Tetrach Tank being unloaded from Hamilcar I.

Illustration 17. The Albemarle.

Illustration 18.   The Halifax.

Illustration 19.   The Stirling.

Illustration 20.   The Whitley.

Illustration 21.   British Parachutist wearing " X " type
Parachute (Sten gun carried).

Right hand pulls
quick release after
jumping and pays
out rope until
valise is suspended
20 ft. below man.

Illustration 22.   British Parachutist with L.M.G. valise.

Quick release
(pulled by left
hand after
jumping).

Paying out rope.

When quick release
is pulled right hand
pays out rope until
valise is suspended
20 ft. below man.

Illustration 23.   British Parachutist with rifle valise
(high position).

Illustration 24.   Parachute troops with kit-bags waiting to jump from a Dakota Aircraft.

Illustration 25.   A parachutist with kit-bag about to land.

Illustration 26a.   The Jump (No. 1).

Illustration 26b.   The Jump (No. 2).

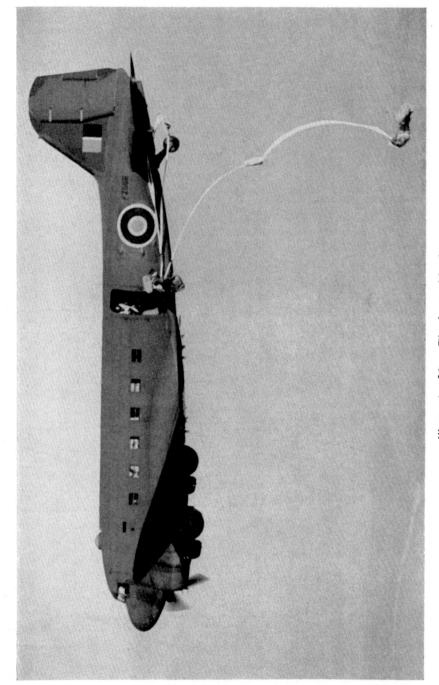

Illustration 26c.   The Jump (No. 3).

Illustration 26d.   The Jump (No. 4).

1 Corps. On the whole the medical plan was successful during the initial drop though, like the remainder of the Division, many of the personnel were scattered. The airborne medical liaison officer with 3 British Division was wounded immediately on the beach, but Major MacDonald of 8th Field Ambulance in 3 British Division made contact with 6 Airborne Division medical units at 2100 hours on " D " day. Evacuation of casualties started forthwith, continuing smoothly thereafter, although the lack of ambulance cars caused frequent anxiety. This was relieved to some extent by transport being provided by 3 British Division and 1 Corps.

During the period of static warfare the divisional medical staff was reduced to the Assistant Director of Medical Services, one officer and two orderlies, the Deputy being killed and the Deputy Director of Hygiene and the Chief Clerk both being wounded. During this period all battalions were made up to full establishment of medical personnel from field ambulance resources and each battalion was given an ambulance car, jeeps and a certain number of additional medical personnel to enable casualties to be evacuated quickly from regimental aid posts to main dressing stations. Mobile ambulance convoy cars were allotted to the Division by 1 Corps to evacuate casualties from main dressing stations direct to the hospital area at La Deliverande, while 224th Parachute Field Ambulance manned the divisional rest camp at Riva Bella for the latter part of the period. During the advance to the Seine, each field ambulance was made up to equal strength by re-distribution of vehicles and personnel within the Division, the medical resources of the Royal Netherlands Brigade and the Belgian Brigade coming under command of the senior medical officer of 6 Air-landing Brigade. As the advance progressed field ambulances were leap-frogged forward so that two units were always in action in the forward areas.

A total of 397 major operations were performed by the divisional medical units, and 802 officers and 13,444 other ranks were treated as casualties, including civilians and prisoners of war.

67. The salvage of airborne equipment, with the exception of glider recovery, was carried out by 6 Airborne Division, R.A.S.C., under orders of the Commander, R.A.S.C. Of the airborne equipment which formed part of the initial effort, only comparatively few parachutes were recovered owing to the impossibility of organizing any collection in the opening stages of the battle. Later, considerable numbers of containers and panniers were collected and stacked by units of the Division and were removed in accordance with arrangements made by 1 Corps salvage officer. Heavy damage was caused to gliders by enemy artillery and mortar fire and by the movements of our own armour through the landing zone areas, but despite this it was eventually possible to repair and fly back to the United Kingdom approximately 50 gliders. With regard to equipment forming part of the supply drops, the efficiency of the salvage of material from these missions increased as time went on. In the initial phases, when the supply dropping-points were under enemy observation, salvage was extremely difficult, but later as much as 100 per cent of some drops was handed in to the beach-head salvage organization through 1 Corps salvage officer.

Lessons

68. In the following paragraphs are given the main lessons of the Normandy airborne operations carried out by 6 Airborne Division. These were the first full scale airborne operations that had ever been undertaken on a divisional

level and there were many lessons to be learnt. The subsequent airborne operations at Arnhem and on the River Rhine were based to a large extent upon the conclusions drawn from Normandy.

69. The lines on which the Division had been organized and trained were sound in most respects. Certain adjustments had to be made to some war establishments and these were chiefly in order to allow the Division to function as such for periods longer than a few days.

70. The detailed rehearsals which were carried out in the United Kingdom for the operations to capture the bridges and the Merville battery paid a very high dividend, and proved that if time permits, such rehearsals should always be carried out in the greatest detail.

71. In the initial stages of planning a mistake was made in being too strict over security in planning. Originally, only a few people, members of the divisional headquarters planning team, were permitted to know the details of the plan with the result that the planning team was greatly overworked dealing with items which could have been performed easily by subordinate staff officers. For example, some senior staff officers and heads of arms and services could have been given assistance without any additional risk to security. Another lesson learnt in planning was that airborne staffs must be brought in at the earliest opportunity. By the time that 6 Airborne Division began to plan with 1 Corps the latter had already reached an advanced stage and the two sea-borne assault divisions, 3 British and 3 Canadian Divisions, had already left London to do their detailed planning. It was not until a month had passed that 6 Airborne Division's plan caught up with that of 1 Corps, and this was only achieved by the help given by the Corps staff. Airborne planning should be carried out in step with that of the formations with which the airborne division is co-operating. This would be even more essential in the case of operations carried out at short notice. The accommodation allotted for planning was insufficient and where planning goes on over a period of months it should be on a generous scale.

72. However strong an airborne division is in small arms, once the enemy has recovered from his initial surprise it is essential to obtain artillery support on a scale at least comparable to that likely to be available for a normal division. Apart from anything else, requirements of mortar and gun ammunition will be far in excess of anything that can be brought in by air and, therefore, effective arrangements should be made beforehand with the co-operating ground formations for the use of their artillery. On many occasions during the operations of 6 Airborne Division, such as the attacks by the enemy on the Ranville position from the south and the attack by 12th Parachute Battalion at Breville, it was the assistance of artillery from outside the Division which either saved the situation or enabled the operations to be carried out. This external artillery amounted to the divisional artillery of 3 British Division, a battery of 4 A.G.R.A., two cruisers, and two destroyers. Initially, the only airborne artillery available was one light battery and one anti-tank battery, plus one troop, though the remainder of the air-landing light regiment was brought in on " D " + 7 day. The original support for the Division was by forward observation bombardment parties, who were dropped by parachute or landed in gliders and, in general, the system worked well. The fire from 3 British

Division's artillery and 4 A.G.R.A. was obtained by means of parachute and glider-borne forward observation officers who were all connected by wireless link through a common airborne support net direct, in some cases to the field batteries and in others to the field regiments of 3 British Division and to the medium regiment of 4 A.G.R.A. In addition, the Commander, Royal Artillery, 6 Airborne Division, had a link with the Commander Corps Royal Artillery, 1 Corps. This system worked excellently while 6 Airborne Division was sharing 3 British Division artillery and calls for fire were answered generously and rapidly. Subsequently, 6 Airborne Division always had two field regiments and one heavy anti-aircraft regiment in a ground role under command, in addition to its own air-landing light regiment.

On occasions the Division had a battery or a regiment of medium artillery, and after 12th August, 12 and four guns belonging respectively to the Belgian and Royal Netherlands Brigades. 12 Centaur tanks (*ex* Royal Marine Armoured Support Group) were placed under command of the Division in the early stage of the campaign. These guns were used primarily in a counter-mortar role and took the place of 4·2 inch mortars, the lack of which was felt by the Division.

73. The Normandy operations proved that, no matter what undertakings are given as to its length of stay in the area, an airborne division flying into an operation must be backed up by sea/land element and that the scale of administrative units must be the same as for an infantry division. This is necessary to bring it up to full strength in administrative units as early as possible. To accept that a unit or a part of a unit can be left at base is to accept an administrative drag in the field.

74. These points all aimed at the same mark—that the organization of an airborne division must be the same as that of an infantry division or the former could not be expected to function efficiently in battle. There was also a requirement for corps troops to be increased to provide for an airborne division when it came under command of a corps on the ground.

75. It was agreed that, given surprise and air supremacy, both of which were achieved in Normandy, it is possible, though not desirable, to land an airborne division successfully at night. Provided there is time for specialized training, small *coup de main* parties have a reasonable chance of carrying out what would appear to be the most daring operations.

76. To end this chapter some of the reasons will be considered which caused the scattered dropping of parts of the Division, especially 3 Parachute Brigade. A detailed " inquest " was held soon after the operation and the following points were brought out :—

(*a*) One of the pathfinder teams for dropping zone " V " (1st Canadian and 9th Parachute Battalion), although dropped reasonably accurately, had its Eureka sets so badly damaged in the drop that they were unworkable. The other team for this area came down well away from the dropping zone and did not get its beacons into action until much too late. The result was, as we have already seen, that the marking on the dropping zone consisted of only two lights.

(*b*) Greater accuracy might have been achieved if there had been more insurance in the shape of more pathfinder teams for each dropping zone. It has already been mentioned that surprise was essential and depended on the timing of the operation. The time allowed for the pathfinders to erect their beacons had to be kept to the minimum in order not to prejudice the surprise of the glider assault on the River Orne bridges. Therefore the pathfinders could only be given half an hour, which was time enough if they were dropped accurately. But it was taking a risk if they were even a short distance away from the dropping zone, as they would have to find their position before making their way to the correct place   However, the risk had to be accepted, though more teams would have increased the chances of success

(c) The aircraft carrying out the drop of 3 Parachute Brigade, which were the comparatively hastily trained crews of 46 Group, were instructed to fly in loose formation and release on a signal from the leading aircraft

Thus if the leading aircraft missed its mark, and in the absence of Eureka many of them did, the whole drop went wide   This method which was the same as that adopted by the Americans, differed from the standard procedure. In the latter each aircraft navigated singly, which increased the chance of isolated aircraft dropping wide but it did ensure that there would be no wide mass drops. The experience of one Dakota aircraft of 46 Group which had got off course illustrates how things can go wrong. After it had crossed most of the Channel it encountered flak put up, as it transpired later, by ships of an Allied navy who were stationed some five to eight miles off the coast. The pilot of the Dakota thought he was over the coast, and as he had promised the stick commander the privilege of releasing the small bombs carried, he called him forward and away went the bombs. This convinced the ships that the aircraft was hostile and the anti-aircraft barrage increased. The pilot immediately took evasive action so that one moment the troops were piled up at the forward end of the aircraft, and the next moment at the rear. In the meantime the green light had gone on and the first three men had jumped into the sea, never to be seen again. The remainder of the stick got out as and when they could, but were scattered over a huge area.

Finally, a note of caution should be sounded. A few seconds flying time will carry the aircraft well away from the dropping zone. It must be remembered that it is difficult for a man dropped at night in strange country to say accurately where he is, especially when there are standing crops and such obstacles as floods to contend with. Distances become exaggerated and multiplied by each detour made to avoid an obstacle. To the lay-man the expression " dropped wide " probably conjures up a distance of several miles, but to the parachutist it may mean only 1,000 yards or so—which takes a long time to cover on foot under conditions such as prevailed in Normandy.

CHAPTER XVI

FIRST ALLIED AIRBORNE ARMY AND PROJECTED AIRBORNE OPERATIONS, JUNE TO SEPTEMBER, 1944

General

1. While 6 Airborne Division had been committed in Normandy, 1 Airborne Division was standing by in England as a reserve for 21 Army Group. This necessitated the investigation and preparation of a number of plans for airborne operations which varied almost from day to day as the ground troops advanced. Throughout, 1 Airborne Division received their instructions on these planned operations from Headquarters, 1 Airborne Corps, who, in turn, at the beginning of the Normandy invasion, took their orders direct from Headquarters, 21 Army Group, or S.H.A.E.F. However, two months after the landings, First Allied Airborne Army was formed to co-ordinate all airborne operations directly under S.H.A.E.F. and from then on orders for all Allied airborne formations in the European theatre were issued by the new Army to Headquarters, 1 Airborne Corps, or Headquarters, XVIII U.S. Airborne Corps. This chapter deals with the formation of First Allied Airborne Army and will cover briefly some of the many projected airborne operations that were planned, but did not take place, between the Normandy landings and the airborne operations in the Arnhem–Nijmegen–Grave area, including a short reference to the Airborne Forward Delivery Airfield Group. Other possible operations were, of course, considered by Headquarters, First Allied Airborne Army, both during this period and after the Battle of Arnhem, but they are too numerous to cover in a history of this description. It does not touch on the activities of First Allied Airborne Army in connection with operations that did occur, as these are dealt with in the appropriate operational chapters.

First Allied Airborne Army

2. For some time before the launching of the invasion of North-West Europe much thought had been given to the best ways of achieving the maximum co-ordination between the American and British airborne forces and the air forces to carry them. Although the Normandy plans involved the carriage of American troops by American aircraft and British troops by British aircraft it was realized that this would not necessarily be so in future operations. It was realized also that the best results would only be obtained if there were the closest co-ordination of planning and training between the two nations. The first step in this direction was taken in March, 1944, when S.H.A.E.F. issued a Standard Operating Procedure for Airborne and Troop Carrier Units (*see* Appendix F), the object of which was :—

> " to provide a common basis upon which the training and operations of allied airborne and troop carrier units can be conducted, and to define the responsibilities of (' the First Allied Airborne Army and . . . ' was inserted here later) airborne and troop carrier commanders."

3. Just before " D " day, on 2nd June, 1944, S.H.A.E.F. issued outline proposals for a combined British and American Headquarters, Airborne Troops, for the control of airborne troops after the Normandy operations. On

20th June, the Supreme Commander approved the organization for such a headquarters and on 28th July he stated his reasons in a message to General George C. Marshall, Chief of the General Staff, United States Army :—

" . . . . Experience has proved that in preparing to utilize large airborne forces there is at present no suitable agency available to the High Command to assume responsibility for joint planning between the troop carrier command and the airborne forces. This planning includes joint training, development of operational projects and logistical support until this function can be taken over by normal agencies. It includes also co-ordination with ground and naval forces. Another important function is that of assuring sufficiency of technical equipment and supplies both as to type and quantity. My idea of setting up an airborne commander directly under this headquarters is to give him these responsibilities. It is for these vital purposes that I need the man requested from General Arnold. He would not command troops actually fighting on the ground but would be responsible for providing them all logistical support until normal lines of communications could be established. Assuming that an airborne attack by two or three divisions took place within a single area, a temporary corps commander would be designated to conduct the fighting on the ground. He would operate under directives issued by this headquarters until his forces could join up with the nearest army, whereupon he would be taken over by the army commander both operationally and logistically."

" . . . for this purpose I assure you that we need an officer of real ability, leadership and experience. The job is a tough one, and the great reason that I want an American air officer is so that I can give him the necessary operational and training control over troop carrier command and assure the closest kind of co-operation with tactical air-forces. This whole activity has been too loosely organized and I want to tighten it up under an energetic man who will do the job properly."

4. On 17th July, Lieutenant-General Lewis H. Brereton, Commanding General Ninth U.S. Air Force, was informed by General Eisenhower that he had been selected to command the new Allied Airborne Headquarters, and on 2nd August Supreme Headquarters issued the formal order for the formation of the new army and stated that it would be made up of the following :—

(a) Army Headquarters.
(b) 1 British Airborne Corps, consisting of 1 and 6 British Airborne Divisions, 1 Special Air Service Brigade, and 1 Polish Independent Parachute Brigade Group.
(c) XVIII U.S. Airborne Corps, consisting of 17, 82 and 101 U.S. Airborne Divisions and certain Airborne Aviation Engineer Battalions. Later 13 U.S. Airborne Division joined the Corps.
(d) IX U.S. Troop Carrier Command.
(e) 38 and 46 Groups R.A.F., which were only to be under the operational control of the new headquarters as and when placed under command for specific operations by Headquarters, Allied Expeditionary Air Forces. This was because 38 Group was at that time engaged on a considerable amount of S.A.S. and S.O.E. work, 46 Group being the only air transport group available to the Allied Expeditionary Air Forces. In practice this meant that First Allied Airborne Army would undoubtedly have first call for any major operations.

In addition, though not officially part of 1 Airborne Corps, 52 (Lowland) Division, which had been training as a mountain division before 6th June, was shortly afterwards re-organized as an air transported division but never employed as such. It was later used in an amphibious landing at Walcheren Island—which was below sea level.

5. The functions of the headquarters as laid down by S.H.A.E.F. were :—

(a) To supervise training and allot facilities.

(b) To study and recommend improvements in airborne equipment.

(c) To co-ordinate supply.

(d) Consult with the C.-in-C., Allied Expeditionary Air Forces, concerning his requirements.

(e) To assemble troops, equipment and supplies at designated air bases.

(f) The preparation and examination in conjunction with the S.H.A.E.F. planning-staff of the outline plan for the employment of airborne troops, and preparation of detailed plans for the employment of airborne troops in conjunction with the ground force and air force commanders. In fact First Allied Airborne Army only dealt with outline plans, all details being decentralized to lower formations.

(g) Direction and control of the execution of such plans until the ground force commander takes command of such units.

(h) To establish resupply requirements, arrange for delivery to departure air bases and to supervise supply by air.

(i) When arrangements for the release of airborne units by the ground force command have been made, to provide for the return to their home bases.

(j) To reconstitute airborne forces.

The operational channels of command are shown at Appendix L.

6. Air Chief Marshal Sir Trafford Leigh-Mallory, Air Commander-in-Chief, Allied Expeditionary Air Force had some criticisms of the new organization, the chief of which were :—

(a) Increases in personnel, time and labour would be inevitable with yet another headquarters, resulting in a loss of efficiency.

(b) There would be a division of responsibility on purely air problems.
    Previous events—the invasion of Normandy—had not shown the present organization to be a failure and therefore any re-organization involving such division of air forces was illogical and unsound.

(c) Troop Carrier Command aircraft would remain under the control of the new organization in between airborne operations and would therefore not be available for other purposes.

7. General Eisenhower considered that the one criticism that carried weight was the utilization of Troop Carrier Command between operations. He felt that the need for the organization existed and that if it were to carry out its functions efficiently, troop carrier units must be under operational control of the airborne headquarters. In between operations they would concentrate on training with airborne troops to maintain or improve air-crew standards. He did not agree

that airborne operations had been satisfactory from the dropping point of view. This was especially so in Sicily and in the operations of the American divisions in Normandy where one divisional commander had reported that his troops had no faith in the troop carrier air-crews.

8. On 4th August, Lieutenant-General Brereton recommended to the Supreme Commander that the new formation should be known as the First Allied Airborne Army and to this General Eisenhower agreed, and on the same day Lieutenant-General F. A. M. Browning was appointed as deputy commander in addition to his duties of commanding 1 Airborne Corps. The formation of the new army was not made public until a week later when on 10th August, General Eisenhower announced it while addressing units of IX U.S. Troop Carrier Command at Membury, England.

9. The early part of August was spent in getting the headquarters organized and in picking up the threads of the various operational plans which had already been made and which are dealt with later on in this chapter. During the month the majority of the staff joined, and the following list, which shows all the British officers and the chief American officers, gives some idea of the establishment :—

Appointment.	Name.	Nationality.
Commanding General ..	Lt.-Gen. L. H. Brereton.	American.
Deputy Commanding General.	Lt.-Gen. F. A. M. Browning.	British.
Chief of Staff	Brig.-Gen. Floyd L. Parks.	American.
Deputy Chief of Staff ..	Brigadier R. F. K. Goldsmith.	British.
G.1 Section	Colonel Frank Ward.	American.
Assistant	Captain Chapman.	British.
G.2 Section	Colonel J. A. Cella.	American.
Assistant	Lt.-Col. A. E. Tasker.	British.
G.3 Section	Brig.-Gen. Ralph E. Stearley.	American.
Assistant	Colonel W. T. Campbell.	British.
Assistant	Group Captain Abrahams.	British.
Assistant	Wing Commander Atkinson.	British.
Assistant	Captain P. C. Fielder.	British.
G.4 Section	Colonel J. H. Whalley-Kelly.	British.
Assistant	Lt.-Col. W. Howard.	British.
Planning Section	Brig.-Gen. Stewart Cutler.	American.
Assistant	Lt.-Col. N. J. L. Field.	British.
Communications Section	Colonel E. C. Gillette.	American.
Assistant	Lt.-Col. B. Donald.	British.
Assistant	Wing Commander Fahie.	British.

Early in December, 1944, Major-General R. N. Gale was appointed Deputy Commander of First Allied Airborne Army in place of Lieutenant-General Browning who had been appointed as Chief of Staff to the Supreme Allied Commander South-East Asia. Brigadier Flavell was appointed as Deputy Chief of Staff as successor to Brigadier Goldsmith who was taken ill.

10. The airborne army headquarters was originally established at Sunninghill Park, Ascot, alongside rear headquarters of Ninth U.S. Air Force, but an advanced headquarters was set up at Maison Laffitte on the outskirts of Paris

on 30th September, the main component of which was the planning section so that they could work closely with S.H.A.E.F. who were in Versailles. The main headquarters remained at Ascot, taking over the rear headquarters of Ninth U.S. Air Force in the meantime, until the end of February, 1945, when the majority moved to Maison Laffitte.

11. The activities of First Allied Airborne Army were controlled by a series of directives, issued by General Eisenhower, by which the airborne army's resources were placed at the disposal of a particular army group for specified periods. Thus all its resources were allotted to 21 Army Group during the pursuit from Normandy to the River Rhine, and again for the crossing of the River Rhine. The intention behind this was to free S.H.A.E.F. from tactical planning, the idea being that requirements for the employment of an airborne force should be initiated at army group level and then planned direct with First Allied Army. The original requirement was examined in outline, both from the Army and Air Force point of view, by First Allied Airborne Army and if considered suitable by them was passed on to the corps headquarters concerned for more detailed planning. Thus 1 Airborne Corps had passed to it a number of suggestions from 21 Army Group, Allied Expeditionary Air Forces and S.H.A.E.F. for the employment of 1 Airborne Division. All those ideas had to be examined at corps headquarters which therefore acted as a " planning filter ", and reduced the number of requirements that were passed on to 1 Airborne Division. With them 1 Airborne Corps were able to hand over much valuable planning material as a result of their own examinations.

12. After the successful airborne operations connected with the crossing of the Rhine, Lieutenant-General Brereton received on 8th April, 1945, the following letter from Field Marshal Sir Alan Brooke, Chief of the Imperial General Staff. It was a tribute to the team work of the joint Anglo American staff of the First Allied Airborne Army, which was in fact the only joint British and American combat command :—

" Major-General Gale has just been to see me and has given me an account of the recent successful airborne operations carried out under your direction by the XVIII U.S. Corps with 6 British and 17 U.S. Divisions under command. I had the pleasure of witnessing this force go into action from a viewpoint on the west of the Rhine, and it was a most impressive and inspiring spectacle.

" I should like to congratulate you most heartily on the great results achieved by what has been perhaps the most successful airborne operation carried out up to now. At the same time I should like to take the opportunity of thanking you for all you have done for British airborne troops since the formation of the First Allied Airborne Army.

" I realize that our contribution has necessarily been limited in quantity, and that owing to our inability to provide trained reinforcements rapidly for 1 Airborne Division, we have latterly been able to put only one division at your disposal. Nevertheless I know that you have invariably given full support, encouragement and credit to our airborne commanders and troops. The leadership which you have exercised with such sympathy and understanding has resulted in a most happy fusion of the airborne forces of our two nations, and has made them into one team in a manner which must be very nearly unique in military history."

13. After the Germans had been defeated there was no further need for the continued existence of the headquarters and so on 20th May, 1945, First Allied Airborne Army was dissolved. The British element, with one or two exceptions returned to the United Kingdom and the United States element, re-named the First Airborne Army, took over command of the United States Sector of Berlin.

Projected Airborne Operations—June to September, 1944, and the Airborne Forward Delivery Airfield Group

14. Apart from the operations of 101 U.S. Airborne Division at Bastogne*, which are not dealt with in this history, First Allied Airborne Army planned many operations but only two actually took place, those in the Arnhem–Nijmegen–Grave area and those in connection with the crossing of the River Rhine. These are dealt with fully in Chapters XX and XXI. A further 16 or so operations were planned but, for various reasons, they were all cancelled, and as some of them were planned before the formation of First Allied Airborne Army we must now go back to the month of June, 1944. In some cases they have been described only in outline as detailed information is not available.

" Tuxedo "

15. The object of this operation was to maintain the build-up of troops on the ground if the Normandy beach landings did not go according to plan. It was to have taken place anywhere as required within the bridgehead, Second Army being responsible for choosing the dropping zones and informing 1 Airborne Corps and Combined Troop Carrier Command Post, and was to have consisted of one parachute brigade only. For this purpose 4 Parachute Brigade were placed at four hours' notice from " D " day and were to stand by to drop with bare operational requirements only.

" Wastage "

16. The object and landing areas were to be the same as for " Tuxedo ", but it was to consist of the whole of 1 Airborne Division. It became quite a strong possibility when the weather off the Normandy beaches took a turn for the worse as there was a prolonged danger of sea-borne reinforcements and supplies not being able to get ashore.

Reinforcement of 82 U.S. Airborne Division
7th to 10th June

17. The whole or part of 1 Airborne Division was to take part in this task at any time between 7th–10th June, to reinforce 82 U.S. Airborne Division immediately after their landings should the enemy gain the upper hand, because of the vital necessity of gaining control of the Carentan Peninsula. The area was St. Sauveur-le-Vicomte, but planning was stopped as it was decided that landing zones were entirely unsuitable for Horsa Gliders.

" Wild Oats "

18. The object of " Wild Oats " was to prevent the arrival of enemy reinforcements by landing 1 Airborne Division just south of Caen in the vicinity of Carpiquet airfield with the plateau at Evrecy as the centre of the divisional

---

* See " Rendezvous with Destiny ", a History of the 101st Airborne Division, by Leonard Rapport and Arthur Northwood, Jnr., published by the Infantry Journal Press, Washington, U.S.A.

perimeter. A planning team from 1 Airborne Division spent some 24 hours with Headquarters, 1 Corps in Normandy co-ordinating arrangements. The original planning was done in some detail from old and out-of-date photographic cover, but when new cover was received it showed that there were a considerable number of anti-aircraft guns on the dropping zones. It became obvious that the operation would be costly but luckily it was overtaken by events and was not required.

"Beneficiary," 22nd June to 3rd July

19. At one time it was thought that airborne troops would be required to assist in the capture of St. Malo and to establish a bridgehead sufficiently large to permit the clearance and development of the port for the landing of troops and stores for the occupation of Brittany. The bridgehead was to be cleared by an airborne assault which was to be followed by a sea-borne landing. The troops available were :—

Airborne
> H.Q. 1 Airborne Corps.
> 1 Airborne Division.
> One Squadron 1st Special Air Service Regiment.
> 504 U.S. Parachute Regimental Combat Team.
> 878 U.S. Airborne Aviation Engineer Battalion.
> 1 Polish Independent Parachute Brigade.

Sea-borne
> Headquarters XX U.S. Corps.
> 28 U.S. Division.
> 80 U.S. Division.

20. The commander of the airborne troops was to command all troops until Headquarters XX U.S. Corps was ashore. 1 Airborne Division was to land east of the River Rance to destroy the beach defences and capture St. Malo, sending one brigade into St. Malo, one to cut the two main roads leading to the south out of the peninsular and keeping the air-landing brigade in reserve. It is interesting to note that the plan envisaged landing the whole of 1 Air-landing Brigade directly on to the sandy beach and that the landing zones were chosen below the high water mark so that the tides had an effect on both the airborne and sea-borne landings.

21. 504 U.S. Regimental Combat Team, with under command 1 Polish Independent Parachute Brigade, was to land west of the River Rance to annihilate the beach defences and to capture Dinan and Dinan airfield. The capture of the airfield before the sea-borne landing was not essential but it had to be captured within 24 hours so that, if the build-up over the beaches was prevented by bad weather or enemy action, the airfield could be used for air maintenance of the sea-borne force. 878 U.S. Airborne Aviation Engineer Battalion was to be held in immediate readiness in the United Kingdom until the Dinan airfield was captured and would then be responsible for repair and maintenance of the airfield.

22. One squadron of 1st Special Air Service Regiment was to drop 25 small parties in the area Dol-Pontorson–St. Aubin–Montauban–Plancoet–Dinan, to harass the movement of enemy reserves towards the airborne and sea-borne landing areas. After they had completed their tasks the Special Air Service troops were to withdraw into the beachhead.

23. Forward observation officers and forward observation bombardment parties were to control supporting fire from corps artillery and also naval gunfire, but there was to be no bombing before the airborne landings although certain targets were to be attacked by heavy, light and fighter-bombers after first light on " D " day, and after that on call.

24. All parachute drops were to take place as soon as possible after darkness on " D " — 1 day and were to be followed immediately by the glider landings, while the sea-borne landings were not to take place before the evening of " D " day.

25. Much has often been said about the capture of heavy beach defences by airborne troops. On this occasion the naval forces were only to sail into St. Malo if the enemy defences had been captured and the airborne troops could guarantee that no shot would be fired at our craft. Somewhat naturally they could not give this guarantee, and so the operation was cancelled.

The Airborne Forward Delivery Airfield Group

26. Consideration of the first five projected operations and study of some that might be required in the future had shown Lieutenant-General Browning that in many cases it might be necessary to fly-in air-transportable troops and indeed several operations of this type were planned, though none actually took place.

27. On 3rd July, 1944, therefore, Headquarters, 1 Airborne Corps pointed out to 21 Army Group that should an air-transported division be flown in to an airstrip which had been captured by an airborne division, it would be necessary to provide machinery to ensure that the forces could be maintained adequately by air. They emphasized that if airborne forces operated alone they would not have the benefit of the administrative installations which are normally available to them when operating in conjunction with a land or sea-borne force. The necessary administrative organization should consist of three parts :—

  (a) R.A.F. air control and maintenance.
  (b) Main headquarters of the organization with full Services representation which would be found from Headquarters, 1 Airborne Corps.
  (c) Signal sections of administrative units and installations.

The purpose of such an organization would be to :—

  (a) Receive troops, transport and stores arriving by air.
  (b) Keep one or more airfields in working order.
  (c) Receive, hold and forward stores of all descriptions to the fighting force.
  (d) Receive, hold and return to the United Kingdom by air all casualties.
  (e) Salvage.
  (f) Control the whole airhead.

21 Army Group were asked to earmark the personnel and equipment for the above, and to this they agreed, the organization being formed a fortnight later. The organization would function, of course, equally on an airstrip which had been constructed, but in this case an airborne aviation engineer battalion, which would have to be American as the British had none, would be landed in

gliders. The battalion would form part of the forward delivery airfield group and would be responsible for the construction, maintenance and enlarging of the airstrip. The whole group would be increased considerably in size, with a particular increase in the air commitment because of the large numbers of gliders necessary to lift troops and stores of the engineer battalion.

To assist in the Break-out of the Normandy Bridgehead—Mid-July

28. At one time a possibility arose that 1 Airborne Division would be required to drop on the Falaise–Caen road about half-way between the two towns, with Bretville as the centre of the divisional area, with the object of assisting the break-out from the bridgehead by our armour, which had been delayed for about a month.

"Swordhilt"—20th July to 4th August

29. The R.A.F., despite several attacks, had failed to destroy the Morlaix Viaduct and it was considered imperative that Brest should be cut off. Therefore, 1 Airborne Division was warned to stand by to drop in the area between Morlaix and Lannion to destroy the viaduct.

"Hands-up"—15th July to 15th August

30. As it became likely that General Patton's Third U.S. Army was going to break out of the southern extremities of the Normandy bridgehead, plans were made to assist his advance and to prepare for the maintenance of his army by cutting off Quiberon Bay and the Brittany Peninsula. The strategic planners had calculated that Cherbourg would be incapable of maintaining all the American armies once they landed on the Continent. An additional major port would be necessary and it was decided that one was to be established in Quiberon Bay on the general lines of the artificial Port Winston at Arromanches.

31. The decision was taken to assist General Patton with an airborne operation which would have the following objects :—

    (a) The capture of the Quiberon Bay area so that initial surveying and perhaps even construction work could be started.

    (b) To provide a base for the development of the " resistance " movements in the area.

The dates of the operation remained fluid for about a month and it was not to be launched until the Third Army had reached the approximate line St. Malo–Rennes–Laval, was ready to attack towards Brest and Quiberon Bay, and would be able to join up with the airborne forces within four days. 1 Airborne Division and 1 Polish Parachute Brigade were to capture Vannes airfield, 52 (L) Division was to be flown in, and the Airborne Forward Delivery Airfield Group was to be used for the administrative build-up. There was to be no sea-borne assault but sea-borne convoys, which included 1 S.S. (Commando) Brigade were to be brought in to carry out preliminary reconnaissance and work for the new harbour. The responsibility for securing beach-heads was given to the airborne forces. The operation was to be controlled by 12 U.S. Army Group through Third U.S. Army and Headquarters 1 Airborne Corps under Lieutenant-General Browning would command all Allied troops in the Quiberon Bay area until the main land forces joined up, when they would come under command of Third Army.

32. The operation was finally cancelled because the speed with which Third Army advanced made it unnecessary. In any case Cherbourg was rehabilitated more quickly than was anticipated and it was found that it could deal with a greater tonnage than was expected so that with the assistance of minor capacity ports such as St. Malo and Brest it would be possible to maintain Third Army.

" Transfigure "—7th to 17th August

33. " Transfigure " was the code name for the airborne operation that was planned to take place in conjunction with " Lucky Strike B " which was to have been a sweeping armoured movement around the southern flank of the German forces in Normandy. On 6th August, the original plan was revised and the airborne task was then given as being to close the Paris–Orleans gap and cut off the enemy's retreat. The landing and dropping zones were centred on Rambouillet, the area surrounding which was ideal country, and 1 Airborne Corps was to take part consisting of :—

1 Airborne Division.
52 (L) Division.
101 U.S. Airborne Division.
1 Polish Parachute Brigade Group.
878 U.S. Airborne Aviation Engineer Battalion.
2nd Air-landing Light Anti-Aircraft Battery.
Airborne Forward Delivery Airfield Group.

34. The operation envisaged the capture of an air-strip area by the airborne troops and, as soon as it was made serviceable by the engineer battalion, the fly-in of 52 (L) Division and the establishment of an airhead. By doing this it was hoped to provide a forward base and pivot from which Allied armour could go forward into Paris.

35. Headquarters, 1 Airborne Corps was responsible for the mounting of the operation and for the maintenance of all troops until contact with the ground forces had been established, when responsibility for the maintenance of the American troops was to be transferred to 12 U.S. Army Group, who commanded the whole operation. A large sea-borne element was catered for and was to concentrate in France and the United Kingdom, where it would be the responsibility of 21 Army Group, and was to join up with the airborne troops as soon as possible, coming under command of 12 U.S. Army Group as soon as it started to move. The sea-borne elements of 1 Airborne Corps and 1 Airborne Division crossed over to France before the operation was cancelled, but in anticipation of it, and remained there until joining up with them at Nijmegen at the end of September. This caused much inconvenience to all concerned for the sea-borne elements contained most of the transport and everyone's kit.

36. The airborne plan was based upon two parachute lifts followed by an air-portable lift and was as follows :—
    (a) *First lift*
        101 U.S. Airborne Division to land in the area south of Sonchamp to capture the road centre of St. Arnoult-en-Yvennes and dominate the surrounding country and roads in that area without prejudice to the retention of the main road Chartes–Dourdan–Paris. The alternative task of the division was to protect the landing strips for the fly-in of 52 (L) Division.

1 Polish Parachute Brigade less a glider element to land in the area west of Rambouillet to protect the landing strips which were to be constructed along the route Rambouillet–Ablis.

(b) *Second lift*

1 Airborne Division to land south of Rambouillet to capture the town and dominate the roads radiating from it without prejudice to the retention of the road Chartres–Rambouillet–Paris. The glider element of 1 Polish Parachute Brigade Group to join its brigade.

878 U.S. Airborne Aviation Engineer Battalion to construct up to four air strips north of the road Orphin–Sonchamp.

(c) *Subsequent lifts* were to bring in 52 (L) Division, which was to concentrate east of Rambouillet in the area of Le Foret de Yvennes as corps reserve.

(d) *G.H.Q. Liaison Regiment* (Phantom) was to provide patrols for Headquarters 1 Airborne Corps and each division, and these patrols were to maintain direct communication with 12 U.S. and 21 Army Groups.

(e) *United States Armoured formations* were to seize the Dourdan road centre and dominate the area south of Dourdan as far as and inclusive of Chartres-Etamps.

(f) *The operation* was to take place not before 16th August ; it was to be an evening drop and the American armoured forces were to make contact with the airborne troops within 24 hours after they had landed.

37. On 13th August, all units were moved to their airfields and the force stood by at 48 hours' notice from 15th August, the day on which the Allied invasion of Southern France took place, but by 17th August, General Patton had again moved so quickly that the airborne operation was no longer necessary and it was cancelled. There was another factor which may have influenced the decision not to use the airborne troops, and which is borne out by S.H.A.E.F.'s decision to use all available transport aircraft to maintain Third Army. General Patton had plenty of troops but insufficient supplies and long lines of communication. It would have been unsound to use aircraft which were needed to carry supplies to drop more troops who would increase the supply problem.

AVAILABILITY FOR OPERATIONAL USE OF BRITISH AIRBORNE
FORCES IN AUGUST, 1944

38. By the beginning of August so many operations had been planned that Lieutenant-General Browning decided that higher authority must be told what troops could be expected to take part in operations at short notice and so informed Headquarters, First Allied Airborne Army that the availability of British Airborne Forces, which included Allied airborne forces, under command of 1 Airborne Corps, was as given below. The S.A.S. Brigade is not included as they were directly under S.H.A.E.F. for operations.

(a) *Availability at seven days' notice :—*

1 Airborne Division.
52 (L) Division.
1 Polish Parachute Brigade.

(b) *Availability in addition to (a) at from seven to fourteen days' notice :*—
Headquarters, 1 Airborne Corps.
Airborne Forward Delivery Airfield Group.

(c) *Availability two months after return from present location :*—
6 Airborne Division.

For an occupation or a police role, which would not involve offensive operations, all those units mentioned in sub-paragraph (a) above could be ready at five days' notice, but for any air-portable operation at least one airborne aviation engineer battalion would be necessary, but was not available from British resources. Up to date this had been 878 U.S. Airborne Aviation Engineer Battalion. For the above timing it was assumed that an outline plan and photographs had been prepared and were ready. The following was the position of the availability of British aircraft and gliders :—

Bomber type	..	..	..	..	..	..	248 } 398
C.47	..	..	..	..	..	..	150 }
Horsa Gliders	..	..	..	..	..	..	920
Hamilcar Gliders		..	..	..	..	..	72
Glider pilot crews—Horsa		..	..	..	..	453 } 504
—Hamilcar ..		..	..	..		51 }

Therefore, there were insufficient British aircraft for a divisional operation in one lift and Lieutenant-General Browning advocated the continuation of the pooling system for British and United States aircraft for operations and training.

" Boxer "—August

39. Immediately after operation " Transfigure " was cancelled, S.H.A.E.F. ordered First Allied Airborne Army to stand by for an operation known as " Boxer " which was to be launched as soon as possible and which would have the following objects :—

(a) To capture Boulogne.

(b) To operate in a south or south-easterly direction against the right flank and rear of the enemy.

(c) To attack the area from which flying bombs (V.1) were being launched against England.

(d) To draw off enemy forces from the main front by creating a diversion in the Boulogne area.

The force allotted was the same as for " Transfigure " and troops remained in their marshalling areas but, though plans were completed by 17th August, the operation was finally cancelled on 26th August.

" Axehead " and " Linnet "—15th August to 3rd September

40. Before the cancelling of and in parallel with the planning for " Boxer," two other operations were being worked out. The first was " Axehead " which was one of many planned to assist 21 Army Group in crossing the River Seine by capturing and holding bridgeheads or a bridgehead on the general line Les Andelys–Villerest–Douville sur Andelle–Anfreville sous les Montes. Planning for this operation was to be completed by 25th August, and it was to have been undertaken by 1 Airborne Division with under command 1 Polish Parachute Brigade.

41. The other operation was " Linnet ", the object of which was to seize a firm base in the vicinity of Tournai, to secure and hold a bridgehead over the River Escaut at Tournai and to control the principal roads leading north-east from the front through Tournai–Lille–Courtrai, thereby cutting off the German withdrawal.   The troops to take part were :—

Headquarters 1 Airborne Corps.
1 Airborne Division.
82 U.S. Airborne Division.
101 U.S. Airborne Division.
52 (L) Division.
1 Polish Parachute Brigade.
878 U.S. Airborne Aviation Engineer Battalion.
2nd Air-landing Light Anti-Aircraft Battery.

42. The tasks in detail were as follows :—

(a) 101 *U.S. Airborne Division*

    (i) To seize the road centre of Tournai and capture intact the Tournai road bridges over the River Escaut.
    (ii) To dominate the area surrounding Tournai ;
    (iii) To capture any airfields in the vicinity, especially those with hard runways.

(b) 82 *U.S. Airborne Division*

    (i) To seize and hold the high ground north of Tournai in the area of Mont St. Aubert, and in the event of any heavy enemy attack developing against 101 U.S. Airborne Division, to support that formation.
    (ii) To dominate the area in the vicinity of Mont St. Aubert.
    (iii) To capture any airfields, especially those with any hard runways.

(c) 1 *Airborne Division* with under command 1 Polish Parachute Brigade.

    (i) To seize the area from inclusive the high ground at Mont de L'Enclus to inclusive of the crossroads at Kerkhove.
    (ii) To seize Courtrai or the exits from it, *i.e.* the road Courtrai–Deynze and the road Courtrai–Bruges.
    (iii) To dominate all the surrounding country.
    (iv) To capture the airfield west of Courtrai and Bisseghem.

The troops were to be ready to take off as from 3rd September, but eventually the operation was cancelled.

43. An alternative to " Linnet ", known as " Linnet II ", was planned to be mounted on or after 4th September, with the object of landing in the area Aachen-Maastricht in order to block the gap.   It was to be mounted at 36 hours notice but was cancelled on 5th September and troops were then permitted to stand down from their marshalling areas.

" Infatuate ", " Comet " and " Market "

44. At the beginning of September, S.H.A.E.F. placed the entire effort of First Allied Airborne Army at the disposal of the Commander-in-Chief, 21 Army Group, until a bridgehead was secured across the Lower Rhine, with the result that two operations, " Comet " and " Market ", were planned.   At the same time, First Allied Airborne Army was requested by 21 Army Group to examine the possibilities of an airborne operation, " Infatuate ", against the Walcheren

Islands to assist in opening up the port of Antwerp by cutting off and hastening the German retreat across the Scheldt estuary. However, the examination never really turned into a plan as, on the strong recommendation of Lieutenant-General Brereton, the operation was turned down on 21st September, because of the heavy enemy flak on the island and the lack of suitable landing zones. Such as there were had the sea at either end and a large number of deep dykes filled with water across their centre.

45. When " Linnet II " was cancelled 1 Airborne Division was ordered to plan operation " Comet ", the object of which was to secure the bridges over the River Rhine from Arnhem to Wesel, in order to facilitate the advance on the Ruhr basin from the north, but only 1 Airborne Division and 1 Polish Parachute Brigade were to be used. Division Headquarters, 1 Polish Parachute Brigade and 1 Air-landing Brigade were to land at Nijmegen, 1 Parachute Brigade at Arnhem and 4 Parachute Brigade at Grave. " D " day was to be 10th September and take off at 0600 hours, but at 0200 hours on 10th September, senior officers at division headquarters were awakened and told that the operation was cancelled. By 1500 hours that same day the Commander, 1 Airborne Division, Major-General R. E. Urquhart and his staff had received fresh instructions and were at work planning the Division's part in operation " Market ", which was to take place a week later. In the " Market " plan two airborne divisions out of the three to be used, plus a parachute brigade, were allocated to the tasks given above which a few hours before had been considered within the powers of one division and one parachute brigade.

Lessons

46. It has been stated that the idea behind First Allied Airborne Army was that requirements for airborne operations should be initiated on the army group level. Nevertheless, in order to be ready for any requirement presented to them the Airborne Army Headquarters had to keep a constant eye on the progress of the battle and had to have a plan in mind for almost any eventuality. Although details have been given of the more important operations and the minor ones have been described in outline only, an equal amount of planning on all of them had to be done by the headquarters concerned. The command and staff problems were not very much less because an operation did not take place, and staff officers had to work on the assumption that the troops would go into action as planned.

47. However, probably owing to overkeenness, on occasions officers of Headquarters, First Allied Airborne Army made two important mistakes. More than once they attempted to " sell their wares " by suggesting airborne operations to army groups or armies, and they also passed on some operational plans to lower airborne formations before they had received even the provisional approval of the army group or army commander concerned. The result was that the time of commanders and staffs was taken up with unnecessary planning when it could have been spent in much needed training of the troops. The troops themselves, both British and Allied, suffered from a sense of frustration with a consequent effect on morale caused by frequent postponements and living for long periods in transit camps, often not as complete units. It would have been of great assistance to formation commanders if they had been told whether an operation had been planned in case it might be required or whether it had been asked for by a ground formation commander.

48. The planning period brought out the necessity for a senior airborne formation headquarters which was in the closest touch with the ground operations and at the same time could ensure that everything was done to maintain a high standard of morale and training in the army and air force formations under its command. There would be many competitive calls for the services of the transport aircraft and to keep them tied up for long periods in case of projected operations might be endangering other operations. A good example of this was operation " Transfigure ".

49. Better results might have been achieved if Headquarters, First Allied Airborne Army had consisted only of a small planning staff and just sufficient " G " and " Q " staffs for co-ordination purposes. Almost all other aspects of airborne operations had to be worked out in any case at army group, army or airborne corps headquarters, and unnecessary duplication could have been avoided. It has also been suggested, and is for consideration, that there should have been only one Allied airborne corps headquarters, commanded by the best available general, irrespective of nationality, the advantage being that the few available experienced airborne planners on the corps level would have been concentrated.

50. On the other hand, First Allied Airborne Army did a great deal of very good work in improving the training of certain Air Force units, and this was evident in the excellent drops achieved at Arnhem. This in itself is a big factor, for scattered dropping, whether or not it is the fault of the aircrews, may cause mistrust among the soldiers which might impair the close co-operation needed to achieve success. Headquarters, First Allied Airborne Army, was able to knit this co-operation even closer.

(C29259)

CHAPTER XVII

2 INDEPENDENT PARACHUTE BRIGADE GROUP FROM NOVEMBER, 1943, TO OCTOBER, 1945

The Brigade Group in an Infantry Role in Italy

1. As related in Chapter XI, 2 Independent Parachute Brigade Group, commanded by Brigadier C. H. V. Pritchard, remained in Italy after 1 Airborne Division sailed for England in November, 1943, and received their official title as an independent brigade group on 22nd November, 1943. They were required by the Supreme Allied Commander in the Mediterranean for future airborne operations and as an integral part of his balanced forces. For the time being they were placed under General Alexander, who was Commander-in-Chief of 15 Army Group in Italy, as that seemed to be the theatre in which they would most probably be required. They relied for their air training and for their air transport during operations on the resources of the United States Troop Carrier Command, equipped entirely with Dakota aircraft.

2. The detailed order of battle of the brigade group is given at Appendix O. Generally speaking the brigade suffered from a lack of really adequate R.E.M.E., and Ordnance resources in the order of battle, and a lack of good war estabments and equipment tables for some of the units which were hurriedly formed.

3. No airborne base was provided for the brigade and though it was very necessary it was not authorized until about the beginning of March, 1944. In the meantime an organization was improvised from within brigade resources, chiefly first reinforcements under the brigade deputy commander, who acted as base commander with the staff captain and supervising officer, parachute training, as staff officers. It was located with Troop Carrier Command and in addition to the organization for operations, it had to cater for all parachute and glider training of recruits and personnel undergoing refresher training, even when the main body of the brigade was engaged in ground operations. No. 2 Mobile Parachute Servicing Unit, R.A.F., was part of the base but no R.A.F. Parachute Jumping Instructors were provided until about September, 1944. In the meantime parachute training instruction was carried out by the brigade Army Physical Training Corps personnel.

4. In addition to 2 Independent Parachute Brigade Group, 1st Air-landing Light Regiment, R.A. (Lieutenant-Colonel W. F. K. Thompson), also remained behind in Italy. Although not part of the brigade, and although it had been left behind chiefly to gain battle experience before returning to England, it was also intended to provide a reserve of air-landing light artillery available for the brigade for any airborne operations required while it was in the theatre. It left Italy in January, 1944, but was only replaced by 64th Light Battery from Malta in April, 1944. In June, 1944, a forward observation bombardment troop was formed from volunteers for parachute duties in Central Mediterranean Forces and consisted chiefly of Canadian officers.

5. Before 1 Airborne Division left Italy, 2 Parachute Brigade relieved 1 Parachute Brigade in the area of Bari and Barletta. While reorganizing there in November they sailed up the eastern Italian coast in locally-conscripted fishing vessels, in a feint operation which was part of a larger cover plan. No

landings were planned or executed for this operation. However, 5th Parachute Battalion and 2nd Parachute Squadron, R.E., did some amphibious training with the object of disrupting rail communications, but they did not carry out any operations of this sort. For the remainder of their time in a ground role in Italy their operations fall naturally into three phases, as described below, until operation " Hasty " at Toricella on 1st June, 1944.

29TH NOVEMBER TO 28TH DECEMBER, 1943

6. On 29th November, 1943, one week after becoming an independent formation, the brigade was warned by General Montgomery, Eighth Army, that they might have to serve as infantry in the line north of the River Sangro. In the meantime the brigade moved south to Gioia and started arrangements there for airborne training for which 15 Army Group had arranged for two wings of Troop Carrier Command to be available. However, at 1930 hours on 30th November, orders were received from Eighth Army that the brigade must move in 48 hours into the line as infantry and by the evening of 2nd December, they had re-organized for their new role and were moving north by train and road. The brigade consisted of the three battalions, 2nd Parachute Squadron, R.E., 127th Parachute Field Ambulance, L.A.D., and a detachment of provost. Each battalion had 19 jeeps and 14 three-ton lorries which were acquired from various sources and collected *en route* and all 3-inch mortars and medium machine-guns were carried on jeeps. First reinforcement personnel remained behind to continue airborne training.

7. Thus, in addition to being able to carry out its primary role as a parachute formation, the brigade group was established as a formation capable of undertaking ground operations efficiently when not required for airborne operations. They were, of course, still equipped on a very light scale and were in no sense a " motorized " or " mobile " ground formation, nor did they have any light or field artillery as a permanent component of the brigade group, though arrangements were made for light artillery to be made available for particular airborne operations if required. But they were better organized for ground operations than 1 Parachute Brigade had been in Tunisia.

8. During the evening of 2nd December, the brigade came under command of 2 New Zealand Division (Lieutenant-General Sir Bernard Freyberg) and was allotted the task of protecting their left flank while advancing towards Orsogna. In atrocious weather, along a bad mountain road inches deep in mud, they moved north of the River Sangro to the area just south of Castelfrentano, and by 6th December, they held a front 25 miles wide north of the river. On the way there was some strong opposition south of Guardigrele but this was overcome fairly quickly.

9. The enemy were known to be in Torricella, nearby, and were in some cases only some 600 yards north of the brigade. Successful patrols showed that he was holding the high ground south of Orsogna and an attack by 2 New Zealand Division on 8th December, failed to dislodge him. The attack was repeated, successfully this time from the east, on 13th December, and was assisted by strong and numerous brigade patrols operating from the south. In the meantime 2nd Parachute Squadron R.E., was engaged in repairing and improving roads and bridges in the area. Offensive patrol activities continued and there was considerable enemy artillery fire which caused heavy casualties.

10. Realizing that the ten-day stay which had been indicated originally would probably extend to many weeks, Brigadier Pritchard decided that his command must be as self-supporting as possible and arranged for his R.A.S.C. Company and Light Aid Detachment R.E.M.E., to join him and for reinforcements to replace casualties. This was completed by 25th December. At 1000 hours on that day, however, 2nd Battalion The Royal Inniskilling Fusiliers (Lieutenant-Colonel J. P. O'Brien-Twohig) from 13 Infantry Brigade of 5 Infantry Division relieved 6th Parachute Battalion and came under command of the brigade, whose frontage was now extended to 30 miles, as 6th Parachute Battalion in turn relieved 24th New Zealand Battalion south of Orsogna. The problem of control was considerable but was solved satisfactorily by mobile No. 22 wireless sets and improvised line sections which were organized most efficiently by the Signal Company under Major Roberson. A third attack by 2 New Zealand Division on Orsogna was only partially successful in bad weather and exploitation was impossible, but the brigade held some of the southern outskirts of the town and continued active patrolling, and on 28th December, 2nd Battalion The Wiltshire Regiment, of 5 Infantry Division, relieved 5th Parachute Battalion. This ends a period during which the brigade had fought its first actions as such and had, at the same time, become an efficient infantry formation which was guarding the left flank of Eighth Army.

11. During this period, too, Allied Forces Headquarters authorized the concentration of 1st Independent Glider Pilot Squadron, 1st Independent Parachute Platoon and 300th Air-landing Anti-Tank Battery in Sicily for airborne training with Troop Carrier Command. Simultaneously, the airborne base was made responsible for supply dropping for 15 Army Group on the scale of one battalion at a time and for recruiting and training parachute volunteers. They also established and staffed their own convalescent depot in order to concentrate wounded parachutists and rehabilitate them, and thus prevent a large wastage of trained men, for otherwise there was no guarantee of getting them back. Some 50 recruits were selected and trained during December, and it is worth recording that from the time 1 Airborne Division left Italy until 2 Independent Parachute Brigade returned to the United Kingdom not one reinforcement joined the brigade from England. All were recruited from and trained within Central Mediterranean resources. It was not until a year later that a proper depot was authorized for the brigade.

28TH DECEMBER, 1943 TO 26TH MARCH, 1944

12. The brigade remained under command of 2 New Zealand Division in approximately the same area for the first fortnight of 1944. The weather was very bad with snow blizzards and snow drifts up to six feet deep, the supply of food and ammunition was difficult and sometimes was reduced to small manloads, reliefs were not easy to accomplish and the brigade was holding an extended front with little depth, the forward troops being on mountain ridges in front of an almost impassable river. The defensive system was based on a series of strong points, supported by concentrated fire on demand from the divisional and corps artillery. Having had little opportunity for training with artillery on this scale, the brigade found they had plenty to learn. Enemy artillery activity was increasing but otherwise, although he had good observation over our positions, there was little active fighting. However, from 10th January, onwards, the brigade carried out a series of successful patrols and raids which gave them ascendancy in the battle area.

13. On 16th January, 2 New Zealand Division was relieved by 8 Indian Division, who took over command of 2 Independent Parachute Brigade Group in the same area. 4 Indian Division were now in position on their left.

14. On 29th January, General Sir Oliver Leese, Bart. who had by this time taken over command of Eighth Army, visited the brigade. He said that although he would like to release them for airborne training and operations he was unable to do so yet because of the necessity for concentrating all available formations to gain a decision on the front opposite Rome, and for giving all possible rest to 8 Indian Division after their hard fighting of the past months. In the meantime airborne training of recruits and first reinforcements, as well as of the glider pilots, continued at the airborne base. General Leese had to accept the fact that continued employment in the line as infantry would retard the eventual availability of the brigade as an airborne formation.

15. On 16th February, still in atrocious weather, the brigade moved out of the line into local reserve nearby, in the general area of Castelfrentano, being relieved by 17 Indian Infantry Brigade. Their role was now that of a counter-attack formation and they were still under command of 8 Indian Division, who were part of 13 Corps. On 23rd February they moved again, back to the area of Casoli where they had been in December, and a detachment of Italian parachute troops with the title of ' 'F '' Force were placed under their command. Activity was confined to patrols and assistance to escaping Allied prisoners and refugees, but once again they gained ascendancy over their opponents and made several minor advances to improve their positions.

16. On 1st March, Brigadier Pritchard left the brigade for a few days to visit Headquarters Allied Armies in Italy and to inspect his units and recruits still training in the back areas. He wanted a definite policy on the future role of his brigade, a clarification of the system of command for airborne operations and training, and information regarding the future availability of aircraft. Although fighting under the command of 15 Army Group in Italy, the brigade was still administered and trained partly by Allied Forces Headquarters, who retained the right to remove them from 15 Army Group in Italy if they thought fit. There was no airborne staff at the latter headquarters and no one except Brigadier Pritchard to give advice on airborne affairs. This was very unsatisfactory as he could not advise a senior headquarters many miles in rear and at the same time command his brigade in action. But at Allied Forces Headquarters there was a small airborne staff under Lieutenant-Colonel D. V. Phelps known, for deception purposes, as 5 Airborne Division (Plans). They were responsible for advising the staff on all aspects of airborne affairs and were permitted direct contact for liaison purposes with the Director of Air at the War Office. It was the lack of a similar link at Headquarters 15 Army Group in Italy that gave Brigadier Pritchard such a difficult task at that time.

17. As the result of his visit and subsequent agreement between the two senior headquarters concerned, it was decided that he would remain as the airborne adviser to the Commander-in-Chief 15 Army Group in Italy, that Lieutenant-Colonel Phelps would maintain close liaison with that head-quarters, and that every effort would be made to provide aircraft for training and in ample time for any airborne operations planned. This was a step

219

forward, but Brigadier Pritchard was still left with far greater and wider responsibilities than those of a normal brigade commander, especially as very few commanders or staff officers had any experience in handling airborne troops. Every effort was made by Central Mediterranean Forces to assist him and the situation was eased temporarily by the fact that the weather, the shortage of aircraft and the somewhat static nature of the campaign made airborne operations unlikely for some months. The shortage of aircraft did, however, have a detrimental effect on airborne training, particularly with regard to the glider pilots, in spite of the efforts of Brigadier General Beverley, Commanding General 51 U.S. Troop Carrier Wing. The lack of assistance from the United Kingdom made Brigadier Pritchard decide that his brigade should be self-supporting in all respects. With the liberal assistance of 15 Army Group he reorganized it completely as both an airborne and light brigade. In addition, by extensive recruiting the war establishments were supplemented to provide a parachute school and an airborne base. The latter was opened at Rome in the autumn under Major J. W. Pearson, and with a staff of about 15 officers and 100 other ranks was capable of holding and training 50 officers and 750 other ranks. Officer reinforcements were obtained by direct recruiting from certain formations and about 28 South African officers joined the brigade.

18. Brigadier Pritchard returned to his brigade on 5th March, to find the situation there had changed little. The Allied troops were being gradually thinned out on this sector of the front, to release extra formations for the major thrust to be developed towards and beyond Rome. The emphasis changed from offence to active defence and, although there were many minor actions, there were no major attacks by either side. By 19th March, the ground had dried considerably and the weather had become much milder, so much so that for the first time dust showed signs of becoming a problem, though there was still considerable snow on the mountains.

19. On 26th March, the brigade left the command of 8 Indian Division on the Sangro front and withdrew into reserve for four days at Guardia, near Benevento, under 13 Corps, which was behind the western sector of the Allied front, still in the mountains. So ended another phase, one that had provided excellent battle experience under hard conditions of weather and terrain, and had introduced the troops to heavy enemy gun-fire and to static warfare using our own artillery support. In addition they had proved their fighting ability and gained confidence, and had become an efficient field formation administratively.

26TH MARCH TO 28TH MAY, 1944

20. Headquarters, 15 Army Group confirmed that early airborne operations were unlikely, because the enemy's defences were growing in strength, a quick and successful break-through by the Allies was unlikely, and the aircraft necessary to lift the brigade were needed elsewhere for the next six weeks. In these circumstances the Commander 13 Corps agreed to use the brigade, if possible, in a light role on the ground.

21. On 4th April 2 Independent Parachute Brigade Group, less 300th Air-landing Anti-Tank Battery R.A., and the other units still training at the airborne base, moved forward under command of 2 New Zealand Division of 13 Corps

and took over, with 10th Battalion the Rifle Brigade under command, a part of the Cassino front from 1 Guards Brigade and units of 2 New Zealand Division. They held a sector which included Cassino station, and was overlooked completely by the enemy on the high ground to the north. All ranks lived in a permanent smoke-screen that was maintained in an effort to conceal movement by day which would have been impossible otherwise. Although there was only minor activity at the time the defences on both sides had been developed considerably and minefields were extensive. On 8th April, 6 Armoured Division relieved 2 New Zealand Division in the line, 2 Independent Parachute Brigade Group passing to their command. The brigade remained there, patrolling and gaining all possible information about the enemy, until relieved by 21 Indian Infantry Brigade of 8 Indian Division on 16th April.

22. After two days rest, on 18th and 19th April, using mule transport by night as day movement was overlooked by the enemy, they relieved 6 New Zealand Brigade in the line just north-east of Cassino and once more came under command of 2 New Zealand Division in 10 Corps. 300th Air-landing Anti-Tank Battery R.A. had now joined them and acted in an infantry role as the mountainous country made anti-tank guns unnecessary. The brigade was told that they were likely to remain in that sector for some four or five weeks no advance being likely or practicable, but that they were to carry out intensive offensive patrolling and worry the enemy to the maximum extent possible. This they did, but the weather broke on 26th April and for some days there was heavy rain and mist, the cold was severe, the biting winds in the mountains penetrated all kinds of clothing, and to add to the discomfort there was incessant shelling and mortaring by both sides. Although casualties in the brigade were few life was very unpleasant but the troops were compensated somewhat by the knowledge that their active patrolling made the enemy very nervous regarding a future offensive on this sector.

23. On 12th May, the main Allied offensive against Rome by the Fifth U.S. and Eighth Armies started successfully and enemy activity opposite the brigade diminished, but increased patrolling was initiated to act as a cover plan so that the enemy would get the impression of an impending attack on this front. The object was achieved and he retained his troops there for a considerable time, but such operations were not popular with our unit commanders. On 21st May, 6th Parachute Battalion was withdrawn out of the line and by 27th May the whole brigade, less 5th Parachute Battalion which remained under command of 6 New Zealand Brigade was concentrated in reserve at Portecagnano and Filignano, near Salerno. 5th Parachute Battalion rejoined the brigade there on 28th May, the enemy on their front having withdrawn.

Airborne Operation " Hasty "

24. Meanwhile the initial German withdrawal towards the line Pisa–Rimini was being followed up closely by the Fifth U.S. and Eighth Armies. Fifth U.S. Army was approaching Rome, with Eighth Army advancing on its right east of Rome. The enemy withdrawal was planned and deliberate and he was expected to make use of large-scale demolitions. General Sir Oliver Leese decided that the prevention of some of these demolitions was a very suitable task for airborne troops and on 30th May he issued orders to 2 Independent Parachute Brigade Group to provide harassing parties on the German

221

withdrawal route from Sora to Avezzano.   The parachute troops were to land in 48 hours' time, during the night of 1st/2nd June.   The original orders suggested one parachute battalion but having studied the project, Brigadier Pritchard stated that he considered that the operation did not justify using a battalion singly thus breaking up the brigade.   His advice was accepted and he allotted a force of 60 all ranks of 6th (Royal Welch) Parachute Battalion to the task, with detachments of 127th Parachute Field Ambulance and brigade signals included. Captain L. A. Fitzroy Smith was nominated as the commander.

25. A conference was held at brigade headquarters at 1900 hours on 30th May, with the commander 62 U.S. Troop Carrier Group, and a staff officer of Eighth Army.   The outline plan was approved by Eighth Army next morning.   A further conference at 1800 hours on 31st May, at which the Tactical Air Forces were also represented, fixed the time of take-off at 1930 hours and the drop at 2010 hours on 1st June, which was one hour before last light. Photographic cover of the area, near Torricella, was flown on 31st May and by 0600 hours on 1st June, the brigade operations room was fully prepared with photos, maps and other intelligence.   The personnel of the task force began briefing at 0800 hours and by midday they were fully prepared and equipped.

26. Take-off was completed successfully on time, three Dakotas being used for the troops and eight for dummies, and fighter escort was picked up *en route* to the dropping zone.   The flight of about one and a half hours, *via* Caserta and Venafro, in good weather, was unopposed and dropping was accurate at about 2030 hours.   Dummies were dropped both before and after the real drop in an effort to make the enemy believe that a large force was being used. Captain Fitzroy Smith had concentrated his force unopposed at the rendezvous, by 2100 hours, and by 0200 hours 2nd June had reported to 2 New Zealand Division, due to advance that way, that all was well and that supplies were to be dropped as arranged.   There was one casualty on the dropping zone, a medical orderly with a broken rib.

27. For some reason, instead of keeping his small force concentrated so that it could not be defeated in detail, Captain Fitzroy Smith split it into three parties under Lieutenant Ashby, Lieutenant Evans and himself.   For a week these parties harassed the road with a certain amount of success but with considerable casualties to themselves.   By about 7th June, they had completed their task and the problem then was to get the survivors back to our lines, since all communications had broken down.   Captain J. Awdry, the company second-in-command had gone to Headquarters, 2 New Zealand Division, and as this was known to the troops pamphlets were dropped in the area with the words " Return to Awdry " and some 50 per cent of the survivors returned, the remainder being captured.

28. Although the operation had been carried out at short notice and although the actual damage to the Germans was not great it caused alarm out of all proportion to the size of the force.   The use of dummies exaggerated the number of troops dropped, and apprehension spread throughout the rear areas forcing the Germans to deploy troops that were urgently required elsewhere. In the meantime the remainder of the brigade at Salerno had been carrying out airborne exercises in readiness for further operations.

The Invasion of Southern France

29. When 2 Independent Parachute Brigade Group were withdrawn from the line to Salerno at the end of May, the Allied forces in England were due to invade Normandy within a few days, though this was not known, of course, to the brigade. The strategic plan included a subsidiary and delayed Allied attack through southern France, which would synchronize with the advance of the main forces from Normandy. This operation would be carried out by Seventh U.S. Army, with certain British and French formations under command, under the direction of Allied Forces Headquarters, then commanded by General Sir Maitland Wilson. It involved an assault landing from the sea between Frejus and St. Raphael, about halfway between Toulon and Cannes, followed by the most rapid advance possible up the valley of the River Rhone. Little opposition was anticipated in the initial assault, but it was known that the Germans had considerable reserves inland and it was essential to delay their movement to the coastal area until a firm footing had been obtained. For this task an airborne force was required and during June, 1944, it was decided to organize such a force from all available British and American resources in the theatre. Five American parachute battalions, one American air-landing regiment, and 2 Independent Parachute Brigade Group were formed into First Airborne Task Force under the command of Major-General Robert T. Frederick, United States Army. The brigade was released from all commitments with the Eighth Army and moved from Salerno to the Rome area, its future airborne operational base on 12th July. The next four weeks were spent in preparing for the operation.

30. The task allotted to the brigade, as part of the airborne task force, was to seize the area between La Motte and Le Muy, destroy all the enemy in that area, deny the enemy access to it and hold it for further airborne landings later in the day. The area lay some ten miles west-north-west from St. Raphael, and included three important roads which German reserves might use. Dropping zones were enclosed, rough and difficult, but the best available. Opposition on the dropping zones was not expected to be in any force but enemy reserves could attack within a few hours. The time of the main drop was to be at 0445 hours, pathfinders of 1st Independent Parachute Platoon dropping at 0334 hours, to mark the dropping zones for the whole force ; the sea-borne assault was to start at 0700 hours. The brigade was to be prepared to operate for 48 hours before contact with the sea-borne forces and to seize Le Muy and operate to the north and east in the second phase. The third phase would include the arrival of the sea-borne element on " D "+ 10 day and any operations ordered subsequently. Automatic supply by air of arms and ammunition was arranged for the morning of " D "+ 1 day. Thereafter supply by air was available on demand by brigade headquarters by wireless for the next six days, from one of the base airfields near Rome.

31. The air plan allotted 125 aircraft of 51 U.S. Troop Carrier Wing, for the parachute troops, with 35 Horsa and 26 Hadrian Gliders towed by 51 Wing for 64th Light Battery and 300th Air-landing Anti-Tank Battery, R.A., which would start landing in daylight at 0814 hours on " D " day, some three and a half hours after the main parachute force. Five departure airfields near Rome were allotted. Owing to the high ground features in the assault area, it was

decided to adopt the unusual course of dropping the parachute troops from about 1,500 to 2,000 feet, the gliders being released at similar heights. The route was *via* Elba and Corsica, thence direct over the sea with the aid of three Naval beacon ships and the time of flight averaged three and a quarter hours for all parties, only the last few minutes being overland. The Allied Air Forces were to provide fighter escort by day, together with other assistance, and a dummy parachute drop, which proved to be very successful was arranged for an area just north of Toulon.

32. " D " day was fixed for 15th August, 1944, and by 0323 hours that day 1st Independent Parachute Platoon had landed unopposed and had set up on the dropping zone the first Eureka wireless beacon to guide in the main parachute force. The first Allied parachute troops to land in southern France, they had been dropped correctly by their American pilots in spite of cloud and thick ground mist, which had developed quickly and unexpectedly. The main brigade parachute force started to make landfall at 0440 hours and flew on towards the dropping zones without opposition. Unfortunately the cloud and mist with visibility of only about half a mile then confused many of the pilots and only 73 aircraft dropped their troops on the correct dropping zones, the remaining 53 being as far apart as Cannes and Fayence, 20 miles or more away. However, the pilots had to drop their troops without seeing the dropping zones, they had to rely almost entirely on the wireless direction beacons, which were not all accurate, and in any case Major-General Frederick had issued an order, which had been agreed by Allied Forces Headquarters, that no aircraft would return with troops on board. On assembly on the ground it was found that brigade headquarters was complete, with 4th, 5th and 6th Parachute Battalion Groups at about 40, 25 and 60 per cent respectively of full strength. But there was very little enemy opposition and first objectives were soon captured. One of the two small German garrisons in the area surrendered to 6th (Royal Welch) Parachute Battalion, and the other was powerless to intervene.

33. While the battalions occupied their positions, 1st Independent Parachute Platoon and 2nd Parachute Squadron R.E. cleared the glider landing zones of hundreds of poles erected as anti-airborne defences. At 0920 hours 64th Light Battery R.A. in the Hadrian Gliders landed successfully, after spending over an hour circling above Corsica *en route* waiting for the visibility to clear. The remaining German garrison then surrendered. 300th Air-landing Anti-Tank Battery R.A. in the Horsa Gliders, with less spare flying-time owing to their greater size, had returned to Italy where they landed at 1030 hours. The tugs refuelled, hooked up and took off again almost at once, releasing their gliders over France at 1630 hours. They had not been expected back in Italy and the chief credit for the speedy and efficient organization of their second take-off must go to Major W. H. Ewart-James, The Glider Pilot Regiment, who had been sent out from England as an observer and was luckily on the airfield.

34. By 1015 hours the brigade had accomplished all its first tasks. The only fighting had resulted in 4th Parachute Battalion killing 16 Germans and taking 29 prisoners, at a cost to themselves of seven killed and nine wounded. Brigade headquarters had been in wireless communication with 36 U.S. Division, the leading sea-borne assault division, since 0615 hours and it was known that

the sea-borne assault was going well. During the day many troops of the brigade joined again after having been dropped wide and there was no indication of a major enemy counter-attack, though several small actions were fought *en route* by troops rejoining. At 1630 hours the second air lift arrived with more troops of the airborne task force, including 300th Air-landing Anti-Tank Battery R.A., and by that night Allied airborne troops to the strength of about a division were well established across all the enemy's possible counter-attack routes to the sea.

35. Next morning, 16th August, the pre-arranged supply drop was made to the brigade and, although it was somewhat scattered in rough country, most of it was collected. During the morning, too, Colonel T. C. H. Pearson, now deputy commander of the brigade, who had accompanied 36 U.S. Division by sea, landed in the brigade area in a light Auster aircraft. He brought the news that Frejus and St. Raphael had been captured and that 142 Regimental Combat Team of 36 U.S. Division would start to advance towards Le Muy that afternoon. They reached Le Muy and made contact with the airborne task force early on the next morning 17th August.

36. Apart from a few minor local actions against a rapidly retreating enemy, the brigade's operations in southern France were now ended. The main sea-borne invasion forces passed through in pursuit and on 20th August, Brigadier Pritchard was recalled to Italy to see General Wilson who said that the brigade would be required for operations in Greece, and asked him how soon they could be ready. The Brigadier replied that if they left France immediately they could be ready in the heel of Italy by 7th September. On 26th August, the Brigade embarked to return to Italy and the large sea-borne element, who were in various stages of embarkation at Naples to go to southern France, were moved back to the base at Rome.

Operations in Greece

37. The brigade returned to the airborne base near Rome on 3rd September, having travelled *via* Naples. Preparations were started immediately for operations which were expected to start within a few days, and the brigadier and unit commanders began planning. The situation, as outlined by Allied Forces Headquarters, was that Athens was to be occupied as quickly as possible after the Germans had withdrawn from the city, so as to bring supplies and relief to the Greek people, to maintain law and order and to. establish a régime in Athens favourable to Western Europe before the Communists took control. The force allotted for these tasks consisted of 2 Independent Parachute Brigade Group and 23 Armoured Brigade who were to leave their tanks behind and act as infantry. The parachute brigade were to be the first to land, some by parachute, others air-transported and the remainder by sea, the 23 Armoured Brigade landing at Piraeus on the following day. The Germans were expected to withdraw before the end of September, the actual date depending on the speed of the Russian advance in the Balkans, but Brigadier Pritchard was told that he was to avoid a major battle and that his troops were not to pursue the Germans.

38. On 8th September, the brigade moved to a camp near San Pancrazio, some 20 miles east of Taranto in the heel of Italy, so as to be able to use the three airfields nearest to Athens. These were already being used by Allied bombers and it was difficult to base 51 U.S. Troop Carrier Wing's aircraft on them as well, but there were no suitable alternative airfields available.

39. The Germans, in fact, did not withdraw from Athens until October. The brigade had been ready to operate in September so they utilized the extra time to complete final details of the move of their transport by sea and the organization on the departure airfields. They were given the additional task of securing Kalamaki airfield on the outskirts of Athens, so that supplies could be flown in to the whole force. In fact, Megara airfield, 40 miles to the west, which in the original plan had been the only airfield not required by us, was substituted for Kalamaki at the last moment and could be identified only from a 1/100,000 map of the area. No fresh photographic cover of the dropping zone there could be obtained in time, and only one old photograph of it was available.

40. At 1200 hours on 12th October, some two and three quarter hours after take-off, one company group of 4th Parachute Battalion personally commanded by Lieutenant-Colonel Coxon dropped on Megara airfield in a 35 miles an hour wind, the decision to drop having been left to a naval officer who had gone ahead on special duties. However there was no opposition and although the company had suffered 50 per cent landing casualties they secured the airfield quickly. The weather deteriorated and prevented the main part of the brigade from dropping there on the next day, 13th October, as intended, but they jumped successfully on 14th October (less 5th (Scottish) Parachute Battalion). The Germans had blown the road to Athens and as the brigade had orders to get there quickly they commandeered local transport including sailing caiques and entered the city on 15th October, 5th (Scottish) Parachute Battalion joining them later by air, and 23 Armoured Brigade arriving on 17th October.

41. For the next three months the brigade were very busy following up the retreating Germans, establishing and maintaining law and order, and helping the Greeks in every possible way to reorganize their country. Their activities ranged from Thrace to Salonika and the Bulgarian border, but their most important task lay in Athens itself. Here there were continuous and serious riots and battles between the rival Greek political parties, involving the British troops in considerable trouble and in serious warfare against the Greek rebels during the whole of December The situation was so serious that although 4 Indian Division had arrived in Greece by the end of November, and although 2 Independent Parachute Brigade Group were required by Eighth Army for airborne operations in Italy, the brigade was retained in Athens until the rebels were defeated about 4th January, 1945. The scope of the brigade's activities may be illustrated by the fact that at one period during serious rioting they were feeding 20,000 Greek civilians, and on one day during the final battle in Athens they killed 170 rebels, wounded 70 and took 520 prisoners at considerable cost to themselves.

42. This fighting was not popular with the troops but they disliked even more the criticism levelled at them by certain sections of the press and public in England. These criticisms accused the troops of killing Communists who were

alleged to be backed and aided by our ally Russia, but they entirely overlooked the atrocities committed by the Communists against the remainder of the population. As a result of public opinion at home a Trades Union Congress Delegation, led by Sir Walter Citrine visited Athens to investigate the charges. Volunteers to see the delegation were called for and a party of 400 other ranks and some officers assembled in the brigade cinema. Here they were split into parties of 50 other ranks and one party of officers, each party being interviewed by a separate member of the delegation. The delegates then learned the true facts of the case from the men who had to deal with some of the unpleasant situations in Greece, and, whether or not as a result of this visit, criticism ceased.

The Offensive in Italy, Spring, 1945

43. In January, 1945, the brigade returned to Italy and spent a period of intensive planning and preparations for airborne operations which never in fact materialized. Between 6th March and 4th May, 1945, 32 airborne operations were initiated and cancelled by Eighth Army and one by 15 Army Group.

44. The main reason for the brigade not being used in these operations was that the ground over which the advance was made was unsuitable for the employment of airborne troops. However, it is worth recording that in November, 1944, while the brigade was in Greece, Brigadier Pritchard with a planning staff had been recalled to Italy. It was expected that the Germans would retreat through Milan fairly soon, and that they would blow up all roads and railways leading into the city. Although the ground troops would be able to follow them up, it would be difficult to get up supplies. The plan was to drop the parachute brigade near Milan so that an air-strip could be constructed and supplies flown in, but the operation never got beyond the planning stage, although all arrangements for a base were made at Rome. When the brigade returned from Greece they went back to Rome, but were then moved to Foggia to plan for operations in support of Eighth Army. A base was opened at Foggia, but in case they had to support Fifth U.S. Army the Rome base was also maintained.

45. At one period the brigade staff was planning in detail 11 different possible brigade operations, all due to take place during the following fortnight. Between the beginning of March and the first week in May they handled 90,000 photographic prints and 36,000 maps, and planned about 33 different operations, all of which were cancelled. For long periods the brigade planning staff, located with Headquarters, Eighth Army, were 260 miles from the brigade, and the brigade commander completed some 40 hours of flying time in his efforts to co-ordinate planning between the various field force commanders, air force commanders and his own units. The provision of the planning staff was entirely from the brigade's own resources with a consequent effect on the efficiency in the actual command and administration of the brigade itself.

46. As a result of his experience during this planning, the brigade commander with the agreement of the commanding general 51 U.S. Troop Carrier Wing, reported that his brigade could undertake operations at the following notice. He assumed that the brigade could plan simultaneously up

to 12 possible operations, provided that number was reduced as the date of the operations approached and provided that the supply of briefing material was adequate.

Hour of take-off for operations minus 5 days—number of possible operations reduced to 5.

Hour of take-off for operations minus 36 hours—number of possible operations reduced to 3.

Hour of take-off for operation minus 6 hours—order issued to operate on one of the three operations.

Return to the United Kingdom

47. On 6th May, 1945, at the conclusion of the final offensive in Italy, 15 Army Group reported to Allied Forces Headquarters that they had no further employment for the brigade in an airborne role in Italy. So ended many weeks of planning and for the first time for a month the brigade itself was released from readiness for an operation within 48 hours. In June they returned to England. It was not long, however, before changed circumstances required another move and in October they went to Palestine to join 6 Airborne Division, having been re-organized as a normal parachute brigade.

CHAPTER XVIII

THE BACKGROUND TO THE SPECIAL AIR SERVICE
BRIGADE (S.A.S.)

Introduction

1. The need for airborne troops for special duties, in addition to those included within the airborne divisions, has already been mentioned and it will have been seen that although the first requirement in the early days was to produce the major fighting formation of the division, there was also a definite requirement for airborne troops designed to operate in small parties behind the enemy lines, for such purposes as cutting communications and harassing rear areas.

2. Although resources had not permitted the raising of such a special force in the United Kingdom up to the end of 1943, and in fact there had been little opportunity for their use in Western Europe up to that time, several small units had been formed and operated successfully with much the same object in view in the Middle East and in South East Asia Command. Except in a few isolated cases, they had not operated from aircraft. In the Middle East the Long Range Desert Group and " L " Detachment S.A.S. had shown the practicability and value of small forces operating behind the enemy's lines and wide on his flanks (*see* Chapter X). While in South East Asia Command Major-General Orde Wingate had demonstrated what could be done by similar methods in Burma and had followed this up by glider landings behind the Japanese lines in 1944 (*see* Chapter XXV).

3. Reference has been made to the Special Raiding Squadron, the Special Boat Squadron and 2nd S.A.S. Regiment in the Mediterranean, having established a close liaison with Headquarters, Major-General Airborne Forces, with the object of eventual co-operation in the assault on the western front (*see* Chapter X). These units, already experienced in operations behind the enemy lines, would provide an excellent nucleus on which to form the completely " guerilla " force required for eventual operations in Western Europe. Strong representations resulted in the return to the United Kingdom of the Special Raiding Squadron at the end of 1943, when it was reformed as 1st S.A.S. Regiment (Lieutenant-Colonel R. B. Mayne) and the arrival of 2nd S.A.S. Regiment (Lieutenant-Colonel W. S. Stirling) in the United Kingdom in March, 1944.

4. After much discussion and considerable delay, approval was given in January, 1944, for the formation of Headquarters, Special Air Service Troops, under Lieutenant-General Browning's command, and Brigadier R. W. McLeod was appointed to command a brigade about 2,000 strong consisting of 1st S.A.S. Regiment, 2nd S.A.S. Regiment, 3rd and 4th French Parachute Battalions, (later renamed 2me and 3me Regiments de Chasseurs Parachutistes) and a Belgian Independent Parachute Squadron (later, in 1945, The Belgian S.A.S. Regiment). " F " Squadron General Headquarters Reconnaissance Regiment (" Phantom ") was attached under command as a brigade signal section.

5. In addition a special branch of the staff at Headquarters Airborne Troops was formed under Lieutenant-Colonel I. G. Collins, who had had great experience in planning previous commando and S.A.S. operations and in co-ordinating their activities with those of special agents operating under such organizations as the Special Forces Headquarters. It was found by experience that such a special branch of the staff was essential to compete with the very diverse and particular needs of the S.A.S., and very specialized experience was required to deal with the many Allied political and civilian bodies which were closely concerned with their activities. The wishes of these bodies were frequently opposed to military necessities either because of incomplete knowledge of the course of the campaign or because their political views differed slightly from those of the Supreme Allied Command. Operations behind the enemy lines in countries whose populations were basically friendly to the Allies depended for their success to a great extent on the co-operation of the exiled governments in Great Britain, who were in touch with and controlled to a greater or lesser extent the activities of the various " resistance " movements in enemy-occupied territories.

6. Although policy was laid down by S.H.A.E.F. and by 21 Army Group' the carrying-out of that policy in day-to-day affairs required a knowledge and tact which only experience could give. Lieutenant-Colonel Collins worked directly under the Brigadier, General Staff, and was responsible to him for all staff work in connection with the S.A.S. This included :—

(a) Initial, strategic and high level planning (before the outline was presented to the S.A.S. Brigade for detailed planning and execution).

(b) Staff duties arrangements for raising and equipping the brigade.

(c) The training requirements of the brigade.

Lieutenant-Colonel Collins remained as the officer immediately responsible for these affairs until the end of the war with Germany, at times being attached to S.H.A.E.F. for direct consultation and being in general control of several liaison missions working between Headquarters, 1 Airborne Corps, and the French and other allied nations. At times, also, in order to quicken plans and decisions, the Commander, S.A.S. Brigade, was allowed direct contact with army and corps commanders in the field. On these occasions Lieutenant-Colonel Collins co-ordinated such plans with the resources and plans of the airborne corps.

7. The tasks for which the S.A.S. Brigade was originally formed may be described briefly as follows :—

(a) *Strategical.*—The harassing of selected headquarters and attacks on enemy rail and telegraph communications so as to cause the maximum delay and confusion to the movement of troops and stores, the provision of an ever-present threat to security in rear areas, thereby forcing the enemy to employ troops on guard duties which would otherwise not be required, assistance to any " resistance " or other movement by patriots in enemy-occupied countries and the provision of information to the Allied commanders.

(b) *Tactical* —The harassing of enemy movement towards a particular battle area or during retreat, the spreading of false information or rumours, the provision of guides and information ; diversionary raids and small-scale attacks on particular objectives.

8. The emphasis on any one of these tasks varied, of course, throughout the campaign, according to the general directions of S.H.A.E.F. and 21 Army Group, but they were all carried out at some time or other. The S.A.S. personnel needed a very wide training and unusual powers of initiative and personal resource to be able to tackle any of them at short notice. The normal British and American airborne divisions could not be employed in this manner as they were required for major operations as divisions or corps and could not be broken up for small-scale tasks as well. It must be emphasized that S.A.S. troops always operated in uniform and were not saboteurs in the ordinary meaning of the word. They were soldiers employed on special missions, they were entitled, if captured, to treatment as soldiers, and their uniform was frequently of use in raising the morale of local patriot forces. Clandestine sabotage tasks were carried out by other personnel under the aegis of Special Forces Headquarters and similar organizations, whose personnel were frequently of the greatest assistance to S.A.S. troops but whose tasks and methods of operation were quite separate.

9. In designing the organization of the S.A.S. Regiments, the base from which they would work, and the system of control in the field, it was essential to encourage extreme flexibility, to enable operational parties to remain in action for considerable periods behind the enemy lines, and to base plans on the use of only such resources as were likely to be available in the time. It will be remembered that the formation of the brigade was not authorized until January, 1944, that many of its personnel and one complete regiment were still overseas, and that they had to be ready to play their part in the invasion of France, which was then planned for May, 1944. Regimental war establishments suitable for European warfare were drawn up, governed by what the War Office could make available in the time. They were not ideal but they did incorporate the essential feature of a large proportion of officers, thus providing the leaders for many small operational parties varying in size from three or four men up to platoons and squadrons.

10. At this stage the necessity and diversity of S.A.S. requirements for supply in the field were not fully realized, and it was proposed that the airborne corps base should undertake most of the S.A.S. requirements. In practice these arrangements were found inadequate and a separate S.A.S. base organization had to be improvised, arrangements for supply by air being co-ordinated by 1 Airborne Corps Headquarters with 38 Group R.A.F., and Special Force Headquarters. Control of parties in the field was complicated and elaborate owing to the technical limitations of long range wireless communication. The system was based upon low-power portable field wireless sets working to high-power base wireless sets. These in turn worked to the wireless broadcasting plant installed at Headquarters, 1 Airborne Corps by the British Broadcasting Corporation. The wireless system, with the equipment available, depended almost entirely on the efficiency of the base signal personnel. It could not have worked successfully without the expert and untiring efficiency provided by " F " Squadron, General Headquarters Reconnaissance Regiment and the backing and support at the outset of 1 Airborne Corps Signals.

11. It is a debatable point whether or not the S.A.S. Brigade should have been placed under command of the airborne corps. The reasons for doing so at the time were that Lieutenant-General Browning took the initiative in getting approval for their inclusion in the order of battle for the invasion

of western Europe, that no other suitable headquarters existed to look after them, and that 21 Army Group and S.H.A.E.F. were not prepared to have them under direct command owing to the detailed work entailed. It was also expected that in western Europe, at least in the early stages of the invasion, the S.A.S. troops would normally have to move to their operational area in the same parachute aircraft and gliders as used by the airborne troops. On the other hand, although Headquarters, 1 Airborne Corps, were usually well informed regarding the projected course of operations in western Europe, they were not in full possession of all the facts, political as well as military, that would enable them to suggest the most valuable employment of S.A.S. troops on strategical objectives. Furthermore, when airborne operations on a large scale became imminent, it was not possible for the commander and all the staff at Headquarters, 1 Airborne Corps to spare sufficient time to look after the interests of the S.A.S. to the full extent. In fact, on these occasions the Commander, S.A.S. Brigade, was given very considerable latitude in direct dealings with 21 Army Group and S.H.A.E.F. as regards operational plans.

12. There is no easy solution to the proper command of S.A.S. troops but certain principles were evolved during 1944 and 1945. These were :—

    (a) The general policy of operations and the extent to which the regular armed forces, agents and patriots in enemy-occupied countries are to co-operate, and through what channels of command, must be laid down by the Supreme Commander concerned.

    (b) The Supreme Commander and his staff must not be worried by details of command and administration.

    (c) The number of links in the chain between the S.A.S. troops doing the job and the headquarters controlling the strategy of the campaign must be reduced to the minimum.

    (d) The allotment and use of aircraft must be co-ordinated with the senior airborne headquarters in the theatre and with the R.A.F.

    (e) The existence of a special operations section at Supreme Allied Headquarters, on which all three Services are represented, is almost essential to co-ordinate the plans and operations of Special Forces both military and secret services.

13. Apart from the organization and equipment of units, the first requirements of the S.A.S. Brigade were parachute training and a suitable training area for ground operations. Parachute training with a special shortened course was done at No. 1 Parachute Training School, Ringway, simultaneously with recruits for the airborne divisions, candidates being allotted vacancies on high priority. Training areas were found in Ayrshire in Scotland with Headquarters at Sorn and the brigade really formed and trained there during the spring of 1944.

14. It was difficult to post enough young officers to complete units to war establishment owing to the competing demands of 21 Army Group and in fact units were never quite up to strength in officers. Other rank recruits were found mainly from amongst those volunteering for the Parachute Regiment, though a special auxiliary force being disbanded at the time provided nearly 300, and a high standard and a regular intake was maintained. The war establishment for brigade headquarters was quite insufficient and it could compete only by the undesirable method of borrowing extra officers from operational units, until it was expanded many months later.

Planning for the Invasion of France

15. There were many difficulties encountered in getting the S.A.S. Brigade ready for war in time to take part in the invasion of France, but they were all overcome eventually and many and very varied methods were suggested for employing the brigade. However, 21 Army Group laid down four principles which governed their use in all operations :—

(*a*) For reasons of security no S.A.S. personnel would be landed in western Europe before the assault landings by the main invasion force started.

(*b*) The main object of all S.A.S. operations in the earlier stages of the invasion must be to delay the movement of enemy reserves towards the invasion area.

(*c*) About half the strength of the S.A.S. Brigade should be held in reserve in England ready for any operations required as the main battle progressed.

(*d*) No diversion of the limited troop-carrying aircraft could be allowed to interfere with the vital operations of the one British and two American airborne divisions in the initial landings.

16. It was decided eventually by 21 Army Group that the S.A.S. operations proposed in the coastal belt from Normandy to the Pas de Calais could not assist the main assault sufficiently to be worth the casualties expected and in this decision the principle laid down in sub-para. (*a*) above was a major factor. The decision was reinforced by the fact that the airborne divisions would require all available aircraft on and immediately after " D " day and therefore these could not be spared at that time for the S.A.S. Planning therefore re-started on new lines early in May, by which time the invasion date had been postponed to June, and the only tactical operation by S.A.S. troops on " D " day was the provision of a very small parachute party to act in conjunction with a dummy airborne landing designed to confuse the enemy. However reconnaissance parties for operations " Samwest ", " Dingson ", " Bul-basket " and " Houndsworth " left on night 5th/6th June (*see* Chapter XIX).

17. The new plans were based on operations in rear of the coastal belt, behind the German army areas. Used there in a strategic role, they would be able to obtain the assistance of the French " resistance " movement and the agents working under Special Forces Headquarters. Such operations were very suitable for S.A.S. troops, who were also expected to encourage and assist the " resistance " groups to a great extent, and their depth would be limited only by the range of aircraft, the short hours of summer darkness and by semi-political requirements, such as the avoidance of premature action resulting in the defeat and dispersal of local patriots before the main Allied armies could assist them. It was still desired to delay the movement of enemy reserves from a distance, to disrupt his communications, to cause the maximum dispersal of his resources and to harass him by continual threats to his security. In general, S.A.S. operations were now planned to take place from 50 to 400 miles in advance of the main Allied armies. In the inner area roughly bordered by just south of the River Loire in a circle round Paris and north-west on the line of the River Somme to Abbeville, 21 Army Group had control, operations in the outer area of France and Belgium being controlled by S.H.A.E.F. both exercising their control through Headquarters, 1 Airborne Corps.

18. A major problem was the necessity to supply and evacuate, if necessary, the S.A.S. troops after they had achieved their initial tasks.   Supply by air would nearly always be required and only in special circumstances would it be possible for the troops to return by land or sea routes to the safety of the Allied bases.   It was therefore decided to establish special bases behind the enemy lines, where S.A.S. operational parties of varying strengths could be concentrated and concealed, re-supplied, re-organized for further operations in the locality, and from which it might be possible to evacuate them by air. This system was adopted successfully throughout the campaigns in France, Belgium and Holland, the greatest help being given by the " resistance " movements in all three countries.   All operations were co-ordinated with those of Special Forces Headquarters and representatives from this headquarters usually accompanied S.A.S. operational parties so that immediate contact could be made with the " resistance " groups.   In Brittany the whole task of organizing and equipping the resistance forces was eventually given to the Commander, 4th French Parachute Battalion.

19. In general, one of two tactical methods was employed, the first method involving the landing of advance parties, if possible duplicated in two aircraft with signalling teams with each party, either to pre-arranged reception parties or dropped blind in a selected area.   Liaison personnel, known as " Jedburgh " teams, or guides were usually provided by Special Forces Head-quarters to accompany them so that immediate contact could be made with the resistance groups, the "Jedburgh" teams also being responsible for organizing and arming the resistance groups.   The advance parties then called for reinforcements so that a proper base could be formed from which operational parties worked outwards on targets within a radius of 25 to 50 miles.   Additional parachute dropping zones, to which supplies and reinforcements were sent, were selected in the area of the base and small local store dumps were then built up.

20. The second method was used when targets had to be attacked at short notice.   It meant that small operational parties had to be dropped blind near their targets and, after completing their task, make their way to the nearest S.A.S. base.   For example, 18 small parties were dropped blind in Brittany on the night 7/8th June in their target areas to attack enemy lines of communication and delay movement of enemy reserves towards Normandy.   Their instructions were then to join the nearest S.A.S. base which would have been established by that time.

21. Of the two methods the former was the most satisfactory when there was time, for on dark nights blind drops were sometimes inaccurate and there was difficulty in organizing on the ground after landing.   Nevertheless, considerable success was achieved by blind dropping during the " Amherst " operations in Holland in 1944, as will be seen later.

The Administrative Organization

22. The administrative problems involved in the maintenance of Special Air Service operations were considerable and contained many unusual features. Before considering these problems in detail and going on to see how the administration was finally organized it is as well to have the original background clear.

(a) The brigade headquarters, when first formed, contained a very high proportion of personnel with no previous experience of S.A.S. work or even of airborne formations.

(b) The British regiments were used to working independently.

(c) The French battalions had been previously organized as parachute battalions, had no previous experience of S.A.S. work, contained a very low percentage of administrative personnel and in any case were used to the French system of administration on a brigade basis.

(d) The Belgian company had no previous experience of S.A.S. work, though its administrative personnel were excellent.

(e) In February, 1944, the administrative staff at S.A.S. Brigade Headquarters consisted of :—

One D.A.A. and Q.M.G.
Two Staff Captains.
One D.A.D.O.S. plus two other ranks R.A.O.C.
One E.M.E.

23. Inevitably no S.A.S. plan could be made until the details of the main operational plan were firm, and so practically all S.A.S. planning was done comparatively late. The following factors usually remained unknown until the last minute :—

(a) The size of the party.

(b) The distance of operational areas from the main battle.

(c) The probable duration of the operations.

(d) The type of initial equipment required.

(e) The action by personnel after operations—*i.e.*, whether they would remain where they were and be maintained by air, or whether they would make their own way through our lines.

(f) The intentions and preparations of other organizations involved, such as the Special Operations Executive and French Forces of the Interior   There was no one headquarters co-ordinating all activities of these special organizations from which information could be obtained.

24. The S.A.S. Brigade was formed under Headquarters 1 Airborne Corps, and although this had the initial advantage of facilitating parachute training and the provision of airborne equipment it had several disadvantages amongst which were :—

(a) It was possible that after the first airborne operations there might be scope for S.A.S. sea-borne or land infiltration for which the airborne corps might not be the most suitable controlling headquarters as they would probably be busily engaged in planning further airborne operations.

(b) Although there was a small special " G " Staff at 1 Airborne Corps Headquarters to deal with S.A.S. matters, there was no special " Q " Staff. The normal " Q " staff had all its work cut out to deal with ordinary airborne operations.

(c) Before the invasion of Normandy, Headquarters 1 Airborne Corps was under 21 Army Group, whereas S.A.S. Brigade was directly under S.H.A.E.F. for all operational requirements. Nevertheless 21 Army Group remained the channel for administrative requirements.

25. Until operations began, the availability of communications with operational parties was an unknown quantity. Great distances were involved, the enemy might jam broadcasts, the parties might not be able to open up their wireless sets for fear of giving away their positions, etc. At the same time communications would be obviously the vital factor in operational maintenance, which would have to be by air, usually by night, and on demand as automatic air supply would seldom be possible. Maintenance would therefore be dependent on clear, accurate and comprehensive demands being received, and quick notification to the operational parties of air supply plans so that reception could be arranged. In the event, all communications were first-class.

26. It was not possible for a permanent allocation of aircraft to be made to the S.A.S. Brigade and so bids had to be made each day. As a result, the staff did not know until noon at the earliest on the day of a supply operation from which airfield containers were to be sent. Furthermore, the troops in the field were never sure whether aircraft would be available to meet their demands.

27. Units were mobilized on an equipment scale prepared at the end of 1943 before the real scope of S.A.S. activities was known. The tables attempted to provide a fixed scale of equipment which would include that required for all possible types of operations, including airborne, sea-borne and jeep-borne. As a result it was found in practice that there was always a deficiency of that equipment actually required for a particular phase of operations, together with a surplus of other equipment, but this is likely to be the case in any unusual type of operations.

28. For the reasons that have been given it was possible to plan operations for any length of time ahead on broad principles only and these were designed to cover three main aspects :—

(a) The provision of initial equipment for parties, based on the load that one man could carry to enable him to exist on his own resources for as long as possible.

(b) The formation of some sort of organization for holding and providing equipment and supplies to maintain parties after they had dropped. Originally it was considered that the dumps formed in the Cirencester area by 1 Airborne Corps for maintenance of the divisions would be sufficient to cover the S.A.S. as well. This was not the case and the formation of a separate S.A.S. dump was agreed to, subject to the following limitations :—

(i) It was to hold only those items considered peculiar to S.A.S. All "common user" items were to be drawn from 1 Airborne Corps, R.A.S.C. and Ordnance dumps.

(ii) No extra staff was to be provided for it. Personnel had to be provided from S.A.S. Brigade Headquarters and unit resources.

(iii) It was to be considered as a part of 1 Airborne Corps base organization, and was therefore dependent on them for transport, communication and channels of supply.

This dump was later known as Station 1090 and was established initially at Williamstrip Park near Down Ampney, Gloucestershire.

(c) Liaison to avoid duplication or conflict with Special Forces, especially in cases of supply to mixed parties of S.A.S. and Resistance Forces.

29. As time went on and more experience was gained, an adequate administrative organization began to be evolved and by September, 1944, had achieved very efficient results. One of the most noteworthy is the case of an S.A.S. officer who, from the middle of German-held France, requested a pair of boots size eight, medium. He received them from England four and a half hours later by air. The development of the administrative organization followed on as a result of, and parallel to, the canalization through Headquarters S.A.S. Brigade of " G " planning and contact with units in the field. Owing to the limited numbers of wireless sets and operators available, all parties in the field were in communication with the base at Tactical Headquarters, S.A.S. Brigade, Moor Park. More often than not, unit commanders were in the United Kingdom while some of their troops were operating on the Continent and therefore tended to lose touch with them after they had dropped, as their only means of communication was through brigade headquarters. Units were very scattered and the delay in referring queries to them would not have been justified. As a result the brigade staff took a number of decisions on its own and was rapidly becoming overworked until it was decided to establish at tactical headquarters, unit detachments who had the authority to make decisions for their own units.

30. It was soon obvious that a similar organization was needed on the " Q " side so that decisions on re-supply could be taken immediately—in other words a proper S.A.S. base was required. It was undesirable that this base should be in the same place as tactical headquarters, but the facilities at Station 1090 were quite inadequate on account of almost non-existent accommodation, no direct communications and an almost complete lack of transport. Also it was badly placed in relation to 38 Group airfields. The ideal S.A.S. base would have to conform to the following requirements, if possible all in one place :—

(a) Be large enough to accommodate residues, reconstituting units and Station 1090 ;

(b) contain permanent accommodation for troops returning from operations ;

(c) be suitably placed as regards 38 Group airfields and the training of reinforcements ;

(d) have direct communications with both Tactical Headquarters S.A.S. Brigade and 38 Group airfields ;

(e) contain a small administrative staff, under a responsible " Q " Staff Officer. This staff would be responsible for the administrative side of the mounting and control of operations, especially air re-supply, in conjunction with unit administrative staffs.

31. The answer to the problem was provided by the move of 38 Group to airfields in Essex in September, 1944. Although it was not possible to achieve the ideal of having the S.A.S. base in one location in Essex the facilities provided were good. Station 1090 was established at Mushroom Farm Camp, which also provided a transit camp. Here there were hard standings, permanent accommodation, good storage facilities, packing bays and office accommodation. An R.A.S.C. Detachment from the Air Despatch Group was also in the camp and included a transport platoon. Headquarters S.A.S. Brigade was about eight miles away, the British regiments were some 15 to 20 miles away and the French regiments somewhat further, about 40 miles. But excellent direct line communication was provided to the War Office, Headquarters 1 Airborne Corps, 38 Group, S.A.S. Brigade, Special Forces, 20 Liaison Mission (with the French regiments) and the British regiments. The base was finally approved in November, 1944, and is shown in diagrammatic form at Appendix M, Part 1 : Part 2 gives the final composition of the " Q " staff and services at Headquarters, S.A.S. Brigade. The next chapter will describe some of the operations the base served.

CHAPTER XIX

THE S.A.S. OPERATIONS IN FRANCE, BELGIUM HOLLAND AND ITALY, 1944-45

Operations in France, Belgium and Holland from June to October, 1944

1. There were no less than 43 separate operations carried out by the S.A.S. Brigade during the period 6th June to 31st October, 1944. It is thus quite impossible to describe them all even in outline in a history of this length. Maps Nos. 9 and 10 show the areas where each of the parties operated and in many cases these alone indicate the role and task of the party concerned. Base areas from which the parties operated were chosen with reference to the following factors in order of priority :—

(*a*) proximity to the target area,

(*b*) suitability of terrain,

(*c*) strength of the enemy,

(*d*) strength and resources of " resistance " groups,

(*e*) accessibility to the R.A.F.

2. The importance of the part played by 38 Group R.A.F., sometimes assisted by 46 Group R.A.F. under command and by the R.A.F. Station Tempsford in delivering men and supplies to these various places, in every kind of weather, usually by night and in face of enemy opposition, cannot be over-stated. It was a great display of team work with the Army, of determination to overcome all difficulties, of gallantry on the part of the aircrews and of expert navigation with or without radar and other technical aids. Their story cannot be told in this volume but it is expected and hoped that full justice will be done to them elsewhere. One example is given to indicate the scope of their problems ; it occurred during a period when airborne operations on a large scale were also being planned. During the night 4th/5th August, 42 aircraft of 38 Group were detailed to go to 22 different dropping zones from five departure airfields with a total load of over 150 troops, four jeeps and 700 parachute containers of arms, stores and supplies, the weight being about 100 tons. In the same 24 hours eleven gliders with 45 troops and eleven jeeps were landed in Britanny behind the enemy lines. As usual, the location of many of the dropping zones could not be finally decided until the day of take-off, owing to enemy activities, yet about 95 per cent of all these air operations were successful—a fact which speaks volumes for the efficiency and co-operation of all ranks of the R.A.F. formations concerned.

3. A description by an S.A.S. officer of a scene on one of the dropping zones is repeated below to give an idea of the local conditions that sometimes prevailed. It is not intended to cast any doubt on the efficiency or helpfulness of the French Maquis, but it shows what may happen when new methods of warfare are introduced by night to friendly irregular forces in a foreign country.

" UN PARACHUTAGE "

" There was nothing either quiet or clandestine about my first what the French call ' un parachutage '.

" Once the containers were released from the aircraft there was considerable drama. Albert (the local Maquis chief) began the proceedings by shouting 'Attention everyone, the bidons descend '. Everyone present repeated this, adding advice to Bobo or Alphonse or Pierre, or whoever was nearest to ' have a care that the sacred bidons do not crush thee '.

" Once the containers had landed the parachute stakes were on. The winner was whoever could roll and hide away the most parachutes before being spotted by someone else.

" The bullock carts then came up with much encouragement from the drivers such as ' But come, my old one, to the bidons advance '. Then began the preliminary discussions as to how the first container would be hoisted on to the cart and who should have the honour of commencing. I found I had to go through the actions of beginning to hoist one end myself before, with loud cries of ' But no, my Captain, permit ' or, for example, ' My Captain, what an affair ', would my helpers then get on with the job.

" Once, however, the drill of clearing the dropping zone was understood these helpers were of the greatest value and we succeeded one night in clearing the dropping zone in 70 minutes. This was very good as it included four containers that had fallen in trees."

4. Special mention should also be made of No. 2 Group R.A.F., under Air Vice-Marshal Embry, who carried out at short notice many successful operations on targets whose locations were sent by wireless to them through S.A.S. headquarters from parties in the field.

The following are very brief descriptions of the major S.A.S. operations during this period. The code names were used at the time to preserve secrecy.

The map shows the locations.

Phase One

(Operations in Brittany and the establishment of a ring of S.A.S. bases from which attacks could be carried out on the communications leading to the Normandy Bridgehead.)

OPERATION " HOUNDSWORTH ", NEAR DIJON

5. This operation, carried out by "A" Squadron, 1st S.A.S. Regiment, during the period 6th June to 6th September, had as its main object the disruption of communications on the railway lines Lyons–Châlon sur Saône–Dijon–Paris and Le Creusot–Nevers. A force totalling 18 officers and 126 other ranks was maintained for three months behind the enemy lines with the loss of only about 18 casualties of whom 14 were lost in one aircraft which apparently hit a hill in low cloud. Continuous offensive operations were carried out with considerable success, the railway lines being blown up on 22 separate occasions 220 Germans being confirmed as killed or wounded, 132 taken prisoner, and 30 bombing targets being reported to the R.A.F. In supply by air operations 1,129 containers, 73 panniers, nine jeeps and two 6-pounder anti-tank guns were dropped by parachute. Relations with the Maquis were excellent and of mutual advantage. However, operations were sometimes limited by a shortage of transport, and the rather large base could not be permanently sub-divided owing to the shortage of signallers to communicate with brigade headquarters in England.

Operation " Gain ", near Orléans and Paris

6. This operation, carried out by nine officers and 49 other ranks under Major I. Fenwick of 1st S.A.S. Regiment during the period 14th June to 19th August, was designed to cut the German lateral railway communications in the bottle-neck area Rambouillet–Provins–Gien–Orléans–Chartres and to continue interfering with them. Considerable damage was done, at a cost of ten killed, including Major I. Fenwick and one missing. 250 containers and five jeeps were dropped during re-supply. In all, some 1,500 miles were covered behind the German lines in the jeeps, including six trips between the Forêt d'Orléans and a base camp near Fontainebleau, which involved crossing level-crossings 12 times, and opening the gates each time, the heavily festooned jeeps being mistaken for German vehicles. The lax methods of the German security arrangements were confirmed ; no checks of identity cards appeared to be made, no road blocks were manned and railway lines were guarded by uninterested Frenchmen. As a variation to demolitions of railway lines, trains known to be carrying German troops were attacked by machine-gun fire from stationary jeeps.

Operations in Brittany

7. These operations were carried out by 4th French Parachute Battalion with British S.A.S. liaison officers attached and reinforced in one particular operation (" Derry ") by ten officers and 74 other ranks of 3rd French Parachute Battalion. Brittany was considered to be an area where the " resistance " movement, though at the time severely weakened by arrests and large scale infiltration by Gestapo and Milice,* might be able to crystallize into an effective force capable of paralysing enemy movement, as the country was thick and broken, offering good concealment. Furthermore, an apparently major effort in this direction might help to conceal the real axis of advance of the main Allied armies. 21 Army Group decided therefore to employ sufficient S.A.S. troops in Brittany to harass the Germans severely—but not to such an extent that they would be forced to undertake major operations against the civilian population before the Allies could come to their aid effectively—to cut communications and to organize resistance so as to be ready to assist the Allied armies destined eventually to capture Brest and Lorient, and to protect their flanks in the drive eastwards. 4th French Parachute Battalion (Commandant Bourgoin) were given this task which was particularly suited to them as the battalion contained a large number of Bretons.

8. Operations started on the night of 5th/6th June, when two officers and 16 other ranks were dropped successfully to reconnoitre the base for "Samwest," eventually located in the Forêt Duaut, west of St. Brieuc. By 11th June, the force had grown to 115 all ranks assisted by some 30 locally recruited franc-tireurs ; it was in touch with the " resistance " movement and had located some 500 Germans not far from the base. It was found that the " resistance " movement consisted of several different organizations who were not working together and who were distrustful of each other. This led to many complications and some jealousy, particularly as regards priority of allotment of arms and supplies. The security of the base was compromised by careless

---

* A French police force, operating under Admiral Darlan, who worked with the Gestapo.

action on the part of a few of the parachute troops taking meals in restaurants, and on 12th June, the burning by the Germans of a farmhouse within a mile of the base necessitated counter-measures to maintain local morale. The result was an attack on the base by considerable German forces, of whom it was estimated that about 55 were killed and 100 wounded. However, there were 15 casualties amongst the parachute troops, about 17 amongst the " resistance " personnel and the base was dispersed. The survivors broke up into small parties with orders to join another base (" Dingson ") which had already been established in Morbihan, in southern Brittany as soon as possible, some 30 parachute troops remaining as instructors to local " resistance " units. In a few weeks, with the aid of a " Jedburgh " team they formed and armed a strong, well organized " resistance " group in this area.

9. Simultaneously with the establishment of the " Samwest " base, another party set up a further base known as " Dingson " in a wood near St. Marcel, not far from Vannes. By 18th June, Commandant Bourgoin was in command in that area of a force of three " resistance " battalions, reinforced by about 150 parachutists of 4th French Parachute Battalion with a few jeeps, a company of *gendarmes* and a considerable liaison element engaged in organizing and recruiting more local units. These " resistance " battalions had been armed, mostly with rifles, Brens and Stens and their total strength was some 2,500 men. However, they were not capable of cohesive action as units, being generally untrained, ill-equipped and without transport or signal equipment. The whole force was attacked by the Germans in strength on 18th June, and by that night Commandant Bourgoin was compelled to order the dispersal of his base. It is probable that the size of his force was too great and it was too concentrated to avoid detection at this stage, although it was not strong enough to fight a continuous major action. The " resistance " personnel mostly returned to their home areas, the parachute troops dispersing into smaller groups some further to the north-west.

10. Meanwhile 18 small parties of between three and six men had been dropped blind during the night 7th/8th June, and dispersed on a general line from St. Malo to Vannes with the task of attacking selected objectives on the German lines of communication and thus delaying the movement of enemy reserves towards Normandy. This was known as Operation " Cooney ". Each party was ordered to join the nearest S.A.S. base on completion of their task. They were generally successful in accomplishing their tasks and made their way to one or other of the previously established S.A.S. bases.

11. From these accounts it will be realized that although much had been done it was not yet possible, nor was it desirable at this early stage of the campaign, to conduct major operations in Brittany. Both S.A.S. bases had been dispersed although two parties with wireless communications were in daily touch with Headquarters S.A.S. Brigade and most of the troops were scattered in small parties without much central control. In the end this had advantages, as they all trained and organized the " resistance " units wherever they found them and it was not long before a reasonably efficient airborne supply system was working again. Many minor operations were staged against German detachments and on all their lines of communications. During this period two officers were successfully evacuated by sea to report on the exact position in Brittany, which was somewhat obscure, to headquarters in England.

12. An additional party (" Grog ") was formed south-west of Pontivy and by 28th June, was established there with a strength of some 40 men. Organization, training, and equipping of " resistance " units continued throughout Brittany and Commandant Bourgoin was recognized, in fact if not at first in theory, as the Allied leader in the province. He concentrated on minor operations while preparing the way for large scale operations later. His position was recognized and confirmed later from England by General Koenig, Commander of the French Forces of the Interior. By the end of July it was estimated that some 15,000 " resistance " personnel, at varying stages of military efficiency, were organized and armed, and that the enemy had suffered between 1,400 and 2,000 casualties. Many bombing targets were reported to the Allied Air Forces and effective action taken. On 5th August, the only S.A.S. glider operation took place, when 11 jeeps with crews of 4th French Parachute Battalion were landed in support of Commandant Bourgoin.

13. As a final comment on all these operations, it is worth quoting General Eisenhower in his " Report by the Supreme Commander to the Combined Chiefs of Staff on the Operations in Europe of the Allied Expeditionary Force " :—

" Special mention must be made of the great assistance given us by the F.F.I. in the task of reducing Brittany. The overt resistance forces in this area had been built up since June around a core of S.A.S. troops of the French 4th Parachute Battalion to a total strength of some 30,000 men. On the night of 4th/5th August the Etat-Major was despatched to take charge of their operations. As the Allied columns advanced, these French forces ambushed the retreating enemy, attacked isolated groups and strong points and protected bridges from destruction. When our armour had swept past them they were given the task of clearing up the localities where pockets of Germans remained, and of keeping open the Allied lines of communication. They also provided our troops with invaluable assistance in supplying information of the enemy's dispositions and intentions. Not least in importance, they had, by their ceaseless harassing activities, surrounded the Germans with a terrible atmosphere of danger and hatred which ate into the confidence of the leaders and the courage of the soldiers."

As soon as scattered detachments could be collected again 4th French Parachute Battalion was re-equipped and recruited many of the local Maquis personnel to bring the battalion up to strength for their next operations.

OPERATION " BULBASKET "—SOUTH OF CHÂTEAUROUX

14. This operation was carried out by 1st S.A.S. Regiment and by 3rd Patrol S.A.S. " Phantom " (from " F " Squadron, G.H.Q. Liaison Regiment) during the period 6th June to 7th August, under command of Captain J. E. Tonkin, 1st S.A.S. assisted by Captain R. J. McC. Sadoine, 3 Patrol Phantom. It was to attack the railway lines Limoges–Vierzon–Poitiers–Tours. Confirmed casualties of 20 killed and wounded were inflicted on the enemy, the railways were cut 12 times, one train was destroyed and two derailed, and one bridge was destroyed. As the result of information sent to the Allied Air Forces, amongst other targets, 11 petrol trains and 35 locomotives were destroyed. In addition, the immediate support given to the Maquis by the R.A.F. when they were being attacked by a large force of German S.S. troops had a most heartening effect. Out of a total strength of 56 S.A.S. troops 34 were missing, one killed and one wounded. Owing to treachery the bulk of the missing were captured and later

shot, and the number of survivors was insufficient to carry out further tasks. Arrangements were therefore made to withdraw them and replace them by fresh troops and the whole party were flown out by Hudsons and Dakotas at the beginning of August (*see* para. 23).

OPERATION " HAFT "—SOUTH OF MAYENNE

15. This was a small but very successful operation by four officers and six other ranks of 1st S.A.S. Regiment during the period 8th July to 11th August. The object was to obtain for 21 Army Group information in general and bombing targets in particular, in the area Mayenne–Laval–Le Mans. Forty targets were reported and many of them were attacked successfully. In this instance co-operation with contacts provided by Special Forces Headquarters was particularly good and effective.

OPERATION " DICKENS ", NEAR NANTES

16. This operation was carried out by 64 all ranks of 3rd French Parachute Battalion during the period 16th July to 7th October. The object was to attack the railway lines Saintes–Parthenay–Saumur and Saintes–La Roche–Nantes, to delay and report all enemy movements from the south, and to assist in organizing the " resistance " units, so as to harass the German withdrawal from St. Nazaire and Nantes at a later stage. It was claimed that the S.A.S. and the " resistance " units together cut the railways 83 times, destroyed 20 engines and killed 453 Germans ; seven bombing targets were reported. Their presence prevented a German withdrawal from St. Nazaire and the S.A.S. party for a time formed part of the " resistance " forces surrounding St. Nazaire. They nearly succeeded in persuading them to surrender. S.A.S. casualties were three killed and 14 wounded.

Phase Two

(The period of the breakout from the bridgehead—short time operations designed to harass the retreating enemy)

OPERATION " DUNHILL ", NORTH OF NANTES

17. This operation was also originally planned to provide information of the withdrawal, and was carried out by ten officers and 44 other ranks of 2nd S.A.S. during the period 3rd to 24th August. However, events moved so fast that by the time the party was on the ground the Germans were withdrawing from the whole area as fast as possible. Party " Dunhill " were landed south of Laval with tasks similar to those of " Haft," being instructed to seize any opportunity of harassing the German withdrawal. In the short time at their disposal before the American armies arrived, they passed back much information and inflicted 20 confirmed casualties on the enemy, at a cost of one killed, three missing and two wounded.

OPERATIONS " BUNYAN ", " CHAUCER " AND " SHAKESPEARE "

18. These were carried out by 31 all ranks of the Belgian Independent Parachute Company, during the period 3rd to 15th August, with the object of causing the greatest possible confusion during the enemy retreat eastwards, north of the River Loire and west of Paris, by attacks on enemy troops and transport. About 30 Germans were killed and some transport destroyed at a cost of four wounded.

19. By the beginning of August, it was clear that the German Armies were beginning to break and that the time had come when the forces in Brittany should come out into the open and take all possible steps against the enemy. The American armies were beginning their swift advance, and it was most important to capture the port of Brest intact. To assist in this, a party of ten officers and 74 other ranks of 3rd French Parachute Battalion were dropped on 5th August as party " Derry " in the department of Finisterre to protect the viaduct at Morlaix and the bridges at Landivisiau and to strengthen and encourage resistance in the area. We have already seen in Chapter XVI that an operation was planned for 1 Airborne Division to destroy this viaduct at the end of July, but with the changing situation, it was decided to keep it intact.

OPERATIONS " GAFF " AND " TRUEFORM ", SOUTH OF ROUEN

20. This tactical operation was carried out by two forces including three officers and 57 other ranks of the Belgian Independent Parachute Company, three officers and 37 other ranks of 2nd S.A.S. Regiment, and five other ranks of 1st S.A.S. Regiment. The objects were to destroy German petrol supplies for their retreating mechanical transport, to harass the enemy and to provide information, in the area between the Rivers Seine and Risle. In spite of very hurried mounting arrangements, the operations were comparatively successful and some damage was done, for a total of five casualties, while the enemy was withdrawing from Normandy. It was found that, owing to the conditions of retreat, the enemy was too pre-occupied to search for reported parachutists even in the immediate area of the battle. It was possible for S.A.S. parties to operate and lie up very close to the German troops. It is of interest to record that of five sections dropped from Stirling aircraft of 38 Group to complete the party, two were dropped accurately on the selected zones, two were dropped two miles away and one was dropped 11 miles away. This is a fair indication of the error that has to be accepted in a blind drop at night in operations of this nature.

OPERATION " BENSON ", NORTH-EAST OF PARIS

21. This was carried out by one officer and five other ranks of the Belgian Independent Parachute Company during the period 28th August to 1st September, with the object of reporting on the enemy's movements and dispositions. A great deal of reliable information was produced including the capture of the German order of battle on the River Seine and there is no doubt that if the Allied advance had not progressed so quickly, the results obtained would have been greater. A similar operation (" Wolsey ") about the same time but further west was carried out by one officer and five other ranks of S.A.S. Phantom with similar results.

Phase Three

(The establishment of a series of bases in central France designed to harass the withdrawal of the German Forces south of the River Loire. For various reasons these operations were all mounted rather too late, and were not as effective as they might have been had the troops been on the ground a month or two earlier.)

OPERATION "HAGGARD", EAST OF VIERZON

22. Operation "Haggard" was carried out by 79 all ranks of 1st S.A.S. Regiment, some being dropped by parachute and some infiltrated in jeeps through the now incoherent enemy lines, during the period 10th August to 23rd September. The object was to report on enemy troop movements and to operate against the railways Vierzon–Tours and Orléans–Vierzon, and to harass the German withdrawal. The S.A.S. claimed 233 Germans killed or wounded and a considerable amount of motor transport destroyed. This operation, like the majority of those mounted in central France during August, might have paid a better dividend if the requests of Headquarters, 1 Airborne Corps to drop them a month earlier could have been approved, but 21 Army Group considered there were good reasons against such proposals.

OPERATION "MOSES", NORTH AND NORTH-WEST OF LIMOGES

23. Forty-six all ranks of 3rd French Parachute Battalion carried out this operation during the period 3rd August to 5th October, taking over from the "Bulbasket" party who had been evacuated by air. They maintained particularly good wireless communications with the base in England and consequently received efficient supply by air and achieved control and effective passing of information. The object was to attack the railways Montauban–Brine–Limoges and those running laterally to the Rhône valley, and to harass Germans withdrawing from Bordeaux and La Rochelle. Nine bombing targets were submitted, of which two were confirmed to have been engaged successfully. Some 330 containers and 19 panniers were dropped in supply by air and four jeeps were infiltrated through the lines to join the party.

Phase Four

(The establishment of a series of bases designed to harass the withdrawal of the German forces from the South of France)

OPERATIONS "BARKER", "HARRODS" AND "JOCKWORTH", NORTH OF LYONS

24. These operations were carried out by seven officers and 95 other ranks of 3rd French Parachute Battalion during the period 13th August to 24th September. The probability of an enemy withdrawal from southern France provided an opportunity to intensify action along the routes which he was expected to follow, particularly in the Le Creusot–Châlon area (Saône et Loire). There is no doubt that in conjunction with the Maquis much damage and many casualties were inflicted before American and French armies from the south reached the area. Many Germans surrendered in disorder and S.A.S. casualties were light. Some 240 containers and 16 panniers were dropped in supply by air. The presence of these S.A.S. parties in conjunction with organized " resistance " groups undoubtedly speeded up very considerably the advance of the Allied Armies up the Rhône valley after their landing in southern France.

OPERATIONS IN THE LIMOGES AREA—" SAMSON " (HAUT VIENNE)—
" MARSHALL " (CORRÈZE) AND " SNELGROVE " (CREUSE)

25. These operations of a similar nature to " Harrods " and " Barker " were carried out by approximately 78 all ranks of 3rd French Parachute Battalion in three groups of about 25 each, during the period 9th August–mid-September. All three parties were particularly well placed in suitable

terrain to harass the Germans retreating from the south and south-west.
" Samson " later joined for a short time in the investment of La Rochelle, and
" Marshall " and " Snelgrove " carried out very successful ambushes showing
great courage, sometimes of almost too reckless a nature, in their attacks on
heavily armed German troop trains and convoys. " Samson " eventually
joined up with " Moses " and proceeded to block St. Nazaire and all western
escape routes.

Operation " Abel ", East of Dijon

26. This operation was intended to encourage resistance in the area and to
harass the German withdrawal from the south of France. It was carried out
by 16 officers and 116 other ranks of 3rd French Parachute Battalion, the
personnel being the same as for " Derry ", during the period 15th August to
22nd September. The party was eventually employed to carry out some particularly dangerous reconnaissance in the Belfort Gap, under the commanding-
general of 45 U.S. Infantry Division.

Phase Five

(The establishment of an outer ring of bases from which to attack communications between Germany and France).

Operation " Rupert ", North of Dijon

27. This operation, originally planned soon after " D " day on 6th June,
was delayed owing to the limited hours of darkness for the flight and the
likely enemy resistance *en route*, and because Special Forces Headquarters
objected to having uniformed troops in the area. It was not until 23rd July
that these objections were overcome, but unfortunately the aircraft carrying
the first advance party crashed, with the result that the second reconnaissance
party did not drop until 5th August. By the time the main S.A.S. party arrived
the American armies were within a few days march of that area. The operations were carried out by nine officers and 49 other ranks of 2nd S.A.S. Regiment, during the period 23rd July to 10th September, with the object of cutting
the main railways in the strategically important area between Châlons sur Marne
and Dijon. Major Symes was the original commander, but was killed when
his aircraft was shot down. The eventual Force Commander was Major
O. B. Rooney. The tasks were not accomplished as the S.A.S. were established
in the area too late. Their casualties were two killed, nine missing and one
wounded.

Operation " Loyton ", in the Vosges

28. Operation " Loyton " was carried out by about 90 all ranks of 2nd
S.A.S. Regiment under command of Lieutenant-Colonel B. M. F. Franks
during the period 13th August to 16th October, and was part of the plan to
establish an outer ring of bases from which to attack German communications.
It was appreciated that the communications leading from the area of Strasbourg
–Saarbrucken towards Paris were of considerable importance to the enemy
but airborne operations there were at the extreme operational range of 38
Group's aircraft and the country was difficult for navigation. However, the

247

" resistance " units in the area, although ill-armed and equipped, were reported to be active and it was decided to reinforce them as much as possible. A number of successful ambushes were laid, considerable damage was done and 32 enemy were killed or wounded. About 20 bombing targets were reported, of which two were confirmed as attacked. The " resistance " forces in the area were, however, not well-organized and co-operation with them was difficult. The operation was finally abandoned owing to a major German attack by about 600 infantry, supported by artillery, aircraft and tanks. Although the S.A.S. troops were withdrawn, the Germans took a division out of the line in order to attack the base.

OPERATION " NOAH ", IN BELGIUM, SOUTH-EAST OF NAMUR

29. This was the first S.A.S. operation in Belgium and was carried out by 41 all ranks of the Belgian Independent Parachute Company with two jeeps, during the period 16th August to 13th September. They were dropped with 63 containers and seven panniers. It was anticipated that the enemy would probably withdraw back to the Siegfried Line, the bulk of his army moving through Belgium, and it was therefore necessary to establish S.A.S. bases in readiness. Unfortunately this action had been delayed for reasons which were never clearly established but were probably connected with the fear of premature reprisals if uniformed troops were dropped in Belgium before the Allied armies were near at hand. As far as the S.A.S. was concerned, the delay caused many opportunities to be missed.

30. The objects of "Noah" were to obtain knowledge of local conditions, to report on enemy movements and dispositions and to advise and control the reception of reinforcements. Apart from carrying out these duties, the party also killed 87 and wounded 41 Germans, and destroyed 25 vehicles including three tanks. S.A.S. casualties were one killed and three wounded.

OPERATION " HARDY ", NORTH OF DIJON (LATER COMBINED WITH OPERATION " WALLACE ")

31. These operations were started by " Hardy " on 26th July, when two parties, each of three all ranks and one jeep, from 2nd S.A.S. Regiment were dropped to the " Houndsworth " base. In the next few nights more personnel of 2nd S.A.S. Regiment, with jeeps, were dropped and the total rose to a mobile party of six officers and 44 men under command of Captain Grant-Hibbert. On 1st August, the " Hardy " party left " Houndsworth " for the Plateau de Langres, north-east of Dijon, arrived there on 5th August, without incident, and set up their own base. On 12th August, the base was moved a short distance as the original area was found to be a favourite haunt of German officers who wished to shoot wild boar. The local Maquis were effective and extremely co-operative. On 17th August, a combined S.A.S.–Maquis force surprised a German force which consisted of 300 men with one heavy tank, two light tanks, six armoured cars and two half-track vehicles moving east towards Langres. The two half-tracks were captured, and 12 civilian hostages who had been taken by the Germans from a local village as a reprisal, were re-captured and released. The base was moved again on 19th August. On 21st August, the S.A.S. effected another successful ambush, 30 Germans being killed and wounded and two trucks destroyed without any casualties to the S.A.S. By 24th August, two more enemy trucks had been destroyed and the main railway line from Langres to Dijon had been blown up.

Phase Six

(The series of jeep operations with the object of attacking the large columns of partly demoralized Germans retreating through central France).

OPERATION " WALLACE "

32. In the meantime operation " Wallace " had started on 19th August, with the landing from Dakota aircraft belonging to 46 Group R.A.F. of 60 all ranks and 20 jeeps of 2nd S.A.S. Regiment under command of Major R. A. Farran at Rennes, now held by the Americans. By the same means 40 all ranks and 20 jeeps of 1st S.A.S. Regiment were landed to join " Houndsworth " and " Kipling " in the Morvan mountains. The " Wallace " party immediately started its road journey of 380 miles, 200 of them behind the enemy lines, to join " Hardy ", where they arrived on 24th August, having had several engagements *en route*, six jeeps being destroyed and a party with five other jeeps being detached and failing to get through, though they later returned to England. At least 50 Germans had been killed, more wounded and a train completely burnt. The strength of the " Wallace " party was now 32 all ranks with nine jeeps.

33. " Hardy " and " Wallace " now combined as one squadron of 2nd S.A.S. Regiment under command of Major Farran and many successful ambushes were carried out. On 30th August an operation at full strength against previously located enemy forces at Chatillon resulted in over 100 Germans being killed, many more wounded and 12 enemy vehicles destroyed. S.A.S. casualties were one killed and two wounded. After this " Wallace " broke up into three parties in order to cover as wide an area as possible and to retain freedom of action. Until 17th September, they made a continuous series of attacks on all enemy movements over a wide area stretching some 70 miles from east to west at a cost of three killed and two jeeps destroyed.

34. Certain further points must be mentioned in connection with these operations. 38 Group R.A.F. carried out 36 sorties, only six being unsuccessful, and dropped 485 containers, 12 panniers and 12 jeeps, into very difficult dropping zones, without any casualties to aircraft. The total S.A.S. casualties were 16 personnel and 16 jeeps, 12 by enemy action and two damaged in parachuting. In addition to continual harassing of the enemy and the effect on his morale, the confirmed enemy casualties were 500 killed or seriously wounded, 65 vehicles destroyed, one goods train burnt out, and 100,000 gallons of petrol destroyed. S.A.S. jeeps with extra petrol tanks giving a range of six or seven hundred miles, in some cases with armour plating and armed with from two to five Vickers " K " machine-guns or with Brens, Bazookas or 3-inch mortars, proved invaluable. It was found that it was much better to use them as stationary gun-platforms or to dismount the guns for firing, than to try to fire accurately on the move. Twin-Vickers would cut a truck in half at under 50 yards range. Movement by jeep behind the enemy lines was not only possible but easy, but experienced officers were required for each party. The tactical team was three jeeps, including one in reserve. All German troops who were in the area were harassed ceaselessly and this was undoubtedly one of the most successful S.A.S. operations, the credit being due to the initiative and leadership of Major Farran.

Operation "Newton", South-East of Orleans

35. This was an operation to reinforce existing operational bases with jeep parties, so that guerrilla activities might be intensified during the enemy's withdrawal from south and south-west France. It was carried out by eight officers and 54 other ranks of 3rd French Parachute Battalion with 20 jeeps, during the period 19th August to 11th September, 1944. The party went by sea and crossed the River Loire south-east of Orléans. They then split into several parties, one of which penetrated as far as the " Jockworth " area, the others turning west and joining the " Moses " party.

Operation "Spenser", North-East of Vierzon

36. This was an operation during the period 29th August to 14th September carried out by 317 all ranks of 4th French Parachute Battalion now re-organized from their operations in Brittany with 54 jeeps and trucks, with the object of harassing the enemy's withdrawal through the area Vierzon—Châteauroux—Vichy (Loire et Cher, Cher, Indre and Allier). They infiltrated through the enemy lines and crossed the River Loire south of Orléans. There were perhaps not as many opportunities for action as had been expected, owing mainly to the rapid advance of the American armies. However, in conjunction with " Haggard ", " Moses " and " resistance " groups, the party was responsible for causing a German force, some 18,000 strong, to surrender at Issoudun to a hastily summoned American officer.

Phase Seven

(Operations in Belgium to attack German communications)

Operation "Brutus", in Belgium, South-East of Namur

37. When the German retreat through Belgium really began, emergency steps were necessary to arm and equip the Belgian " resistance " forces and this operation was mounted largely with this object. A total of 20 all ranks of the Belgian Independent Parachute Company were dropped on 2nd September to join " Noah " and to communicate a part of the plan for future operations to " Noah's " commander and the commander of No. 5 Zone of the Belgian " resistance " organization. They found that the most pressing requirement was to drop arms to the Belgian " resistance " units in the Ardennes.

Operation "Bergbang", South-East of Liege

38. This operation was also carried out by the Belgian Independent Parachute Company from 2nd to 12th September, some 40 all ranks being employed. The object was to attack communications east of the River Meuse in the Ardennes. It was seriously handicapped by a shortage of good wireless operators, by the short time available before the main Allied armies arrived, and by the fact that the local population were less co-operative than in other areas. Nevertheless the S.A.S. accounted for a fair number of Germans and they reported that an S.A.S. force dropped there earlier could have achieved a great deal.

Phase Eight

(Operations in Holland)

Operation " Fabian " (originally " Regan ") in North Belgium and Holland

39. This operation was carried out by a small party from the Belgian Independent Parachute Company under command of Lieutenant G. S. Kirschen during an exceptionally long period from 19th September, 1944, to 14th March, 1945. The original object was to obtain information about the enemy on the lines Antwerp–Albert Canal–Maastricht and the rivers Maas and Rhine in Holland, and on their movements from the areas of Amsterdam the Hague and Rotterdam. Much valuable information was sent back daily and 38 bombing targets were reported. From his headquarters in the area between Arnhem and Amersfoort, north of the River Rhine, Lieutenant Kirschen, who lived for some weeks in a chicken coop belonging to a friendly Dutchman, rendered very valuable assistance to men of 1 Airborne Division who escaped back over the Rhine after the main body of the Division had been evacuated. He worked in very close touch with the Dutch " resistance " units who helped most efficiently in every way without actively attacking the strong German forces in the area.

Operation " Gobbo " (originally " Portia ") and " Keystone " in East Holland

40. These operations were of a similar type to " Fabian " and were carried out by the Belgian Independent Parachute Company during approximately the same period. The objects were to instruct and organize " resistance " groups and obtain information of enemy movements from northern Holland and at a later date to harass the enemy retreating through the province of Drente to Germany. (*See* paragraph 59.)

Operations in Italy, December, 1944, to April, 1945

41. As the main battle-front along and west of the River Rhine settled down temporarily to more static conditions, with little hope of a major Allied advance during the winter, so the scope for S.A.S. operations on this front diminished. Operations were therefore sought elsewhere and a request for one squadron S.A.S. was made by the Allied Command in Italy. 3rd Squadron 2nd S.A.S. Regiment were despatched there by air transport arriving in December, 1944.

42. On arrival this squadron, which was commanded by Major R. A. Farran, came under the direct command of 15 Army Group. They were kept for operations of a strategical nature and to work in close co-operation with the Italian " resistance " movement, now enthusiastic and of considerable size but very lacking in leadership and determination. Operational conditions in Italy were in some respects dissimilar to those in France, Belgium and Holland. The Allied air superiority was more marked and even unarmed Dakota aircraft could and did fly behind the enemy lines by day. The country was more broken and mountainous, and roads and railways were fewer, more vital and often more difficult to attack as they were well-guarded.

43. Two major operations were carried out by 3rd Squadron, 2nd S.A.S. Regiment, the first being a normal S.A.S. operation and the second varying from the normal in that the force employed included guerilla units of Russians and Italians under command. In both, weapons carried were heavier than on previous occasions and were used with good effect. The squadron continued to operate in Italy until the German surrender, their last action being an attempt to block the Brenner Pass by causing a landslide.

Operation " Galia ", inland from Spezia

44. This was a successful operation by 33 all ranks during the period 27th December to 15th February. The object was to harass the enemy inland from Spezia, in the area where one of the few roads over the Apennine mountains leads to Parma. Adverse winter weather and the very hilly close country made supply by air difficult but arrangements were good and delays were reduced to the minimum. The troops were armed with 3-inch mortars as well as medium machine guns and lighter weapons and the former proved their worth. Mules for porterage were obtained from the Italian " resistance " organization. The harassing was effective and enemy losses were at least 150 killed, in addition to 22 motor vehicles destroyed. Additional small operations were carried out in this area later on in March and April.

Operation " Tombola ", South-West of Modena

45. On 4th March, 1945, Major Farran was dropped on the northern slopes of the Apennine mountains to contact a British mission from Special Forces Headquarters, who were organizing the local Italian " resistance " personnel, and to investigate the possibility of more active operations against the enemy there. The area was strategically important, as it was within striking distance of the two mountain roads Lucca–Modena and Spezia–Reggio and these roads would become vital enemy withdrawal routes in case of an Allied advance. The Allied line then ran from just north of Ravenna on the east coast to a point about halfway between Lucca and Spezia on the west coast. Major Farran found that the local " resistance division " was about 1,200 strong of whom 1,000 were useless as fighting material. There were also about 100 Russians, who were deserters from the Wehrmacht and escaped prisoners of war. With the assistance of the Special Forces Mission, he organized from these resources and from 42 all ranks of his own S.A.S. Squadron an Allied battalion under his own command and concentrated on training them from 8th to 23rd March, behind the enemy lines and within a defended base area in the mountains. S.A.S. detachments with the heavier weapons, one 75-mm. and one 37-mm. gun, 4·2- and 3-inch mortars, supported the Italians and Russians. All Italian units and sections were stiffened by S.A.S. leaders and in some cases S.A.S. private soldiers led Italian detachments with great success.

46. On 23rd March, Major Farran reconnoitered the positions of the German 51 Corps Headquarters Albinea, which was about 500 strong and attacked it at 0200 hours on 27th March. The German Chief of Staff was killed and at least 60 other German casualties were inflicted. Most of the headquarters papers, files and maps were burnt and the whole district was thrown into a state of alarm. Allied casualties were 17 killed of which two officers and four other ranks were S.A.S.

47. From 28th March to 12th April, the Allied battalion remained on the defensive, in accordance with orders from 15 Army Group, though the last few days were spent in moving from the base to positions from which they could attack all enemy road communications south-west of Modena when 15 Army Group started their advance. During this period the battalion was thrice attacked in position but defeated the enemy decisively each time and caused him heavy casualties, 51 German dead being left on the ground on 10th April alone. Four jeeps were dropped to the battalion later.

48. On 13th April, 15 Army Group ordered the battalion to attack the main German supply and withdrawal routes in the area, to coincide with the advance of the main Allied armies. This the battalion did for the next two days, attacking continuously and effectively shelling bridges and German forces in towns. These operations contributed materially to the panic of three or four German divisions but were only made possible by the drive and energy of the British component of the battalion. At times the German withdrawal was held up for hours on end and thrown into complete confusion. Enemy casualties were probably over 300 killed and 20 motor vehicles destroyed, and 158 prisoners were taken on 22nd April. Total casualties of the Allied Battalion were :— S.A.S. nine, Russians twelve, Italians three.

Operations in Holland, Belgium and France from November, 1944, to March, 1945

49. As mentioned previously, there was little scope for S.A.S. operations behind the enemy lines during the winter of 1944-45. The opposing armies were more or less static or were engaged in deliberate battles with limited objectives. Operations " Fabian " and " Gobbo " in Holland were providing information in German-held Holland. Prolonged operations in the hostile country of Germany, across the River Rhine were not considered to be worth the risk involved at that stage. Experience had shown perfectly clearly that it was quite impossible to conceal supply operations from the local population. Prolonged S.A.S. operations could only be undertaken if the local population were friendly and for this reason they were not possible inside Germany. Means were therefore sought by which the S.A.S. Brigade could help the Allied armies within the immediate theatre of war and it was decided to provide mobile jeep squadrons from 1st and 2nd S.A.S. Regiments. They were used in much the same way as normal divisional reconnaissance regiments, their tasks being limited to suit their strength, and took an effective part in holding and defeating the German offensive in the Ardennes. 2nd and 3rd Regiments de Chasseurs Parachutistes, the former 3rd and 4th French Parachute Battalions, also provided jeep parties some of the time but later were concentrated for further training in an airborne role. Any S.A.S. airborne operations contemplated were handicapped by the fact that the heavy bombers with which 38 Group R.A.F. were equipped were unable to operate during the winter from the airfields in France and Belgium, these being constructed for light or medium aircraft only. Consequently flying distances were long and delays were inevitable. Otherwise there is nothing of particular interest to describe during this period, except that Brigadier J. M. Calvert succeeded Brigadier McLeod as Commander S.A.S. Brigade, when the latter officer was posted to India in March, 1945, as Director of Military Operations General Headquarters, New Delhi.

(C29259)

K*

Operations in Holland and Germany from April, 1945, to the end of the War in Europe

50. The situation changed, however, when the Allies began their advance into North Holland and Germany once the River Rhine had been crossed. S.A.S. operations were now divided into airborne operations in Holland and ground operations in Germany.

OPERATION "AMHERST" IN NORTH-EAST HOLLAND

51. Early in 1945, the Commander S.A.S. Brigade, after consultation with Special Forces Headquarters with regard to the terrain and possible assistance from the Dutch "resistance" organization, had proposed the area of north-east Holland as suitable for airborne S.A.S. operations when the main Allied offensive took place. On 28th March, 21 Army Group instructed that such operations should be discussed with First Canadian Army, in whose area any such operations would be. Plans were drawn up on 30th March, subject to approval by the Allied Air Forces, which was given on 3rd April, after a conference with 38 Group R.A.F. and 84 Group, 2 Tactical Air Force, R.A.F. The operation was expected to be required on or after 14th April, but on 5th April their rapid rate of advance caused First Canadian Army to give a warning order for the night 6/7th or 7/8th April. On 6th April they confirmed the latter date. Thus the operation had to be mounted extremely quickly and, as previously indicated, from airfields in England. On landing, the S.A.S. troops would come under command of 2 Canadian Corps.

52. The tasks allotted to the S.A.S. were :—

(a) To cause the maximum confusion throughout the area by continually harassing the enemy and thus preventing him from taking up any fixed positions or forming any sort of line to oppose the advance by 2 Canadian Corps.

(b) To prevent the demolition of 18 bridges over the canals by removing the demolition charges. Where routes were impassable owing to bridges being already blown, they were to reconnoitre alternative routes for 2 Canadian Corps.

(c) To preserve Steenwijk airfield for the use of the R.A.F.

(d) To pass all available information regarding enemy dispositions movements and intentions to First Canadian Army and subordinate formations concerned.

(e) To provide guides for the advance of the ground forces.

(f) To raise and assist the "resistance" units in the area.

53. These tasks were different from those in all previous S.A.S. operations as it was intended that the S.A.S. troops should be dropped fairly close in front of the advancing ground armies and be overrun by them within 72 hours of being dropped. Furthermore, the drops would have to be blind night drops, as reception parties were impracticable.

54. The S.A.S. forces employed were 41 officers and 298 other ranks of 2nd Regiment de Chasseurs Parachutistes, 42 officers and 315 other ranks of 3rd Regiment de Chasseurs Parachutistes and a Special Force liaison team of three officers and one other rank. This was a total of 700 all ranks organized into about 50 small parties. Aircraft employed were 47 Stirlings of 38 Group R.A.F., for dropping, and other aircraft of 84 Group R.A.F. for re-supply and air support. The enemy forces in the area were estimated as the equivalent of one division, with certain garrison troops in addition ; their morale was not high.

55. 19 dropping zones were selected in the area Groningen–Emmen–Meppel. Each aircraft carried 15 all ranks and four containers, parties dropping in two sticks of seven and eight all ranks. Two or three parties landed on each dropping zone and then split up. Actual dropping was done through 10/10ths cloud from 1,400 feet, errors in dropping varying on an average from two to four miles from the selected dropping zones, and provided a magnificent example of the very great accuracy obtained by 38 Group pilots in extremely unfavourable weather. Six aircraft dropped their parties absolutely accurately. Casualties on dropping were two killed, one by drowning and one through a container fouling his parachute, and three seriously hurt. No aircraft were lost. All except one party which was delayed for 24 hours were landed during the night 7/8th April, and operated for varying periods of three to seven days before being overtaken by our ground troops. A plan to drop jeeps to the S.A.S. one hour after they had themselves dropped had to be cancelled as there was still 10/10ths cloud and reception lights could not have been seen.

56. The ground operations succeeded in their main objects and First Canadian Army reported that they very materially assisted their advance and the disorganization of the enemy. Special emphasis was laid on the offensive spirit displayed by these French troops, though some of their actions, especially attacks on enemy-held villages in daylight with no support except their own small calibre weapons, were possibly too ambitious. In describing them, Brigadier Calvert ended with the words " some other men were last seen disappearing in the direction of Berlin, hot-foot after the enemy ". The whole effect may be described as a net formed by the French, materially assisted by Dutch " resistance " personnel, entangling the enemy for the thrust by 2 Canadian Corps which took them, in a very short time, to the North Sea. The dispersion of a large number of small parties operating over a wide area amongst a failing enemy, even though they were mostly high class German units, proved most successful.

57. Enemy casualties were difficult to assess and in any case they were incidental to the attainment of the main objects, but they were estimated at 270 killed, 220 wounded, 187 prisoners-of-war, 29 motor vehicles destroyed or captured and three railways cut. S.A.S. losses were 29 killed, 35 wounded and 29 missing.

58. One further point to note is a recommendation that in future operations of this nature air support signal unit wireless parties should accompany the S.A.S. for communication with the air forces with regard to bombing targets, supply by air and the general passing of information. These would be in addition to the normal S.A.S. communications.

255

S.A.S. Ground Operations in Germany

OPERATION " ARCHWAY "

59. This operation was carried out by a mixed British force commanded by Lieutenant-Colonel Franks, and was composed of one squadron from each of 1st and 2nd S.A.S. Regiments, with a total strength of about 300 all ranks and 75 jeeps. A few 3-ton lorries and 15-cwt. trucks were provided for administrative purposes. A further party of about 130 all ranks of 2nd S.A.S. Regiment, who were to have taken part in operation " Keystone " (subsequently cancelled) at the same time as "Amherst ", joined the force later on, at the crossing of the River Elbe.

60. The force left their base in England on 18th March, and moved to a concentration area west of the River Rhine in readiness for operations after the main armies had forced the river crossing. From then on they operated in turn with 6 Airborne Division, 11 Armoured Division and 15 (Scottish) Division, ending up as the first British troops to enter Kiel. Their main task was reconnaissance but they were used also in a counter-intelligence role, including the rounding-up of German war criminals. The value of a jeep with machine-guns mounted was proved again and 3-inch mortars carried on jeeps were very effective. In common with all other formations, the force took many prisoners and inflicted heavy casualties while advancing with great speed and determination.

OPERATION " HOWARD "

61. This operation was carried out by one and a half squadrons of 1st S.A.S. Regiment under the command of Lieutenant-Colonel R. B. Mayne, being a force of about 180 all ranks with 40 jeeps and a few administrative vehicles. They operated under command of 4 Canadian Armoured Division of First Canadian Army, in a reconnaissance role ahead of the Division. The country in north-east Holland, where most of their operations took place, is however very cut up with canals and dykes and unsuitable for jeep operations. Furthermore there were numerous prepared enemy strong-points along the roads, with many minefields. The result was that casualties were fairly heavy and the operations unsatisfactory, in spite of the experience and great gallantry of the force commander. S.A.S. troops were not sufficiently heavily equipped for operations of this nature.

OPERATION " LARKSWOOD "

62. This operation was carried out by the Belgian S.A.S. troops, now expanded into a regiment of two squadrons but still under its original commander, Major Blondeel. Its strength was about 300 all ranks, with 45 jeeps and some troop-carrying trucks and administrative vehicles. The regiment operated with 2 Canadian Corps from 5th April and subsequently with the Polish Armoured Division. They were amongst the first troops to contact the French S.A.S. taking part in "Amherst ". They were used energetically and successfully, mainly in a reconnaissance role, and undoubtedly caused the enemy many casualties, though their own were not light. Later, when used on internal security duties they captured von Ribbentrop and prevented him from committing suicide.

Statistical Summary of all S.A.S. Operations in France, Belgium and Holland from June to November, 1944

63. The following figures are as reliable as possible, but must be treated with reserve. The enemy casualties shown are based on claims by parties and are therefore liable to be exaggerated. They include those inflicted by " resistance " units acting directly with the S.A.S. However, they serve to give a useful picture of the material results achieved during the period when most operations of the true S.A.S. type took place, and the cost of those results.

S.A.S. Brigade

Total approximate strength, all ranks	2,000
Casualties (a proportion of these, especially 4th French Parachute Battalion, were recovered, having been captured or gone into hiding with the " resistance ").	330

38 Group R.A.F.

Total operational and supply-by-air sorties flown	780
Successful	600
Abortive	180
Casualties in aircraft	6
Jeeps dropped and landed by glider	86
6-pounder anti-tank guns dropped	2
Containers and panniers dropped	10,370

Enemy

(*a*) Personnel killed or seriously wounded	7,733
Prisoners (excluding 18,000 who surrendered at Issoudun in France to nine U.S. Officers partially as a result of being cut off by S.A.S. troops and the French " resistance ").	4,784
Total	12,517
(*b*) Motor vehicles captured	40
Motor vehicles destroyed.. ..	600
Bicycles and motor-cycles destroyed	100
Total ..	740
(*c*) Trains destroyed	7
Railway trucks destroyed	89
Railway locomotives destroyed	29
Derailments	33
Railway lines cut	164
(*d*) Bombing targets reported	400

General Remarks

64. The figures given above speak for themselves but the greatest value of the S.A.S. operations comes under the following headings :—

(*a*) The moral support given to the " resistance " movements and assistance in organizing and arming them.

257

(*b*) The adverse moral effect on the enemy caused by the continued harassing of his lines of communications. He had to hold considerable forces to garrison all important areas and on many occasions he had to deploy field units against the S.A.S. and " resistance " units, to the detriment of his main forces. Enemy traffic and reinforcements to the front were delayed and his retreat was harried continuously.

(*c*) The considerable amount of information gained and transmitted both to senior headquarters such as S.H.A.E.F. and 21 Army Group and to advancing Allied formations in the field.

(*d*) The specific pin pointing of targets for the R.A.F.

65. It is important not to magnify or minimize the value of these operations carried out by such a comparatively small percentage of fighting troops compared to the armies employed in the field.

Although the results achieved as enumerated above were considerable, the experience gained on this, the first large-scale employment of small parties of troops, has shown the immense and increasing possibilities for their future use by Army and Air Force Commanders, who had, by the end of the campaign, acquired knowledge and confidence in their capabilities.

66. It should be emphasized that S.A.S. operations provided an opportunity to exploit the personal independence and initiative of individual leaders who excel in comparatively small actions, apart from the more mass-controlled operations of the main armies. Throughout history the British Empire has produced many such men and it continues to do so. They achieve results out of all proportion to the forces at their disposal and far greater than they would in more regular circumstances. The S.A.S. troops were composed of such types, but owing to their numbers it has not been possible in this short history to mention the names of any except some of the unit commanders.

67. Finally, they were not deterred by the murderous and unlawful treatment of their wounded and prisoners taken by the Germans, who tortured and shot many of them in spite of their right to be treated as normal uniformed prisoners of war under the Geneva Convention. They had to consider, however, the certainty of brutal enemy reprisals against civilians who were in any way suspected of aiding or concealing them and this consideration handicapped their operations on many occasions.

Lessons

68. The S.A.S. operations proved that it is possible and advantageous to infiltrate bodies of uniformed troops with transport behind the enemy lines, either by air, land or sea, and that they can operate successfully for long periods if supplied by air. This is especially true when the front has stabilized and where there is a " crust " of enemy troops. On an average this crust will be about 30 miles thick, and behind it, apart from some reserve formations, there will be few fighting troops and one will be able to travel quite a long way without seeing any troops at all. Here is the happy hunting ground of the S.A.S. The greatest effect can be obtained and the greatest freedom of movement is possible when the " crust " is under the maximum pressure from our troops. Then the enemy administration will be strained and reserves will not be spared to round up small bodies of troops in the rear areas.

69. When a break-through by our troops occurs, opportunity targets and the maximum spreading of confusion will be the main roles. An example of this was Major Farran's use of one gun in northern Italy during the German retreat. This had a very great effect on morale and led to many rumours of " the enemy are on us " variety.

70. The S.A.S. role was complementary to the air force interdiction programme, for they reported many targets and were also able to let the air force know the results of their attacks.

71. The operations showed that " resistance " forces will rally round a small core of uniformed troops and that it is possible to arm and train these " resistance " forces under the very nose of the enemy.

72. An efficient system of communications is vital to the success of S.A.S. operations, and parties should normally be not more than 50 strong. If they are to operate for more than a few days they must have a secure base where they can rest and be supplied by air.

73. All orders for S.A.S. should be issued through normal staff channels but there should be a separate headquarters or a separate branch at Supreme Headquarters to co-ordinate the policies and activities of all special forces dropped behind the enemy lines. There should also be a staff officer at each headquarters as the link between the S.A.S. and the ground formations concerned for all purposes.

CHAPTER XX

THE AIRBORNE OPERATIONS IN THE ARNHEM AREA— SEPTEMBER, 1944

General Situation

1. By the middle of September, 1944, General Hodges' First U.S. Army, in the face of considerable opposition, had thrust to the German frontier and was in contact with the defences of the Siegfried Line. It was planned that the Army should continue its operations to Bonn and Cologne. Further to the South General Patton's Third U.S. Army had established bridgeheads over the River Moselle, and in the extreme north, General Dempsey's Second British Army had completed its rapid advance from the River Seine, and its leading formations were established at small bridgeheads along the general line of the River Meuse—Escaut Canal. During this period the Second Army had taken part in hard fighting against an enemy who, although disorganized, continued to offer stiff resistance with rear guards, mainly composed of infantry supported by Tiger tanks and self-propelled guns. Behind the front he was attempting to organize defensive positions, based on the major water obstacles, such as the Rhine, which would have to be crossed if a continued thrust by the Second Army were to be made through the Netherlands. General Eisenhower agreed to Field-Marshal Montgomery's proposal to secure crossings over the Rivers Rhine and Maas in the general area Grave—Nijmegen—Arnhem, with the object of outflanking the defences of the Siegfried Line and of striking along the main route to Berlin across the plains of northern Germany. This meant a general slow-down along the whole front facing Germany, as all available resources would be required in the north, and a temporary delay in freeing the port of Antwerp. The British line of communication was now 400 miles long, and, although Antwerp had been captured, it was not yet operative, so that any delay in freeing the port meant a consequent delay in the administrative build-up of 21 Army Group. However, General Eisenhower and Field-Marshal Montgomery were prepared to accept this as they considered that the advantages of such an operation, should it be successful, outweighed the disadvantages.

2. The Second Army was allotted the task of carrying out this thrust with the assistance of the newly formed First Allied Airborne Army (Lieutenant-General Lewis H. Brereton), which was responsible for co-ordinating the airborne plans. The airborne operations were to be carried out by 1 Airborne Corps (Lieutenant-General F. A. M. Browning) consisting of three airborne divisions, placed under command of Second Army. Having secured the crossings, operations were to be developed to establish a strong force along the line Arnhem—Deventer—Zwolle, facing east, with bridgeheads on the east bank of the Ijssel River. Preparations were then to be made to advance east on the general axis Rheine—Osnabruck—Munster—Hamm, with the main weight of the right flank directed to Hamm. Thence a thrust would be made along the eastern face of the Ruhr. Field-Marshal Montgomery's instructions to General Dempsey were that the drive northwards to secure the river crossings should be made " with the utmost rapidity and violence and without regard to the events on the flanks ". The corridor of supply was to be widened and consolidated while the main advance continued.

3. Because of the long lines of communication, the administrative build-up of Second Army had to be supplemented by road transport which was provided at the expense of lifting fighting formations. At the same time it was vital to prevent the enemy reorganizing and this could only be done if the time for the administrative build-up were shortened. After careful consideration, it was decided to take this risk, subsequently fully justified, and the actual date of the start of the operation was advanced by six days. The operation entailed the largest task yet undertaken by airborne forces, while three ground corps were to take part, 30 Corps leading in the centre and 8 and 12 Corps echeloned back on each flank. For these reasons it can be said that the proposed operation was unique.

The Second Army Plan and the Airborne Tasks

4. The object of Second Army, with airborne forces under command after landing, was to get astride the rivers Maas, Waal and Lower Rhine, in the general area Grave—Nijmegen—Arnhem, and to dominate the country to the north as far as the Zuider Zee, thereby cutting off communications between Germany and the Low Countries. Of the ground formations within the Second Army, 30 Corps was to advance, at maximum speed, to secure the area Nunspeet —Arnhem, while 8 Corps was to move up with the tasks of protecting the right and rear of 30 Corps and, as the latter advanced, to relieve it of the responsibility for flank protection. To carry out this task 8 Corps was to capture Weert and Soerendonk, subsequently extending as far north as Helmond. The left flank was to be protected by 12 Corps, which was to relieve 30 Corps of the responsibility by capturing initially, Rethy, Arendonck, and Turnhout and subsequently advancing to the River Maas, possibly beyond.

5. The airborne force available consisted of Headquarters, 1 Airborne Corps, with under command 1 Airborne Division, 82 U.S. Airborne Division, 101 U.S. Airborne Division, 1 Polish Parachute Brigade Group, 878th U.S. Aviation Engineer Battalion, 2nd Air-landing Light Anti-Aircraft Battery, R.A., and 52 (Lowland) Division (air-portable). The general task given to this force, which was an essential feature of the overall plan, operation "Market Garden ", was the laying of a carpet of airborne troops across the water-ways of the Lower Rhine culminating in a bridgehead force north of Arnhem,— operation " Market ". Simultaneously, 30 Corps was to link-up with the airborne troops by an advance along the main road through Eindhoven, Uden, Grave, Nijmegen and Arnhem—operation " Garden ". In general terms, within the airborne force, tasks were allotted as follows :—

(a) 1 Airborne Division, with under command 1 Polish Parachute Brigade Group, was to capture the bridges at Arnhem and establish a bridgehead round them so that the land formations could continue their advance northwards.

(b) 82 U.S. Airborne Division was to capture the crossings at Nijmegen and Grave and to hold the high ground between Nijmegen—Groesbeek. Headquarters, 1 Airborne Corps was to land with 82 U.S. Airborne Division.

(c) 101 U.S. Airborne Division was to seize the bridges and defiles between Eindhoven and Grave.

(*d*) 878th U.S. Aviation Engineer Battalion and 2nd Air-landing Light Anti-Aircraft Battery were to be flown in by glider, if the situation permitted, to prepare and defend landing strips north of Arnhem.

(*e*) 52 (Lowland) Division was to be flown in to the prepared landing strips in Dakota aircraft.

The two American airborne divisions were to be withdrawn as soon as the ground forces had joined up, but 1 Airborne Division might be required to fight on in a ground role. Our resources in transport aircraft made it impossible to fly the whole of the airborne corps in one lift, and, in fact, four days were required to convey the corps to the battle area together with the provision of supply by air.

1 Airborne Division Plan

6. As was seen in Chapter XVI, Headquarters, First Allied Airborne Army and 1 Airborne Corps had spent the period between June and September, 1944, in planning a series of airborne operations to keep pace with the advance of the land armies. One of these, Operation " Comet ", was cancelled on 10th September, and on the same day Major-General Urquhart received his orders for " Market ". By this time units of 1 Air-landing Brigade and divisional troops were in transit camps alongside the airfields of 38 and 46 Groups, R.A.F. 1 Parachute Brigade and 4 Parachute Brigade, with parachute elements of divisional troops, were in their normal locations in the Grantham area from which they could move direct to the northern group of airfields being used by IX U.S. Troop Carrier Command. 1 Independent Polish Parachute Brigade Group was in the Stamford area and 21st Independent Parachute Company was at the 38 Group Station at Fairford, which was providing the pathfinder aircraft. A tactical divisional headquarters was established at Headquarters, 1 Airborne Corps at Moor Park. The Commander, 1 Airborne Division, issued his orders to the divisional "O" Group at Moor Park at 1700 hours on 12th September, and on that evening information was received that " D " day for the operation would be 17th September. Certain readjustments in transit camps, consequent upon a fresh allotment of gliders and troops to airfields, were carried out on 12th September. On 14th September the divisional commander, accompanied by the Commander, Royal Artillery (Lieutenant-Colonel R. G. Loder Symonds), visited the three British brigade commanders and the Commander, 1 Polish Parachute Brigade Group and co-ordinated any outstanding points in the plan. The loading of gliders and briefing of troops began on 15th September.

7. The detailed tasks given to Commander, 1 Airborne Division, in order of priority, were as follows :—

(*a*) *First Task.*—The capture of the Arnhem bridges, or a bridge.

(*b*) *Second Task.*—To establish a sufficient bridgehead to enable the follow-up formations of 30 Corps to deploy north of the Lower Rhine.

(*c*) *Third Task.*—Immediately after the landing of the first lift, to destroy enemy anti-aircraft defences in the area of the dropping zones and landing zones, and in the area of Arnhem, to ensure the passage of the subsequent lifts of the division.

In addition to the tasks given above, the divisional commander was told that in order to preserve the southern bomb line, no attempt was to be made to effect a junction with 82 U.S. Airborne Division to the south. At the southern-most point held by 1 Airborne Division on the main axis of 30 Corps, whether this was north or south of the Lower Rhine, 1 Airborne Division was to establish a liaison party which would organize the reception and pass-through of the follow-up formations, who were expected to link up not later than 48 hours after the airborne landings.

8. Information supplied to the Division concerning the enemy was scanty, but it was known that the whole of the operational area was being prepared for defence as quickly as possible and he was expected to fight hard on the line of the River Rhine. There was little up-to-date news of the actual enemy formations in the area, but from figures available before June, 1944, it was known that the area of Arnhem—Zwolle—Amersfoort was an important training area, particularly for armoured and motorized troops including units from the Hermann Goering S.S. division and reinforcement units. The following is an extract from 1 Parachute Brigade Intelligence Summary No. 1, dated 13th September, 1944 :—

"To sum up : There is no direct recent evidence on which to base an estimate of the troops in the immediate divisional area. The capacity of the normal barracks in Arnhem, Velp and Ede is nearly 10,000 and billet-ing possibilities are considerable ; moreover Arnhem itself, if the enemy's main defensive line is on the Waal, will be a vital centre on his line of communication and will inevitably contain a number of troops which are out of the line ; it will be strongly defended as soon as the line is manned, but at present may be emptier while the available troops are digging trenches or conducting their fighting withdrawal from the Albert Canal."

The general picture painted was that major enemy resistance would be of a strength of not more than a brigade group, supported by some tanks.

9. Commander, 1 Airborne Division was faced with one outstanding problem. With the air forces available, the lift of the Division could not be completed until the second day of the operation. By this time strong enemy reaction would be developing, and it would be necessary to concentrate the Division within a fairly short perimeter about the Arnhem bridges, preferably on both sides of the river. However, at the time the terrain was thought to be unfavourable for this purpose. South of the bridges, between the Rhine and Waal Rivers was a belt of low-lying polder (fen) land with numerous deep ditches and few roads, very exposed, and considered unsuitable for mass glider landings or for rapid deployment. About four miles north of Arnhem, beyond a dense belt of woods, was some rough heath and dune land, fit for parachute dropping and for limited glider landings, but not for mass glider landings. The airfield at Deelen, in the centre of the area, was heavily ringed by ground and anti-aircraft defences. The only good air-landing terrain near Arnhem appeared to be west-north-west of the town. In Holland, an elevation of a few feet greatly affects the nature of the ground. In this part the level rose above 250 feet, and in large clearings in a wooded belt there were extensive, open, firm areas offering excellent dropping and landing zones. But when sufficient of this area had been chosen to accept the first lift, the line of dropping and landing zones extended from two and a half to eight miles, measured in a straight line, from the main objective of the road bridge at

Arnhem.   Although the initial force, with the advantage of surprise, might assemble successfully, the protection of dropping and landing zones for the second and third days would involve a risk of the forces becoming too thin on the ground.   Moreover the second lift troops would have to advance a considerable distance against rapidly developing opposition to link up on the final objective, and this was liable to cause further delay and casualties.   This fear of the enemy splitting the Division was very real indeed to the divisional commander and was constantly at the back of his mind.

10. However, as no acceptable alternative appeared to exist, the area west-north-west of Arnhem was chosen by 1 Airborne Division and 38 Group.   One dropping zone was in an enemy training area, and the most easterly landing zones were within heavy flak range from Arnhem and from Deelen airfield. Some days before the operation, reconnaissance showed that flak covered all the dropping and landing zones.   The railway running west-north-west from Arnhem intersected the landing zone with a high embankment carrying a power line, but the surface was good, and the map-reading features distinctive.   The allotment of forces to the dropping and landing zones for the various days was designed to conform as far as possible with the final advance towards Arnhem. " S," " X," " Y " and " Z " (see Map 12) would not be used after " D "+1 day.   On " D "+2 day gliders would be landed only on the nearest landing zone " L " and troops dropped only on dropping zone " K " immediately south of the river at Arnhem, accepting the unfavourable terrain for the sake of concentration.   A small but distinctive supply-dropping point " V " on the outskirts of Arnhem was chosen for use on " D "+2 day.   It was hoped that by then, or soon after, contact would have been established with the ground forces.

11. The Commander, 1 Airborne Division, based his plan on three lifts, all landings to take place in daylight.   He intended to form a firm bridgehead round Arnhem with a false front position and standing patrols pushed well out in front of the main position.

(a) *First Lift—" D " day.*—Tactical Divisional H.Q., 1st Airborne Reconnaissance Squadron, 1st Air-landing Light Regiment, R.A., 1st Parachute Squadron, R.E., 9th Field Company, R.E., 1 Parachute Brigade, 1 Air-landing Brigade less certain sub units, 16th Parachute Field Ambulance and 181st Air-landing Field Ambulance.

1 *Parachute Brigade Group,* commanded by Brigadier G. W. Lathbury and consisting of 1st, 2nd and 3rd Parachute Battalions, 1st Airborne Reconnaissance Squadron less one troop, 3rd Air-landing Light Battery, R.A., 1st Air-landing Anti-Tank Battery, R.A., 1st Parachute Squadron, R.E., and 16th Parachute Field Ambulance, were given as first priority the capture of the main road bridge at Arnhem.   As a second priority they were to capture the pontoon bridge to the north-west.

1 *Air-landing Brigade,* commanded by Brigadier P. H. W. Hicks, consisting of 1st Battalion The Border Regiment, 2nd Battalion The South Staffordshire Regiment, and 7th Battalion The King's Own Scottish Borderers, were to protect the dropping and landing zones until the arrival of the second lift on the afternoon of " D "+ 1 day, when the brigade was to concentrate and form a perimeter defence line on the western outskirts of Arnhem.

(b) *Second Lift—" D "+ 1 day.*—4 Parachute Brigade, 2nd Anti-Tank Battery, R.A., one battery of 1st Airborne Light Regiment, R.A., 4th Parachute Squadron, R.E., 133rd Parachute Field Ambulance, the balance of Divisional Troops and of 1 Air-landing Brigade.

4 *Parachute Brigade*, commanded by Brigadier J. W. Hackett, and consisting of 156, 10th and 11th Parachute Battalions were to move eastwards and continue the perimeter line on the high ground just north of Arnhem, linking up with 1 Parachute Brigade midway between the roads Arnhem-Apeldoorn and Arnhem-Ede.

(c) *Third Lift—" D "+ 2 day.*—1 Polish Parachute Brigade Group commanded by Major-General S. Sosabowski, were to land south of the river immediately opposite Arnhem. They were to cross the river by the main bridge and occupy a position on the eastern outskirts of Arnhem.

The Air Plan and Operations

12. On 5th September, General Eisenhower ordered the First Allied Airborne Army to co-operate with 21 Army Group in a northward advance. Lieutenant-General Brereton was to have at his disposal the complete resources of IX U.S. Troop Carrier Command, 38 Group, and 46 Group which was to be under command of 38 Group. Air Vice-Marshal Hollinghurst and Major-General Williams used the Combined Troop Carrier Command Post at Eastcote as a combined headquarters from which all transport operations were controlled. All initial decisions as to route, air cover, weather, etc., were made by Lieutenant-General Brereton and were co-ordinated at the Combined Troop Carrier Command Post. The available air forces were as follows :—

(a) *38 Group.*—Ten Squadrons (two Albemarle, six Stirling, two Halifax) with Horsa and Hamilcar Gliders.

(b) *46 Group.*—Six Squadrons (Dakota) with Horsa Gliders.

(c) *IX U.S. Troop Carrier Command.*—42 Squadrons and one Pathfinder School (Dakota) with Hadrian (C.G.–4A) Gliders.

13. In choosing the aircraft routes the following factors were taken into consideration :—

(a) The shortest distance to target area with due regard to prominent land features.

(b) Traffic control in the air.

(c) Inner anti-aircraft artillery zone and balloon areas in the United Kingdom.

(d) Enemy anti-aircraft and searchlight batteries.

(e) Avoidance of "dog-leg" turns over the sea.

(f) Choice of prominent irregular coast for making land fall.

(g) Shortest distance over hostile territory.

In the same way that the military tasks in the three sectors were inter-dependent, so the air tasks were also inter-dependent. A joint flight plan was necessary to ensure complete co-ordination, and by combining the Arnhem-

Grave–Nijmegen Air Forces into one for the greater part of the flight, fighter cover and ground aids could be shared. It was decided, therefore, to choose two routes, one to the north, travelling over enemy territory from the coast to the target area, and the other to the south travelling over friendly territory from the coast onwards and through a corridor held by our own forces. This was done to provide greater security and to improve the flexibility in the execution of the whole plan. By the simultaneous use of both routes troop carrier forces were subjected to a minimum of ground fire and caused the enemy to divert aircraft over a far greater area. Proof of the wisdom of such a plan was given on " D "+ 1 day when, with the southern route rendered impassable by weather, that to the north was unaffected. Great care was taken in marking the routes, so that navigation was made simple. At the air formation assembly points were radar beacons and searchlight cones. Departure points on the English coast where aircraft started their North Sea crossings were also marked with Eureka beacons and lights flashing code letters. Along the routes, approximately half way between friendly and enemy coasts, were stationed two marker boats, each of which carried Eureka beacons and coded lights.

14. Offensive air support was provided by Eighth and Ninth U.S. Air Forces, Air Defence of Great Britain, Coastal Command and Bomber Command, whose tasks were as follows :—

(a) *Eighth U.S. Air Force and Air Defence of Great Britain.*—On " D " day to attack all flak positions along the route immediately before and during the operation.

(b) Eighth U.S. Air Force to provide light escort over the North Sea throughout the operation and the heaviest possible cover for the remainder of the route to and from the dropping and landing zones.

(c) *Ninth U.S. Air Force* to maintain cover for the landing area by day after the landings, and the Air Defence of Great Britain was to maintain cover by night.

(d) *Bomber Command* to attack enemy day fighter airfields and fixed flak positions on " D " day.

(e) *Bomber Command* to drop dummy parachutes in three areas (west of Utrecht east of Arnhem and at Emmerich), on the night of " D " day/" D "+ 1 day. 2 Group to attack barracks in the landing area, completing its task at " H "— 25 minutes.

(f) *2nd Tactical Air Force R.A.F.* to carry out armed reconnaissances in the landing area.

(g) *Coastal Command* to carry out diversionary missions outside the area of airborne operations.

15. In the Arnhem area 38 and 46 groups would undertake all pathfinder dropping and glider towing, and IX U.S. Troop Carrier Command would carry out all main parachute drops and the later fly-in of airfield engineers and defence units. 38 and 46 Groups would be responsible for supply by air. In the Nijmegen–Grave sector, IX U.S. Troop Carrier Command would be responsible for all tasks except towing of the glider-borne Headquarters, 1 Airborne Corps, which was allotted to 38 Group. In the Eindhoven sector, IX U.S. Troop Carrier Command would be responsible for the complete lift.

16. The flight plan for 1 Airborne Division and 1 Polish Parachute Brigade Group was as follows :—

(a) *1st Lift :* " *D* " *day*
   D.Z. " *X* "
      " *H* " — 20 *minutes*—six aircraft of 38 Group to drop pathfinders of 21st Independent Parachute Company.
      " *H* " *Hour*—149 aircraft of IX U.S. Troop Carrier Command to drop 1 Parachute Brigade.
   †*L.Z.* " *S* "
      " *H* " — 20 *minutes*—six aircraft of 38 Group to drop pathfinders of 21st Independent Parachute Company.
      " *H* " *Hour*—153 aircraft of 46 and 38 Groups to release Horsa Gliders carrying 1 Air-landing Brigade Group.
   L.Z. " *S* "
      " *H* " *Hour*—167 aircraft of 38 Group to release 154 Horsa and 13 Hamilcar Gliders carrying elements of 1 Air-landing Brigade Group.
   Total First Lift
      161 parachute aircraft.
      320 towing aircraft.
      320 gliders.

(b) *Second Lift :* " *D* " + 1 *day*
   D.Z. " *Y* "
      126 aircraft of IX U.S. Troop Carrier Command to drop main body of 4 Parachute Brigade.
   L.Z. " *X* "
      208 aircraft of 38 and 46 Groups to tow 189 Horsa, four Hadrian and 15 Hamilcar Gliders carrying elements of 1 Air-landing Brigade Group.
   L.Z. " *S* "
      62 aircraft of 46 Group to tow Horsa Gliders carrying elements of 1 Air-landing Brigade group.
   D.Z. " *L* "
      35 aircraft of 38 Group to drop supplies.
   Total Second Lift
      126 parachute aircraft.
      305 tug aircraft.
      305 gliders.

(c) *Third Lift :* " *D* " + 2 *day*
   D.Z. " *K* "
      114 aircraft of IX U.S. Troop Carrier Command to drop the main body of 1 Polish Parachute Brigade Group.
   L.Z. " *L* "
      45 aircraft of 38 Group to tow 35 Horsa and 10 Hamilcar Gliders carrying elements of 1 Polish Parachute Brigade Group, and 878th U.S. Airborne Aviation Engineer Battalion.

---

* Dropping Zone.   † Landing Zone.

*S.D.P. " V "

    163 aircraft of 38 and 46 groups for supply by air.

Total Third Lift

    277 parachute and supply aircraft.

    45 tug aircraft.

    45 gliders.

17. Station commanders were briefed at the Combined Troop Carrier Command Post, Eastcote, on 15th September, 1944, and aircrew briefing followed immediately. On 17th September, 1944, there was fog in the early hours of the morning, but this cleared later and the weather at all bases was fit for take off at 0900 hours, the first take-off of the main lift being at 0945 hours. Of the 359 gliders detailed, only one failed to take off, having been damaged on the airfield. One glider combination returned to base early with engine trouble, took off again but was forced to return again. Both these loads were transferred to the second lift. Visibility soon improved to between four and ten miles, but there were patches of thick cloud at about 800 feet which cleared between 1000 and 1100 hours. Before the English coast had been crossed 24 gliders had broken adrift, at least half of them owing to difficulties in cloud. Of these, one crashed seriously, but the remainder made forced-landings and their loads were all returned to base and transferred to the second lift. Over the sea there was little cloud and good visibility. Four gliders were forced to ditch, two by broken tow ropes and two because of tug engine trouble. All glider crews were rescued although one glider was shelled for two hours by enemy coastal guns, the rescue launch coming alongside under fire. A fifth glider was forced down by tug engine trouble and landed on Schouwen Island. Little flak was met on the route to the target area and no enemy fighters were seen by the airborne formations, though some enemy aircraft were engaged by our high fighter cover.

18. The aircraft carrying 1 Airborne Division and 82 U.S. Airborne Division followed two northern routes over Schouwen Island to the interception point at Boxtel where they turned left to their dropping and landing zones. 101 U.S. Airborne Division flew by the southern route over friendly territory from Ostend to the interception point at Gheel where they also turned left to their objective. Over the target area the weather was fine and generally as forecast. On the Nijmegen route one glider landed with a broken tow rope in enemy territory some miles short of the landing zone. On the Arnhem route eight more gliders were lost over Holland, probably owing to difficulties in the wake of the aircraft ahead. Flak of all types was met near the target area, but only one pathfinder aircraft and six tug aircraft were damaged and none was shot down. Dropping and landing zones were clearly recognized in the good visibility and all the ground aids set up by the pathfinders of 21st Independent Parachute Company (Major B. A. Wilson) were operating. Most of the gliders landed first, followed by 1 Parachute Brigade. The parachute drops were extremely accurate but in the light wind prevailing some gliders tended to overshoot. There were very close concentrations of gliders at the north end of landing zone " Z " and at the west end of landing zone " S " but only a few gliders were damaged. Two Hamilcars landed on soft ground on landing zone " Z," bogged their wheels, nosed in and overturned, and their 17-pounder gun loads were lost. The total aircraft and glider losses sustained were small,

---

* Supply Dropping Point.

all parachute aircraft carrying British troops arriving at the target area and only 39 British gliders failing to arrive out of a total of 358. In fact, the dropping and landing of the first lift was outstandingly good. Of the aircraft and gliders carrying the American airborne divisions, 35 American troop carrying aircraft were lost and 16 American gliders were destroyed, most of these as a result of enemy anti-aircraft fire.

19. The take-off on the morning of 18th September for the second lift was delayed by morning fog until 1100 hours. Thick rain cloud at low altitude was spreading slowly north across Belgium towards the target area, making the southern route impassable so that the northern route was used. One glider crashed on take-off owing to tug engine failure but its crew took part in the next lift. Owing to weather conditions, seven gliders made forced landings before crossing the English coast and two gliders were forced to ditch in the North Sea, one breaking up on impact. Heavy flak was encountered over the Dutch coast, but caused no casualties, and all along the route anti-aircraft opposition was stiffer than on the previous day. 15 gliders were lost over Holland and of these it is known that three tow ropes were cut by flak, one glider was shot down and three were forced to release owing to flak damage to glider. or tug. One tug aircraft was unaccounted for. One particular air crew showed outstanding initiative—they belonged to 575 Squadron of 46 Group. The pilot was killed by flak. The second navigator, who was slightly wounded, immediately took control and agreed with the glider pilot to attempt to complete the mission. Shortly afterwards the glider's ailerons were shot away but it was towed back to friendly territory. After releasing, the tug attempted to land at Brussels but failed owing to low cloud and with the help of the first navigator was flown back to Martlesham Heath in England. There, despite the fact that he had never before attempted to land an aircraft, the second navigator made a perfect landing.

20. Again the weather over the dropping and landing zones was fine and again they were easily recognizable, the pathfinders once more having set up their ground aids despite meeting opposition. The drop of 4 Parachute Brigade on dropping zone " Y " was successful, but over the landing zones gliders were released in heavy and medium flak, in spite of which the majority got down successfully. A supply drop was put down on dropping zone " L " and was 80 per cent. successful. Of the total Anglo-American transport air effort for the second lift, 24 British gliders failed to reach the landing zones, two supply aircraft were unaccounted for and 20 American aircraft and 19 American gliders were lost.

21. On 19th September, 1944, the ground battle was becoming increasingly ferocious and the proposed fly-in of 878th U.S. Airborne Aviation Engineer Battalion and 2nd Air-landing Light Anti-Aircraft Battery, and the drop of the Polish Parachute Brigade on dropping zone " K " immediately south of the river at Arnhem were postponed. Only the supply mission and the glider mission to carry some of the heavy weapons and equipment of the Polish Parachute Brigade were ordered. The weather forecast indicated that the northern route might offer better flying conditions, but it was thought unwise to use it for the third successive day and so the southern one was adopted. The weather in England did not lift until after mid-day and take-off was consequently postponed. Seven glider tow ropes were broken, two of these in a cloud over

the sea. Anti-aircraft fire over the enemy coast was not serious but one tow rope was cut by flak and the glider ditched, and in another glider both pilots were wounded in the legs but insisted on completing the flight to the landing zone where they landed successfully. In the latter stages of the flight a second glider was shot down out of control and a further five gliders landed in Belgium or Holland owing to broken tow ropes. Owing to an error of timing at the rendezvous as a result of inadequate communications with the fighter base on the continent, no fighter escort was in evidence when the transport aircraft arrived. It was learned later that they had made the rendezvous earlier, but meeting no transport aircraft assumed that the operation was cancelled and returned to base. The failure of the fighters to keep the rendezvous may have been partly responsible for the marked increase in losses due to flak on that day. Of a total of 44 glider combinations despatched, 14 failed to reach the target area, and of 163 supply aircraft, 13 were shot down. When the supply aircraft appeared over the supply dropping point " V " it was in enemy hands, but although a message containing this information was sent out from divisional headquarters it was never received by higher formations. Consequently the situation was not known to the aircrews. A new dropping zone was marked out near divisional headquarters and every effort was made by the troops on the ground to attract the attention of the aircrews. But the clearings in the woods were small and as the aircraft were flying low the markings could only have been recognized at the last moment in any case. But the markings were not seen by the aircrews, and, in the words of the divisional commander—" We on the ground were only too well aware of the consequences of this signal failure and it was quite pathetic to watch these low flying aircraft being hit."

No history would be complete if it did not pay a tribute to the great gallantry of the supply aircrews who refused to take any evasive action until their drop had been completed and concentrated all their energies on getting supplies to the hard pressed troops of 1 Airborne Division, without any thought of their own lives. One report tells of a Dakota aircraft of 46 Group which, after being hit on its first run in and with its port engine on fire, made a second run in through " fearful flak ". Observers on the ground could see the crew throwing out the supply panniers from the burning aircraft before it went out of control and crashed. In another case a Stirling aircraft of 38 Group was seen to complete the dropping of its supplies, although one engine had been hit, before the crew baled out.

22. On 20th September, it was evident that the situation of 1 Airborne Division was becoming serious and that their supply and early relief was urgent. It was therefore decided to carry out a large supply mission and to transport the parachute element of the Polish Parachute Brigade and the remaining glider element. However, low cloud persisted and at the last moment the drop of the Polish parachutists was again postponed and only the glider and supply missions were undertaken. The glider mission was carried out successfully, but of the 164 supply aircraft despatched, nine were shot down, the remainder reporting successful drops.

23. On 21st September, the weather improved in the morning over England and in the afternoon over the Continent. The opportunity was seized to send troops and supplies to the British Division and to despatch the remaining glider lifts of 82 and 101 U.S. Airborne Divisions. The supply mission was undertaken

by 123 aircraft of 38 and 46 Groups, but the drop was not a success, most of the supplies being recovered by the enemy. 12 aircraft were shot down over the battle area. 41 United States aircraft dropped the Polish Parachute Brigade on to a dropping zone south of the River Rhine, and two miles west of the area originally planned. The drop was successful but seven aircraft were lost. Glider missions for the American airborne divisions were highly successful, including the landing of 325 U.S. Glider Infantry Regiment at Grave to reinforce 82 U.S. Airborne Division.

24. Between 22nd and 26th September, both British and American aircraft concentrated on supply missions with varying success, and the only large scale mission undertaken, other than supply, was the fly-in on the afternoon of 26th September to the air strip west of Grave, of 1st Light Anti-Aircraft Battery and the Airborne Forward Delivery Airfield Group.

The Operations of 1 Airborne Division and 1 Polish Parachute Brigade Group

25. The ground operations of 1 Airborne Division and the Polish Parachute Brigade Group have been divided into four phases which deal with distinctive stages of the battle rather than periods of time. These are :—

(a) The capture of and attempts to hold Arnhem bridge.

(b) The formation of the divisional perimeter.

(c) The withdrawal.

(d) The activities of those left behind.

Both glider and parachute landings of the first lift took place practically without opposition and almost 100 per cent. were put down on the correct landing and dropping zones, starting at 1300 hours 17th September, 1944. Glider landings took place before the parachutists dropped. Casualties on the landing and dropping zones were slight. The concentration at the rendezvous was quick and units moved off from 80 to a 100 per cent. strong. It is worth noting that the time taken to concentrate at the rendezvous was less, and the numbers arriving at the rendezvous were higher, than anything previously achieved in any exercise or operation.

THE CAPTURE OF AND ATTEMPTS TO HOLD ARNHEM BRIDGE

26. The plan of Commander, 1 Parachute Brigade was for 1 Airborne Reconnaissance Squadron less one troop to capture the bridge by a *coup-de-main* advancing on to the town of Arnhem from the west and north. 2nd Parachute Battalion was to move *via* Heelsum along the road running close to the north bank of the River Rhine, relieve the reconnaissance squadron and hold both ends of the bridge facing west and north-west. In the event of the reconnaissance squadron not having reached their objective, 2nd Parachute Battalion was to attack and capture the bridge. 3rd Parachute Battalion was to move *via* the road Heelsum–Arnhem to aid 2nd Parachute Battalion by approaching the bridge from the north and was then to assist in holding the north end of the bridge by facing north-east and east. Meanwhile 1st Parachute Battalion was to move on orders of brigade headquarters to occupy the high ground just north of Arnhem, when it was clear that 2nd and 3rd Parachute Battalions were satisfactorily on their way.

27. By 1530 hours, 17th September, the greater part of 2nd Parachute Battalion, less " B " Company, had moved off from their rendezvous at Heelsum towards Arnhem. They encountered only light opposition on the way which caused some delay and casualties, but by 2030 hours that evening they had occupied some buildings the top storeys of which overlooked the north end of the main bridge across the Rhine, and the road viaduct leading up to it. They were also without " C " Company who had been detached to capture the railway bridge south of Oosterbeek, but this had been blown up in their faces. Some men were actually on the bridge when it went up, but they escaped with wounds. They had then tried to follow the remainder of the battalion but were surrounded in a hotel by enemy tanks and self-propelled guns. They were forced to break out and never re-formed. Later the same night Headquarters, 1 Parachute Brigade arrived at the bridge but without its commander, Brigadier Lathbury.

28. During the night 17/18th September, 2nd Parachute Battalion, with the assistance of 1 Parachute Brigade Headquarters Defence Platoon, made two attempts to capture the south end of the main bridge, once by a direct assault by " A " Company across the bridge, which failed, and once by the defence platoon which was to cross the river lower down by a pontoon bridge, but this had been destroyed. During the night about one and a half platoons of " C " Company, 3 Parachute Battalion, reached the bridge.

29. On the morning of 18th September, the battalion was reinforced by its own " B " Company less one platoon, and by about 25 sappers. After these parties, no other personnel of 1 Parachute Brigade managed to reach the area of the bridge and Lieutenant-Colonel Frost assumed command of the whole force there, about 700 men. During that morning, enemy armoured vehicles attempted to cross the bridge from south to north, but 11 armoured cars and half tracks were knocked out and several others damaged. In the afternoon a strong attack developed along the river bank from the east, but this was held after house to house fighting, at the expense of some casualties. Just before dark several of the houses occupied by the bridge force were burnt down and a little later an enemy attack from the south end of the bridge was repulsed.

30. Meanwhile, 1st and 3rd Parachute Battalions had started to move towards Arnhem along the Ede–Arnhem road and the Utrecht–Arnhem road respectively. Both battalions, however, were held up by enemy opposition and by dark on 17th September had only managed to reach the western edge of Oosterbeek. Major-General Urquhart and Brigadier Lathbury had come forward independently and met at Headquarters 3rd Parachute Battalion. They were prevented by enemy action from returning to their own headquarters that night. During the night of 17/18th September, both battalions had moved south, disengaging from the enemy, in an attempt to link up with the bridge force. 1st Parachute Battalion less " R " Company which had become separated, was held by enemy forces, whom they failed to dislodge, in the area of the road and railway crossing south of Koepel. In the early morning of 18th September they received a message from 2nd Parachute Battalion asking urgently for reinforcements and so they by-passed the enemy and headed for the bridge. Shortly afterwards they picked up Headquarters Company of 3rd Parachute Battalion, which had become separated from its parent unit, and then they met the enemy in strength along the railway and on Den Brink. The battalion attacked immediately but was only partially successful. They were then joined by " A " Company,

3rd Parachute Battalion which had also become separated, and a second and successful attack was made. The whole force reached a point just west of the Elizabeth Hospital where it was held up.

31. In the meantime 3rd Parachute Battalion, with the divisional and brigade commanders, had also reached a point just west of the Elizabeth Hospital, arriving on the morning of 18th September. Then they discovered that " A " and Headquarter Companies, all the transport, three out of the four anti-tank guns and the general's and brigadier's wireless jeeps were missing. For the remainder of the morning the battalion was attacked constantly. That afternoon they were joined by the remnants of " A " Company, who had been with 1st Parachute Battalion, and the battalion, about 140 strong attempted to move through the town towards the bridge. They failed, however, and only managed to make about 300 yards progress before being held up. The divisional commander, brigade commander and brigade intelligence officer attempted to reach the bridge but on the way Brigadier Lathbury was wounded and they all had to remain hidden in a house during the night. While they were in the house a German appeared at a window and the General despatched him with his revolver. The next morning the General and the intelligence officer had to leave Brigadier Lathbury in a cellar while they themselves managed to get back to divisional headquarters in a jeep.

32. On the morning of 18th September, Brigadier Hicks took over the duties of acting divisional commander as nothing had been heard of Major-General Urquhart since the previous evening. He decided to send 2nd Battalion, The South Staffordshire Regiment, less two companies, to reinforce the 1st and 3rd Parachute Battalions and to assist them in their advance towards the Arnhem bridge. By the afternoon 2nd Battalion South Staffordshires, less two companies, had been held up about a quarter of a mile west of where the railway crosses the Utrecht–Arnhem road. The acting divisional commander decided that the other companies of this battalion should join them as soon as they arrived, and that 11th Parachute Battalion should also be diverted as soon as it arrived to assist 1st and 3rd Parachute Battalions to get through to the bridge. The remainder of 4 Parachute Brigade was to carry on with the original plan of securing the high ground north of Arnhem.

33. The second lift was due about 1000 hours on 18th September, but owing to weather conditions in England it did not begin to arrive until 1500 hours. The dropping and landings were successful despite the fact that 7th Battalion The King's Own Scottish Borderers, whose task included the security of the dropping zones, had only just succeeded in dominating the landing zones by a spirited bayonet charge a few minutes before the second lift came in. Fighting continued there to a lesser degree for some time afterwards especially near 10th Parachute Battalion's rendezvous. The battalion was in action almost at once against opposition better organized than itself. Two Germans gave themselves up to Brigadier Hackett " within two minutes after I was out of my parachute harness and I had a couple of prisoners even before I had a command post." Lieutenant-Colonel C. B. Mackenzie, who was General Staff Officer, 1st Grade, (Operations) of the Division, met Brigadier Hackett on the dropping zone at 1515 hours, and told him of the change of plans owing to the strong opposition that 1 Parachute Brigade was meeting.

34. 11th Parachute Battalion moved off at once and by the early hours of 19th September the commanding officer had contacted the commanding officers of the South Staffordshires and 1st Parachute Battalion on the western outskirts of Arnhem. An attempt was then made to carry out a co-ordinated advance along the road and the river bank. The air-landing battalion started to advance towards the bridge through the main street of Arnhem, followed by 11th Parachute Battalion, and at the same time the remnants of 1st and 3rd Parachute Battalions, under Lieutenant-Colonel Dobie, moved along the river bank. As soon as Major-General Urquhart arrived back at divisional headquarters at about 0730 hours that morning and learned the situation he sent Colonel Hilary Barlow, Deputy Commander, 1 Air-landing Brigade and former battalion commander of 7th (Light Infantry) Parachute Battalion, from divisional head-quarters to co-ordinate this movement, but he did not arrive nor was he ever seen again. About two hours after they started, the South Staffordshires were held up at the Monastery in the main street of Arnhem and suffered heavy casualties, and 11th Parachute Battalion owing to enemy counter-attacks had failed in their efforts to dislodge the enemy from the high ground north of the railway.

It was not long before the South Staffordshires had exhausted all their P.I.A.T. ammunition and had been overrun by tanks which inflicted heavy casualties. The battalion therefore withdrew up the road for about half a mile to the west, reorganized and immediately attacked the high ground of Den Brink to secure a pivot for an assault by 11th Parachute Battalion on to the line of the road running north from Den Brink. The South Staffordshires attack succeeded but they were heavily mortared before they could dig in and were again attacked by tanks and overrun. The 11th Parachute Battalion were also attacked by tanks with the result that their own attack never started. The two battalions, which had suffered heavy casualties, then fell back to the area of Oosterbeek Church where they formed a composite force with what was left of the 1st and 3rd Parachute Battalions whose attempts to advance had also failed. This force, some 500 strong, became known as Lonsdale Force under command of Major R. J. H. Lonsdale, second in command of 11th Parachute Battalion. Lieutenant-Colonel Fitch had been killed and Lieutenant-Colonels McCardie, Dobie and Lee had all been wounded and captured. So ended a gallant attempt to get reinforcements through to 2nd Parachute Battalion at the bridge.

35. Meanwhile 2nd Parachute Battalion was still holding on to the north end of the bridge over the river and were being heavily mortared and shelled, the German attacks from the east being resumed with increased violence· throughout 19th September. By that evening five of the houses occupied by our troops had been burnt down, including a key one just east of the bridge. The enemy had occupied areas north and west of the position and, although he did not attempt infiltration from these areas, he was able to keep our positions covered by automatic fire. 2nd Parachute Battalion could not afford to reply to this owing to shortage of ammunition, which by now was acute. The numbers of wounded had assumed serious proportions and they were all evacuated to the cellars of force headquarters.

36. On the morning of 20th September, enemy attacks from the east were resumed once more. The bridge force had dug alternative positions in the gardens of the ruined houses, but these were now shelled at point blank range

by enemy tanks. The 6-pounder anti-tank guns could not be manned as they were under direct enemy small arms fire. A party of the enemy attempted to set charges under the bridge but was counter-attacked and the attempt was foiled. Lieutenant-Colonel Frost was wounded, and Major C. F. H. Gough, Commander of 1 Air-landing Reconnaissance Squadron, who had arrived in the area, took active command of the force, referring all matters of importance to Lieutenant-Colonel Frost. The force was still in touch with divisional headquarters through the Arnhem civil telephone system, as the exchange was operated by Dutch patriots. During the afternoon some of the enemy tanks crossed the river from the north to south, but nevertheless our positions held firm and the bridge was covered by fire through gaps between the burning houses.

37. By that evening the situation was very serious, nearly all the houses occupied by 2nd Parachute Battalion having been burnt down. Just after dark force headquarters house was set on fire and the wounded, now very numerous, were moved to another house but this was also set on fire before the move could be completed. Lieutenant-Colonel Frost ordered the headquarter party to move out and the wounded to be surrendered. By this time the strength of the bridge force had been reduced to about 140 and a further 50 or 60 were lost during the night. Darkness and enemy infiltration made the position worse, and when at 0500 hours on 21st September, an attempt to re-take some houses failed, it was obvious that this was the end. Force headquarters and the remnants of 2nd Parachute Battalion split into small parties and attempted to break out, but the majority became casualties or were taken prisoners during the day.

38. All British opposition at the bridge now ceased, but the troops of 1 Parachute Brigade had carried out the task that had been set them of seizing and holding the bridge and had held it for three days against overwhelming enemy strength until they were physically incapable of further resistance.

THE FORMATION OF THE DIVISIONAL PERIMETER

39. As in the case of 1 Parachute Brigade, the remainder of the first lift concentrated rapidly after landing and moved almost without opposition to its initial position. Divisional headquarters opened up at 1430 hours on 17th September, south-west of Wolfheze. Communication was established between the divisional commander's rover set, 1 Parachute Brigade and 21st Independent Parachute Company, but later was lost with 1 Parachute Brigade. The remainder of the day was uneventful for divisional headquarters, except for occasional firing in the woods and salvoes of rocket-projected mortar bombs, which had the beneficial effect of speeding up the digging of slit trenches. After 1 Airborne Reconnaissance Squadron had been prevented from carrying out their initial *coup de main* on the bridge, Major Gough reported back to divisional headquarters and was told to report to Major-General Urquhart for further orders. In doing so he and his escort were cut off and joined up with Lieutenant-Colonel Frost's force at the bridge as already mentioned. The remainder of the squadron made a determined effort to get through on the night 17th/18th September but failing to do so was pulled back into divisional reserve and occupied a position in the woods south of Reijersheide, on the Arnhem–Ede road. Shortly after dark divisional headquarters moved into four gliders on landing zone " Z."

40. Headquarters, 1 Air-landing Brigade opened in the area of Wolfheze Station by 1600 hours, 17th September. The brigade was deployed for the protection of the landing and dropping zones for the second lift, with 2nd Battalion The South Staffordshire Regiment (less two companies due to arrive in the second lift) at Reijers Camp, 7th Battalion The King's Own Scottish Borderers at Planken Wambuis and 1st Battalion The Border Regiment at Renkum. The night was uneventful except for one platoon of the King's Own Scottish Borderers, which was attacked repeatedly, and for patrols of this battalion which penetrated into Ede.

41. At about 0700 hours on 18th September, divisional headquarters moved to the cross-roads on the Utrecht road a mile south of Wolfheze Station. Shortly afterwards enemy were reported in Heelsum and one company of the Borderers was reported to be surrounded. During the morning, Brigadier Hicks took over the duties of divisional commander and the decision was taken to send the South Staffords to the bridge. The Border company, which had been surrounded, managed to withdraw, but had to leave its supporting weapons behind, and the King's Own Scottish Borderers were engaged in stiff fighting to the north to protect the dropping zones. At about the same time as the second lift was coming in about 35 aircraft carried out a small supply drop which was scattered, but the R.A.S.C. managed to collect a fair proportion. At about the same time divisional headquarters began to move to the Hartestein Hotel, where it was dug in by the evening of 18th September. There was still no news of the General, but divisional headquarters had suffered no casualties. Divisional headquarters was established at the hotel under the impression that it was to be a temporary headquarters only, pending a move to the next bound, when according to the original plan, it moved into Arnhem itself. At first the whole building was occupied with offices on all floors, and slit trenches in the grounds. As the battle progressed and things grew more dangerous the headquarters was gradually reduced, first to the ground floor and then to the cellars in which it spent the last five days of the battle. All those not operationally necessary were moved into the grounds and dug themselves in. A local defence scheme was put into operation and various staff officers and clerks, such as the D.A.A.G. and others, with no particular jobs to do, formed themselves into anti-sniper patrols with a certain amount of success. The German snipers showed great enterprise, one covering the back door of the hotel for the whole of one day.

42. Meanwhile, Brigadier Hackett had been informed of the modification to the plan and ordered 156 Parachute Battalion to lead the advance of the brigade along the line of the railway to the high ground north of Arnhem. 10th Parachute Battalion was to remain for the time being in the area of South Ginkel on the Arnhem–Ede road. Brigade headquarters was to move as soon as possible to a track junction in the woods half a mile east of there and 133rd Parachute Field Ambulance was to follow along the axis of advance as soon as the casualty situation permitted. That evening 4 Parachute Brigade took over the protection of the dropping zones from the King's Own Scottish Borderers who reverted to command of 1 Air-landing Brigade. By dark 156 Parachute Battalion had reached Wolfheze station, 10th Parachute Battalion had halted at the track junction one mile north-west of Buunderkamp, and brigade headquarters had moved to the railway halt immediately south of Buunderkamp. Later that night the brigade commander came into divisional

headquarters and operations were discussed for the following day. It was decided that the brigade should secure the high ground at Koepel, a mile north-west of the outskirts of Arnhem, and was to keep a firm left flank on the road Arnhem–Ede.

43. On the evening of 18th September, the Borders withdrew from Renkum and took up positions with a company each at Graftombe north-west of Hartestein, the crossroads between Oosterbeek church and Heveadorp, astride the Utrecht road south-west of Hill Oek, and at Zilverenberg south of Hill Oek, positions which had been allotted in the original plan and which remained practically unaltered throughout the battle. The King's Own Scottish Borderers started to move towards the high ground between Johanna Hoeve and Koepel, bounded by the railway and the Ede road. These positions were strongly held, and the battalion, after suffering casualties, took up positions at Johanna Hoeve just before dawn on 19th September.

44. Brigadier Hackett's plan for 19th September, was for 156 Parachute Battalion to capture Koepel, while 10th Parachute Battalion formed a firm base on the Ede road about 1,000 yards north of Johanna Hoeve, and 4th Parachute Squadron with one anti-tank troop was to remain north of Johanna Hoeve as a backstop. The King's Own Scottish Borderers were placed under command of 4 Parachute Brigade. Early on the morning of 19th September, 156 Parachute Battalion made two unsuccessful attacks on the Lichtenbeek feature but established themselves firmly half-way between Lichtenbeek and Johanna Hoeve. .

45. In the afternoon, Major-General Urquhart, who had managed to get back to his headquarters that morning, visited 4 Parachute Brigade. It was obvious that they would not make headway on their present axis. It was decided that the brigade would disengage from the enemy and move through 1 Air-landing Brigade's area to form the eastern flank of a division perimeter on a line running through the road and railway crossings south of Koepel, west of Den Brink, and at Oosterbeek Laag. The King's Own Scottish Borderers were to revert to command of 1 Air-landing Brigade. It was still hoped that 4 Parachute Brigade would join up with 1 Parachute Brigade in the town, thus giving the Division a box-like perimeter, the western and eastern flanks held by 1 Air-landing and 1 Parachute Brigades respectively, and the centre by 4 Parachute Brigade. The southern flank would rest in the open ground just north of the river.

46. During the afternoon of 19th September, 4 Parachute Brigade began to disengage from the enemy and to move south-east. The units of the brigade found some difficulty in withdrawing, which they had to do under considerable fire from small arms, mortars, and self-propelled guns from north of the area. While they were attempting to get clear, the Polish glider element arrived, causing violent enemy reaction, an immediate increase in the volume of fire, some congestion, splitting up of sub-units and loss of direction. When darkness fell that night 10th Parachute Battalion and 4th Parachute Squadron, R.E., had reached Wolfheze station, and 156 Parachute Battalion, approximately 270 strong, was on the railway immediately west of Johanna Hoeve. Two companies of this battalion became separated and did not cross the railway. During the night they were attacked and overrun, and only the quartermaster and six

men ever reappeared. Brigade headquarters was near the railway north-east of Wolfheze Hotel. Meanwhile, the Scottish Borderers, after considerable difficulty, concentrated at their rendezvous north of the Wolfheze Hotel. They could find no representative of 1 Air-landing Brigade and eventually they were ordered by divisional headquarters to occupy a position in some woods at Ommershol.

47. Major-General Urquhart returned to divisional headquarters early on the morning of 19th September and Brigadier Hicks then went back to 1 Air-landing Brigade. Divisional headquarters had a quiet morning on this day. In the afternoon an air-supply drop took place but failure in communications meant that the Division was unable to warn the airborne corps, or the base in England, that the dropping zone was in enemy hands. Every effort was made with all types of indicators to attract the attention of the pilots but they had to contend with very heavy flak, and all supplies fell into enemy hands. In any case it is doubtful whether the pilots would have been justified in dropping on to a different point merely on the authority of signs which might well have been placed out by the Germans. The latter, incidentally, did not keep the supplies themselves but distributed them to the local Dutch population.

48. 1 Air-landing Brigade then only consisted of brigade headquarters, 1st Battalion The Border Regiment, and the glider pilots, and were disposed with brigade headquarters at Bilderberg, the Borders in the area from Bilderberg to Heveadorp and the glider pilots in the area of Graftombe. 7th Battalion The King's Own Scottish Borderers did not revert to command of 1 Air-landing Brigade until midnight of that day.

49. The drop of the parachute element of 1 Polish Parachute Brigade Group which was due to form the major part of the third lift did not take place on 19th September, and it was now clear that they could not carry out their original task of landing south of the main Arnhem bridge, crossing it and occupying positions east of Arnhem. It was therefore decided to arrange a new dropping zone for their parachute element, north-east of Driel and to give them the task of holding a firm bridgehead on the south bank of the river in that area.

50. At about 0600 hours on 20th September, the whole of the divisional area was heavily shelled and mortared and this was continued for some time. At the same time 4 Parachute Brigade began to move towards the divisional perimeter. 156 Parachute Battalion was leading the brigade and they came under heavy fire almost at once north-east of the Wolfheze Hotel, but by about 1000 hours they had overcome most of the initial opposition and had reached a point on the main road at the road junction south of Bilderberg. By now the battalion strength was only about 90 all ranks, enemy opposition was becoming considerable, it was difficult to find his flanks and it was obvious that he was in some strength between 4 Parachute Brigade and 1 Air-landing Brigade. Brigadier Hackett's orders were to link up with the Division as soon as possible and he did not wish to become involved in a major action. He therefore tried another line of approach and ordered 10th Parachute Battalion to move round to the east of 156 Parachute Battalion and take the lead, while 156 Parachute Battalion remained in contact with the enemy as rearguard. Although they met a certain amount of enemy opposition, by mid-day 10th Parachute Battalion had reached the road passing Graftombe and were moving south. In the meantime the enemy fire had been growing in intensity with attacks which were pressed home

strongly and by 1115 hours at least two enemy tanks had appeared on the scene. Owing to a misunderstanding 10th Parachute Battalion increased the pace and began " to move in what developed into something like a bayonet charge through the trees " and just after 1300 hours Lieutenant-Colonel Smyth and Major Warre, the commanding officer and second in command of the battalion, with about 60 all ranks, which was all that was left, arrived at divisional headquarters.

51. The remainder of 4 Parachute Brigade could not keep up as 156 Parachute Battalion was still fighting as rear-guard, and brigade headquarters found itself leading the column. The brigade continued to be attacked in a very determined manner by German infantry supported by tanks, which were only prevented from being successful by immediate counter attacks and grenade throwing. Casualties had been heavy, particularly in officers. Among those killed were Lieutenant-Colonel des Voeux, Major C. W. B. Dawson, the brigade major, Captain James, temporarily commanding the Defence Platoon, and Captain G. L. Blundell, the brigade intelligence officer ; the wounded included Lieutenant-Colonel Smyth who died later, Captain R. R. Temple, a member of the brigade staff, and Lieutenant-Colonel Heathcoat-Amory, attached to the brigade. The fighting was almost all at close quarters and everybody from brigade commander to clerk was using whatever weapons he could find. As ammunition was very short many of these were now German. Water was scarce, as there had been no opportunity to fill water-bottles the morning before ; signal communications had failed ; medical attention was non-existent ; rations were exhausted and nothing had been known of events in the rest of the Division since the morning. It appeared to the remnant of 4 Parachute Brigade that the enemy was determined to liquidate their positions before dark. The brigade commander therefore decided to break out and make a dash for the main divisional position. This was successful and by about 1900 hours brigade headquarters, 156 Parachute Battalion, some 70 strong, and 4th Parachute Squadron, R.E., some 50 strong, were in positions on the main road in the area of Hartestein. What was left of the brigade was then placed in position covering the approaches to Hartestein along the main road from Arnhem. By this time the enemy was astride the railway and road approaches between Arnhem and Oosterbeek and prevented all efforts to supply or make contact with 1 Parachute Brigade in Arnhem. Although the remnants of 4 Parachute Brigade were on the main road, there was little or nothing at this stage to stop the enemy if he attacked in the direction of Oosterbeek from the east.

52. In the remainder of the divisional area, 20th September, was chiefly remarkable as being the day when intense mortaring and shelling really started, followed by determined infantry attacks supported by tanks or self-propelled guns. The eastern perimeter could only be thinly held and the result of this was that the main dressing station on the main road east of Hartestein fell into enemy hands, so that the Germans were not far from divisional headquarters. The light regiment was very actively engaged all day in support of 1 and 4 Parachute Brigades. The speed and accuracy with which support was given both now and later prevented many enemy attacks from developing. A supply drop took place at 1700 hours, and, although opposition was again intense, it was more successful than the last and several containers and panniers fell in unit lines.

53. On the morning of 21st September, it became obvious that the stage had been reached in the battle when the plan had to be entirely recast and efforts made to save what remained of the Division. 4 Parachute Brigade had, for all practical purposes, ceased to exist and there was now no question of being able to move offensively. There was little or nothing at this stage to have prevented a strong German attack westwards out of the town of Arnhem towards Oosterbeek. Major-General Urquhart decided to stand firm on the perimeter which had been forming slowly and to build this up with the maximum numbers that were available. He divided his remaining troops into two forces. The force under Brigadier Hicks was to be responsible for the west side of the perimeter and that under Brigadier Hackett for the east side. Brigadier Hicks had under his command the reconnaissance squadron on the main road at Hartestein, The King's Own Scottish Borderers in the woods due north at Ommershol, 21st Independent Parachute Company on the high ground south of Ommershol, the glider pilots to their left at Graftombe, 1st and 4th Parachute Squadrons and 9th Field Company, R.E., in the woods south of Graftombe, and the Borders from there to Heveadorp. Brigadier Hackett had what was left of 156 Parachute Battalion at the cross roads south-east of Ommershol, the remnants of 10th Parachute Battalion, augmented by glider pilots, at the cross roads east of Hartestein, the Lonsdale force at Oosterbeek Church, and 1st Air-landing Light Regiment combined with the South Staffordshires and known as Thompson force, west of the church.

During the morning there was heavy mortaring and shelling, and that afternoon heavy attacks developed against the eastern perimeter. 10th Parachute Battalion was overrun, and most of the houses they were occupying were set on fire. All officers in this battalion had been either killed or wounded and few men were left, but those few appeared again and went back into some of their old houses, where they stood up to constant attack for the next two days. During the day Lieutenant-Colonel Thompson was wounded, Brigadier Hackett was slightly wounded and his second brigade major, Major D. J. Madden, normally on the air staff at divisional headquarters, was killed by the same shell. Units of Brigadier Hicks' force were also heavily attacked during the morning and again in the afternoon, The King's Own Scottish Borderers driving the enemy Units of Brigadier Hicks' force were also heavily attacked during the day and again in the afternoon, The King's Own Scottish Borderers driving the enemy out by a vigorous bayonet charge, which although successful, cost them four officers killed and eight wounded. One company of the Borderers was driven from their position and despite gallant efforts to retake it were forced to fall back. A mid-day air supply drop was not very successful, but one which took place in the afternoon was better. By now there was very little food throughout the Division and scarcely any water, and ammunition was also running very low. The main wireless net to other formations was still working, except to 1 Airborne Corps.

54. The Polish anti-tank battery had landed by gliders on 18th/19th September, and had been allotted tasks within the divisional perimeter. During the evening of 21st September, the parachute element of the Polish Brigade dropped on to the new dropping zone south of the river. That night patrols from the brigade discovered that the Heveadorp ferry had been sunk and that the north bank of the river at this point was in enemy hands. The brigade

was instructed to cross the river and to do this it was planned that the Division would attack the north end of the ferry and send over boats and rafts. When the Poles reached the river they found that neither boats nor rafts had arrived and the brigade commander therefore decided to move to Driel and to establish defensive positions there.

55. Before first light on 22nd September, the divisional perimeter was contracted on the north face. The reconnaissance squadron, 21st Independent Parachute Company, 4th Parachute Squadron, R.E., and an R.A.S.C. party were moved over to the eastern flank, and placed under command of 4 Parachute Brigade, as 10th Parachute Battalion had ceased to exist, and the other two battalions only had a few officers and men each. The ground included in the divisional perimeter was an odd combination of thickly wooded country and built-up areas. The west and centre were well wooded and the northern and eastern flanks were streets and houses. The south flank was the River Rhine. During 22nd September, Lieutenant-Colonel Mackenzie, and Lieutenant Colonel E. C. W. Myers the Commander, Royal Engineers, crossed the River Rhine to contact 1 Polish Brigade, 1 Airborne Corps and 30 Corps, the former returning to 1 Airborne Division during the night 23rd/24th September. The British Liaison Officer of the Polish Brigade arrived at divisional headquarters on this day. On the night 22nd/23rd September, approximately 50 men of 1 Polish Parachute Brigade were ferried across as reinforcements and on the following night another 150 got across, all of them being placed under command of Brigadier Hicks. During the evening of 23rd September, a supply drop took place, but only a very small quantity was picked up, though this did slightly relieve the food shortage for the wounded.

56. On the night 24th/25th September, 250 men of the 4th Battalion The Dorsetshire Regiment of 130 Infantry Brigade (43 Infantry Division) made a very gallant attempt to cross the River Rhine, led by their commanding officer, Lieutenant-Colonel G. Tilly. The landings made were very scattered, owing to enemy fire and the swift river current, a large proportion being in the area of the Heveadorp Ferry which was in enemy hands. The battalion never concentrated as a fighting unit after crossing. This unit deserves a tribute for the brave and determined efforts it made to get through to the airborne troops in the face of stiff opposition.

57. From 22nd September until the morning of 25th September, for those in the perimeter it was a question of withstanding continuous attacks of mortaring and shelling. The force was dwindling steadily in numbers and strength owing to casualties and it was becoming increasingly short of ammunition. Despite this, little or no ground was lost, and the general layout remained the same. From now onwards, rations and water were very short and the evacuation and care of the wounded was always a problem, the main dressing station being in enemy hands for most of the time, though it changed on occasions. Movement became very restricted owing to the infiltration of enemy snipers and, latterly, medium machine guns. The blocking of roads and tracks by fallen trees and branches and by damaged vehicles made the use of the few surviving jeeps almost impossible. The Germans did everything they could to lower the morale of the troops, including the use of a tank fitted with a loudspeaker. It is best described in the words of one of our officers :—" It used to come up, at night usually, very close, and after a burst of ghastly music give us the works over a loud speaker. It told us about our wives and children, the

uselessness of further resistance, the hopelessness of relief from the Second Army and the imminence of attack from at least one armoured division. It was pretty depressing, but the way the boys gave it the bird was most heartening ".

THE WITHDRAWAL

58. In the early hours of 25th September Major-General Urquhart received a letter from the Commander, 43 Infantry Division which was brought across the river by Lieutenant-Colonel Myers. The colonel had remained on the south bank since 22nd September to advise possible reinforcements about crossing the river, and then himself crossed with the Dorsets. The letter explained that the Second Army's intention was not now to form a bridgehead over the Rhine near Arnhem. It also gave the plan for the withdrawal of the Division south of the river on whatever date should be agreed. The divisional commander therefore informed 43 Infantry Division by wireless that the withdrawal must take place on the night of 25th/26th September, and this was agreed. That morning he gave out his orders for the withdrawal. The plan was based on those furthest from the river going first, by two routes which were the best possible, though it was not expected that either of them would be free from enemy interference. They were to be marked as far as possible. Units were to move to the river in parties of 14, which was approximately a boat load. Boots were to be muffled and if possible troops were to avoid fighting on the way to the river and on arrival were to lie down in the mud and wait their turn for a boat. A comprehensive artillery programme to cover the whole withdrawal was arranged with 30 Corps involving the shooting of every available weapon from medium machine guns upwards, and the efficiency of this undoubtedly contributed very largely to the success of the operation. By the time the withdrawal had been ordered the enemy had closed in on either side of the perimeter on the line of the river, with their positions only some 800 yards apart—a very narrow gap to withdraw through.

59. Things were quieter than usual on 25th September until the end of the day, when enemy infiltration increased and became considerable. Brigadier Hackett was seriously wounded and handed over command of 4 Parachute Brigade to Lieutenant-Colonel I. A. Murray of the Glider Pilot Regiment. The enemy was firmly established in a wood in the centre of the division's position and to neutralize them as much as possible a very effective shoot was carried out on to this wood by 64th Medium Regiment of 30 Corps Artillery despite the risk to 1 Airborne Division. At many places, snipers and medium. machine guns were in position inside our lines and most units were to some extent encircled and cut off from their neighbours. Such was the position when the withdrawal began. At 2145 hours the first units to withdraw crossed the starting line, which was the road running east and west alongside Oosterbeek church. The enemy was mortaring and shelling very heavily at this time. However, by 2200 hours his fire slackened and, though there was a considerable amount of spasmodic shelling and other fire, it did not seriously interfere with the movement. The night was dark with an overcast sky, heavy rain and a strong wind. The enemy himself made no move to prevent the withdrawal and, no doubt, 30 Corps artillery concentrations were largely responsible for this. The shooting of 64th Medium Regiment was particularly praiseworthy. Their support, once contact had been made, was almost continuous and targets were engaged rapidly and with great effect. Once ranging had taken place scale 10 was usually asked for, sometimes with many repeats. The C.R.A. of 1 Airborne

Division, Lieutenant-Colonel Loder-Symonds, directed the fire of the guns. In some cases targets were between the C.R.A. and the guns. The fire was so accurate that some targets were engaged within 100 yards of our own troops.

Ferrying across the river began at 2200 hours and continued throughout the night. The behaviour of the troops during the withdrawal and the long wait in the cold rain beside the river was exemplary. This was particularly so as they had been fighting continuously for 9 days, had had practically no sleep or food and only very little water. By dawn on 26th September, when the withdrawal operations had to cease, approximately 1,700 all ranks of the Division and 420 glider pilots had been ferried across. About 300 men still remained, all who could swim having already done so. After crossing, all ranks marched to a rendezvous south of Driel, where tea, hot food and a blanket were supplied by 43 Infantry Division—a very welcome reception. With the assistance of 43 Division, what remained of 1 Airborne Division was concentrated at Nijmegen at 1200 hours on 26th September, having suffered the following casualties during the operation :—

	Killed.	Wounded.	Missing.
Officers	52	27	394
Other ranks	275	229	6,190

These casualties are the figures as they were after the operation, A number of missing returned through our own lines, and others were found later to be in prisoner of war camps.

60. The land/sea element of the Division was already in Nijmegen and had been able to prepare for the arrival of the survivors. This meant that the great majority received their large packs containing a complete change of clothing. 27th September was spent in re-organizing, cleaning and resting. On 28th September the Division moved to Louvain, and on 29th and 30th September it was flown back to the United Kingdom from Brussels airfield.

The Activities of Those Left Behind

61. After the survivors from the divisional perimeter had been evacuated there still remained between 300 and 400 who could not get across the River Rhine to the safety of the Allied Lines. Most of these were men who had been cut off early in the battle or who had been captured and escaped, several from German hospitals and dressing stations. Some of them were wounded and others killed but many escaped into the woods and farms of the surrounding country-side. There they lived for several weeks, looked after by the local civilians who took their lives in their hands, for if the Germans had caught them it would have meant certain death. Among these were Brigadier Lathbury, Brigadier Hackett, Colonel G. M. Warrack, Lieutenant-Colonel D. T. Dobie, Major H. P. Maguire and Major A. D. Tatham-Warter of the 2nd Parachute Battalion. The latter had been wounded, was captured and had escaped and had deliberately remained behind in order to organize operations against the Germans when, as was hoped, Second Army arrived. However, Second Army sent a message saying that it was no good waiting and plans were then made for a mass escape, which eventually took place a month after the main body of the Division had been withdrawn. Lieutenant-Colonel Dobie was in possession of important information concerning escape routes, so that he returned across the Rhine ahead of the others, finally making contact with 21 Army Group after the utmost difficulty.

62. Brigadier Lathbury and Major Tatham-Warter collected 80 officers and other ranks who had made their way to the rendezvous by various routes. Major J. A. Hibbert, Brigade Major of 1 Parachute Brigade, had collected another 40 other ranks who were too far away to get to the rendezvous in time on their feet. They were taken there in lorries, lying on the floor, wearing their uniforms and carrying their weapons. As they debussed in the dark German troops were walking down the road, but they did not challenge. The whole party of 120 all ranks proceeded to the river, which they crossed after a brief encounter with the enemy. The escape had been organized by Major Tatham-Warter, Lieutenant G. S. Kirschen, a Belgian S.A.S. officer (*see* Chapter XIX, para. 39) and the Dutch " resistance " on one side and by Headquarters 101 U.S. Airborne Division and Lieutenant-Colonel Dobie on the other.

63. Many were left behind and conditions became increasingly difficult for them. Brigadier Lathbury's parties had moved down to the river amongst the traffic moving to and fro during the evacuation of Renkum and were able to do so the more easily as this was the last day on which free civilian movement was permitted down to the river. A prohibition zone was established by the Germans along the river bank extending six miles to the north within which no civilian movement was allowed. Unfortunately a great deal of publicity had been given to the escape of the first parties and a British Broadcasting Corporation report said how splendid the Dutch operators in the telephone exchanges had been in helping with the arrangements for the move out. Within 24 hours they had been replaced by Germans and " that was that."

64. A few weeks later another party was formed under Major Maguire, but his task was almost impossible. The troops were no longer in any sort of condition owing to lack of food and general privation, and there was too much optimism on the part of the Dutch. The party was dispersed and much of it captured as soon as it tried to move through the prohibited zone.

65. From then on those who still remained, including Brigadier Hackett, Colonel Warrack and Captain A. W. Lipmann-Kessel, became increasingly associated with the Dutch underground organization. Escape routes were very difficult, but eventually a party including Brigadier Hackett, Colonel Warrack and Captain Lipmann-Kessel got into a route, using canoes, down the River Waal. For a considerable time after this odd groups of men continued to infiltrate back to our lines.

The Civil Population and the Dutch Underground Movement

66. Throughout the whole operation the civil population and the Dutch " resistance " organization were most helpful in providing information and guides, and in assisting with the wounded. They took many risks and suffered casualties and hardship as a result. They assisted in the final evacuation of the main body and without their help it would have been impossible for those who were left behind to escape. During the battle there were just over 100 civilian casualties in Arnhem, with several times that number in Oosterbeek. Practically every house and farm in the area of the dropping zones and the perimenter was badly smashed, and in Arnhem itself, as a result of this battle and of subsequent Allied action, only 150 houses remained undamaged. Immediately after the battle the whole of Arnhem's population of 98,000 people was compulsorily evacuated by the Germans, who then proceeded systematically

to loot and remove the contents of every building in the town. For helping the airborne troops 50 members of the underground forces were executed by the Germans.

Five Victoria Crosses

67. In an operation in which so much bravery was displayed by every officer and man taking part, both in the air and on the ground, it is, perhaps, invidious to select individuals. However, no account of the Arnhem operations would be complete without reference to the five Victoria Crosses which were awarded for acts of valour performed at Arnhem. Four of these were posthumous—Captain L. E. Queripel, The Royal Sussex Regiment, attached to 10th Parachute Battalion, Flight-Lieutenant D. A. S. Lord, 271 Squadron 46 Group, Lieutenant J. H. Grayburn, 2nd Parachute Battalion, and Lance/Serjeant J. D. Baskeyfield, 2nd Battalion The South Staffordshire Regiment, but the fifth, Major R. H. Cain, The Royal Northumberland Fusiliers, attached to 2nd Battalion The South Staffordshire Regiment, lived to receive his decoration from His Majesty The King.

The Operations of the Remainder of 1 Airborne Corps

68. While 1 Airborne Division had been endeavouring to hold its position round Arnhem, the remainder of 1 Airborne Corps had been operating successfully south of the river. 101 U.S. Airborne Division was dropped and landed between Weghel and Eindhoven and consolidated their positions quickly. By dark on 17th September the divisional headquarters had been established in St. Oederrode, and Weghel to the north and Zon to the south had been occupied. Another force pushed west towards Best. The bridge over the Wilhelmina Canal south of Zon was found to be destroyed, but the force crossed the canal over an improvised bridge and at last light had reached Bokt. At mid-day on 18th September, 101 U.S. Airborne Division had occupied Eindhoven and joined up with the Guards Armoured Division advancing from the south.

69. The headquarters of 1 Airborne Corps landed with 82 U.S. Airborne Division, in the Nijmegen area, and these landings were also successful. By the evening of 17th September, the bridges over the river Maas at Grave and over the Maas–Waal Canal at Heumen had been captured, while the high ground south-east of Nijmegen was occupied as well as that south and south-west of Groesbeek. One force had occupied Nijmegen, and corps headquarters was established just south of that city. The bridge over the Maas–Wall Canal at Hatert was found to be damaged, and that at Malden had been blown up by the enemy.

70. The Germans re-acted quickly to the threat south of the River Rhine and their pressure increased throughout 18th September, forcing troops of 82 U.S. Airborne Division to withdraw to the centre of Nijmegen, but nevertheless the number of German prisoners taken by the Division increased. 101 U.S. Airborne Division and the Guards Armoured Division continued to push northwards during 18th September, the bridge at Zon being repaired to carry tanks, and by the morning of 19th September, Grave was reached and a junction was made with 82 U.S. Airborne Division. That afternoon the Commander 30 Corps, Lieutenant-General B. G. Horrocks, joined Lieutenant-General Browning at his headquarters, south of Nijmegen. By that night our

advanced armoured elements were across the Maas–Waal Canal. The late afternoon of 19th September, and all day on 20th September saw severe fighting for the town of Nijmegen and the road bridge over the Waal just outside the town. After a stiff fight, a very courageous attack on the bridge was carried out in the face of murderous German fire from an old fort on the north bank of the river. The tanks of the Guards Armoured Division rushed the bridge frontally while troops of 504 U.S. Parachute Infantry Regiment made an outstandingly gallant assault in boats across the river and attacked the north end of the bridge from the enemy's side. By that night the bridge had been captured, the German demolition fuse having been cut by a Dutch Boy Scout, Jan van Hoof. Further south the enemy infiltrated across the narrow Allied corridor but was pushed back to Schijndel and there was stiff fighting at Best, which our troops had not yet captured. 43 Infantry Division was moving up behind the Guards Armoured Division according to plan. On 21st September, Air Commodore Darvall, flying in an Auster light aircraft, visited Lieutenant-Generals Browning and Horrocks at Nijmegen to discuss the problems of supply by air before the anticipated join up with 1 Airborne Division. These discussions had the following results :—

(a) The production of an anti-flak plan for aircraft and medium artillery to assist the fly-in of supplies.

(b) The immediate use of Brussels airfield by Dakotas where direct communication with the forward area and the tactical air force was assured, thus permitting the use of fleeting opportunities and facilitating supply.

(c) The opening of Grave airfield for Dakota operations.

71. On the same day the Guards Armoured Division and elements of 43 Infantry Division made a determined effort against stiff resistance, and under the handicap of heavy rain, to reach the beleaguered 1 Airborne Division. By that evening leading units had pushed several miles towards the Rhine north of the Waal and were able to bring artillery fire down in support of the troops at Arnhem. Meanwhile the Germans continued to put in determined counter-attacks from Reichswald to the Nijmegen area, and heavy fighting continued at Best. 506 U.S. Parachute Infantry Regiment attacked in the direction of Wintelre, and Headquarters 101 U.S. Airborne Division was moved from St. Oedenrode north to Uden. 11 Armoured and 3 Infantry Divisions were moving up the right flank of the corridor towards Helmond.

72. On the afternoon of 22nd September, the Guards Armoured Division was held up at Elst, but the leading elements of 43 Infantry Division by-passed this resistance to the west and contacted the Polish Parachute Brigade at Driel, when the ferry service across the Rhine, which has been referred to earlier, was put into operation. At Nijmegen 82 U.S. Airborne Division was consolidating its position by clearing the enemy from the bend of the Waal to the east towards Beek but south-west of Grave the corridor was cut for the second time by the Germans. The enemy reached the main road between Uden and Weghel and were able to maintain their position until the following morning when they were forced to withdraw by an attack by the Guards Armoured Division.

73. The next few days were spent by the American divisions in consolidating their positions and, with the Guards Armoured Division and 43 Infantry Division, in attempting to break through to the rescue of 1 Airborne Division.

However, in the late afternoon of 24th September the corridor was again cut by the Germans between Weghel and St. Oedenrode and again the enemy managed to maintain his position astride the road, this time for 36 hours. As a result, there was no traffic at all on the road on 25th September. That afternoon an attack was launched by 101 U.S. Airborne Division to re-open the road south of Weghel and the following morning the Germans were forced back once more. Nevertheless, the road remained within German artillery range. Meanwhile 82 U.S. Airborne Division was advancing into Germany beyond Beek. This ended the period of fighting so far as the airborne troops were concerned in this particular operation.

74. The battle at Arnhem had been designed to gain quickly, and at relatively cheap cost, a bridgehead beyond the Rivers Waal and Rhine. It had to be undertaken with resources which left very little margin for the ensurance of success in view of the remarkably rapid recovery of the enemy, and at a time of year when it was necessary to expect considerable risks with the weather. Field Marshal Montgomery gave it as his opinion that had 1 Airborne Division received the planned measure of airborne reinforcements and supplies, together with the full scale of support from the air, the result would have been very different. He believed that the link up with 1 Airborne Division would have been effected had it been possible accurately to drop the Polish Parachute Brigade on " D "+ 2 day together with the glider regiment of 82 U.S. Airborne Division. At the same time the normal scale of action by the Allied Air Forces would not only have impeded the enemy pressing in on the Arnhem bridgehead but would have greatly retarded the speed with which he was able to react and bring forward his reinforcements. The Field-Marshal considered that the battle of Arnhem was 90 per cent. successful, that we had undertaken a difficult operation attended by considerable risks and that it was justified because, had good weather held, we should have attained full success. He paid the following compliment to 1 Airborne Division :—

> " A great tribute is due to 1 Airborne Division for the magnificent stand at Arnhem ; its action against overwhelming odds held off enemy reinforcements from Nijmegen and vitally contributed to the capture of the bridge there. Such reinforcements as did reach Nijmegen were forced to use a long detour to the east and a ferry crossing, and there is no doubt that the delays thus imposed were instrumental in enabling us to secure the Nijmegen bridges intact ".

The magnificent fighting qualities of the troops on the ground must not be allowed to overshadow the very staunch and gallant efforts of the airmen in trying to get supplies through in the face of appalling flak. In 46 Group alone for example, some 30 per cent. of the aircraft were lost or so badly damaged as to be " write offs " or contractors' repairs and of the remainder, 80 per cent. were damaged. The airborne troops themselves would be the first to pay a sincere tribute to the airmen for their complete disregard for their own lives. For his part Major-General Urquhart, commander of the Division, in his official report of the operation stated " the operation ' Market ' was not a 100 per cent success and did not end quite as was intended. The losses were heavy, but all ranks appreciate that the risks involved were reasonable. There is no doubt that all would willingly undertake another operation under similar conditions in the future. We have no regrets ".

Administration

75. After 6th June, 1944, the role allotted to 1 Airborne Division was in effect that of standing-by to carry out at short notice operations of widely varying natures anywhere in France or in the Low Countries, as was related in Chapter XVI. As a result it was essential that any administrative plan embodied two principles :—

(a) The plan had to be flexible to cope with the varying types of operation, different orders of battle and the varied numbers of aircraft allotted for administrative purposes.

(b) It had to be simple so that it could be easily digested by units in the short time available for briefing.

The preparation and subsequent cancellation of a series of operations, some at very short notice, enabled the administrative drill to be worked out so that the plan could be thoroughly understood by all concerned. Before 6th June, 1944, two comprehensive administrative instructions, described in Chapter XIV, were issued by 1 Airborne Corps. Subsequent to this, all administrative orders were based on these instructions and the only details sent out for operations were :—

(c) Allotment of troops to transit camps.

(d) Allotment of troop carrying transport to airfields.

(e) Allotment of aircraft to administrative echelons.

(f) Details of supply by air.

(g) Money exchange arrangements.

76. The transit camps occupied varied according to the allotment of units to airfields which, in their turn, were different for each operation. For the Arnhem operation both parachute brigades took off from airfields in the Grantham area and were therefore able to use their own billets. The remainder of the Division occupied camps on airfields in the south of England extending from Manston in Kent to Tarrant Rushton in Dorset. The movement of troops to transit camps and later to airfields required more transport than could be provided from divisional resources. Therefore, three additional War Office controlled R.A.S.C. companies were attached to the division during the preparatory period. However, if the whole division had taken off in one lift, working on an allotment of one vehicle to each parachute aircraft, it is doubtful whether even these would have been sufficient.

77. The maintenance plan was based upon the fact that the ground forces would link up with the division after four days—a deliberate over insurance—and was as follows :—

(a) All troops were to land with two 24-hour rations and one emergency ration for each man, and all gliders were to carry one box of *compo*.

(b) Sufficient petrol was to be carried for 350 miles a vehicle.

(c) First line scales of ammunition plus a considerable amount of certain extra ammunition were to be carried in spare containers by units, airborne vehicles of the R.A.S.C. and bulk loaded Hamilcars. It was appreciated that the following types of ammunition would be particularly required and these formed the bulk of the load of the R.A.S.C. vehicles and Hamilcars—75-mm., 6-pounder, 17-pounder, 3-inch mortar H.E., and P.I.A.T.

(d) Only sufficient Ordnance personnel to receive, list and issue stores received by air were to be taken as a large detachment was not considered necessary. A certain amount of space was allotted to Ordnance stores in the bulk loaded Hamilcars.

(e) All jeeps were supplied with spares in order that repairs could be carried out by drivers. With regard to the men brought by R.E.M.E., it was considered that their main task would be the maintenance of wireless sets and weapons, and that there would be no time or opportunity during the operation for major repairs to vehicles.

(f) One parachute platoon R.A.S.C. was to be dropped or landed with each brigade. Five gliders were allotted to each parachute platoon for jeeps and trailers, which would be used to carry spare ammunition for the brigades in the initial stages, but would later revert to control of Commander R.A.S.C. for use in clearing divisional supply drops. 18 Horsa Gliders were used for one light transport platoon, R.A.S.C., who were to carry divisional spare ammunition and to carry out normal R.A.S.C. duties within the Division.

(g) One section of provost was to be dropped or landed with each brigade and two sections with divisional headquarters.

78. Before the Division took off for Arnhem, lists of ammunition and stores required for supply by air, based on the figures of aircraft available, had been given to Headquarters, 1 Airborne Corps, and certain supply dropping points had been pre-selected. The marking of supply dropping points was to be carried out by personnel of 21st Independent Parachute Company using Eureka equipment (see Appendix D). After the drops, all stores were to be cleared to the divisional maintenance area by R.A.S.C. and issued to units on demand. Any surpluses built up were to be handed over to Headquarters, 1 Airborne Corps on its arrival. The supply by air of the Division was unsuccessful and the main causes of this were as follows :—

(a) In the early stages the lack of communications prevented the changes of supply dropping points being notified to base.

(b) Enemy anti-aircraft defences were strong and caused considerable losses to aircraft.

(c) The lack of communication between ground and air prevented the exact location of dropping points being notified to the aircraft when overhead.

(d) The comparatively small size of the perimeter, combined with (b) and (c) above, caused the major portion of the supplies dropped to fall into enemy hands.

(e) The constant shelling and mortaring and consequent lack of vehicles made collection and distribution on a divisional and even at brigade level impossible in the later stages. Units merely recovered what they could from containers dropping in their own area.

79. Previous operations had shown that a jeep and trailer carried in a Horsa Glider cannot carry economic loads of ammunition and supplies, and it had always been appreciated that a supply drop was an unsatisfactory method of supply. For the operations, therefore, it was decided to experiment in loading three Hamilcars, complete with stores, using R.A.S.C. to clear them to divisional

maintenance area on arrival. All these Hamilcars landed safely and two were completely unloaded, the third falling into enemy hands. Their loads proved invaluable and formed the basis of divisional maintenance centres which were set up early in the operation.

80. The land/sea element of the Division contained some thousand vehicles which were despatched to France about six weeks before the operation. These vehicles were loaded with second line ammunition, explosives, *compo* rations for the whole division, petrol for 50 miles for every vehicle, mess packs, cooking equipment and office equipment. In addition, each vehicle carried 12 rounds of 75-mm. howitzer ammunition, giving a total of 4,500 rounds over and above the normal second line allotment. The land/sea element arrived in the Nijmegen area with the forward troops of the Guards Armoured Division, early in the operation, and had they made contact they would have been invaluable in replenishing the Division. As it was they proved extremely useful to Head-quarters, 1 Airborne Corps, who handed the 75-mm. ammunition over to the American airborne divisions and used the medical stores, rum, rations, etc., for units of the Corps and for maintaining 1 Airborne Division after its withdrawal across the River Rhine.

81. The medical plan was based upon field ambulances being under command of brigades and was as follows :—

(a) 181st Air-landing Field Ambulance (Lieutenant-Colonel A. T. Marrable) was to establish a dressing station in the area of Wolfheze which was to remain open until the evening of " D "+ 1 day, when it was antici-pated that the Air-landing Brigade would withdraw to Arnhem. This dressing station was to deal with casualties from all dropping and landing zones and from 1 Air-landing and 1 Parachute Brigades in their initial tasks. As the dressing station was only to be kept open for 36 hours, surgery was to be kept to a minimum. On arrival in Arnhem a dressing station was to be opened at the Deaconess Hospital.

(b) 16th Parachute Field Ambulance (Lieutenant-Colonel E. Townsend) was to establish casualty clearing posts as required, and was to evacuate casualties to 181st Air-landing Field Ambulance in the early stages. It was to establish a dressing station in Arnhem, probably at the Saint Elizabeth Hospital, as soon as the town had been captured.

(c) 133rd Parachute Field Ambulance (Lieutenant-Colonel W. C. Alford) was to establish a dressing station in the Arnhem area on arrival, probably in the Municipal Hospital.

(d) The Polish Parachute Field Ambulance was to open casualty clearing posts as required, and would be informed of its final tasks on arrival.

82. On 17th and 18th September, the medical services functioned more or less according to plan, and by the evening of 19th September, both 133rd Para-chute and 181st Air-landing Field Ambulances were established side by side in Oosterbeek. On 20th September both these units were captured and the majority of medical officers and other ranks were removed to a prisoner of war cage, though a small number were allowed to remain with some 40 seriously wounded casualties. From 21st September onwards these personnel formed a

small hospital in the Municipal Hospital. Meanwhile, 16th Parachute Field Ambulance, having opened as ordered, had been captured at Arnhem on 18th September, and all but the surgical teams, who also went to the Municipal Hospital, were sent to prisoners of war cages. Thus by 20th September, all three medical units were in enemy hands, and the only divisional medical services remaining were the reserve section of the air-landing field ambulance, Colonel Warrack and his staff, and those regimental medical officers still with units. These were all amalgamated to form an improvised dressing station within the perimeter, which was later captured.

83. In the meantime those medical personnel who had been allowed to remain behind at the Municipal Hospital had their hands full, although they were reinforced by Lieutenant-Colonels Alford and Marrable who were allowed by the Germans to join them. At one time there must have been 300 casualties there, including a large number who had been evacuated by the Germans from the dressing-station which they had captured within the perimeter. A few days later the Germans began to evacuate our wounded from the Municipal Hospital, most of them to Apeldoorn, until finally only 30 seriously wounded cases were left.

84. On 24th September, Lieutenant-Colonel M. E. M. Herford, of 163rd Field Ambulance (43 Infantry Division), organized an attempt to get medical supplies over the river. However, the remainder of his party and his supplies were captured, so that the attempt failed. Nothing daunted, Lieutenant-Colonel Herford contacted the German senior medical officer, and arranged for the barracks at Apeldoorn to become a hospital for British wounded, and for it to be staffed by the medical personnel from Oosterbeek. On 26th September, Colonel Warrack arrived and took command of the hospital. While it was being organized the Germans were evacuating parties of wounded and medical personnel to the interior of Germany. The evacuation arrangements were bad, and as a result of strong protests from Lieutenant-Colonel Herford, who spoke fluent German, they were improved and properly equipped hospital trains were provided. The Dutch gave valuable assistance, providing stores and surgeons. By 30th September, there were some 850 cases in the hospital, a number having been brought in from surrounding German hospitals and the British hospital in Arnhem, which closed on 12th October, and some 250 medical personnel. Evacuation went on until 16th October, when the hospital was almost clear, and that night Lieutenant-Colonel Herford escaped.

85. Collection of casualties into the dressing stations was difficult in the early stages owing to lack of transport, and later owing to the close contact with the enemy. Intercommunication between the divisional medical staff and the medical units was impossible in the early stages, and later was only established by personal contact through the enemy lines under Red Cross protection. The initial supplies landed were adequate for three days working, after which plasma and penicillin became short owing to the failure of the supply drop, the only replacements available being those taken through the lines under the Red Cross. It is worth noting that plasma picked up from the dropping zone three weeks after it had been dropped was in good condition. Supplies were supplemented to a certain extent by German medical services. On the whole the enemy were co-operative and rendered assistance in the care of wounded.

86. In an operation of this sort it is almost impossible to estimate the number of casualties treated, but between 17th September and 16th October it appears to have been over 2,000, all members of the Division. It is known that Captain Lipmann-Kessel alone performed 96 surgical operations up to 12th October while he was at the Municipal Hospital.

Lessons

87. As in any operation there were many lessons of organization and equipment in the Arnhem battle, but as these have all been put right it is not proposed to go into them here. We will only deal with the main lessons which are set out below.

88. An airborne division is designed to fight as a whole, but if, as at Arnhem, it is split and part carried in a second lift some 24 hours later, the effective strength for immediate offensive action will be reduced to that of a brigade, which is what happened. This was because it was necessary to allot part of the first lift to protect the dropping and landing zones of the following troops. In addition, by the time the second lift arrived the enemy had been " stirred up," and the second lift had to land against opposition and fight its way to its objectives, thus prejudicing the success of the whole operation. The lesson learned was that if the greatest advantage were to be taken of initial surprise the division must be landed complete in one operation. This is especially important when the weather on subsequent days may be uncertain, but the rapid concentration of hostile flak which should be anticipated would, in any case, render later air operations increasingly costly. In this connection it is interesting to note that the original air plan suggested by 38 Group was for the first lift to arrive over the target area before dawn, thus permitting a second lift to be brought in later the same day. The land-marks were good and there should have been little difficulty in identifying the dropping and landing zones. However, the proposal was not accepted by First Allied Airborne Army because IX U.S. Troop Carrier Command were not trained up to the standard of night work required.

89. The reasons for the choice of the dropping zones so far from the objectives are not clear. At the time of writing this history a senior airborne and senior R.A.F. officer gave the following points of view. The airborne officer said :—

> " It was appreciated that although small parties of parachutists and some gliders organized in a *coup-de main* role might be put down very near to the objectives and in the actual outskirts of the town, anything in the nature of mass landings, either glider or parachutists, was out of the question. In fact, when operation " Comet " was planned, it was then arranged for some *coup-de-main* parties to go in on the three bridges at Grave, Nijmegen and Arnhem. The impression which is uppermost in my mind, and which I am sure influenced the decision of the choice of actual D.Zs., was that the R.A.F. would not accept the risk of dropping parachutists in mass, or landing a large number of gliders within a light flak radius of Deelen airfield and of the town of Arnhem itself. If a mass landing was to be attempted, then the ground selected must be such that the very large stream of aircraft which was involved could fly straight to the D.Z. area without coming in contact at a low level with light flak. It was this factor, when considered with the actual layout of the ground itself which forced the choice of the actual area chosen."

The R.A.F. officer said :—

" In point of fact there was little accurate information as to the location of active flak ; and in any case, light flak (which was the danger so far as the parachute and tug aircraft were concerned) is not static. It was known that Deelen airfield would probably be heavily defended and that area was ruled out for a day operation in consequence. The overriding factor in the choice of the L.Z.s/D.Z.s, *i.e.*, whether they were to be in the suburbs of Arnhem or west-north-west of the town, was the ability of the gliders to get down in enclosed country. The experience of the U.S. glider pilots in enclosed country on " D " day was still fresh in people's minds. The presence or otherwise of flak was incidental . . . there was no question of avoiding . . . flying in the face of enemy flak."

Whatever the reasons, it seems that more risks might have been justified during the initial stages of the operations. It appears that it would have been a reasonable risk to have landed the division closer to the objectives. Previously it had always been the rule when planning that the maximum distance from the dropping or landing zones to the objective should not exceed five miles. In the Arnhem operation, as has been stated previously in this account, the distance was seven and, in some cases, eight miles. The division did obtain initial surprise but its effect was lost owing to the time lag of some four hours before the troops could attack their objectives. By then the enemy had taken up defensive positions between the dropping zones and the bridge.

90. If the plan had included a whole brigade to be dropped near the Arnhem bridge on " D " day the outcome of the battle might have been very different as a longer delay would have been imposed on the enemy. Similarly, both sides of the obstacles were in enemy hands, and it would almost certainly have paid a big dividend if troops had been dropped or landed at the same time north and south of the Arnhem bridge.

91. Excessive reliance was placed both by R.A.F. and Army, on photographic interpretation of the ground and on intelligence appreciation of the flak defences in the area. In fact these forecasts proved to be pessimistic. Parachute troops could have been dropped in an open area on high ground two miles north-east of the town. Another area immediately east of Arnhem and north of the Rhine, the centre of which was two miles from the bridge, was suitable for parachute troops and probably gliders, as was the area south of the bridge. It would have been possible to have landed a small glider *coup de main* party, near the bridge, as was done for the Normandy operations.

92. The intelligence information supplied to 1 Airborne Division was sketchy and inaccurate ; there was little detailed information of enemy troops in the neighbourhood ; and for security reasons no attempt could be made to maintain liaison fully with the Dutch underground movement. There was no previous knowledge of the presence of II S.S. Panzer Corps, consisting of 9 and 10 S.S. Panzer Divisions, which were refitting in the neighbourhood. This lack of information naturally had an effect on formation commanders' plans, and especially on those of Brigadier Lathbury, Commander, 1 Parachute Brigade. He based his plan on getting the bridge quickly against minor opposition, and took risks, ordering his battalion commanders to advance on a wide front, move quickly and by-pass enemy opposition. He assumed that

any troops in Arnhem would be second-line personnel of poor fighting quality. Such a plan is quite unsuitable against anything like strong opposition as control is lost easily, units tend to get split up and the brigade commander has no reserve. As it was, the strong opposition appeared in the shape of armour, which the brigadier had not catered for, and the plan only succeeded in so far as 2nd Parachute Battalion managed to slip through to the bridge, but the ultimate result was chaos and the defeat of units in detail. Had the brigadier been told the real strength of the enemy he would undoubtedly have adopted a different method. Similarly the reconnaissance squadron would not have become involved in heavy fighting at Wolfheze only a short distance from the landing zone, if our intelligence had been better. The result was that the fighting effectively stopped the *coup de main*.

93. The operation suffered from a lack of close offensive air support throughout and this would have been especially invaluable during the first afternoon. If there had been a " cab rank ", available then and on subsequent days, the effect on the enemy would have been considerable. Offensive support during the period when troops were on the move might easily have turned the scale and allowed the whole of 1 Parachute Brigade to have concentrated near Arnhem bridge. The few sorties that were produced were very effective.

94. The whole question of supply by air needed reorganizing, and this was especially evident from the fact that there was no reliable method of communicating a change of supply dropping points to the aircraft at the last possible minute. The air contact team normally used for offensive support could, in future, also be used for the purpose of controlling supply by air.

95. During the operations there was no really effective overall air command for communication between the air transport groups, the divisions on the ground and the tactical air forces.

96. The operations showed that an elaborate anti-flak plan is necessary during the initial phases and for supply by air. If the enemy build-up round the dropping area is more rapid than the advance of the supporting forces, not only are the dropping zones likely to be overrun before the supply sorties arrive, so that the enemy will receive the supplies, but flak becomes so severe as to be prohibitively costly to the supply aircraft.

97. It was proved again that the principle of an early relief of airborne troops, usually within 48 hours, was sound where the enemy was well organized and that the dropping of air supplies could not be relied upon in conditions of uncertain weather and enemy flak concentrations. But the link-up failed. If this principle were to be successful the build-up of our forces by ground and air should be as fast or faster than that of the enemy.

98. The operations proved that high-powered wireless sets, and more of them, were required. Throughout the battle, communication was bad. The main sets for liaison with aircraft and with the airborne base were damaged on landing and never in fact functioned. There was little or no direct communication with 1 Airborne Corps for the first two or three days and many of the messages that were passed were sent through the British Broadcasting Corporation set *via* London, or over the G.H.Q. Liaison Regiment (Phantom) detachment's set.

The Enemy Point of View

99. From German documents captured later it was learned that the Germans admitted that the Arnhem operations took them by surprise, although the possibility of Allied airborne operations was discussed by General Rauter, the commander of the S.S. troops in the area, and Field-Marshal Model, commander of Army Group " B ". The latter dismissed the likelihood of airborne landings because :—

(a) The Allies would consider parachute troops too valuable for such a hazardous operation.

(b) The distance from Nijmegen to Arnhem was too great.

(c) Antwerp was under German V.2 fire which would make it impossible for the Allies to use the port. He considered that this would stop the Allied administrative build-up, as land lines of communication would be too long.

100. The Germans thought that the attacks against the anti-aircraft positions were an attempt to destroy the bridges. However, they considered that we used too much of our air force in protecting the airborne landings instead of interfering with the movements of German reinforcements. They said that we lost surprise because our troops took so long to get into action against their real objectives. They considered that the Allies' chief mistake was not to have landed the entire 1 Airborne Division at once, and not to have dropped a second division east of Arnhem.

CHAPTER XXI

THE CROSSING OF THE RIVER RHINE AND THE ADVANCE TO THE BALTIC, MARCH TO MAY, 1945

The Land and Air Situation

1. After the defeat of the Germans in the Ardennes it was necessary to strike quickly before they could reorganize. The Supreme Commander therefore accepted Field-Marshal Montgomery's plan to clear up the area between the Rhine and the Meuse from Dusseldorf to Nijmegen and to establish a bridgehead north of the Ruhr. The Ninth U.S. Army (General W. H. Simpson) was to be under command of 21 Army Group for the operations. After clearing the area the Allies were to line up along the River Rhine, Ninth U.S. Army from Dusseldorf to exclusive Mors, Second Army (Lieutenant-General Sir Miles Dempsey) from Mors to inclusive Rees, and First Canadian Army (General H. D. G. Crerar) from exclusive Rees to Nijmegen. The Rhine was to be crossed in the vicinity of Rheinberg, Xanten and Rees. By 13th February, the British and Canadians had completed the first phase of the operations. On the right they were pushing towards Goch, the Reichswald Forest was completely in their hands, and in the north the Canadians had reached the Rhine opposite Emmerich.

2. The attack of Ninth U.S. Army, which had been held up by the flooding of the River Roer by the Germans, began on 23rd February, and by the end of the month they had captured Munchen Gladbach and were advancing towards Neuss.

3. On 7th March, First U.S. Army (General Hodges), which had been advancing with great drive and determination, secured undamaged the railway bridge at Remagen by a display of outstanding initiative, and immediately began to form the first Allied bridgehead on the east bank of the Rhine. Meanwhile, Third U.S. Army (General G. S. Patton) pushed forward to the Rhine at Coblenz, and subsequently established a bridgehead south-west of the city over the River Moselle, and later over the Rhine. On 15th March American troops thrust southwards from this bridgehead and eastwards from Trier, while Seventh U.S. Army (General A. E. Patch) attacked northwards between the Rhine and Saarbrucken. Seventh U.S. Army forced their way through the Siegfried defences and pinned down the German troops there, thus allowing the armoured columns of the Third U.S. Army to drive into the rear of the enemy positions. The result was that all resistance between the Moselle and the Rhine crumbled, the Saar was enveloped and Mainz and Worms were captured so that by the third week in March we were on the banks of the Rhine for the whole of its length.

4. By March, 1945, the Allied armies in the North West European theatre under General Eisenhower had been built up to a total strength of nearly 4,000,000 men. The difficult manpower situation with which these armies had been confronted during the Ardennes battle had been remedied and they were once more at full strength, and were displaying a very high morale and battle effectiveness. The enemy was in an unenviable position. He had thrown all his resources into the battle of the Ardennes, in which he had hoped to split

296

the Allied armies and to drive through to Antwerp. In this he had failed and had been driven back with severe punishment and heavy losses in men and material. On New Year's Day he had carried out a large scale air offensive on the airfields in the neighbourhood of Brussels and elsewhere but, although he had inflicted severe losses upon Allied aircraft, he had suffered much heavier losses himself. He had, as the Allied High Command had hoped, and attempted to compel, elected to stand and fight west of the River Rhine, with results that had been disastrous to him. After his defeat in the Ardennes he had been compelled to retreat behind the Rhine but he was now in no condition to hold fast even in these positions. His powers of resistance had been reduced by an increasing shortage of weapons, ammunition and oil, which had resulted from Allied air attacks against his war economy. His losses in battle had been crippling and these inevitably caused a deterioration in the morale of all but his elite units. More and more he was forced to entrust his defence to the local Volkssturm who would fight courageously enough for the protection of their homes, but as field units, were at times as much a liability as an asset.

Higher Formation Plans and the Airborne Tasks

5. In the meantime preparations were being made to implement Field-Marshal Montgomery's plan for a crossing of the Rhine north of the Ruhr, and on 9th March he issued written orders confirming plans that had already been agreed. (*See* Appendix N for detailed higher planning time-table.) The Field-Marshal's intention was to secure the bridgehead before developing operations to isolate the Ruhr and to advance into the northern plains of Germany. Ninth U.S. Army remained under the command of 21 Army Group. The outline plan was to cross the Rhine on a front of two armies between Rheinberg and Rees using Ninth U.S. Army on the right and Second Army on the left, the principal initial objective being Wesel which was an important centre of communications. It was intended that the bridgehead should extend to the south sufficiently far to cover Wesel from enemy ground action and to the north to include bridge sites at Emmerich, and was to be deep enough to allow large forces to form up for the drive to the east and north-east. The target date for the operation was set as 24th March. The total available Allied forces for this operation were XIII, XVI and XIX U.S. Corps, in Ninth U.S. Army, and 8, 12 and 30 British Corps, 2 Canadian Corps and XVIII U.S. Airborne Corps, all under command of Second Army. The forces in Second Army consisted of three armoured, two airborne (6 British and 17 U.S.) and eight infantry divisions, five independent armoured brigades, one commando brigade and one independent infantry brigade. Those of Ninth U.S. Army totalled three armoured and nine infantry divisions. In addition, there was 79 Armoured Division with its specialized armour and amphibious devices.

6. The object of the first phase of the operation was to secure a bridgehead on the general line Duisberg—Bottrop—Dorsten—Aalten—Doetinchem—Pannerden, the River Lippe being the boundary between the two armies. Ninth U.S. Army was to assault across the river south of the River Lippe, its principal task being to secure the right flank of the operation. Second Army was to assault north of the River Lippe, with the tasks of capturing Wesel so that the Ninth Army could bridge the river at that place, and to secure the initial bridgehead there from exclusive of Dorsten to Pannerden. The second

phase of the operation involved the expansion of the bridgehead to the general line Hamm—Munster—Rheine—Almelo—Deventer—Apeldoorn—Otterloo—Renkum.

7. The responsibility for the airborne plan rested with the First Allied Airborne Army, who co-ordinated the activities of the airborne formations and the Air Forces carrying them. The Commanding General, First Allied Airborne Army was to relinquish his command over the airborne formations as soon as they landed. A combined command post controlling all troop carrier and airborne forces operated at Headquarters, First Allied Airborne Army, near Paris. At this Command Post were the Commanding General, IX U.S. Troop Carrier Command, a representative of the Air Officer Commanding 38 Group, and staff and liaison officers from First Airborne Army, IX U.S. Troop Carrier Command, 38 Group and XVIII U.S. Airborne Corps. A small tactical headquarters of First Allied Airborne Army was established at Headquarters, Second Tactical Air Force, R.A.F., which co-ordinated all offensive support aircraft and which was immediately adjacent to Headquarters, 21 Army Group. The Commanding General, First Allied Airborne Army, was present at the tactical headquarters from 22nd March to 25th March and so he was always on the spot for joint discussions between the three senior commanders concerned. Major-General M. B. Ridgway, Commanding XVIII U.S. Airborne Corps was responsible for detailed planning, for the execution of the operation and for the control of the airborne troops after the drop until contact was established with the forces of the ground commander. He set up an airborne corps command post, from which both he and the airborne deputy commander, Major-General R. N. Gale, kept very close touch with Lieutenant-General Sir Neil Ritchie, whose 12 Corps Tactical Headquarters was close by. Major-General Ridgway also held a planning exercise in England which was attended by Major-General Gale, the two divisional commanders, the three American combat team commanders and the three British brigade commanders. The purpose of the exercise was to study a series of situations which might develop in the operations. Each commander had to give his plans for meeting the situation presented.

8. Opposite Xanten, where 15 (Scottish) Division (Major-General C. M. Barbour) was to cross the River Rhine, was an area that was mostly flat agricultural land, dotted about with groups of farm buildings, the fields being divided by small ditches and wire fences. But there was one relatively commanding feature, high thickly wooded ground, the Diersfordt Wood, which rose to about 200 feet above river level and overlooked the crossing places to be used by 12 Corps. Through this wood ran the main lateral road from Wesel to Rees and Emmerich. Along the eastern edge of the area ran the River Issel, which was not large but flowed between steep banks from 30 to 50 yards apart. It was a tank obstacle, and so it was important to capture and hold the bridges over it as soon as possible. The roads running into the area along which enemy counter-attacks might be expected to develop, all converged on the village of Hamminkeln, so this place was an important initial objective.

9. The defence of the Rhine in the area of the crossing was in the hands of the German First Parachute Army, which had three corps on the river, north 2 Parachute Corps, centre 86 Corps and south 63 Corps. It was believed that the inter-corps boundary between 2 Parachute Corps and 86 Corps was opposite to but slightly north of Xanten, the forward divisions of the two corps being

respectively 7 Parachute Division and 84 Infantry Division, so that the latter would be holding the areas of the Allied airborne landings. After their retreat to the Rhine both these divisions were very weak and did not number more than 4,000 men each, and 84 Division was believed to be supported by only 50 or so medium or field guns. The local armoured reserve consisted of 47 Panzer Corps with 116 Panzer and 15 Panzer Grenadier Divisions. Both these formations had been employed in covering the withdrawal across the Rhine and had suffered badly. However, reliable information pointed to their having been reinforced and by 22nd March, 116 Panzer Division was believed to have up to 70 tanks, and 15 Panzer Grenadier Division 15 tanks and 20 or 30 assault guns. A heavy anti-tank battalion had also possibly arrived in the area. It was thought that First Parachute Army had a total of 150 armoured fighting vehicles at its disposal. There was no doubt that the enemy was expecting an airborne operation of some kind to be staged in connection with the river crossing. On 17th March it was estimated that there were 153 light and 103 heavy flak guns in the Emmerich—Bocholt—Wesel triangle. A week later, just before the operation, these figures had risen to 712 light and 114 heavy guns.

10. The task given to XVIII U.S. Airborne Corps was " to disrupt the hostile defence of the Rhine in the Wesel sector by the seizure of key terrain, by airborne attack, in order to deepen rapidly the bridgehead to be seized in an assault crossing of the Rhine by British ground forces, and facilitate the further offensive operations of Second Army ". The force was to seize and hold the high ground north of Wesel between the Rivers Rhine and Issel, to defend the bridgehead from enemy counter-attacks, to ensure that the enemy was not allowed to seal off the bridgehead before enough troops could be concentrated in it for the advance to continue, and was to prepare for offensive action to the east on orders of Second Army. At all costs the momentum of the advance was to be maintained. To cater for this, phase lines were laid down with times by which they were to be reached.

11. The whole Corps was to be flown in one lift and the troops were to land on top of their objectives. Because previous experience had shown that the best results might not be obtained by night airborne landings, and in order to take full advantage of Allied air supremacy and overwhelming superiority in artillery, the operation was to take place in daylight. As it would be impossible to make full use of our artillery with the ground assault if airborne troops were dropped in the target area before 12 Corps crossed the river, the airborne assault was to follow the amphibious assault. The Commander-in-Chief 21 Army Group agreed to defer the assault for up to 48 hours, should it be necessary to do so, in order to obtain suitable weather conditions for the airborne operation. The commander, Second Army, decided that if it were not possible to carry out the operations as planned, and the river crossing had to be launched alone, then he would request that airborne troops be dropped on the first favourable day in the general area of Erle, thereby deepening the bridgehead. Commander XVIII U.S. Airborne Corps therefore drew up an alternative plan which was not executed.

12. In deciding the landing and dropping zones of the airborne force, the principles employed were that they would be put down within range of artillery sited on the west bank of the Rhine in order to obtain immediate artillery support, and that the link-up with the ground troops should be effected on the first day of the operation.

13. XVIII U.S. Airborne Corps consisted of 6 British and 17 U.S. Airborne Divisions, with 6 Guards Tank Brigade (Brigadier W. D. C. Greenacre) on call, and 1 Commando Brigade was to pass to operational command of 17 U.S. Airborne Division after the commandos had captured Wesel. The tasks of the first three formations in order of priority were :—

(a) 6 Airborne Division (Major-General E. L. Bols) was to drop on the north portion of the area at 1000 hours, 24th March, seize the high ground east of Bergen, the town of Hamminkeln and certain bridges over the River Issel. It was also to protect the north flank of XVIII U.S. Airborne Corps and to establish contact as soon as possible with 12 Corps and 17 U.S. Airborne Division.

(b) 17 U.S. Airborne Division (Major-General W. M. Miley) was to drop on the south portion of the area, at the same time, to seize the high ground east of Diersfordt and certain bridges over the River Issel. It was also to protect the south flank of XVIII U.S. Airborne Corps and to establish contact with 1 Commando Brigade in Wesel, 12 Corps and 6 Airborne Division. As soon as Wesel had been captured 1 Commando Brigade was to come under command of 17 U.S. Airborne Division.

In both cases objectives were to be held at all costs.

(c) 6 Guards Tank Brigade was to supply an early reinforcement to the airborne formations starting with a crossing by the left flank squadron 3rd Tank Battalion, Scots Guards (Lieutenant-Colonel C. I. H. Dunber) to join up with 6 Airborne Division on " D "+ 1 day. The remainder of this unit and the other two battalions in the brigade, 4th Tank Battalion, Grenadier Guards (Lieutenant-Colonel The Lord Tryon) and 4th Tank Battalion, Coldstream Guards (Lieutenant-Colonel A. W. A. Smith) were to cross later at a time and place to be dictated by the development of the battle. The two latter were to be in support of 17 U.S. Airborne Division. The commanding officer and squadron leaders of the Scots Guards flew to England to meet officers of 6 Airborne Division during March, and officers of the other battalions met 17 U.S. Airborne Division.

6 Airborne Division Plan

14. In December, 1944, 6 Airborne Division had been rushed across to north-west Europe to assist in stemming the German advance during the battle for the Ardennes. Earlier the Division had completed planning for an operation for crossing the Rhine under similar circumstances but in a different place, and so when they returned to England at the end of February, 1945, the problem was familiar to commanders, and a great deal of the detailed staff work and organization had been completed. The divisional commander was given his first outline of the operation by Brigadier-General Ralph P. Eaton, Chief of Staff, XVIII U.S. Airborne Corps at Epernay on 18th February, 1945. On 25th February, he was given his detailed task by Major-General Ridgway. The operation had to be mounted from England and therefore the flying element of the Division was withdrawn from Holland, where it was holding part of the line along the River Meuse towards the end of February, leaving the land element, which included the majority of the divisional troops, on the Continent.

15. It was proposed that 250 parachute aircraft and 320 glider tugs should be allotted to the Division. The divisional commander considered that the number of parachute aircraft was adequate but that the gliders were too few to carry essential units, even at the hardest scale. The matter was taken up with the Commanding General, XVIII U.S. Airborne Corps and with the Air Officer commanding 38 Group, and as a result Supreme Headquarters Allied Expeditionary Air Force ordered the number of glider tugs to be increased to 440, which was the number produced on the day of the operation.

16. Detailed tactical planning began immediately after orders had been received from XVIII U.S. Airborne Corps and a large scale model of the area was constructed under divisional arrangements. Major-General Bols issued his provisional outline plan verbally on 2nd March. On 6th March he issued his verbal orders and on 12th March, the divisional operation order was issued. The divisional commander held his final co-ordinating conference on 14th March. A planning headquarters was not established as it was not considered that circumstances warranted it, but a special list showing those people permitted to know all details of the operation was opened and was similar to that used before Normandy. Detailed dates on which commanders and staff officers were briefed were as follows :—

(a) Brigade commanders and Commanders, Royal Artillery, Royal Engineers and Royal Signals = " D " — 22 days = 2nd March.

(b) Heads of services and officers commanding units = " D "— 15 days = 9th March.

(c) Company commanders and equivalent = " D " — 6 days = 18th March.

(d) Platoon commanders and equivalent = " D " — 3 days = 21st March.

The time available for planning and preparation was right in all respects except one in that there was insufficient time for the completion of the glider pilots' orders and their subsequent briefing. Administrative planning was largely carried out in the initial stages by 1 Airborne Corps in conjunction with 21 Army Group and 12 Corps on the Continent, and Home Commands in the United Kingdom.

17. As mentioned in Chapter XX, among the lessons learned from the Arnhem operation was the fact that if possible the complete division should be brought into action in one lift, and that landing and dropping zones should be as close as possible to the initial objectives. In this way there would be little time for enemy reaction to develop and our troops would be able to maintain their initial advantage of surprise. Since the Arnhem operation, the Commander, Glider Pilot Regiment (Brigadier G. J. S. Chatterton) had made a detailed study of the possibility of landing the glider elements of an airborne force in tactical groups. He had come to the conclusion that units of the division could be landed in gliders close enough to their objectives to be able to carry out their tasks immediately the glider had landed. Owing to the losses at Arnhem, and the time taken to train new volunteers for the Glider Pilot Regiment, a large number of R.A.F. pilots had been attached to the regiment, and trained in glider flying. Brigadier Chatterton had included his new theories in the exercise which he set for the glider crews after September, 1944.

By March, 1945, they were well versed in the art of tactical landings. A study of the ground showed that in this particular operation suitable areas for landing zones were available, adjacent to the immediate objectives, and, therefore, Major-General Bols decided to adopt tactical landing as suggested by Brigadier Chatterton. The new method had the additional advantage of dispersing gliders in small groups over a greater area, which would increase the enemy's difficulties in defending it, while quick unloading was made easier by the use of the new Horsa, Mark II, the nose of which swung open in a manner similar to the Hamilcar. This was especially important in view of the fact that the landing was to take place on to the enemy's gun areas and would obviously be subject to heavy fire.

18. Sufficient aircraft were available to carry most of the fighting element of the Division in one lift. It was decided that the operation demanded the maximum infantry resources of the Division, with all anti-tank guns and such field artillery as could be transported in the available air-lift. The parachute brigades were to land first, followed by 6 Air-landing Brigade, divisional headquarters, and the divisional artillery, in that order. The whole Division was to be put down in the shortest possible time in order to minimize the danger of interference by enemy aircraft and the build-up of enemy flak. The glider element of the parachute brigades was increased above that which had been considered normal in the past to allow for the carriage of heavy weapons, jeeps, stores and reserve ammunition. Of divisional troops, only Headquarters, Royal Engineers, three troops of Royal Engineers, the light tanks and 4·2-inch mortars of the Armoured Reconnaissance Regiment, medical units and elements of R.A.S.C., R.A.O.C. and R.E.M.E. were to accompany the Division by air. The remainder were to travel overland.

19. The detailed tasks within the division were as follows :—

(a) 3 Parachute Brigade Group (Brigadier S. J. L. Hill) on to dropping zone " A " at the north-west corner of the Diersfordt Wood to capture the Schnappenberg feature. They were then to clear and hold the western edge of the forest and the road junction at Bergen. They were to patrol out to, and be prepared to hold, the area of the railway line running through the north-east of the forest, and to link up with 5 Parachute Brigade Group.

(b) 5 Parachute Brigade Group (Brigadier J. H. N. Poett) on to dropping zone " B " north-west of Hamminkeln to clear and hold an area astride the main road running from their dropping zone to Hamminkeln. They were to patrol westwards and be prepared to hold the area immediately east of the railway line so that they linked up with 3 Parachute Brigade Group.

(c) 6 Air-landing Brigade (Brigadier R. H. Bellamy) was to land tactically in company groups as close as possible to the objectives or areas they were to seize and occupy. A landing zone was allotted to each battalion within which the exact position for each company was chosen in conjunction with the Commander, Glider Pilots. Headquarters, 6 Air-landing Brigade and 12th Battalion The Devonshire Regiment (Lieutenant-Colonel P. Gleadell) were to land on landing zone " R," south-west of Hamminkeln, with the task of capturing and clearing that town. 2nd Battalion Oxfordshire and Buckinghamshire Light Infantry (Lieutenant-Colonel M. Darell-Brown) were to land on landing zone " O ", north of Hamminkeln, with the task of seizing and holding the road and railway bridges and the bridges over the River Issel between Hamminkeln and Ringenberg. 1st Battalion The Royal Ulster Rifles (Lieutenant-Colonel R. J. H. Carson) were to land on landing zone " U ", south of Hamminkeln, with the task of seizing and holding the bridge over the River Issel on the main road from Hamminkeln to Brunen and the area immediately surrounding it.

(*d*) Divisional headquarters and divisional troops on to landing zone " P ", north-east of the Diersfordt Wood adjacent to Köpenhof, where divisional headquarters was to be established.

(*e*) There were to be supply dropping points immediately west of and adjoining both dropping zones " A " and " B."

20. The combined fire-plan for 12 Corps and XVIII U.S. Airborne Corps was made by the Commander Corps Royal Artillery 12 Corps (Brigadier G. W. E. Heath) in co-operation with the artillery commanders of XVIII U.S. Airborne Corps and the airborne divisions. In direct support of 6 Airborne Division landing, 12 Corps allotted three field regiments and two medium regiments, Roal Artillery. In adition a call could be made on two other medium regiments, and an American group of long range guns was to be available for harassing fire. 3 Parachute Brigade would be within range of the three field regiments and was therefore allotted no support from the air-landing light regiment. However, 5 Parachute and 6 Air-landing Brigades would be out of range of field guns from the west bank of the Rhine, and depended on a medium regiment each, while sharing the fire power of the air-landing light regiment. All fire from the west bank of the Rhine was to be controlled by officers of the divisional Forward Observer Unit who were to land by parachute. This unit would also provide its own rear communications and liaison parties on 12 Corps gun positions. Prearranged support ordered by 12 Corps included the following :—

(*a*) A *counter-battery bombardment* covering 12 Corps and XVIII U.S. Airborne Corps areas by eleven medium regiments, two heavy regiments, one super-heavy regiment, one heavy anti-aircraft regiment and three United States 155-mm. battalions, a total of 280 guns. From 1800 hours to 2000 hours on " D "— 1 day.

(*b*) A *softening bombardment* by nine field regiments, eleven medium regiments, one heavy regiment, four heavy batteries, one heavy anti-aircraft regiment, one super heavy battery and three United States 155-mm. battalions, a total of 487 guns. From 0820 hours to 0920 hours " D " day.

(*c*) *Anti-flak bombardment* by eleven field regiments, eleven medium regiments, two heavy regiments, one super-heavy regiment, one heavy anti-aircraft regiment and three United States 155-mm. batteries, a total of 544 guns. From 0930 hours to 1000 hours on " D " day.

21. In order to make sure that there was no danger of an aircraft or glider of the airborne force being hit by our own guns very careful safety precautions were taken. Headquarters Royal Artillery 12 Corps laid down that

"The overriding principle is that no gun must fire along or across the route taken by any aircraft during the fly-in and fly-out".

The ultimate responsibility for ensuring that this instruction was obeyed lay with the gun position officers who were to stop the fire of their guns if they considered that any aircraft was flying into their line of fire. The anti-flak bombardment was timed to finish just before the leading-aircraft passed over the general line of the gun areas but gun position officers were to be prepared to stop it early if necessary. Once they had been stopped all guns were to remain silent until 12 Corps Artillery Commander authorized them to start shooting again. As an additional precaution an observer on 12 Corps Royal Artillery Commander's net was stationed ten miles behind the gun areas to give advance warning of the arrival of the aircraft and another observer on the same net was posted in an observation tower in Xanten Woods. In practice the leading aircraft did arrive eight minutes early and the latter observer gave the order " Stop " to all the corps artillery. A " No fire " line was laid down between 12 Corps and XVIII U.S. Airborne Corps to be observed from the time that the airborne troops landed. No anti-aircraft fire was allowed in any circumstances between 0900 hours and 1400 hours on " D " day. The complete ban imposed on firing while aircraft were overhead meant that :—

(a) There could be no fire support at the time of the airborne landing.

(b) There could be no major bombardment during the fly-in.

(c) The anti-flak bombardment was only effective for the leading waves of aircraft and thereafter the enemy could shoot undisturbed ; in the event this bombardment had to be stopped before it had been completed.

(d) The 12 Corps artillery, where the trajectory crossed the fly-in or fly-out routes, had to stop firing altogether for two or three hours. (The north fly-in route was expected to be clear by 1110 hours and the south by 1330 hours on " D " day.)

The Air Plan and Operations

22. The air plan was based on the whole of the airborne movement being carried out in one main lift in daylight, with the first drops beginning at 1000 hours, followed by supply-by-air by 2nd Bomber Division, Eight U.S. Air Force. Additional supply-by-air was planned for " D "+ 1 day on request. The available Air Forces consisted of 38 Group (Air Vice Marshal J. R. Scarlett-Streatfield) with ten squadrons of Halifaxes and Stirlings, 46 Group (Air Commodore L. Darvall), with six squadrons of Dakotas, and IX U.S. Troop Carrier Command (Major-General P. L. Williams) with 42 squadrons and one Path-Finder school of Dakota and Commando aircraft.

23. 38 and 46 Groups were to be responsible for all glider towing of 6 Airborne Division, and IX U.S. Troop Carrier Command was to undertake all parachute drops of the Division. The lift of 17 U.S. Airborne Division from the Continent was the entire responsibility of IX U.S. Troop Carrier Command. As in the Arnhem operations, the main military tasks were inter-dependent,

Therefore, a joint flight plan was necessary to ensure complete co-ordination, and by combining the United Kingdom and continental based air forces into one for the greater part of the flight, fighter cover and ground aids could be shared. The initial aircraft resources of 38 and 46 Groups were not sufficient to tow all gliders of 6 Airborne Division in one lift. When the Air Officer Commanding 38 Group was ordered by Supreme Headquarters to increase the numbers of tugs, he solved the problem by building up the squadron aircraft strength from a unit establishment of 24 to 34 aircraft, and by utilizing 20 aircraft from the group Operational Refresher Training Unit for the operation. Similarly, the crew strength in squadrons was increased to 31 crews in each squadron. This was done by keeping tour expired crews in the squadrons and reinforcing with all available crews within the resources of the group. Crews who had just completed their Heavy Conversion Unit course were given special instructions in tug flying at the Operational Refresher Training Unit two weeks before the operation, and took part in it using the 20 Operational Refresher Training Unit aircraft. So 38 Group, with a total of 340 aircraft and 328 crews, were able to produce 320 aircraft for the operation. The Air Officer Commanding 46 Group solved his part of the problem by using some of his Operational Training Unit aircraft and crews and was able to produce 120 aircraft in addition to his other transport commitments. Thus were the 440 tug aircraft made available to 6 Airborne Division for one lift. This would not have been possible had it not been for the efforts of the ground staff who worked unceasingly in many cases until newly delivered aircraft were ready. The total number of aeroplanes employed in lifting 6 Airborne Division was 683 aircraft, and 444 Hamilcar and Horsa Gliders, while 913 aircraft of IX U.S. Troop Carrier Command and 906 Hadrian Gliders were employed to lift 17 U.S. Airborne Division.

24. The task of neutralizing all enemy air forces was given to the Air Officer Commanding-in-Chief, Second Tactical Air Force, R.A.F., who had the complete resources of the Allied Air Forces in the western theatre at his disposal for this purpose. Several days before the operation, enemy airfields were to receive constant attention from our bomber forces. While the troop carrier forces were in flight, in addition to escorting fighters, offensive sweeps were to be maintained over the enemy fighter airfields. It was anticipated that the enemy air forces would be incapable of making an appreciable air effort against the transport aircraft. Special attention was to be paid to neutralizing enemy flak, both by artillery fire and by fighter and fighter-bomber operations. This task was given to Second Army and 83 Group, R.A.F. A special anti-flak committee was set up to study all flak problems and collect all up-to-date information in the area. Artillery fire against flak positions was to be continued until the head of the troop carrier stream crossed the Rhine. At the same time fighter-bombers and fighters were to attack all known flak positions. During the landings a continuous patrol of anti-flak fighters was to be maintained in the area to deal with any flak positions which might open against the airborne aircraft.

25. An automatic supply mission was to be carried out by Eighth U.S. Air Force using 120 Liberators for each division, approximately 15 minutes after the last glider landing. On return to base, six Halifax aircraft were to load six jeeps and six 6-pounder guns, and all other serviceable aircraft in 38 Group were to load containers, and stand-by at one-and-a-half hours call from 0700 hours

on " D "+ 1 day. Three squadrons of aircraft from 46 Group were to land back at Nivelles and were to load panniers. They were to stand-by to supply in an emergency only and were to be at two hours call from dawn on " D "+ 1 day. The supply-by-air of 17 U.S. Airborne Division was the responsibility of IX U.S. Troop Carrier Command. A total of six possible supply dropping points were selected for 6 Airborne Division, but only one was to be used for the entire supply effort. This was to be decided before take off, but air crews were ordered to carry the references of all six in case of alteration when they were airborne. If this occurred, three aircraft of 570 Squadron, 38 Group, were detailed as master supply aircraft and were to be in wireless communication with the ground force. When within 50 miles of the supply dropping point they were to call up the visual control post and were to convey any change to the main body of aircraft by a very high frequency broadcast when within ten minutes of the dropping zone. This broadcast was to be repeated once a minute for ten minutes. In the event of an emergency supply-by-air being required after " D "+ 1 day, a lift of 100 aircraft was to be made available from 38 Group.

26. Three visual control posts were to be flown in to 6 Airborne Division landing zones for the purpose of controlling offensive support aircraft and to provide direct communications with supply aircraft and the group control centre with Second Tactical Air Force, R.A.F. One of these visual control posts was allotted to 6 Airborne Division, one to 17 U.S. Airborne Division, which was to join the Division as soon as possible, and one was kept spare.

27. The combined flight plan was drawn up by the joint planning staff of 38 Group and IX U.S. Troop Carrier Command at the Combined Command Post, Paris. The base airfields for the complete operation formed two distinct groups, a northern group of eight British and three American airfields in the United Kingdom and a southern group of 15 American airfields in France. Aircraft from the northern group were to form up over Hawkinge and those from the southern group over Pontoise, Le Quesnoy and Laon. From there the streams were to proceed to a command assembly point at Wavre and thence in a double stream to the target area, 6 Airborne Division flying on the left, and 17 U.S. Airborne Division on the right, with a space of two miles between the columns. The streams were escorted by R.A.F. Fighters of Fighter Command as far as the Rhine and the route was marked with Eureka beacons and coloured strips with distinctive letter panels. As the battle for the Rhine was already in progress it was not anticipated that air crews would have any difficulty in finding the dropping and landing zones and therefore Pathfinders were not used.

28. The weather on the morning of 24th March, 1945, was fine and even at 0600 hours visibility was good and soon improved to ten miles. Take-off was in darkness. There was no cloud and the whole flight to the target was carried out under perfect flying conditions, no enemy fighters being met *en route*. The parachute drops began a little early, at 0951 hours, and a certain amount of anti-aircraft fire was encountered. Of the 242 parachute aircraft used for 6 Airborne Division, 18 were destroyed or missing and on return 115 were found to be damaged by flak. Of the 440 glider sorties a total of 35 were abortive. Of these, eight were unserviceable because of technical failures, 16 were prematurely released owing to slipstream trouble and nine to broken tow ropes ; one was late in taking off and one failed to take off as the undercarriage of the tug

collapsed before it became airborne. By the time the gliders were released over the landing zones, the whole area was covered literally with the " fog of war ". There was a cloud of smoke and dust caused chiefly by the artillery anti-flak barrage and the Allied bombing of Wesel. There were fires on the ground and the glider pilots had difficulty in judging their height and locating their exact landing positions, with the result that there was a tendency for gliders to overshoot towards the south into 17 U.S. Airborne Division area.

29. The flight, drops and landings of 17 U.S. Airborne Division were equally successful. Of the 913 parachute and glider aircraft which lifted the American division, 28 aircraft were destroyed or missing and 233 were damaged by enemy action. Two American gliders ditched in the Channel, but their crews were picked up successfully by air-sea rescue launches.

30. The time of the supply drop was dictated by the length of time it took the division to fly-in. Whereas the fly-in of 6 Airborne Division was completed in 40 minutes, that of 17 U.S. Airborne Division took two and a half hours.

31. Liberators of the Eighth U.S. Air Force carried out an automatic supply drop as planned, with 239 aircraft for the loss of 14 reported missing. All subsequent supplies for both airborne divisions were cancelled by Second Army on " D " day and " D "+ 1 day.

Operations of 6 Airborne Division

0950 HOURS 24TH MARCH UNTIL MIDNIGHT 24TH MARCH

32. 3 Parachute Brigade landed first according to plan. The drop was nine minutes early but was extremely accurate despite the fact that some 20-mm. flak was encountered. Most of the woods surrounding the area were still held by the enemy who caused a number of casualties on the dropping zone and who fought stubbornly before being cleared out. By 1100 hours the area of the brigade dropping zone was virtually cleared and all battalions were organizing without interference. By 1130 hours 1st Canadian Parachute Battalion had secured all its objectives, and by 1345 hours the main task allotted to the brigade, the capture of the Schnappenberg feature, had been accomplished by 9th Parachute Battalion. 8th Parachute Battalion, having completed its task of clearing the dropping zone, was ordered to move into the area due east of the Schnappenberg feature. Later in the afternoon it was ordered to clear the woods to the west of divisional headquarters, which was established at Köpenhof farm. After the battalion had moved off to carry out this task, the road behind it was cut and communications were not re-established satisfactorily until the following morning. Shortly after 1500 hours the leading elements of 15 (Scottish) Division made contact with 3 Parachute Brigade. Three-quarters of an hour later the ground link was secured and the Commander, 44 (Lowland) Infantry Brigade arrived at the Headquarters of 3 Parachute Brigade. By 1700 hours it was estimated that the brigade had killed some 200 of the enemy and had taken about 700 prisoners. They had lost up to that time about 270 killed, wounded and missing. A number of the original casualties were caused by men being killed while they hung suspended by their parachute harness in trees. Among these was Lieutenant-Colonel J. A. Nicklin, Commanding 1st Canadian Parachute Battalion. The remainder of the day was comparatively quiet.

33. The drop of 5 Parachute Brigade, though not so accurate as that of 3 Parachute Brigade, was good, but the bad visibility caused by the " fog of war " made it difficult for the men to obtain their bearings. The dropping zone came under fire immediately from enemy troops in the neighbourhood, and airburst shelling and mortaring caused casualties in the battalion rendezvous areas. However, despite this, 7th Parachute Battalion was soon in position covering the dropping zone, while the remainder of the brigade were concentrating ready to attack their objectives to the south and west. Practically all the farms and houses were held by the enemy, but they were quickly cleared out by 12th and 13th Parachute Battalions, who attacked with great speed and vigour. By 1530 hours, the whole objective had been captured. Contact with 6 Air-landing Brigade was made by patrols of 13th Parachute Battalion who met 12th Battalion, The Devonshire Regiment just west of Hamminkeln. Enemy shelling and mortaring continued throughout the day but was much reduced during the afternoon.

34. The glider landings of 6 Air-landing Brigade, as related above, were made difficult by the presence of much haze and smoke, and in some instances, considerable anti-aircraft fire. The impression was gained that artificial smoke had been used by the Germans against the landings, but it was established afterwards from the interrogation of the Commander, 84 German Infantry Division that this was not so. Nevertheless, whatever the cause, a very effective unintentional counter-measure against glider landings was constituted either by our own side or by the enemy. Glider pilots had been given air photographs of their landing zones, but in most cases these covered only the immediate area in which they were to land. This resulted in some pilots, who got off course, being unable to pick up their bearings. Many gliders landed in the wrong place, some were destroyed in the air, some crashed badly on landing and others were set alight by enemy fire after landing. The *coup de main* parties landed on their objectives and sufficient of the remainder of the brigade landed close enough to enable the enemy to be overrun in the first rush. By 1100 hours the three bridges over the River Issel had been captured intact and the village of Hamminkeln had been secured. Fairly heavy fire from enemy anti-aircraft guns in a ground role, and mortars, continued for some time after landings, but as further sub-units of the brigade arrived, they quickly mopped up the neighbourhood in conjunction with elements of 513 U.S. Parachute Infantry Regiment who had been dropped in the area by mistake. The only organized enemy force left in the eastern portion of the bridgehead was in the neighbour-hood of Ringenberg where there appeared to be four or five tanks and a considerable number of infantry. The only available battalion to deal with them was 2nd Battalion, The Oxfordshire and Buckinghamshire Light Infantry, who at that time were only about half strength and not strong enough for the job. However, some Typhoons were called up to assist, and kept the enemy quiet. During the remainder of the day there was but little activity on 6 Air-landing Brigade front, though one or two self-propelled guns appeared in front of 1st Battalion, The Royal Ulster Rifles. By that night the total number of prisoners taken amounted to 650 and it was estimated that 6 Air-landing Brigade casualties were approximately 30 per cent of the total strength.

35. Eight light tanks (T.A. Locust) of the Armoured Reconnaissance Regiment were flown into the operation and of these four reached the rendezvous successfully but only two were 100 per cent fit for action. Of the others, one

was missing, another overturned on landing, a third was set on fire, and a fourth was put out of action. The enemy was engaged by the serviceable tanks during the day and, with the support of a platoon of 12th Battalion, The Devonshire Regiment and glider pilots, the Tanks formed a strong point on the edge of the woods west of divisional headquarters. Attempts were made during darkness to link up with the 8th Parachute Battalion, but these were not successful until the following morning.

36. 53rd Air-landing Light Regiment R.A. and 2nd Air-landing Anti-Tank Regiment R.A. were at about half strength as a result of early casualties, and only a small proportion of their 75 mm.s and 6-pounders was got into action on the first day, but otherwise the artillery support worked well. The fire of the two medium regiments was put down at long to extreme ranges and proved effective and surprisingly accurate. The parachuting officers of 2nd Forward Observer Unit were in communication by wireless with their supporting regiments in time that varied from 15 to 40 minutes after landing.

37. The main divisional headquarters was established successfully at the farm at Köpenhof and after this they had no more real trouble. As an example of the new tactical landing method, Major-General Bols was landed safely within 100 yards of his selected headquarters. However, rear divisional headquarters, which was in a farm west of the railway about half a mile away, was subject to sniping and mortaring from the woods to the west, most of the afternoon. That evening rear divisional headquarters joined main divisional headquarters as there were not sufficient forces to protect both during the hours of darkness. That night Major-General Ridgway, accompanied by Major-General Miley, visited Headquarters, 6 Airborne Division and issued orders for 25th March. He said that the Division was to maintain the position it then occupied except that 6 Air-landing Brigade was to be relieved by 157 Brigade of 52 (Lowland) Division during the night 25th/26th March. The Division was to be prepared to advance eastwards at first light on 26th March. On the way back to his command post, which was near Headquarters, 17 U.S. Airborne Division, the airborne corps commander drove into a considerable number of Germans, moving east from 3 Parachute Brigade area. He was fired on and was grazed on the shoulder, and it is said that he accounted for at least one German himself. The majority of this party of Germans were rounded up by 5 Parachute Brigade later in the night.

25TH MARCH–28TH MARCH

38. During the night 24th/25th March, 3 Parachute Brigade spent a noisy but not unduly dangerous period, as the enemy was chiefly concerned with trying to escape from his invidious position in the woods. During that night a considerable amount of traffic from the Rhine started to pass through the brigade area, and soon after first light the enemy launched a counter-attack with infantry and about four tanks against 1st Canadian Parachute Battalion, but were driven off easily. The remainder of the day passed comparatively quietly. 5 Parachute Brigade spent a quiet day watching the battles being waged by 15 (Scottish) Division to the north and west and by 6 Air-landing Brigade to the south-east.

39. During the night 24th/25th March the enemy was active against the northern part of 6 Air-landing Brigade front. At 0230 hours tanks and infantry attempted to rush the bridge immediately west of Ringenberg. Permission was

asked from and granted by divisional headquarters to blow the bridge and this was done by 2nd Battalion Oxfordshire and Buckinghamshire Light Infantry at 0240 hours. Shortly before dawn small parties of enemy infiltrated into the northern edge of the Light Infantry area and set fire to the buildings there. In spite of efforts to clear them out some enemy remained in that area most of the day. Just after first light a gap between 6 Air-landing and 5 Parachute Brigades was closed by fighting patrols from the latter. At 0730 hours, two enemy tanks attempted to rush the bridge in the area held by 1st Battalion, Royal Ulster Rifles, but were driven off, one tank being destroyed and the other damaged by a 17-pounder gun covering the bridge. During the day a continuous air " cab rank " was maintained over the area and about 12 targets were attacked with good results. At 1045 hours one squadron of " D.D." (Duplex Drive—amphibious) tanks arrived in the vicinity of Headquarters, 6 Air-landing Brigade, and one battery of self-propelled anti-tank guns also arrived, a troop being placed to protect each of the bridges over the River Issel.

40. The divisional commander's plan for 26th March, was for 6 Air-landing Brigade, having been relieved during the night 25th/26th March by 157 Brigade of 15 (Scottish) Division, to attack and capture the high ground immediately north-west of Brunen. 5 Parachute Brigade was to remain in its original position while 3 Parachute Brigade was to move south into 17 U.S. Airborne Division area and concentrate temporarily in corps reserve. By 0600 hours, 26th March, the relief of 6 Air-landing Brigade was complete. The brigade, with under command one squadron, 3rd Tank Battalion, Scots Guards and one self-propelled anti-tank battery, attacked east from the southern part of their bridgehead at 0900 hours, 12th Battalion Devonshire Regiment leading. 1st Battalion The Royal Ulster Rifles followed, and after crossing the River Issel came up on the right of the Devons. There was a short sharp fight with approximately two enemy companies, and both battalions then pushed on to their final objectives which they had captured at about 1345 hours, having taken 180 prisoners. That afternoon 3 Parachute Brigade was released from corps reserve and ordered to move forward and take over from 513 U.S. Parachute Infantry Regiment, with a view to advancing early on 27th March.

41. With the remainder of XVIII U.S. Airborne Corps, 6 Airborne Division was ordered to take part in an attack on 27th March, to secure the line Dorsten–Wulfen–Lembeck–Heiden, and the Division's objective was given as Lembeck. Major-General Bols decided to advance with 3 Parachute Brigade leading, and gave it the task of securing the area Kloster–Luktheriem and the high ground south-east of Brunen. For this advance the whole of 3rd Tank Battalion Scots Guards, which was equipped with Churchill tanks, was placed under command of 3 Parachute Brigade.

42. During the night 26th/27th March, patrols from 6 Air-landing Brigade entered Brunen and found it deserted. Patrols from 3 Parachute Brigade found that the line of the River Issel had been left unoccupied by the enemy, so Brigadier Hill decided to seize the bridgehead while he had the opportunity. After this he was granted permission to exploit towards his objective for the next day, and the advance was therefore continued during the night. The original time laid down for the attack to start was 0900 hours, 27th March, but by then 3 Parachute Brigade had secured all their objectives. 3rd Tank Battalion, Scots Guards, was taken away to join 6 Guards Tank Brigade, which

was operating on the right flank of the airborne corps. The divisional commander then ordered 5 Parachute Brigade, which had concentrated during the night just east of the River Issel, to pass through 3 Parachute Brigade and secure Erle. 6 Airborne Armoured Reconnaissance Regiment was responsible for reconnaissance in front of 5 Parachute Brigade.

43. The advance of the brigade began at about 1100 hours, and by 1200 hours they had passed through Brunen, having met no opposition. After this, enemy resistance began to stiffen and at about 1700 hours the reconnaissance regiment was held up some 8,000 yards west of Erle by approximately one enemy company, supported by a number of light flak guns and two or three self-propelled guns. The enemy was astride the divisional axis of advance, which was along a road some two miles south of the main road Brunen–Raesfeld–Erle. However, the advance of 5 Parachute Brigade was not to be stopped by such small opposition. 7th Parachute Battalion attacked and cleared out the enemy on the main axis, killing or capturing some 80 Germans and 11 guns. 13th Parachute Battalion advanced during the night across country, and by 0400 hours, 28th March, had secured its objective, which was the high ground about 2,000 yards west of and dominating Erle. In the meantime 12th Parachute Battalion advanced along the main axis as soon as it was clear and entered Erle from the rear at first light, achieving complete surprise. They killed or captured about 200 enemy and destroyed a large number of vehicles.

29TH MARCH–2ND MAY

44. At midnight 27th/28th March, 6 Airborne Division had passed from command of XVIII U.S. Airborne Corps to 8 British Corps for the advance across Germany to the Baltic, though in fact they reverted to XVIII Corps during the last few days. Across 8 Corps axis lay the Rivers Weser and Elbe which divided the operations into three phases—from the Rhine to the Weser, from the Weser to the Elbe and from the Elbe to the sea.

45. On 28th March, 8 Corps Commander, Lieutenant-General Sir Evelyn Barker, issued his orders for the advance to begin. The first step was to be the capture of Coesfeld. 6 Airborne Division on the right, with one squadron of the Inns of Court Regiment under command, was directed into the town itself, while 11 Armoured Division on the left was to advance on a parallel axis north-east to dominate the town from the north.

46. During the night 28/29th March, 6 Air-landing Brigade occupied Rhade and on the following day the main party of the " land element " and " seaborne tail " joined up with their respective units, with the result that from now on the Division was in a better position with regard to transport. Early that same morning, 3 Parachute Brigade, who had spent the night in the Brunen area, moved up to an assembly area just west of Erle, while 6 Air-landing Brigade moved in behind them and divisional headquarters moved to the Erle area. At 1200 hours the advance began again with 3 Parachute Brigade leading, preceded by elements of the reconnaissance regiment and followed by 6 Airlanding Brigade. No troop carrying transport had yet been made available so the advance was on foot. A sharp engagement took place 2,000 yards east of Erle where a party of flak troops was cleared out of a position covering the road. In a small village, half way between Rhade and Lembeck, heavier opposition was met but was mopped up by 8th Parachute Battalion. It was

apparent that Lembeck, about 6,000 yards further on, was not going to be taken without a battle, so 9th Parachute Battalion moved round in a wide left flanking movement to get behind the town and block the roads to the east of it.

Meanwhile 8th Parachute Battalion continued along the main axis of advance, but the leading company was pinned down by 20 mm. and small arms fire on the hill immediately to the west of Lembeck. Enemy air bursts also inflicted casualties on the follow-up companies. The protection of the main axis was taken over by 1st Canadian Parachute Battalion, and 8th Parachute Battalion put in a right flanking attack, supported by tanks of the armoured reconnaissance regiment. The battle lasted until last light and then the brigade commander decided to limit the extent of 8th Parachute Battalion's attack, and ordered it to seize the high ground immediately south of the town. The leading company of the battalion became detached and was involved in bitter hand-to-hand fighting with two companies of a Panzer-Grenadier training battalion. However, enemy resistance was gradually overcome and by midnight they had all been killed or captured, and the company then got into the western suburbs. Meanwhile, 1st Canadian Parachute Battalion had been preparing to attack down the main axis and get into the town under cover of darkness, but was diverted to join the detached company of 8th Parachute Battalion, to complete the mopping up. Afterwards the Canadians were to occupy the high ground immediately to the south. While all this had been going on, 9th Parachute Battalion had executed a most successful left flanking movement, and after several skirmishes were astride the enemy's back door. The result of the day's fighting was that 3 Parachute Brigade had eliminated the Panzer-Grenadier training battalion and captured or destroyed many vehicles and flak guns. They had covered 15 miles on foot in 24 hours and fought almost continuously for 18 hours. In the meantime 6 Air-landing Brigade passed through 3 Parachute Brigade, reaching Coesfeld in the late afternoon, and clearing it of enemy resistance by midnight.

47. Owing to rubble in the streets of Coesfeld caused by Allied bombing, movement was impossible and the Division had to make a considerable detour through lanes to the south, joining the main road six miles east of the town. The River Ems was reached at 2200 hours that night at Greven by 3 Parachute Brigade, who had covered 23 miles in less than 24 hours and fought several engagements on the way. A small bridge was captured intact, though the main road bridges had been blown up by the Germans, and by midnight on 31st March, the Dortmund–Ems Canal was reached north-west of Schmedehausen. All bridges had been destroyed, and the canal was about 36 yards wide with steep grass and stone banks. After 3 Parachute Brigade had cleared the enemy from the site, bridging operations began at 1130 hours on 1st April, and by 0530 hours the next morning a Class 9 bridge had been constructed, which was completed for Class 40 traffic six hours later.

48. 6 Air-landing Brigade led the advance on foot towards Lengerich which it captured by midday 2nd April, after some hard fighting against considerable opposition. The brigade then took the high ground to the north and east of the town, having marched and fought 15 miles in about 20 hours. By midnight on 3rd April, 3 Parachute Brigade on the right had reached Wissingen, some six miles east of Osnabruck and 6 Air-landing Brigade was in the western outskirts of Osnabruck. On 4th April, with 3 Parachute Brigade still in the

lead, Wehrendorf and Lübbecke were cleared, and the outskirts of Minden on the River Weser were reached. The town was too strongly held for 3 Parachute Brigade to get through to the river, so they took up positions in the western edge where they contacted American troops on the right. 6 Air-landing Brigade were following 3 Parachute Brigade and concentrated north of Lübbecke, 5 Parachute Brigade remaining just west of Osnabruck. It rejoined the Division as soon as Osnabruck had been cleared by 1 Commando Brigade.

49. In the early morning of 5th April, 3 Parachute Brigade attacked Minden and after some fighting cleared it by midday, and that afternoon it was handed over to the troops of Ninth U.S. Army, as it was within their boundary. In the meantime 6 Air-landing Brigade reached the River Weser at Petershagen and crossed slightly upstream from it. By midnight one battalion and one company were over, 5 Parachute Brigade was concentrated south-west of Petershagen, and troops of 11 Armoured Division on the left, who had been level with 6 Airborne Division all the way, had got a small bridgehead at Stolzenau. Measured by the most direct route troops of 8 Corps had advanced 150 miles in eight days.

50. More troops of 6 Air-landing Brigade were ferried across the Weser during the night 5/6th April and by midday the bridgehead had been extended considerably. Two bridges were constructed, protected by 5 Parachute Brigade which beat off two counter-attacks. The Weser was between 80 and a 100 yards wide and the current was flowing fairly fast but nevertheless by the early hours of 7th April one of the bridges was fit for Class 40 traffic and the advance was resumed with 15 (Scottish) Division Reconnaissance Regiment, now under command of the airborne troops, leading, followed by 5 Parachute Brigade. By 1800 hours Wunstorf and Neustadt had been taken after a sharp battle but the bridge over the River Leine at the latter place was blown by a German delayed action charge. The next few days were spent in consolidating the bridgehead and on 11th April, 15 (Scottish) Division took over the lead from 6 Airborne Division, who were given the role of clearing up the axis of advance.

51. On 16th and 17th April, 6 Airborne Division occupied several villages east of Uelzen to cut off the enemy retreat from that town when it was attacked by 15 (Scottish) Division on 18th April. The Scots attack was successful, and 6 Airborne Division was ordered to remain concentrated east of Uelzen carrying out reconnaissance on the roads Uelzen–Luchow and Uelzen–Dannenberg, for which purpose 5 Divisional Reconnaissance Regiment was placed under command. By the morning of 23rd April, 8 Corps was along the line of the River Elbe on a 38-mile front, but no bridges had been captured. An advance of 103 miles had been made in 14 days and 19,000 prisoners had been captured.

52. The River Elbe was a formidable obstacle and had to be taken by an assault crossing. It was about 300 yards wide and the enemy bank opposite Artlenburg was a steep and wooded escarpment. On our side, however, the country was dead flat marshland, totally devoid of cover and was completely dominated by the enemy positions. The operation was to take place in five phases :—

(a) *Phase I.*—15 (Scottish) Division with under command 1 Commando Brigade to assault and secure a bridgehead at Lauenburg to cover bridge and ferry construction. To secure, intact if possible, bridges over the Elbe–Trave Canal east of Lauenburg.

(b) *Phase II.*—15 (Scottish) Division to extend the bridgehead to include Krüzen, about two miles north of Lauenburg.

(c) *Phase III.*—15 (Scottish) Division to extend the bridgehead further to include certain villages in a ring about seven miles north and north-west of Lauenburg.

(d) *Phase IV.*—15 (Scottish) Division to pause and regroup, handing over the eastern sector of the bridgehead to 6 Airborne Division, who would then extend the bridgehead further eastwards to include two villages about five miles from Lauenburg.

(e) *Phase V.*—6 Airborne Division on the right was to secure the final limit of the bridgehead using 15 Brigade of 5 Division to secure that part of their area west of the Elbe–Trave Canal, and to seize two bridges over the canal some eight miles north of Lauenburg. The Division was to come under orders of XVIII U.S. Airborne Corps after crossing the canal. 15 (Scottish) Division was to secure the final limit of the bridgehead on the left.

On about 24th April a plan had been agreed by Lieutenant-General Barker, Major-General Bols and Air Commodore Darvall to drop 5 Parachute Brigade to assist in the river assault. The dropping zone was to be the airfield at Lauenburg, which was about five miles from the objective, but the operation was not required.

53. " D " day was to be 1st May, but was put forward to 29th April in order to forestall the hordes of refugees believed to be converging on Lubeck in front of the Russians. By the evening of 29th April, most of the first two phases had been completed, and Phase III was carried out on 30th April. On the same day 3 Parachute Brigade crossed the Elbe by one of the newly constructed bridges, followed by 15 Brigade. The sappers of 8 Corps did a magnificent job, as one Class 9 bridge was opened for traffic on the evening of 29th April, and a Class 40 by midday on 30th April, despite heavy engineer casualties due to enemy air attacks. 3 Parachute Brigade turned east and reached a point just beyond Boizenberg where they linked up with American troops.

54. On the afternoon of 30th April, 6 Airborne Division with under command the Scots Greys of 4 Armoured Brigade, and 6 Field Regiment, passed to command of XVIII U.S. Airborne Corps once again and learned that its objective was to be Wismar, on the Baltic. The following day the Division covered 50 miles in daylight, driving through large numbers of released Allied prisoners of war, and reached the Baltic, being the first Allied formation to do so.

55. Since 29th March, the Division had covered about 300 miles, which is roughly the distance between Lembeck and Wismar. Apart from a halt of two days on the River Leine for the Americans to clear up the Ruhr and another on the River Elbe, to plan the assault crossing, the operations were continuous except for minor checks by river or canal obstacles. An overall speed of advance of 11 miles a day was achieved from the Rhine to the Elbe, after which it increased considerably. The original instructions to maintain the speed of the advance at all costs had been fully carried out, and the momentum originally gained was never relinquished, to such an extent that most units

reached the phase lines before the time laid down. Five major bridging operations were carried out over the River Ems, the Dortmund—Ems Canal and the Rivers Weser, Leine and Aller, and the following troops were under command of 6 Airborne Division more or less permanently :—

(a) 4th Tank Battalion Grenadier Guards, replaced on 1st May by the Scots Greys.

(b) 6th Field Regiment, R.A.

(c) 25th Field Regiment, R.A., up to the River Elbe.

(d) One self-propelled anti-tank battery.

(e) One medium regiment.

(f) Three platoons troop-carrying transport, R.A.S.C.

56. In his report Major-General Ridgway summed up the result of the operation thus :—

" The airborne drop was of such depth that all enemy artillery and rear defensive positions were included and destroyed, reducing in one day a position that might have taken many days by ground attack only." He came to the following conclusions :—

" (a) Concept and planning were sound and thorough, and execution flawless. The impact of the airborne divisions, at one blow, completely shattered the hostile defence, permitting prompt link-up with the assaulting 12 Corps, 1 Commando Brigade and Ninth Army to the south.

(b) The rapid deepening of the bridgehead materially increased the rapidity of bridging operations which, in turn, greatly increased the rate of build-up on the east bank, so essential to subsequent successes.

(c) The insistent drive of the Corps to the east and the rapid seizure of key terrain in the Dulmen and Haltern areas, were decisive contributions to this operation and to subsequent developments, as by it both British and United States armour were able to debouch into the North German plain at full strength and momentum.

(d) In planning and execution, the co-operation of participating air forces, both British and American, I consider completely satisfactory. There was no enemy air interception. The fighter bombers, in their counter-flak role, were as effective as could have been expected. The air supply by heavy bombers was timely and met a critical need. Troop delivery by IX Troop Carrier Command was on time, and with minor exceptions, in the correct areas.

(e) I wish particularly to record that throughout both planning and execution, the co-operation and actual assistance provided by the Commanders, Staff and troops of the British formations under which this Corps has served, which it commanded, or with which it was associated, left nothing to be desired. For my part I have never had a more satisfactory professional service in combat nor more agreeable personal relations with participating commanders."

Victoria Cross

57. One Victoria Cross was gained by a member of the Division, Corporal F. G. Topham, 1st Canadian Parachute Battalion.

Administration

58. Outline administrative planning for the previous projected Rhine crossing operation had been discussed and planned in broad terms during October and November, 1944, but the administrative plan did not take definite detailed shape until the second week in March. The original " D " day for the operation, for planning purposes, had been 30th March, but the success of the preliminary operations brought this forward to 24th March at short notice. However, this did not affect 6 Airborne Division's plan, though it meant that Second Army had a week less in which to build up stores for the Division east of the River Maas. Two liaison officers were loaned by 1 Airborne Corps to XVIII U.S. Airborne Corps and 12 Corps for the purpose of representing the interests of 6 Airborne Division. The fact that the headquarters of 6 Airborne Division was in the United Kingdom and the corps headquarters in north-west Europe caused inevitable delay in communication and consequent difficulty to the formations concerned. This was especially so in the case of lengthy detailed requirements. The maintenance plan was divided into two parts, the first covering maintenance by air and the second, maintenance by " DUKWS " across the River Rhine. Supply by air was planned as follows :—

(a) Automatic supply by Eighth U.S. Air Force from Liberators to take place two and three-quarter hours after the initial drop. A total of 145 tons was to be dropped.

(b) During the morning of " D "+ 1 day, automatic supply by 38 Group, from Stirlings and Halifaxes, subject to cancellation by Second Army. The total involved in this case was 536 tons.

(c) Automatic medium level supply from 7,000 ft. by 38 Group. This was to consist of 134 tons. It was only to take place if (b) above proved to be necessary, but was not possible owing to the amount of flak opposition at low heights.

(d) One day's supply by 38 Group on call from " D "+ 2 days, a total of 260 tons.

(e) In case weather conditions forbade any supply missions being flown from the United Kingdom, 46 Group was to be responsible for an automatic emergency supply from Dakotas based at Nivelles. The total for this operation was to be 170 tons.

All parachute aircraft which were not carrying unit containers were to carry four " jettison " containers. Twelve Hamilcar Gliders were allotted to the R.A.S.C. for flying in Universal carriers and the spare places in these gliders were packed with 162 panniers of stores.

59. Sixty-nine " DUKWS " were allotted to the Division by 12 Corps and a dump was formed on the west side of the River Rhine under the control of Commander, R.A.S.C., 6 Airborne Division who worked in conjunction with 12 Corps. Initially, the " DUKWS " were pre-loaded with one day's requirements and were to be phased across the river under orders of the bank unit, a dump being formed on the east side of the river. A further two days' requirements were dumped on the west bank, and the " DUKWS " were phased across the river in a similar manner.

60. The problem of collecting, controlling, and issuing the airborne supplies was partially solved by flying in a detachment of 716 Airborne Light Composite Company R.A.S.C. The detachment was commanded by the company commander (Major C. P. R. Crane) and consisted of 80 all ranks, and had with it 12 universal carriers and trailers flown in by Hamilcars. This force was not large enough for the purpose but it was the maximum that the available air-lift would permit. A jeep and trailer platoon, R.A.S.C., was to come overland and be phased across the Rhine, on a high priority, in order to augment the light composite company detachment. Until this platoon arrived, the detachment was to be assisted by the loan of 40 jeeps and trailers from 6 Air-landing Brigade and the Royal Artillery. These jeeps and trailers were to be available from six hours after the initial drop, but were not in fact produced owing to losses.

61. In the medical plan, field ambulances were allotted directly to brigades with the tasks of clearing the brigade's dropping and landing zones to medical dressing stations of brigade areas, clearing and holding casualties from battalions until evacuation was possible, and performing priority one surgery and resuscitation. In addition, 195th Air-landing Field Ambulance, Lieutenant-Colonel W. E. Anderson, was given the task of detailing a medical officer to clear the divisional headquarter landing zones and to reinforce the regimental aid post established by Headquarters, Royal Artillery, in that area.

62. Only two Ordnance personnel were taken in the air lift. They flew with the R.A.S.C. Hamilcar party to assist in the formation of the air supply dump and the recognition of Ordnance stores. The remainder of the divisional Ordnance Field Park came overland. Detachments from R.E.M.E. Light Aid Detachments dropped or landed with their brigades and one " Z " trailer and crew was flown in a R.A.S.C. Hamilcar. No other R.E.M.E. vehicles went in by air. The advance workshop detachment consisting of eight jeeps and trailers came overland and was given a high priority across the river. A detachment of the Postal Unit was detailed to cross with the pre-loaded " DUKWS " carrying outstanding mail to establish an Army Post Office at the " DUKW " dump on the east bank of the Rhine.

63. Before the operation, administrative arrangements, including transporting personnel and stores to transit camps and airfields, drawing of special rations, arrangements within the transit camps and other requirements, went smoothly with one or two exceptions. The difficulties of transit camps being, in some cases, many miles from airfields, and of many units having to take off from two or even three airfields, were overcome by accepting the distance and accommodating complete units together. Troops who were going into the operation by air moved to their transit camps on 20th March, while sea-borne elements moved in three parties on 15th and 12th March from their normal locations and on the evening of " D " day from the airborne transit camps. The Division was allotted 15 platoons of transport for moving troops to the transit camps and these were distributed on the scale of one truck to each aircraft in the case of parachute units, and one truck to 20 men in the case of air-landing units. Units received their transport on the evening of 18th March, and it remained attached until " D " day.

64. The "Jettison" drop containers were packed at Figsbury by the divisional services and were issued to parachute units on the scale of four to each aircraft on 19th March. After this it was a unit responsibility to ensure that they were correctly loaded on to the aircraft. A large number of these containers had been packed for an operation which did not take place, during the autumn of 1944, and thus the packing problems for the Rhine crossing were considerably relieved. The rations required for the operations were issued at Bulford from the static R.A.S.C. units on 19th March direct to units. 1 Airborne Corps had arranged eight transit camps in the vicinity of the airfields for the operation. Each transit camp was staffed by a camp commandant and a small staff, and the facilities included a N.A.A.F.I., accommodation stores, bedding etc. Petrol, oil and lubricants and medical facilities were also arranged. Arrangements for pay, exchange of currency, delivery of incoming and outgoing mail, fatigue and guard duties and provision of security personnel were made by 6 Airborne Division. Traffic control and marking of routes between airfields and camps was the responsibility of Eastern Command.

65. The battle was influenced by the losses in vehicles sustained in the initial landings, and the heavy loss among the R.A.S.C. Hamilcars.

These losses were as follows :—

(a) *Percentages*

Jeeps ..	.. 46 per cent
Trailers	.. 44 ,,
Carriers ..	44 ,,
Light Tanks	50 ,,
75-mm. Howitzers ..	29 ,,
25-pounders	50 ,,
17-pounder anti-tank guns ..	.. 56 ,,
6-pounder anti-tank guns	.. 29 ,,
Dodge ¾-ton weapon carriers	56 ,,

The figures represented by the percentages shown for jeeps and trailers were 140 jeeps lost on 24th March out of 323 taken in by air, and 125 trailers out of 283 taken in.

(b) *Losses from R.A.S.C. Hamilcars*

Taken	12
Landed in the divisional area ..	7
Trailers recovered from	5
Carriers recovered from	7
Stores recovered from	3

A point to note is that the above figures were the final losses for 24th March, and that during the first few critical hours anything up to 20 or 30 per cent of the recovered equipment was still missing. These losses and the subsequent early advance at times nearly overwhelmed the "Q" staff, but owing to the magnificent efforts made by the Services, particularly the R.A.S.C., and the liberal scale of insurance allowed during planning, the divisional commander's plan was never hindered during the first few days.

66. Casualties were moderately heavy during the first day, though not more than was expected considering the opposition that was encountered, and in fact were about the same as for the first day of the Normandy operations. They dropped subsequently and the figures for the first three days were as given below :—

	24th March.		25th March.		26th March.	
	Officers.	*O.Rs.*	*Officers.*	*O.Rs.*	*Officers.*	*O.Rs.*
Killed ..	39	308	—	1	—	6
Wounded ..	48	683	1	6	5	24

Missing	
Officers.	*O.Rs.*
13	300

The majority of the missing were subsequently accounted for. Although only 600 graves had been located by the end of May, 1945, it is estimated that some 700 men lost their lives between 24th March and 2nd May.

67. The supplies which were " jettisoned " from the parachute aircraft remained to a large extent an untapped source. This was chiefly owing to the lack of transport and, in the case of 5 Parachute Brigade, to the fact that the area covered by the " Jettison " drop remained for sometime under enemy fire. 3 Parachute Brigade collected between 15 and 20 per cent of the " Jettison " containers by using the Light R.A.S.C. Platoon, which crossed the river on the afternoon of 24th March and was waiting to get through to the supply-by-air dump. The automatic supply by Liberators arrived as scheduled at 1300 hours, 24th March. It was moderately successful, though as the planes flew rather on the low side, some damage was done to the stores through delays in parachutes opening. The supply dropping point had been marked by personnel of 22 Independent Parachute Company but only a handful of R.A.S.C. personnel with two carriers and trailers were available to collect stores. 6 Air-landing Brigade and the gunners were only able to produce ten jeeps and trailers to assist. Because of this lack of men and transport there was a short period during the afternoon of 24th March when ammunition demands from 5 Parachute and 6 Air-landing Brigades could not be met, but this was rectified during the evening when a small stock was built up. Probably about 35 per cent of this supply drop was recovered by the Division, of which nine per cent passed through the dump, the remainder being collected on the spot by brigades. The land element began to cross the River Rhine during the afternoon of 24th March, and the dump and report centre was established on the east bank. By the morning of 25th March, the Assistant Provost Marshal and R.A.S.C. representative had contacted divisional headquarters and priority land elements had begun to move forward to join units. Late that afternoon it was possible to switch 3 Parachute Brigade to the dump for all maintenance, supplies of petrol, oil and lubricants for the remainder of the Division being taken from this dump. By this time clearance of the air supply was no longer an urgent requirement ; therefore the Light Transport Platoon R.A.S.C. was allotted to the three brigades which were very short of transport.

68. The medical part of the operation went according to plan and by the evening of 26th March it was well under control and evacuation was proceeding smoothly. This was largely owing to the excellent help given by 12 Corps.

Lessons

69. During planning, Headquarters 38 Group, and Headquarters 6 Airborne Division, were about 150 miles apart. This did not prejudice their chances of success, but it did involve inconvenience and extra work. If the available time for the preparation of the operation had been shorter the delays involved by having the two headquarters so widely separated might have been serious. Wherever possible the Army and Air Force Headquarters, on whatever level, should be close together.

70. The fact that careful preparation pays high dividends was proved once again. Not a single situation developed during the initial stages of the battle that had not been foreseen and planned for in Major-General Ridgway's preliminary exercise.

71. Offensive air support for airborne landings should be of an intimate character, and the final wave of bombers and fighters should come in immediately ahead of the first wave of aircraft or gliders. During a landing, attacks should continue on the flanks of and as close as possible to the area in which troops are landing. The object of this offensive air support should not so much be to destroy the defenders, which is difficult to achieve, but to attack their morale and keep their heads down. This could only be achieved by continuous and intimate air support.

72. Although the fly-in of 6 Airborne Division was completed in 40 minutes, it might have taken even less time had the aircraft carrying the Division flown in two streams. From the Army point of view this would have had the additional advantage of enabling both the leading brigades to be put down together, resulting in greater speed on the ground.

73. Both parachute brigades used one battalion to clear their dropping zones in order to neutralize enemy fire and to deal with any enemy counter-attack. It was considered that this was essential when carrying out a mass drop. The arrangements for indicating formation and unit rendezvous varied in each brigade, coloured smoke being used in 3 Parachute Brigade and sounds such as bugles or hunting horns in 5 Parachute Brigade. The latter were quite inadequate and smoke or rocket signals would have been more successful. Easily discernible land marks such as copses should not be used as a rendezvous because the enemy usually knows the range and shells them. In both 3 and 5 Parachute Brigades one battalion allotted their sub-units lanes of aircraft instead of successive aircraft numbers in order to assist rallying. This meant that those men dropped on the left of the dropping zone mostly belonged to one company, those in the centre to another, and those on the right to another.

74. The Rhine crossing operation showed that a mass parachute drop in daylight in enemy defended areas and in the face of considerable flak is an operation which can be carried out successfully, though casualties may be heavy. Casualties caused by flak were light, the majority being sustained on the ground in the period between dropping and assembling at the rendezvous. Brigadier Hill was given the choice of two dropping zones for 3 Parachute Brigade. One measured only a thousand yards by a thousand and was right on the objective. About two miles away was a larger one. The brigade commander knew that the enemy was covering the smaller of the two, and that it would call for very great accuracy on the part of the pilots, but considered speed was vital.

320

The drop was accurate and completed in nine minutes, the aircraft flying in mass formation. It is open to argument whether this could have been achieved by using the " bomber-stream principle ", and whether casualties might not have been heavier.

75. The operation showed again that gliders are vulnerable and are an easy target for light anti-aircraft fire, and that when carrying petrol in cans or in petrol tanks they are highly inflammable. It also showed that glider-borne troops have an advantage over parachutists in that a complete sub-unit lands under its commander. This is an advantage in some circumstances, but it is a serious disadvantage in landing in the face of short-range ground fire as the platoon is caught concentrated and is liable to suffer heavy casualties. Once again the operation proved that gliders are eminently suitable for *coup de main* parties, provided that they are landed sufficiently close to the objective so that a certain measure of surprise or neutralization can be achieved. The operation also showed that parachute troops are better than gliders for landing in daylight in enemy defended territory. Gliders should not normally land until the parachute troops have time to clear the landing zones of the enemy, which may take anything from two to six hours. If gliders must be employed in addition to parachute troops, only those carrying personnel should fly in the first wave.

76. As a result of the enemy anti-aircraft defences met during the operation, a special study of the problem of dealing with such defences was made by the Division when the operation was ended. The study was based on the assumption that the fly-in of an airborne operation was likely to be at a height of about 600 to 900 feet for parachute aircraft and between 1,000 and 2,000 feet for gliders. The three types of flak which would probably give most trouble in an airborne operation, in order of priority, would be light flak (40-mm. and lesser calibre), machine guns and small arms fire, and heavy anti-aircraft guns. Of these, light flak would be the most effective, being liable to destroy aircraft and gliders by setting fire to or exploding loads, as well as causing casualties to personnel and damaging control rigging. Machine guns and small arms would be about as effective as light flak, being specially useful against parachutists and gliders coming in to land. Heavy anti-aircraft guns would probably be the least effective as they were not really efficient below 5,000 feet, though in the future they might be a danger if used from the flank. When the proximity airburst fuze came into universal use for light anti-aircraft guns, aircraft and gliders would become vulnerable. Once gliders had stopped on their landing zone, it was the light weapon that would do the damage, as the heavier gun was soon spotted and destroyed, but the machine gun was difficult to find.

77. In any airborne operation the main source of knowledge of the layout of enemy defences would be photographs, but often they would not disclose the positions of the light or machine-gun, and they were dependent on weather, so their information might be out of date. Therefore, the problem narrowed down to one of dealing with areas which contained the enemy defences. It would not be practical to hope to destroy targets in such areas, but all resources should be devoted to their neutralization. There appeared to be two methods of successfully counteracting enemy flak opposition. The first was by delivering the airborne force in " packets " at intervals, supported by heavy counter-flak bombardment and strafing, as opposed to one long " armada ". The first

method might not be practicable owing to the time required, and therefore, the second method should be used. This was to " drench " the area with parachute troops so that the enemy defences would be overrun at once.

78. Despite the fact that in this operation very little use was made of the " Jettison " drop, it was considered that all available additional lifts of parachute aircraft should be used for this purpose in future. When making the air plan, every effort should be made to drop the containers on top of or as near as possible to the final objective. " Jettison " containers dropped at a distance from the objective would rarely be of any use unless it were known that there would be no opposition. The use of Hamilcars as storage gliders was found to be not worth while until a landing zone was known to be free of the enemy, when this method was an economical and easy means of supply by air.

79. Two other lessons emerged from this operation. The first being the tremendous advantage gained by the Division from the fact that the men went into operation fresh, having been home to the United Kingdom after the Ardennes operation, and from the strong divisional spirit which imbued all the services. The length and speed of the advance was evidence of the excellence of their work. Without quite exceptional efforts on the part of all services, the great success of the Division might have been jeopardized. Deserving special mention is the achievement of the R.A.S.C. in producing four platoons of troop carrying transport for the last day's operations. The second lesson was that the establishment and maintenance of the closest and most friendly relations at an early stage with the corps under which the airborne division is to operate is of the greatest importance. The administrative task of 6 Airborne Division was greatly lightened by the magnificent support accorded by the administrative staff and services of both 8 and 12 Corps, and the fact that XVIII U.S. Airborne Corps command post and 12 Corps tactical headquarters were so close together during the planning stage made all the difference to the tactical control of the administrative build-up.

A German Commander's Opinion

80. Major-General Fiebig, Commander 84 Infantry Division, who was captured later and interrogated, made some interesting observations. He claimed that the Germans were not unaware of our preparations for an airborne operation in support of the Rhine crossings and appreciated that no fewer than four Allied airborne divisions were available, although he confessed he had been badly surprised by the sudden advent of two complete divisions in this particular area, and throughout the interrogation reiterated the shattering effect of such immensely superior forces on his already badly depleted troops, which did not number more than 4,000 in all.

Major-General Fiebig had no exact advance information about landing and dropping zones, or times although he had fully appreciated the likelihood of a landing somewhere in his area. He rather expected the landing farther from the Rhine, in the area east of the River Issel and thought it would take place either at dusk before the land assault or else simultaneously with it.

CHAPTER XXII

BRITISH AIRBORNE FORCES, MAY TO DECEMBER, 1945

General

1. In Chapter XVI a study was made of the operations that were planned but never carried out between June and September, 1944. After the Arnhem operations First Allied Airborne Army continued to examine various projected operations, among which was the crossing of the River Rhine. Although this chapter deals with the period May to December, 1945, it will be advisable to return to the beginning of the year to obtain a clear picture of the planning that took place just before the German collapse, and led to 1 Airborne Division's air-transported operation in Norway.

2. Among plans prepared by First Allied Airborne Army after the Arnhem operations, in case they were wanted, were one east of Aachen to assist in penetrating the Siegfried Line, one to assist in crossing the Rhine between Neuwied and Coblenz, and yet another to breach the Siegfried line at Saarbrucken. None of these plans got very far as they were never requested but they were followed by a proposed operation named " Choker II " to assist in crossing the River Rhine between Mainz and Mannheim in co-operation with General Patch's Seventh U.S. Army. Originally it was to be carried out by 17 U.S. Airborne Division but when this formation was earmarked for the Second Army Rhine crossing operation, 13 U.S. Airborne Division was selected, and went to transit camps on 27th March, 1945. However, the operation was cancelled on 4th April.

3. Operation " Varsity ", as the assault on the River Rhine by XVIII U.S. Airborne Corps was called, was followed by several more projected airborne operations, one of which was the largest ever considered. General Eisenhower cancelled it owing to the rapid advance of the land armies that made it unnecessary. The operation was called " Arena ". Briefly, the plan was to :—

   (a) Invade the Cassel–Fritzier–Hofgeismar area with First Allied Airborne Army.

   (b) Establish a fortress from which would be launched a decisive offensive at the east end of the Ruhr.

   (c) Seize the high ground east of Paderborn to deny the enemy the use of this natural defensive position.

   (d) Provide an airhead to which the southern group of armies could advance.

The troops to take part were :—

Headquarters, First Allied Airborne Army.
1 Airborne Corps—1 and 6 Airborne Division
XVIII U.S. Airborne Corps—13, 17, 82 and 101 U.S. Airborne Divisions.
U.S. Air-transported Corps—2, 84, 103 and one other U.S. Infantry Division (Air-transported).
Three U.S. Airborne Aviation Engineer Battalions.

4. Other operations were planned just before the end of the war, among them being one for 13 U.S. Airborne Division to seize an airhead in front of Seventh U.S. Army in the vicinity of Bisingen to surround the Black Forest, and one in the Cassel area to seize the airfields and the Eder River Dam. Various situations were catered for in the event of the Germans surrendering, such as the general seizure of important areas (" Talisman "), the seizure of Berlin by 82 and 101 U.S. Airborne Divisions (" Eclipse "), the protection of Allied prisoners of war if the Germans got " tough " (" Jubilant ") and the seizure of the port of Kiel by the parachute brigade group and the glider-borne element of 1 Airborne Division in the liberation of Denmark.

1 Airborne Division and the S.A.S. Brigade in the Occupation of Norway

PLANNING

5. During the latter part of 1944 and the early part of 1945, plans had been under consideration to provide an operational and reconstruction force in Norway on the unconditional surrender of Germany. This force was to be known as Force 134, composed of all three Services, with the military element consisting of all Norwegian troops who had been training in Scotland, certain American troops, and a British element which included 52 (L) Division, the whole Force being commanded by Headquarters Scottish Command. When the time came in May, 1945, for this force to be employed, 52 (L) Division was committed in Germany and so 1 Airborne Division was nominated to take its place. The code-word for the operation was "Apostle ".

6. By May, 1945, 1 Airborne Division, still under Major-General R. E. Urquhart, had recovered from Arnhem and, though mainly made up of young and inexperienced personnel, had reorganized into a normal airborne division establishment less one parachute brigade, whose place was taken by 1 Polish Independent Parachute Brigade. The Division was carrying out an exercise called "Amber ", in Suffolk at the end of which it was hoped that it would be fit once again to take part in an active operation, so long as it was of simple nature and did not entail prolonged action. On 4th May, the Polish Parachute Brigade was ordered to return to base pending a move overseas, 1 Parachute Brigade was also returned to its locations to fly-in to Denmark to maintain order in that country, and on the next day the remainder of the Division was warned that it would be employed at short notice in an air-transported role in Norway. Within a few days of receiving its orders, 1 Parachute Brigade, less 2nd and 3rd Parachute Battalions, was in Denmark, the other two battalions remaining in England. Although they were never called forward they were not available for Norway as they were kept in reserve. The Special Air Service Brigade, who were operating in Germany with 21 Army Group were concentrated as quickly as possible and flown to England as aircraft became available to join 1 Airborne Division, taking the place of 1 Parachute Brigade.

7. As soon as the warning order was received Exercise "Amber " was closed down by stages, as the units were returned either to transit camps in Essex or to their normal locations in Lincolnshire, according to the preliminary plan for " Doomsday ", which was the name for the air-transported part of "Apostle ". Major-General Urquhart and some of his staff caught the night

train to Edinburgh on 5th May, and spent all the next day at Headquarters, Scottish Command discussing the details of the operation. Major-General Urquhart informed Command Headquarters that his Division only required three days to get ready for the operation, which was much less than the headquarters had expected. The divisional planning party travelled south again on Sunday night, 6th May, spent Monday and Tuesday on the final plans, and by 9th May the Division was ready to take off.

8. The tasks of the Division, with the Special Air Service Brigade under command, were :—

(a) To maintain law and order.

(b) To prevent sabotage of the most important civil and military installations, dumps and communications.

(c) To maintain the security of operational airfields.

(d) To ensure observance of the surrender terms by the Germans.

There were two main factors which affected the employment of the Division, the first being the lack of information regarding the enemy in Norway. It was not known whether the orders from the German High Command for total surrender would be obeyed by their subordinate formations, though it was hoped that the landing would be unopposed. The second factor was the necessity for speed in mounting the operation, the total time from the receipt of the warning order until the take-off of the advance parties from their airfields being only four days.

9. Because information was so scanty, and because briefing had to be done with materials and information provided by higher headquarters at short notice, the plan was essentially simple. The division was organized into three brigades (one an artillery brigade) each having its proportion of divisional troops, to land in three lodgement areas, selection of which was based on the following :—

(a) Military importance with regard to control of the German Forces.

(b) Political significance.

(c) Suitability of airfields for landing four-engined aircraft.

(d) Limitation of areas to be liberated initially owing to the size of the forces available.

(e) Distance from bases in the United Kingdom and feasibility of air and naval support.

10. The operation was to take place in two stages :—

(a) *Stage* 1

The occupation of :—

(i) Oslo by 1 Air-landing Brigade under Brigadier R. H. Bower who was appointed Commander, Oslo area, which would also contain Headquarters 1 Airborne Division and a large proportion of attached troops from Force 134, Civil Affairs, Disarmament Units, etc.

(ii) Stavanger by the Artillery Brigade under Brigadier R: G. Loder-Symonds, who was also Commander, Stavanger area. This stage was to be completed by 14th May.

(b) *Stage* 2

The fly-in of the Special Air Service Brigade, under Brigadier J. M. Calvert, to Stavanger, from where it would be sent to Kristiansand, which area it would take over.

11. Oslo was chosen as one lodgement area because it was the capital of Norway and was the centre of both Norwegian and German administration, Stavanger because it had a good airfield which was also suitable for the operation of fighter aircraft and was one of the nearest points to the United Kingdom with a good harbour, and Kristiansand because of its importance to the Royal Navy as a minesweeping base for sweeping the Skagerrak.

12. In accordance with the surrender terms, German delegates had been sent to the United Kingdom, and Allied representatives of all three Services, known as " Heralds " were to accompany them back to Norway. They were to take with them small parties who were to ensure the neutralization of anti-aircraft defences, withdraw airfield demolition charges, and report on the condition of the ports concerned from the point of view of the early arrival of reinforcements by sea. As soon as the " Heralds " reported the airfields as fit to land on, advance parties of Army and R.A.F. personnel were to fly in to establish airfield security and control.

13. Headquarters, 38 Group, still under Air Vice-Marshal J. R. Scarlett-Streatfield, was to control the air operations. In addition to having four Halifax and six Stirling Squadrons of its own, it would have under command 52 Wing (Brigadier-General Harold L. Clark) of IX Troop Carrier Command, with 80 C.46 (Commando) aircraft, and 80 Group R.A.F. (Air Vice-Marshal J. R. Boret) with Mosquitos and Mustangs. 52 U.S. Wing gave a good example of efficiency and " hustle ". They were warned for the operation by First Allied Airborne Army on the Saturday, were taken off their transport task in Germany on Sunday, flew to Lincolnshire on Monday and were ready for their Norway task on the Tuesday. They chose to operate 80 of their aircraft from one airfield.

14. Two airfields were to be used for landing the airborne troops, Oslo/Gardermoen and Stavanger/Sola. It was not considered that there would be fighter opposition to the transport aircraft, but as a " show of force " 12 Mustangs were detailed to cover Gardermoen airfield and six to cover Sola airfield during the initial landings of the advance parties. The air movement was divided into four phases :—

Phase I

Ten Halifaxes and five C.46 aircraft from Earls Colne and Barkston Heath to carry the advance parties and their jeeps and equipment to Gardermoen and Sola, and 18 Mustangs from Peterhead as fighter cover.

Phase II

(a) Seventy Halifaxes from Earls Colne and Tarrant Rushton and 140 Stirlings from Great Dunmow, Rivenhall and Shepherds Grove to carry personnel of Headquarters, 1 Airborne Division, divisional and attached troops and 1 Air-landing Brigade Group to Gardermoen.

(b) Seventy-six C.46 aircraft from Barkston Heath to carry personnel of the Artillery Brigade Group, and 20 tons of supplies, to Sola.

Phase III

This was to be a repeat of Phase II, except that personnel of the Special Air Service Brigade were to be taken to Sola.

Phase IV

Thirty C.46 aircraft from Barkston Heath to carry jeeps and stores to Gardermoen and Sola.

Phase I was to take place on 8th May, and the remaining phases on successive days. The shortest possible route was to be taken by all aircraft.

EXECUTION

15. Loading of aircraft began on the evening of 7th May, and was hampered because too little was known about the loading and lashing of stores into aircraft, and because the non-parachute elements knew nothing about the packing and loading of containers. Despite this the loading of the first lift was completed by 1100 hours on 8th May. No news came through from the " Heralds " on 8th May and so Phase I was postponed for 24 hours. One aircraft failed to take off owing to engine trouble but the remainder made a successful flight on 9th May.

16. By the evening of 9th May, the decision had been taken to launch Phase II with take-off times varying from 0200 hours to 1330 hours. By 0700 hours the weather had deteriorated badly and many aircraft signalled that they were returning to base because of weather over Oslo. At 0915 hours Gardermoen was unfit for landing, but Stavanger remained clear. By this time 116 aircraft had taken off for Gardermoen, of which 84 returned to base, 21 landed on other airfields in the United Kingdom, one landed on the Continent, seven landed on airfields in Norway, one crashed in Sweden and one was missing. The net result was that on 10th May only about 21 aircraft landed at Gardermoen, though all the C.46 aircraft bound for Sola arrived safely. Phase II was repeated on 11th May and was completed successfully, except for one aircraft crashing on take-off at Gardermoen, and one aircraft missing on the return flight. Of the missing aircraft one was eventually discovered to have landed at Eggemoen, and the remains of the other were found three weeks later in a thick wood about 30 or 40 miles outside Oslo. Unfortunately Air Vice-Marshal Scarlett-Streatfield was a passenger in this machine—a great loss to Army/Air co-operation in airborne activities.

17. Phase III took place on 12th May and was successful except that 27 aircraft from Barkston Heath were unable to take off owing to fog. Phase IV took place on 13th May, together with 49 sorties that had been abortive previously, and was successful. Between 13th and 28th May additional troops, chiefly S.A.S., were flown in, and supplies dropped to Kristiansand as requested by the Division and as weather permitted.

18. So the main part of the operation was completed successfully though it took 36 hours longer than planned. The casualties suffered by 1 Airborne Division (some days after the general cease fire, it should be remembered) were one officer and 33 other ranks killed and one other rank injured, and by the R.A.F., six killed and seven missing. Apart from the maintenance plan to build up a reserve of five days' supplies and petrol by " D " + 3 day the air-

transported part of the operation was now ended, and it is not intended here to go into details of the Division's role in Norway. However, a few examples will be given for the sake of interest.

19. The original plan had catered for a triumphal march by two battalions, plus attached troops, into Oslo on 10th May. However, as only a few aircraft managed to land this was curtailed somewhat drastically, and the actual march consisted of two small parties of 2nd Battalion The South Staffordshire Regiment, each about 30 strong, with Major-General Urquhart's car in the middle surrounded by four military policemen on motor-cycles. The party was somewhat apprehensive as they were not sure what attitude the Germans would adopt, but all was well, and they were given a terrific reception by the Norwegians—everyone seemed to be in the streets. Until the arrival of Headquarters, Allied Land Forces, Norway, some days later, Headquarters, 1 Airborne Division was in control of affairs in Norway. As a result Major-General Urquhart welcomed His Royal Highness the Crown Prince when he came ashore with advanced elements of his Government. The Division also took part in the ceremonies which welcomed His Majesty The King of Norway on his return to his country.

20. In addition to their main tasks the airborne troops gave every possible assistance to Russian and other Allied ex-prisoners of war, in rounding up war criminals, in segregating German troops to reservations, and in making the Germans " prove safe " buildings, minefields, etc. The latter was done under R.E. supervision and was not popular with the Germans as the " proving " consisted of German troops walking across the minefields shoulder-to-shoulder after the mines had been lifted. In the early days there were one or two accidents.

21. On the whole the Germans were found to be orderly and still under the discipline of their officers. They accepted Allied orders quietly and there were no serious cases of disobedience. To say the least of it the position was unusual. There were about 350,000 Germans and not more than 6,000 British troops. The Germans collected themselves in their camps, disarmed themselves, fed themselves and finally made arrangements for evacuating themselves. The morale of the Luftwaffe and Kriegsmarine remained high but there was no question of organized continuance of hostilities. In all areas the Germans were living in considerable comfort, having plenty of food and transport, and they did not regard themselves in any way as a beaten army.

22. The co-operation of the Norwegian Underground Organization " Milorg " was at all times very valuable and great assistance was rendered. They carried out their guard duties with great enthusiasm and maintained very close liaison with the British troops. Everywhere a great welcome was given to all ranks by Norwegian civilians and everything was done to make the soldier's stay in Norway a happy one. Civilian morale was high and strict law and order was maintained at all times.

23. 1 Airborne Division and the Special Air Service Brigade remained in Norway until the end of the summer and during their stay they were able to piece together the story of the operation " Freshman ", which was described in Chapter VII, and to bring to justice the Germans responsible for the murder of our men.

6 Airborne Division is Ordered to the Far East

24. As the German war drew to an end, plans were being drawn up for the invasion of Malaya in the Far East—operation " Zipper ".   The target date for this operation was 31st August, 1945, and it envisaged the use of one British airborne division, as 44 Indian Airborne Division would not be ready in time.   General Sir Oliver Leese, Commander-in-Chief, Allied Land Forces South East Asia, also required an airborne corps headquarters and he asked that both the division and the advanced elements of the corps headquarters should be deployed in India in time to take part in operation " Zipper ".

25. The world strategic plan for the positioning of British forces, after Germany had been defeated, included an airborne division as Imperial Strategic Reserve which would probably be based on the United Kingdom or North-West Europe for the first nine months after the end of the war in Europe, and thereafter in the Middle East.   1 Airborne Division was already committed to the Norway undertaking and in any case was not strong enough and required further training for sustained operations overseas, whereas 6 Airborne Division had not suffered too heavily in the Rhine crossing and pursuit across Germany and could be ready for operations again in a comparatively short time.   The decision was taken, therefore, to retain 1 Airborne Division as the Imperial Strategic Reserve and to send 6 Airborne Division to the Far East.

26. On 17th May, the Division returned to England where the men were sent on leave and reorganization took place, troops due for early demobilization being transferred to 1 Airborne Division which sent younger men in their place. By 1st June, however, General Leese had changed his plan and no longer required an airborne division for " Zipper ", but he wanted a parachute brigade which was to arrive in Bombay by 9th August for the capture of Singapore, while 6 Airborne Division, less the parachute brigade, was to concentrate in India in case it was needed later.

27. By 11th June, Major-General Bols had selected 5 Parachute Brigade as the one for the Singapore operation and in the first half of July about 600 all ranks of the brigade flew to India, the remainder going by sea.   Lieutenant-General Gale with some 500 personnel of Headquarters, 1 Airborne Corps, and the divisional commander and planning staff of 6 Airborne Division had flown out in July.   As will be seen in Chapter XXIV, corps headquarters concentrated at Gwalior where the staff studied plans for airborne operations against Singapore and Bangkok.

28. On 15th August, after the Japanese surrender, the War Office ordered 5 Parachute Brigade to remain in the Far East, but it cancelled the move of the remainder of 6 Airborne Division.

1 Airborne Division and the S.A.S. Brigade are Disbanded and 6 Airborne Division goes to Palestine

29. When 1 Airborne Division was retained as Imperial Strategic Reserve it was due to move to the Middle East at the end of 1945, but this plan was based on the supposition that 6 Airborne Division would be in the Far East. The post-war order of battle of the British Regular Army only included one airborne division and no S.A.S., and so when 6 Airborne Division's move was

cancelled there were two divisions to fill one role.   From the historical and sentimental point of view it would appear that if one formation had to disappear it should be the youngest and junior—6 Airborne Division, but the problem was not so simple as that.   Even if 2 Parachute Brigade, which had returned to England from Italy in June, were included, 1 Airborne Division was weak in numbers, having sent a large number of men to 6 Airborne Division, and included among its personnel were many due for early demobilization.   In addition, the Division had not had time to become fully trained before it went to Norway and had not had any training while in that country, so that it would have taken a considerable time to bring it up to the standard required for an Imperial Strategic Reserve.

30. It was therefore decided that 6 Airborne Division should be retained in the post war army.   1 Airborne Division and the Special Air Service Brigade returned to England at the end of August and went on leave, while 6 Airborne Division, consisting of 6 Air-landing Brigade, 3 Parachute Brigade with a new 17th Parachute Battalion taking the place of the Canadians, and 2 Parachute Brigade as its third formation, proceeded to Palestine.   1 Airborne Division spent the last two months of its existence preparing more drafts for 6 Airborne Division and generally " winding up ", and was finally disbanded on 15th November, 1945.

CHAPTER XXIII

AIRBORNE FORCES IN INDIA FROM DECEMBER, 1940 TO OCTOBER, 1943

General

1. The story of airborne forces in India from their beginning up to the end of 1945 falls naturally into two distinct phases, from October, 1940, until October, 1943, and from October, 1943, until December, 1945. The first period which was one of uncertainty, indecision, lack of volunteers and equipment and of frustration for those whose job it was to build up airborne forces in the country, will be dealt with in this chapter. We shall follow the higher policy discussions over the whole period in order to provide a background and then retrace our steps and see how each part of airborne forces developed in detail. The second period began immediately after, and as a direct result of Major-General Browning's visit to India in the autumn of 1943, and will be covered in Chapter XXIV. When reading these chapters the reader should bear in mind the great distances involved. To move a parachute brigade from Secunderabad to Rawalpindi is no ordinary move as we know it in England, for it is the equivalent of going from Kiel in Western Germany to Syracuse in Sicily. To assist the reader Map No. 17 shows Europe superimposed on India.

High Level Discussions

2. It was in June, 1940, that Mr. Churchill laid the foundation stone of British airborne forces, as we have already seen, and it was in October of that year that His Excellency the Commander-in-Chief in India, General Sir Robert Cassels, authorized the formation of a cadre of parachute troops. This cadre was intended to carry out experiments with the R.A.F. and to provide a nucleus of trained parachutists from which a mixed brigade of British, Indian and Gurkha parachute troops could be formed.

3. It turned out, however, that the experimental cadre was overtaken by events and was never formed, though the commander designate, Lieutenant-Colonel W. H. G. Gough, was sent to England to attend a course at the Central Landing Establishment, Ringway. Two other Indian Army Officers, Captain P. Hopkinson and Captain B. E. Abbott who were attending a staff course in England, also completed the parachute course at Ringway, and all three had returned to India by September, 1941.

4. On 2nd December, 1940, the Commander-in-Chief authorized the formation of three parachute battalions which were to be organized into a parachute brigade later, and asked for War Office approval. However, on 30th January, 1941, a signal was received by General Headquarters from the War Office stating that the policy for airborne forces was being considered and suggesting that the raising of parachute battalions in India should be postponed until it had been decided, but General Cassels was not prepared to accept the delay. On 16th April, an Airborne Troops Committee was formed under the Senior Air Staff Officer, Air Commodore Claude-Wright, of Air Headquarters (India) with the following terms of reference :—

"(a) To draw up proposals on all points affecting the formation, organization, equipment, location and training of an airborne brigade and an air-landing school ;

331

(*b*) to work out details and further procedure of the scheme when it is approved."

On 15th May, 1941, the Commander-in-Chief decided to proceed with the raising of the parachute brigade. Approval in principle to the formation of the brigade was given by the United Kingdom in June, subject to one battalion being British, and in the same month the Secretary of State for India, Mr. L. S. Amery, in a letter he sent to the Viceroy, showed that the project had his backing :—

> "I believe that India might do a really big thing by going ahead on her own, developing an airborne force that might turn the scale anywhere in these countries of open spaces, great distances and relatively weak forces at any one point."

It was not realized by everyone at that time that whereas airborne troops were normal fighting troops the aircraft to carry them were in many degrees specialized. The provision of specialized aircraft at that time could be made only at the expense of other forms of air power. Detailed instructions followed from the War Office in August and India was instructed to form an airborne brigade, for which she was to provide and train 2,500 parachute troops.

5. In October, 50 Indian Parachute Brigade was formed at Delhi and at the same time Air Headquarters authorized the setting up of the Air-landing School. For the remainder of the year, General and Air Headquarters concentrated their efforts on trying to obtain equipment and aircraft for the brigade and school, at the same time considering the possible expansion of airborne forces in India to include some air-landing troops and more parachute troops. The only aircraft available were unsuitable for parachuting and there were few of these. They investigated the possibilities of producing small ten-seater gliders in India, which would be towed by light aeroplanes, and also the possibilities of manufacturing statichutes in India, in which they had little success, for in December, 1941, it appeared that no Indian statichutes would be ready for a considerable time. At the end of 1941 India offered its parachute brigade to the British Government for overseas service and this offer was accepted.

6. In January, 1942, the Secretary of State for India, in keeping with the desire to expand, asked Mr. Winston Churchill for more airborne troops for India, upon which the Prime Minister suggested to the Chief of the Air Staff that there should be an extra airborne division—or better, its equivalent in brigade groups—raised in India as soon as possible, and asked him for his proposals for this.

The Chief of the Air Staff pointed out that we were already raising one airborne division in the United Kingdom, and a parachute brigade in India with a view to expanding it to a division. He said that the limiting factors were the shortage of instructors, parachute aircraft and glider tugs and that for the two latter we relied on bombers at home. India was in a different position and would have to "start from scratch" as there was no chance at present of increasing the facilities there. He concluded by saying that to start a second division in India then would only delay the formation of the first.

7. By the end of March, 1942, little progress had been made and discussions between India and the United Kingdom began to grow somewhat acrimonious. It appeared that on the one hand the home authorities felt that India was

trying to go too fast and was putting the war against the Japanese in front of operations in the west, and on the other hand India thought that Whitehall was not supporting her in the matter of airborne forces and was rather disinterested. It must be said, however, that the General Staff at New Delhi did not appreciate the complexity of the problems involved as the whole question of air support generally was dealt with by an inadequate staff for some considerable time, as will be seen later. The situation as pointed out by India on 30th March, was :—

(a) No Indian statichutes had yet passed tests and only 200 had been received from the United Kingdom against an order of 2,200 ; in Chapter X it was shown how some of these had arrived in the Middle East, either through misdirection or mis-appropriation.

(b) The six Hudsons promised six months previously to assist in air training had not yet arrived.

(c) The manufacture of ten-seater gliders was held up owing to the lack of timber and the delay in erecting a factory.

(d) There were no tug or troop carrying aircraft in India or in sight.

(e) No policy had been received from the United Kingdom on glider pilots ; therefore, no training was taking place.

At the same time Defence Headquarters, New Delhi, sent a signal to the Secretary of State in which they said :—

" . . . no doubt parachute and air-landing troops operating from India Command will be of greatest value in future operations. But useless for us to continue effort to provide these forces in present atmosphere of lethargy and indifference. Forces can be provided if we receive help and guidance asked for . . . ."

On the following day General Wavell, who had become Commander-in-Chief in India, sent the following signal to the Chief of the Imperial General Staff :—

" I am now planning possible operations in Burma in autumn and essential to know whether any prospect of being able use parachutists or airborne troops. We have now been waiting fifteen months for definite policy."

8. These complaints from India were answered a week later by the Secretary of State for India who made the following points :—

(a) Four thousand five hundred man-dropping statichutes had been ordered for India, of which 250 left the United Kingdom in mid-February, 700 were awaiting shipment, and the remainder would be delivered at the rate of 100 a week, rising to 150 a week in two months.

(b) Two thousand two hundred and fifty containers had been ordered with statichutes fitted, of which 80 were awaiting shipment and the balance would be delivered at the rate of 50 a week.

(c) The despatch of the six Hudsons, promised in October, 1941, had been delayed because one, captained by Flight-Lieutenant E. B. Fielden with Wing Commander F. M. Benito, commanding officer designate of the Air-landing School, as second pilot, crashed at Gibraltar, one crashed in England and weather conditions had been bad. The entry of Japan into the war had altered all priorities so that operational aircraft for India and the Far East had been put first. The first aircraft of the new six had left in mid-March, the crews of two had completed training by the end of March, one was being prepared for the Far East and the other two had not yet been allocated by 41 Group for modification purposes.

(d) The numbers of parachute operational aircraft would be included within the ceiling of heavy and medium bombers in India.

(e) It was impossible to ship Hotspur gliders to India as they could only travel as deck cargo.

(f) Glider pilots would have to be trained in the United Kingdom and their provision for India would be a long-term policy.

(g) The conclusion was that the provision of an air-landing brigade was a long-term project.

The Secretary of State ended by suggesting that officers should be sent home to discuss the above points, to which India replied that they could not spare officers to discuss matters on which they had expressed their views for the last 15 months.

9. From India's point of view the position was far from satisfactory as, allowing for the time taken on the voyage, she could not hope to receive the full quantity of statichutes before the end of December, 1942, or the containers before April, 1943, though this could be explained by the acute world shortage of shipping.

10. By June, the situation had improved somewhat. Deliveries of Indian statichutes had begun at the rate of 300 a month, and were expected to rise up to 1,750 a month by October, 1942. The first ten-seater glider produced by the Hindustan Company (*see* para. 32) had completed its tests satisfactorily, and the Tata Aircraft Company said that they would be able to begin production of Horsas in January, 1943, but there were many technical " snags " to be overcome which will be discussed later. However, India pointed out that if the six Hudsons were to be the only aircraft available, the target date of 1st September, 1942, set for the readiness of 50 Indian Parachute Brigade could not possibly be achieved and they repeated that :—

" . . . little advance will be made without His Majesty's Government's whole-hearted co-operation and assistance . . . ."

11. In September, India again returned to the charge and said that the supply of volunteers for parachute troops was dwindling because of the lack of air training and naturally this news had spread to troops of other formations. Besides this there was no Airborne Forces Experimental Establishment in India and all experiments had to be done by borrowing the Air-landing School aircraft, which interfered with their training programme. At the same time General Headquarters asked again if India was to provide air-landing troops, and if she was to provide a parachute battalion to replace 151 Parachute Battalion which was being withdrawn to the Middle East. The Chiefs of Staff replied that Indian airborne forces should be limited to parachute troops with glider-borne supporting arms, all of which were to be provided by India, and they confirmed that 151 Parachute Battalion was to be replaced.

12. Two months later the Commander-in-Chief, India, said that it was unlikely that a brigade of airborne troops would be required as a formation against the Japanese, and that therefore he was going to train battle groups of about a hundred each as he foresaw a possibility of their use in South-East Asia. He also said that if India was going to train parachute troops she must have another squadron of aircraft. In replying to Field-Marshal Wavell in December, the Chiefs of Staff pointed out that a brigade could be carried in several lifts, a principle which was accepted at home as inevitable until sufficient aircraft were available. They agreed to the formation of battle groups but suggested that headquarters should still be kept for the brigade and for the battalions. They also stated that aircraft would be despatched to India on the following programme :—

June, 1943	One Halifax squadron.
September	One Halifax squadron.
	One Wellington squadron.
December	One Halifax squadron.
	One Wellington squadron.

13. India did not form the battle groups but spent the first part of 1943 concentrating on the training of 50 Indian Parachute Brigade despite the shortage of equipment and aircraft. The period covered in the above paragraphs was undoubtedly a very difficult one for airborne forces in India, but responsibility lies on both sides. The authorities in the United Kingdom were concentrating on the war against the axis powers, and when Japan entered the fray, India and South East Asia were treated as subsidiary and something to which full attention would be given after Germany and Italy had been beaten. Shipping was desperately short among the Allies, the route to India lay round the Cape of Good Hope so long delays were inevitable, and every aircraft counted for a great deal. With this background in mind we shall now go back to 1941 and follow in more detail the fortunes of the various elements of airborne forces in India.

50 Indian Parachute Brigade

14. 50 Indian Parachute Brigade was formed at Delhi in October, 1941, under Brigadier W. H. G. Gough, to consist of the following units :—

Brigade Headquarters.
50 Indian Parachute Brigade Signal Section (Captain E. J. Buirski).
151 Parachute Battalion (Lieutenant-Colonel M. A. Lindsay).
152 Indian Parachute Battalion (Lieutenant-Colonel B. E. Abbott).
153 Gurkha Parachute Battalion (Lieutenant-Colonel F. J. Loftus-
Tottenham).
411 (Royal Bombay) Parachute Section Indian Engineers (Captain M. J. J.
Rolt).

Volunteers were obtained from all active units in India and the response was good. Brigade Headquarters was mixed, British, Indian and Gurkha, but the Signal Section was entirely British. 151 Parachute Battalion was also British and was formed from volunteers from about 23 infantry battalions, some 30 or 35 other ranks being accepted from each unit. Because of the very strict medical examination it was estimated that during its stay in 50 Parachute Brigade the battalion handled about 2,000 men. The Commanding Officer was only allowed to accept a maximum of nine regular officers, though scores volunteered. Most of the volunteers, both officers and other ranks, consisted of regulars who had been caught in India at the beginning of the war and who visualized their future part in it as a series of endless garrison and frontier duties. They saw in parachuting an opportunity to get some fighting and excitement. The only aircraft available at the time were five Valencias. Although they were obsolete and unsuitable for parachuting, one was used for the first experimental jump in India made at Karachi on 15th October, 1941, by Flight Lieutenant Brereton, Chief Instructor of the new Air-landing School, which is described later, and Captains Abbott and Hopkinson. Unfortunately the pilot misjudged the dropping zone, and all three landed on the concrete runway of the airfield and were injured.

15. During the next two months all units in the brigade began basic parachute training and collective training. Unfortunately it had been decided that the medical test for parachute duties would be the same as that for R.A.F. aircrews, and this resulted in a number of so-called " unfit " men being rejected, chiefly on the grounds of colour-blindness, which lengthened the " settling-down " process. In February, 1942, the first stick of parachute troops was dropped in India on an exercise, Major R. M. C. Thomas, the intelligence officer, and a section of 151 Parachute Battalion being used. Unfortunately, of the ten men dropped, one was killed and one was seriously injured.

16. In the summer, three small airborne operations were carried out (*see* Chapter XXV), one in Sind against the Hurs, and two in Burma, and tactical training continued steadily, an endurance test being undertaken in April by 151 Parachute Battalion who marched 50 miles in 22½ hours, only five men dropping out. Parachute training also continued but only slowly, and some men had to wait four or five months in their unit before being sent on a parachute course. The need for airborne exercises and refresher jumps became urgent—in some cases those who had qualified as parachutists on the original courses in November, 1941, had not jumped again as late as June, 1942. During June and July the whole brigade did a two months intensive course in combined operations at the Combined Training Centre, Poona. In August, large scale rioting broke out all over India, instigated by Congress. The brigade was employed on internal security duties in Delhi city. Thanks largely to its efforts, and especially those of 151 Parachute Battalion, the riots in Delhi were suppressed rapidly. It was probably the first time the parachute troops had been used in an internal security role and the Germans made much use of the fact for propaganda purposes. There was a considerable amount of firing during the rioting and this, coupled with the Sind operations, caused quite a sensation throughout India.

17. Lieutenant-Colonel Lindsay returned to England and was succeeded in command of 151 Parachute Battalion by Lieutenant-Colonel H. C. R. Hose, while Brigadier M. R. J. Hope Thompson took over the brigade from Brigadier Gough. The brigade moved north to Cambellpore near Rawalpindi in the Punjab, during October, where there were better training areas and better climatic conditions for parachuting. Just before they left Delhi, 151 Parachute Battalion was withdrawn for service in the Middle East (*see* Chapter X) and in December, 3rd Battalion 7th (3/7) Gurkha Rifles arrived to take their place. The Gurkhas had taken part in the Burma campaign of 1942 and the battalion was con-

siderably depleted by casualties and sickness, but despite this it had volunteered as a unit for parachute duties. The name of the unit was later changed to 154 Gurkha Parachute Battalion.

18. Throughout the period the system of holding reinforcements for the brigade was most unsatisfactory. In March, 1942, training companies had been authorized for each parachute battalion and later these were incorporated in the Parachute Troops Training Centre at Delhi, which was unsuitable from all points of view, but despite protests and much discussion the centre had to remain there for over a year. It then moved to Rawalpindi where it occupied a badly built camp with primitive drainage, leaking roofs and no electric light or power, and the camp remained in this condition until June, 1945. The Training Centre was treated as part of 50 Indian Parachute Brigade and held reinforcements on the scale of 30 per cent. for each parachute battalion, instructors being provided by the brigade and transfers being arranged mutually.

19. Training continued throughout the summer and autumn of 1943, but the strength of the brigade gradually became less through normal wastage and few replacements were available, as has been explained earlier, because of the generally discouraging conditions. Such was the situation when Major-General Browning arrived.

The Air-landing School (later No. 3 Parachute Training School)

20. On 1st October, 1941, Air Headquarters authorized the formation of an Air-landing School which would be responsible for :—

(a) The technical training of parachute troops in their parachute duties.

(b) Experiments in connection with and tests of special equipment required for :—

    (i) Parachute troops.

    (ii) Their maintenance by air.

(c) The training in glider drill and duties of glider-borne troops.

The school was established at Willingdon Airport, New Delhi, directly under Air Headquarters, and only had five Valencia aircraft. The Valencia was a remarkable aircraft. It had a cruising speed of about 85 miles an hour and a maximum speed of a little over 90 miles an hour. Instead of slowing down, full throttle was given just before the troops jumped, but in spite of this the delay in the development of the statichute was more comparable with that experienced in a balloon than in an aircraft. The first commanding officer was Wing Commander J. H. D. Chapple, with Flight-Lieutenant Brereton as his Chief Instructor, assisted by Captain P. Law as Chief Ground Instructor, Flight Serjeants Roberts and Oakes, and five Army warrant officers and staff serjeants. They brought with them a total of 14 statichutes in their personal baggage and set up their somewhat primitive equipment in two hangars.

21. In the first week of March, 1942, Wing Commander Benito arrived at Delhi. After the first Hudson had crashed at Gibraltar he had continued his journey *via* West Africa and the reinforcement route across Africa to Egypt, and so to India. He took over command of the Air-landing School from Wing Commander Chapple on 9th March, some six months after he was first selected for the appointment in September, 1941. At this time there were no aircraft available at the school as all five Valencias had been sent to assist in the evacuation of refugees from Burma. The staff consisted of eight R.A.F.

officers, five Army officers, four R.A.F. fabric workers from Ringway who also acted as Parachute Jumping Instructors and a number of Army non-commissioned officer instructors who had been trained at Ringway. The parachute packers were British and Indian Army other ranks who were trained and supervised by the R.A.F. fabric workers. Later the Army instructors were supplemented by Indian Viceroy's commissioned officers, Gurkha officers and Indian and Gurkha non-commissioned officers.

22. It will be remembered that the War Office and Air Ministry had agreed at the end of 1941 that all Army instructors at Ringway should be replaced by R.A.F. personnel, but the implications of this decision were not fully understood in India. When he arrived Wing Commander Benito began to implement the new policy on behalf of the R.A.F. and met a certain amount of resistance from Army authorities, though he was successful in the end.

23. The five Valencias returned to Delhi during the second week in April, but were nearly all severely damaged by a tropical storm a few days later. On 11th April, Flight Lieutenant Fielden, who had gone back to the United Kingdom from Gibraltar, arrived with the first Hudson. Like the others which followed, it had been modified in England by the addition of a wooden slide leading from the centre of the fuselage through the under gun hatch. Later in the month 16 descents were made from this aircraft without accident. Nevertheless, they were bad aircraft for parachute training, whether slide, aperture, which super-seded the slide, or door exit, which was developed later, were used. They were too fast, so that exit faults were aggravated, and only held a stick of eight men. At about this time Mr. L. L. Irvin, the parachute manufacturer, was visiting India on behalf of the Ministry of Supply to establish a parachute factory for the Indian Government at Cawnpore. He brought several prototype-X-type parachutes to Delhi, where satisfactory drop tests were made.

24. Accommodation for the Parachute Training School had never been very satisfactory, and in October, 1942, Willingdon became overcrowded so the school moved to Chaklala, near Rawalpindi, in the Punjab. Here was an airfield which was " off the beaten track " and therefore not liable to receive many visiting aircraft, where there was a spare hangar suitable for ground training, reasonable accommodation for the troops close to the airfield and good dropping zones in the vicinity. At the same time 215 Squadron R.A.F. moved into Chaklala and began training in dropping parachute troops, using personnel of 50 Indian Parachute Brigade. Up to date, Valencia, Hudson and one Lodestar aircraft had been used, but the new squadron was equipped with Wellingtons.

25. Courses lasted for 14 days but the output was limited to 30 parachutists each course, until April, 1943, when it increased to 60 a course. Despite the limited output, however, the casualty rate was far higher than in the United Kingdom. In October an officer and a serjeant were killed, in November there were four fatal accidents and in December a havildar was killed. In an effort to stop these accidents orders were issued that troops were not to be dropped below 700 feet, with the immediate result that at least one man's life was saved as his parachute remained unopened for the first 500 feet. Careful checks were carried out on all parachutes, and some Indian X-types were found to be not up to specification. But in January, 1943, another

man was killed and so Air Headquarters asked for Wing Commander M. Newnham, the commanding officer of No. 1 Parachute Training School, Ringway, to come out to India to advise on means of preventing fatal accidents.

26. He arrived in February and went into the problem thoroughly, especially the question of parachute maintenance. An immediate result of his visit was that Flight Serjeant Minter was sent out from Ringway in March with the up-to-date training syllabus. He was accompanied by Flight Sergeant Campbell who took over parachute maintenance. In this month an incident occurred which showed the Gurkha's attitude to flying. A Valencia, heavily laden with Gurkhas, crashed on taking off at Chaklala. Fortunately no one was hurt and the Gurkhas, who had never flown before, apparently thought this was the normal drill. They deplaned from the crashed aircraft, fell in and marched smartly back down the run-way, emplaned in another aircraft and went off quite happily to complete their air experience.

27. Improvements continued to be made to the synthetic training equipment and the running of the Parachute Maintenance Section during the next few months. 99 Squadron R.A.F., with Wellingtons, arrived for training in April, stayed for a month and were replaced by 62 Squadron with Hudsons. In June the first Dakota was allotted to the Air-landing School as part of a re-equipment programme. It was modified at Chaklala and was in use for jumping by the beginning of August.

28. In the period between the opening of the school and October, 1943, it had endeavoured to carry out the basic training of 50 Indian Parachute Brigade and had made good progress despite the many obstacles to be overcome. The chief of these were the difficulty of obtaining essential instructional apparatus, the shortage of R.A.F. instructors, for although 11 out of the 13 on the establishment had arrived they were always being taken for other jobs, and the scarcity of parachute packers and packing facilities, which alone would have made it impossible to carry out collective training, initial parachute training and operations at the same time. In addition aircraft, aircrews and packers were continuously being taken for operations, and from August, 1942, onwards an increasing proportion of the school effort was expended on training secret agents.

The Directorate of Army/Air Liaison, General Headquarters

29. As the war in the Far East developed, not only on the ground but in the planning, it became increasingly evident that air support would play a vitally important part—in fact a far greater part than in the war in Europe, especially on the supply side. Until the end of 1943, however, the staff at General Headquarters was much too small and the staff officers dealing with air support were much over-worked and naturally had little experience of airborne affairs.

30. By 1942, India was faced with a rapidly expanding Air Force, and on the airborne forces side the situation was most unsatisfactory as the complications of the problem were not realized. By the end of the year, a new commitment had appeared in the shape of supply by air on a large scale. In June, 1942, an organization was set up under a Lieutenant-Colonel who was known as the Deputy-Director of Staff Duties (Air). The establishment of his staff was two Majors, a Squadron Leader and a Flight Lieutenant, with seven clerks, but the R.A.F. appointments were never filled. In August the Air Force posts were deleted, and a Captain was substituted. This branch had to deal with all Army

aspects of air organization, training and equipment. In November the designation of the Lieutenant-Colonel was changed to Director of Army Air Liaison.

31. In December, an additional Lieutenant-Colonel was authorized for six months on the air liaison side, and a Lieutenant-Colonel and a Captain on the airborne side, forming two sections known as A.A.L.1 and A.A.L.2. Both sections were under the control of the original Lieutenant-Colonel and thus they remained, with the addition of five Indian clerks, for another year.

Efforts to obtain Gliders and Glider Pilots

32. Throughout the struggle to get 50 Indian Parachute Brigade equipped and trained, General Headquarters, India, always had in mind the eventual formation of an air-landing brigade, as has been seen when considering higher policy discussion. As early as September, 1941, an order was placed with the Tata Aircraft Company, Bombay, for the manufacture of 400 Horsa Gliders, and two months later the Hindustan Aircraft Company was asked to produce a wooden ten-seater glider which would probably be towed by a light aircraft such as the Audax or Lysander. Enquiries were also made as to the possibility of manufacturing Dakotas in India, but the blue-prints being taken out by Mr. Vincent, a representative of Tata's, were lost *en route* when his aircraft disappeared. By March, 1942, little progress had been made in the production of the Hindustan glider owing to a shortage of the correct timber, but Treasury sanction had been obtained for a further 400 Horsas to be constructed in India, though the order was not to be placed until the first 400 had been completed.

33. By May, the Hindustan glider prototype was ready and the first tests were satisfactory despite the fact that the wings had warped. In the same month India asked the United Kingdom if a nucleus of trained glider pilots could be sent out to train others in the country. In June, the Tata Aircraft Factory said they could begin production of Horsas in January, 1943, and would reach a production level of 40 a month by April, completing the order of 400 by December, 1943. The cost would be £12,500 a glider, which was a total of £5,000,000 as against the total of £500,000 sanctioned for the construction of a new glider factory, etc. In addition there was the problem of moving the gliders from the factory as there were no tugs and no glider pilots.

34. It was beginning to look as though the production of any type of glider in India was impracticable, and so in July, 1942, the Ministry of Aircraft Production, London, asked Washington for 200 Hadrians (CG4A) for India, with technicians to assist in assembling them. The Americans said that none would be available before January, 1943. A programme was then laid down for 20 Hadrians and ten glider pilots to arrive in India in January, 1943, a further 200 in June, 1943, with the necessary glider pilots from the United Kingdom, while an additional 470 gliders were to be held in America. When this arrangement was made the Ministry of Aircraft Production cancelled their contract with Tata's for the manufacture of gliders in India. Three months later the Hadrian programme was accelerated to allow 18 to be shipped in November, 1942, 100 in February, 1943, and 100 in March, 1943. By the beginning of 1943, however, the shipping situation was so bad that Field-Marshal Wavell was forced to ask Washington to postpone the shipping of gliders so as to concentrate on more essential war materials, and the question was not raised again until after Major-General Browning's visit to India in October, 1943.

340

CHAPTER XXIV

AIRBORNE FORCES IN INDIA FROM OCTOBER, 1943, TO DECEMBER, 1945

Major-General Browning's Visit to India, September/October, 1943

1. In September, 1943, the Vice-Chief of the Imperial General Staff, Lieutenant-General Sir Archibald Nye, instructed Major-General Browning to visit India, telling him that the objects of his visit were :—

(a) To report on the situation of 50 Indian Parachute Brigade.

(b) To advise on the plans for the operational use of the Indian parachute brigade in the campaign of 1943–44.

(c) To obtain from the Supreme Commander, South-East Asia Command, an agreed requirement with the Commander-in-Chief, India, for airborne forces for the prosecution of the war against Japan after the defeat of Germany.

(d) To advise the Commander-in-Chief, India, and the Supreme Allied Commander on the necessary build-up of formations, depots and operational bases.

2. Major-General Browning arrived at New Delhi on 17th September, 1943 accompanied by Lieutenant-Colonel Walch who, it will be remembered, was General Staff Officer, First Grade, at Headquarters, Major-General Airborne Forces, Major Bradish, Deputy Assistant Quartermaster-General at the same headquarters, and Lieutenant-Colonel A. B. Harris, an American liaison officer. On the way he had visited Allied Forces Headquarters at Algiers, Headquarters 15 Army Group at Bizerta, 1 Airborne Division at Taranto on the day that Major-General Hopkinson was killed, and General Headquarters, Middle East Forces, at Cairo.

3. Major-General Browning had his first discussion on 22nd September, with Major-General O. C. Wingate on the use of airborne troops in Burma, with special reference to co-operation between 50 Indian Parachute Brigade and Special Force in the forthcoming operations during the winter of 1943–44, which will be described in the next chapter. A complete identity of views was established. His next discussion was with the Commander-in-Chief, General (later Field-Marshal) Sir Claude Auchinleck, who agreed to issue an order to bring 50 Indian Parachute Brigade up to strength immediately as they were 1,200 short.

4. During the first week in October, Major-General Browning accompanied General Auchinleck and the Air Officer Commanding-in-Chief, Air Chief Marshal Sir Richard Peirse, on a visit to the brigade and to No. 3 Parachute Training School. The Commander-in-Chief was impressed with the brigade and promised that he would personally ensure that the very best material from the Indian Army would be made available in future for Indian airborne formations. He never went back on this promise and always maintained a personal interest in the formations, paying many visits in later days, visiting all units and getting to know all officers. One immediate result of this visit was that General Auchinleck ordered 30 British officers to be posted to the brigade.

5. In the next two weeks Major-General Browning had three important meetings, the first with Air Chief Marshal Sir Richard Peirse, the second with General Sir Claude Auchinleck, Admiral Lord Louis Mountbatten, General Sir George Giffard, General Officer Commanding in Chief Eastern Army and the third with General Auchinleck, Air Chief Marshal Peirse and Lieutenant-General E. L. Morris, Chief of the General Staff, India. As a result of these meetings the following requirements were agreed :—

(a) The despatch of one mobile parachute servicing unit from North Africa to Chaklala to augment the parachute packing facilities.

(b) A small number of experienced R.A.F. officers from 38 Group to assist in forming an airborne wing of C.47s (Dakotas) at Chaklala.

(c) An airborne staff officer to be appointed at Air Headquarters, India, as well as an R.A.F. staff officer with airborne experience.

(d) The provision of R.A.F. equipment for airborne operations during 1943–1944.

(e) The formation of an airborne forces depot at Rawalpindi.

(f) The upgrading of the Director of Army/Air Liaison at General Headquarters to Director of Air with the rank of brigadier, who would be found from outside India.

(g) The formation of an Indian Army Air Corps on the same lines as that in England.

(h) The raising of an Indian airborne division for operations in the winter of 1944–45 on the following conditions :—

(i) The provision from airborne resources outside India of the divisional commander, G.S.O. 1, G.S.O. 2, and D.A.Q.M.G.

(ii) The provision of a British parachute brigade as and when one could be released from European or Mediterranean operations, the brigade to arrive in India by 1st July, 1944.

6. The need for an Indian airborne division had been agreed in discussions with Admiral Lord Louis Mountbatten on long-term requirements of airborne formations for future operations in South-East Asia. His view, subject to review from time to time, was that for 1944–45 four airborne divisions would be necessary, two being American, one British from the United Kingdom and one from India. The latter would be made up of 50 Indian Parachute Brigade, 2 Parachute Brigade from the Mediterranean and an air-landing brigade and divisional troops to be formed in India. The War Office were therefore asked to approve the formation of an air-landing brigade and divisional troops in India, and to agree to move 2 Parachute Brigade to India by the spring of 1944. They agreed to the formation of the division, including the air-landing brigade and divisional troops, but emphasized that, with the exception of 2 Parachute Brigade, it would have to be found from within Indian man-power resources. They pointed out that the despatch of 2 Parachute Brigade from the Mediterranean must be dependent on events in that theatre, and that it must not be assumed that any additional aircraft would be provided for the division for training or operations until Germany had been defeated and the aircraft could be spared from other theatres.

The Expansion of 50 Indian Parachute Brigade and the Formation of 44 Indian Airborne Division

7. The expansion of 50 Indian Parachute Brigade followed on quickly after Major-General Browning's visit. By December some units had been expanded and re-organized, and several new units had joined (*see* Appendix O). The signal section was now mixed, but the independent parachute platoon was entirely British. Almost immediately orders were issued for the formation of what was originally called 9 Indian Airborne Division, but was later redesignated 44 Indian Airborne Division, and Major-General E. E. Down, from 1 Airborne Division, was appointed as the commander. The division was to form at Secunderabad. Major-General Down was given two tasks—to raise the airborne division and to act as airborne adviser to Lord Mountbatten. In the latter capacity he had considerable liaison with Major-General Wingate concerning the air aspect of the mounting of the Chindit operations. 50 Indian Parachute Brigade was to be incorporated in the new division and further units were provided by disbanding 44 Indian Armoured Division, the divisional troops of which were most enthusiastic about their new role.

8. In April, 1944, South-East Asia Command decided that the employment of a whole airborne division would not be necessary for operations in Burma, and in any case the air force units were not available then. However, in June, General Headquarters (India) suggested to the War Office that though this might be the situation then, it would not necessarily be so in the future, and that it might be advisable to have a nucleus for expansion. This was agreed, so those airborne troops that already existed remained in being.

9. In the meantime while discussions had been taking place, 50 Indian Parachute Brigade less 154 Gurkha Parachute Battalion had been sent to Assam to gain battle experience, and became involved in very heavy fighting in a ground role. Shortly after this operation Brigadier E. G. Woods assumed command of the brigade from Brigadier Hope Thomson who was invalided home. 154 Gurkha Parachute Battalion which had been sent to Secunderabad in May moved to Rawalpindi in August, by which time the remainder of 50 Indian Parachute Brigade had arrived there from Imphal to re-organize and to carry out air training, as many of the troops had not done a jump for nine months. It was the intention to use the whole brigade in operations in Burma in 1945, but the plan was eventually abandoned and only one composite battalion was used (*see* Chapter XXV). While at Rawalpindi the brigade received a visit from the Director of Air at the War Office, Major-General Crawford, who did a jump with a stick of Indian troops, using an Indian statichute, which greatly impressed all concerned. It was also in that period that the first jumps in India were made with the valise and kit-bag.

10. In October, 1944, the Supreme Allied Commander, South-East Asia asked India to go ahead with the raising of 44 Indian Airborne Division, and in the next month this was agreed by the War Office, though they said they could not state yet whether the British parachute brigade would be available. Part of the air-landing brigade was found from General Wingate's Special Force, and 14 Infantry Brigade was selected and renamed 14 Air-landing Brigade. It was commanded by Brigadier T. Brodie, Colonel F. W. Gibb being posted as deputy commander shortly after it joined the Indian airborne division. The

latter assumed command early in 1945 when Brigadier Brodie was invalided home. Owing to the low state in numbers and health of the British units in Special Force it was only possible to provide one British battalion, 2nd Battalion The Black Watch (Royal Highland Regiment). 4th Battalion (Outram's) The Rajputana Rifles, which had served with 4 Indian Division throughout the war, and 6th Battalion 16th Punjab Regiment, which at the time was the demonstration battalion at the Tactical School, Dehra Dun, therefore joined 14 Air-landing Brigade in Secunderabad early in 1945.

11. In January, 1945, the War Office stated that they would not be able to provide a British brigade for the division, and it was then decided that, in addition to the air-landing brigade, there would be two Indian parachute brigades, each of one British, one Indian and one Gurkha parachute battalion. As 50 Indian Parachute Brigade already consisted of one Indian and two Gurkha parachute battalions, this meant that an Indian parachute brigade headquarters, two British and one Indian parachute battalions would have to be raised. Special Force was about to be broken up and so Headquarters 77 Indian Infantry Brigade moved from Malthone (Central Provinces) to Rawalpindi and became Headquarters 77 Indian Parachute Brigade, under Brigadier C. J. Wilkinson with Colonel W. P. Scott as deputy commander. The two British battalions were to be formed from volunteers in Special Force, and 2nd Battalion The Queens Royal Regiment and 1st Battalion The Essex Regiment were to be reduced to cadre, with their own volunteers used as a nucleus for the two battalions. Later it was discovered that these regiments contained a large number of men with only a short overseas tour to complete before qualifying for repatriation, and so 1st Battalion The King's Regiment and 1st Battalion The South Staffordshire Regiment were substituted, and their volunteers were formed into 15th and 16th Battalions The Parachute Regiment.

12. In the meantime recruiting for divisional troops had been " stepped up," but considerable difficulty was encountered in finding British artillery, engineer and signals volunteers, and most of them were obtained from incoming drafts from the United Kingdom. 123rd Field Regiment R.A. left the division, being replaced by 159th Parachute Light Regiment R.A., and 23rd Light Anti-Aircraft Regiment R.A. came from the armoured division, and was redesignated 23rd Light Anti-Aircraft/Anti-Tank Regiment R.A. A reconnaissance squadron had been obtained by converting the Viceregal bodyguard, which was redesignated 44 Indian Airborne Division Reconnaissance Squadron (Governor-General's Bodyguard) and the men took to parachuting extremely well. In March, 1945, Special Force was disbanded and 12 Field Company R.E. became 12 Parachute Squadron R.E., the Special Parachute Company provided the foundation for 44 Indian Airborne Division Pathfinder Company, 51st and 58th Indian Composite Platoons R.I.A.S.C. became 58th Indian Parachute Composite Platoon R.I.A.S.C., and medical personnel were formed into 60th Indian Parachute Field Ambulance.

13. By April, 1945, the majority of the Division were concentrated at Secunderabad, except for 50 and 77 Indian Parachute Brigades, the engineer units and one company of the R.I.A.S.C., who were completing basic parachute training in the Chaklala–Rawalpindi area, and in May the Elephant Point operation took place near Rangoon and is described in Chapter XXV.

14. While the Division was assembling Major-General Down had to consider the problems of training it and getting it ready for war. He kept in close touch with the Air Directorate at General Headquarters and with the Airborne Operations Division at Headquarters South-East Asia Command which had been set up in December, 1944, under Brigadier Walch to study the technique of airborne operations in South-East Asia, to advise on the policy of airborne training, and to advise the command planning staff on airborne operational planning. Major-General Down had been told that his Division should be ready for operations by 1st November, 1945, and on 8th March he sent a letter to General Headquarters in which he set out a very concentrated training programme of the division which could not be compressed unless the standard of training was to be affected. He based his programme on beginning combined collective training with the R.A.F. on 1st August, but this was dependent on whether both parachute brigades had completed their basic training and joined the division by 1st July, and on a minimum of six squadrons each of 20 aircraft plus the necessary gliders being available by 1st August. Even then the target date would not be achieved, for the air training period coincided with the monsoon, so that there would be only about 17 flying days in August, and it appeared that the earliest date by which the combined force would be ready would be 25th December. Major-General Down also pointed out that while the combined training was being carried out the divisional staff would have to be doing preliminary operational planning and he therefore asked for a special training team to be provided to assist the staff. Major-General Down's recommendations were accepted and the target date for the Division was postponed to 1st December, 1945.

15. By July the training team under Lieutenant-Colonel G. H. Lea had joined, the Division was pretty well up to strength (see Order of Battle at Appendix O) and had moved from Rawalpindi and Secunderabad to Bilaspur, where conditions were extremely bad. Bilaspur is in the Central Provinces, about 450 miles west of Calcutta, and 200 miles from Ranchi. The nearest town of any size is Nagpur, which is about 150 miles away. The country was a curious mixture of very thick, at times almost impenetrable jungle, paddy and wide open fields that reminded one of Richmond Park. The area was one of the worst malarial areas in India, and elephantiasis, cholera and other diseases abounded in the local villages. The weather was pleasantly cool and dry in the winter but in the early part of the summer it became unbearably hot. The monsoon rains came in the late summer and the temperature then dropped. However, it was near five airfields, good dropping zones and suitable country for jungle training.

16. Before the Division moved to Bilaspur there had been much argument about the area, those against it, including Major-General Down, claiming that it was unsuitable country in which to prepare a division for war hurriedly, that the facilities were bad and that sickness would interfere with training. On the other hand, a great deal of money had undoubtedly been spent on the camps and even more on the airfields. These airfields included such technical buildings as special parachute drying rooms and tow rope stores which were not available and could not be reproduced rapidly elsewhere. Had it been necessary for the Division to move elsewhere the air force could not have provided the airfields necessary for the lift which was then planned. After some argument

it was decided that Bilaspur would remain the airborne training area. In fairness to the R.A.F. it should be mentioned that this was an Army decision made without any pressure from the Air Force.

17. Camps were built in some places literally in the jungle which had to be cut down between buildings. When the rains came, roads were quagmires, living areas morasses and administration a nightmare. Vehicles could scarcely get out of their lines, let alone from one camp to another and units were forced to spend much valuable training time in making places habitable and combating the effects of damp on weapons and equipment. The Division had to put up with a bad outbreak of skin disease—probably due to training through paddy-fields flooded to a depth of four feet in places, as it did not affect R.A.F. personnel. The disease was particularly bad among Gurkha and British units who were about 1,200 strong, and in several instances some 350 in a unit were ineffective from this cause. In addition to this, the two British parachute battalions were new units still " shaking down " and the shortage of aircraft was acute—a company drop was treated as an unusual event of great significance. The problem that Major-General Down and his staff had to face would have been a big one in normal circumstances but in the four months allowed it was immense.

18. Despite all the difficulties the Division persevered, encouraged by the drive and enthusiasm of its untiring commander and his officers, and by the long hours and hard work put in by the divisional staff in their efforts to help units. Conditions improved gradually and disease was got under control. Training was concentrated and continuous in all weathers and all temperatures, and sickness was not allowed to affect the intensity of exercises. Hours of work were long for the men, but for the officers they were endless, for very careful attention had to be paid to the troops' welfare so that the monotony of the existence could be relieved as much as possible.

19. By the end of the war a high standard of training had been achieved, the divisional commander had personally conducted test exercises for one company in each unit and at least one parachute brigade group exercise had been held, though without aircraft. Others were on the programme and would have taken place but for the Japanese capitulation. It was not easy to keep up the spirits of the parachute troops when they could not jump, but at least they had completed their parachute course. In the case of the air-landing troops it was even more difficult, and to offset the lack of gliders all air-landing troops were encouraged to volunteer for parachute duties and still remain in their units, an opportunity many gladly accepted. For the remainder of its stay in Bilaspur the Division took advantage of the better weather to relax and put its house in order, looking forward to the day when it would move to a more civilized station.

The Air Component

20. A few days before Major-General Browning landed in India, in September, 1943, Group Captain Donaldson arrived to take over command of R.A.F. Station Chaklala, and Wing Commander Benito, who had been acting in the dual capacity of station commander and Officer Commanding the Air-landing School, was able to devote all his energies to the latter. Later in the month No. 177 (Airborne Forces) Wing was formed consisting of wing headquarters

and Nos. 31, 62, 117 and 194 Transport Squadrons, two of which had Dakota aircraft. The following month Group Captain Donaldson took command of the new wing, and Wing Commander Benito became station commander at Chaklala.

21. It was in October, too, that the largest formation drop up to that time took place. Headquarters, 50 Indian Parachute Brigade, the Signal Section and 153 Gurkha Parachute Battalion took off in about 32 aircraft at Chaklala and after a three and a half hour flight across India dropped at Raiwala just north of the River Ganges, near Dehra Dun. A number of high-ranking officers including General Giffard watched the drop and a short exercise followed. After the exercise 153 Gurkha Parachute Battalion reported to the Jungle Warfare School, Raiwala, for a three weeks' course—a novel method in those days of joining a course of instruction.

22. In the meantime discussions had been proceeding concerning the necessity for a transport support group for India and South East Asia. In December, Headquarters Air Command, South East Asia received a signal ordering the formation of 229 Transport Group, and Air Commodore C. E. N. Guest arrived out from England to command it. The group was to be responsible for all transport support in India, including the training of airborne troops, though the greater part of its work would be the maintenance of communication trunk routes and the ferrying of aircraft. By the end of January the group headquarters staff, which included an army staff officer, Lieutenant-Colonel Wagstaff, had assembled at New Delhi in buildings very close to the Air Directorate of General Headquarters.

23. By the beginning of March, 1944, the whole of 50 Indian Parachute Brigade had completed its basic parachute course. The output of trained parachutists from each course had increased, largely owing to the arrival of Nos. 3 and 5 Mobile Parachute Servicing Units, and it was to go on increasing so that by December, 1944, it had risen to 160 a course and by August, 1945, to 450. By then some 20,000 all ranks had been trained and there had been 31 fatal accidents. The comparison of trainees who passed the course, as between British, Indian and Gurkha, and of refusals, is interesting, especially in relation to the performances of the R.A.F. Iraq Levies Parachute Company (Chapter X) :—

(a) *Passed Basic Course*

British	..	..		85·5 per cent.
Indian	..	..		90·8 per cent.
Gurkha	..	..		89·9 per cent.

(b) *Refusals*

British	..	..	..	..	5·3 per cent.
Indian	..	..	..	..	4·9 per cent.
Gurkha	..	..	..	..	4·5 per cent.

However, to revert to the situation in March, 1944, although the basic training of the brigade had been completed the situation was far from satisfactory, as parachute training had to be suspended in March, because all aircraft were taken away for operations in Burma, and did not recommence until May.

24. At the end of April, the R.A.F. Station, Chaklala, including the Air-landing School and the R.A.F. component of the Airborne Forces Development Centre, were transferred to 229 Group, and the station was reorganized as No. 1333 Transport Support Training Unit. The new unit included the Air-landing School, renamed No. 3 Parachute Training School, a flying training unit, a servicing wing, a glider servicing repair flight and a " satellite " or two, and was to be responsible for :—

(a) The conversion of crews to Dakota aircraft.
(b) The training of parachute troops.
(c) The advanced training of glider crews.
(d) The training of aircrews in supply dropping, parachute troop dropping and glider towing.

25. By September, the situation was that four squadrons were earmarked for work with airborne forces when not required for supply dropping, etc., in Burma. Of these 31 and 62 Squadrons each had 30 crews to be trained in airborne work, 31 Squadron had 19 aircraft, 62 Squadron had 11 aircraft, and Nos. 435 and 436 Squadrons, R.C.A.F., were being formed. A month later the situation had improved as there were six squadrons available, Nos. 31, 62, 194, 353, 435 and 436. However, at a strength of 20 each, these squadrons could only produce a total of 120 aircraft whereas the minimum required for a brigade group drop was 154 plus a reserve of 15. This situation continued for over a year until aircraft were either withdrawn from the Burma front or transferred out from England.

26. By January, 1945, it had been practically decided that an airborne assault force of more than one division would be used in South East Asia that year. This necessitated the formation of a group headquarters on the lines of 38 Group in the United Kingdom. 238 Group was formed, therefore, under Group Captain D. E. Cattell, with the following functions :—

(a) The mounting and training of air forces for airborne assault operations.
(b) The air training of airborne forces for airborne assault operations.
(c) The detailed planning for operations under Headquarters, Air Command, South East Asia.
(d) Liaison with Headquarters, 44 Indian Airborne Division on all matters of airborne training and operations.

No. 3 Parachute Training School, all glider squadrons and certain R.A.F. squadrons were placed under the control of the new group. The next six months were chiefly taken up by 238 Group in planning for the recapture of Malaya, and for the reception of the numerous Dakota squadrons that were expected in India from the United Kingdom. The end of the Japanese war found group headquarters about to move to Bilaspur but this move was cancelled. Instead they joined the airborne division at Karachi where a combined divisional/wing headquarters was set up with Army and Air Force " opposite numbers " working closely together, sharing offices at times, with all facilities pooled and a common officers' mess ; it was not long before the President of the Mess Committee of the divisional headquarters mess was a squadron leader. Soon after the end of the war the group was reduced to a wing as part of 229 Group and as officers were posted home so the wing became smaller until only one or two R.A.F. officers remained as advisers to the divisional commander.

The Indian Parachute Regiment

27. The Commander-in-Chief took a little time to implement his decision to form an Indian Airborne Forces Depot and an Indian Army Air Corps, and it was also some time before the Glider Pilot Regiment was put on a proper footing.   At the beginning of 1944, the designation of the Parachute Troops Training Centre was changed to the Indian Airborne Forces Depot and it was placed under the control of the old Directorate of Army Air Liaison, now re-named the Directorate of Air, with Brigadier O. L. Jones at its head.   Instructors continued to be drawn chiefly from 50 Indian Parachute Brigade though a certain number were supplied from elsewhere and the scale of reinforcements was fixed at 20 per cent with units and 20 per cent at the depot.

28. In March, 1945, the existing Indian and Gurkha parachute units were formed into the Indian Parachute Regiment, the Colonel of which was Lieutenant-General Browning.   These were 152 Indian and 153 and 154 Gurkha Parachute Battalions, but additional units were required for the new Division and so an extra battalion and four defence companies were raised, one for division headquarters and one for each brigade headquarters.   Up to that date mixed Mohammedan and Hindu battalions had been the general rule of the Indian Army, although there had been a number of Hindu regular units. The new battalions were to be reformed into one-caste units, including the first and only all-Mohammedan unit in the Army, and were re-designated as follows :—

1st Battalion The Indian Parachute Regiment	..	Hindu.
2nd Battalion The Indian Parachute Regiment	..	Gurkha.
3rd Battalion The Indian Parachute Regiment	..	Gurkha.
4th Battalion The Indian Parachute Regiment	..	Mohammedan.
14th Company The Indian Parachute Regiment	..	Hindu.
44th Company The Indian Parachute Regiment	..	Gurkha.
50th Company The Indian Parachute Regiment	..	Hindu.
77th Company The Indian Parachute Regiment	..	Mohammedan.

2nd and 3rd Battalions were formed from 153 and 154 Gurkha Parachute Battalions respectively, and between them they formed 44th Company.   The Hindus and Mohammedans of 152 Parachute Battalion formed the nucleus of 1st and 4th Battalions and of 14th, 50th and 77th Companies.   The majority of men for both the battalions and the companies were produced as a result of recruiting tours to units of North-West Army.   As these units were merely garrison troops, the men had little conception of the style or conditions of modern warfare.   As recruiting was barely completed by June, 1945, the proposed date of readiness left very little time for thorough training to battalion level.   Nevertheless all the battalions and companies rapidly became first class units.   The Hindu units were composed of Mahrattas, Rajputs, Dogras, Kumaonis Gharwalis and Jats, the Mohammedan units of Pathans, Punjabi Mussalmen, Rajputana Mussalmen and Mohammedan Rajputs and the Gurkha units of all castes of Gurkha.

The Glider Pilot Regiment and the Glider Situation

29. After Major-General Browning's visit and the subsequent decision to raise an air-landing brigade the question of gliders and glider pilots for India was raised once again.   At the end of 1943, the Air Ministry informed South East Asia Command that there was a possibility of 150 Hadrian Gliders each

349

month being delivered during 1944. To this South-East Asia replied that the gliders would have to go to India, that there would be not more than one squadron of aircraft available for airborne forces and that manpower resources in India would not permit them to receive so many gliders a month, though they would accept up to 100 for trials at Chaklala. But they made it clear that at least 200 gliders were required as a long-term policy for operations during 1946. However, it was impossible to stop the first consignment which began to arrive at Chaklala at the end of February and were assembled by R.A.F. personnel, the first being ready to fly in April. By May a number were ready and by August the manpower situation had so improved that South-East Asia asked for a further 650 Hadrian Gliders, stating that they were hoping to work up to the assembly of seven gliders a day by November, 1944.

30. Meanwhile, General Headquarters was trying to get pilots to fly the gliders. They asked the United Kingdom for 80 crews in January, 1944, but were told that until after the invasion of North-West Europe only 30 crews could be spared and that these would be sent from North Africa, so they asked the Middle East for 40 non-commissioned officers to be trained as second pilots. The first glider pilots to reach Chaklala were those from North Africa consisting of four officers and 24 non-commissioned officers, under Major P. F. Stancliffe, all trained and experienced. They were sent to Ambala for a three weeks refresher course on flying light aircraft, a small amount of Tiger Moth flying was available at Chaklala, and when not actually flying the pilots were given intensive training in instrument flying on the Link Trainer.

31. In April, 40 volunteer non-commissioned officers arrived from the Middle East and as vacancies were not available until August at Elementary Flying Training Schools in India they had to be content with theoretical instruction, and at the beginning of May as no Dakotas were available for towing, the detachment went up to the cool of the Murree Hills, leaving only one section at Chaklala. However, shortly afterwards the Transport Support Training Unit was formed at Chaklala, and glider towing was included in the syllabus. During June, in the very great summer heat of Rawalpindi, training became intense and much glider flying was carried out, including long night cross-country trips.

32. In August a war establishment was published for the detachment and it was designated " 10 Independent Glider Pilot Squadron," consisting of squadron headquarters and three flights, with a strength of ten officers and 133 other ranks, but it was only at half-strength and recruits had to be obtained from units in India.

33. It was then decided that a considerable further expansion was required and as there was a shortage of manpower the majority of the additional glider pilots were to be provided from the R.A.F. These were sent out from the United Kingdom with 200 Army glider pilots, and in December the R.A.F. glider wings were formed :—

Headquarters	*Headquarters*
343 *Glider Pilot Wing.*	344 *Glider Pilot Wing.*
668 Glider Pilot Squadron.	671 Glider Pilot Squadron.
669 Glider Pilot Squadron.	672 Glider Pilot Squadron.
670 Glider Pilot Squadron.	673 Glider Pilot Squadron.

The wings were commanded by R.A.F. wing commanders with army majors as seconds-in-command, and in squadrons where there was an army squadron commander there was an R.A.F. second-in-command. Unfortunately someone had made some very rash promises to the R.A.F. glider pilots before they left the United Kingdom. The pilots alleged that they had been told that :—

(a) They would take part in operations very soon, probably within six weeks of arriving in India.

(b) Glider Squadrons would be entirely an R.A.F. " show " and not under the Army at all.

(c) No pilot would be kept on gliders for more than 18 months and on arrival in India they were threatened with a longer time.

(d) There would be no army training other than small arms weapon training which was normally carried out by other R.A.F. personnel.

However, nothing could be done about the complaints except to devise expedients to keep the pilots employed.

34. In March, 1945, 10 Independent Glider Pilot Squadron was disbanded, a decision which did a certain amount to alleviate the inter-service " warfare " and spread the experience. All qualified pilots were transferred to 670 Glider Pilot Squadron, which also took in the army trainees after they had finished their elementary flying training school courses at Jodhpur and Begumpet. From now on until the end of hostilities intensive training was carried out, but was hampered because, although a number of Horsa Gliders had reached India in addition to Hadrians, trials had proved that in the eastern climate the Dakota/Horsa combination was not operationally possible, and that four-engined aircraft were necessary. There were few of these available and so massed glider exercises were never achieved.

44 Indian Airborne Division Changes its Name and Reorganizes

35. While 44 Indian Airborne Division was at Bilaspur, plans had been drawn up and preparations made for large-scale operations in Burma and Malaya involving the use of airborne troops, which are described in the next chapter. Part of these preparations was the arrival of Headquarters, 1 Airborne Corps at Gwalior under Lieutenant-General R. N. Gale. The Indian Airborne Division was placed under command of 1 Airborne Corps in August, 1945, but two weeks later the Japanese capitulated and the need for an airborne corps no longer existed. It was disbanded on 23rd October, 1945.

36. The first effect of the end of the war on 44 Indian Airborne Division was that they had to supply several teams of officers and non-commissioned officers, both British and Indians, who were dropped into Japanese held territory to assist in the Relief of Allied Prisoners of War and Internees (R.A.P.W.I.). Each team consisted of a medical officer, a medical orderly, one combatant officer and one combatant other rank, the last two for protection and to organize administration. They were dropped over wide areas ranging from Sumatra, Malaya, Java and French Indo–China to Hong Kong, they did invaluable work in helping the prisoners and attending the sick, and in more than one case the initial surrender of a Japanese Army was accepted by a handful of men.

351

37. Much progressive thought was given to the employment of airborne troops, parachute training of the Division continued and by the autumn was going ahead far better than it ever had done during the war, but there was no glider training for the air-landing brigade, as the R.A.F. glider pilot squadrons were disbanded and the army glider pilots were either sent home or dispersed among R.A.F. airfields in ground roles.

38. During October and November, the Division less one parachute brigade moved to Karachi, Sind, one parachute brigade group went to Quetta, in Baluchistan, and the name of the Division was changed to 2 Indian Airborne Division. At the end of the year decisions were made on the future of the Division which eventually resulted in its complete reorganization and Nationalization,* though the formation of separate states of India and Pakistan was not foreseen. The main decisions were :—

(a) The Division was to be Nationalized as soon as possible.

(b) All British troops were to be withdrawn from the Division and formed into 6 British Independent Parachute Brigade (Brigadier C. J. Wilkinson), which would remain under command of the Division.

(c) All British staff officers were to be replaced by Indian officers, working from the junior ranks upwards.

(d) The Indian Parachute Regiment was to be disbanded and all members of it, where possible, except Gurkhas, transferred to other parachute units.

(e) Gurkhas were to be withdrawn from the Division.

(f) The Division was to consist of three parachute brigades, 14 Air-landing Brigade (Brigadier R. B. Scott) being re-organized as a parachute brigade, and divisional troops. Parachute battalions were to be regular units of the Indian Army and certain regiments were detailed to provide a parachute battalion. For example, one such regiment was the Rajputana Rifles whose parachute unit was the 4th (Parachute) Battalion, the Rajputana Rifles. A complete order of battle of the Division as it was two years later, on 1st January, 1947, is given for the sake of interest at Appendix " O."

39. This ends the story of Indian airborne forces leaving 2 Indian Airborne Division preparing for a vast re-organization and training programme for new units, still under Major-General Down, though he was to be replaced shortly by an Indian Army Officer, Major-General C. H. Boucher. Did they but know it, the Division was about to take part in the quelling of the Royal Indian Naval mutiny and civilian riots at Karachi, the rescue of stranded villages on a flooded island at the mouth of the River Ganges, demonstration jumps for the Staff College at Quetta and one of the biggest air-transported deployments of troops in India in connection with widespread disturbances at Multan, Jacobabd, Lahore, Ambala, Rawalpindi and throughout the Punjab. They also had to stand by for operations against the Pathans on the North-West Frontier. The Indian Airborne Division had achieved full status at last after many difficulties, but it is doubtful if it would have done so without the original drive, energy and determination of Major-General Down and his officers who overcame every obstacle in their way despite setbacks and lack of interest shown on occasions.

---

* " Nationalization " was the term used to describe the replacement of all British personnel by Indians, as they were then.

CHAPTER XXV

OPERATIONS, IN THE FAR EAST

General

1. Although there were no operations in the Far East, except those of General Wingate, on anything approaching the scale of those that took place in Europe, there were several that varied in size from brigade groups downwards, some of these being by parachute and others by glider. In addition, there were a number of large-scale air-transported operations, for South-East Asia Command used air transport for strategical moves of troops and equipment from one point to another far more than did the armies in Europe. The majority took place under somewhat unusual conditions and each one has a peculiar interest of its own. In this chapter some of these operations will be studied in outline, all those that were carried out by troops of Indian airborne forces being dealt with and also the more interesting of those undertaken by other forces. One operation that will be described is that of 50 Indian Parachute Brigade in a ground role in Assam, between February and July, 1944. There were no airborne aspects to this fighting, but in the same way as the operations of 1 Parachute Brigade in North Africa in 1942–43 showed what could be done by determined British troops, those of 50 Indian Parachute Brigade show the very heavy fighting that well trained troops with a high morale can undertake even in the worst conditions. On the other hand the ground operations of Major-General Wingate's Special Force, 3 Indian Division, will not be covered, as only the air-landing tasks are of interest to this history. The only British airborne formation in the Far East was 5 Parachute Brigade which was not used in an airborne role but took part in ground operations in the Dutch East Indies that are not described here.

Operations " Drab ", " Puddle ", and " Firepump ", July to August, 1942

2. These operations were the first that were undertaken by Indian airborne forces and, small though they were, they are interesting for this fact alone. In the Sind Desert in North-Western India, there was a tribe known as the Hurs, who belonged to a fanatical Moslem sect and who were ruled by a leader who was regarded by his people as almost a god, to such an extent that the Hurs would carry out any outrage at his request. All men of the tribe were armed, and by 1942 they had established a reign of terror in a large area of the Sind Desert. Despite the fact that many punitive expeditions had been taken against them and that a number of their minor leaders had been branded as outlaws and criminals and thrown in jail, they continued with their outrages. The Hurs were extremely difficult to catch and so in July, 1942, it was decided to deal with them by dropping one company of 152 Indian Parachute Battalion in co-operation with other forces in the area. However, the tribesmen's intelligence was very good and, although the actual drop was successful, no contact was made with them.

3. In the same month it was known that the Japanese were constructing airfields in the Myitkyina area of Burma and it was suspected that they were moving troops up on the two main roads of Myitkyina–Fort Hertz and Myitkyina–Mogaung–Maingkwan, but information in such close country was difficult to obtain. It was therefore decided to drop in a reconnaissance party

of one British officer, Captain J. O. M. Roberts, three British other ranks, three Gurkha Viceroy Commissioned Officers, one Gurkha Havildar and three Gurkha Lance/Naiks, all except the British other ranks being from 153 Gurkha Parachute Battalion. On 3rd July, the party was dropped from a Lodestar aircraft about 40 miles from Myitkyina and it remained in enemy territory collecting information for some 42 days. While they were behind the lines the only member who remained free from fever throughout the operation was Captain Roberts, and to add to their difficulties they found that none of the local inhabitants could speak either Hindustani or Gurkhali. However, by chance they met some British officers of the Burma Levies who had also remained behind the Japanese lines with their troops, and as a result a considerable amount of information was eventually obtained.

4. On 13th August, 1942, a party consisting of two officers, Captain G. E. C. Newland, 153 Gurkha Parachute Battalion and Lieutenant R. A. McClune, an Engineer officer, four British other ranks, one Gurkha Viceroy Commissioned Officer and four Gurkha other ranks, was dropped at Fort Hertz to join up with the " Puddle " force and to start draining and repairing the landing ground at Fort Hertz so that an infantry company could be flown in subsequently to act as a garrison. The operation was entirely successful and the company was later flown in, the same aircraft being used to evacuate the " Puddle " and " Firepump " parties.

Operations at Wau, New Guinea, 29th–31st January, 1943

5. In January, 1943, Wau was being used as an outpost for Port Moresby and it was realized that it was only a question of time before the Japanese attacked, for it overlooked their bases at Lae and Salamaua, possessed an air strip and could be used by us as a base for future attacks on to Lae and Salamaua. The 2/5th and 2/7th Australian Independent Infantry Companies, with a detachment of the New Guinea Volunteer Rifles, the whole known as the " Kanga Force ", were moved to Wau as a garrison with the tasks of reconnoitring the jungle trails forward towards the Japanese bases. Thorough as the Australian reconnaissance was in the very thick country, although they found two tracks, they missed one which had been partially surveyed before the war by a German and then forgotten by everyone except the Japanese, who moved their main force along it to attack the Australians, at the same time sending token forces along the other two. Parties were sent out to deal with the Japanese feints, the main attacks still being unsuspected, but by 28th January, the direction of the main attack became apparent and the enemy managed to work to within 800 yards of the air strip.

6. Reinforcements had been waiting at Port Moresby but owing to the weather it had been impossible to fly them in. On the morning of 29th January, at 0700 hours, the situation at Wau was becoming desperate and the valley was covered with dense clouds so that it did not appear possible that there would be any chance of obtaining reinforcements that day. However, luck was with the Australians for quite suddenly at 0800 hours the clouds rolled back and at 0830 a high flying fighter on weather reconnaissance passed over the town. Half an hour later C.47s began to come in and unload, bringing with them the remaining troops of 2/5th and 2/7th Australian Infantry. 57 aircraft landed on that day, bringing in a total of approximately 1,400 men with their weapons,

354

ammunition and three days' emergency rations. On the following morning 30th January, the Japanese launched a strong attack directed against the air strip but it was held and thrown back by our counter-attack, and at 0930 hours transports arrived again, this time bringing 25-pounder guns of the 2/1st Australian Field Regiment. 54 aircraft arrived on this day and on the following day more troops, equipment and ammunition were flown in. The Japanese were so taken aback by the arrival of these troops and heavy equipment under their very noses that not only did they suffer severe casualties, but they were unable to reorganize for another attack.

7. This operation which marked the beginning of the counter-offensive that drove the Japanese back to the coast of New Guinea had many interesting features. The aircraft landed under enemy small arms and mortar fire and the troops deplaned straight out into their defensive positions. In fact in some cases they came out of the aircraft shooting and immediately engaged the enemy. Not more than two planes were able to land on the air strip at any one time as it was only 1,100 yards long and there was a difference of 300 feet in elevation between one end of the air strip and the other, so that the aircraft had to land uphill, unload, turn round and take off down hill. Despite this there were no crashes which speaks highly for the skill of the American pilots.

Markham Valley, New Guinea, 5th September, 1943

8. It has already been mentioned that the operations at Wau were the beginning of a general Australian counter-offensive against the Japanese in New Guinea toward Lae. One of the first steps in this counter-offensive was the capture of Lae, which would provide a forward base that could be supplied by sea for further advances against the Japanese, and the control and improvement of the Markham Valley for the establishment of advance airfields. The valley of the River Markham varied in width from five to twenty miles and consisted chiefly of coarse sand and alluvial gravel which was easy to drain. Being covered only with grass it was possible with a limited amount of labour to construct airfields of any size wherever required. The main enemy bases of Rabaul, Wewak and Madang and his airfields in the west of New Britain were within range of medium bombers operating from Dobadura, but there were no airfields near enough to give adequate fighter protection to these bombers and therefore it was necessary to establish landing strips further north, for which purpose Markham Valley was ideal.

9. The plan catered for a combined operation that included an amphibious landing by 9 Australian Division east of Lae, an overland thrust from Tsili-Tsili to Nadzab by the 2/2nd Pioneers and the 2/6th Pioneer Company, Signals and Ambulance personnel, a parachute drop at Nadzab by 503 U.S. Parachute Infantry Regiment with under command one troop of 2/4th Australian Field Regiment and, finally, the fly in of 7 Australian Division.

10. Planning for the operation began in 1943 and intensified training by all the troops taking part was carried out on the mainland of Australia, including a complete dress rehearsal. Port Moresby was to be the take-off area for the parachute troops and 503 Parachute Infantry Regiment arrived in August but the troop of 2/4th Australian Field Regiment was not warned for the operation until one week before it. They had never done any parachute training before

and they underwent a very short course, which was long enough for each man to make one jump before the operation in which they were to drop with two Q.F. 25-pounder Light (Australian) Mark I guns, four officers, four non-commissioned officers and 26 other ranks.

11. The tasks of 503 Parachute Infantry Regiment were to drop on " D " day to :—

  (a) capture the area Nadzab–Gabmatzung–Gabsonkek, with the object of covering the preparation of the Nadzab emergency landing field ;

  (b) establish a road block across the Markham Valley road to prevent enemy movement into Nadzab ;

  (c) begin the work of preparing the Nadzab emergency landing field as soon as they had landed and before the arrival of the 2/2nd Australian Pioneer Battalion.

12. Two air strips in the Port Moresby area were to be used for take off and " D " day was to be 5th September, with the time of take off as soon after 0800 hours as the weather permitted. By 0730 hours a weather reconnaissance plane had reported that it was clear and the first plane took off punctually at 0800 hours, arriving over the target area by 1030 hours, not having met any enemy activity *en route*. So that their approach could not be detected so easily, after crossing the mountains the planes used a low approach to the dropping zones, pulling up to the jumping height of 500 feet just before reaching them. The dropping zones were large enough to allow the aircraft to fly in elements of six. A total of 303 aircraft were used in the operation, and in the parachute lift 81 aircraft dropped all their troops in four and a half minutes.

13. The landing, which was covered by bombing attacks on the villages of Gabmatzung and Gabsonkek and the Markham Valley road, was unopposed except for a few small enemy patrols which were encountered during assembly. Two hours after landing had taken place all parachute units were in position covering the area of the airfield, and work on Nadzab emergency landing ground had begun by burning the Kunai grass with flame-throwers. The Australian Pioneers and Field Company crossed the Markham River at Kirklands Dump by rubber boats and folding-boat bridge as soon as the forward airborne troops had landed. With their assistance such good progress was made on the development of the air strip during the night that by 1000 hours the following morning the first transport aircraft landed with American engineers and heavy engineering equipment. Two more air strips were begun immediately and on the morning of 7th September, Headquarters, 7 Australian Division and part of 25 Australian Infantry Brigade Group was flown in. They were complete in the area a few days later.

The Operations of 3 Indian Division (Major-General Wingate's Special Force)—March, 1944

" Granted the power to maintain forces by air and direct them by wireless, it is possible to operate regular ground forces for indefinite periods in the heart of enemy occupied territory to the peril of his war machine. This is because the value of such forces is disproportionate to their cost. One fighting man at the heart of the enemy's military machine being worth many hundreds in the forward battle areas." (WINGATE, 1943.)

Illustration 27.   Container, C.L.E., Mk. 3, less parachute, but with cradle ready for bombing up.

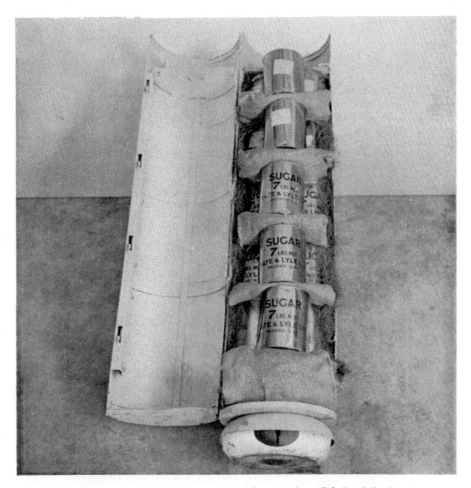

Illustration 28.   Rations packed in container C.L.E., Mk. 3.

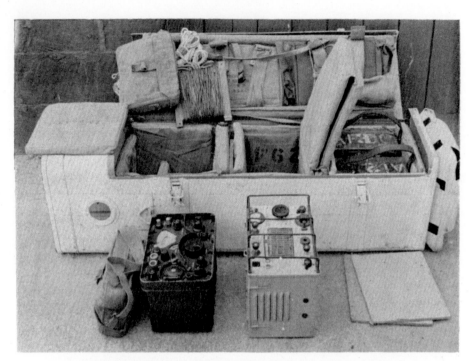

Illustration 29.　W.S. 76/R.209 ready for packing in type " F " container.

Illustration 30.　Method of packing ammunition in pannier.

Illustration 31. Method of despatching panniers from Dakota 3 Aircraft on roller conveyor using " Daisy-Chain " principle.

Illustration 32. Car, 5 cwt., 4 × 4, dropped by a cluster of four parachutes.

Illustration 33. Two Cars, 5 cwt., 4 × 4, on Halifax Bomb Beam.

Illustration 34.   Two Cars, 5 cwt., 4 × 4, " bombed-up " for take-off under Halifax Aircraft.

Illustration 35. Dakota Aircraft assembled for quick take-off.

Illustration 36. Halifax Tug Aircraft assembled for take-off with Hamilcar Gliders.

EFFECTS OF 1943 WINGATE OPERATION

14. The first Wingate Expedition in 1943 showed clearly the scope offered for applying new methods in the Burma theatre. The tactical effect of the operation was small. The morale effect was, however, enormous. The result of the operation was to make the Japanese High Command change their plan which aimed at sealing the Burma Road and extinguishing the air lift from Assam across the "Hump", as the danger of such an operation with lines of communication bared to attack by Long Range Penetration Groups was clearly seen. The plan was changed, therefore, to that which was mounted in 1944.

15. The first operation proved that the power of supply and control was limited only by the number of aircraft and trained crews available. After the 1943 operation, General Wingate, under Lord Louis Mountbatten who was Supreme Commander Designate, South East Asia Command, was told to go ahead and develop all forms of air supply and air transportation including mules, horses, and guns, using Dakota aircraft and gliders.

OBJECT OF 1944 OPERATIONS

16. Wingate's objective was to capture and dominate all the Indaw–Kaha area down to the 24th parallel, which he would hold until relieved by the joining up of the Chinese under Stillwell, the Yoke Force then facing the Japanese 56 Division on the Salween River, and the Fourteenth Army. This area would then be the springboard for the autumn offensive as soon as the monsoon ended. For this purpose his requirements were six Long Range Penetration Brigades plus certain ancillaries. These were as follows : 72 and 111 Indian Infantry Brigades, 14, 16 and 23 British Infantry Brigades ex-70 Division, and 3 West African Brigade. Wingate accepted gratefully the offered support of an American Task Force—the No. 1 Air Commando under the joint command of Colonel Philip Cochran, U.S.A.A.F. and Colonel John Alison, U.S.A.A.F. This was to include bomber, fighter, transport and glider elements and also, most important, perhaps, of all, a large number of light aircraft (L.1 and L.5). One of the major drawbacks to the 1943 Long Range Penetration operations had been the necessity of leaving behind any wounded men who could not march.

ORGANIZATION OF SPECIAL FORCE

17. Wingate returned to England and hastily gathered together the nucleus of his headquarters earmarking others who would fly out later, both for the staff and for service in the field. Lieutenant-Colonel Rome in 77 Brigade and Major Eric Kite, R.E. on the staff of Special Force had both had experience in airborne operations and their services were of great value.

18. Operations were due to start in early March, 1944. It was mid-September when Wingate with a nucleus of his staff arrived in India and during the initial period of formation contracted typhoid fever and was on the D.I. list for a considerable time. Brigadier D. D. C. Tulloch, Brigadier General Staff to General Wingate, had a difficult task during this period, but on 28th October Headquarters Special Force was opened at Gwalior and the units and formations comprising the Force had by that date concentrated in Central India with the exception of 3 West African Brigade which did not arrive until late November.

19. The Force was given the title of " Special Force " and to disguise its real strength and components it was given, during operations, the code name of " 3 Indian Division ". The units consisted of fifteen British battalions, two gunner regiments converted to infantry, four Gurkha battalions, three West African battalions, one Burma rifle battalion, a battery of 25 pounders and a battery of Bofor 40 mm. R.A.

The operation itself was called " Operation Thursday ".

TRAINING

20. During the training period the following techniques had been practised assiduously in conjunction with No. 1 Air Commando, a section of 117 Squadron, R.A.F. and 81 (Dive Bomber) Squadron, R.A.F. :—

(a) *Air supply by night.*

(b) *Casualty evacuation by light aircraft.*—American L.5 aircraft were used for this purpose. This was a new idea evolved from the 1943 Wingate Expedition.

(c) *Close air support.*—This was directed from the ground using a new technique and controlled by R.A.F. officers with the ground troops. At that time this was not accepted by the R.A.F.

(d) *Double-tow gliders.*—This was carried out both by day and by night, and had not been previously attempted.

(e) *Construction of airfields.*—The construction of airfields and strips for Dakotas and light aircraft by glider borne Engineers, which had never been attempted before, was undertaken.

(f) *Air-transportation of horses and mules in Dakotas.*—At that time this was stated to be impossible.

(g) *Loading and packing of equipment and vehicles.*—This was undertaken in gliders and Dakotas, with artillery equipments (25 prs. 40 mm. and 2 pr. A. tk.) and scout cars, jeeps and mortars.

21. During this period too, the air base layout and packing procedures were perfected. Wireless codes for supplies (QQ) were evolved out of the experience gained in the 1943 Expedition by Lieutenant-Colonel Lord and Squadron-Leader Burberry.

22. All the above were to have far-reaching effects on the subsequent tactics employed by Fourteenth Army in their defeat of the Japanese forces in Burma.

PLANNING

23. Two of the major principles of Long Range Penetration tactics are flexibility and surprise. Of all methods of waging war this is one where decisions must be made with the utmost speed and must be capable of immediate implementation.

24. It was proposed to mount an airborne lift of 77 Brigade into Paoshan, an airfield east of the Salween in China. Wingate firmly believed that the Chinese Yoke Force in that area would follow a British brigade across the Salween and might do some fighting which so far they had shown no signs of attempting on that front. Mainly for political reasons this plan was dropped and it was finally decided to fly two brigades (77 and 111) direct to the operational areas where they would form strongholds in suitable places which

could be used as a firm base for their operations. The plan for 16 Brigade was unchanged. As strongholds are of such vital importance in Long Range Penetration operations it is necessary to explain what they are.

The Stronghold

25. .The essentials of a Long Range Penetration Stronghold as laid down by General Wingate are as follows. It must be sited far enough from any form of road to prevent its attack by other than pack-supported enemy. It must have a suitable space to allow for the construction of a fair-weather strip for transport aircraft. There must be an inner defence area (with an adequate water supply) which is capable of being heavily fortified and from which the garrison can repel attacks. Floater columns, which are an essential to all strongholds, operate outside ; these attack the attackers and prevent them from having any firm base. To allow for the landing of fortress stores and the preparations of fortifications, it is essential, in the early days of occupation, that the enemy should not be aware of the existence of the stronghold.

" Broadway " which was commanded by Colonel Rome during the operation forms a classic example of a stronghold.

26. The outline plan was completed at the end of January and Wingate decided to site one stronghold later known as " Piccadilly ", in the Kyaukkwe Valley, where a Dakota had previously landed to pick up casualties. Two more landing strips were needed for the initial air lift, one of which was to be held in reserve and used later. A fourth was also needed in the Sinlam Kaba area where the Dah Force were to land and organize a revolt among the Kachins to support the advance of Yoke Force.

27. The possibility of employing double-tow gliders was considered, and in spite of the inherent risks Wingate decided to use the double-tow from the base rather to use it from an advance air strip which though safer from the air aspect was exposed to the risk of Japanese ground attack.

28. General Old, U.S.A.A.F., who commanded Transport Command, took Brigadier Tulloch and Colonel Rome on an aerial reconnaissance to make a final choice of these sites which had previously been selected both from the map and from personal ground reconnaissance in 1943. The new sites chosen were given the code names of " Broadway " and " Chowringhee ". " Piccadilly " was visited and pronounced suitable. Later all brigade and column commanders were give the facility to reconnoitre their areas from the air. These flights invariably concluded with ground straffing attacks on trains in order to disguise their real object.

Fourteenth Army Operation Instructions

29. On 4th February, Fourteenth Army and Eastern Air Command issued a Joint Operation Instruction to General Wingate giving his tasks in order of importance as follows :—

(*a*) To hold the advance of combat troops (Ledo Sector) to the Myitkyina area by drawing off, and disorganize the enemy forces opposing them, and to prevent the reinforcement of those forces.

(*b*) To create a favourable situation for the Chinese to advance westward across the Salween.

(*c*) To inflict the maximum confusion, damage and loss on the enemy forces in Burma.

30. General Wingate intended to implement these orders by compelling the enemy to withdraw from all areas in Burma north of the 24th parallel. This was the objective he had pledged himself to attain when the proposition was first discussed at Quebec. At that time he relied on three factors :—

(a) A determined advance by General Stillwell from the north.

(b) An attack by the Chinese Yoke Force across the Salween from the east.

(c) A follow-up division from Fourteenth Army to take over Indaw.
None of these was fulfilled.

31. Such was the Commander's intention which never changed up to the time he was killed on 24th March.

OPERATIONS

32. Training for the forthcoming operations had to break entirely new ground for which there was no precedent. Deliberate calculated risks were taken which have been unwittingly referred to as mistakes. It is of the utmost importance that this should be realized.

33. The penetration of 3 Indian Division into Burma may conveniently be divided into three clear phases :—

Phase I. The approach march of 16 Infantry Brigade under Brigadier Fergusson.

Phase II. The fly-in of 77 Indian Infantry Brigade under Brigadier Calvert and 111 Indian Infantry Brigade under Brigadier Lentaigne.

Phase III. The follow-up air lift of 14th Infantry Brigade under Brigadier Brodie, and 3 West African Brigade under Brigadier Gilmore.

PHASE I.—GROUND APPROACH—16TH INFANTRY BRIGADE

34. On 5th February, just a month before the airborne operation was due, Brigadier Fergusson left the road head at Hamtung and moved across the most difficult country possible to imagine ; hacking steps up and down hillsides and revetting each step to enable men and animals to follow, *via* Hkalak Ga to Kanglai on the banks of the Chindwin where they were met, on 29th February, by General Wingate, who landed on a sandbank in the Chindwin in an American U.C. 64 aircraft, without incident, and accompanied by Brigadier Fergusson's second-in-command who was in charge of the air base. Shortly afterwards four gliders landed safely, loaded with river-crossing equipment. This was swiftly assembled and the Brigade, after a short rest, completed the crossing by 5th March. Two gliders had already landed on sandbanks south of the crossing place a couple of days before 16 Brigade arrived, carrying patrols of the Black Watch who blocked and booby-trapped the approaches from which Japanese reinforcements might be expected to appear and interfere with the river crossing. These gliders all went in single-tow, there being no necessity to use double-tow. Valuable supply dropping experience had been gained during Brigadier Fergusson's approach march by 231 Squadron, U.S.A.A.F., which had had no previous experience of dropping supplies in bad country. The dropping zones were invariably of knife edge width and about 60 yards long on occasions, and anything which missed this zone was lost. The first, badly bungled, drop to 16 Brigade gave the U.S.A.A.F. a sharp lesson and they then came into line with the drill which had been evolved by the R.A.F. with Special Force during training, so that by the time the Chindwin was crossed their efficiency had increased tremendously.

35. The initial airborne movement was a fully integrated effort employing both R.A.F. and U.S.A.A.F. Squadrons. The following took part :—

44 Dakotas
{
31 Transport Squadron R.A.F.
62 Transport Squadron R.A.F.
117 Transport Squadron R.A.F.
194 Transport Squadron R.A.F.
}

39 Dakotas
{
27th Troop Carrier Squadron U.S.A.A.F.
315th Troop Carrier Squadron U.S.A.A.F.
No. 1 Air Commando Troop Carrier Squadron U.S.A.A.F.
}

Three landing areas had been chosen by air reconnaissance and photographs. These were given code names as follows :—

" Broadway " .. .. 96° 45′ E., 24° 45′ N.
" Piccadilly " .. .. 96° 46′ E., 24° 29′ N. (*See* Sketch Map)
" Chowringhee " .. 96° 24′ E., 23° 57′ N.

Three airfields were to be used for the fly-in as follows :—

77 Brigade from Hailekandi and Lalaghat
111 Brigade from Lalaghat (2 columns)
} In Assam.

Tulihal (less 2 columns). In the Imphal Plain.

All glider operations were to be carried out from Lalaghat, using 120 W.A.C.O. gliders of the No. 1 Air Commando, U.S.A.A.F.

Distances from base

Lalaghat Hailekandi area to target airfield .. 270 miles.
Tulihal to target airfield .. .. .. 180 miles.

36. The order of insertion was—first 77 Brigade, second 111 Brigade.

The glider element was to include :—

American Engineers with jeeps, bulldozers, graders.

Air Control Party—Colonel J. Alison, U.S.A.A.F., Colonel Olsen, U.S.A.A.F.

Brigade Headquarters, 77 Indian Infantry Brigade—Brigadier M. Calvert.

Ground protection troops (1 Kings)—Lieutenant-Colonel Scott.

37. It was arranged that aircraft on the outward trip should fly at 8,000 feet the minimum safe altitude to clear the mountains. On the return trip to fly at 9,000. 50 R.A.F. fighters were massed by 3rd Tactical Air Force during the immediate concentration period to counter an air attack on bases, should this develop. Colonel Philip Cochran, U.S.A.A.F., Commander No. 1 Air Commando U.S.A.A.F., was in charge of the operations on " D " day since the entire lift on that day was to be by the W.A.C.O. gliders of his Force. As the double-row procedure was to be used and his pilots alone had had experience in this, it was arranged that each of the 26 Dakota pilots under his command should act as first pilot and that Troop Carrier Command should provide, for that night, 26 pilots to act as second pilots for the occasion.

38. The maximum strength of the tug aircraft was thus limited to 26. The plan was, therefore, to conduct the operation in two stages, a total of 40 gliders being towed to each of the target air strips " Piccadilly " and " Broadway " in two separate lifts, 26 gliders to each air strip in the first stage and 14 to each subsequently. The date, 5th March, 1944, was fixed so that the maximum value of moonlight could be obtained for the whole operation. Operations into Chowringhee were not to begin until D + 3.

39. The first glider was due to take off at 1700 hours on 5th March. At 1630 hours one of Cochran's L.1 aircraft approached the strip, landed, and the pilot was brought in a jeep down to where Wingate and Colonel Cochran were standing at the head of the line of gliders. He unrolled a " blown-up " air photo of " Piccadilly " which revealed the fact that the entire landing zone had been blocked by large sawn-down trees littered so as to leave no possible space for landing anywhere.

40. The subsequent events are best described in General Wingate's own words in his official report of 19th March, 1944.

As is revealed in the accompanying report, on " D " day at the very moment when the first gliders were due to take off, the Commander was presented with a photograph taken two hours before by a B.25 of No. 1 Air Commando which showed that the entire landing ground at " Piccadilly " had been covered with obstacles. Only two days before it had been clear.

In view of the fact that a large number of people had necessarily been informed of the operation it was only too possible that the design had been penetrated by the Japanese. This photograph appears to afford definite evidence that such was the case. I therefore consulted at once with the Army Commander who agreed with my arguments and left me to decide for myself so far as I myself was concerned.

The arguments I presented were as follows :—

Of the four airfields which it was proposed to use, only one could have been known to the Japanese by any means other than direct revelation of the details of the plan. That one was " Piccadilly ", for the simple reason that photographs of this airfield had appeared in " Life " in June, 1943, and apart from this the Japanese were well aware at the time that the place had been used in the manner described in that periodical.

Therefore the blocking of " Piccadilly " by the enemy did not necessarily imply any knowledge of the plan and the fact that none of the other three had been blocked (as far as we were aware) entitled one to hope that this interference of the enemy was merely a routine measure taken in consequence of a general scare of airborne landings.

It can be imagined, however, how ominous at that moment the discovery appeared and how considerable was the risk taken.

The Army Commander and the Air Marshal were both in full agreement with me that the plan should proceed, cutting out " Piccadilly ". The next decision was one for 3rd Indian Division alone.

It was decided to divide up the sorties between " Broadway " and " Chowringhee " for I had already directed that in the event of any obstruction being found at the last minute on any one airfield, then the airfield immediately south (Chowringhee) would be used. It was, therefore, logical and in accordance with my plan to switch the sorties from " Piccadilly " to " Chowringhee ".

This however was opposed by Commander 77 Brigade. He presented strong arguments against the putting down of his Brigade at " Chowringhee ". He stated that if his Brigade was put down half to the north and half to the south of the Irrawaddy he considered his plan was likely to fail even though 111 Brigade was similarly divided. As this was plainly the case I agreed to reload half the gliders with personnel of 111 Brigade for " Chowringhee ".

There was also a serious obstacle to the use of " Chowringhee " by large numbers of troops on the grounds of the Irrawaddy which would have to be crossed immediately after landing. I therefore decided to start with " Broadway " alone. It was probably fortunate that we did so since lessons we learnt in the glider landings on " Broadway " were put into practice the following night when " Chowringhee " was utilized. (Wingate's Report, 19th March.)

41. The news had been received at 1630 hours. The first pair of gliders took off at 1812, after some changes had been made in the Timetable to cope with the new plan. A little over an hour of moonlight had been lost by the delay and the number of gliders was reduced from 80 to 60. Eventually 61 were airborne.

42. This last minute change of plan had necessitated certain changes. There was a threat of immediate ground attack when the first gliders touched down. (This was subsequently proved to be baseless but at the time it seemed eminently possible), therefore the initial party of gliders was changed to a total of eight. These contained engine stores, communications, strip lighting and control parties with a small specially selected ground protection party headed by Lieutenant-Colonel Scott, Commanding Officer of the King's Regiment, which were the spearhead of the attack.

43. The Pathfinding Team, consisting of Colonel Alison, U.S.A.A.F., his control staff and covering troops of the King's Regiment under Lieutenant-Colonel W. P. Scott, landed at " Broadway " after an uneventful flight of two and a half hours. This party was followed fifteen minutes later by Brigadier Calvert and Advance Headquarters, 77 Indian Infantry Brigade.

The strip lighting, oil burning duck lamps, was set up by pacing along compass bearings from a central light. This was completed just before the arrival of the main body.

The first two gliders of the main body landed safely and rolled clear as was the intention. The next three pairs of gliders unfortunately fouled a drag ditch which knocked their wheels off and caused them to swing round and block the strip. Before the lights could be moved on another alignment one of the next pair crashed in to the wreckage. Two men were killed and six seriously injured.

The gliders which followed succeeded in avoiding this obstacle, two by taking off again and clearing it, the remainder landing in the newly marked landing zone.

The method of approach was for the tug aircraft to fly low along the line of lights and the gliders to " cut " at a pilot light half a mile short of the landing zone. This method was adopted because it was believed that the landing was likely to be opposed and they would therefore be vulnerable to small arms fire for a shorter period. The first four gliders were cut off at height and landed at a normal speed.

When the first flight of gliders was completed it was decided to accept no more gliders that night and the codeword agreed for the cancellation of the operation was sent to Lalaghat. This message was not received until 0227 hours by which time nine gliders of the second wave, now flying at single tow, were already on their way. Eight were recalled and landed safely at base. The ninth, containing a bulldozer, was released over " Broadway ". This one, landing at speed, overshot the strip, discharging its load into the jungle as it stuck between two trees. The co-pilots were lifted bodily as the nose raised to emit the bulldozer, they were unhurt. The bulldozer was destroyed.

By first light the obstructions on the landing zones had been dragged clear. The five tracks leading into the " Broadway " area were blocked by strong standing patrols. A mobile reserve was in position commanding the strip. Inner ring patrols were operating round the strip and the airfield engineers were busy preparing the Dakota strip assisted by a working party of 100 men from the covering troops using picks and shovels.

A summary of the results of the first night is as follows :—

First wave .. .. 4 broke loose near Lalghat.
(52 gliders).

2 returned to Imphal when the tug cut them off owing to petrol trouble.

2 returned to base as the tug developed electrical trouble.

8 landed in enemy territory east of the Chindwin. Personnel of two returned to the Chindwin and arrived safely. Personnel of another two marched on to join their unit at " Broadway ", and those of another two were taken prisoner. The remaining two were never traced.

2 were prematurely released near " Broadway " by the tug aircraft and crashed half a mile from the landing zone in the jungle, all but two being killed.

34 landed safely on the dropping zone. Total casualties : two killed, 34 wounded.

Second wave .. 8 recalled.
(9 gliders).

1 landed across the strip—containing a bulldozer and a crew of two who had a remarkable escape.

At dawn on 6th March some 400 all ranks were in " Broadway ".

44. 12 light aircraft flew in from Ledo under the command of Captain Rebori, U.S.A.A.F., at midday on 6th March, a small strip having been cleared, and removed the wounded. This was the first occasion that these aircraft had operated over enemy territory.

45. By dusk that evening a 1,600 yards strip had been completed.

46. The first Dakota, piloted by General Donald Old, U.S.A.A.F., who commanded Troop Carrier Command, carrying a modified load of 4,500 lb., flew into " Broadway " at 2000 hours on 6th March, approaching, to the consternation of ground control, from the wrong end, but landing without difficulty. The strip was pronounced so good that the second wave of Dakotas from Hailikandi landed with the full load of 6,000 lb.

47. The same night an advance party of 111 Brigade and American engineers in 12 gliders landed at single-tow at " Chowringhee " at intervals of 12 minutes between gliders. The interval of five minutes between gliders on " Broadway " had proved too fast for ground control. One glider overshot through misjudgment, its crew of three were killed and the tractor it was carrying was damaged beyond repair. The tractor was replaced, also by glider, from " Broadway " which by then had no further use for it, and some additional engineer stores were also sent across. The two strips were only some 40 miles apart. A tremendous effort was put in on the " Chowringhee " strip the next day, and at 2315 hours the codeword " Roorkee " was received; this meant that the strip was ready to receive fully-loaded Dakotas, and 20 of these were promptly despatched. Movement Control were suspicious, however, and sent a signal to check that the strip was really sufficiently long for full loads. To their horror the answer came back that the strip was only 2,700 feet long. A signal was promptly sent out recalling all aircraft to base. Seven aircraft which did not receive this signal landed without incident, and returned after clearing their loads—the remainder returning to base in a very bad temper !

48. On D + 4 (9th March) General Wingate, after a discussion at the morning planning conference, decided to land only four columns at " Chowringhee " and to divert the rest of 111 Brigade to " Broadway ". " Chowringhee " had served its purpose well but it was only 15 miles from Katha airfield and also near a good motor road so that the Japanese were likely to react very quickly. It had served its purpose also to draw attention away from " Broadway ". The Brigadier, General Staff flew in on the last plane to " Chowringhee " that night and explained the Commander's change of plan to Brigadier Lentaigne, who made immediate arrangements to leave at dawn the following day. By 1100 hours " Chowringhee " was empty except for some damaged gliders and, just two hours later, it was heavily bombed and strafed by Zeroes and light bombers who repeated the attack at 0600 hours on the following day. The timing had been good.

49. By D + 6 (11th March) the first airborne landing was complete. Four gliders were landed that night on the banks of the Irrawaddy with equipment for Lentaigne's crossing. Two of these were snatched safely and returned with four prisoners who were being interrogated at base within a few hours of their capture, the other two gliders were abandoned and destroyed.

50. The approach of the initial striking force was now complete (12th March). These Long Range Penetration Brigades were embedded behind the enemy's lines and more or less at the centre of four Japanese divisions. The stronghold at " Broadway " was firmly established and Brigadier Calvert was within two

days' march of Henu where he was to impose a complete stranglehold for weeks on the main lines of communication leading to 18 (Japanese) Division which faced General Stillwell in the Hukawng. Morris Force (4/9 Ghurkha Regiment) was well on its way to block the Bhamo–Myitkyina road and 111 Brigade were crossing the river Irrawaddy to attack and destroy the Japanese supply dumps and to block the lines of communication to 31 (Japanese) Division.

51. On 17th March a strong patrol under Major Blain (code name BLADET) was landed in five gliders to operate against the Japanese lines of communication in the Kawlin-Wuntho area and to direct our bombers on to worth-while targets. These gliders were subsequently snatched and returned to base.

PHASE III.—THE FOLLOW UP

52. The next air-landing operation was the insertion of 14th British Infantry Brigade and 3rd West African Brigade into the Meza Valley which Fergusson's 16 Brigade had now reached after their long march.

53. 23 Infantry Brigade was removed from 3 Indian Division and put under command 33 Corps where it operated in a short range penetration role. General Wingate was afraid that the remainder of his force might be removed so he committed them earlier than he had intended.

54. General Wingate landed on 21st March, in a light aircraft, and met Brigadier Fergusson near Mahnton. He completed the reconnaissance of this new strip (code name " Aberdeen ") himself on a borrowed pony. As there was no necessity in this case for ground protection the advance glider-borne element was reduced to six gliders which contained the American engineers and the tools of their trade. These landed without difficulty at first light on 22nd March and the strip was ready for Dakotas by the following evening. It was planned to complete the Dakota lift in a series of 360 sorties over a period of six nights. However during this period the Japanese offensive against 4 Corps had developed alarmingly and things were going very badly for Fourteenth Army who were beginning to realize the magnitude of the Japanese attack and needed all available supply-dropping aircraft in their own emergency. Consequently only 15 Dakotas could be guaranteed by Troop Carrier Command for this operation, and not more than 10 could be relied upon from No. 1 Air Commando.

55. The air lift of these two Brigades, though finally successful, dragged on over a period of 20 days. Bad weather, which put both home and target air strips out of action for considerable periods, and the constant risk of inter-ference by enemy fighters, which necessitated fighter cover by day, added to the difficulties encountered. The strip at " Aberdeen " could only be approached from one end, which made night landings extremely hazardous. Since surprise was now lost, daylight operations of the very vulnerable Dakota sorties invariably needed fighter cover. The Japanese made several air attacks on " Aberdeen " and on one occasion the last Japanese fighter going home was over the strip when the first of 12 Dakotas came in view. Fortunately they did not meet.

56. On 24th March, one of Cochran's Dakotas reported that it had seen an aircrash near the village of Pabram, between Imphal and Silchar, during a thunderstorm. The following day it was learned that General Wingate had left Imphal—which he had visited on his way back from " Broadway "—to return to his Headquarters at Lalaghat the previous evening. Fears for his safety were finally confirmed on 27th March when a ground reconnaissance party from Main Headquarters 3 Indian Division, sent out to investigate, reached the crashed aircraft. The signal they sent stated that the wreckage was that of a B.25 aircraft, in which type it was known General Wingate had been travelling. The aircraft had exploded and there was no hope of identification of bodies. But some papers found, and most important of all the Commander's characteristic Wolsely topee, unique in itself and known to every man in Special Force, discovered thrown aside from the debris, showed that there was no doubt that General Wingate had been killed, and his death cast a deep gloom over the whole Force.

GROUND SITUATION—APRIL

57. By the beginning of April, 77 Indian Infantry Brigade had established a blockade firmly astride the road and rail communications from Indaw to Mogaung and Myitkyina, and also the River Irrawaddy. The road and rail block was called " White City ". This block had had precisely the effect which General Wingate had expected. Considerable efforts had been made to dislodge it but failed with great loss to the enemy, who were now faced, for the first time in the Burma Theatre, with the problem of attacking well dug-in troops of high morale instead of adopting their usual technique of infiltration. It was fully realized that the enemy effort would increase as this line of communication was absolutely vital to the Japanese 18 Division facing the now comparatively inert Stillwell, and it was decided by General Lentaigne—who had now assumed command of 3 Indian Division—at a conference with Brigade Commanders of 16, 77 and 3 West African Brigades, to close down " Aberdeen " as a stronghold and to reinforce " White City ", strengthening the garrison's defence by the addition of 25 prs., Bofors, and 2-pr. A. tk. guns. This of course implied the construction of a Dakota strip, where at that time only a small strip for light aircraft existed, and so on 3rd April five single-tow gliders with American engineers and their equipment were safely landed at " White City " and work immediately began on this strip. Six Japanese aircraft watched this work proceeding with interest but strangely made no effort to interfere.

58. It was at this stage that on 4th April Cochran had another inspired raid, this time on Aungban airfield, destroying 25 aircraft (confirmed by photos.) on the ground, one in the air and many others damaged. His air commando losses were nil.

59. On the night of 5th April, a storm broke out over " White City " and the newly constructed air strip became very soggy. Control was by Aldis lamp that night for security reasons, for the Japanese were strong in the vicinity and a major attack was expected at any moment. 26 sorties landed at " White City " that night, carrying 250 men, four 25 pr. guns, six Bofors and two 2-pr.

A. tk. guns. The Japanese striking force was actually on the spot at the time and must have observed the whole proceedings, but made no effort to interfere, a fact which they came to regret bitterly shortly afterwards. This was a typical example of the total lack of initiative invariably displayed by the Japanese during operations.

60. The following day reports received at Main Headquarters, 3 Indian Division indicated that a heavy Japanese attack on "White City" had started, but definite news as to the situation was not received until three of the night's sorties were airborne. They and the rest of the sorties that night were diverted to "Aberdeen". The reinforcement of "White City" had been timed to nicety.

61. The enemy attack on "White City" continued with a force using tanks, artillery and heavy mortars, until 15th April when they put in a final effort which also failed at great loss. From that time until "White City" was voluntarily evacuated no further serious effort was made to dislodge the garrison. Between 1,500 and 2,000 Japanese had immolated themselves against the most efficient Japanese killer of the whole Burma Campaign. The Direct Air Support throughout was superb, and a note on the methods used appears later.

SITUATION AT END OF PHASE III

62. 27th April marks the end of Phase III, and with it all hopes of realizing General Wingate's strategical objective, although his tactical objectives had now been fulfilled, *i.e.* :—

(*a*) The country in a 40-mile radius of Indaw was dominated by Long Range Penetration Brigades.

(*b*) A clamp had effectively been placed on all main road and rail-borne communications with 18 Japanese Division facing Stillwell, since 9th March.

(*c*) The lines of communications Bhamo–Myitkyina, although not firmly closed as in the case of (*b*), was nevertheless dominated by Morris Force which had destroyed bridges and roads and constantly ambushed enemy movement along that route.

(*d*) A small force was planted in the Kachin country to the east of the Irrawaddy, prepared to lead a Kachin revolt as soon as Yoke Force Force showed any signs of forward movement.

(*e*) The supply dumps in the base area of the Japanese 31 Division had been effectively destroyed and the lines of communication through Banmauk–Humalin cut.

63. However, through force of circumstances which had been temporarily imposed on the Allies by the Japanese High Command :—

(*a*) Stillwell had *not* yet put in a serious attack, consequently 18 Japanese Division had had no need to call on their 3rd Line ammunition and supplies as they could live on their "hump".

(*b*) Yoke Force was totally immobile.

368

(c) Fourteenth Army, so far from being in a position to exploit the successful situation by putting in a division to take over from 3 Indian Division, had been forced to take away 23 Infantry Brigade, the only remaining reserve brigade to Special Force, at an early stage, in order to protect the railway running from India to Assam. This task proved unnecessary and 23 Brigade then swept round in a short range penetration movement, cutting the Japanese supply lines one after the other. This action started the disintegration of 31 Japanese Division, proving the first weight in the scales which then started to turn in our favour at last. Being trained to move and fight off roads their value was above price to 33 Corps, as their Corps Commander gave testimony.

3 INDIAN DIVISION COMES UNDER COMMAND CHINESE ARMY IN INDIA

64. It was clear that at this stage Special Force was now an embarrassment to Fourteenth Army, since Fourteenth Army were unable to exploit the situation. The troops surrounded in Imphal needed every Dakota, and more, that was available, and at a conference which was held at General Stillwell's Headquarters on 1st May, and which was attended by Fourteenth Army Commander and General Lentaigne, it was arranged that 3 Indian Division was to act in future entirely in support of the Chinese Army in India and would come directly under their command at a date to be notified later. The tactics practised in the ensuing period bear little or no relation to the principles laid down by General Wingate for Long Range Penetration operations.

65. Briefly, the plan now was, first, to evacuate 16 Brigade which had now been operating for more than three months and were exhausted, secondly to give up all existing strongholds and road blocks, and, lastly for 111 Brigade to establish a new block (code name " Blackpool ") between Pinbaw and Hopin in the Mogaung Valley, and nearer to Stillwell's army. 77 and 14 Brigades were to act as floating brigades to protect this new block from attacks from the east and west.

66. This plan was contrary to Long Range Penetration principles and in fact it never resulted in blocking the communications to any appreciable extent. It annoyed the Japanese, however, and fresh Japanese troops were attacking it from the very first day that advance elements of 111 Brigade started to invest the area, and a swift enemy build-up was subsequently made. Consequently no surprise was obtained and there was no opportunity to fortify and strengthen the perimeter before a major build-up occurred. In addition the monsoon had by now broken properly and night supply was too hazardous to attempt. The Japanese quickly realized this and brought up anti-aircraft guns in addition to the ground artillery already there which eventually rendered day supply equally impracticable. On the last attempt every aircraft which took part was hit and severely damaged, and only a very small percentage of supplies fell inside the perimeter. Direct Air Support under monsoon conditions from Hailekandi and Lalaghat was impossible and in any case No. 1 Air Commando was due for a refit, and on 20th May ceased to operate in the support of 3 Indian Division. On 25th May, " Blackpool " was evacuated after heavy fighting,

having almost run out of ammunition and supplies. The evacuation took place at 0550 hours and all wounded were taken out over the hills and down to the Lake Indawgwi. The route was blocked and booby trapped, and the Japanese did not follow. Without air support or air supply Long Range Penetration operations could not succeed and localized blocks on main arteries would have been suicidal under such conditions.

AIR MOVEMENT, WITHDRAWALS AND RE-POSITIONING

67. During this period (27th April–25th May) the following tactical moves were made by air, some of which may be of interest to the students of air movement.

(a) "*Aberdeen*" *closes down*.—On 5/6th May, "Aberdeen" closed down, all guns and heavy equipment being withdrawn to the air base at Sylhet without incident. This true stronghold had lived up to its name throughout, the only blot on its escutcheon being that the Dakota strip could be approached from one end only and to over-shoot spelt disaster. Only one bad crash had occurred, however, and on that occasion the pilot made a bad approach across the strip and tried to take off again without success.

(b) "*White City*" *evacuated*.—On 9th May, the complete evacuation of "White City" was smoothly carried out though it was three-quarters surrounded by the Japanese. A troop of 25 prs., a troop of Bofors and one 2 pr. anti-tank gun were all evacuated that night by Dakota. Lights were left on in the perimeter throughout the proceedings. This appeared to persuade the enemy that reinforcements and supplies were coming in instead of an evacuation being carried out. "White City" block had been held for seven weeks and was now evacuated voluntarily for tactical reasons after the Japanese had completely failed to lift it. The troops had been in action almost continually for a period of two months.

(c) *Glider landing at* "*Blackpool*".—At first light on 9th May, four gliders (note the number now considered sufficient) with American engineers and equipment arrived over "Blackpool". These were fired at on landing, one glider stalled at 50 feet, the crew being killed and the load destroyed. The following day five Dakotas landed but the strip was very rough, two were damaged and one over-shot and burst into flames. Eventually, at intervals, Dakota sorties were landed on "Blackpool" strip. Many landed under fire, on one occasion several landed and discharged their loads successfully while an attack was actually going on on the north side of the block. This was the eleventh glider landing operation in Operation "Thursday".

(d) *Evacuation of* "*Broadway*".—Meanwhile on 13th May, the evacuation of "Broadway" stronghold was completed. This evacuation took two nights and 16 Brigade were flown out from here to base at Sylhet in addition. The oldest of the strongholds, "Broadway", had existed since the first night of the fly-in, a period of ten weeks, and in

370

spite of three periods of ground attack, and fairly heavy air attacks initially, had reigned supreme. It had vindicated all General Wingate's theories on strongholds and had, with the help of an extensive intelligence system and two floater columns, controlled an area for miles around within which little could have happened without the stronghold commander being informed. The light anti-aircraft troop from " Broadway " was ferried over to " Blackpool ".

DIRECT SUPPORT OF CHINESE ARMY IN INDIA

Move of Air Supply Base, Special Force

68. General Lentaigne, with Tac Headquarters Special Force, moved on 2nd May to Shadazup where Stillwell had his Headquarters, and the difficult situation then arose of the switch of the administrative air base from Sylhet to the Dinjan area. Logically it was far more sensible to be supplied from the north now that our centre of gravity was moving towards Stillwell. In addition nine-tenths of the flights would be over friendly country, and country moreover where the monsoon did not rage quite so fiercely. The distance between Dinjan and Sylhet was however nearly 300 miles, and, while normal stores such as " K " rations and certain types of ammunition were homogeneous with those of our Allies, most of our specialist stores and other types of ammunition were stockpiled at Sylhet. At this time Fourteenth Army were in the direct need of the R.A.F. Squadrons, including 117 Squadron, for their own use, and it was only because of the " Nelsonic " attitude adopted by 117 Squadron towards orders from 3 Tactical Air Force that Special Force did not go dangerously short of supplies for a period of a fortnight while the changeover occurred.

69. The air base at Dinjan with an improvised staff were able to start supply dropping on 27th May, working under the greatest difficulties imaginable through lack of any suitable accommodation at all. The wireless set-up made this switch even more difficult and the daily " QQ " demands had still to be decoded at Sylhet where the main W/T was sited and where priorities were determined. Requirements were then passed on to Dinjan on R/T. The specialist stores difficulty was overcome by holding three aircraft of 117 Squadron at Sylhet until 4th August for this purpose.

Final Operations of Special Force

70. The final operations carried out by 14 and 77 Brigades and 3 West African culminated in the capture of Mogaung (taken by 77 Brigade) and the link-up of these Brigades with Stillwell's force at last. Land battles of great ferocity were fought and three V.Cs. were gained during this period. Direct Air Support continued when weather permitted, and this switch to different American squadrons with which no training had taken place showed that the methods evolved were foolproof. Two flying boats came to the rescue of many sick and wounded men in the area of Indawgyi Lake and two separate parties of parachutists were dropped in ; one party to 77 Brigade with flame-throwing equipment subsequently used at the capture of Mogaung and the other, a party of an Airborne Brigade R.A.M.C., dropped in to organize a field hospital.

71. The main lesson which emerged from these operations was that Wingate's theories on Long Range Penetration, and his assessment of the probable Japanese reaction to such tactics, had proved correct in detail. He had forced the Japanese to attack on ground chosen by himself. His Force had gnawed a hole in the entrails of three Japanese divisions which had weakened them to such an extent that their eventual collapse was complete.

72. Night operations by glider-borne troops under moonlit conditions in jungle country are entirely feasible, but double-tow should *not* be used over high mountains. A reasonable interval between gliders landing at night on virgin strips was found to be 12 minutes.

73. In this type of operation, if a ground reconnaissance has not been made of the target air strip this should be carried out by parachute reconnaissance party—at the last possible moment, in order not to prejudice surprise.

74. Sufficient engineering personnel and equipment can be carried in four glider loads to build a fair weather Dakota strip in paddy or grass country in 12 hours under normal conditions. The work carried out by 900th Engineer Squadron (Airborne) U.S.A.A.F. was above all praise.

75. Central control during the planning stages of such an operation is essential. During the planning of this operation there were four separate entities other than Special Force involved—Fourteenth Army, 3rd Tactical Air Force R.A.F., Troop Carrier Command U.S.A.A.F., and No. 1 Air Commando U.S.A.A.F. To get these four together in order to discuss planning was a super-human task which was accomplished for very short periods, very occasionally. This severely handicapped the Brigadier, General Staff and Staff of the 3 Indian Division during the planning stages. General Old, U.S.A.A.F., Commander Transport Command, states in this connection— " Results can be obtained through co-operation when individuals concerned do not permit personal jealousies to interfere ".

76. The morale value of light aircraft in direct support for casualty evacuation cannot be too highly stressed, nor can the work during these operations of the pilots of No. 1 Air Commando be too highly praised.

77. The myth which was current in India in 1943 that a Japanese soldier was superior to our own was exploded as a result of the first Wingate Operation. He was proved to be brave but exceedingly stupid.

78. In operations of this type a " single ejection " apparatus for supply-dropping aircraft is an operational necessity and would have saved many casualties. Even the roller type of fitting, permitting the release of the entire load in two runs, would have been of vital assistance on occasions.

79. With regard to close support aircraft, bombers and fighter-bombers can be controlled from the ground by R/T without difficulty and with great accuracy when comparatively small land forces—*i.e.* up to two brigade strength—are involved. The methods used were simple and foolproof.

80. The need for careful drill in supply-dropping procedure was proved. There was constant danger to the "chuckers-out" of getting caught and dragged out with the containers, but fortunately this never occurred.

If a container is pushed out late there is a danger to the tail fin. One was removed bodily in this way but the aircraft reached base safely.

81. Free drops are, and were on occasion, lethal. This is not generally recognized.

82. The snatch gear fitted to the C.47 (Dakota) aircraft of No. 1 Air Commando weighs approximately 1,000 lb., and this reduces the payload considerably. The chief use of the snatch glider is to bring back pilots, wounded or prisoners. Only a few aircraft need to be fitted and these can be allocated to such special tasks.

83. A helicopter was used operationally with success. The development of this technique may do away with the importance of glider-snatching in future to some extent. This was the first occasion of such use in operations. The type used was a Y.R.4 (two place), and 23 operational sorties were flown.

84. Two months is the maximum period for which troops should be employed in Long Range Penetration operations. After this period a marked deterioration takes place.

85. When landing by night on unreconnoitred landing zones, gliders should be released sufficiently high to allow them to lose speed, unless there is a serious threat of immediate enemy ground action. This lesson is borne out by the number of gliders which were cut adrift during the initial glider landing and made good landings at slow speeds.

50 Indian Parachute Brigade in the Imphal Operations, February–July, 1944

86. In Chapter XXIII it was seen how 151 British Parachute Battalion had been withdrawn from 50 Indian Parachute Brigade to the Middle East, and had been replaced by 154 Gurkha Parachute Battalion. By the beginning of 1944, 154 Gurkha Parachute Battalion was not yet ready for operations owing to its recent conversion and the assimilation of large numbers of young recruits, and when it was decided to move 50 Indian Parachute Brigade to an operational area for training in patrolling and jungle warfare the battalion did not go. Since October, 1942, plans had been put forward continually for the use of the brigade in an operational parachute role. In some cases they reached an advanced stage but each was successively cancelled for one reason or another, usually because of the lack of aircraft or because of the cancellation of the connected ground operations. They included a plan to capture Indaw airfield in co-operation with 25 Indian Division and Special Force, an assault on the Mayu peninsula with 33 Corps and finally the capture of Akyab which was originally to be undertaken by one of the battle-groups mentioned in Chapter XXIII and which re-appeared with increasing frequency. Once again, as in Europe and North Africa, here is a picture of a parachute formation endeavouring to compete with planning for operations and training its units at one and the same time. The result was that most time was given to planning and training for specific operations while basic training suffered, with a consequent

slowing up in the state of readiness of the brigade as a whole. In addition there was the inevitable problem of maintaining the troops' morale when operations were being planned and cancelled in rapid succession. It was with bitter disappointment and a sense of injustice that they heard later of the Special Force operations.

87. At the end of February, 1944, brigade headquarters, 152 and 153 Parachute Battalions, the Brigade Medium Machine Gun Company, 411th Parachute Squadron R.I.E. and 80th Parachute Field Ambulance moved to the neighbourhood of Kohima. For the next fortnight patrolling was carried out and the brigade transport was re-organized on a mule basis. At the same time reports started to come in that the Japanese were beginning to cross the River Chindwin in the Homalin area in the preliminary moves for their attempted invasion of India.

88. About 14th March, the brigade was ordered to take over from another brigade a position in the area Ukhrul-Sheldon's Corner–Sangshak, and moved in at once. 152 Indian Parachute Battalion were the first to arrive, and started to take over positions from the 5th Mahratta Light Infantry. Before these positions could be effectively occupied much work was necessary since they were unfinished and had been designed for a four company battalion.[1] Moreover the two forward company areas were too far apart to be mutually supporting. By 18th March, the remainder of the brigade, less a company of 153 Parachute Battalion and 411th Parachute Squadron, had concentrated near Finch's Corner, which was between Ukhrul and Sangshak, and the machine gun company was holding Ukhrul. During that day a message was received that a party of 200 enemy were advancing on Pushing, a village six miles in front of 152 Parachute Battalion and 5th Mahrattas.

89. The enemy attacked on the following day against one of the forward companies of the parachute battalion and kept up their attacks throughout the day and the following night. They tried to break into the position from all sides. Fierce hand-to-hand fighting took place and all efforts to reinforce or supply the company failed as it was isolated by enemy road blocks and completely surrounded. On the morning of 20th March, the company reported very heavy casualties and that ammunition was running short. A short while later the only British officer left alive sent a wireless message saying that he had not enough men and ammunition to hold on against another determined attack. At 1100 hours the Japanese overran the position, where there was insufficient wire to form an adequate obstacle and after most of the garrison had been killed or wounded. Only some 20 men returned to our lines a few weeks later. They had all infiltrated through the Japanese lines and were all wounded. During the action Lieutenant J. A. Faul and Havildar Makmad Din particularly distinguished themselves by bringing up ammunition under fire, putting wounded men under cover and leading hand-to-hand attacks against the enemy who had penetrated the perimeter, until both died of their wounds. From documents captured after the action it was established that the company was attacked by 3 Battalion 58 Regiment, and that at least 450 Japanese had been killed.

---

[1] Parachute battalions only had three rifle companies in those days.

90. On 21st March, it was decided to concentrate the whole force at Sangshak, a position which was partially held by two companies of the Kali Bahadur Regiment. The village was built on the top of a narrow ridge 6,000 feet above sea level, with heavy jungle coming right up to the huts on the north, the whole area being covered with scrub and grass. There was a magnificent view of steep jungle-covered ridges down to the River Chindwin to the south and to Ukhrul to the north. 152 Indian Parachute Battalion, with 582 Jungle Field (Mortar) Battery, which had joined the battalion at Sheldon's Corner, and 5th Mahrattas were ordered to withdraw to Sangshak during the night 21st/22nd March. There was a well-concealed jungle track from Sheldon's Corner towards Sangshak which was to be used for bringing up reinforcements and supplies. Lieutenant-Colonel Hopkinson, commanding 152 Battalion, and the commanding-officer of the Mahrattas believed that the Japanese did not know of the track and so they decided to use it for the withdrawal. They also decided not to cancel a supply drop which was to take place just before dusk. The mortar battery was moved back first, while it was still light. The supply drop took place as ordered and it seems that the Japanese therefore assumed that no withdrawal was intended that night. Their patrols were reasonably active up to 2200 hours, but when the withdrawal began later it took them a long time to realize what was happening and their efforts to follow the force were made chiefly along the main track. They did not discover the path through the jungle.

91. On 22nd March, as 152 Indian Parachute Battalion and the Mahrattas were moving into the Sangshak position, a Japanese column approaching from the north put in an attack against the western end of the brigade position. Without hesitation one company of the Mahrattas, commanded by Captain Steele, attacked the Japanese as they were themselves attacking and prevented them from gaining a ridge which partially overlooked the main position, holding it until the concentration of the brigade was completed. Besides the Mahrattas, 15 Mountain Battery and 582 Jungle Field (Mortar) Battery were also under command of the brigade.

92. It was now obvious that the only road from Sangshak to Imphal was cut and that the brigade was isolated. A considerable amount of digging in the position was required and there was little barbed wire. There were no water points within the perimeter and even if those outside could have provided enough for the garrison they were coming increasingly under enemy fire. Had there not been heavy rain on 23rd March, water would have presented a serious problem.

93. During the night 22nd/23rd March, the Japanese made heavy attacks against the whole perimeter, but as they were not supported by artillery they were repulsed and suffered considerable losses. On the following morning our patrols reported large enemy columns with motor transport and elephants moving up from the east and about mid-day enemy artillery fire was directed on to our position in support of an attack of considerable strength. In response to a call for air support Hurricanes came over and engaged the enemy with cannon fire but owing to the heavily wooded nature of the country targets were difficult to engage. In places fierce hand-to-hand fighting took place but the enemy were driven back at all points. Nevertheless our difficulties were now mounting as the perimeter was so congested that nearly every shell was

bound to inflict some damage. Artillery and mortar ammunition and grenades were running short and supply by air was not very effective as the dropping area was very small and it was almost impossible to collect loads which fell outside. In addition one of our 3·7 guns was knocked out by enemy shell fire.

94. Throughout 25th March, there were spasmodic attacks and shelling, and water began to run very low, what little there was left being required by the wounded. Just before dusk 152 Parachute Battalion was attacked very heavily, but the enemy were driven back with many killed and wounded after several counter attacks. By this time the troops were becoming exhausted through lack of sleep. 152 Parachute Battalion was already depleted through the action at Sheldon's Corner and tired through having withdrawn 12 miles over very difficult country to reach Sangshak. Nevertheless worse was to come.

95. At 0400 hours on 26th March, a large scale attack started, preceded by the heaviest shelling to date and accompanied by intense small arms and grenade fire. One of our outposts was driven back near the American Missionary Church and the position changed hands several times, grenades actually being thrown at point blank range inside the building itself. The Church dominated the remainder of the position but notwithstanding desperate resistance our troops holding it were all killed or wounded. From here, in spite of our counter attacks, the enemy launched an attack which penetrated still further into 152 Parachute Battalion position. As soon as it was light counter attacks were put in from our meagre reserves but were unsuccessful. The type of fighting can be realized by the fact that both the Mountain and Mortar Battery commanders were killed in hand-to-hand fighting with the Japanese alongside their guns but nevertheless the guns and mortars were kept in action continuously, the steadiness of the British and Indian gunners being an example to all. The position was not finally restored until a risk was taken in withdrawing a company of 153 Parachute Battalion from their lightly held perimeter to put in the counter attack against the Japanese. Even then the church position remained in enemy hands. Our casualties were now very heavy and so congested was the area that enemy shells were disinterring bodies that had been buried. However the enemy had not had everything his own way and was obviously badly shaken, and except for sniping, his activities during the day were confined to a little patrolling. This was just as well as the brigade's water and ammunition of all sorts were almost finished.

96. By now, however, 5 Indian Division had been flown into Imphal from Arakan and at 1800 hours on 26th March, a message was received ordering the brigade to break out and fight its way back to Imphal. Guns, mortars and all possible stores were destroyed and at 2230 hours the position was left. Evacuation was carried out without any enemy interference and, as all roads and tracks were known to be blocked, the brigade was split up into small parties which were ordered to make their way south through the jungle for 12 miles, and thereafter west to the Imphal road. Little imagination is required to visualize what a journey these exhausted troops had when one remembers that they had to bring their wounded, that the night was pitch black, that the jungle was very thick in most places with high grass in others, the country hilly for the most part with the streams in the valleys deep and swift and with what tracks that existed only very narrow. Food was scarce and there was not much to be obtained on the way for the enemy had looted

most of the villages. Many of the parties had encounters with the enemy, some were taken prisoner and escaped and some of the men who were badly wounded took up to ten days before they reached Imphal but despite all this the majority got through. It was estimated that during these actions of 50 Indian Parachute Brigade the enemy suffered a total of over 2,000 casualties.

97. The brigade immediately concentrated, rested and re-organized and for the next few weeks was employed in the close defence of Headquarters, 4 Corps at Imphal. In May, Brigadier E. G. Woods took over command from Brigadier Hope Thomson and units of the brigade were employed as and when required under command of other formations for the next few months. Brigade headquarters with the signal company, pathfinders and defence platoons went forward to join Headquarters, 17 Indian Division and took command of a miscellaneous force which had been got together to drive back the enemy who were threatening divisional headquarters itself. 411 Parachute Squadron was employed on bridge construction work with 5 Indian Division, while 152 and 153 Parachute Battalions assisted various formations. During June and July both battalions operated against the Japanese lines of withdrawal between Ukhrul and the Chindwin river, co-operating closely with the R.A.F. They ambushed many enemy parties, and besides killing many enemy, took a fair number of prisoners—highly prized specimens in those days.

98. In July, 1944, the whole brigade was concentrated and withdrawn from Imphal to Secunderabad having completed five months of continuous action, which included some periods of very heavy fighting and which demonstrated the power of well-trained parachute troops with a high morale to hold out under very difficult conditions against superior enemy forces. In his report to the Combined Chiefs of Staff the Supreme Allied Commander, South East Asia, Admiral Lord Louis Mountbatten, said, " The defence of Ukhrul was left to 50 Indian Parachute Brigade (at that time consisting only of two small battalions, which had been flown in at the beginning of March). This force fought a fierce and current action against strong enemy forces. On the 29th March, it began to fall backwards towards Imphal but it had inflicted heavy casualties and by its defence of Ukhrul it had held up the Japanese advance down the Ukhrul–Imphal Road for several days giving the leading units of 5 Indian Division (which had just arrived from Arakan) time to concentrate at Imphal ".

Noemfoor, July, 1944, Corregidor and Los Banos, February, 1945

99. Leaving Burma for the present a brief examination will now be made of three American parachute operations that took place in the Pacific. The first was at Noemfoor Island in July, 1944, the second the capture of Corregidor Island, in Manila harbour, the capital of the Philippine Islands, on 16th February, 1945, and the third the rescue of Allied Prisoners of War at Los Banos near Manila on 21st February, 1945.

NOEMFOOR ISLAND

100. Noemfoor Island is about halfway between Biaks and the western tip of New Guinea, and was strategically important because of the Japanese landing fields there. Its capture would enable the Allies to construct advance air strips from which they could extend the blockade by air of Japanese shipping lanes.

101. The initial bridgehead on the island which was to include Kamiri air strip, was to be captured by an amphibious assault, and parachute troops were then to be dropped in as reinforcements. 503 U.S. Parachute Infantry Regiment was selected as the parachute formation.

102. The sea-borne operation took place on 2nd July with very little opposition, as the defences had been thoroughly neutralized by air and naval bombardment, and the bridgehead was secured with few casualties. At 1030 hours regimental headquarters and 1st Battalion 503 Regiment dropped on to Kamiri air strip. The dropping zone was long and narrow and so the planes were forced to fly in line astern, and the pilots did not stick to the planned jumping height, some parachutists being dropped from as low as 200 feet. The sea-borne troops had not cleared the dropping zone and it was cluttered up with bulldozers, half-tracks, jeeps and other vehicles. This, combined in some cases with the low dropping height, and the surface of the airfield which was made of crushed coral rock and was rather like cement, caused many injuries. However, despite the injuries to the first lift, on the next day 3rd Battalion, part of regimental headquarters company and the service company, dropped on the air strip as scheduled, using the same flight-plan as before, but again several men were hurt, though not quite as many as on the previous day. The third lift was cancelled, the troops being brought in by sea, and for the next six weeks the regiment took part in heavy ground fighting against the Japanese until all resistance on the island ceased on about 22nd August.

103. Although this was a small airborne operation mistakes were made and some valuable lessons brought out. Many of the Air Force pilots had never dropped parachutists at all and some had not done so for over a year, which probably accounts for the difference in heights of the first lift. The airmen were not the only ones who suffered from a lack of practice, as many parachutists had not made a jump for over six months because of the lack of aircraft. The aerial photographs taken were not supplemented by aerial reconnaissance, and the difficult nature of the dropping zone was not shown on the photographs. Information about the dropping zone does not appear to have been sent back to base by either the sea-borne troops or the first lift, and the dropping zone should have been cleared by the sea-borne troops.

CORREGIDOR

104. By February, 1945, the Americans were advancing across the Philippine Islands and 6 U.S. Army was driving down towards Manila from the north, while 8 U.S. Army were pushing up from the south and were attacking the Japanese at Nichols Field. As soon as the city of Manila was liberated, the Americans wanted to use the port, and to do this the entrance to Manila Bay had to be captured. Corregidor Island was the key to the harbour defences as it could support land-based batteries on Bataan or batteries on Caballo and El Fraile. In 1942, during the gallant and historic defence of the island by the troops under General MacArthur and Major-General Wainwright, the Japanese had shown just how costly a purely amphibious assault could be, and so this method had to be avoided. It was decided to make a combined amphibious and airborne attack. Information on the strength of the garrison was scanty as the Japanese had not permitted any civilians on the island since they occupied it, and what information there was had to be assessed from water traffic from

the mainland to the island. It was estimated that the garrison was a minimum of 850, but it transpired in the event that it was about 6,000. From 23rd January, the island got a daily pounding from the Air Forces, and over 3,000 tons of bombs were dropped in an area of less than one square mile. For the last two days this was increased in conjunction with the Navy.

105. On 3rd February, 1945, 503 U.S. Parachute Infantry Regiment was warned to stand-by to drop and seize Nichols Field, Luzon, but this operation was cancelled on 5th February, and on the following day the regiment was warned for the operations against Corregidor, due to begin on 16th February. There were only three possible dropping zones on the island one of which was the emergency landing field at the east end, and this was ruled out as the island here was very narrow, bounded by sheer cliffs some 300 or 400 feet high. This left the parade ground and the golf course, both of which were small.

106. Very careful planning was necessary because of the small size of the island and the dropping zones, and most of the jumpmasters were able to make reconnaissance flights with the bombers. At that time of year prevailing winds averaged a speed of 15 or 20 miles an hour, and special arrangements had to be made to ensure that all troops got on to the islands, let alone the dropping zones. Aircraft were to fly in line astern, dropping sticks of only six to eight men on the first run and going round again until all were out. Jumpmasters were to count three after the green-light before allowing the troops out. Control of jumping was to be from a command aircraft which was to carry the regimental commander.

107. Sixty C.47 (Dakota) aircraft were available and a force of roughly 3,000 men was to be transported in three lifts, as follows :—

(a) *First Lift.*—51 aircraft carrying 3rd Battalion, Detachment of Regimental Headquarters, 161st Engineer Company, Detachment of Headquarters Battery, "A" Battery complete and one platoon of " D " Battery of 462nd Field Artillery Battalion (·50 calibre heavy machine guns).

(b) *Second Lift.*—51 aircraft carrying further elements of Regimental Headquarters, 2nd Battalion, Survey Company, " B " Battery and another platoon of " D " Battery of the artillery battalion.

(c) *Third Lift.*—43 aircraft carrying the remainder of Regimental Headquarters, 1st Battalion, " C " Battery and the remaining platoon of " D " Battery of the artillery battalion.

12 aircraft were allotted to re-supply daily which was to begin as soon as the third lift was completed and continue until replaced by sea-supply.

108. The first lift took off at 0715 hours and began dropping at 0833 hours at a height of 600 feet above ground level in a wind of 18 knots. As the first troops began landing the regimental commander in the command aircraft noticed that some of the men were being carried over the edge of the island, and so he ordered all other planes down to 500 feet and jumpmasters to count six after the green light. As a result troops began to land on the dropping zone and by 1000 hours the first lift was on the ground. The Japanese, most of whom had been driven underground by the preliminary air and naval bombardments, confined their activity to small arms fire into the aircraft and

descending parachutists, but numbers of men were injured on landing because of the wind and the rough ground. However, about 75 per cent were effective, and all objectives were taken.

109. The second lift took off at 1100 hours and began dropping at 1244 hours, but the wind had increased to 20 knots. Jumpmasters were told to count ten after the green light and despite the wind, the proportion of men landing on the dropping zone, was greater than in the first lift, as the pilots were more familiar with the ground. The lift was completed by 1400 hours but again many men were hurt on landing. Owing to the numbers of men injured in the first two landings, which totalled just over 200, it was decided not to drop the third lift but to fly them to Subic Bay, Bataan and bring them in by sea. At 0830 hours on 17th February, the third lift flew over Corregidor, dropped their equipment bundles and flew on to San Marcelino air strip to land. They arrived on Corregidor at 1630 hours, but not before they came under heavy automatic fire from caves in the cliffs.

110. For the next ten days 503 Parachute Regiment was engaged in heavy fighting with the Japanese who went to desperate lengths to hold out. On one occasion a fortress, located in an old power and refrigerator plant, was only subdued after all sorts of inflammable material, including Japanese petrol and oil, had been dropped down the ventilating shaft and set on fire by throwing grenades after it. On another occasion the Japanese attempted to blow up the south portion of the American perimeter by setting off explosives stored in some vaults in which the Phillipine Government gold used to be kept. The explosion occurred at 0130 hours on 19th February, rocked the island, threw debris for thousands of yards and caused casualties on both sides. Two days later the Japanese went one better. Underneath Malinta Hill, the top of which was occupied by 34th U.S. Infantry Battalion, were stored vast quantities of explosives and everyone, particularly the men of the 34th, were wondering what would happen if the Japanese blew these up. On 21st February, they found out. At 2130 hours the Japanese set off an explosion at Malinta Tunnel which not only rocked Corregidor, but was also felt in the Bataan Peninsula. Flames shot out of all tunnel entrances and air vents and a landslide was formed on the south of the hill which buried some of the American troops, many Japanese being killed by the explosion.

111. A few days after this the Japanese caused an even greater explosion which was their last act of desperation. 1st Battalion, 503 Regiment was about to attack the landing strip when the Japanese detonated a huge arsenal which was located in an underground radio city beneath a hill. The explosion made a crater where the hill had been previously, and caused 196 casualties to the American troops. The force of the explosion was so great that it blew a Sherman Tank 50 feet in the air and showered debris on a destroyer nearly a mile from the shore.

112. The total casualties to the airborne troops were between 800 and 900 killed, wounded and injured. More than 4,700 enemy dead were counted, and only 24 prisoners were taken.

Los Banos

113. While the Corregidor battles were being fought, another parachute operation of an entirely different nature took place. On 4th February, 1945, the Commanding General of 17 U.S. Airborne Division was warned to prepare

plans to rescue some 2,200 Allied internees at Los Banos internment camp which was about 20 miles inside territory then held by the Japanese. It was believed that if the internees were not rescued the Japanese would kill them rather than surrender them to Allied troops.

114. The plan was for " B " company of 1st Battalion, 511 U.S. Parachute Infantry Regiment and the Divisional Reconnaissance Platoon to drop near the internment camp where, assisted by guerrillas, they would destroy the guards and organize the internees into two groups, those capable of marching and those not capable of marching. The remainder of 1st Battalion, supported by artillery and engineers would land at Los Banos from the lake by amphibious tractor, secure a beachhead and move inland to the internment camp guided by some 200 guerrillas. Internees would then be evacuated by amphibious tractor, after which 1st Battalion would fight its way back to our ground forces.

115. The whole operation was entirely successful, all internees being rescued and over 250 Japanese being killed for the loss of two Americans killed and three wounded. Moreover, the 1st Battalion did not have to fight its way back but was evacuated in the second amphibious tractor lift.

The Elephant Point Operation, Rangoon, May, 1945

116. From the South West Pacific we must now move back to South East Asia. Operation " Dracula " was the code-name for the capture of Rangoon which was to be taken by an amphibious assault. The first consideration in the planning was the clearance of the 24 miles of the River Rangoon which had been heavily mined by both the Japanese and our own aircraft. Before minesweepers or landing craft could enter the river the coastal defences on the west bank, especially those at Elephant Point, would have to be eliminated. Owing to the difficulties of approach to the mouth of the river it was not practicable to neutralize these by fire, and a sea-borne landing on the Point itself was most difficult at this time of year. By far the best solution was to seize Elephant Point by an airborne operation.

117. One of the main difficulties was the short time available for preparation, coupled with the situation in 50 Indian Parachute Brigade. The old 152 Indian Parachute Battalion had been split to form the new 1st and 4th Indian Parachute Battalions, half of 2nd Gurkha Parachute Battalion was on leave and half of 3rd Gurkha Parachute Battalion was just moving to join 77 Indian Parachute Brigade, while the other half was on leave. Therefore an improvised Gurkha Parachute Battalion had to be got together, which was done as follows :—

Battalion Commander	Major G. E. C. Newland—2nd Gurkha Battalion.
Battalion Staff	2nd Gurkha Battalion.
Battalion Headquarters and Headquarter Company.	50 per cent from 2nd and 3rd Gurkha Battalions.
A and B Rifle Companies ..	2nd Gurkha Battalion.
C and D Rifle Companies ..	3rd Gurkha Battalion.
Support Company—3-inch Mortars	50 per cent from each Battalion.
Support Company—M.M.Gs. ..	2nd Gurkha Battalion less half one gun team from 3rd Gurkha Battalion.

O•·

In his despatch on the operations Lieutenant-General Sir Oliver Leese, Commander-in-Chief, Allied Land Forces South East Asia, said " It was very much to the credit of the Indian Airborne Division that this was efficiently organized and carried out up to time. The consideration which limited the size of the airborne operation was the available lift. To find enough aircraft to lift the battalion the two American Air Commandos had to be taken from 4 Corps."

118. The battalion concentrated at Chaklala, India, where it was expanded to a battalion group and joined by one section of 411 Parachute Squadron, Indian Engineers, a detachment of 80 Parachute Field Ambulance, two Pathfinder teams from 50 Indian Parachute Brigade Pathfinder Platoon, and detachments from 50 Indian Parachute Brigade Signal and Intelligence Sections. At Chaklala three air exercises were carried out and on 14th April, 1945, the force moved to Midnapore, where it arrived on 18th April, and where it spent ten days collecting equipment and carrying out a rehearsal. On 29th April it was flown to Akyab arriving at midday, and the remainder of the day and all the next day were spent in briefing. On the same day a reserve party of 200 all ranks also arrived at Akyab. This party was drawn from 1st Indian Parachute Battalion, 2nd Gurkha and 3rd Gurkha Parachute Battalions.

119. The battalion group was to be carried in 40 aircraft from 1st and 2nd U.S. Air Commandos whose crews had not previously carried out any dropping of parachute troops. It was necessary, therefore, to have jumpmasters who had experience of handling Indian and Gurkha troops, and these were obtained from 435 and 436 Squadrons, Royal Canadian Air Force. In addition the American crew chiefs were given a short course. Parachute racks modified for British containers had to be fitted to the aircraft and these were obtained from 31 and 117 Squadrons, R.A.F. The force was to be dropped in two lifts five miles due west of Elephant Point :—

> (a) *First Lift*
>> H — 30 mins. Two aircraft carrying Pathfinders, Visual Control Posts, Force 136 agents, members of the press and a protective platoon.
>> H Hour. Thirty-eight aircraft carrying the main body.
> (b) *Second Lift*.—Eight aircraft carrying the reserves organized as a company group.

Last-minute information showed that it was unlikely that there would be any opposition, as it was believed that the Point had been evacuated.

120. The first lift took off at 0310 hours on 1st May in rain, and after a flight of about four hours dropped on time at the right place. There was no opposition and assembly was completed quickly. The advance for the first two and a half miles was also fast and consequently got ahead of schedule so that there was a long wait while the Strategical Air Force bombed targets on Elephant Point. Although the troops were more than 3,000 yards from the bomber's target one company was bombed and machine-gunned by Allied aircraft and suffered over 40 casualties.

121. The second lift dropped successfully at 1530 hours, and there were no container failures in either lift. This speaks highly of the work of the air force armourers who had been working continuously for 48 hours, first in dust and then in heavy rain.

122. The leading company reached the Point at 1600 hours and was fired on from the north by enemy in a bunker and some small ships. Aircraft were called and the ships were set on fire, but the bunker was more obstinate, so that a company attack was put in with flame throwers. Eventually it was also set on fire. At 1600 hours there was a successful automatic supply drop, and at 2000 hours it started to rain and continued to do so for three days. That night there were very high spring tides which rose 19 feet so that the whole battalion area was covered with 3 feet of water.

123. The following day was spent in watching the sea-borne convoys go past and in searching all bunkers and ship-wrecks. On 3rd May, the battalion group moved to Sadhaingmut, which was half-way up the west bank of the river, leaving a detachment at Elephant Point. To get to Sadhaingmut involved carrying out an extremely difficult march over flooded paddy fields in pouring rain, and crossing seven deep, wide, flooded ditches. This march took eleven hours. On 6th May, the battalion less one company, which joined them a week later, was moved by sea to Rangoon where they operated in anti-looting patrols. On 17th May, the complete battalion embarked for India, reaching Bilaspur on 25th May.

124. During their stay in Burma the battalion had killed 43 Japanese and taken one wounded prisoner. Apart from losses in the bombing incident their casualties were one British officer killed and one wounded, and two Gurkha other ranks killed, two wounded and one drowned.

CHAPTER XXVI

A SUMMARY OF THE LESSONS OF AIRBORNE OPERATIONS
(1939–45)

This chapter summarizes the main lessons of airborne operations that took place during the 1939–45 war. Before dealing with them a note of warning should be sounded. The reader should remember that in World War II it was not until 1944, in the fifth year of war, that sufficient allied aircraft were available to carry a large airborne force into action at one time. In any future war limitations in the numbers of transport aircraft that we can afford to maintain in peace will probably restrict the employment of airborne forces in the initial stages. War-time production may not make itself felt for some time and in any case priority may have to be given to types of combat aircraft essential to the survival of the United Kingdom and overseas bases. Civil aircraft may not be suitable for airborne assault, though they may be employed to carry personnel in air transport operations.

This chapter is based on the airborne operations of the 1939–45 War. Most of these operations were in the nature of deliberate assaults and took place after much planning. The lessons of the war as a whole, however, have shown that there were, during World War II, and will be again, occasions and conditions when " the way over the top " could have been exploited with tremendous effect by small airborne forces applied quickly. There may be a danger that the reader will gain the impression that the only way to use airborne troops is in mass, in perfect conditions after long and cumbrous planning—in short that airborne troops are a massive, unwieldy instrument capable only of a long deferred, final act. This is far removed from the truth for, though a large-scale operation may need much preparation, there is an urgent need to develop speed and flexibility to the utmost, to " stream-line " planning and by so doing to forge a weapon of opportunity second to none, available as required from the outbreak of war.

General

1. A major airborne operation is an air operation of the first magnitude. Before it can take place at all, therefore, a favourable air situation must be created. We must have local air supremacy and the plan must provide for the neutralization of the enemy ground defences at least for the period immediately before, during and immediately after the airborne operation.

2. An airborne operation and its subsequent supply and build-up are dependent on suitable weather. This factor must be considered by commanders when planning the scope and timings of any operation.

3. The morale effect on the enemy of dropping airborne forces in their rear areas is out of all proportion to the number employed.

Roles

4. Airborne operations can be divided into two main types :—

    (*a*) Operations carried out in close proximity and in direct relation to the battle on the ground.

    (*b*) Deep penetration operations, not immediately concerned with the ground battle and probably involving prolonged maintenance by air.

5. Possible roles might be :—

(*a*) Capturing and holding vital ground.

(*b*) Forming a bridgehead in a river crossing assault.

(*c*) Turning the enemy's flank.

(*d*) Quick reinforcement.

(*e*) Securing a flank.

(*f*) Securing a defile.

(*g*) To gain and hold an airhead for the fly-in of air-transported forces.

(*h*) Raids for a specific purpose, such as obtaining vital information or destroying a key objective.

(*i*) The rapid deployment of troops for the maintenance of law and order in liberated territories.

(*j*) Use of small parties such as the Special Air Service, for rallying resistance forces, for cutting the enemy communications or for sabotage. Such parties can operate for long periods if supplied by air and if suitable bases are established behind the enemy's lines from which harassing operations can be carried out. There is also a definite tactical role for small parties, such as creating general confusion amongst a withdrawing enemy, and for deception purposes.

Training

6. The highest morale, initiative and a high standard of physical fitness are required for airborne troops all of whom, irrespective of arm or service, must be prepared to take their place in the battle.

7. Glider-pilots, in addition to being trained airmen, must also be fully trained soldiers, and must be prepared to fight on the ground beside the occupants of their glider. This applies equally to Air Force pilots attached to the Glider Pilot Regiment. On the other hand glider pilots, whether they are Air Force or Army, are highly trained men and they should be withdrawn from fighting on the ground as soon as possible.

8. It is of the utmost importance that the Air Forces should put the troops down at the right place and the right time. Without this the operation may be a failure.

9. All airborne personnel must be trained in the loading and unloading of gliders, the packing and loading of containers, the loading and unloading of transport aircraft, and in crating and lashing.

10. All airborne personnel must understand the organization of the transport air forces with whom they work and the procedure for airborne operations at their airfields.

11. All commanders and staffs should have a basic knowledge of the planning and technique of airborne and air transported operations. They should consider that the employment of airborne forces is a normal operation of war.

Command

12. There must be one overall Army airborne commander through whom all requests for airborne troops are passed. This commander should be the adviser on airborne matters to the army group or army commanders concerned.

13. The overall command of the air side of an airborne operation should be centralized in the hands of one air commander at the highest possible level. It is essential that this headquarters should have full knowledge throughout the campaign of airborne plans and technique. It should be capable of immediate absorption of the Air Staff officers from the Troop Carrying Air Force Group. It is of paramount importance that the Air Headquarters made responsible for airborne operations should handle all Air Forces throughout the battle.

Inter-service Co-operation

14. It is vitally important that the co-operation between the airborne personnel and the air forces should be the closest possible on all levels.

15. It is desirable that the airborne force headquarters and the corresponding air force headquarters should be located together for training and planning.

16. The closest liaison should be maintained between glider pilots and the air crews towing them, and whenever possible between parachute troops and the aircrews who will drop them. In the case of glider-pilots they should be stationed permanently on the airfields from which their tug-pilots are operating.

Launching

17. To ensure correct launching a combined Army/Air Force base organization is essential. If full value is to be obtained from an airborne strategic force, *i.e.*, maximum range, mobility and flexibility, this base organization should itself be mobile and self-contained.

Planning

18. It is essential that airborne commanders, both Army and Air Force, are kept in touch with the planning of the ground forces whom they may be called upon to support.

19. In order to ensure that airborne operations can be mounted at the minimum notice and thus take advantage of any suitable tactical situation during mobile operations, it is essential that a careful " drill " is worked out for the combined planning of the operations between the three commanders and staffs concerned, *i.e.*, the Air Force, the airborne force and the formation with which the airborne force will join up on the ground. This drill must include arrangements for the rapid distribution of maps and the quick moves of troops. Personal liaison is essential and when distances are large special means of inter-communication by air will be required.

20. When airborne formations are kept at immediate readiness for opportunity roles it should be remembered that it may be necessary to tie-up large numbers of transport aircraft that might be required elsewhere.

21. It is the task of senior airborne headquarters to keep themselves up to date with the progress of the battle and the latest information about the enemy, so that they can plan at short notice operations as required by the army group or army headquarters concerned.

22. Planning should be kept at the highest level consistent with the efficient conduct of the proposed operation. Division headquarters should not be required to plan in detail until there is a good chance of the operation taking place. They in turn should not issue orders, thereby initiating planning at lower levels, until the operation is practically certain. Although every consideration must be given to the effect on morale and training of all ranks, airborne troops, just as aircrews, must get used to being continually " stood-to " and " stood-down ". This is a trying but inevitable accompaniment of air operations.

23. A branch of the General Staff should co-ordinate the activities of the Special Air Service and other special bodies at the senior headquarters controlling their operations. Orders for these organizations should be issued through normal staff channels.

24. Dropping and landing zones should be chosen as close as possible to the objectives so as to obtain the maximum amount of surprise and because airborne troops on the ground are comparatively immobile. If it is necessary, it is possible to make mass parachute drops in enemy defended areas, though this adds to the difficulty of assembly on the ground and a heavy casualty rate must be accepted. Risks are sometimes justifiable in the early stages of an operation for such tasks as a *coup-de-main*. In this type of operation well trained troops can carry out with success what at first may seem an impossible task, but if time permits rehearsals are advisable.

25. Night landings on a large scale have been proved possible and largely successful in half moon conditions for parachute troops. They add to surprise but in order to achieve concentration a very high standard of training must be achieved especially by the Air Forces. In similar conditions it is possible to land small numbers of gliders.

26. The plan should, if possible, cater for an airborne formation to be carried in one lift. The rate of build-up, on which depends the period within which the the airborne force must be relieved, should at least equal that of the enemy.

27. Dummy parachutists and battle simulators are an effective means of drawing enemy reserves away from the real landings and of bewildering the enemy command, especially at night.

28. Parachute troops are always vulnerable for some time after landing and careful arrangements must be made for their concentration and assembly. Air-landing troops have an advantage in this respect over parachute troops as they land in complete sub-units, but they are more vulnerable during descent and while leaving the planes.

Artillery and Air Support

29. As it is unlikely that airborne formations will have adequate artillery support of their own, arrangements must be made for this support to be provided by the link-up troops as soon as possible after the airborne troops have landed.

30. All major airborne operations should include close offensive air support which should be of an intimate character, just ahead of the first wave. It should continue until after the force is on the ground, even at the risk of casualties to our own troops, and should take the place of additional artillery support until this is available.

31. A detailed and careful anti-flak plan must be prepared so that as many as possible enemy anti-aircraft guns are unable to fire during the airborne landing.

32. Tactical air reconnaissance should always operate in conjunction with airborne troops to report their movements in case communications break down.

Organization and Administration

33. The basic airborne formation is the division. Its organization should be as nearly similar to a standard infantry division as possible. It must be divided into " airborne " and " follow-up " elements, the latter containing the essential equipment to permit the division to take part in prolonged fighting. However, there may be occasions on which an independent brigade group or even less will be required without committing part of a division.

34. Automatic supply by air should be arranged for as soon as possible after the drop on " D " day of the airborne operation, in case the weather should break on " D "+ 1 day, or ground formations do not manage to link up. In addition, arrangements must be made for supply by air on subsequent days, even when a quick link-up is planned.

35. All available spare space must be used for supplies, *i.e.*, spare racks in parachute aircraft for " jettison " containers, and surplus pay-load in gliders.

36. All administrative requirements for the Special Air Service and other similar organizations should be supplied through the normal " A " and " Q " staff channels. All " Q " staff officers must be trained in dealing with specialist, and quite probably top secret equipment.

Communications

37. Wireless sets of the highest possible power must be taken by airborne formations for rear communications to the link-up troops, airborne base, etc. During the period of the actual landing and immediately after, it may be necessary to give the airborne forces and their Air Forces considerable, if not complete, wireless priority.

38. There must be good communications between the airborne troops and the " supply by air " aircraft so that if necessary the latter can be diverted to new dropping zones at the last moment.

39. Communications within the airborne base organization to all units, airfields, dumps, etc., are essential.

Note

On 15th August, 1945, the Chief of the Imperial General Staff, Field-Marshal Sir Alan Brooke wrote to Field-Marshal The Honourable Sir Harold Alexander and to Field-Marshal Sir Bernard Montgomery and asked them for their views on the value of airborne forces during the 1939–45 war. Their replies are given at Appendix P.

EPILOGUE

The following is an extract from the speech of the Rt. Hon. Winston Spencer Churchill, C.H., F.R.S., M.P., on 21st May, 1948, on the occasion of the unveiling, in the cloisters of Westminster Abbey, of a combined memorial to the fallen of the Airborne Forces, the Commandos, and the Submarine Branch of the Royal Navy :—

" This memorial with all its grace and distinction does not claim any monopoly of prowess or devotion for those to whom it is dedicated. We all know the innumerable varieties of dauntless service which were performed by His Majesty's soldiers and servants at home and abroad in the prolonged ordeals of the Second World War for right and freedom. Those whose memory is here saluted would have been the first to repulse any exclusive priority in the Roll of Honour. It is in all humility which matches their grandeur that we here today testify to the valour and devotion of the Submarine Service of the Royal Navy, in both wars, to the Commandos, the Airborne Forces and the Special Air Service. All were volunteers. Most were highly-skilled and intensely-trained. Losses were heavy and constant, but great numbers pressed forward to fill the gaps. Selection could be most strict where the task was forlorn. No units were so easy to recruit as those over which Death ruled with daily attention. We think of the forty British submarines, more than half our total submarine losses, sunk amid the Mediterranean minefields alone, of the heroic deaths of the submarine commanders and crews who vanished for ever in the North Sea or in the Atlantic Approaches to our nearly-strangled island. We think of the Commandos, as they came to be called—a Boer word become ever-glorious in the annals of Britain and her Empire—and of their gleaming deeds under every sky and clime. We think of the Airborne Force and Special Air Service men who hurled themselves unflinching into the void—when we recall all this we may feel sure that nothing of which we have any knowledge or record has ever been done by mortal men which surpasses the splendour and daring of their feats of arms.

Truly we may say of them as of the Light Brigade at Balaclava, ' When shall their glory fade ? ' "

APPENDIX A

THE GLIDER

Introduction

1. This Appendix contains descriptions of the main types of gliders used by airborne forces during the war—Hotspur, Horsa, Hamilcar, Hadrian—but does not deal with those types such as the Hengist, which were not used. Detailed specifications are given in the Annexure.

Hotspur

2. The original conception of the Hotspur was for an eight seater glider capable of a very long approach, the idea in those days being to cast off at a considerable altitude and glide in, so that the sound of the tug aircraft would not give warning of the attack. A best gliding angle not steeper than 1 in 24 was required for this purpose, and it was intended that each aircraft should be used for one flight only. Thus an aircraft of considerable aerodynamic refinement was required, but it also had to be cheap and simple to construct. These requirements were put to the designers, The General Aircraft Company Ltd. in June, 1940, during the Dunkirk evacuation and the Hotspur Mark I was produced to meet them. This had a wing span of 62 feet and an aspect ratio[1] of 12, a fuselage of the best known shape, a "jettisonable" undercarriage, and a gliding angle very little inferior to a high performance sailplane. The first flight of this aircraft took place on 5th November, 1940, a little over four months from its original conception.

3. The Hotspur Mark I had a "lid" type fuselage. The whole of the fuselage top, or lid, could be thrown off in a few seconds by the troops, who then jumped out over the sides of the boat-shaped lower half. However, in October, 1940, the official view had changed somewhat, and it was thought that parachute troops might be dropped from gliders. A new type of fuselage was therefore introduced, of more conventional type, with two side doors for jumping.

4. At about the same time, there was another most important change in policy, and it was decided that the tug aircraft would go right in to the landing zone at low altitude and that a very steep approach would be made. This was of course a complete reversal of the original requirements, necessitating a more robust aircraft, with little emphasis on good gliding qualities. The Mark II glider was therefore introduced, having a reduced wing span of 46 feet, which raised the strength factors by 50 per cent and caused a 20 per cent increase in the minimum gliding angle. The second type of fuselage was used on this mark. A further increase in angle of glide was obtained by using a brake parachute, but this method did not get beyond the experimental stage.

5. As far as is known, no operational flights were made with Hotspurs, as the Horsa came along soon after, and the Hotspur was relegated to training. This represented a further change of the original policy as the glider had been designed for a very short flying life. There was a scheme to use Hotspurs as freighters on a quick turn round basis, using pre-packed freight trains for the Normandy invasion, but this did not take place.

---

[1] The ratio between the wing span and the width of the wing.

6. When work was started on the Hotspur, little was known about multiple towing, but the gliders were originally fitted with nose and tail hooks, for towing in trains. This was soon found impracticable, as there was no known solution to the dynamic stability problem.[1] They were sometimes towed in threes, each glider having a separate tow rope to the tug.

7. In 1942 an attempt was made to introduce an interim 15-seater glider by joining two Hotspur fuselages, 12 feet apart, by means of a new wing centre section, the outer wings being standard Hotspur. A prototype was built but the project was dropped, largely owing to the unpopularity of the arrangement with pilots.

8. In all, 1,000 Hotspur gliders were built.

Horsa

9. The first Horsa glider was the Horsa Mark I which was originally developed as a means of increasing the capacity of bomber aircraft to carry parachute troops. Evidence of this is to be seen in the two passenger doors, one in either side of the fuselage, which are widely separated for simultaneous exits and which are designed to be opened in flight by being slid round the inside of the fuselage. A further tactical use of this arrangement was the ability to fire guns at attacking aircraft. Other such firing points were the aperture in the roof aft of the main spar and a trap-door in the tail. The firing points were never used in action. The method of attachment of the parachutist's static line to the fuselage was to be a short rail just over each parachute door. The parachutist was to hook his line to this rail on approaching the door just before making his exit. Supporting arms and supplies were to be dropped by containers and panniers.

10. Originally six containers could be carried in wing cells. As four of these were located over the undercarriage, it was necessary to drop this first, but this was to be the normal technique, as it would decrease the glider's drag and so increase the radius of action. The undercarriage was to drop soon after take-off, on parachutes. On the return to base the glider was to land on its skids. Later, when the undercarriage was normally retained, the use of these four cells was discontinued and the bomb-releases removed from them. For discharging the panniers from the parachuting doors a double roller conveyor was designed, but was not a great success and was not used.

11. The means of access to the Horsa I, apart from the two passenger doors, was by means of a rectangular loading door in the port side just aft of the nose. This measured 7 ft. 9½ ins. by 5 ft. and was hinged at the bottom edge, so that it provided an unloading platform when dropped on to the separate light-weight unloading trestle. A pair of troughs 11 ft. 8 ins. by 6 ins. were used as ramps to ground level. These troughs were used in flight under the wheels of heavy equipment to spread the weight over the lightly constructed floor. The use of the door as a platform was restricted to unloading when it was of little consequence if it was damaged slightly in the process. For loading, however, a large, heavy and robust loading ramp was used which spanned the complete path from the ground to the glider floor.

---

[1] Stability of the aircraft in flight.

12. Originally the only vehicles required to be carried with the air-landed troops were solo and combination motor-cycles : it was a remarkable piece of luck that the jeep could be loaded with so little modification. With the necessity to manœuvre heavy equipment round the corner of the door leading from the interior, which was barely wide enough, the unloading time was lengthy and means were sought to reduce it. Experiments were carried out by Messrs. Airspeeds Ltd. in early 1944 to remove the tail by means of a band of cordtex explosive round the fuselage at the rear of the load carrying compartment. This was successful, and this surcingle, as it was termed, was carried on the Normandy operations. Meanwhile the R.A.F. Air Transport Technical Development Unit devised a means of making the tail as a separate unit, which was bolted to the main fuselage by eight bolts with ingenious quick-release nuts. A pair of powerful wire-cutters was carried to sever the control cables. A large number of Horsa Mark I gliders were modified in this manner and used in Normandy, the surcingles being carried for emergency use. To distinguish between the modified and unmodified Horsas Mark I they were termed " Red " and " White " Horsas respectively.

13. A development of this quick method of unloading was the design of the Horsa Mark II glider—at first termed the " Blue " Horsa—which would carry 29 passengers and two glider pilots. It had a hinged nose to give straight access for both loading and unloading, the controls to the pilot's cockpit in the nose being ingeniously coupled together by pairs of push rods butting together so that no lock was required. The nose is, of course, a part of any glider which is particularly vulnerable to damage on landing under difficult conditions, and the loading door may therefore become jammed. To provide against this eventuality the detachable tail feature of the Red Horsa Mark I was retained in the Horsas Mark II.

14. With the use of the Horsa glider as a means of landing men and heavy equipment, rather than dropping them by parachute, it became normal technique to retain the undercarriage where the range permitted and to land on the wheels. This lengthened the landing run but gave greater control of the glider and enabled a large number of gliders to be parked fairly compactly to avoid obstructing the landing zone. An endeavour was made to shorten the landing run required by developing an arrester parachute system. This system used a pair of 14-feet parachutes which were released from a stowage under the tail just before touch-down. A fully-laden Horsa could be stopped in less than 100 yards with this device. Twelve Horsas were fitted with it and used for *coup de main* assaults on the River Orne bridges and the Merville battery on the night before " D " day of the Normandy operation.

15. Another device carried for the coastal battery assault was a Rebecca position indicator, but it is believed that this was not used owing to the loss of the Eureka beacon on the ground. Altogether 600 of these Horsa Mark I Rebecca sets were produced but only a few were fitted in gliders.

16. The speed with which the Horsa was originally produced is interesting. Mock-up conferences were held on 15th and 30th January, 1941. The first official prototype flight was on 10th September, 1941, piloted by Wing Commander Wilson of the Royal Aircraft Establishment. The development flying was done by Mr. G. B. S. Errington of Messrs. Airspeeds. The first production

model was made in June, 1942, and in all, about 5,000 Horsa Mark I gliders were made. Some of these were flown in North Africa and in India. As the wood shrank in tropical countries renovation kits were produced. On 17th April, 1942, Mr. Errington, at a demonstration flight at Netheravon, flew a " Very Important Personage " load which included Admiral Lord Mountbatten, General Marshall, Major-General Browning, Major-General Sir Hastings Ismay, Wing Commander Sir Nigel Norman, Sir James Grigg, then Secretary of State for War, Sir Arthur Street, Captain Harold Balfour, Mr. Duncan Sandys, with Sir Archibald Sinclair as second pilot—a responsible load.

17. The Horsa glider was largely built by furniture manufacturers all over the country and the parts were assembled by 41 Group R.A.F. storage units. It is of interest to note that the Horsa chain lashings were developed by Airspeeds Ltd. at the same time as the glider, and seven years later were still the standard cargo lashing gear for aircraft and gliders.

Hamilcar

18. The Hamilcar glider was the second contribution made by General Aircraft Ltd. during the war period to meet the requirements of airborne troops. It was preceded by the Hotspur, which had an "all up" weight of 3,600 pounds. The Hamilcar, which weighed 36,000 pounds fully loaded, therefore constituted a major development in design.

19. After preliminary conferences and design studies the general lay-out for the Hamilcar was finally agreed early in 1941. It was considered advisable to design and construct a half-scale flying model. A design team of over 100 draughtsmen and 20 technicians was allocated to the complete task, and the resources of the Royal Aircraft Establishment and the National Physical Laboratory were made available to provide structural and wind tunnel test data. The prototype was designed and built in 12 months and successful test flights were made in the early spring of 1942. Flight trials were completed in three weeks.

20. The Hamilcar was the largest wooden aircraft constructed during the war. It was designed to carry heavy armoured vehicles, or combinations of vehicle equipments. For this to be done with structural and aerodynamic efficiency, it was necessary to select a wing loading much greater than anything previously contemplated for a glider—21·7 lb./sq. ft.—and it took on itself more the character of an aircraft without engines as opposed to the popular conception of the lightly loaded sailplane of pre-war years. With it was developed the technique now so well appreciated in airborne operations— that the time taken to land after release from the tug aircraft should be a minimum, so that the glider is exposed to fire from the enemy ground defences for as short a time as possible. One noteworthy feature of the Hamilcar design was, therefore, the large and powerful wing flaps, operated by servo-pneumatic means, which enabled the pilot to control at will the angle of glide, and to effect a landing in a confined space.

21. Because of its great size, the Hamilcar needed the largest and most powerful four-engined bombers available to act as tug aircraft, and the Halifax had an excellent operational record in this capacity. Apart from the engine

power available in the tug, the successful take-off of a heavily loaded glider depends on the total weight of the tug-glider combination. Consequently every effort had to be made during the design to keep the Hamilcar structure weight within strict limits. This was done with such effect that the glider came out 800 pounds lighter than the original estimate. The Hamilcar was able to carry almost its own weight in the form of military load.

22. The decision to design the Hamilcar as a high-wing monoplane with a nose-opening door was to ensure that, with the aircraft lowered on to its skids, armoured track vehicles could be driven straight out without needing special ramps. They could, therefore, be in action in as little as 15 seconds after the aircraft had come to rest. To assist in this rapid exit, the vehicle engine was started up in the air before landing, the exhaust pipes having temporary extension pipes to the outside of the aircraft, which disengaged as the vehicle moved forward. In the case of tank and Bren gun carrier loads the anchorages, which held the vehicles securely in place in the aircraft, could be discarded instantaneously by pulling a lanyard from inside the vehicle. The forward movement of the vehicle then operated a mechanical device which freed the nose-door lock and automatically opened the door.

23. Originally the Hamilcar was intended to make skid landings when used for military operations. For this purpose it had a special chassis for take-off which could be dropped by parachute (the chassis weighed three quarters of a ton). For more normal purposes the aircraft was fitted with a permanent undercarriage. Developments in the tactics of airborne landings, however, caused a change in technique. The possible landing sites during an operation are usually very restricted, and, in order that they may be used by the maximum number of gliders, they must be kept clear. It was, therefore, desirable that the aircraft should land on its normal chassis and use its speed, combined with separate wheel brake operation, to steer itself clear of the landing strip. Immediately it came to rest, high pressure oil in the chassis shock absorber struts was released, causing them to telescope and permit the aircraft to sink on to its skids for the vehicle inside to drive out.

24. The variety of equipment which the Hamilcar could carry presented a formidable list and was continually being augmented. Up to a military load of 17,500 pounds (7·8 tons) it included :—

(a) Tetrarch Mark IV tank.

(b) Locust T.9 tank.

(c) Two Bren gun universal carriers.

(d) Three Rota Trailers.

(e) Two armoured scout cars.

(f) 17-pounder anti-tank gun with tractor.

(g) 25-pounder gun with tractor.

(h) Self-propelled Bofors guns.

(i) Jeep with universal carrier with slave batteries.

(j) Universal carrier for 3-inch mortars and eight motor cycles.

(k) Bailey pontoon bridge equipment.

(l) 48 panniers containing equipment and ammunition.

(*m*) D.4 tractor with angledozer.

(*n*) Scraper with Fordson tractor.

(*o*) Grader.

(*p*) H.D.10 bulldozer (carried in three Hamilcars).

(*q*) H.D.14 bulldozer (carried in three Hamilcars).

The design and construction of the basic aircraft was only part of the whole problem. Each variation of load required special study in respect to anchorage equipment, as with heavy loads there could be no movement during flight.

25. Special praise is due to the expert team of works personnel who operated up and down the country on the various aerodromes to which Hamilcars were allotted. It was their task to install the formidable series of modifications entailed by the variety of military loads and to be on hand at all times to advise and instruct the R.A.F. and airborne personnel. During the period before the Normandy operations they played a considerable part in the final preparations.

Hamilcar, Mark X

26. The Hamilcar Mark X Air Freighter was a development of the Hamilcar tank-carrying glider. It was a twin engine, high-wing monoplane of wooden construction, having a fixed undercarriage. It owed its existence to the necessity for an increase in the operational range and an improvement in the take-off performance of the tug-glider combination, to enable operations to be undertaken in conditions less favourable than those afforded in England. At the time of the Japanese surrender the prototype powered Hamilcars were undergoing exhaustive tests in the hands of the Airborne Forces Experimental Establishment, and quantity production of the aircraft had begun.

27. The reports of the machines' performances and flying qualities were favourable in all respects. Carefully balanced control surfaces and the provision of servo-trimmers (mechanically assisted trimmers) ensured that the aircraft was comfortable to fly throughout its speed range. The Hamilcar's stability was such that its easy flying qualities were maintained either empty or fully loaded and at various centre of gravity positions. The pilot's cockpit was arranged in tandem and was above the cargo cabin ahead of the main plane. All controls were duplicated, the rudder bars being adjustable. Trimmer controls for elevator, rudder, and ailerons were combined in a single unit. Engine controls were grouped on the starboard side. The high-lift flaps were pneumatically operated : the control was progressive, it being possible to stop the movement of the flap in any desired position. The air system was fed by engine-driven compressors which supplied air reservoirs capable of storing enough to operate all air services in the event of it being desired to use them with the engines stopped.

28. Access to the cargo space was through the front of the fuselage. The streamlined nose, which had transparent plastic windows, was hinged on the starboard side of the fuselage. The entrance so formed was the full height and width of the cargo space, and was 6 ft. 8 in. high by 8 ft. wide. The stowage space was 27 ft. 2 in. long giving an area of 1,440 cu. ft. The maximum weight carried was 17,500 pounds, when in towed flight, or 3,000 pounds with full fuel tanks when operating under the aircraft's own engine power.

29. To facilitate the loading of vehicles and heavy cargo, the undercarriage oleo struts were used as hydraulic jacks which, when deflated, allowed the fuselage to come in contact with the ground, where it rested on skids which were permanently attached to the underside of the fuselage. When loading operations had been completed the aircraft was raised to its normal position by recharging the oleo struts by means of hand pumps which were permanently fitted to the axle struts. When not in use the pumps were isolated by stopcocks.

30. The materials used were, for the most part, highest grade spruce timbers and birch plywood joined with waterproof synthetic resin cement. The plywood skin was covered with cotton fabric and protected with a doping scheme suitable for tropical conditions. Highly stressed metal parts were of stainless steel. Mild steel parts were protected against corrosion. All the materials of construction conformed to the specifications adopted by the Ministry of Aircraft Production.

Hadrian (U.S.C.G.–4A)

31. The Hadrian was the standard medium glider for American airborne forces, and was used on a number of occasions by British air-landing troops as a result of the close co-operation between them, and the pooling of resources which was treated as a matter of course throughout the war. The name Hadrian, applied to it by British airborne forces, was in keeping with the existing series of names for British gliders—Hotspur, Hengist, Horsa and Hamilcar, but it was known by its owners, the Americans, as the C.G.–4A (Waco), being made by the Waco Aircraft Co., U.S.A. It was a 15-seater troop and cargo carrying high-wing monoplane with rectangular wings, manually operated flaps to assist landing and conventional landing gear. Two types of undercarriage were designed. The first, known as the " training " gear, was fitted with pneumatic-tyred wheels equipped with hydraulic brakes and a spring oleo shock absorber. The second type, the " tactical " landing gear, could be jettisoned after take-off in the same manner as that fitted to the early Horsa glider.

32. The pilot's compartment and the cargo compartment were hinged together along the roof, so that the nose of the glider could be raised up, and locked in the open position. In addition the tail could be supported on a jack, so that two hinged loading ramps at the front of the cargo compartment were tipped forward and touched the ground. By this means the cargo compartment could be loaded to full capacity, and jeeps, artillery and motor cycles could be easily run into it. To unload a jeep after landing, a cable and pulley system from the nose of the glider was attached to the rear bumper of the vehicle. On driving the jeep forward this cable pulled the nose up, and was then automatically uncoupled as the jeep moved on. Apart from this device, the nose could be opened and closed by hand.

APPENDIX A

ANNEXURE

GLIDER SPECIFICATIONS

Glider Mark.	Wing Span.	Length.	Passengers.	Internal Dimensions of Fuselage.	All-up Weight.	Military Load.
HOTSPUR I	61 ft. 11 in.	39 ft. 3 in.	8	—	3,600 lb. (1·6 tons)	
II	45 ft. 11 in.					
HADRIAN (U.S.C.G.—4A)	83 ft. 8 in.	48 ft. 4 in.	15	13 ft. 2 in. 5 ft. 10 in. 5 ft. 6 in.	7,500 lb. (3·3 tons)	3,750 lb. (1·7 tons)
HORSA I	88 ft.	67 ft.	29	34 ft.	15,500 lb. (6·9 tons)	6,900 lb. (3·1 tons)
II				4 ft. 6 in.	15,750 lb. (7·0 tons)	
HAMILCAR	110 ft.	68 ft.	40	27 ft. 8 ft. 6 ft. 8 in.	36,000 lb. (16·1 tons)	17,500 lb. (7·8 tons)
HAMILCAR X Towed flight	"	"	"	"	47,000 lb. (21 tons)	17,500 lb. (7·8 tons)
Solo flight	"	"	"	"	32,000 lb. (14·5 tons)	3,000 lb. (1·3 tons)

APPENDIX B

THE AIRCRAFT

Introduction

1. During the period 1940–1945 many different types of aircraft were employed in connection with airborne forces. This appendix gives a brief general description of the main types, and lists others which were used or which were considered for use in connection with airborne forces. In each case the name of the maker is given in brackets. Where details are given in the Annexure the figures relating to speed and range are taken from the makers' specifications and bear no relation to those actually obtained under operational conditions. Too many factors—full load, altitude, cargo, etc.—would have to be taken into account to give a constant figure.

Aircraft which were in general use by Airborne Forces
Albemarle (Armstrong–Whitworth)

2. The Albemarle was designed as a medium bomber and was first delivered to the R.A.F. in January, 1943. From that date onwards it played a major role in airborne training and operations, being employed by 38 Group R.A.F. for towing Horsas or smaller types of gliders and for dropping parachute troops and supplies.

3. Marks I and II were used primarily as glider tugs and had an " all up " weight of 35,000 pounds. The practical range for this purpose varied between 350 and 900 miles and the radius of action was 230 miles.

4. The Mark V was used mainly for dropping parachute troops, ten of whom could be carried. They were stationed forward of a large dropping hole in the floor of the rear fuselage. Rails were fitted to the sides of the fuselage for the parachute static strops. Bomb racks were retained and containers could be carried.

5. The extreme practical range at which troops could be dropped varied between 360 and 820 miles according to the weight of equipment carried by the troops, climatic conditions, and whether or not a beam gun, firing to either side of the aircraft, was fitted to the aircraft. The weight of the turret affected considerably the range and speed of the aircraft. The radius of action as a glider tug was 345 miles and the normal cruising speed was 130 knots.

6. The Mark VI Albemarle was introduced into 38 Group R.A.F. in June, 1944, and differed only from its predecessors in having a large pair of cargo doors on the starboard side.

Commando (Curtis Co., U.S.A.)

7. The Commando, or C.46, transport aircraft was first used in airborne operations during the crossing of the River Rhine in March, 1945, by IX U.S. Troop Carrier Command.

In appearance it was similar to the Dakota, but carried 40 parachute troops in two sticks of 20 jumping simultaneously from two doors in either side of the fuselage. It had a radius of action of 500 miles with full payload.

Dakota (Douglas Co., U.S.A.)

8. The Dakota, or C.47, proved itself to be the outstanding all purpose transport aircraft of the war and was used in all theatres. Although designed as a civil transport aircraft it was easily modified for dropping parachute troops and glider towing. When 46 Group was formed in January, 1944, the five squadrons of the group were completely equipped with Dakotas. Three Marks—I, III and IV—were used by the R.A.F. and U.S. IX Troop Carrier Command for their operations in Europe.

9. The aircraft carried 20 fully equipped parachute troops who jumped out of a door forward of the tail on the port side. It could tow a Horsa or smaller type glider, and for this purpose had a radius of action of 325 miles towing a Horsa, or an additional 25 miles with a Hadrian (U.S. CG4-A). For dropping parachute troops its radius of action was 450 miles.

Halifax (Handley Page)

10. From early in 1943, when 295 Squadron R.A.F. began to re-equip with the Halifax Mark V in place of the Whitley Mark V, until the cessation of hostilities, this aircraft took part in all major operations. The first airborne operation in which Halifaxes were used was the ill-fated " Freshman " in November, 1942, and it also undertook the first long range ferry of gliders in July, 1943, when Horsas were towed to North Africa from the United Kingdom.

11. The Mark A III, and A VII and A IX were designed and modified to be the airborne forces versions of the original heavy bomber. Instead of the Merlin engines used in the Halifax Mark A V, Hercules VI and XVI were fitted. Marks A III and A VII were similar and used in the operations in Europe, but the Mark A IX with an extended wing span, redesigned fuel system and larger dropping aperture was not in service until after the war.

12. During the war the Halifax was the only aircraft in service with airborne forces that was capable of towing the Hamilcar glider, and it was used extensively for glider towing generally. It was an uneconomical aircraft for dropping parachute troops, despite its size, because owing to its internal construction the earlier Marks would only carry ten troops and the Mark A IX sixteen. However, the bomb-racks were retained and the aircraft was used for dropping heavy equipment, such as jeeps and 6-pounder anti-tank guns.

13. When towing a Hamilcar glider the radius of action was 400 miles and with a Horsa 600 miles.

Stirling (Short)

14. Towards the end of 1943, the Stirling became obsolete as a heavy night bomber with the result that many were transferred to 38 Group early in 1944. From then on a glider towing hook and remote control release were fitted during production of all Stirlings. Larger and more powerful than the Albemarle, the Stirling Mark IV gradually superseded the former until in 1945 six squadrons had been equipped with it.

15. The Mark IV Stirling was the long range troop transport conversion from the Mark III. The nose and mid-upper turrets were removed and replaced by fairings, but the four-gun tail turret was retained. It was used for towing the Horsa and smaller gliders, and for dropping parachute troops, 22 jumping through a large opening in the underside of the rear fuselage. The bomb cells were retained and used for containers, 12 of which could be dropped with a stick of 22 men, or 27 when no parachute troops were carried.

16. When carrying parachute troops, the Stirling had a range of between 1,500 and 2,000 miles, and a radius of action of over 800 miles, which was reduced to 525 miles when towing a fully-laden Horsa.

Whitley (Armstrong-Whitworth)

17. When the War began the Whitley was Britain's largest bomber but because of its slowness and vulnerability it soon became obsolete for this purpose. It was then handed over to airborne forces, being used for training parachute troops until superseded by the Albemarle. It took part in the raid (operation " Colossus ") in Italy, in February, 1941, and the Bruneval raid in February, 1942. The rear turrets were removed and a circular aperture was cut in the floor of the fuselage and fitted with hinged doors. The aircraft could carry a stick of ten parachute troops, but it was not a suitable aircraft for the purpose, being dark, gloomy and uncomfortable. It was also used as a tug to tow Horsa and smaller gliders, but it was incapable of towing a fully laden Horsa.

18. The radius of action of the Whitley carrying parachute troops was at least 500 miles.

Other Aircraft Connected with Airborne Forces

19. The following types of aircraft were all used or adapted for use in conjunction with airborne forces.

504N (Avro) .. .. A single engine aircraft used for training in the very early days of airborne forces.

Hart (Hawker) .. .. A single engine bi-plane used in the infancy of No. 1 Parachute Training School for towing civilian type elementary gliders.

Hector (Hawker) .. A variant of the Hart used for towing Hotspur gliders at the Glider Exercise Unit when 38 Wing was first formed.

Hudson (Lockheed) .. Twin-engined reconnaissance medium bomber —it was never used in European airborne operations but took part in minor operations in the Middle and Far East. It was also used for experimental purposes at Ringway and for training in India.

Hurricane (Hawker) .. Single engine fighter capable of dropping supplies in two 300-lb. containers.

400

Lancaster (Avro)	..	Most successful British four engined heavy bomber of the war, capable of carrying six or seven thousand pounds of supplies. Adapted for glider towing though never used on operations.
Lodestar (Lockheed)		Twin engine aircraft smaller than the Hudson and used occasionally in Far East for dropping troops.
Master (Miles) ..	..	Fast single engine trainer adapted for glider towing.
Typhoon (Hawker)	..	Single engine fighter also capable of dropping a similar load to the Hurricane.
Valencia (Vickers)	..	Very early type twin engine bi-plane bomber. Used for parachute training in the Middle East in 1941 and at the Air Landing School, India. Its very slow speed made it ideal for basic training.
Ventura (Lockheed)	..	Twin engine reconnaissance aircraft intended for use by 299 Squadron R.A.F., but replaced immediately by Stirlings in January, 1944.

AIRCRAFT SPECIFICATIONS

Aircraft Mark.	Engines.	Wing Span.	Length.	Height.	Maximum Speed.	Range.	Maximum All-up Weight.
ALBEMARLE I II V VI	Two Hercules XI Mark I	77 ft.	59 ft. 11 in.	15 ft. 7 in.	250 m.p.h.	1,350 miles	36,500 lb.
COMMANDO C.46	Two Pratt and Whitney R2800—51 Double Wasp	108 ft. 1 in.	76 ft. 4 in.	21 ft. 9 in.	265 m.p.h.	2,800 miles	45,000 lb.
DAKOTA C.47 I C.47 A III C.47 B IV	Two Twin Wasp R. 1830—92 or 90 C.	95 ft.	64 ft. 5½ in.	16 ft. 11 in.	229 m.p.h.	1,500 miles	31,000 lb.
HALIFAX II V III VII IX	Four Merlin XX or XXII. Four Hercules VI or XVI.	104 ft.	71 ft. 7 in.	21 ft. 7 in.	270 m.p.h.	3,000 miles	65,000 lb.
STIRLING I III IV V	Hercules XI Hercules VI or XVI	99 ft. 11 in.	87 ft. 3 in.	22 ft. 9 in.	280 m.p.h.	3,000 miles	70,000 lb.
WHITLEY I II III V	Two Tiger IX Two Merlin X	84 ft.	72 ft. 6 in.	15 ft.	230 m.p.h.	2,400 miles	33,500 lb.

APPENDIX C

THE PARACHUTE

1. As was seen in the introduction to this volume, the Germans were quick to realize the possibilities of parachute troops after they had seen the Russian demonstration in 1936. By the spring of 1937 they had decided to use an automatic parachute for their new parachute forces. By the outbreak of war, this type of equipment had been produced by both American and British manufacturers. Previous R.A.F. parachutes, required only for emergency use, were operated by the wearer pulling a rip cord after he had jumped out of the aircraft. He had to estimate when to open his parachute and needed his hands free to operate it. Such a method was used in the summer of 1940 by the Central Landing School, but was found to be unsuitable for army parachute troops, who would be required to jump in groups instead of singly, and from the lowest height consistent with safety, carrying heavy equipment. So the school soon changed to a parachute of American design.

2. This parachute was securely attached to a strong point on the aircraft by a length of material known as a static line. The other end of this line was attached to the apex or top of the parachute canopy by a weak line, the slack or lazy cord. As the jumper fell from the aircraft, the parachute was pulled from the pack on his back, canopy first, followed by the rigging lines, the cords connecting the canopy to the harness. The jumper's weight then broke the lazy cord, and he was left with a fully developed canopy over him, the static line remaining attached to the aircraft.

3. This method had many advantages over the rip cord type, as the parachute opened automatically at the correct moment without any action on the man's part, thus eliminating the possibilities of failure through the human factor. As it developed more rapidly, a lower jumping height was possible, making the drop on to a pin pointed area more accurate and leaving the parachutist exposed to small arms fire for a shorter time. But after only 57 descents had been made with this type, a fatal accident showed that, although the method was good, the inherent fault lay in the ballistic instability of the human being. A man jumping from an aircraft twists and somersaults in a peculiar manner. If, as the canopy emerged, the man were twisting, it could catch under his arm, or if he were somersaulting, on his leg, and the resulting friction would break the lazy cord, before the canopy was withdrawn from its pack. The man and tangled parachute would then drop free to the ground.

4. The remedy for this was found by Mr. Raymond Quilter of the G.Q. Parachute Co., Woking. He produced a static line parachute named the " X " type, which reversed the process. When the man jumped, the parachute pack containing the canopy and rigging lines was broken from his back by a series of progressively stronger ties, and hung from the aircraft. As he fell, the rigging lines were dragged from this pack and by the time the canopy appeared, the man was the length of the rigging lines, 20 feet below. A final tie, holding the apex of the canopy to the pack, then broke and the parachute was fully extended leaving the pack and static line attached to the aircraft. This method of deployment was an improvement upon that of the American pattern being more controlled and simpler, and giving approximately only a fifth of the shock previously experienced.

5. The device was immediately adopted, and despite the somewhat haphazard but extremely keen methods of servicing, and the lack of technical knowledge on the part of the parachute troops, 24,000 drops were made without a single accident. It was then found that such was the confidence in the apparatus, that the parachutes were being packed with the rigging line loops broken and in a damp condition, because of the previous continued success under apparently any conditions, and were therefore thoroughly unserviceable.

6. This excellent start proved that, as the parachute troops were working from a very low altitude, and only wearing one parachute, the system employed was good and worth while perfecting. As the quantity of parachutists was increased from the small numbers originally required, a very determined and methodical approach was made to the problem both at the Airborne Forces Experimental Establishment, under Group Captain L. G. Harvey, and at the Royal Aircraft Establishment, Farnborough, under Mr. W. D. Brown, both parties working in the closest co-operation with Mr. Quilter. It was found that a number of trained observers to each descent was essential. These observers noticed that whereas a parachutist leaving the hole beneath an aircraft from the front edge always turned round and round, the man jumping from the rear side always tended to somersault. Two reasons have been advanced to explain the first case. It may have been that when the static strop came out of the pack on the man's back it hit his shoulder, and so started him twisting, or possibly it was owing to the effect of the slip stream on him. In the second case, the man from the rear side was struck on the shins by the airstream, which made him somersault.

7. Both of these failings were remedied by a new design of pack. In this the strop emerged at the back of the man's neck instead of from waist level, and so was well clear of his shoulder. This strop, too, required more tension to pull it out, and so counteracted the somersaulting tendencies previously experienced. The methods of jumping and landing were improved, and accidents were reduced to a minimum. There were accidents, however, caused by faulty canopy fabrics, particularly noticeable with silk, and this material was largely superseded by nylon, and finally by ramex which proved very satisfactory. In addition, tests were introduced to detect material which was too porous.

8. In the original pack, the rigging lines were carried on a flap at its mouth, A second design (which was used after the end of the war) was produced in which they were on one side, but for a time a combination of old and new was used, the strop in the high position with the rigging lines on the flap.

9. The " X " type of parachute, or statichute, was the standard type employed by British airborne forces throughout the war, and, apart from its role as a man dropping parachute, it was used in clusters of up to 12 for dropping heavy equipment. Though statistics may often be misleading, out of over half a million descents made in training at No. 1 Parachute Training School with this statichute up to August, 1948, only 42 fatal accidents had occurred, an average of under one in 12,000.

APPENDIX D

RADAR HOMING DEVICES

1. In the early days of airborne forces, two of the most difficult tasks of the air forces in an airborne operation were first to locate the exact dropping zone for each unit, and then to ensure that all aircraft dropped their troops on their correct areas. The R.A.F. presented this problem to their Telecommunications Research Establishment, Great Malvern, who already had equipment which, with very little modification, would solve a great many of the difficulties.

2. The first aid to direction was a navigational device named " Gee ", from which an aircraft could deduce its exact position. Before the formation of 38 Group in the autumn of 1943, this apparatus was only fitted to aircraft in Bomber and Coastal Commands, but after the group was formed, airborne forces were allowed to use it. The second aid was a homing device named " Rebecca/Eureka ". " Eureka " was a beacon, set up on the ground and set to receive on one fixed frequency, and transmit on another fixed frequency. " Rebecca " was carried in an aircraft and transmitted on the Eureka receiver frequency and received on the Eureka transmitter frequency. On receiving the impulse from the aircraft " Rebecca " set, " Eureka " on the ground automatically replied, which gave the captain of the aircraft his bearing to, and distance from, the beacon. This in outline was the " Rebecca " Mark I. The beacon, a rectangular box with a collapsible aerial, was to be carried by the pathfinders of the independent parachute companies, and being set up on their dropping zones would lead subsequent formations to the correct places. It had a morse key fitted to it, so that the operator could send the code letter designating his particular dropping zone to the " Rebecca " in the aircraft. With this arrangement, however, it was found that an aircraft approaching adjacent dropping zones where several beacons were in use, would react with all within range, thus making it almost impossible to identify the correct dropping zone. Rebecca Mark II and Eureka Mark II were developed to overcome this difficulty. In these equipments five separate frequencies were provided, common to both receiver and transmitter portions of Rebecca and Eureka. It was now possible to arrange combinations of transmitter and receiver frequencies which prevented both the action of beacons one on the other at close ranges, and reaction with more than one beacon by the aircraft. The increased channels available, of course, gave additional security. The different combinations could be selected in flight on the Rebecca, and by the operator of the Eureka on the ground, though normal practice was for the Eureka to be issued pre-set and tested.

3. The original " Rebecca/Eureka " was sent to the United States, where similar equipment working on the same frequencies was produced. This equipment, known as " AN APN2 " (Rebecca) was fitted to all aircraft of United States Troop Carrier Commands. American Eureka equipment was also produced, known as AN PPN. 1. The Horsa gliders carrying part of 9th Parachute Battalion to Normandy were fitted with a battery-powered " Rebecca Mark III ", to enable them to home on to their objective, the Merville battery. At the same time, a light-weight beacon, carried in webbing pouches, " Eureka Mark III " was produced for Special Forces Headquarters. The " Eureka Mark II " beacon, used by pathfinder companies of the airborne divisions, fitted into a normal leg kit bag ; complete with battery and collapsible

aerial it weighed only 28 pounds, and was powered by a 12-volt battery. In an emergency any 12-volt battery, say from a jeep or civilian car, could be used. The weight of Eureka compared favourably with the 100-lb. " Rebecca " in the aircraft. Best results were obtained where a direct line of sight existed between the aircraft and the beacon. A hill between the two would drastically diminish the range, but a hill behind the beacon relative to the approaching aircraft acted as a " reflector " and produced a greater range forward of the hill. Wooded country or buildings close at hand resulted in fading and poor results, but with reasonable country for siting the beacon, an aircraft flying at 2,000 feet would expect to home on it from eight to twelve miles away. For a low-flying plane the range would be less.

4. The only operational use of " Rebecca–Eureka Mark I " was for the abortive attack on the Norwegian heavy water plant in November, 1942. During the summer of 1943 the Mark II equipment was hurriedly sent to North Africa for use by 38 Wing in the invasion of Sicily. However, it was felt to be too difficult a task in the short time available to fit this new equipment, and it was not used. For the invasion of Normandy 90 per cent of aircraft using " Gee " got satisfactory results. " Eureka " beacons were successfully used to mark group rendezvous, but on the dropping zones several were damaged and others were set up in the wrong areas, and a number of aircraft were misled. More successful results were obtained on the first two days of the Arnhem operations, and in March, 1945, over 95 per cent of the aircraft used it successfully on crossing the Rhine.

5. One other use was made of radar in an airborne role. This was a ground radar set produced as a result of the Arnhem operation and designed as a link between airborne forces on the ground and aircraft. The set, known as a " Dinner Wagon ", was carried in three Horsa gliders, and was used by the visual control posts with complete success for the Rhine crossing. It incorporated facilities to control day and night fighter cover, and beacons to enable fighters to orbit dropping and landing zones, and could be used to give warning of the approach of enemy aircraft, as well as provide communications with our own supply planes.

APPENDIX E

EQUIPMENT FOR DROPPING STORES FROM AIRCRAFT

Introduction

1. This appendix shows how the problems of delivering stores and equipment to troops were solved and the reasons why certain types of dropping equipment were produced. It does not go into the technical considerations connected with the development of the equipment.

2. In all the operations undertaken by the British airborne forces during the war, most heavy loads such as transport, artillery and engineer equipment and medical stores had to be landed by glider. But before the gliderborne air-landing battalions were formed, the original parachute battalions had to devise their own methods of dropping with their small arms and equipment, as at that time, no suitable equipment existed.

Containers

3. At the outbreak of war, the Royal Air Force had two types of equipment for dropping stores, the first was a cylindrical metal container two and a half feet long and one foot in diameter, opening at one end. The second consisted of a wooden beam to which packing cases could be strapped. The limits for both of these types were 150 lb. weight and an aircraft speed of 120 miles an hour, and they were dropped from the bomb cell of an aircraft by a 10-ft. or 14-ft. parachute. These methods were obviously not suitable for parachute troops, as not even a rifle could be fitted into the container, and by the box method, it was impossible to unpack the equipment quickly on the ground, quite apart from the difficulties due to the restriction in weight.

4. As a result, the Central Landing Establishment experimented with various designs for dropping stores. The first, produced by the Elliot Equipment Company, was a quilted mat, stiffened with bamboo rods, fitted with pockets in which rifles and other equipment were carried. The mat was rolled up, strapped to a steel bar, and had a 28-ft. parachute attached to one end. This canopy, similar to that in the X-type man-carrying parachute, had to be fitted into a pack the same diameter as the rolled mat, so that it could be carried in the bomb cell of an aircraft. It controlled the design of many subsequent containers, as each type has had to employ existing pack specifications. The limitations of the roll soon became obvious. Only a very restricted range of arms could be carried, and insufficient of those. In addition, it was difficult to unpack on the ground, and did not stand up to rough usage.

5. The development of the next container, designed to fit into the bomb cell of the Whitley aircraft, was given to the G.Q. Parachute Company, who produced a number for the Special Operations Executive. These were 6 ft. long and 15 in. in diameter, and again opened at one end only. The first to be packed was stood on end between two pairs of steps. Mr. Quilter and Squadron Leader Miles then held a boy employee of Mr. Quilter's by the ankles and lowered him into the container ; in this position he was handed rubber padding and the equipment to pack. When he had had enough he was hauled up for air. Despite its " Heath Robinson " aspect, the container worked in

407

practice but showed the need for some other form of opening. Further types were made to open longitudinally, and eventually a satisfactory model of metal-skinned construction was produced which was able to carry 600 lb.

6. However, a difficulty arose over certain stores which would not fit into a cylindrical container of 15 in. diameter, notably wireless sets. Accordingly, two containers were designed, to fit the No. 11 and No. 22 set respectively. Owing to modifications to the sets, these containers rapidly became useless, which showed very clearly the error of designing merely " one-purpose " equipment. Later, working on the principle that any container should be designed to the maximum size of the bomb cell in which it is to fit, one was constructed for the 2,000-lb. bomb cell in Halifax, Stirling and Lancaster aircraft 11 ft. 6 in. long by 1 ft. 6 in. square.

7. An example of the problems of the design of containers is shown by the requirements put forward by the Special Operations Executive in one case :—

" (1) A container which can be carried in the bomb racks of any Bomber Command aircraft.

(2) To be released at approximately 1,000 ft. for dropping into water.

(3) To have a negative buoyance so that it will sink immediately, and remain submerged, to be capable of remaining submerged in fresh or salt water up to six months in a depth up to 15 fathoms and to have an anchorage system to withstand a two-knot current.

(4) The parachute to be automatically detached from the container on striking the water and to sink when detached.

(5) A marker buoy to be released immediately on touching the water, or at any time up to one hour thereafter.

(6) The container to be capable of being raised by the buoy cable and unpacked by one man in a small boat."

Crates for Loads unsuited to Containers

8. Although the container system was the most desirable for stores and equipment dropping, certain loads could not be carried by this method. Special crates and a range of different sized parachutes were consequently produced for these. Many of these crates could be suspended from a single parachute such as the 3-inch mortar base plate and camouflet sets, although certain light and bulky loads tended to somersault in the air, thus collapsing their parachutes, and had to be fitted with fins to stabilize them. Use was also made of the standard cradle used for the normal container. By fitting wooden blocks of various shapes, a variety of different stores could be carried, including Bangalore torpedoes, and spare barrels for the 75-mm. pack howitzer. In most cases the 28-ft. canopy was sufficient but in the case of the gun barrels three 38-ft. chutes were used in a cluster.

9. More complicated crates were required for loads such as motor cycles, which were not only bulky, but had several weak spots that had to be protected for landing. For the 350-c.c. motor cycle an overall framework was needed to prevent damage on the ground, but such a crate had to be instantly detachable. It also had to give support to various components of the cycle which could not take parachuting inertia stresses in their own structure. The motor cycle proved one of the most awkward loads to crate and carry as it had to lie flat in a bomb cell for the bomb doors to be closed, then had to be turned in mid-air to enable it to land the right way up.

10. Certain loads, by reason of their shape or size, could not be stowed in the bomb cells but had to be carried inside the aircraft and dropped through the jumping hole or thrown out of the door. A good example of this was the folding bicycle, of very low weight, but inconvenient shape. It covered three bomb positions if placed in the bomb racks and also called for a special crate to be provided. To drop it through the door needed only a parachute and an attachment strap. Some experiments were needed to find the best way of landing it. The obvious way, to make use of the shock-absorbing capacities of the wheel tyres, was found to be wrong. In nearly all tests the wheels were buckled, and the cycle useless. It was found that to drop it for final impact on its handlebars was the best. Normally there would be no damage, and although in bad cases, where landings were made on hard ground or in high winds, there might be a bent handlebar, the cycle would still be ridable.

11. The success of this means of dropping and the coming of the Dakota aircraft, which at first had no bomb racks, led to the introduction of the pannier, a rectangular wicker basket into which a very large variety of arms and equipment could be packed, and which could be thrown from the door of the aircraft. With the introduction of the Dakota in quantities this method was standardized, and roller conveyors and other means were introduced into the aircraft to enable the largest possible number of panniers to be ejected in a short time.

Ancillary Equipment

12. The growth and development of parachute dropping led to the need for several items of ancillary equipment to be used with parachute canopies and crates.

LOCATION DEVICES

13. One of the most important of these was the need for locating equipment that had been dropped at night. Containers were at first camouflaged, and even in broad daylight were difficult to locate, and though later a white finish was given this was very little help at night. Four lamps were fitted to light up on touching the ground, so that whichever way the container lay one was showing on each side. Further, the lights had coloured discs over them, so that certain containers could be readily identified. These lights worked well on flat unobstructed ground, but undulations, however slight, bushes, walls or crops made them ineffective. Alternative methods varied from the use of illuminated jets of water to the scenting of containers and the dropping of dogs to find them. Electric bells could not always be heard in the general noise, and pyrotechnics were discarded as too dangerous in that they were a fire hazard. The final design was a collapsible frame, made up of three legs of equal length, hinged together at one end, which when closed could be stowed in a 2-inch tube on the container, and when open formed a pyramid with lights and flags at three of the apices, and an impact switch at the fourth. The device was also fitted with a triangular parachute between the legs, arranged so that it hung with the impact switch downward. It was connected to the container by a cord attached to the centre of the upper side of the canopy on the device. The natural springiness of the framework caused it to give when striking an obstruction and to " dance " over rough ground. Radio methods were given extensive trials before they were finally rejected, and by the end of the war, no satisfactory answer had been found, in spite of exhaustive research into the problem.

DELAY DEVICES

14. Various delay devices were evolved, to facilitate dropping containers and men together on the ground. It was soon found that the best dropping order for men and equipment was for half the stick to jump, followed by the containers which were released by the action of the last man to jump in the first half. The remainder of the stick then jumped so that on the ground the containers were in the centre of the pattern. This system meant that the man jumping after the containers had to estimate the pause necessary to allow the containers to clear the aircraft. An unnecessary strain was placed on this man, and he might in his enthusiasm jump early and collide with the containers, or for safety delay too long and make a very long stick on the ground. The device adopted eventually allowed the containers to be dropped together and fall free for a period, clear of the men. Their parachutes then opened by a delay action device, with an interval between each to avoid entanglement. A second type allowed equipment to be released at a high altitude, about 15,000 feet, and to fall freely to 500 feet from the ground when the parachute opened. The object was to allow supplies to be dropped accurately on to a point without forcing the aircraft to fly low, exposed to fire from ground weapons.

CANOPY RELEASE DEVICES

15. It had long been known that it was highly desirable for the parachute to be separated from its load immediately upon landing, to avoid dragging in the wind. No really satisfactory device was produced, but designs have been used with some success in dropping heavy standard loads like the jeep and 6-pounder anti-tank gun.

WHEELED EQUIPMENT

16. It is well known that the parachutist is most vulnerable directly after landing. His arms and stores may be several yards away in a container, and even when he is armed he is encumbered with heavy loaded containers to hamper his movements. Several devices have helped to minimize this weakness, the earliest being a folding trolley. This was a useful vehicle for carrying stores but was not big enough to transport loaded containers, and in any case took some minutes to assemble after it had been dropped. Accordingly, equipment was designed to fit wheels on to containers, and after "teething" troubles were overcome, an axle and rubber tyred wheels, were produced and dropped attached to the container. It could then be manœuvred by two men over rough ground, or towed on roads at up to 30 miles an hour without overturning.

KIT BAGS AND VALISES

17. At this point it is worth considering the object of all these devices—to deliver a soldier on the ground armed and ready for battle. The parachutist was, up to now, dropped parted from his arms. At the worst the container holding his arms might get stuck in the aircraft, and be flown home again. It might collide with him during his descent, or at the other extreme, land miles from him. He might spend half an hour on landing looking for his rifle or his wireless set. The ideal of dropping the man with his arms was achieved with the development of the kit-bag, a landmark in the early days of airborne forces.

It rapidly became an indispensable part of the parachutist's equipment and the design, in various guises, was modified to take a variety of stores. The kit-bag was made of canvas reinforced with leather, two and a half feet long and a foot in diameter, opening at one end. Inside it could be packed any stores of that size, such as wireless sets, suitably padded, or a Sten gun in two sections owing to its length, up to a weight which the parachutist could lift—60 to 80 pounds. The opening was then roped up, and the bag strapped around the man's leg or both legs depending upon the type of door or hole through which he was to jump. As soon as his parachute had opened, the leg straps were freed by the parachutist operating a quick release device, and he then lowered the bag on a 20 foot length of rope, until it dangled below him, secured to his parachute harness by the rope. The bag on hitting the ground first lessened the weight on the parachute, and enabled the man to land unencumbered with his stores, but yet attached to them by a length of rope. In the same fashion, valises to carry a rifle or bren gun were designed and proved invaluable.

PERCUSSION HEADS

18. Investigation was carried out to find the best type of percussion head to absorb landing shocks. Some designs used springs and rubber but both of these mediums proved unsuitable as the container tended to bounce and somersault on landing. Other designs absorbed the shock by the bending of mild steel members or using aerated plastics which broke and crumbled, thereby dispersing the shock.

Heavy Dropping

19. The dropping of loads heavier than the standard container, at that time 350 pounds, started with the airborne lifeboat, weighing 800 pounds. On account of the fragile nature of the boat, three 32-ft. canopies joined together in a cluster were used. After development in this field, including the dropping of a 6,000 pound midget submarine with a crew of one, it was found that a cluster of 12 32-foot canopies could be satisfactorily released. This system was used for the first jeeps dropped in operations. In dropping the jeep it was found that the chassis itself could not possibly take the landing shocks. To rectify this, a sub-frame was fitted under the vehicle and a top frame above, the two connected by rods so that the jeep was sandwiched between two strong structures, which supported it at many points, holding the various heavy units such as engine and axles in relation to each other, a function the normal chassis could not perform under parachute strain. Under this sub-frame were fitted crash pans.

20. The 6-pounder gun was fitted with extra supports to hold up certain heavy items, but the whole design was simpler owing to the gun's very robust construction. In the case of both jeep and gun, all projections were faired off by metal fittings or wire rope guards so that in the event of somersaulting any rigging line that became wrapped around the load would slip off. To reduce the somersaulting, both jeep and gun were tilted forward as they fell from the bomb cell of the aircraft; this caused each to somersault against the force of the slipstream, which gave the opposite effect. It also positioned the load at right angles to the parachute rigging lines and produced more satisfactory results.

Free Dropping

21. A certain amount of work was also done on the dropping of stores from aircraft without the use of parachutes. The first method tried was free dropping—in general not found to be a successful system, being applicable to only a restricted range of loads such as bundles of blankets, and sacks of rice double sacked, with tins of food in among the grain. Liquids were free dropped, but a flexible double container, complicated and expensive, was needed. The inner container was almost invariably broken and the whole useless for further work. Attempts to fit " wings " to boxes, resulting in a " sycamore seed " effect were made, but proved to be a complete failure, and this method was not pursued.

Summary

22. The development of supply dropping equipment through the war was unfortunately carried on almost entirely on a " trial and error " basis. This was because of the almost complete lack of any knowledge on the subject at the outbreak of hostilities and also because the need to produce equipment under the pressure of operational requirements precluded any long term basic research. In general the system produced good results as equipment was ready as needed but it resulted in a lack of planned development, and the information obtained was largely in the form of trial reports in development files, not an easy form of reference.

23. The various items of ancillary equipment, releases, lighting sets and time lag devices were produced as needed and were capable of almost infinite variety to suit special conditions. Work on other methods of dropping showed that free dropping was of very limited application, that vanes provided suitable retardation for small loads but were difficult to launch, and that rocket deceleration was possible, but much work was needed to bring it to a state of development fit for service use.

24. All the work was carried out at the Royal Aircraft Establishment, Farnborough, Hampshire, or at the Airborne Forces Experimental Establishment, Sherborne-in-Elmet, near Harrogate, Yorkshire, these units either testing equipment put forward by contractors or designing and testing their own items. Particular mention should be made of the following names among many people who contributed largely to the work :—

Squadron Leader Pitkethley of A.F.E.E.—General supply dropping.
Capt. Tillett of A.F.E.E.—Heavy load dropping.
Dr. Gibbs of R.A.E.—Heavy loads and containers.
Mr. Billett of R.A.E.—Heavy loads and containers.
Mr. Brown of R.A.E.—Parachute canopies.
Mr. Anderson of R.A.E.—Containers.
Mr. Morley of R.A.E.—Heavy load crates.
Major Smith of Trianco Ltd.—Heavy load crates.
Mr. Pollard of Trianco Ltd.—Heavy load crates.
Mr. Thomas of Evenlite—Location devices and other ancillary equipments.
Mr. Quilter of G.Q.—Parachute clusters and specialized equipment.
Mr. Cooper of Cunliffe Owen—Release devices.

STANDARD OPERATING PROCEDURE FOR AIRBORNE AND TROOP CARRIER UNITS—SUPREME HEADQUARTERS, ALLIED EXPEDITIONARY FORCE

OPERATION NUMBER	MEMORANDUM 12	13th March,1944 (amended 8th June, 1944, and 4th November, 1944)..

STANDARD OPERATING PROCEDURE FOR AIRBORNE AND TROOP CARRIER UNITS

SECTION I   LIAISON.

SECTION II   STAFF PROCEDURE.

SECTION III   OPERATING PROCEDURE.

SECTION IV   JOINT RESPONSIBILITIES OF AIRBORNE AND TROOP CARRIER COMMANDERS.

SECTION V   RESPONSIBILITIES OF TROOP CARRIER UNITS.

SECTION VI   RESPONSIBILITIES OF AIRBORNE UNITS.

ANNEXURE I   SCHEDULE OF PLANNING FOR AIRBORNE OPERATIONS.

ANNEXURE II   NAVIGATION AND EMPLOYMENT OF PATHFINDER UNITS.

1. Object

The object of this memorandum is to provide a common basis upon which the training and operations of allied airborne and troop carrier units can be conducted, and to define the responsibilities of the First Allied Airborne Army and the Airborne and Troop Carrier commanders.

SECTION I

LIAISON

2. General

Upon receipt of directives or orders to participate in training or combat missions, the commanding officers of the airborne and troop carrier units concerned will immediately exchange experienced and competent liaison officers to act as advisors and co-ordinators on all matters of common interest. Such exchange of liaison officers will prevail through all echelons as soon as assignments are issued down through the commands.

3. Duties

Duties of the liaison officer will be :—

(1) To represent his unit commander at the Headquarters to which he is assigned.

(2) To act as advisor to the commanding officer to whom he is assigned on matters pertaining to his own command.

(3) To co-ordinate all matters involving dual responsibility such as—
　　(*a*) Joint staff meetings.
　　(*b*) Joint briefings.
　　(*c*) Availability of equipment.
　　(*d*) Provision and implementation of plans, marshalling, and parking and loading diagrams.
　　(*e*) Examination of all parallel orders to insure complete agreement of plans and arrangements.
　　(*f*) Procurement of equipment and facilities belonging to his own command which are required by the command to which he is assigned.
　　(*g*) In the case of lower echelons, to act as airfield co-ordinator in conjunction with his opposite number.
　　(*h*) Preparation of joint reports.

SECTION II

STAFF PROCEDURE

4. Planning

(*a*) The sequence of planning and detail of matters requiring decision are set out in the SCHEDULE OF PLANNING attached at Annexure I.

This Schedule will be adhered to throughout all stages of planning.

(*b*) At the earliest possible date after receipt of directives or orders to participate in joint training or combat missions, the commanding officers involved will meet in a joint planning conference, accompanied by such staff officers, unit commanders and liaison officers as are necessary, and will arrive at complete agreement on all matter pertaining to the mission and its accomplishment.

5. Air Movement Table

The issuance of the completed Air Movement Table with the associated assignments of transporting and transported units to airfields must be accomplished at this stage in order that detailed planning and arrangements of lower echelons may be completed at the earliest possible date.

6. Planning and Conference Centre

A combined planning and conference centre will be established with the necessary communications to units concerned.

7. Forms

(*a*) Common forms for air movement tables, loading tables, and load manifests will be employed. Additional forms for internal and domestic procedures may be used at the discretion of the Formation Unit commanders concerned.

(*b*) Standard Forms to be employed are listed below :—
　　(1) Form A　　..　Air Movement Table.
　　(2) Form B　　..　(Parachutes)—Load Manifest for Parachute Units.
　　(3) Form B　　..　(Glider)—Load Manifest for Glider Units.

(*c*) An inspection form listing the points to be checked will be posted in each airplane.

SECTION III

OPERATING PROCEDURE

8. Airfield Organization

(*a*) An airfield command post, plainly marked, will be established at each airfield for the use of the commanders involved. It will normally be in close proximity to the flying control building. Both liaison officers and two air force despatch riders will be located at this command post.

(*b*) The command post will be connected by telephone with the troop billeting areas, the loading areas, the traffic control officer, and the airfield Private Branch Exchange.

(*c*) The command post will be provided from air force sources with a radio equipped vehicle, tuned on flying control channels, for the use of the troop carrier commander or his liaison officer.

9. Loading of Aircraft

(*a*) The troop carrier unit commander will provide the airborne unit commander, through the liaison officer, with a parking diagram of all aircraft, including gliders, which will show by number the location of aircraft and the sequence of take-off.

(*b*) All aircraft, including gliders, will be numbered on both sides of the fuselage.

(*c*) Guides will be provided from airborne units and will be posted at a convenient place, on or near each airfield, under the control of the airborne liaison officer, to direct each truck-load of airborne troops to its respective aircraft. Each truck will be numbered to correspond with the aircraft for which it is intended.

(*d*) A reserve of planes and gliders will be maintained at each airfield. Priority allotment will be made by the airborne liaison officer. The time of take-off of allotted reserve aircraft is dependent on the situation at the moment and is the responsibility of the troop carrier unit commander.

10. Tug Glider Marshalling

(*a*) Airfields from which gliders will be launched will be predesignated and will be equipped with additional working and marshalling areas.

(*b*) Marshalling and take-off procedures will be standardized for all airfields in order to provide for complete interchangeability of equipment and crews.

11. Despatching Arrangements

(*a*) Each airfield will adopt the standard dispatching system outlined in the following paragraphs :—

(*b*) *Para-dropping operations*

    (1) The Control Officer will be positioned to the port side and forward of the aircraft so as to be plainly visible to the pilot. The Control Officer will give executive signals to the pilot to taxi and take-off. Light or flag signals will be given by day and light signals by night

        (white—taxi, green—take-off, red—stop).

415

(2) An Assistant Control Officer will be stationed along the runway at a position estimated to be that at which the aircraft will become airborne. The Assistant Control Officer will signal to the Control Officer by white light as each aircraft becomes airborne.

(c) *Glider operations*

(1) The Control Officer and Assistant Control Officer will be stationed as for para-dropping operations and will use the same signals.

(2) The Assistant Control Officer will have telephone communication with the Control Officer and the Control Officer with the airfield command post.

(3) A towmaster will be stationed at the position of glider " hook-up." He will signal to the Control Officer by pre-arranged flag signal or white light as each glider is prepared for take off. As soon as the runway is clear the Control Officer will give the white signal to taxi forward. The towmaster will give a green signal to the Control Officer when the rope slack has been taken up. When the Control Officer has received this green signal from the towmaster and the signal from the Assistant Control Officer that the preceding combination has become airborne, he will give the green signal to the pilot to take-off. Thereafter the Control Officer stands clear and moves to the next combination, takes up position, and repeats the process.

(d) All Control Officers will be operationally qualified officers. They will be furnished with the necessary enlisted or other rank assistants.

12. Pathfinding and Navigation

Navigation and pathfinding activities will be in accordance with Annexure II to this memorandum.

13. Formation

(a) Standard formations are prescribed in order to expedite training and to simplify procedures. However, it is recognized that special situations may demand a variation from the standard. Such variations will be mutually agreed to by airborne and troop carrier commanders concerned and approved by the next higher headquarters.

(b) *Parachute dropping formation*

(1) BRITISH aircraft, by day, will fly in a column of 3 ship Vs. BRITISH aircraft, by night, will fly by single ships on concentrated accurate timing.

(2) AMERICAN aircraft will fly 3 ship Vs. in V, day and night.

(c) Jump altitudes will be not less than 400 feet by day and 500 feet by night above the highest terrain in the drop zone. During the drop, the C–47 aircraft will fly in the " tail-up " position.

(d) *Glider tug formation*

(1) BRITISH combinations, by day, will fly in 3 " streams " aircraft line astern. BRITISH combinations, by night, will fly in single units on concentrated accurate timing.

(2) AMERICAN combinations will fly in a column of two to four units echeloned to the right or left, both day and night.

14. Troop Procedure aboard aircraft, including Signals

(a) *C.47 type troop carrier*

(1) Twenty (20) minutes from the D.Z. (dropping zone), pilot will alert the jump-master/(U.S.)/stick-commander (BR), who will make an initial check of men and equipment.

(2) Four (4) minutes from the D.Z., pilot will turn on RED light.

(3) When over the D.Z. with the aircraft in the proper attitude the pilot will turn on the GREEN light as the " go " signal. The flashing on of the GREEN light is a command to " go " at that instant.

(4) The jump will be made on the green light unless some condition in the aircraft precludes a safe exit.

(5) Prior to take-off, the jump-master (U.S.)/stick-commander (BR) will instruct the crewchief (U.S.)/bomb-aimer or navigator (BR) in the correct procedure for the release of the parapacks. When the red light is flashed on, the crewchief (U.S.)/bomb-aimer or navigator (BR) will take his position forward of the door, wearing his interphone helmet, so as to provide alternative means of communication in the event of failure of the green light.

(b) *BRITISH bomber type troop carrier.*—For troops jumping from BRITISH bomber type aircraft there will be a 20 minute warning as in 14 (a) (1) above. A final warning will be given when there are five minutes to go. The red light will be turned on fifteen (15) seconds before reaching the D.Z. Troops will jump upon the green light being turned on.

15. Procedure for Signalling to Glider

(a) Ten (10) minutes warning of cast-off will be given to the glider pilot by the tug pilot.

(b) Command to cast off will be given by the tug pilot when at appropriate position on the approach leg.

(c) Warning and order to cast off will be given over the intercom system and confirmed by Aldis lamp. In the absence of intercom facilities, complete reliance will be placed in the Aldis lamp.

(d) If, in the opinion of the tug pilot, the glider pilot has not released when he should have done so, the tug pilot will release the glider so that it will land in the landing area.

SECTION IV

JOINT RESPONSIBILITIES OF AIRBORNE AND TROOP CARRIER COMMANDERS

16. General

Unit commanders will be jointly responsible for reaching complete agreement and understanding on all points contained in the Planning Schedule (Annexure I) and will issue the necessary orders in such detail as to enable commanders of lower units to proceed to training and arrangements with the fullest understanding of the problems involved.

17. Requirements

Commanding officers of units on battalion and group level will require that :—

(a) Pilots and troop commanders understand and prepare the appropriate parts of all forms.

(b) Each pilot signs his copy of Form B and has it available upon the arrival of the airborne troops. Each troop commander will have his copy of the form completed upon arrival at the aircraft and will compare with the pilot for correctness of assignment.

(c) Pilot and jump-master (U.S.)/stick-commander (BR) carry out the prescribed inspection of aircraft and equipment and complete Form B by signing in the proper place certifying that the inspection has been made.

(d) Upon completion of the Form B, two copies are left with the Airborne Liaison Officer, one for air records, and one for ground records. Additional copies will be furnished as required by higher headquarters in each situation. One copy will be retained by the troop commander in order that he may make a check of his personnel after landing on the D.Z. or L.Z.

SECTION V

RESPONSIBILITIES OF THE TROOP CARRIER COMMANDER

18. Troop Carrier Commanders

A troop carrier commander will be responsible for the execution of all items contained in the check list of the planning Schedule (Annexure I attached), in so far as they apply to his level. He will reach a complete agreement with his opposite airborne commander on all matters.

19. Group and Squadron Commanders

Commanding officers of groups and squadrons will be responsible for :—

(a) Taping of doorway and projections.

(b) Proper functioning of lights, accessories, bundle or bomb racks, radio, Rebecca/Eureka intercom, visual signals, etc.

(c) Providing all airforce accessories and special equipment required by an airborne unit for a particular operation, e.g., Rebecca/Eureka equipment.

(d) Providing emergency equipment including air/sea rescue equipment.

(e) Conducting air/sea rescue drills and ditching procedure.

(f) Completion of all forms applicable to their units.

20. Prior to Emplaning

(*a*) The first pilot will accompany the jumpmaster (U.S.)/stick-commander (BR) in the inspection of the aircraft as outlined on the aircraft inspection card posted in the aircraft. He will also be present during the loading of the containers.

(*b*) The crew chief (U.S.)/bomb-aimer or navigator (BR) will check the correct functioning of the container release mechanism and will be present when the containers are loaded by the parachute troops, to ensure correct loading. He will receive detailed instructions from the jumpmaster (U.S.)/stick-commander (BR) regarding the time of release of the containers.

(*c*) The pilot will make final mechanical check of the aircraft thirty (30) minutes prior to time of emplaning.

(*d*) The pilot will immediately advise his commanding officer and the airborne liaison officer if his aircraft will not be able to take off on schedule, and will assist in the transfer of the load to the spare aircraft assigned.

21. During the Drop

(*a*) The pilot will maintain the prescribed altitude, attitude and speed prescribed for each type of aircraft.

(*b*) The pilot in C-47 aircraft/bomb-aimer in BRITISH bomber type aircraft will give the warning and jump signals.

(*c*) The crew chief (U.S.)/bomb-aimer or navigator (BR) will comply with instructions concerning the release of containers and will determine that containers have been released. He will notify the pilot when all men have jumped and when the containers have been dropped. The pilot will then release the automatic salvo switch.

(*d*) The crew chief (U.S.)/bomb-aimer or navigator (BR) assisted by the radio operator or other designated crew member will pull in static lines and will turn them and any equipment left in the aircraft over to the parachute unit upon landing.

22. Gliders

The loading, inspection and handling of gliders will be accomplished as outlined for the airplane in so far as it applies.

SECTION VI

RESPONSIBILITIES OF THE AIRBORNE COMMANDER

23. Airborne Commanders

The airborne commander will be responsible for the execution of all items contained in the check list of the Planning Schedule (Annexure I attached) in so far as they apply to his level. He will reach complete agreement with his opposite troop carrier commander on all matters.

24. Parachute Battalion Commanders

Commanding officers of parachute battalions will be responsible for :—

(a) Packing of equipment containers, and loading to prevent incorrect distribution of weight and improper balance of the aircraft.

(b) Loading of the aircraft and container racks in the presence of the pilot and crew chief (U.S.)/bomb-aimer or navigator (BR).

(c) Completion of airborne portion of Form B—(Parachute).

(d) Procuring and fitting of parachutes for both troops and containers.

(e) Briefing of parachute troops.

(f) Movement of troops to take-off airfields.

25. Glider Unit Commanders

Commanding officers of Glider units will be responsible for :—

(a) Preparation of loads for gliders in accordance with approved published practices.

(b) Loading of gliders in the presence of the glider crew.

(c) Completion of the Form B—(Glider).

(d) Briefing of glider troops.

(e) Movement of troops to take-off airfields.

By command of General Eisenhower.

A.1

```
┌─────────────────────────────────┐
│       INITIAL PLANNING          │
│          CONFERENCE             │
│   by F.A.A.A. with Airborne and │
│   Air Commanders involved.      │
│                                 │
│ (a)  General plan of whole operation
│                                 │
│ (b)  Mission of the airborne units
│      to include general destination
│      date and approximate hour of
│      landing.                   │
│                                 │
│ (c)  Command and composition of │
│      airborne units.            │
│                                 │
│ (d)  Command of and composition │
│      and equipment of Air Force │
│      units to provide lift.     │
│                                 │
│ (e)  Operational control.       │
│                                 │
│ (f)  Outline plan for supply and│
│      resupply.                  │
│                                 │
│ (g)  Air support plan for convoy│
│      and for ground operations. │
│                                 │
│ (h)  Airfields available for operation
│      and route limitations.     │
│                                 │
│ (i)  Plan for co-ordination with│
│      other forces.              │
│                                 │
│ (j)  Cover plan.                │
│                                 │
│ (k)  Security plan.             │
│                                 │
│ (l)  Planning and responsibility for
│      rehearsal.                 │
│                                 │
│ (m)  Intelligence and sources of│
│      intelligence including photo-
│      graphs, maps, models and   │
│      priorities for obtaining them.
│                                 │
│ (n)  Signals and communications │
│      arrangements.              │
│                                 │
│ (o)  Special equipment and admin-
│      istration arrangements including
│      air/sea rescue equipment.  │
│                                 │
│ (p)  Navigational aids.         │
│                                 │
│ (q)  Arrangements for altering or
│      cancelling operation.      │
└─────────────────────────────────┘
```

```
┌──────────────┐
│  DIRECTIVE   │
│    FROM      │
│  S.H.A.E.F.  │
└──────────────┘

┌──────────────┐      ┌──────────────┐
│ CONFERENCE   │      │ ISSUANCE AND │
│ F.A.A.A. WITH│      │ DISTRIBUTION │
│ APPROPRIATE  │─────▶│ OF A PLANNING│
│ ARMY GROUP   │      │ STUDY BY     │
│    ON        │      │ F.A.A.A.     │
│  OUTLINE     │      └──────────────┘
│   PLAN       │
└──────────────┘
```

```
┌─────────────────────────┐
│      INITIAL            │
│      AIRBORNE           │
│                         │
│ (a)  Mission an         │
│      Unit upon          │
│                         │
│ (b)  Strength  a        │
│      Unit.              │
│                         │
│ (c)  Equipment          │
│      taken with         │
│      tions.            │
│                         │
│ (d)  Composition        │
│      all subordir       │
│      commitmen          │
│                         │
│ (e)  Lift require       │
│      ate Units.         │
│                         │
│ (f)  Training an        │
│      ments.            │
│                         │
│ (g)  Supply and         │
│      ments.            │
│                         │
│ (h)  Amphibiou          │
│                         │
│ (j)  Intelligence       │
│      reconnaissai       │
│                         │
│ (k)  Movements          │
│      quirements.        │
└─────────────────────────┘
```

```
┌─────────────────────────┐
│    INITIAL ST           │
│    CARRIER              │
│                         │
│ (a)  Availability       │
│      craft, equip       │
│                         │
│ (b)  Condition          │
│      available air      │
│                         │
│ (c)  Intelligence       │
│      further  in        │
│      ments, rec         │
│                         │
│ (d)  Meteorolog         │
│      information        │
│                         │
│ (e)  Restrictions       │
│      for co-ordi        │
│      Services.          │
│                         │
│ (f)  Tentative fl       │
│                         │
│ (g)  Air support        │
│      ments.            │
│                         │
│ (h)  Arrangemer         │
│      fields to in       │
│      and service        │
│                         │
│ (j)  Provision          │
│      craft to ir        │
│      marking lan        │
│      grounds.           │
└─────────────────────────┘
```

IX F

OR AIRBORNE OPERATION

S.H.A.E.F. Op Memo No. 12
dated 13th March 1944
(issued 4th November 1944)

B.1

STUDIES —
COMMANDER

d plan of action of
anding.

nd composition of

and weapons to be
in weight limita-

n and equipment of
ate Units and their
t priority.

ments of subordin-

d rehearsal require-

l resupply require-

lift requirements.

requirements,
ice.

and bivouac re-

B.2

JDIES — TROOP
COMMANDER

and status of air-
ment and crews.

and equipment of
fields.

information and
telligence require-
nnaissance.

ical   astronomical

imposed by plans
nating with other

ight plans.

plan and require-

ts at departure air-
lude traffic control
facilities.

of pathfinder air-
clude system for
ding and dropping

C.1

CONFERENCE BETWEEN THE AIRBORNE AND TROOP CARRIER COMMANDER

(a) Number and types of available aircraft.

(b) Load capacity of each type of aircraft.

(c) Definite selection of L.Zs and D.Zs.

(d) Pathfinder methods and requirements.

(e) Size and shape of aerial formations.

(f) Order of arrival at D.Zs and L.Zs.

(g) Air Movement Tables.

(h) Allotment of aircraft and airfields to each Airborne Unit.

(j) Communications arrangements in departure areas.

(k) Supply and resupply plans.

(l) Plans for movements to and billeting at airfields.

(m) Plans for loading to include parking diagrams, timing, and motor transport traffic control.

(n) Disposition of glider pilots, parachutes and containers after landing in combat zone.

(o) Training and rehearsals.

(p) Briefing arrangements.

(q) Reconnaissance arrangements.

(r) Signals arrangements.

(s) Security arrangements.

D.1

PLANS AND ORDERS OF AIRBORNE COMMANDER

(a) Training programme.

(b) Rehearsal plans.

(c) Initiation of steps necessary to obtain special equipment required.

(d) Movement to departure bases and occupation of base bivouacs.

(e) Loading plans.

(f) Air Movement Table.

(g) Field orders for operation to be conducted immediately upon landing.

(h) Supply and resupply plan.

(j) Final briefing, issue counter sign, exact destination made known to all ranks.

D.2

PLANS AND ORDERS OF TROOP CARRIER COMMANDER

(a) Training programme.

(b) Rehearsal programme.

(c) Procurement of rehearsal facilities.

(d) Procurement of additional service facilities.

(e) Loading plans.

(f) Movement Table.

(g) Intelligence.

(h) Flight plan.

(j) Preliminary briefing of key personnel.

(k) Traffic control, air and ground.

(l) Plan for servicing and replacement.

(m) Field Orders.

(n) Security arrangements.

(o) Final briefing.

(p) Forced landing and air/sea rescue procedure.

(q) Escape procedure.

APPENDIX F

ANNEXURE II

NAVIGATION AND EMPLOYMENT OF PATHFINDER UNITS

1. Organization

(a) *Ground*

(1) Each Airborne Division will constitute, train and maintain :—
    BRITISH   ..   Eighteen (18) Parachute Pathfinder teams.
    U.S.   ..   One (1) Parachute Pathfinder team per battalion.

(2) Teams will consist of one (1) or two (2) officers and nine (9) to fourteen (14) men, and will be reinforced by such protective personnel as the division commander may deem necessary under the circumstances. The teams will be equipped with radar and other navigational ground aids as may be specified from time to time for a particular operation.

(b) *Air*

(1) 38 Group R.A.F. will have all crews trained for Pathfinder Operations and approximately 75 per cent. of its aircraft equipped with the necessary navigational aids.

(2) IX Troop Carrier Command will constitute, train and maintain a Pathfinder Force on the basis of 6 crews per Group and 3 aircraft per Group.

2. Procedure

(a) Two (2) or three (3) aircraft with two (2) or three (3) identical pathfinder teams for each D.Z. or L.Z. will precede the first Serial of the main effort, the exact time interval being established by both airborne and air commanders. The leading group of the 1st serial of the main effort into each D.Z. or L.Z. will be prepared to drop as scheduled even though the Pathfinder teams may have been neutralized, and will, in addition, be prepared to re-establish Pathfinder aids for subsequent groups.

(b) *Marking of Drop Zones*

(1) *By Day.*—The standard day marking for each D.Z. will consist of a panel " T ", a code letter, and smoke signals. Both the " T " and the code letter (which letter is to identify the D.Z. and distinguish it from others in the same area) will be constructed from panels or ground strips, each panel measuring three (3) feet by about fifteen (15) feet. The colour and size of the " T " and of the letter will be dependent upon the size of the cleared area, vegetation, and any trees obstructing vision, and will be agreed upon by the airborne and air commanders. White smoke will be employed to indicate the position of the " T ". The " T " will be positioned with due regard to wind speed and direction, shape and size of D.Z., the formation being flown, so as readily to be observed from aircraft running in from Target R.V. to D.Z. The identifying letter will be placed in any suitable position in close proximity to the " T ". The Eureka will be placed within a radius of 100 yards from the head of the " T ". Smoke signals will be placed near the base of the stem of the " T ", with due regard to the wind so that smoke will not obscure

the " T " or the identifying letter. The axis of the " T " will be parallel to the line of flight, with approach up the stem. The jump signal will be given when the leader of the formation is over or level with the head of the " T ". Six panel strips will be used, three (3) across the top of the " T ", and three (3) forming the stem. Panels will be spaced one panel length apart (*see* A below).

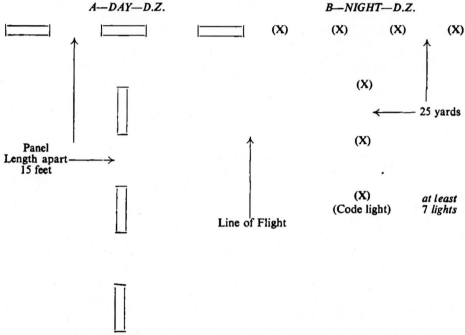

A—DAY—D.Z.   *B—NIGHT—D.Z.*

Line of Flight

(2) *By Night.*—The standard night marking for each D.Z. will consist of lights forming a " T ", with at least four (4) Holophane lights across the top and at least three (3) Holophane lights forming the stem, all lights being twenty-five (25) yards apart. Lights to be red, green or amber, and with 180° screening. The number and colour of the lights in the " T " at each D.Z. to be agreed between the airborne and air commanders, to meet conditions encountered. The tail light of the " T " will be the code light. The Eureka will be placed within a radius of 100 yards from the head of the " T ". (*See* B above.)

(c) *Marking of Landing Zones*

(1) *By Day.*—The day marking of glider L.Zs. will be by panel " Ts ", panel code letters and coloured smoke. Panels will measure twelve (12) to fifteen (15) feet by three (3) feet. The " T " for L.Zs. will be laid with the stem parallel to the line of glider landing, and so as to be readily observed from aircraft running in from Target R.V. to L.Z. The direction of landing so indicated will be not more than 90° out of wind, the amount depending on wind strength and on configuration and shape of L.Z., the best compromise being adopted. White smoke will be placed in the same manner as for a D.Z. The Eureka will be placed in such a position relative to the direction of run in of aircraft from Target R.V. to L.Z. that gliders can be brought

in to a point where they can execute a 90° (or not more than 180°) turn, preferably left hand, to land into the wind. Code letters marking L.Zs. will be prepared from panels similar to those used for marking "Ts". (*See* below.)

DAY—L.Z.

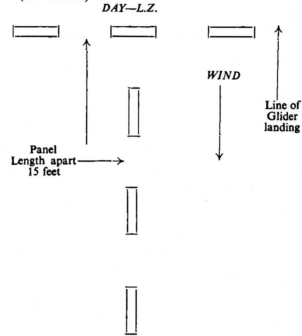

Panel
Length apart——→
15 feet

WIND

Line of
Glider
landing

(2) *By Night.*—(The following marking system for glider L.Zs. by night presupposes sufficient light for glider pilots to distinguish individual fields for landing as briefed.) Night marking of glider L.Zs. will be a "T" formed of Holophane lights, two (2) across the top fifty (50) yards apart and at least five (5) lights forming the stem, twenty-five (25) yards apart. The tail light of the stem to be the code light. Lights to be red, green or amber and with 180° screening. The position of the "T" and of the Eureka will be the same as in the marking of L.Zs by day (*see* below).

NIGHT—L.Z.

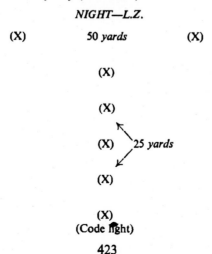

(X)   50 *yards*   (X)

(X)

(X)

(X)   25 *yards*

(X)

(X)
(Code light)

423

(*d*) *Marking of subsequent Group.*—It will be the responsibility of the Airborne Unit Commander to make provision for maintaining and securing Pathfinder teams and their equipment in operation until all serials have arrived.

3. Methods of Navigation

(*a*) Initial Pathfinder aircraft will employ accurate dead reckoning (D.R.) and map reading, closely checked by Radar aids and the use of special D.Z. maps, for the location of Drop Zones and Landing Zones.

(*b*) Main serials will be led to the Drop Zones and Landing Zones by accurate D.R. and Radar aids, and utilize REBECCA/EUREKA for the exact location of the areas.

4. Airborne Resupply Dropping Zones

Resupply D.Zs. will normally be marked in the same way as paratroop D.Zs. Where correct equipment is not available, the same configuration will be used with improvised equipment.

8th June, 1944.

APPENDIX G

THE FUNCTIONS OF THE AIRBORNE FORCES DEPOT AND DEVELOPMENT CENTRE

12th June, 1943

1. The Airborne Forces Depot and Development Centre is under the control of Major-General Airborne Forces.

2. *The purposes of the Depot are :—*
   (a) To train personnel on joining airborne forces.
   (b) To train and accommodate reinforcements of units of airborne forces.
   (c) To carry out rehabilitation courses for casualties and certain other personnel.
   (d) To provide a liaison centre for the various units of airborne formations.
   (e) To carry out training in battle drill and other courses for parachutists and airlanding troops.
   (f) To co-ordinate and standardize training in airborne forces.

3. *The purposes of the Development Centre are :—*
   (a) *Policy.*
       (i) To advise upon airborne forces tactical and technical doctrine. Final decisions and dissemination of tactical doctrine will remain a War Office responsibility.
       (ii) To study the military problems of air transport and supply.

   (b) *Liaison.*
       (i) To maintain liaison with all airborne formations in United Kingdom and overseas.
       (ii) To co-operate with Airborne Forces Experimental Establishments and give such assistance as required in such matters as the preparation of aircraft drills.

   (c) *Research and Experiment.*
       (i) To conduct experiments designed to develop the technique of Airborne Forces in all its aspects.
       (ii) Subject to prior concurrence of the War Office, to construct mock-ups of new or modified items of equipment which may be found to be a requirement of Airborne Forces.
       (iii) To examine medical problems of airborne forces in all their aspects and to maintain liaison with the Sub-Committee (on Airborne Troops) of the Military Personnel Research Committee of the Medical Research Council.
       (iv) To examine the needs of airborne forces in relation to provision of special or modified weapons, vehicles, equipment, ammunition, clothing and stores of all types.

(v) To investigate and collate data regarding the use (both technical and tactical) of equipment peculiar to airborne forces.

(vi) To prepare and circulate technical data such as vehicle loadings, container loads and tactical loadings of gliders.

(vii) To prepare and circulate all type of staff tables for all airborne units.

(viii) To collate and disseminate technical doctrine other than that lying within the province of the Air Ministry and the Ministry of Aircraft Production.

(ix) To examine and formulate necessary changes in War Establishments and equipment tables of Airborne Units.

(x) To act as the repository for all information of a technical nature regarding airborne forces and airborne supply.

HEADQUARTERS 1 AIRBORNE CORPS—JUNE, 1944,

G.O.C.

Liaison Officer
U.S. Army Air Force

P.A.

B.G.S.   Staff Secretary

D.A. and Q.M.G.

G.S.O. I (Ops.)   G.S.O. I (S.A.S.)   Umpire Grade "A"   C.S.O.   Commander Glider Pilots   A.Q.M.G.   A.A.G.   D.D.S.T.   D.D.M.S.   D.D.O.S.   D.D.M.E.   D.A.Ch.G.

G.S.O. I (Air)
1 Airborne Division

G.S.O. I (Air)
6 Airborne Division

ATTACHED FOR Airborne Control Sections
IX U.S. T.C.C.   38 Gp. R.A.F.

G.S.O. II (S.A.S.)   G.S.O. II   A/ C.S.O.   G.S.O. II   D.A.Q. M.G.   D.A. A.G.   D.A.D. S.T.   D.A.D. M.S.   D.A.D. O.S.   D.A.D. M.E.

G.S.O. III (S.A.S.)   I.O. 1A (S.A.S.)
I.O.(Photo) (S.A.S.)   S.O.R. Sigs.   G.S.O. III   S.C. "Q"   S.C. "A"   Psychiatrist   I.O.O.

G.S.O. II (Int.)

G.S.O. II (S.D.)

G.S.O. III
I.O. 1B
I.O.(Photo)

G.S.O. II (Ops.)

G.S.O. III (Ops.)

Camp Commandant

APPENDIX J

AIRBORNE CHANNELS OF COMMAND FOR THE INVASION OF NORTH-WEST EUROPE

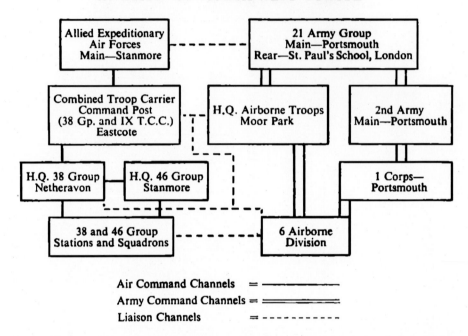

Air Command Channels   = ——————

Army Command Channels = ═══════

Liaison Channels   = - - - - - - - - - -

Note.—Liaison between 46 Group and 6 Airborne Division was through the General Staff Officer, 1st Grade (Air) at Headquarters, 38 Group, although in the later stages minor points of administration were settled direct.

APPENDIX K

PART 1

THE NORMANDY OPERATIONS
COMMANDER 6 AIRBORNE DIVISION'S PLANNING INSTRUCTIONS
FOR COMMANDER 3 PARACHUTE BRIGADE

1. Your primary task is to ensure that the battery 800 yards south of Merville is silenced by 30 minutes before dawn. No other commitment must jeopardize success in this enterprise.

If, as appears possible, the battery is being made into a positive fortress, your plan should include a *coup de main* assault by glider on the position itself.

2. While your attitude of mind must be that you cannot contemplate failure in the direct assault, you must be prepared to have to deal with the battery by naval gunfire. Therefore the first priority of all naval support allotted to 6 Airborne Division is the neutralization of this battery, if it is not captured by 30 minutes before dawn ; in the event of casualties to F.O.Bs. allotted primarily to this task, the alternative F.O.B. waves at my disposal will be earmarked for this task by me.

The detailed arrangements which have been made regarding—

(*a*) signals to be displayed on capture of the battery,

(*b*) wireless messages and codewords to be sent on capture of the battery,

(*c*) the time naval ships will open fire in the event of non receipt of these signals,

will be issued as soon as they have been confirmed.

(These detailed arrangements are given in Part I (*a*) of this Appendix.)

3. If neither of the above signals get through to the headquarters ship or the allotted cruiser, the cruiser will engage the battery with air observation in the absence of any definite calls for fire from F.O.Bs. (Forward Observers, Bombardment).

4. As soon as the battery is silenced you will secure the Le Plein feature which you will hold until relieved by 1 Special Service Brigade.

5. In addition to the task of silencing the Merville battery you will demolish the bridges at Troarn, Bures, Robehomme and Varaville by 0930 hours. You will leave detachments to cover these demolitions. 1 Special Service Brigade will relieve your detachment at Varaville.

6. On completion of these tasks the role of your brigade will be to hold the area Bois de Bavent–Troarn with the object of—

(*a*) denying this high ground to the enemy,

(*b*) interfering with any attempted enemy movement west from Troarn.

If circumstances permit you will send out patrols as far south as La Ramée.

In the event of your being unable to hold Troarn you will withdraw to the high ground to the north. You will not withdraw further north than the road junction " Triangle " without orders from me.

APPENDIX K

PART 1 (a)

Arrangements regarding passing of information concerning the Merville Battery position

1. The following arrangements have been made to ensure that information regarding the capture of the battery position is passed quickly to those who are required to know it.

2. *Code Words*

Battery captured	Hammer
Battery NOT captured and still in action	Hugh

3. *Wireless*

By any of the following means in order of priority :—

(*a*) On spotting wave to H.M.S. Arethusa by F.O.Bs.

(*b*) On B.C.W. (Bombardment Command Wave) to Headquarter Ship Forward Observer Force " S " by F.O.Bs.

(*c*) Divisional command net to divisional headquarters by Commander 3 Parachute Brigade.

(*d*) Divisional headquarters to headquarter ship on corps "A" net.

(*e*) Divisional headquarters to Headquarter Ship Forward Observer Force " S " on lateral to 3 British Division.

(*f*) Through S.O.B. (Senior Officer, Bombardment) at divisional headquarters to headquarter ship on B.C.W. or to H.M.S. Arethusa on spotting wave.

Note.—Method (*c*) will in any event be used in addition to other methods.

4. *Smoke Signal* (To be used if wireless fails)

Yellow smoke will be let off at the battery position at intervals of NOT less than 5 minutes from 30 minutes after dawn. Spotting aircraft will be over approximately 30 minutes after dawn and every effort must be made to ensure that the smoke is displayed when this aircraft is overhead.

5. In the event of all the above signals failing to reach H.M.S. Arethusa or H.M.S. Largs, wearing the flag of Forward Observer Force " S," the former will not engage the battery before 30 minutes after dawn, and then only if it is clear from air observation or other means that the battery is still active.

APPENDIX K

PART 2

FOR COMMANDER 5 PARACHUTE BRIGADE

Your task is—

(*a*) to seize and hold the crossings over the Canal and river Orne at Benouville and Ranville,

(*b*) secure the area Benouville–Ranville–Le Bas de Ranville against infantry or armoured assault.

The seizing of the crossings intact is of the utmost importance to the conduct of future operations. As the bridges will certainly have been prepared for demolition the speedy overpowering of the bridge defences should be your first object. The bridges must therefore be seized by a *coup de main* party landed in gliders as near actually on the bridges as is humanly possible. You must accept risks to achieve this object.

Surprise will, of course, be the essence of this operation. The *coup de main* gliders must therefore be the first troops to land in the divisional area. The operations to be undertaken by 3 Parachute Brigade demand the landing of dropping zone parties five hours before dawn. Thus your *coup de main* party must plan to land at this hour and not a moment after this hour.

Apart from the area between the two bridges all the ground within reasonable assault distance of the bridges is being obstructed by posts. The landing of gliders in these areas is thus impracticable until landing strips have been cleared.

The *coup de main* party will therefore be followed by parachute troops who will consolidate the bridge positions and at the same time clear landing strips for the glider element containing divisional headquarters and 4th Anti-Tank Battery.

You must land the parachute element of your force not later than half an hour after the arrival of the *coup de main* party.

In order to ensure that you are in a position to hold the area Benouville–Ranville–Le Bas de Ranville by first light, the landing strips must be prepared so as to allow 70 gliders to land at two hours before dawn.

It is imperative that you should hold this area. The framework of your defensive plan must rest on the anti-tank and medium machine gun layout. This layout must cover the open ground to the south and the open ground which forms the landing zone to the north. The more enclosed country nearer the banks of the river and the orchards to the east must be covered by infantry in depth and P.I.A.Ts. You will wire and mine the belt of orchards between Herouvillette and Le Mariquet to a depth of 100 yards. This minefield will be well signposted and covered by fire from infantry posts. No 6-pounder anti-tank guns will be dispersed in the Benouville area.

The whole of this area must be held. Infantry positions will be fought to the last round and anti-tank guns to the muzzle.

Defensive fire tasks will include the eastern approaches to your positions and the dead and enclosed ground on the river bank both to the south and north of your position.

It is anticipated that leading elements of 3 British Infantry Division will reach Benouville by 1230 hours. One battalion from 8 Infantry Brigade of 3 British Infantry Division will then relieve you on the bridge. That portion of your force which has been deployed on the actual crossings and on the Benouville bank will then come into brigade reserve in the Le Bas de Ranville area.

1 Special Service Brigade (less one commando) will pass through the bridge positions at approximately 1130 hours. You will be responsible for the smooth passage through of this formation.

6 Air-landing Brigade will land in the late afternoon or evening of " D " day on your landing zone and on a landing zone to the west of the canal. You will be responsible for clearing sufficient space for the glider landings on your landing zone by 2000 hours at the latest. 3 British Infantry Division is to be responsible for clearing the area west of the canal.

On arrival, 6 Air-landing Brigade will take up positions on the line Saint Honorine La Chardonnerette–Escoville. Commander 6 Air-landing Brigade will then be responsible for the holding of the area St. Honorine–Escoville–Le Bas de Ranville.

The battalion holding the Le Bas de Ranville sector and 4th Anti-Tank Battery will come under command 6 Air-landing Brigade.

Your brigade (less one battalion) will then come into divisional reserve in the area Herouvillette–Ranville. Your task will then be to cover the Herouvillette–Le Mariquet minefield and be prepared to counter attack:—

(*a*) St. Honorine La Chardonnerette.

(*b*) High feature 1,000 yards south of Le Bas de Ranville.

(*c*) Le Plein.

APPENDIX K

PART 3

FOR COMMANDER 1 SPECIAL SERVICE BRIGADE

1. On coming under my command your role will be to mop up and subsequently secure the coastal area Franceville Plage–Cabourg–Varaville–Le Plein.

2. It is essential that the Le Plein feature should be denied to the enemy. Your plans will therefore envisage the holding of Le Plein. You will not lock up your force in the static defence of this feature.

3. Working from the Merville–Varaville areas the remainder of your command will operate offensively in the coastal belt, so infesting this area as to make its retention by the Germans impossible or, if this is impracticable, hazardous and difficult. Should you not be able to dislodge, destroy, or capture all German positions in this area, your aim must be so to worry them that they will be incapable of interfering with the beach landings on the front of 3 British Infantry Division. You must be prepared to infest this area over a period of days. Your plan should therefore envisage a series of reliefs for the more actively engaged troops.

4. Such a role as has been allotted you cannot be fulfilled by any form of static defence ; this indeed is not required of you. As a corollary it is appreciated that German infiltration through your screen may well be possible. This risk I accept. You should, however, be able generally to give me information of such movement, and even though you may be unable to stop it, the information is all I require of you.

The bridge at Varaville will have been demolished by 3 Parachute Brigade. You will relieve the 3 Parachute Brigade detachment which will be covering this demolition.

5. Should your detachments be severely attacked from the east they will withdraw, fighting a rearguard action, on to Le Plein and Breville.

6. In the event of 3 Parachute Brigade failing to silence the Merville battery you will be required to undertake this task.

7. It will be my responsibility to instruct you on the suitability of crossing one commando down stream at a point about a mile below the Ranville bridge. This decision will of course depend on local enemy activity, the bridge over the river being intact, and the state of water in the canal.

APPENDIX K

PART 4

FOR COMMANDER 6 AIR-LANDING BRIGADE

Your task is to occupy and hold the area Longueval-St. Honorine-La Chardonnerette-Escoville-Le Bas de Ranville with the object of—

(a) denying all approaches to the crossings of the River Orne and the canal to the enemy, and

(b) providing a firm base from which 6 Airborne Division can operate offensively in the area between the Rivers Orne and Dives.

It is not possible to forecast with accuracy the tactical situation which will prevail on the arrival of your brigade. In order that you should be placed in the picture with a minimum of delay a senior officer will accompany divisional headquarters on the night " D " — 1/" D " day.

Broadly one of two situations will face you. Either the positions held by 5 Parachute Brigade will be closely engaged, or German reaction will have been slow and the 5 Parachute Brigade battle outposts at St. Honorine La Chardonnerette and Escoville will still be in position. In the former circumstances it will be my intention to fight with your brigade to secure the St. Honorine-La Chardonnerette-Escoville position early on " D " + 1 day. In the latter case I shall push your battalions out rapidly and as they arrive, to secure their defence positions. 4th Anti-Tank Battery will come under your command, as will the parachute battalion holding the Le Bas de Ranville position. This latter battalion will revert to 5 Parachute Brigade on the arrival of 12 Battalion Devons.

The framework of your defence plan must rest on the anti-tank and medium machine gun layout. This layout must cover the open southern flank and must further include alternative positions to cover the open ground north of Ranville.

You must wire and mine the area Longueval to the river, St. Honorine La Chardonnerette and Escoville. Mining will not be resorted to in the open country. The area Herouvillette-Le Mariquet will be strongly wired and mined by 5 Parachute Brigade.

APPENDIX K

PART 5

FOR COMMANDER, ARMOURED RECONNAISSANCE GROUP

It is my intention to constitute a force which will be known as the Armoured Reconnaissance Group. You will command this force.

The task of the Armoured Reconnaissance Group will be to form a small firm base outside the 6 Airborne Divisional area from which it will—

(a) carry out deep reconnaissance,

(b) impede and delay any enemy movement from the east and south-east on Caen.

The force will consist of :—

One company of infantry transported in jeeps.
Airborne Armoured Reconnaissance Regiment.
One battery 75-mm. pack howitzers.
Troop 6-pounder anti-tank guns.
Detachment R.E.
Detachment R.A.M.C.

The force must be prepared to operate without support from the division. It will not be withdrawn at night.

You will bear in mind that your task cannot be carried out if your force is liquidated. While you must be prepared to fight to achieve your object, you will avoid static battle in circumstances which in your opinion will result in the annihilation of your force.

The force will land by glider in the late afternoon of " D " day. In order that you should be in the picture when your force arrives, you will accompany me on the night of " D "—1/" D " day.

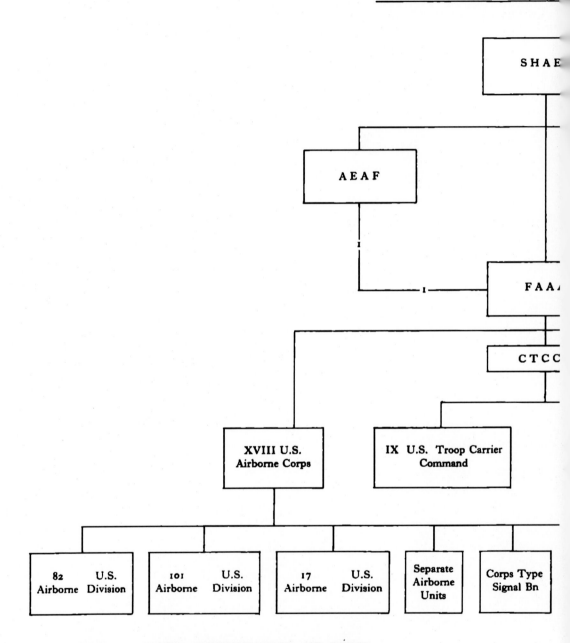

SHAE

AEAF

FAA

CTCC

| XVIII U.S. Airborne Corps | IX U.S. Troop Carrier Command |

| 82 U.S. Airborne Division | 101 U.S. Airborne Division | 17 U.S. Airborne Division | Separate Airborne Units | Corps Type Signal Bn |

A.E.A.F.   ALLIED EXPEDITIONARY AIR FORCE
A.N.C.X.F.   ALLIED NAVAL COMBAT EXPEDITIONARY FORCE
C.T.C.C.P.   COMBINED TROOP CARRIER COMMAND POST
F.A.A.A.   FIRST ALLIED AIRBORNE ARMY
S.F.H.Q.   SPECIAL FORCES HEADQUARTERS
S.H.A.E.F.   SUPREME HEADQUARTERS ALLIED EXPEDITIONARY FORCE

C.B.H. 17972 - Wt. 33701 - Dd. 8719 -400-7/51

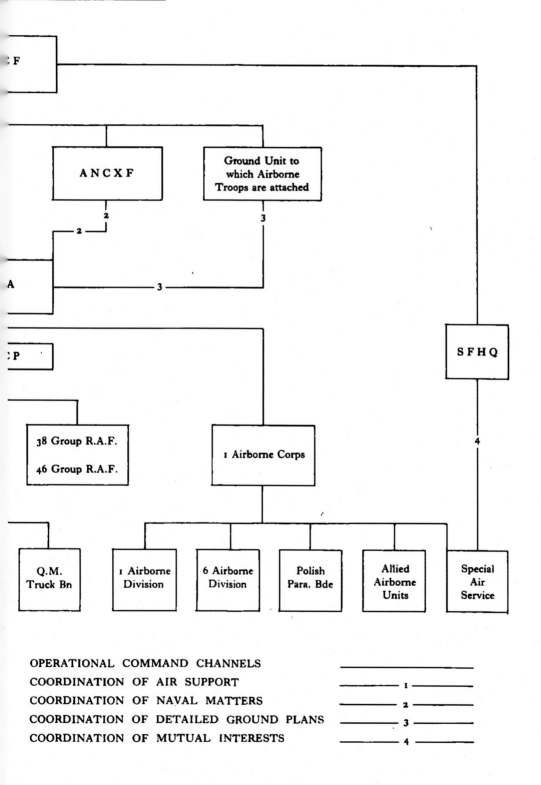

CF

ANCXF

Ground Unit to which Airborne Troops are attached

2

2 2

3

A

3

CP

SFHQ

38 Group R.A.F.

46 Group R.A.F.

1 Airborne Corps

4

| Q.M. Truck Bn | 1 Airborne Division | 6 Airborne Division | Polish Para. Bde | Allied Airborne Units | Special Air Service |

OPERATIONAL COMMAND CHANNELS
COORDINATION OF AIR SUPPORT —— 1 ——
COORDINATION OF NAVAL MATTERS —— 2 ——
COORDINATION OF DETAILED GROUND PLANS —— 3 ——
COORDINATION OF MUTUAL INTERESTS —— 4 ——

APPENDIX M

PART 1

THE S.A.S. BASE

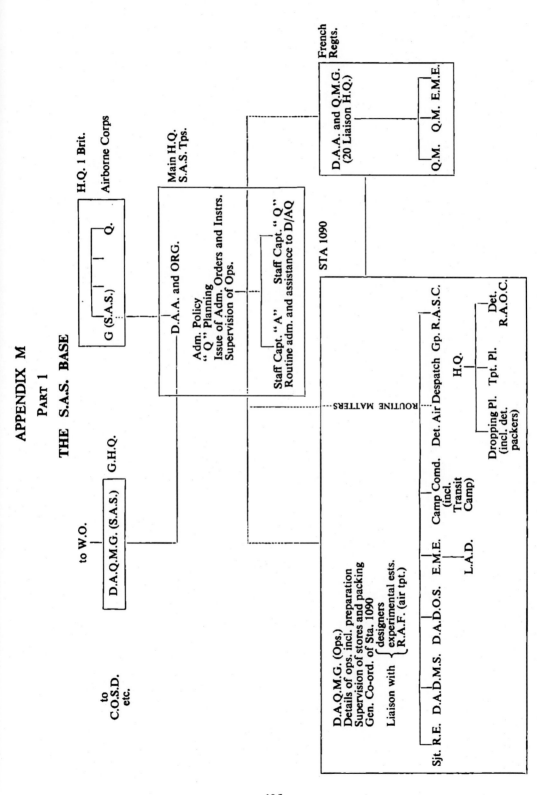

435

APPENDIX M

PART 2

ADMINISTRATIVE STAFF AT H.Q. S.A.S. TROOPS—MAY, 1945

1. *On War Establishment, H.Q. S.A.S. Tps.*   *Total*

D.A.A. and Q.M.G.	1	
D.A.Q.M.G. (Ops.)	1	
Staff Captain "A"	1	
Staff Captain " Q "	1	
" Q " Liaison Officer	1	
D.A.D.M.S. and 4 O.R.s	5	
D.A.D.O.S. plus B.O.W.O. and 8 O.R.s ..	10	
E.M.E. plus L.A.D. and 5 O.R.s	18	
Camp Comd.	1	
Total H.Q. S.A.S. Tps. (exclusive 20 Liaison)	39	
	—	39

2. *20 Liaison*

D.A.A. and Q.M.G.	1	
2 Q.M.s	2	
E.M.E. and 8 O.R s	9	
	12	
	—	51

3. *Det. Air Despatch Group R.A.S.C.*

H.Q., 1 Offr. and 8 O.R.s ..	9	
Tpt. Pl., 1 Offr. and 62 O.R.s ..	63	
Dropping Pl., 1 Offr. and 69 O.R.s	70	
Det. R.A.O.C., 15 O.R.s ..	15	
	157	
	—	208

4. *Det. Pioneer Corps*

1 Offr. and 23 O.R.s	24	
	—	
Total Adm. Personnel		232

APPENDIX N

HIGHER PLANNING TIME-TABLE FOR THE RHINE CROSSING OPERATIONS

4th February. Field Marshal Montgomery met the Commanders of Second British, First Canadian and Ninth U.S. Armies and Second Tactical Air Force at Tactical Headquarters 21 Army Group, Zonhoven, and said that Second Army would carry out the main crossing.

7th February. Headquarters 12 Corps and 79 Armoured Division commenced planning the technique of the assault.

14th February. Commander Second Army met Commander XVIII U.S. Airborne Corps and told him in outline how his corps was to be used.

20th February. Commander Second Army met Commander First Allied Airborne Army and XVIII U.S. Airborne Corps at Epernay. He discussed the whole operation with them and told them in greater detail what he wanted them to do.

21st February. Commander Second Army gave Commander 12 Corps his task.

22nd February. Commander Second Army gave Commander 83 Group, R.A.F., the Army plan.

23rd February. Commander Second Army met the Commander of First Allied Airborne Army, 12 Corps and XVIII U.S. Airborne Corps at Main Headquarters, Second Army, Neerfelt. He gave them the final plan and they discussed details which affected the co-operation of the two Corps.

27th February. Conference at Main Headquarters Second Army at which Commander Second Army gave the full plan to the Commanders of First Allied Airborne Army, 8 Corps, 12 Corps, XVIII U.S. Airborne Corps, 83 Group R.A.F. and their staffs.

ORDERS OF BATTLE

A.	1 Parachute Brigade	North Africa	November, 1942
B.	1 Airborne Division	Sicily	July, 1943
C.	2 Parachute Brigade	Italy	June, 1944
D.	1 Airborne Corps		June, 1944
E.	6 Airborne Division	Normandy	June, 1944
F.	S.A.S. Brigade		1944
G.	1 Airborne Division	Arnhem	September, 1944
H.	6 Airborne Division	Rhine	March, 1945
I.	50 Indian Parachute Brigade		October, 1943
J.	44 Indian Airborne Division		July, 1945
K.	2 Indian Airborne Division		January, 1947
L.	6 Independent Parachute Brigade Group		January, 1947
M.	Australian Airborne Forces		August, 1942
N.	Canadian Officers at No. 1 Parachute Training School		

Shown down to Lieutenant Colonels Commands, and independent units.

A. 1 Parachute Brigade Group. North Africa. November, 1942

Comd.	Brig. E. W. C. Flavell.
1 Para. Bn.	Lt. Col. S. J. L. Hill.
2 Para. Bn.	Lt. Col. J. D. Frost.
3 Para. Bn.	Lt. Col. R. G. Pine-Coffin.
1 Para. Sqn. R.E.	Maj. S. L. Dorman.
16 Para. Fd. Amb.	Capt. C. G. Robb.

B. 1 Airborne Division. Sicily. July, 1943

G.O.C.	Maj. Gen. G. F. Hopkinson.
G.S.O.I. (Ops.)	Lt. Col. R. F. K. Goldsmith.
G.S.O.I. (Air)	Lt. Col. W. T. Campbell.
A.A. and Q.M.G.	Col. J. A. Goschen.
A.D.M.S.	Col. A. A. Eagger.
A.D.O.S.	Lt. Col. G. M. Loring.

1 Para. Bde.

Comd.	Brig. G. W. Lathbury.
1 Para. Bn.	Lt. Col. A. S. Pearson.
2 Para. Bn.	Lt. Col. J. D. Frost.
3 Para. Bn.	Lt. Col. E. C. Yeldham.

2 Para. Bde.

Comd.	Brig. E. E. Down.
Deputy Comd.	Col. C. H. V. Pritchard.
4 Para. Bn.	Lt. Col. J. A. Dene.
5 Para. Bn.	Lt. Col. C. B. Mackenzie.
6 Para. Bn.	Lt. Col. J. Goodwin.

4 Para. Bde.

Comd.	Brig. J. W. Hackett.
10 Para. Bn.	Lt. Col. K. B. I. Smyth.
11 Para. Bn.	Lt. Col. R. M. C. Thomas.
156 Para. Bn.	Lt. Col. Sir W. R. de B. des Voeux.

21 Indep. Para. Coy.

	Maj. J. Lander.

1 Air-landing Bde.

Comd.	Brig. P. H. W. Hicks.
Deputy	Col. O. L. Jones.
1 Borders	Lt. Col. R. G. Britten.
2 S. Staffs.	Lt. Col. W. D. H. McCardie.

Recce.

1 Air-landing Recce. Sqn. ..	Maj. C. F. H. Gough.

R.A.

C.R.A.	Lt. Col. C. H. F. Crawford.
1 Air-landing Lt. Regt. R.A. ..	Lt. Col. R. W. McLeod.
1 Air-landing A. Tk. Bty. R.A. ..	Maj. W. F. Arnold.
2 Air-landing A. Tk. Bty. R.A. ..	Maj. H. Wilson.
1 Air-landing L.A.A. Bty. R.A. ..	Maj. The Lord Hardwick.

R.E.

C.R.E.	Lt. Col. M. C. A. Henniker.
1 Para. Sqn. R.E. ..	Maj. D. C. Murray
2 Para. Sqn R.E. ..	Maj. C. D. H. Vernon.
4 Para. Sqn. R.E. ..	Maj. A. J. Hardiman.
9 Fd. Coy. R.E. ..	Maj. B. Beasley.
261 Fd. Pk. Coy. R.E. ..	Maj. J. N. Chivers

C.R. Signals	Lt. Col. R. J. Moberley.

R.A.S.C.

C.R.A.S.C... ..	Lt. Col. T. H. Jefferies.
250 Airborne Lt. Comp. Coy. ..	

R.A.M.C.

16 Para. Fd. Amb. ..	Lt. Col. P. R. Wheatley.
127 Para. Fd. Amb. ..	Lt. Col. M. J. Kohane.
133 Para. Fd. Amb. ..	
181 Air-landing Fd. Amb. ..	Lt. Col. G. M. Warrack.

R.A.O.C.

1 Airborne Div. Ord. Fd. Pk. ..	

R.E.M.E.

C.R.E.M.E. ..	Lt. Col. R. T. L. Shorrick.
1 Airborne Div. Wkshp.	

Provost

1 Airborne Div. Pro. Coy.	

Glider Pilots

md. Glider Pilot Regt. ..	Lt. Col. G. J. S. Chatterton

Misc.

No. 4 Army Film and Photo. Sec.

C. 2 Parachute Brigade. Italy. June, 1944.

Comd.	Brig. C. H. V. Pritchard.
Deputy Comd.	Col. T. C. H. Pearson.
4 Para. Bn.	Lt. Col. H. B. Coxen.
5 (Scottish) Para. Bn. ..	Lt. Col. D. Hunter.
6 (Royal Welch) Para. Bn. ..	Lt. Col. V. W. Barlow.
300 Air-landing A. Tk. Bty. R.A. ..	Maj. O. Orr.
2 Para. Sqn. R.E. ..	Maj. C. D. H. Vernon.
2 Para. Bde. Gp. Sigs. Coy. ..	Maj. R. S. Roberson.
127 Para. Fd. Amb. ..	Lt. Col. J. P. Parkinson.
2 Para. Bde. Gp. Comp. Coy. ..	Capt. L. Cornish.
R.A.S.C.	
2 Para. Bde. Gp. R.E.M.E. ..	Capt. R. Watson.
1st Indep. Glider Pilot Sqn. ..	Maj. G. A. R. Coulthard.
1st Indep. Para. Pl. ..	Capt. P. Baker.
2 Para. Bde. Gp. Provost Sec. ..	
No. 2 Mobile Para. Servicing Unit	Flt. Lt. J. Blackford.
R.A.F.	

D. 1 Airborne Corps, June, 1944.

G.O.C.	Lt. Gen. F. A. M. Browning.
B.G.S.	Brig. A. G. Walch.
G.SO. I (Ops.) ..	Lt. Col. C. B. Mackenzie
G.S.O. I (S.A.S.) ..	Lt. Col. I. G. Collins.
C.S.O. ..	Col. R. J. Moberley
Comd. Glider Pilots ..	Col. G. J. S. Chatterton.
D.A. and Q.M.G. ..	Brig. R. H. Bower.
A.Q.M.G. ..	Lt. Col. J. M. B. Cowan.
A.A.G. ..	Lt. Col. G. H. N. Wilson.
D.D.S.T. ..	Col. T. H. Jefferies.
D.D.M.S. ..	Brig. A. A. Eagger.
D.D.O.S. ..	Col. G. M. Loring.
D.D.M.E. ..	Col. R. T. L. Shorrock.
Umpire Grade "A" ..	Col. H. O. Wright.
Liaison Officer U.S. Army Air Force.	Lt. Col. A. B. Harris (U.S.)

439

E. 6 Airborne Division, Normandy, June, 1944.

Divisional Headquarters

G.O.C.	Maj. Gen. R. N. Gale.
G.S.O.I. (Ops.)	Lt. Col. R. H. N. C. Bray.
G.S.O.I. (Air)	Lt. Col. W. B. P. Bradish.
A.A. and Q.M.C.	Lt. Col. W. S. F. Hickie.
A.D.M.S.	Col. M. MacEwan.
A.D.O.S.	Lt. Col. J. Fielding.
Senior Umpire	Lt. Col. D. C. A. Shepard.

3 Para. Bde.

Comd.	Brig. S. J. L. Hill.
8 Para. Bn.	Lt. Col. A. S. Pearson.
9 Para. Bn.	Lt. Col. T. B. H. Otway
1 Cdn. Para. Bn.	Lt. Col. G. F. P. Bradbrooke.

5 Para. Bde.

Comd.	Brig. J. H. M. Poett.
7 Para. Bn.	Lt. Col. R. G. Pine-Coffin.
12 Para. Bn.	Lt. Col. A. P. Johnston.
13 Para. Bn.	Lt. Col. P. J. Luard.

22 Indep. Para. Coy.	Maj. Lennox Boyd.

6 Air-landing Bde.

Comd.	Brig. The Hon. H. K. M. Kindersley.
Deputy	Col. R. G. Parker.
12 Devons	Lt. Col. R. Stevens.
2 Oxf. and Bucks.	Lt. Col. M. W. Roberts.
1 R.U.R.	Lt. Col. R. J. H. Carson.

Divisional Troops

Recce.

6 Airborne Div. Armd. Recce. Regt.	Lt. Col. G. R. de C. Stewart.

R.A.

C.R.A.	Lt. Col. J. S. L. Norris.
53 (W.Y.) Air-landing Lt. Regt. R.A.	Lt. Col. A. D. M. Teacher.
3 Air-landing A. Tk. Bty. R.A.	Maj. W. R. Cranmer.
4 Air-landing A. Tk. Bty. R.A.	Maj. T. H. P. Dixon.
2 Air-landing A. Tk. Bty. R.A.	Maj. W. A. H. Rowat.
2 Forward Observer Unit R.A.	Maj. H. J. B. Rice.

R.E.

C.R.E.	Lt. Col. F. H. Lowman.
3 Para. Sqn. R.E.	Maj. J. C. A. Roseveare.
591 Para. Sqn. R.E.	Maj. P. A. Wood.
249 Fd. Coy. R.E.	Maj. A. H. Rutherford.
286 Fd. Pk. Coy. R.E.	Maj. J. H. Waters.

C.R. Signals	Lt. Col. D. Smallman-Tew.

R.A.S.C.

C.R.A.S.C.	Lt. Col. J. L. Watson.
716 Lt. Comp. Coy.	Maj. A. Jones.
398 Comp. Coy.	
63 Comp. Coy.	Maj. A. C. Bille-Top.

R.A.M.C.

224 Para. Fd. Amb.	Lt. Col. D. H. Thompson.
225 Para. Fd. Amb.	Lt. Col. E. I. B. Harvey.
195 Air-landing Fd. Amb.	Lt. Col. W. M. E. Anderson.

R.A.O.C.

6 Airborne Div. Ord. Fd. Pk.	Maj. W. L. Taylor.

R.E.M.E.

C.R.E.M.E.	Lt. Col. R. V. Powditch.
6 Airborne Div. Wksp.	Maj. E. B. Bonniwell.

Pro. Coy.	Capt. Irwin.

A.A.C.

No. 1 Wing Glider Pilot Regt.	Lt. Col. I. A. Murray.
No. 2 Wing Glider Pilot Regt.	Lt. Col. P. Griffiths.

Under Command 6 Airborne Division, June, 1944

1 Special Service Brigade.

Comd.	:: ::	Brig. The Lord Lovat.
No. 3 Commando	::	Lt. Col. P. C. Young.
No. 6 Commando	::	Lt. Col. D. Mills-Roberts.
No. 45 (Royal Marine) Commando		Lt. Col. N. C. Ries.
(No. 4 Commando		Lt. Col. R. W. F. Dawson under Comd. 3 Brit. Inf. Div.).

4 Special Service Brigade.

Comd.	::	Brig. B. W. Leicester.
No. 41 (Royal Marine) Commando		Lt. Col. E. C. E. Palmer.
No. 46 (Royal Marine) Commando		Lt. Col. C. R. Hardy.
No. 47 (Royal Marine) Commando		Lt. Col. C. F. Phillips.
No. 48 (Royal Marine) Commando		Lt. Col. J. C. Moulton.

F. S.A.S. Brigade. 1944.

Comd.	:: ::	Brig. R. W. McLeod.
1 S.A.S. Regt.	::	Lt. Col. R. B. Mayne.
2 S.A.S. Regt.	::	Lt. Col. W. S. Stirling.
20 Liaison	::	
French Demi-Bde.		
3 French Para. Bn.	::	Comdt. P. Puech-Samson.
4 French Para. Bn.	::	Comdt. J. de Bollardiere.
1 Belgian Indep. Para. Coy.		
F. Sqn. G.H.Q. Liaison Regt.		Maj. J. J. Astor.
(Phantom).		

G. 1 Airborne Division, Arnhem. September, 1944.

Divisional Headquarters

G.O.C.	:: ::	Maj. Gen. R. E. Urquhart.
G.S.O. I (Ops.)	::	Lt. Col. C. B. Mackenzie.
G.S.O. I (Air)	::	Lt. Col. E. H. Steele-Baume.
A.A. and Q.M.G.		Lt. Col. P. H. H. H. Preston.
A.D.M.S.	:: ::	Col. G. M. Warrack.
A.D.O.S.	:: ::	Lt. Col. G. A. Mobbs.

1 Para. Bde.

Comd. ..	:: ::	Brig. G. W. Lathbury.
1 Para. Bn.	::	Lt. Col. D. T. Dobie.
2 Para. Bn.	::	Lt. Col. J. D. Frost.
3 Para. Bn.	::	Lt. Col. J. A. C. Fitch.

4 Para. Bde.

Comd. ..	:: ::	Brig. J. W. Hackett.
156 Para. Bn.		Lt. Col. Sir W. R. de B. des Voeux.
10 Para. Bn.		Lt. Col. K. B. I. Smyth.
11 Para. Bn.		Lt. Col. G. H. Lea.

21 Indep. Para. Coy.	::	Maj. B. A. Wilson.

1 Air-landing Bde.

Comd.	::	Brig. P. H. W. Hicks.
Deputy Comd.	::	Col. H. N. Barlow.
7 Border	::	Lt. Col. T. Haddon.
7 K.O.S.B.	::	Lt. Col. R. Payton-Reid.
2 S. Staffords.	::	Lt. Col. W. D. H. McCardie.

Divisional Troops

Recce. Sqn.	::	Maj. C. F. H. Gough.

R.A.

C.R.A.	::	Lt. Col. R. G. Loder-Symonds.
1 Air-landing Lt. Regt. R.A.	::	Lt. Col. W. F. K. Thompson.
1 Air-landing A. Tk. Bty. R.A.	::	Maj. W. F. Arnold.
2 Air-landing A. Tk. Bty. R.A.	::	Maj. A. F. Haynes.
1 Forward Observer Unit R.A.	::	Maj. D. R. Wight Boycott.

R.E.

C.R.E.	::	Lt. Col. E. C. W. Myers.
1 Para. Sqn. R.E.	::	Maj. D. C. Murray.
4 Para. Sqn. R.E.	::	Maj. Ae. J. M. Perkins.
9 Fd. Coy. R.E.	::	Maj. J. C. Winchester.
261 Fd. Pk. Coy. R.E.		Maj. J. N. Chivers.

C.R. Signals	::	Lt. Col. T. C. V. Stephenson.

R.A.S.C.
C.R.A.S.C. .. :: Lt. Col. M. St. J. Packe.
93 Comp. Coy. .. :: Maj. F. Tompkins.
250 Lt. Comp. Coy. :: Maj. J. L. Gifford.
253 Comp. Coy. .. :: Maj. R. K. Gordon.

R.A.M.C.
16 Para. Fd. Amb. :: Lt. Col. E. Townsend.
133 Para. Fd. Amb. :: Lt. Col. W. C. Alford.
181 Air-landing Fd. Amb. :: Lt. Col. A. T. Marrable.

R.A.O.C.
Ord. Fd. Pk. :: Maj. C. C. Chidgey.

R.E.M.E.
C.R.E.M.E. :: Lt. Col. E. J. Kinvig.
Div. Wkshps. :: Maj. W. S. Carrick.

A.P.M.
Pro. Coy. .. :: Maj. O. P. Haig.

A.A.C.
No. 1 Wing Glider Pilot Regt. :: Lt. Col. I. A. Murray.
No. 2 Wing Glider Pilot Regt. :: Lt. Col. J. W. Place.

H. *6 Airborne Division, Rhine. March, 1945.*

Divisional Headquarters
G.O.C. :: Maj. Gen. E. L. Bols.
G.S.O. I (Ops.) :: Lt. Col. M. W. Roberts.
G.S.O. I (Air) :: Lt. Col. C. R. W. Brewis.
A.A. and Q.M.G. :: Lt. Col. G. H. D. Ford.
A.D.M.S. :: Col. M. MacEwan.
A.D.O.S. :: Lt. Col. J. Fielding.

3 Para. Bde.
Comd. .. :: Brig. S. J. L. Hill.
8 Para. Bn. :: Lt. Col. G. Hewetson.
9 Para. Bn. :: Lt. Col. N. Crookenden.
1 Cdn. Para. Bn. :: Lt. Col. J. A. Nicklin.

5 Para. Bde.
Comd. .. :: Brig. J. H. N. Poett.
7 Para. Bn. :: Lt. Col. R. G. Pine-Coffin.
12 Para. Bn. :: Lt. Col. K. T. Darling.
13 Para. Bn. :: Lt. Col. P. J. Luard.

22 Indep. Para. Coy. :: Maj. M. G. Dolden.

6 Air-landing Bde.
Comd. :: Brig. R. H. Bellamy.
Deputy Comd. :: Lt. Col. D. E. Salis.
12 Devon :: Lt. Col. P. Gleadell.
2 Oxf. Bucks :: Lt. Col. M. Darrell-Brown.
1 R.U.R. .. :: Lt. Col. R. J. H. Carson.

Armd. Recce. Regt. :: Lt. Col. G. R. de C. Stewart.

R.A.
C.R.A. :: Brig. W. Mc. C. T. Faithfull.
53 (W.Y.) Air-landing Lt. Regt. R.A. :: Lt. Col. R. A. Eden.
2 Air-landing A. Tk. Regt. R.A. :: Lt. Col. F. E. Allday.
2 Fwd. Observer Unit R.A. :: Maj. H. J. B. Rice.

R.E.
C.R.E. :: Lt. Col. J. R. C. Hamilton.
3 Para. Sqn. R.E. :: Maj. J. C. A. Roseveare.
591 Para. Sqn. R.E. :: Maj. A. J. Jack.
249 Fd. Coy. R.E. :: Maj. A. H. Rutherford.
286 Fd. Pk. Coy. R.E. :: Maj. J. H. Waters.

C.R. Signals :: Lt. Col. P. E. M. Bradley.

R.A.S.C.
C.R.A.S.C. :: Lt. Col. R. A. Lovegrove.
398 Airborne Comp. Coy. :: Maj. M. E. Phipps.
63 Airborne Comp. Coy. :: Maj. D. J. Bradley.
716 Airborne Lt. Comp. Coy. :: Maj. C. P. R. Crane.

R.A.M.C.
224 Para. Fd. Amb.   ..   ..   Lt. Col. A. D. Young.
225 Para. Fd. Amb.   ..   ..   Lt. Col. N. J. P. Newlings.
195 Air-landing Fd. Amb.   ..   Lt. Col. W. M. E. Anderson.

6 Airborne Div. Ord. Fd. Pk.   ..   Maj. W. L. Taylor.

R.E.M.E.
C.R.E.M.E.   ..   ..   Lt. Col. R. V. Powditch.
Div. Wkshp.   ..   ..   Maj. E. B. Bonniwell.

Pro. Coy.   ..   ..   Capt. K. G. Wells.

I. 50 Indian Parachute Brigade. October, 1943.

Comd.   ..   ..   Brig. M. R. J. Hope Thomson.
Signal Section   ..   ..   Maj. E. J. Buirski.
152 Indian Para. Bn.   ..   Lt. Col. P. Hopkinson.
153 Gurkha Para. Bn.   ..   Lt. Col. H. R. E. Willis.
154 Gurkha Para. Bn.   ..   Lt. Col. G. H. W. Bond.
Medium Machine Gun Coy.   ..   Maj. J. E. Ball.
411 (Royal Bombay) Para. Sqn. I.E.   Maj. M. J. J. Rolt.
80 Para. Fd. Amb.   ..   ..   Lt. Col. R. B. Davis.
50 Indep. Para. Pl.   ..   ..   Lt. E. B. L. Hill.

J. 44 Indian Airborne Division. July, 1945.

G.O.C.   ..   ..   Maj. Gen. E. E. Down.
G.S.O. I (Ops.)   ..   ..   Lt. Col. C. B. Mackenzie.
G.S.O. I (Air)   ..   ..   Lt. Col. P. Cleasby Thompson.
G.S.O. I (Trg.)   ..   ..   Lt. Col. G. H. Lea.
A.A. and Q.M.C.   ..   ..   Lt. Col. D. L. Powell Jones.
A.D.M.S.   ..   ..   Col. P. R. Wheatley.
A.D.O.S.   ..   ..   Lt. Col. P. A. A. Leir.

50 Indian Para. Bde.
Comd.   ..   ..   Brig. E. G. Woods.
Deputy Comd.   ..   ..   Col. B. E. Abbott.
16 Para. Bn.   ..   ..   Lt. Col. A. W. E. Daniell.
1 Ind. Para. Bn.   ..   ..   Lt. Col. J. Martin.
3 Gurkha Para. Bn.   ..   Lt. Col. J. White.

77 Indian Para. Bde.
Comd.   ..   ..   Brig. C. J. Wilkinson.
Deputy Comd.   ..   ..   Col. P. Hopkinson.
15 Para. Bn.   ..   ..   Lt. Col. T. B. H. Otway.
2 Gurkha Para. Bn.   ..   Lt. Col. H. R. E. Willis.
4 Ind. Para. Bn.   ..   ..   Lt. Col. G. E. A. Beale.
44 Brit. Indep. Pathfinder Coy.   Maj. F. E. Templer.

14 Air-landing Bde.
Comd.   ..   ..   Brig. F. W. Gibb.
2 Black Watch   ..   ..   Lt. Col. J. E. Benson.
4 Rajputana Rifles (Outram's)   ..   Lt. Col. T. E. Williams.
6/16 Punjab Regt.   ..   ..   Lt. Col. R. Steward.

Recce.
44 Ind. Airborne Div. Recce. Sqn.   Maj. P. Marriott.
  (Governor General's Bodyguard).

R.A.
C.R.A.   ..   ..   Brig. R. A. Kirton.
159 Para. Lt. Regt. R.A.   ..   Lt. Col. F. E. Powell Brett.
23 L.A.A./A. Tk. Regt. R.A.   ..   Lt. Col. V. E. de S. Le Marchant.

R.E.
C.R.E.   ..   ..   Lt. Col. E. F. Kyte.
40 Indian Airborne Fd. Pk. Sqn.   Maj. R. E. Holden.
33 Para. Sqn. I.E.   ..   ..   Maj. G. B. Napier.
411 Para. Sqn. I.E.   ..   ..   Maj. P. F. Cooke.
12 Para. Sqn. R.E.   ..   ..   Maj. R. J. Hindmarsh.

C.R. Signals   ..   Lt. Col. D. A. Pringle.

R.I.A.S.C.
C.R.I.A.S.C.   ..   ..   Lt. Col. H. V. S. Müller.
Parachute Supply Company   ..   Maj. D. C. Brooke-Taylor.
610 Airborne Light (Jeep) Company.   Maj. D. S. Jones.
604 Airborne G.T. Company   ..   Maj. G. Pliva.
165 Airborne G.T. Company   ..   Maj. J. E. Canin.

Recce.
3 Cavalry .. .. .. Lt. Col. K. M. Idris.

R.I.A.
C.R.A. .. Brig. W. G. H. Pike.
9 Para. Fd. Regt. R.I.A. .. Lt. Col. R. A. Eden.
12 Para. Fd. Regt. R.I.A. .. Lt. Col. P. P. Kumaramanglam.
17 Para. Fd. Regt. R.I.A. .. Lt. Col. D. H. N. Baker-Carr.
28 (Punjab) Para. L.A.A. Regt. Lt. Col. C. E. Godby.
  R.I.A.
36 (Mahratta) Para. A. Tk. Regt. Lt. Col. A. S. Jarvis.
  R.I.A.

R.I.E.
C.R.E. .. .. Lt. Col. M. C. A. Henniker.
33 Para. Sqn. R.I.E. .. Maj. P. H. James.
36 Para. Sqn. R.I.E. .. Maj. M. L. Khetarpal.
411 Para. Sqn. R.I.E. .. Maj. J. S. R. Shave.
40 Airborne Fd. Pk. Sqn. R.I.E. .. Maj. R. C. Tweddel.

C.R. Signals .. .. Lt. Col. D. R. Horsfield.

R.I.A.S.C.
C.R.I.A.S.C. .. Lt. Col. P. Miller.
601 Para. Sup. Coy. R.I.A.S.C. .. Maj. T. E. J. Willsher.
621 Airborne Lt. Jeep Coy. .. Maj. C. W. Mullineux.
622 Airborne Tpt. Coy. (3 Ton) Maj. Kartar Singh Singhota.
  R.I.A.S.C.
623 Airborne Tpt. Coy. (3 Ton) Maj. F. N. Meaker.
  R.I.A.S.C.

I.A.M.C./I.M.S.
60 Para. Fd. Amb. .. .. Lt. Col. J. F. A. Forster.
80 Para. Fd. Amb. .. Lt. Col. A. G. Rangaraj.
3 Airborne Fd. Hyg. Sec. Maj. V. S. Mahadevan.

R.A.O.C.
2 Ord. Fd. Pk. .. .. Maj. J. E. L. Furr.

I.A.M.C./I.M.S.
7 Indian Para. Fd. Amb. .. Lt. Col. D. G. C. Whyte.
80 Indian Para. Fd. Amb. .. Lt. Col. J. Young.
60 Indian Para. Fd. Amb. ..

I.E.M.E.
C.I.E.M.E. .. Lt. Col. H. S. J. Jelf.
44 Indian Airborne Div. Wkshp. Maj. A. G. L. Collen.
A.P.M. .. .. .. Maj. Wilson.

K. 2 Indian Airborne Division. *January, 1947.*

Divisional Headquarters
G.O.C. .. .. Maj. Gen. C. H. Boucher.
G.S.O. I (Ops.) .. Lt. Col. T. B. H. Otway.
G.S.O. I (Air) .. Lt. Col. W. A. C. Collingwood.
A.A. and Q.M.G. Lt. Col. D. L. Powell-Jones.
A.D.M.S. .. .. Col. E. C. Jackson.
A.D.O.S. .. .. Lt. Col. J. C. Northey.
1 Para. Bn. Kumaon (Div. H.Q. Lt. Col. J. Trotter.
  Bn.).
3 Para. Bn. 15 Punjab Regt. (M.G.)

14 Para. Bde.
Comd. .. .. Brig. R. B. Scott.
4 Para. Bn. Rajputana Rifles Lt. Col. C. G. Butcher.
  (Outram's).
1 Para. Bn. Frontier Force Regt. Lt. Col. W. I. Moberley.
3 Para. Bn. 16 Punjab Regt. .. Lt. Col. R. C. Robinson.

50 Para. Bde.
Comd. .. .. Brig. E. G. Woods.
3 Para. Bn. 1 Punjab Regt. .. Lt. Col. E. A. G. Wakefield.
3 Para. Bn. The Baluch Regt. Lt. Col. D. Carroll.
2 Para. Bn. The Madras Regt. Lt. Col. A. H. Roosmale-Cocq.

77 Para. Bde.
Comd. .. .. Brig. P. Hopkinson.
1 Para. Bn. 2 Punjab Regt. .. Lt. Col. Y. S. Paranjpe.
3 Para. Bn. Mahratta L.I. Lt. Col. W. H. M. Fawcett.
3 Para. Bn. Rajput Regt. (D.C.O.) Lt. Col. F. W. Collard.

I.E.M.E.

C.I.E.M.E.	Lt. Col. H. S. J. Jelf.
2 Inf. Wkshp. Coy. I.E.M.E.	Maj. A. G. L. Collen.
63 Inf. Wkshp. Coy. I.E.M.E.	Maj. B. W. Harvey.
134 Inf. Wkshp. Coy. I.E.M.E.	Maj. J. Long.
2 Airborne Div. Rec. Coy. I.E.M.E.	Maj. N. K. Ahmed.
2 Airborne Div. Pro. Coy.	Capt. Desai.

L. 6 Independent Parachute Brigade Group. *January, 1947.*

Comd.	Brig. C. J. Wilkinson.
2 Black Watch	Lt. Col. J. E. Benson.
15 Para. Bn.	Lt. Col. P. G. F. Young.
16 Para. Bn.	Lt. Col. G. H. Lea.
2 Brit. Indep. Pathfinder Coy.	Maj. F. E. Templer.
158 Para. Fd. Regt. R.A.	Lt. Col. V. E. de S. Le Merchant.
159 Para. Lt. Regt. R.A.	Lt. Col. M. I. Gregson.
12 Para. Sqn. R.E.	Maj. R. J. Hindmarsh.
7 Para. Fd. Amb.	Lt. Col. D. G. C. Whyte.
Pro. Coy.	Capt. King.

M. Australian Airborne Forces.

1st Australian Parachute Battalion

Commanding Officer	Lt. Col. J. W. Overall.
Second in Command	Maj. J. M. Atkinson.
Company Commanders	Maj. A. C. Smith.
	Maj. D. I. H. McClean.
	Maj. W. D. Clark.
	Maj. S. L. Morse.
Adjutant	Capt. A. L. Stephenson.
Quartermaster	Capt. M. Peachey.
Medical Officers	Maj. V. E. Sampson.
	Capt. J. M. Allingham.
Planning Staff	Maj. J. F. Nagle.
R.A.A.F. Liaison Officer	Flt. Lieut. Utbermid.

1st Australian Parachute Troop R.A.E.

Commanding Officer	Capt. E. C. Burt.
Second in Command	Lieut. W. A. Riggs.

1st Australian Parachute Training Centre.

Chief Instructor Infantry Wing and Parachute Wing.	Maj. H. S. Roberts, succeeded by Maj. R. S. Freeman.
Officer Commanding Holding Wing	Maj. A. E. Shepherd.

Parachute Troop 1st Australian Mountain Battery.

Officer Commanding	Capt. E. V. Haywood.

N. Canadian Officers at No. 1 Parachute Training School. *August, 1942.*

Maj. C. F. P. Bradbrooke.	The Saskatoon Light Infantry (M.G.).
Maj. J. P. L'Esperance	Le Regiment de la Chaudiere.
Capt. J. A. Nicklin	The Royal Winnipeg Rifles.
Capt. D. H. Taylor	The Black Watch (Royal Highland Regiment) of Canada.
Capt. D. J. Wilkins	The Toronto Scottish Regiment (M.G.).
Lt. R. M. Baxter	Royal Canadian Army Service Corps.
Lt. F. C. Boyd	The Perth Regiment.
Lt. F. W. Cooper	The Royal Regiment of Canada.
Lt. D. L. Fraser	The Corps of Royal Canadian Engineers.
Lt. N. A. Garland	5th Armoured Regiment (9th Princess Louise's (New Brunswick) Hussars).
Lt. J. M. Girvan	The Corps of Royal Canadian Engineers.
Lt. J. P. Hanson	The Royal Montreal Regiment.
Lt. B. B. Hart	The Saskatoon Light Infantry (M.G.).
Lt. W. R. Hick	The Seaforth Highlanders of Canada.
Lt. W. G. Kersey	The Cameron Highlanders of Ottawa (M.G.).
Lt. A. A. J. Liddiard	1st Armoured Car Regiment (the Royal Canadian Dragoons).
Lt. R. MacDonald	
Lt. F. S. MacLean	The Corps of Royal Canadian Engineers.
Lt. R. J. MacLean	The Calgary Highlanders.
Lt. R. M. MacLeod	The North Nova Scotia Highlanders.
Lt. R. M. Millette	Le Regiment de Maisonneuve.
Lt. J. D. Poupors	The Toronto Scottish Regiment (M.G.).
Lt. R. A. Smith	The Hastings and Prince Edward Regiment.

445

APPENDIX P

THE VALUE OF AIRBORNE FORCES

The following are the replies sent to Field-Marshal Sir Alan Brooke, C.I.G.S., by Field-Marshal Sir Bernard Montgomery and Field-Marshal The Hon. Sir Harold Alexander, in the autumn of 1945, giving their views on the value of airborne forces.

1. From Field-Marshal Sir Bernard Montgomery

General

Airborne forces form an essential part of a modern army, and there will often be occasions in which they can play a vital role : *particularly in deliberate operations.* Apart from their participation in the battle, the threat of the use of airborne forces can also be used to great advantage, and experience has shown that the enemy can be led by these means to make considerable and even vital dispersion of his front line forces ; in addition, there is always the need to lock up troops in guarding vital areas and installations when an opponent is known to have airborne troops at his disposal.

Under European conditions of warfare, employment of airborne forces during *highly mobile* operations has been shown to be limited ; large airborne operations require considerable time to plan, and the ground troops are liable to overrun Dropping Zones before the airborne project matures.

In undeveloped countries, especially against a second-rate enemy, airborne forces may play a highly important role, particularly since conditions may sometimes permit of their being dropped and maintained in areas well in rear of the enemy's main front.

Airborne Forces in Deliberate Operations

The employment of airborne forces has proved a battle winning factor in deliberate operations such as the major sea-borne assault and the assault across a major obstacle.

In Sicily (July, 1943), in spite of mistakes and disorganization due to the inexperience of those early days, airborne troops played an important part in the capture of Syracuse and of the group of airfields in south-east Sicily.

In the Normandy invasion, British airborne forces secured intact crossings over the Orne river and canal, which were to prove of great importance in the subsequent development of operations, and their action in the first days of the invasion caused confusion and delay to enemy forces at the most vital time.

U.S. airborne forces played an essential part in the establishment of the Utah beaches, by drawing enemy forces to themselves while the sea-borne troops were establishing a foothold, and their employment greatly facilitated cutting off the Cotentin Peninsula and launching the assault northwards to Cherbourg.

Airborne forces were employed in Holland in September, 1944, to seize a series of crossing over the water obstacles between the Meuse–Escaut Canal and the Neder Rhin. By their action a series of crossings were seized intact, and although the Arnhem bridge was subsequently lost, possession of the other bridges, and particularly those at Grave and Nijmegen, had a decisive bearing on the subsequent development of our operations.

At the crossing of the Rhine, airborne forces greatly facilitated the seizure and rapid expansion of the bridgehead, and the speed of the subsequent breakout.

In all these examples the chief advantages which accrued from the employment of airborne troops were secured as a result of their descent from the air. In the case of seizure of intact bridges, no alternative method could have ensured success.

Value of the Threat of Airborne Forces

It has been shown that the threat of employing airborne troops can be made a major factor in determining both the strategical and tactical layout of the enemy's forces.

The airborne threat, used in conjunction with other factors, was material in causing the Germans to retain major formations in the Pas de Calais area during the initial period after our landing in Normandy.

Uncertainty as to our intentions, combined with the use of dummy paratroops, caused the enemy considerable alarm and despondency in the tactical area of the landings, and delayed the arrival on the battlefield of some of his forces at the most vital time.

Both during the Battle of the Rhineland and the Crossing of the Rhine, the airborne threat was again used to inspire uncertainty and confusion in the enemy's mind, and to upset his planning.

We have learnt that the Germans always believed us to have more airborne formations than we actually had, and the possible use of them had constantly to be considered and guarded against.

In the early days of the war, it will be recalled that the Germans made much of the threat of airborne invasion, and that this greatly affected our dispositions in the United Kingdom between 1940 and 1942, and led to a vast expenditure of material and effort.

In north-west Europe even the threat of a small suicidal drop by enemy paratroops in the Antwerp area caused us to maintain troops there in a constant state of readiness.

Limitations to the use of Airborne Forces

Airborne forces are subject to the limitations in their use, the chief of which is the uncertainty of the weather.

The degree, however, to which weather will influence airborne operations in the future is a matter of speculation ; the rapid development of scientific methods designed to facilitate the use of aircraft under adverse weather conditions will undoubtedly continue. It may be expected therefore that this factor will become less important in the future.

Conclusion

A nation without airborne forces will be severely handicapped and at a great disadvantage in future warfare. There can be no doubt that airborne forces will continue to have an important role in battle, and they definitely justify the expenditure of effort which they involve.

447

Notes on Organization of Airborne Divisions

It is considered that the Air-Landing Brigade as such should be abolished. Once on the ground, all airborne brigades have to fight, often for considerable periods, in the normal infantry role. It is therefore desirable to simplify the organization and avoid having two different types of brigades. I consider that we require three homogeneous Para. Bdes. in the airborne division, each brigade having three strong battalions on a four-company basis ; within the brigade there should be a glider element for heavy weapons and other equipment.

It appears desirable that the power glider should be developed, as it would make a valuable addition to existing methods of carriage of airborne troops and their heavy equipment.

2. From Field-Marshal The Hon. Sir Harold Alexander

Future of Airborne Forces

The only airborne operations of any size which have been launched in this theatre are those carried out as part of the invasions of Sicily and the South of France.

The airborne operations that formed part of the Sicily landings were the first large-scale airborne landings to be launched by the Allies during the war. The object of the British airborne forces was to capture the canal and railway bridges near Syracuse, and, if possible, to exploit into the town. The American airborne forces were to be dropped about four miles inland and six miles East of Gela, with the task of seizing the high ground and the road junctions controlling the exits from the beaches on which the 1st U.S. Div. was to land. The failure of navigational aids, combined with a high wind, prevented all but a small proportion of the aircraft from reaching their proper areas, while heavy flak added to the dispersal. Of 137 gliders transporting the British forces, about 12 reached the correct dropping zone, 75 landed ashore, scattered over the south-east part of Sicily, and the remainder came down in the sea. The parachutists of the U.S. 82 Airborne Div. were dispersed over an area of some 50 to 60 miles astride their dropping zone.

In spite of these difficulties, a party in the British sector prevented the demolition of the canal bridge South of Syracuse, although they were unable to hold it until the arrival of troops landed from the sea ; while, in the Gela area, parties of parachutists got to their correct zones and succeeded in holding the high ground and preventing the reinforcements from reaching the landing beaches.

By the time that the operations in the South of France were launched, great strides had been made in the provision of navigational aids, with the result that, in spite of bad visibility and a 90° error in wind forecast, a very high proportion of the troops engaged were landed in their proper dropping zones. The casualties in dropping sustained by the parachutists were less than 2 per cent. and many of these were only minor injuries of a very temporary nature. Many of the gliders landed were severely damaged as the enemy had sown all likely landing areas with stakes, but casualties of men and equipment from the gliders were very low. The operations were entirely successful and the enemy reinforcement routes to the landing beaches were effectively cut.

There is very little in the way of concrete evidence of the German reaction to the possibility of airborne operations in this theatre. It appears that the German General Staff believed that there was an airborne division somewhere in Southern Italy, but, as the campaign progressed, belief in its existence faded. It does not appear that German dispositions were at any time conditioned by the fear of airborne operations. From interrogation reports of P.O.Ws. there is no indication that the German soldier was worried about airborne operations in Italy ; this is probably because his only experience of them was at the Sicily landing and so their effect had not been sufficiently brought home to him.

In the Balkans, considerable help was given to Partisan movements by dropping leaders, liaison missions, weapons and supplies of all kinds. Later, landing grounds were constructed in Partisan held territory so that larger quantities of stores could be handled and casualties evacuated by air.

During the E.L.A.S. rebellion in Greece in December, 1944, two infantry brigades were flown in to provide the necessary reinforcements to deal with the situation. At the rate at which the position was deteriorating, it is probable that a very serious situation would have arisen if it had been impossible to transport troops by air.

It will be seen that airborne operations have played a comparatively small part in this theatre, but the difference in the results of the Sicily and the South of France operations shows the strides that have already been made in ensuring the precision with which these operations can be carried out. Future developments in navigational aids and in flying generally will continue to add to the reliability of this means of getting troops to the battle.

As to the future development in airborne forces : Commanders, throughout history, have always been seeking the open flank round which to launch their decisive operations ; failing this, they have been forced into attempting to create one by the staging of heavy frontal attacks, designed to break through and so afford them the opportunity of envelopment. In the British Empire, the open flank of the enemy land forces has often been found by the proper employment of sea power and amphibious operations. With the development of airborne forces, a further way, over the top, is opened. We shall always require a strong Navy and a strong Air Force and consequently shall be unable to maintain a large Army. If we are to get the fullest value from the Army we must be ready to take advantage both of command of the sea and of the air so that we can strike at the open flank, going round by sea or over by air, without having to cripple our Army by the preliminary delivery of break through blows, the complete success of which becomes more and more difficult to achieve as the power of mechanized movement increases the mobility of the defence.

Apart from carrying troops tactically into battle, as parachutists and glider-borne units, the air can provide the most rapid means for switching our resources to any threatened point. It will also often be necessary to fly in the follow up troops after an airborne assault. It should therefore be considered no more out of the ordinary for units to be carried to battle by air than to travel by motor transport. If this is accepted, design and development of equipment should always have air-portability as a requirement.

With progress in the design of rockets and similar weapons, it is possible that the role of heavy aircraft as bomb carriers will disappear, so that the task of transporting airborne forces, instead of being one which is in competition with the requirements for bombing, may well become the primary task of the heavy aircraft, while the task of the fighter becomes that of maintaining command of the air for the passage of airborne forces.

There is, therefore, in the future Army, a need for airborne divisions to form the spearhead of airborne operations, while all formations must be trained to air movement, both as the means of providing the follow up to the airborne assault and for rapid movement to any part of the world where British troops may be required.

AIRBORNE FORCES

Index

451

453

458

468

MAP 1

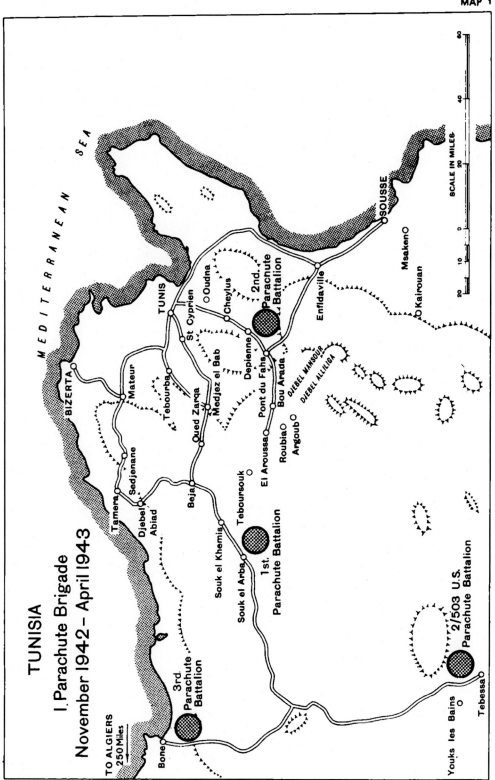

TUNISIA
I. Parachute Brigade
November 1942 - April 1943

MAP 2

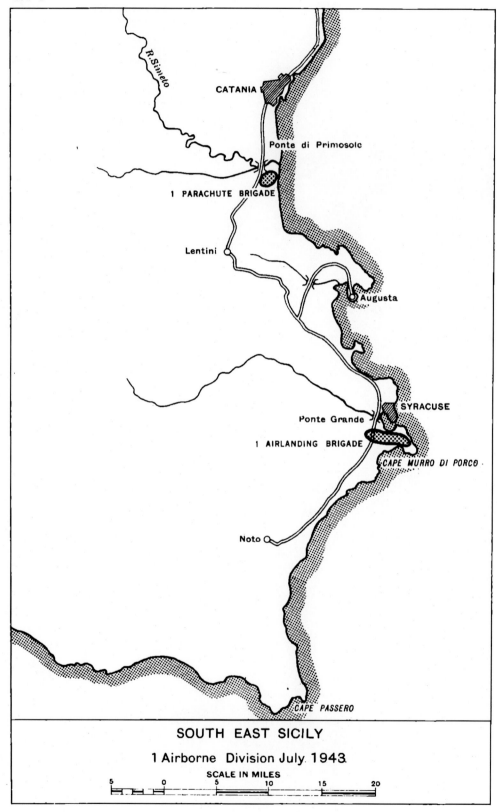

R.Simeto

CATANIA

Ponte di Primosole

1 PARACHUTE BRIGADE

Lentini

Augusta

SYRACUSE

Ponte Grande

1 AIRLANDING BRIGADE

CAPE MURRO DI PORCO

Noto

CAPE PASSERO

SOUTH EAST SICILY

1 Airborne Division July 1943

SCALE IN MILES

5   0   5   10   15   20

MAP 3

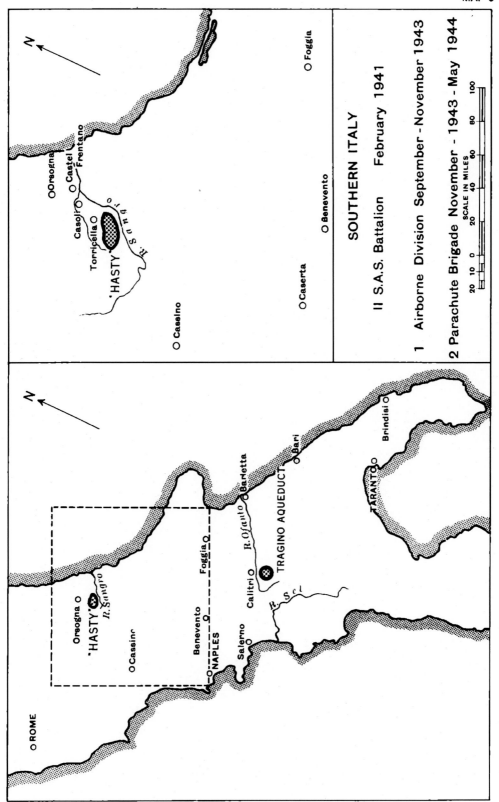

SOUTHERN ITALY

II S.A.S. Battalion   February 1941

1 Airborne Division September - November 1943

2 Parachute Brigade November - 1943 - May 1944

SCALE IN MILES

20 10 0   20 40 60 80 100

MAP 4

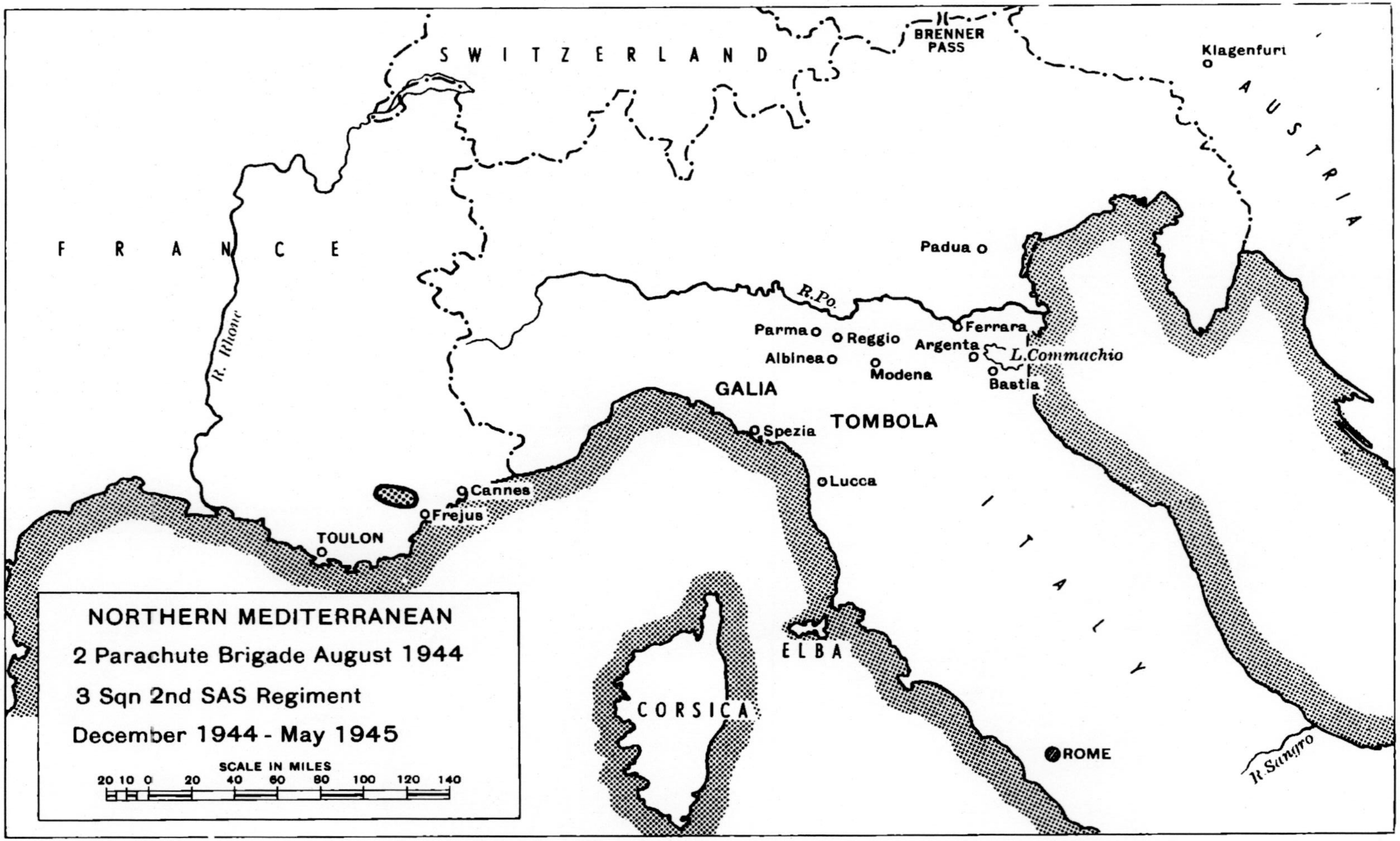

AUSTRIA

Klagenfurt O

BRENNER PASS

SWITZERLAND

FRANCE

R. Rhône

TOULON O

Cannes O

Fréjus O

Padua O

R. Po

Parma O O Reggio

Albinea O

O Ferrara

Argenta O

Modena O

GALIA

TOMBOLA

O Spezia

O Lucca

L. Commachio

Bastia O

ITALY

O ROME

R. Strumov

ELBA

CORSICA

NORTHERN MEDITERRANEAN

2 Parachute Brigade August 1944

3 Sqn 2nd SAS Regiment

December 1944 – May 1945

SCALE IN MILES

20 10 0   20   40   60   80   100   120   140

MAP 5

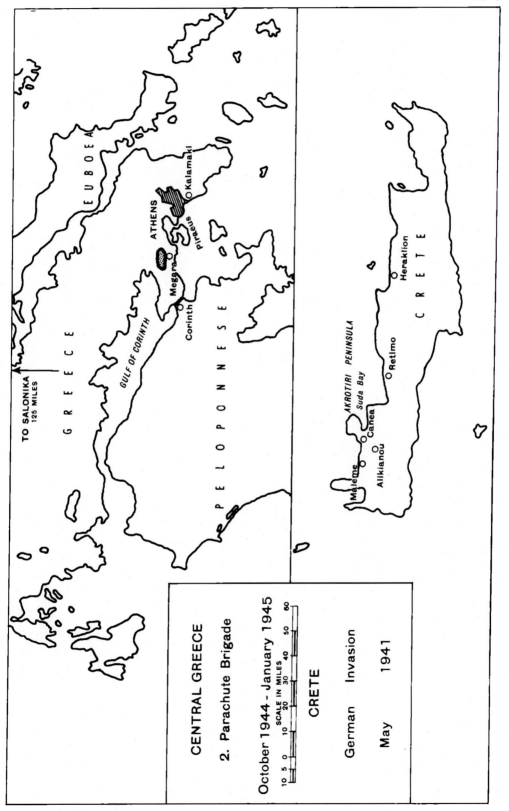

TO SALONIKA
125 MILES

GREECE

GULF OF CORINTH

EUBOEA

ATHENS

Megara

Kalamaki

Piraeus

Corinth

PELOPONNESE

AKROTIRI PENINSULA

Suda Bay

Maleme

Canea

Alikianou

Retimo

Heraklion

CRETE

CENTRAL GREECE

2. Parachute Brigade

October 1944 - January 1945

SCALE IN MILES

10 5 0   10   20   30   40   50   60

CRETE

German   Invasion

May   1941

MAP 6

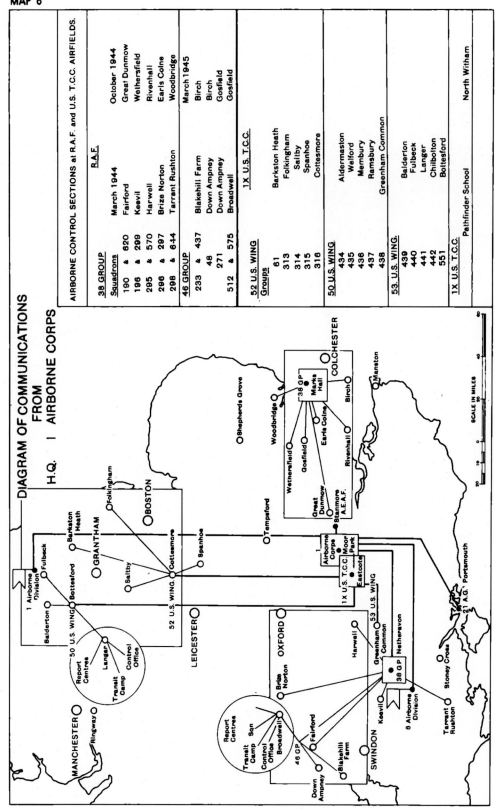

DIAGRAM OF COMMUNICATIONS FROM
H.Q. I AIRBORNE CORPS

AIRBORNE CONTROL SECTIONS at R.A.F. and U.S. T.C.C. AIRFIELDS.

R.A.F.

38 GROUP

Squadrons			March 1944	October 1944
190	&	620	Fairford	Great Dunmow
196	&	299	Keevil	Wethersfield
295	&	570	Harwell	Rivenhall
296	&	297	Brize Norton	Earls Colne
298	&	644	Tarrant Rushton	Woodbridge

46 GROUP

				March 1945
233	&	437	Blakehill Farm	Birch
48			Down Ampney	Birch
271			Down Ampney	Gosfield
512	&	575	Broadwell	Gosfield

1X U.S. T.C.C.

52 U.S. WING

Groups	
61	Barkston Heath
313	Folkingham
314	Saltby
315	Spanhoe
316	Cottesmore

50 U.S. WING

434	Aldermaston
435	Welford
436	Membury
437	Ramsbury
438	Greenham Common

53. U.S. WING.

439	Balderton
440	Fulbeck
441	Langer
442	Chilbolton
551	Boltesford

1X U.S. T.C.C.

Pathfinder School	North Witham

MAP 7

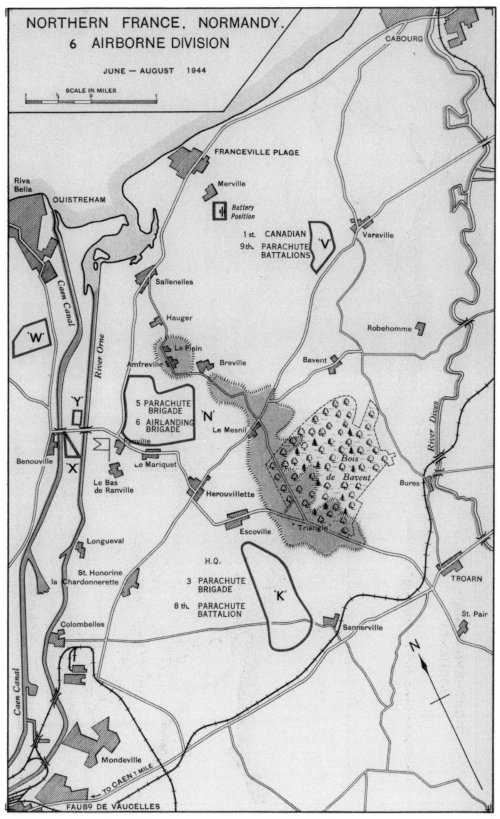

NORTHERN FRANCE, NORMANDY.
6 AIRBORNE DIVISION

JUNE — AUGUST 1944

SCALE IN MILES

CABOURG

Riva
Bella

OUISTREHAM

FRANCEVILLE PLAGE

Merville

Battery
Position

1st. CANADIAN
9th. PARACHUTE
BATTALIONS

'V'

Varaville

Caen Canal

River Orne

Sallenelles

Hauger

Robehomme

'W'

Le Plein

Amfreville

Breville

Bavent

'Y'

5 PARACHUTE
BRIGADE
6 AIRLANDING
BRIGADE

'N'

Le Mesnil

River Dives

Benouville

'X'

Ranville

Le Mariquet

Bois
de Bavent

Bures

Le Bas
de Ranville

Herouvillette

Longueval

Escoville

'Triangle'

St. Honorine
la Chardonnerette

H.Q.

3 PARACHUTE
BRIGADE

8th. PARACHUTE
BATTALION

'K'

TROARN

St. Pair

Colombelles

Sannerville

N

Caen Canal

Mondeville

TO CAEN 1 MILE

FAUBG DE VAUCELLES

MAP 8

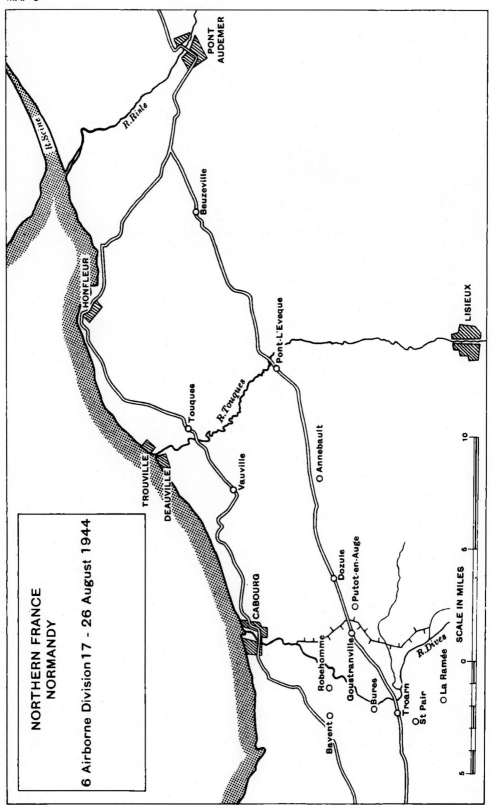

NORTHERN FRANCE
NORMANDY

6 Airborne Division 17 - 26 August 1944

PONT AUDEMER

R. Rinle

R. Seine

Beuzeville

HONFLEUR

Pont-L'Eveque

LISIEUX

Touques

R. Touques

TROUVILLE

Vauville

DEAUVILLE

Annebault

CABOURG

Dozule

Putot-en-Auge

Robehomme

Goustranville

R. Dives

Bayent

Bures

Troarn

St Pair

La Ramée

SCALE IN MILES

5   0   5   10

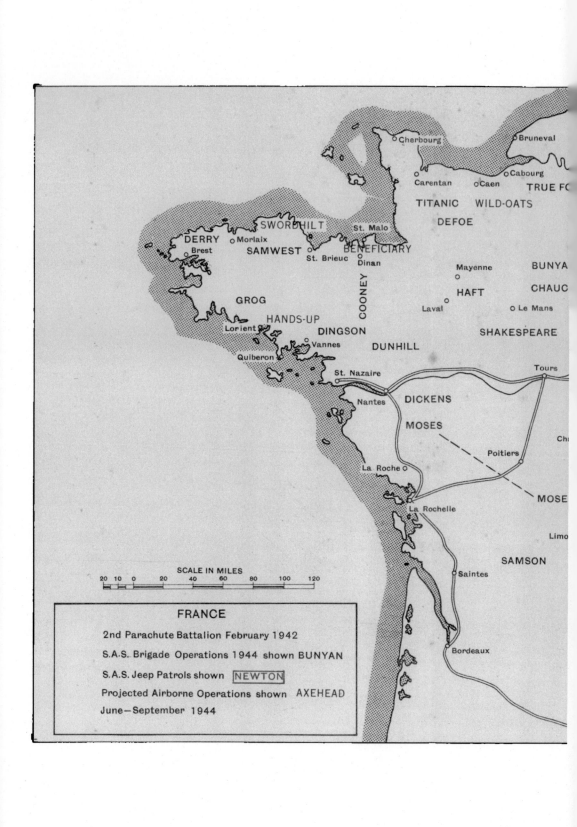

Cherbourg ○   ○ Bruneval

○ Cabourg

TRUE FC

Carentan ○   ○ Caen

TITANIC   WILD-OATS

DEFOE

St. Malo

SWORDHILT

DERRY ○ Morlaix   BUNYA

○ Brest   SAMWEST ○ BENEFICIARY   Mayenne   CHAUC

St. Brieuc ○ Dinan   ○

COONEY   HAFT

GROG   Laval ○   ○ Le Mans

HANDS-UP

Lorient ○   DINGSON   SHAKESPEARE

Vannes ○ DUNHILL

Quiberon ○

St. Nazaire ○   Tours ○

Nantes ○   DICKENS

MOSES

Poitiers ○   Ch

La Roche ○   MOSE

La Rochelle ○   Limo

SAMSON

○ Saintes

○ Bordeaux

SCALE IN MILES

20 10 0   20   40   60   80   100   120

FRANCE

2nd Parachute Battalion February 1942

S.A.S. Brigade Operations 1944 shown BUNYAN

S.A.S. Jeep Patrols shown [NEWTON]

Projected Airborne Operations shown AXEHEAD

June—September 1944

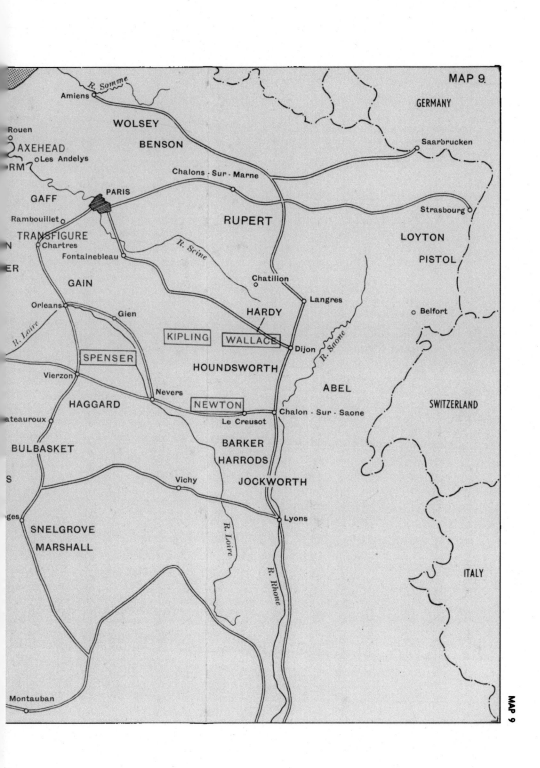

MAP 9.

MAP 9

MAP 10

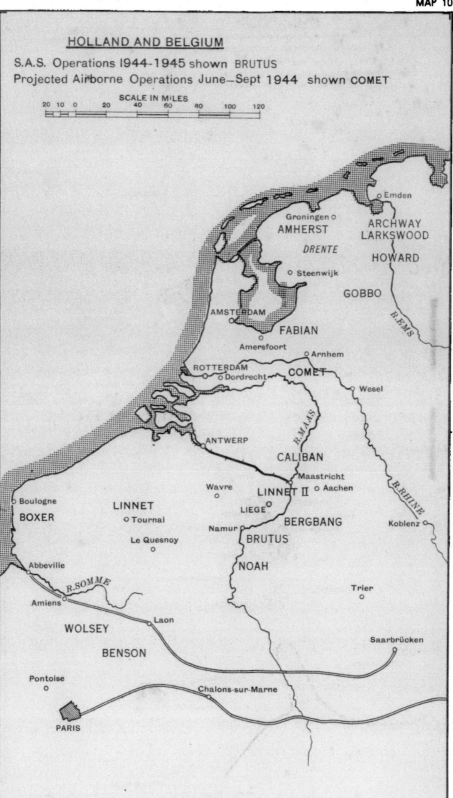

HOLLAND AND BELGIUM

S.A.S. Operations 1944-1945 shown BRUTUS
Projected Airborne Operations June—Sept 1944 shown COMET

MAP 11

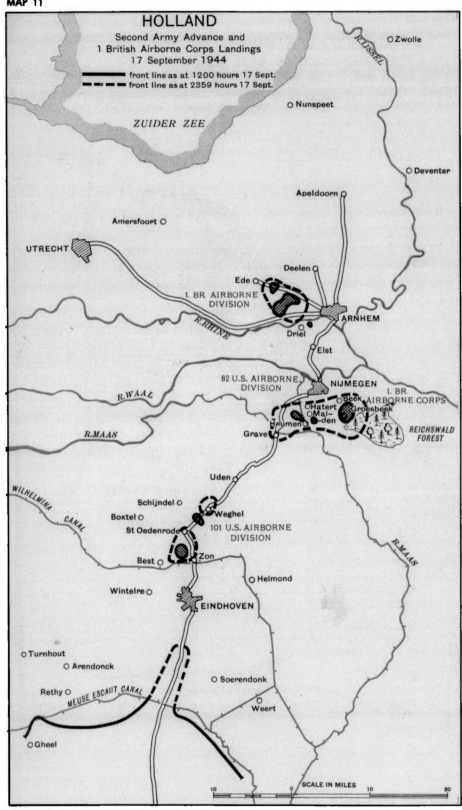

HOLLAND
Second Army Advance and
1 British Airborne Corps Landings
17 September 1944

━━━━━━ front line as at 1200 hours 17 Sept.
╍╍╍╍╍ front line as at 2359 hours 17 Sept.

ZUIDER ZEE

R.IJSSEL

○ Zwolle

○ Nunspeet

○ Deventer

Apeldoorn ○

Amersfoort ○

UTRECHT

Deelen ○

Ede ○

1. BR. AIRBORNE
DIVISION

R.RHINE

Driel ○

ARNHEM

Elst

82 U.S. AIRBORNE
DIVISION

NIJMEGEN

1. BR.
AIRBORNE CORPS

R.WAAL

Beek
○ Hatert   Groesbeek
○ Mal—
den

R.MAAS

Heumen ○

Grave

REICHSWALD
FOREST

Uden ○

Schijndel ○

Boxtel ○

St Oedenrode ○

Weghel ○

101 U.S. AIRBORNE
DIVISION

R.MAAS

Best ○   Zon

Wintelre ○

Helmond ○

EINDHOVEN

○ Turnhout

○ Arendonck

Rethy ○   MEUSE ESCAUT CANAL

WILHELMINA CANAL

○ Soerendonk

○
Weert

○ Gheel

SCALE IN MILES

10   0   MILES   10   20

MAP 12

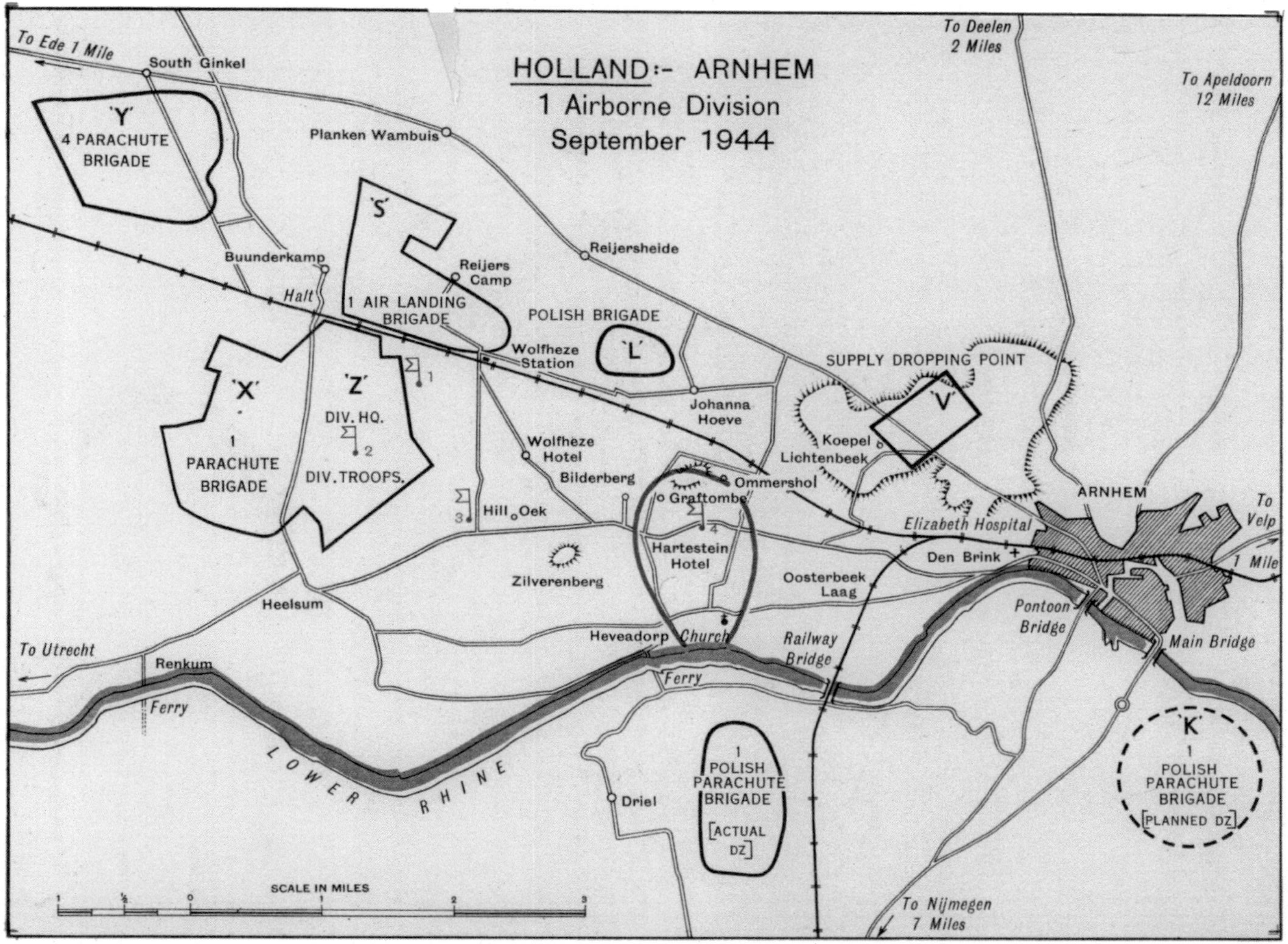
HOLLAND:- ARNHEM
1 Airborne Division
September 1944
To Ede 1 Mile
South Ginkel
'Y' 4 PARACHUTE BRIGADE
Planken Wambuis
'S'
Buunderkamp
Reijersheide
Reijers Camp
Halt
1 AIR LANDING BRIGADE
POLISH BRIGADE
'L'
Wolfheze Station
'X'
1 PARACHUTE BRIGADE
'Z'
DIV. HQ.
DIV. TROOPS.
1
2
3
4
Johanna Hoeve
Wolfheze Hotel
Bilderberg
Hill Oek
SUPPLY DROPPING POINT
'V'
Koepel
Lichtenbeek
Ommershol
Graftombe
Hartestein Hotel
Zilverenberg
Heelsum
To Utrecht
Renkum
Ferry
Heveadorp
Church
Railway Bridge
Oosterbeek Laag
Den Brink
Elizabeth Hospital
ARNHEM
To Deelen 2 Miles
To Apeldoorn 12 Miles
To Velp
1 Mile
Pontoon Bridge
Main Bridge
LOWER RHINE
Driel
1 POLISH PARACHUTE BRIGADE [ACTUAL DZ]
'K' 1 POLISH PARACHUTE BRIGADE [PLANNED DZ]
To Nijmegen 7 Miles
SCALE IN MILES
1
½
0
1
2
3

MAP 13

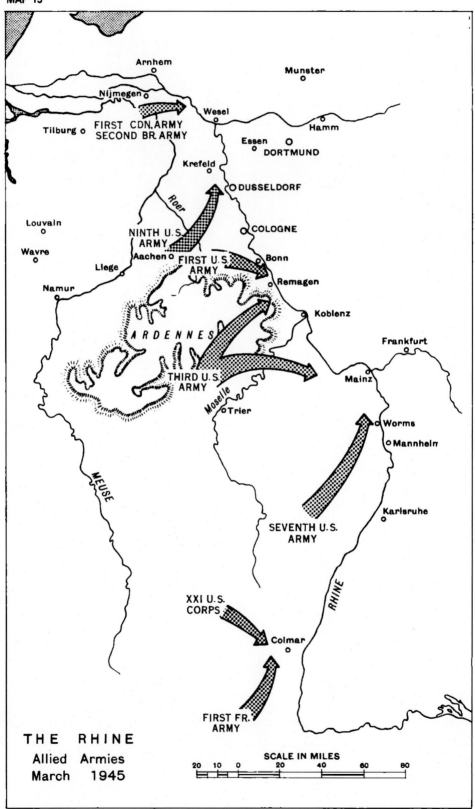

THE RHINE

Allied Armies
March 1945

MAP 14

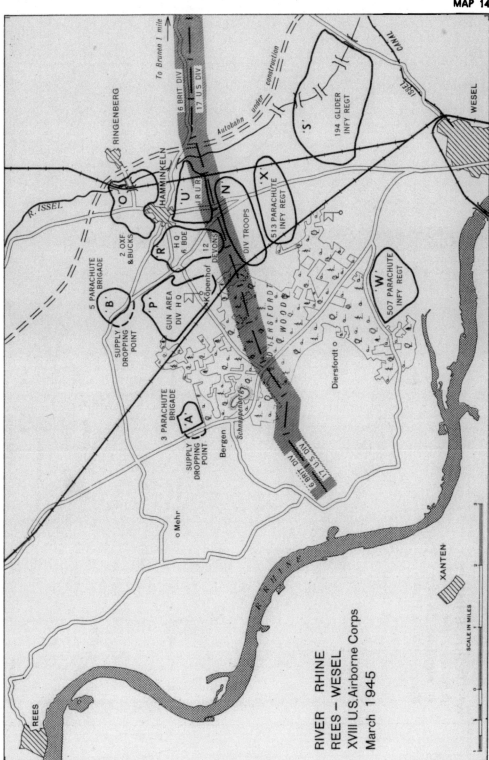

RIVER RHINE
REES – WESEL
XVIII U.S. Airborne Corps
March 1945

MAP 15

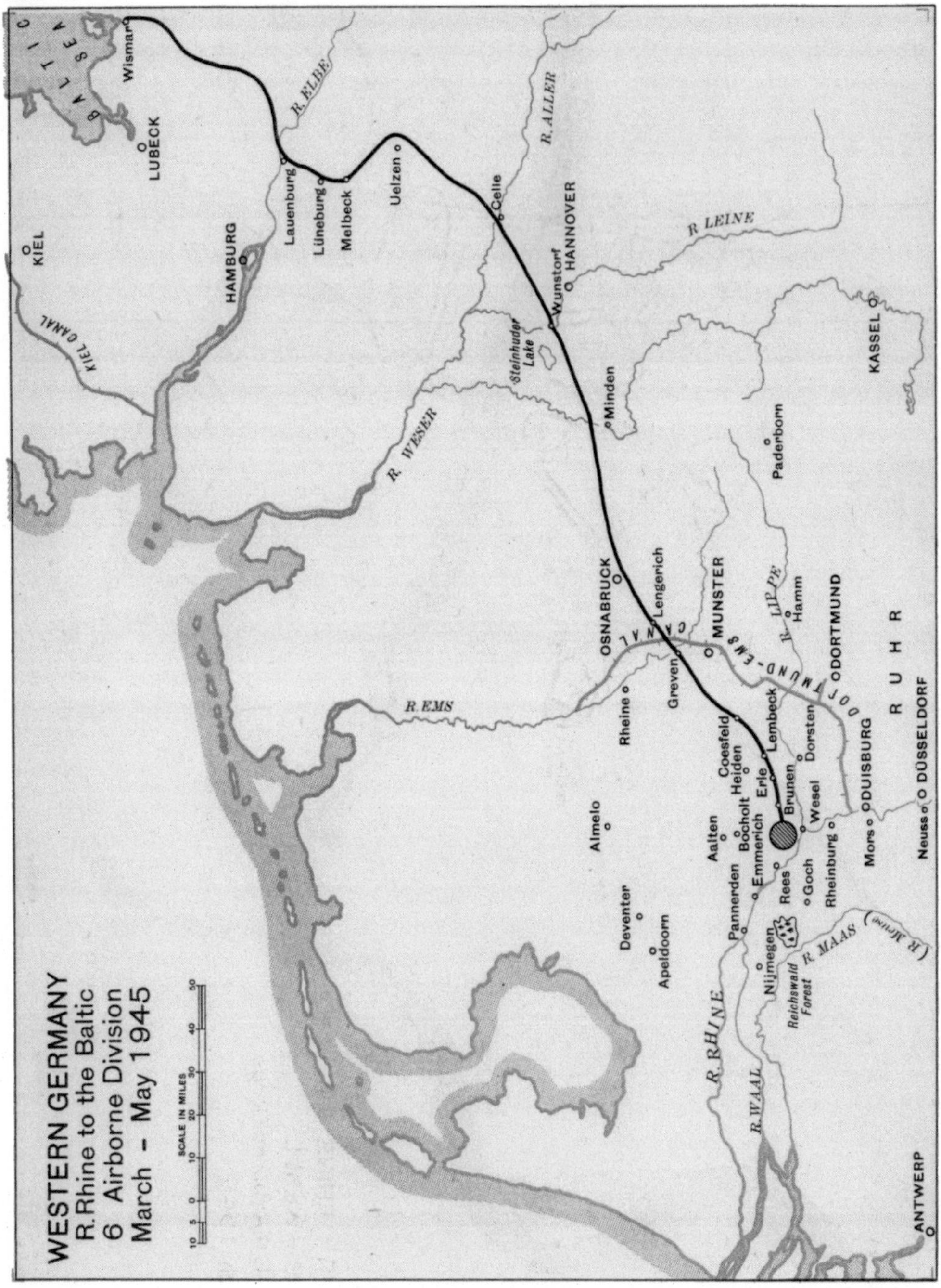

WESTERN GERMANY
R. Rhine to the Baltic
6 Airborne Division
March - May 1945
SCALE IN MILES
10 5 0 10 20 30 40 50
BALTIC SEA
Wismar
LUBECK
KIEL
KIEL CANAL
HAMBURG
Lauenburg
Lüneburg
Melbeck
Uelzen
Celle
R. ELBE
R. ALLER
HANNOVER
Wunstorf
R. LEINE
Steinhuder Lake
Minden
R. WESER
KASSEL
Paderborn
OSNABRUCK
Lengerich
MUNSTER
R. LIPPE
Hamm
DORTMUND
DORTMUND-EMS CANAL
R. EMS
Rheine
Greven
Coesfeld
Lembeck
Heiden
Dorsten
Erle
Brunen
Wesel
R U H R
DUISBURG
DÜSSELDORF
Neuss
Mors
Rheinburg
Goch
Rees
Emmerich
Bocholt
Aalten
Almelo
Deventer
Apeldoorn
Pannerden
Nijmegen
Reichswald Forest
R. MAAS
(R. Meuse)
R. RHINE
R. WAAL
ANTWERP

MAP 16

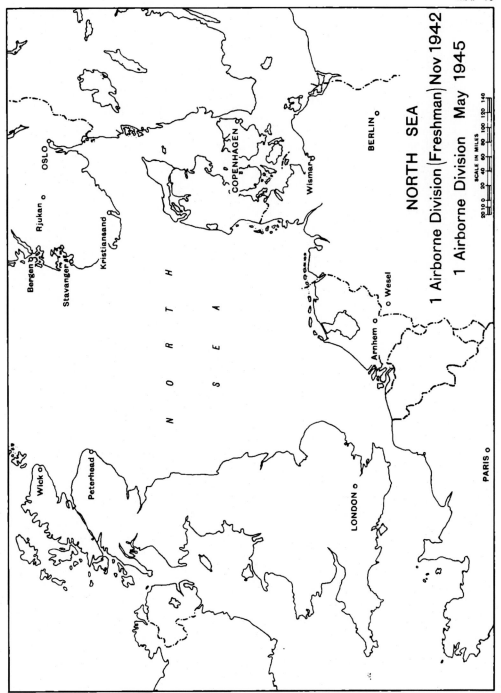

NORTH SEA

1 Airborne Division (Freshman) Nov 1942

1 Airborne Division May 1945

SCALE IN MILES
20 10 0   20   40   60   80 100 120 140

MAP 17

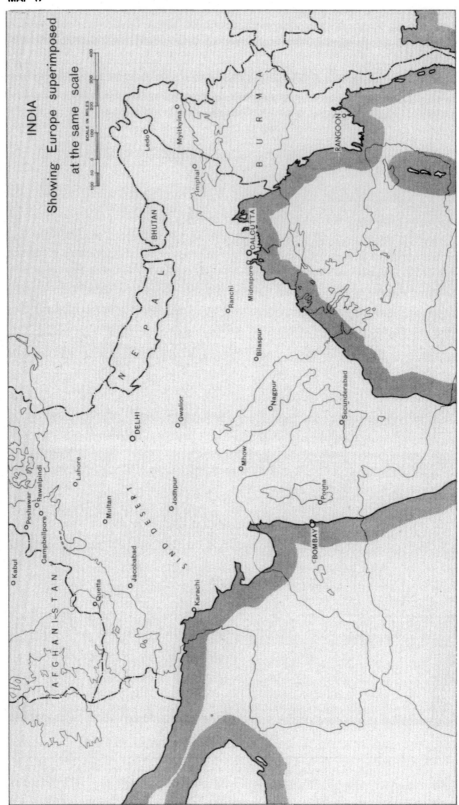

INDIA

Showing Europe superimposed

at the same scale

MAP 18

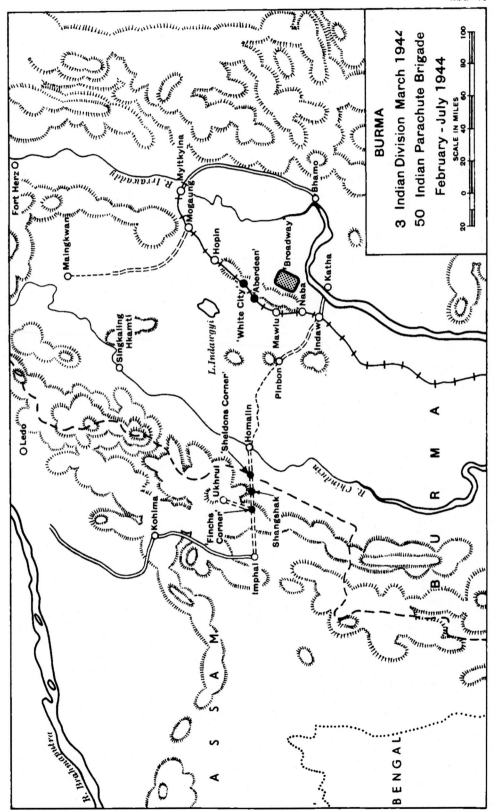

BURMA

3 Indian Division March 1944

50 Indian Parachute Brigade
February - July 1944

SCALE IN MILES

0   20   40   60   80   100

MAP 19

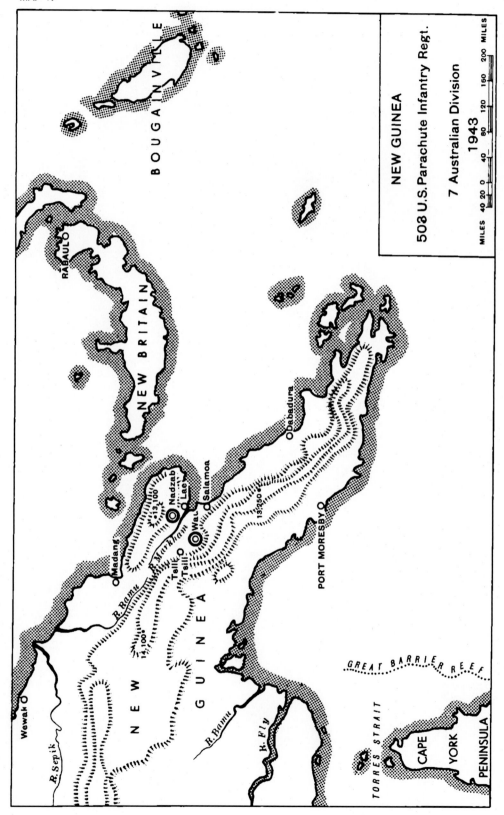

NEW GUINEA

508 U.S. Parachute Infantry Regt.

7 Australian Division

1943

MAP 20

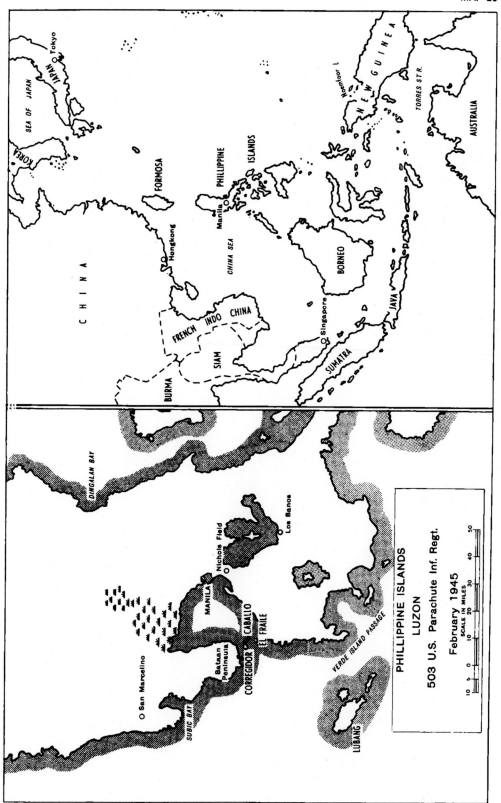

PHILLIPPINE ISLANDS

LUZON

503 U.S. Parachute Inf. Regt.

February 1945

SCALE IN MILES

MAP 21

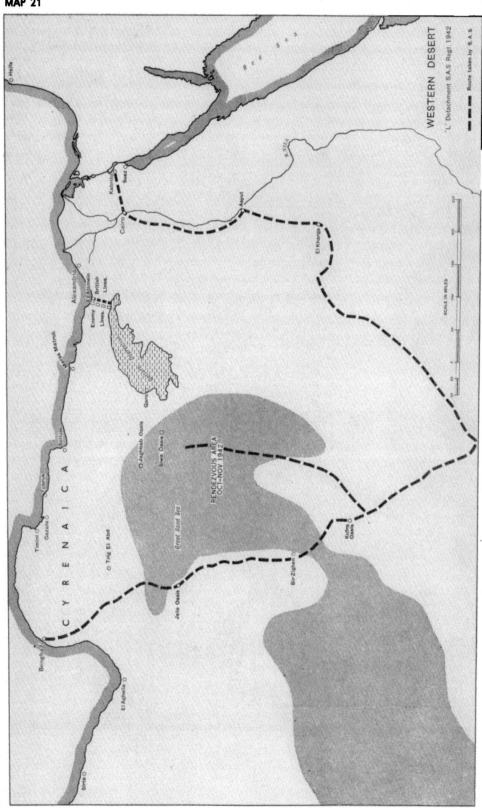